D1179554

THE COLLECTED LETTERS OF
JOSEPH CONRAD

GENERAL EDITOR:
FREDERICK R. KARL

VOLUME 4

THE COLLECTED LETTERS
OF JOSEPH CONRAD

VOLUME 4 1908–1911

EDITED BY

FREDERICK R. KARL

AND

LAURENCE DAVIES

The right of the
University of Cambridge
to print and sell
all manner of books
was granted by
Henry VIII in 1534.
The University has printed
and published continuously
since 1584.

CAMBRIDGE UNIVERSITY PRESS

CAMBRIDGE

NEW YORK PORT CHESTER

MELBOURNE SYDNEY

Published by the Press Syndicate of the University of Cambridge
The Pitt Building, Trumpington Street, Cambridge CB2 1RP
40 West 20th Street, New York, NY 10011, USA
10 Stamford Road, Oakleigh, Melbourne 3166, Australia

First published 1990

Printed in Great Britain at the University Press, Cambridge

British Library cataloguing in publication data
Conrad, Joseph, 1857–1924
The collected letters of Joseph Conrad.
Vol. 4, 1908–1911
1. Fiction in English. Conrad, Joseph – Correspondence, diaries, etc.
I. Title II. Karl, Frederick R. (Frederick Robert) 1927–
III. Davies, Laurence 1943–
823'.912

Library of Congress cataloguing in publication data
(Revised for vol. 4)
The collected letters of Joseph Conrad.
English and French.
Includes bibliographical references and indexes.
Contents: v. 1. 1861–1897 – v. 2. 1898–1902 – v. 3 1903–1907 – v. 4 1908–1911.
1. Conrad, Joseph, 1857–1924 – Correspondence.
2. Novelists, English – 20th century – Correspondence.
I. Karl, Frederick Robert, 1927– .
II. Davies, Laurence, 1943– . III. Title.
PR6005.04Z48 1983 823'.912 82-14643

ISBN 0 521 24216 9 (vol. 1)
ISBN 0 521 25748 4 (vol. 2)
ISBN 0 521 32387 8 (vol. 3)
ISBN 0 521 32388 6 (vol. 4)

CE

This volume is dedicated to a new generation of curators:

Aileen Cahill (The Rosenbach Foundation)
Cathy Henderson (University of Texas)
Saundra Taylor (University of Indiana)

CONTENTS

PLATES

between pages 238 and 239

These illustrations appear by kind permission of: The Humanities Research Center, University of Texas at Austin (1 and 10); Cambridge University Library (2); Aldington Parish Council (3); Dartmouth College Library (4, 5, and 7); The Berg Collection: Astor, Lenox and Tilden Foundations, New York Public Library (6); The National Portrait Gallery, London (8); The Henry E. Huntington Library (9).

ACKNOWLEDGMENTS

We offer our warm thanks to the individuals and institutions listed as guardians of the letters. Although we have been treated with great kindness by all the librarians we have burdened with our questions and our presence, we particularly wish to honour the memory of Dr Lola Szladits, of the Berg Collection, New York Public Library, who as overseer of by far the largest assembly of Conrad letters bore the edition's curatorial brunt for over twenty years. In her passion for the treasures in her charge she was inimitable.

Many of the people acknowledged in the first volume gave us help that benefits the entire edition; we render them all our redoubled gratitude. For particular help with Volume Four we thank Dr Krystyna Dietrich and Professors Walter Arndt, Andrew Busza, David Leon Higdon, Yvonne Howell, Paul Kirschner, Wiesław Krajka, Jeffrey Meyers, Seiji Minamida, Thomas C. Moser, Takahisa Nishimura, Sharon O'Brien, Walter Putnam, Esther Rashkin, S. W. Reid, Virginia Swain, and Cedric Watts.

We owe a particular debt of gratitude to the energy and cooperative spirit of those determined scholars who have found new letters: Professor Allan Hunter, Dr Janet Jellard, Dr Owen Knowles, Professor Donald Rude, and Dr J. H. Stape.

This volume was much fortified by Professor Keith Carabine, joint editor of the Cambridge *Under Western Eyes*, who showed us his chronology of that novel's composition and gave the typescript of the 1908–1911 letters his expert, not to mention lively, scrutiny.

As ever, Mr Hans van Marle has been extraordinarily kind and extraordinarily patient: he steers us all with care.

The preparation of Volume Four has been made possible in part by a grant to Laurence Davies from the National Endowment for the Humanities, a federal agency which supports the study of such fields as history, philosophy, literature, and languages.

HOLDERS OF LETTERS

Berg
: The Berg Collection: Astor, Lenox and Tilden Foundations, New York Public Library

BL
: The British Library

Bryn Mawr
: College Archives, Bryn Mawr College, Bryn Mawr, Pennsylvania

Buffalo
: The Poetry/Rare Books Collection, State University of New York at Buffalo

Clifford
: Mr Hugo Clifford-Holmes

Colgate
: Colgate University Library, Hamilton, New York

Columbia
: Special Collections Division, Columbia University, New York

Cornell
: Cornell University Libraries, Ithaca, New York

Dartmouth
: Baker Library, Dartmouth College, Hanover, New Hampshire

Duke
: William R. Perkins Library, Duke University, Durham, North Carolina

EAG
: Mr Edward Alexander Garnett

Forbes
: The late Malcolm Forbes, Jr

Free
: The Free Library of Philadelphia

Gide
: Mme Catherine Delavigne-Gide

Harvard
: The Houghton Library, Harvard University, Cambridge, Massachusetts

Illinois
: University of Illinois Library, Champaign-Urbana

Indiana
: Lilly Library, University of Indiana, Bloomington

Jellard
: Dr Janet Jellard

Lohf
: Mr Kenneth Lohf

Lubbock
: Special Collections, Texas Tech University, Lubbock

Macpherson
: Mr Kenneth Macpherson

Morgan
: The Pierpont Morgan Library, New York

Mursia
: The late Ugo Mursia

Newberry
: The Newberry Library, Chicago

NLS
: The National Library of Scotland, Edinburgh

NYPL
: Miscellaneous Manuscripts Division, New York Public Library

Ozarks
: Ralph Foster Museum, School of the Ozarks, Missouri

POSK	The Polish Library, London
Princeton	Princeton University Libraries
Queen's	Queen's University Archives, Kingston, Ontario
Read	Mrs Diana Read
RLF	The Royal Literary Fund, London
Rosenbach	The Philip H. and A. S. W. Rosenbach Foundation, Philadelphia
Sprott	Mrs Freda Sprott
Syracuse	George Arents Research Library for Special Collections, Syracuse University, Syracuse, New York
Temple	Temple University Library, Philadelphia
Texas	Harry Ransom Humanities Research Center, University of Texas at Austin
Vaugelas	Mme Charles Armand de Vaugelas
Virginia	Tracy W. McGregor Collection, Alderman Library, University of Virginia, Charlottesville
Warsaw	The National Library of Poland, Warsaw
Weber	Mr David C. Weber
Wellington	The Honourable Company of Master Mariners, H.Q.S. *Wellington*, London
Yale	The Beinecke Rare Book and Manuscript Library, Yale University, New Haven, Connecticut

PUBLISHED SOURCES OF LETTERS

Angeleri	Carlo Angeleri, ed., 'Una lettera inedita a Carlo Placci', *Paragone*, 8 (1957), no. 88, 55–9
Baines	Jocelyn Baines, *Joseph Conrad: A Critical Biography*. Weidenfeld & Nicolson, 1960
Blackburn	William Blackburn, ed., *Joseph Conrad: Letters to William Blackwood and David S. Meldrum*. Durham, N.C.: Duke University Press, 1958
Cap	Jean-Pierre Cap, ed., 'A Conrad Letter to Henri Ghéon', *Conradiana*, 8 (1976), 219–24
Danilewiczowa	Maria Danilewiczowa, ed., *Joseph Conrad: Listy do Johna Galsworthy'ego*. B. Świderski, 1957
G.	Edward Garnett, ed., *Letters from Joseph Conrad, 1895–1924*. Nonesuch Press, 1928
G. & S.	John A. Gee and Paul J. Sturm, trans. and ed., *Letters of Joseph Conrad to Marguerite Poradowska*. New Haven: Yale University Press, 1940
Guérin	Yves Guérin, ed., 'Huit lettres inédites de Joseph Conrad à Robert d'Humières', *Revue de Littérature Comparée*, 44 (1970), 367–92
Hidaka	Tadaichi Hidaka, ed., *Some Reminiscences and Amy Foster*. Tokyo: Eibungakusha, 1929
Hunter (1985, 2)	Allan G. Hunter, ed., 'Letters from Joseph Conrad, 2', *Notes and Queries*, 230 (September 1985), 500–5
Hunter (1985, 3)	Allan G. Hunter, ed., 'Some Unpublished Letters by Conrad to Arthur Symons', *Conradiana*, 17 (1985), 183–98
Illg	Jerzy Illg, ed., '"Polish Soul Living in Darkness": Letters . . . to Wincenty Lutosławski', *Conradiana*, 14 (1982), 3–22
J-A	G. Jean-Aubry, ed., *Joseph Conrad: Life & Letters*. 2 volumes. Heinemann, 1927
Jellard	Janet Jellard, ed., 'Joseph Conrad to His Doctor: Nine Unpublished Letters 1909–1921', *Conradiana*, 19 (1987), 87–98
Knowles	Owen Knowles and G. W. S. Miskin, ed.,

'Unpublished Conrad Letters: The H.Q.S. *Wellington* Collection', *Notes and Queries*, 230 (September 1985), 370–6

Letters Frederick R. Karl and Laurence Davies, ed., *The Collected Letters of Joseph Conrad*. Cambridge University Press, 1983, etc.

L. fr. G. Jean-Aubry, *Lettres françaises*. Paris: Gallimard, 1929

Listy Zdzisław Najder, ed., Halina Carroll-Najder, trans., *Joseph Conrad: Listy*. Warsaw: Państwowy Instytut Wydawniczy, 1968

Marrot H. V. Marrot, ed., *The Life and Letters of John Galsworthy*. New York: Scribner's, 1936

Maser Frederick E. Maser, ed., 'A Collection of the Books of Joseph Conrad', *Temple University Library Bulletin*, 2 (1957), no. 2, 1–21

Najder Zdzisław Najder, ed., Halina Carroll-Najder, trans., *Conrad's Polish Background: Letters to and from Polish Friends*. Oxford University Press, 1964

Najder (1970) 'Joseph Conrad: A Selection of Unpublished Letters', *Polish Perspectives* (Warsaw), 13 (1970), no. 2, 31–45

Najder (1983) *Joseph Conrad: A Chronicle*. New Brunswick, N.J.: Rutgers University Press, 1983

Randall Dale B. J. Randall, ed., *Joseph Conrad and Warrington Dawson: The Record of a Friendship*. Durham, N.C.: Duke University Press, 1968

Rapin René Rapin, ed., *Lettres de Joseph Conrad à Marguerite Poradowska*. Geneva: Droz, 1966

Rude (1982) Donald W. Rude, ed., 'An Unpublished Letter from Joseph Conrad to Edward Garnett', *Notes and Queries*, 227 (1982), 328

Rude (1988) Donald W. Rude, ed., 'Two Unpublished Letters in the Texas Tech University Conrad Collection', *Conradiana*, 20 (1988), 159–62

Schwab Arnold T. Schwab, ed., 'Joseph Conrad's American Friend: Correspondence with James Huneker', *Modern Philology*, 52 (1955), 222–32

Symons Arthur Symons, *Notes on Joseph Conrad, with Some Unpublished Letters*. Myers, 1925

Szczpien	J. Szczypien, 'New Light on the Composition of Joseph Conrad's *A Personal Record*', *Notes and Queries*, 232 (March 1987), 50–1
Tobin	*Agnes Tobin: Letters, Translations, Poems*. San Francisco, Grabhorn Press, 1958
Watts	C. T. Watts, ed., *Joseph Conrad's Letters to R. B. Cunninghame Graham*. Cambridge University Press, 1969
WR	Sir William Rothenstein, *Men and Memories, 1900–22*. New York: Coward, McCann, 1932

OTHER FREQUENTLY CITED WORKS

Beckson, Karl	*Arthur Symons: A Life*. Oxford: Clarendon Press, 1987
Carabine, Keith and David Leon Higdon, ed.	*Under Western Eyes*. Cambridge University Press, forthcoming
Conrad, Borys	*My Father: Joseph Conrad*. New York: Coward, McCann, 1970
Conrad, Jessie	*Joseph Conrad and His Circle*. Jarrold's, 1925
Conrad, Jessie	*Joseph Conrad as I Knew Him*. Garden City, N.Y.: Doubleday, Page, 1926
Dupré, Catherine	*John Galsworthy: A Biography*. New York: Coward, McCann, 1976
Garnett, Edward, ed.	*Letters from John Galsworthy, 1900–1932*. Cape, 1934
Higdon, David Leon, and Robert F. Sheard	'Conrad's "Unkindest Cut": The Cancelled Scenes in *Under Western Eyes*', *Conradiana*, 19 (1987), 167–81
Holloway, Mark	*Norman Douglas: A Biography*. Secker & Warburg, 1976
Jean-Aubry, G., ed.	*Twenty Letters to Joseph Conrad*. First Edition Club, 1926
Jefferson, George	*Edward Garnett: A Life in Literature*. Cape, 1982
Karl, Frederick R.	*Joseph Conrad: The Three Lives*. New York: Farrar, Straus, Giroux, 1979
Ludwig, Richard M., ed.	*Letters of Ford Madox Ford*. Princeton, N.J.: Princeton University Press, 1965

Mizener, Arthur *The Saddest Story: A Biography of Ford Madox Ford.*
 New York: World Publishing Co., 1971
Najder, Zdzisław, *Conrad under Familial Eyes.* Cambridge Univer-
ed., and Halina sity Press, 1983
Carroll-Najder,
trans.
Sherry, Norman *Conrad's Eastern World.* Cambridge University
 Press, 1966
Sherry, Norman *Conrad's Western World.* Cambridge University
 Press, 1971
Sherry, Norman *Conrad: The Critical Heritage.* Routledge &
 Kegan Paul, 1973
Wright, H., ed. *Letters from Stephen Reynolds.* Richmond:
 Hogarth Press, 1923

Unless otherwise noted, references to Conrad's work come from the Kent Edition, published by Doubleday, Page in twenty-six volumes (Garden City, N.Y., 1925). Books cited without place of publication originated in London.

CHRONOLOGY, 1908–1911

Unless otherwise stated, dates give book publication in Britain rather than North America; dates and locations for stories and magazines note only the earliest appearance.

12 September 1907	The Conrads moved to Someries, near Luton.
19 September 1907	Borys Conrad began to board at St Gregory's School, Luton.
By 4 December 1907	Conrad began 'Razumov', later *Under Western Eyes*.
January–May 1908	'The Duel' in the *Pall Mall Magazine*.
c. 22–27 January 1908	Work on 'The Black Mate' (*London Magazine*, April 1908), whose earliest version was written in 1886.
April 1908	Grant of £200 from the Royal Literary Fund.
August 1908	'Il Conde' in *Cassell's Magazine*.
6 August 1908	*A Set of Six* published.
September 1908	Conrad began *Some Reminiscences*, later *A Personal Record* (1912).
29 August–21 September 1908	Visit to Aldington, Kent, to be near the Hueffers.
c. 2 October 1908	*The Point of Honor* (US book form of 'The Duel') published.
Autumn 1908	Fear that Jessie Conrad's knee might need another operation.
25 November 1908	Inaugural (December) issue of the *English Review*: it included 'Anatole France, "L'Ile des Pingouins"', and the first part of *Some Reminiscences*, which ran until the issue of June 1909.
14 February 1909	Move to Aldington.
Late March 1909	Conrad finished 'Razumov', Part II.
April–May 1909	'The Nature of a Crime' (a collabor-

	ation with Ford written in May 1906) published pseudonymously in the *English Review*.
April–September 1909	A series of quarrels with Ford as his marriage collapsed and the *English Review* slipped from his grasp.
25 August–10 October 1909	French translation of *The Nigger* serialised in *Le Correspondant*.
18 September 1909	'The Silence of the Sea' in the *Daily Mail*.
September 1909	A visit from Captain Marris awoke memories of the Malay Archipelago.
c. 4–14 December 1909	Conrad wrote 'The Secret Sharer' (*Harper's Magazine*, August–September 1910).
22 January 1910	Conrad finished *Under Western Eyes*, then worked until the 26th on a revised ending.
27? January 1910	Conrad delivered the last of *Under Western Eyes*, and quarrelled with Pinker.
30 January 1910	Physical and mental collapse.
Mid March 1910	Conrad began a hesitant recovery. Robert Garnett had taken temporary charge of his literary as well as legal affairs.
11 May 1910	Conrad finished revisions of *Under Western Eyes*.
c. 18 May 1910	Conrad began 'A Smile of Fortune'.
24 June 1910	The Conrads took up the tenancy of Capel House (during the move itself, Joseph Conrad stayed with the Gibbons).
16, 23, and 30 July 1910	Book reviews published in the *Daily Mail*.
August 1910	Offer from Gordon Bennett, proprietor of the *New York Herald*, for a serial novel.
9 August 1910	Conrad awarded a Civil List Pension of £100 a year.

c. 2 September 1910 Conrad finished 'A Smile of Fortune' (*London Magazine*, February 1911).

25 September 1910 Conrad finished 'Prince Roman' (*Oxford and Cambridge Review*, October 1911), originally part of *A Personal Record*.

October? 1910 Conrad began 'The Partner'.

December 1910–October 1911 *Under Western Eyes* serialized in the *English Review*.

1 or 8 December 1910 Conrad finished 'The Partner' (*Harper's Magazine*, November 1911).

26 December 1910 Conrad began 'Freya'.

By 28 February 1911 Conrad finished 'Freya' (*Metropolitan Magazine*, April 1912).

c. 29 April 1911 After a blank period of seven weeks, Conrad resumed *Chance* at the point where he had left off in 1905 or 1906.

August 1911 Norman Douglas very ill at Capel House; work on *Chance* at a virtual standstill until at least the end of September.

August 1911 The collector John Quinn made his first offers to buy MSS.

August or September 1911 Conrad wrote 'A Familiar Preface' to *A Personal Record*.

22 September 1911 Borys joined HMS *Worcester* as a cadet.

5 October 1911 *Under Western Eyes* published.

INTRODUCTION TO VOLUME FOUR

When Joseph Conrad delivered the last batch of *Under Western Eyes*, he quarrelled with J. B. Pinker. The quarrel was no surprise; both men were exasperated by the text's painful two-year growth from a brief, almost anecdotal story to one of Conrad's most intensely seen – and heard – novels. At the beginning of December 1909, Conrad had interrupted his work on the novel to spend eight or ten days on another project. Nellie Lyons, the Conrads' maid, had been suffering the agonies of an untreated gastric ulcer in loyal but ill-advised silence. Her hospital bills, when the inevitable collapse arrived, could be settled if Conrad wrote and sold a short story. The result was a tale of concealment, risk, and solidarity, a tale also of a captain who endangers his crew with inexplicable manoeuvres:

For titles I suggest *The Secret Self* or *The other Self* An episode from the sea[.] It could be also *The Secret Sharer* but that may be *too* enigmatic.
(To Pinker, [c. 18 December 1909])

Pinker, already annoyed by *A Personal Record*, a previous venture on to the sidetracks, did not seem impressed by this gesture of what some people would call noblesse oblige and others simple decency. Conrad owed more than £2,700, and a short story might fetch fifty. On the 18th he received a letter from his agent threatening to cut off funds if the rest of the novel did not appear within the fortnight. 'If he does that', Conrad wrote of the threat, 'I shall fling the MS of Raz[umov] in the fire – and see how he likes that' (To Gibbon, 19 December). After his initial reply to Pinker on the 20th ('I am not a confounded hypoc[h]ondriac in search of sympathy'), Conrad maintained a studied politeness in his reports on the novel's final stages, but it was not until 27 January, after a bout of 'flu, a rewriting of the final pages, and a scattering of letters and telegrams announcing imminent conclusion, that he took his work to London. There, in Pinker's office near Charing Cross station, author and agent saw each other for the first time in almost a year. During their interview, Pinker scraped a nerve already abraded by certain reviews of *The Secret Agent* and *A Set of Six*. Several months later the encounter still chafed:

[I]t can't have escaped your recollection that the last time we met you told me that I "did not speak English" to you. (23 May 1910)

Conrad returned to his family's cramped lodgings, four rooms in a Kentish cottage next to a slaughterhouse, on 28 or 29 January. On the 30th, he retreated to a couch where he huddled like an unborn baby. His neck had bloated abominably, his voice was hoarse, his speech incoherent. For the next six weeks, like the delirious husband in 'Amy Foster', he rambled in his native tongue, reverting to English only to curse Pinker, converse with characters from his barely finished and still disorderly novel, or recite the service for burial at sea. On 19 May, in the course of a slow convalescence, now able to hobble a few yards and work for a few minutes at a time, Conrad explained his (and Jessie Conrad's) ordeal to Sir Hugh Clifford:

It seems I have been very ill. At the time I did not believe it, but now I begin to think that I must have been. And what's more I begin to see that the horrible nervous tension of the last two years (of which even my wife knows nothing) had to end in something of the sort.
Perhaps it was the only way of relief?

Inescapably, the making of *Under Western Eyes*, the dramatic sequel to its completion, and the gradual recovery from physical and mental illness dominate this volume as they dominated Conrad's life. Even the solace of his family – his wife's ministrations, Borys's transformation from the invalid who 'wished "he had never been borned"' to a short-sighted but agile naval cadet, Jack's 'spritelike' pursuit of rabbits across flower-beds and his 'morals ... distinctly of the pagan kind' (To Galsworthy, 28 July 1911) – was darkened by the fear that without a frequent supply of well-received novels his family's future would be desperate. In this context, writing *A Personal Record* for the incipient *English Review* was a luxury, a literary holiday from the often grim demands of Petersburg and Geneva. All the same, the holiday brought little refreshment:

How to guard myself against the most deplorable prosiness is my difficulty—the thing itself, my haunting fear, and the necessity of writing my despair.
 (To Ford, [12 October 1908])

I fear it is a silly enterprise besides (what with the stirring up of all these dead) being a somewhat ghoulish one. (To Wells, 3 November 1908)

The very process of making 'Polish life enter English literature' (To Pinker, [7] October 1908) had conjured up the demons he might for a while have hoped to forget.

Between 1908 and 1910, Conrad dwelled on and in his memories. As if therapeutically, 'A Smile of Fortune', the first story after the break-

down, recapitulated (with a little help from Maupassant) an old love-affair in Mauritius. With its amiable manner, *A Personal Record* masks more than it reveals, but still it shows more of Conrad than any of the quasi-autobiographical essays from *The Mirror of the Sea*. And whereas *Nostromo* and *The Secret Agent* had reflected the Korzeniowski and Bobrowski experience of autocracy and fanaticism, *Under Western Eyes* revealed it face to face.

That this confrontation hurt Conrad is evident in his letters, which have even more than usual to say about the painfulness of writing:

Two years! Of which surely one half has been illness complicated by a terrible moral stress. Imagine yourself painting with the Devil jogging your elbow *all the time* ... you will know what a torture that sort of thing is when the effort and hindrance are mental.

(To Rothenstein, 17 December 1909)

It saddens me to hear that You too are subject to these moments of cruel blankness when one's writing life seems to come to an end. I live in the constant dread of these visitations. They have been too frequent of late.

(To Lucas, 23 June 1909)

Thus the feeling of exhaustion, the revulsion from writing, predate *Chance, Victory, The Rescue,* and *The Arrow of Gold,* those books where critics, although disagreeing over the time at which it happened, have sensed the faltering of Conrad's powers. Yet *Under Western Eyes* is not an exhausted book; it is the product not of faltering but of reluctant powers, and the reluctance surely came from the nature of the book's materials.

Whatever caused the compulsion to reiterate – a conviction that here was a rift in the moral universe, remorse for leaving Poland, or some secret misdemeanour quite unknown to us – Conrad returned again and again to the subject of unmalicious betrayal. In *Under Western Eyes* this topic has fallen among Russians, whose government and whose revolutionary sects Conrad despised with equal fervour. He asserted in the Author's Note of 1920 that 'The obligation of absolute fairness was imposed on me historically and hereditarily, by the peculiar experience of race and family, in addition to any primary conviction that truth alone is the justification of any fiction which makes the least claim to the quality of art.' In other words, a Polish *szlachcic* and a disciple of Flaubert should show his moral superiority by striking a more generous attitude to the Russians than Dostoevsky had to the Poles. Conrad took a similar line to Edward Garnett, insisting that he had not put his 'hate into a novel. If You seriously think that I have done that then my dear fellow let me tell you that you don't know what the accent of hate is' (20

October 1911). The effort that alarmed and exhausted Conrad was an effort of restraint rather than release.

Conrad's difficulties, however, did not all come from the necessity of avoiding political puppet-shows. The book's energies spring from its contradictions, its way of setting phobias off against their opposites: claustrophobia against agoraphobia, fear of speech against fear of silence. With the significant exception of 'Amy Foster', no work since 'Heart of Darkness' concerns itself so much with the insufficiency of language and the human yearning for talk. The teacher of languages has lost any artistic gifts 'under a wilderness of words' (Part I, Chapter 1) and writes of 'those futile phrases that give the measure of our impotence before each other's trials' (II, 1). Before denouncing Haldin, Razumov 'longed desperately for a word of advice, for moral support. Who knows what true loneliness is – not the conventional word, but the naked terror?' (I, 2). Images of emptiness and isolation abound in the novel as they do in the correspondence. In the early days of composition, Conrad told Ford 'I am stuck dead with R[azumov]. Inventions dead. And yet the imagination works dans le vide' (31 March 1908). The snow covers Russia 'like a monstrous blank page awaiting the record of an inconceivable history' (I, 2). Lu Ki, in his *Essay on Literature (Wen Fu)*, praises literature's ability to call existence from the void and sound from silence. In *Under Western Eyes* silence and the void always seem waiting to gobble up speech and writing again. It is as though Conrad and his language teacher surrogate were alarmed both by the empty sheet and by what could fill it up.

In Conrad's writing from this time, a renewed linguistic scepticism is tied to a renewed obsession with isolation. The motif of isolation figures also in his personal circumstances. Although the move to Someries in the autumn of 1907 had been intended to bring him closer to town, Conrad rarely took advantage of this closeness. The subsequent move to Aldington was an escape from the gloom of the Bedfordshire house, but again Conrad steered clear of London. When he did go to see Galsworthy's *Strife*, the outcome was unpleasant:

In the theatre I felt that peculiar nervousness I know so well—a sort of shock and gasp it is—and by the time we got home my back was full of "small-shot" feeling and now eczema has broken out from neck to tail.

(To Mackintosh, [26? March 1909])

Making matters worse, the other purpose of moving to Aldington had been to live nearer Ford. Ford, however, was more than a little deranged, blown about by paranoid suspicions and manic schemes.

That the former collaborators should fall out was sad but predictable. Only in the most single-minded of psychoanalytic interpretations could it be seen as the sole or even the principal factor in Conrad's collapse, but without a doubt the quarrel increased his isolation. Perhaps he even wanted to increase it. The dispute over Willa Cather's sudden visit suggests that Conrad, an author in the midst of an ambitious novel, 'a man who *can't afford* to be disturbed by casual visitors' (To Ford, 20 May 1909), needed relief from the hurlyburly of life as managed or mismanaged by the Hueffers. Moreover, as the letter to Chalmers Roberts of 1 May shows ('my own feelings with regard to your firm will continue as they are at present,—inexpressible'), Conrad was in a particularly touchy humour.

A combination of will and circumstance brought physical, but not necessarily emotional, separation from other close friends. Addressing Rothenstein in terms that recall both *Lord Jim* and 'The Secret Sharer' (finished only three days earlier), Conrad wrote:

I speak to you here as to a second self . . . to-day in the second week of my 52[nd] year, a failure from the worldly point of view and knowing well that there can be no change—that this must go on usque ad finem—I may perhaps be allowed a little unreason . . . I will only mention that I haven't seen you for more than a year, Galsworthy for nine months, that I have been in town for about six hours in march* last and not since. (17 December 1909)

The concentration demanded by work on a difficult major novel was only one of the reasons. The narrowness of the quarters in Aldington denied Conrad the opportunity to entertain in the generous manner he preferred. In any case, his spirits were depressed, and he was laid low by onslaught after onslaught of eczema and gout. The very medicines he took for gout could have worsened his plight. 'CBQ' made him 'imbecile for a time' (To Ada Galsworthy, 17 January 1909), while overuse of colchicum can induce temporary vertigo and deafness – an intimation of Razumov's fate.

Nevertheless, Conrad was not entirely deprived of company. Norman Douglas came down to visit; the Gibbons and Dr Mackintosh made various boisterous appearances; despite the Hueffers' campaign against him, Marwood often walked over from his farm. Nor, in the four rented rooms, was Conrad denied intimacy with his family. He lacked not simply company, but like-minded company.

Conrad's suggestion that Garnett might not 'know what the accent of hate is' epitomizes the problem. The novel in progress was one that not even his friends might understand. They were too inexperienced and,

with the possible exception of Cunninghame Graham (who was suspect on ideological grounds), too much conditioned by life in Britain. To someone contemplating the knout, Siberia, and the assassin's bomb, Galsworthy's concern with making solitary confinement a more humane experience and his commitment to orderly reform by Parliament could have seemed at best too bland, too inconsequential. At worst, well-intentioned social planning reinforced 'officialism' of the kind that took a pauper to court for not contributing to the relief of pauperism: 'Have you seen it? It's terrible. Summoned for his *poor rate!*' ([15 November 1909]). When signing a 'memorial' that urged Parliamentary action for women's rights, Conrad noted that he could not 'share' its 'beautiful optimism' (11 [14?] May 1910). Western eyes, Conrad must have concluded, could not stand much moral glare.

Galsworthy's liberal reformism and Garnett's theoretical anarchism were not, however, the only ingredients of contemporary British politics. The evidence in the letters is scattered and scanty, but it seems likely, given the nature of debate in the newspapers Conrad read, that he at least suspected he was singing his songs of experience in a country where innocence was under attack. Fierce disputes over the welfare of the unemployed, the sick, and the elderly, over women's rights, industrial pay and organization, Ireland, and the very nature of the constitution divided the nation. In July 1909, ten thousand demonstrators sang 'The Red Flag' in Whitehall; in the same month, militant suffragettes carried out the first of many assaults upon property, and David Lloyd George turned Limehouse (close to the heart of the East End slums) into a synonym for class-hatred; the forcible feeding of suffragette hunger-strikers began in September; in November the Lords threw out the budget. While these events could not seem terrible by the standards of Poland in 1863 or Russia in 1905, they were widely regarded as signs and portents. To put it in the terms that Razumov shared with orators and editorialists, Unity, Direction, and Evolution were losing out to Disruption, Destruction, and Revolution. The leader-writers began to hint at civil war. Whether or not Conrad took the spine-tingling rhetoric of journalists and politicians seriously, he could hardly have ignored its ubiquity. Either to disparage or to endorse the tocsin-ringers was to emphasize the authority of his own distinctive background.

Quite apart from their general relevance to British, Polish, or Russian society, Razumov's other two opposing principles have a particular bearing on Conrad's own plight: 'History not Theory', 'Patriotism not Internationalism'. These maxims exist on 'a square sheet of paper' in a

book by an author who had shown, above all in 'Heart of Darkness' and
Nostromo, that histories are multiple and inseparable from belief, that
patriotism may be no less factitious than internationalism. Neverthe-
less, the knowledge that other fields exist is not always enough to lift us
over the hedgerows – even if we want to be lifted. Conrad had been born
in an area that to the Russians was part of the Russian Empire, to the
Poles was part of Poland, and to the Ukrainians was the Ukraine. Given
the dramatic fluctuations of Poland's borders in better times and their
total obliteration in worse, Polishness might be described as a convic-
tion rather than a physical or metaphysical condition. That conviction
Conrad did not lose when he exchanged Russian citizenship for British
in 1886. Over twenty-one years later, when he began 'Razumov', he
embarked upon a work that, unlike *The Nigger* or *Lord Jim*, was bound to
make him know his continued apartness from British society. What was
A Personal Record if not Conrad's attempt, in the midst of producing the
novel, to stitch the British and Polish sides together again?

It so happened that while working on his novel Conrad was made to
feel particularly alien. *The Secret Agent* had not sold well: 'I suppose there
is something in me that is unsympathetic to the general public ...
Foreignness I suppose' (To Galsworthy, 6 January 1908). Reviewers of
The Secret Agent and *A Set of Six* detected exotic flavours in Conrad's
English, and some of those reviewers disliked the taste. The most
offended – or from Conrad's point of view the most offensive – was the
Irish journalist Robert Lynd:

But there is a fellow in the *D[ai]ly News* who calls me—God only knows on what
provocation—a man without country and language. It is like abusing a
tongue-tied man. For what can one say. The statement is simple and brutal; and
any answer would involve too many feelings of one's inner life, stir too much
secret bitterness and complex loyalty to be even attempted with any hope of
being understood. (To Garnett, 21 August 1908)

Conrad's decision to adopt the voice of an English teacher of languages
made a thoroughly ironic revenge.

The motif of separation echoed through Conrad's experience,
growing louder as his life and art converged. Writing about loneliness
made him feel more lonely. In his delirium he talked to the characters he
had invented rather than to the people around him. Metaphorically the
equivalent of the man in Lawrence's story, Conrad had been retreating
to ever smaller islands.

But he did return to the world outside. Jessie Conrad nursed him back
to physical health, Robert Garnett managed his affairs, Galsworthy

supplied the income lost by the quarrel with Pinker. Helped by Borys, Conrad sorted out the chaotic text of his novel and set about revising it. He started to write again. In the spring of 1911, Conrad resumed *Chance* and soon was working at notable speed. Despite a relapse into despondency during late summer and early autumn, the book was done by the following spring. Its quality relative to the earlier novels has been vigorously debated ever since its publication. It is not the sea story that Conrad originally meant it to be, yet in all but its scrutiny of feminism (and the spirit of that scrutiny too is debatable) it moves away from the political terrain of the three preceding novels. Curiously, if we think of its narrative imbrications, understandably if we think of its turn away from the 'Dostoevskian' mode that many reviewers, no doubt to Conrad's fury, recognized in *Under Western Eyes*, it became his first commercial success.

Thus the letters gathered here belong to a context of strain, crisis, and tentative recovery. All these stages are vividly present in the letters to Pinker and Ford and vividly described in the letters to other correspondents.

The arrangement worked out the previous autumn, whereby Conrad received a weekly allowance for living expenses, had run into difficulties by January 1908. Finding himself short of ready money, Pinker delayed settling an urgent coal bill; on behalf of his shivering family, Conrad rushed to London. He was only able to reassure Pinker, whom he owed £1,572, with a promise to end 'Razumov' forthwith and finish *Chance* by mid July. When July came, *Chance* had been set aside and 'Razumov' was growing indeterminately. The opening of the note written in Pinker's office, probably on the 16th, speaks for itself:

My dear P.
You must not treat me as a journeyman joiner. Am I to understand that if the book is not finished by say 10–15 then You will drop me on the 15th of Augt. I don't inquire whether it is You *can't* or *won't*. From the practical point of view it amounts to the same thing.

Thanks perhaps to Galsworthy's intervention, Pinker had withdrawn his ultimatum by the end of the month, but from then on the possibility that he might cut his client adrift always loomed on the horizon of the correspondence. In the very revealing letter of 18 September [1908], for instance, Conrad wrote:

To go on as I am is impossible. But to go on surely *is* worth while. Jack told me ... that you believed in me. I told him that I was only too willing to believe this

but that the only man who has spoken of *failure*, who had uttered the very word was you.

When the worst happened, Pinker, now 'Dear Sir' rather than 'My dear Pinker', did not rush to take Conrad in tow again; the eventual arrangement was strictly an exchange of cash for work delivered, four pounds per thousand words. Nevertheless, Conrad's defiant tone – 'I beg you to take notice that I shall write "Chance" when it suits me, exactly' (20 August 1910) – was gradually replaced by a tone of conciliation, as if having once been cast away he did not wish to repeat the experience: 'Whatever I might have thought of publishers there could never have been in my mind any thought of the "stupidity" of my agent. You know that I am invariably guided by you' (12 December 1911).

Beyond the scope of this volume, the relationship between Conrad and Pinker developed into a friendship warmer than it had ever been before. The opposite is true of relations with Ford. The murmurs of discontent during the early days of the *English Review*, audible for example in the letter of 17 December 1908, became outright anger during the spring of 1909: 'Stop this nonsense with me Ford. It's ugly. I won't have it' (20 May). Over the missed instalment of *A Personal Record*, the anger turned to ice: 'If I have discredited the R[eview], well I must bear the disgrace' (31 July 1909). When at last the thaw came, the two wrote as convalescents after psychic turmoil: 'I can't tell you how happy we are to know you are at peace at last ... I was very seriously ill last year for some 3 months' (29 March 1911). By the end of the year, the friendly gestures were multiplying. Conrad sent his compliments to Violet Hunt on 'the fine work you both are doing' (To Ford, 21 December), while finding the few miles that separated him from Elsie Hueffer, whom he apparently considered the major culprit in the 'execution' of Marwood, a formidable distance. Conrad also welcomed Ford's study of him for the *English Review*:

I am infinitely touched by what you say and by the accent you have found to express what may be critically just and true but to a certainty is the speech of a friend. What touches me most is to see that you do not discard our common past.

(21 December)

Yet the intimacy never fully returned. In the years to come, the 'common past' of the former collaborators and conspirators against the 'nuvvle' was all that could sustain them in the present.

Conrad made the fullest and liveliest commentary on his life in the

bulletins to John and Ada Galsworthy. The Galsworthys were honorary members of the family, keenly interested in the boys' progress, and always ready with loans, commiseration, and advice. We realize the strength of their sympathy, though, precisely because meetings had become so rare. Apropos of John Galsworthy's fable 'The Windlestraw', Conrad wrote:

> It seems to me at times as though I had, to some small extent, lost intellectual touch with you. Why it should be so, unless from the general weak[en]ing of my grasp on things, of which (rightly or wrongly) I have a dismal consciousness, I don't know. Perhaps it is only that of late we have been physically apart for long stretches of time? There is something in personal contact which clarifies the mists of preconceived ideas each of us carried* about him like a sort of private atmosphere. ([8 November 1910])

This dearth of 'personal contact' can be thanked for the extended critique of Galsworthy's 'Shadows' spread over letters written in August and September 1908. Conrad objected above all to Hilary Dallison (an independently wealthy author in his forties, like his creator), who was too feeble a character to sustain the weight of the book's polemic against class distinctions – too feeble and too much a moral freak:

> I don't think my dearest Jack that in the glow of inspired composition (I am speaking with the utmost seriousness, I am under the charm of it) you have realized the harrowing atrocity of his conduct. You have refined and spiritual-ized that poor wretch into a remote resemblance to those lunatics—there are such—who try to cut of[f] locks of women's hair in the crowds.
> ([2–3 September])

Harking back to Richard Shelton, the character in *The Island Pharisees* who spends his time being appalled by injustice, Conrad warned:

> Beware of *Sheltonism* You understand me? I love Shelton with an exceeding love—but beware of him—I mean of that side of him which is purely and exclusively Sheltonian. No—don't abandon Shelton; he's your creation, your embodied conscience you[r] wistful spirit going about on the earth. Hold him. Stick to him—but don't let him write your novels. ([4 September])

Galsworthy had gone against the grain of his material, thinking in overly schematic terms, failing to explore the moral implications of his characters' conduct, and trying to preach on inadequate texts. His book held no mystery. Conrad's severe but not entirely disheartening criti-cisms point quite openly to the aesthetic gap that separated him from his friend (and by extension from Wells and Bennett); these criticisms fascinate all the more because Conrad too was struggling with a novel of ideas in action, a novel that could aptly have taken either of Gals-

worthy's titles, 'Shadows' or *Fraternity*. When Conrad called his response 'talk between you and me brother' ([4 September]), he had written over twenty pages about the manuscript and was not yet done. Neither in Galsworthy's work nor in Conrad's is brotherhood – or sisterhood – an easy or a simple condition, but its very existence as other than blood relationship is a triumph over social entropy.

Coaching him in the ways of publishers, interceding with editors and agents, Conrad continued to encourage Norman Douglas. Douglas, whose gratitude could extend to a 'romantic gift of sauerkraut and Frankfort sausages' ([19 March 1909]), was a frequent and welcome visitor undeterred by primitive domestic arrangements, although his illness at Capel House in August 1911 gravely alarmed the family and threw Conrad himself off course for many weeks. While still at Someries, Conrad had acquired another protégé, Stephen Reynolds:

> In the midst of my sordid (and befogged) worries I spared a thought now and then for the burly form of *one* who pervades the West Country nursing the dreams of great deeds and cruel books for the discomfiture of the harried bourgeois. (30 January 1909)

When Reynolds allowed, for he could be as quick to take offence as his mentor, Conrad chided him for squandering his talents on journalism instead of attempting an English *Nostromo*, 'a great seaboard novel ... with the whole of our civilisation, social & political for a background' (27 October 1910).

Another of Conrad's new friends, Perceval Gibbon, was both a novelist and a journalist. He and Maisie, his wife, introduced R. D. Mackintosh, doctor, metallurgist, and 'Buccaneer' (5 May 1909). This trio gave Conrad much-needed entertainment, whisking him around Kent in the side-car of Gibbon's motor-bike, spinning traveller's yarns of Africa and inventor's tales of wonderful new alloys. Gibbon, be it noted, had not only travelled in Russia as a foreign correspondent but used his knowledge of the country to write stories about police and revolutionaries; the role of these stories as stimulus or foil to *Under Western Eyes* remains, like so many questions opened up by Conrad's correspondence, to be established.

Many correspondents familiar from earlier times recur in this volume: the Sanderson, Rothenstein, Colvin, and Garnett families, Cunninghame Graham, Harriet Capes, Sir Hugh Clifford. The letter to Sidney Colvin about *A Personal Record* (28 December 1908) merits particular attention for its anticipations of the 'Familiar Preface'; so does the brace of letters to Edward and to Olivia Garnett (both 20

October 1911) for the attention to the allegedly 'Slav' nature of *Under Western Eyes*. One can not be sure whether the rarity of letters to Henry James reflects the loss of manuscripts or the dwindling of a never intimate friendship. With H. G. Wells one is more certain; Wells marked the letters of 25 September and 3 November 1908 'n[ot] a[nswered]': he told Edwin Pugh (MS Berg, undated) that Conrad had become too respectable.

Arthur Symons did not think so. As editor of the *Savoy*, the scandalous (by English standards) magazine of the nineties, he had taken 'The Idiots', Conrad's first story. In 1908, he wrote an essay hailing Conrad as a celebrant of darkness, violence, and death. Even in the diluted version published in 1915, Symons portrays Conrad 'Like a spider in his web ... discussing human affairs with a calm and cynical ferocity'. Symons's extraordinary piece certainly lit up a shadowy side of Conrad that more squeamish critics had ignored, but the hysterical tone said more about the author than his subject. The author, indeed, was on the verge of madness. Conrad responded calmly: 'Death is a fact, and violent death is a fact too. In the simplicity of my heart, I tried to realize these facts when they came in' ([3, 10, or 17 August 1908]). The refusal to take umbrage suggests that he sensed his critic's wretched mental state. In any case, when Symons was sane enough to read again, Conrad wrote to him with great sympathy and understanding, as to a fellow-sufferer:

I understand you are all alone for a few days so I drop you this note en camarade for company's sake, tho' indeed I have nothing memorable and nothing new to say ... I was glad to see you more alert, more hopeful and altogether better this time. I expect many fine things from you in the future. (7 February 1911)

Symons introduced Conrad to Agnes Tobin, a San Franciscan poet and translator 'who brought to our door', as the dedication of *Under Western Eyes* puts it, 'her genius for friendship from the uttermost shore of the west'. The Sandersons introduced Warrington Dawson, a South Carolinan novelist and journalist whose tiresome bigotry and insinuating ways with the great some readers will find less than attractive. J. G. Huneker wrote appreciations of Conrad. Bliss Carman wanted to publish him. John Quinn, the great patron and collector, began the timely purchase of his manuscripts. James Gordon Bennett, Junior, bought the serial of *Chance* for his *New York Herald*. Often to his financial benefit, sometimes to his displeasure, North America now figured more boldly in Conrad's life, inscribing fresh complexities on his cultural map.

In France, and Belgium too, his reputation continued to wax. Negotiating over translation rights, Conrad corresponded with the Abbé de Smet, Robert d'Humières, and H.-D. Davray. Through Davray, he had already become a familiar of the *Mercure de France* circle. Largely thanks to Agnes Tobin, he was now introduced to the brilliant group of writers that had founded the *Nouvelle Revue Française* in 1908. Among them was Gide, who paid an exuberant call at Capel House in the summer of 1911 with Agnes Tobin and Valery Larbaud. Although Conrad's delays in writing to Gide, a phenomenally energetic correspondent, led to talk of public penance – 'je vais me présenter à sa porte un de ces jours, en chemise de nuit, pieds nus et la corde au cou' (To Ghéon, 22 November 1911) – their friendship became lasting and significant. In later years, Gide was the most artistically ambitious of all Conrad's friends.

During his convalescence, Conrad wrote from Aldington:

To get away from this hole here is my ardent wish. We have found a home in the woods within 4 1/2 miles. It is picturesque and roomy. I *must* have space and silence—silence! I shall get that last there if anywhere outside the grave—which has no space. (To Rothenstein, 20 May 1910)

Capel House proved the happiest of the Conrads' lodgings. It was quiet but not claustrophobic, well supplied with room for congenial visitors. After *Chance* was completed Conrad saw more of his circle, and his letters became less anguished for a while. He had his silence, but a silence on his own terms, broken, when he was ready, by the sound of friends and family. His deafness was no longer the deafness of panic and despair. One may regret the retreat from the intensities of *Under Western Eyes*, but one can hardly grudge Conrad his moment of peace.

Laurence Davies

Dartmouth College

CONRAD'S CORRESPONDENTS
1908–1911

A Vermonter, Henry Mills ALDEN (1836–1919) was appointed managing editor of *Harper's Weekly* in 1863, at the height of the Civil War. In 1908 he became editor of *Harper's Magazine*.

Ralph Wolfe ASHCROFT, a Liverpudlian (1875–1947), was Samuel Langhorne Clemens's business adviser, travelling companion, and secretary. Ashcroft created the Mark Twain Company to make the most of his elderly employer's name, but a series of financial and personal misapprehensions led to their parting company.

As 'Lewis Melville', Lewis Saul BENJAMIN (1874–1932) wrote the lives and edited the letters of many authors, among them Lady Mary Wortley Montagu, Smollett, Sterne, Beckford, and Cobbett. His two-volume biography of Thackeray appeared in 1899.

A Scotsman, David William BONE (1874–1959; knighted 1946) began his career in sailing-ships. In 1899 he joined the Anchor Line, whose senior commander he eventually became. He was captain of the *Tuscania* when Conrad made his voyage to the United States in 1923. Conrad also knew his brothers, Muirhead and James Bone.

Jeanne or Janina, Baronne de BRUNNOW (née Taube, 1854–1943) was a friend from Conrad's boyhood in Cracow when she had been a ward of his uncle, Tadeusz Bobrowski.

Harriet Mary CAPES (1849–1936), who lived in Winchester, wrote inspirational stories for children. A great admirer of Conrad's works, she 'selected and arranged' *Wisdom and Beauty from Conrad* (1915); he dedicated *A Set of Six* to her.

The Canadian poet William Bliss CARMAN (1861–1929) came from New Brunswick. After moving to the U.S., he wrote for *Current Literature*, the New York *Independent*, and the *Atlantic Monthly*. Among his collections of verse were *Sappho* (1902) and *Songs from Vagabondia* (with Richard Hovey, 1894); collections of essays included *Kinship of Nature*

(1904) and *The Poetry of Life* (1905). When he wrote to Conrad, Carman was editing the *Gentleman's Journal*.

Sir Hugh Charles CLIFFORD (1866–1941; knighted 1909), a colonial administrator, was serving as British Resident in Pahang, Malaya, when he wrote one of the earliest general appreciations of Conrad's work. Later, he was appointed to the governorships of Labuan and North Borneo, the Gold Coast, Nigeria, Ceylon, and the Straits Settlements. He published many volumes of stories and sketches, collaborated on a Malay dictionary, and produced a Malay translation of the colonial penal code.

The Rev. Samuel Randal Sproule COLQUHOUN was the curate of Kilmore, Co. Cavan, from 1908 to 1911; beginning in 1930, he was for many years incumbent of St John's, Sandymount, in the seaside suburbs of Dublin.

Sir Sidney COLVIN (1845–1927; knighted 1911) became a good friend to Conrad, as he had been to Stevenson. Colvin had been Slade Professor of Fine Arts at Cambridge and director of the Fitzwilliam Museum; from 1884 to 1912 he was Keeper of Prints and Drawings at the British Museum. Among his literary works were editions of Stevenson's letters and biographies of Landor and Keats.

Jacques COPEAU (1879–1949) was an actor, director, and playwright bent on ridding the Parisian stage of triviality and banality. He founded the Théâtre du Vieux-Colombier; for a brief period in 1940–41, he was administrator of the Comédie Française. Like Gide and Ghéon, he was one of the founders of the *Nouvelle Revue Française* and a contributor to *L'Ermitage*.

Cora CRANE (née Howorth, 1865–1910) had travelled as Stephen's wife. A Jacksonville brothel-keeper, she wrote short stories and had been the first woman war-correspondent to see active service.

Henry-Durand DAVRAY (1873–1944) encouraged French and British writers to know each other better. He appeared regularly in the *Mercure de France* and edited its Collection of Foreign Authors. Among those he translated were Kipling, Meredith, Wells, and Conrad.

Captain, later Major Ernest DAWSON, brother of A. J., was introduced to Conrad by Henley and Wells. Dawson contributed reminiscences and

stories of Burma and Australia to *Blackwood's*; he served in Burma as a magistrate and an officer in the Rangoon Volunteer Rifles.

Francis Warrington DAWSON (1878–1962) came from Charleston, S.C.; his father was a newspaper publisher, and his mother, who followed her son to Paris when he made it his headquarters, belonged to a family of faded plantation-owners. Throughout his life Dawson wrote prolifically: fiction, essays, newspaper stories. He covered strikes, wars, peace conferences, the French Senate and the Chamber of Deputies. In 1909, while on safari in East Africa with Theodore Roosevelt, Dawson met Conrad's old friends the Sandersons. When Dawson came to England in May 1910, intending to report the funeral of Edward VII, he carried an introduction to Conrad.

George Norman DOUGLAS (1868–1952), traveller, polyglot, polymath, wit, and former diplomat, first met Conrad in 1905, on Capri. Douglas's oeuvre, ranging from 'The Herpetology of the Grand Duchy of Baden' (1891) to *Venus in the Kitchen* (1952), includes *South Wind* (1917) and *Old Calabria* (1915).

In his novels and his memoirs, Ford Madox FORD (1873–1939) created some of the best English fiction of the twentieth century. He was also a poet and an inspired editor. At the time of his collaborations with Conrad, however, his list of publications was still short. For consistency's sake, he is called Ford throughout this edition, even though he did not change his surname from Hueffer until 1919.

Ada Nemesis GALSWORTHY, born Ada Pearson (1864–1956), was adopted by Ernest Cooper, a Norwich doctor. As a teenager she studied the piano in Dresden; later, she wrote songs. Officially, she remained married to John Galsworthy's cousin Arthur until the end of 1904, when the death of John, Senior, eased the threat of family sanctions.

John GALSWORTHY (1867–1933) met Conrad in the *Torrens* in 1893. The early work was tentative, but in 1932 he won a Nobel Prize (an honour denied his friend) for his fiction and his plays. Like the Forsytes, his family was well supplied with money, and he helped Conrad with many gifts and loans.

David GARNETT (1892–1981), the future author of *Lady into Fox* (1923) and many other novels, was the son of Constance and Edward.

Edward William GARNETT (1868–1937), a publisher's reader and critic, was the husband of Constance, the translator. Edward lived some and Constance all of the time at the Cearne, a meeting-place for writers, artists, anarchists, socialists, and Russian refugees. Edward's encouragement of Conrad was typical of his generous attention to new writers.

Olivia (or Olive) Rayne GARNETT (1871–1957) was Edward's sister. She published *Petersburg Tales* (1900). As a friend of Stepniak and other political refugees, she was familiar with the background to *Under Western Eyes*.

Robert Singleton GARNETT (1866–1932), Edward's elder brother, was senior partner in the law firm of Darley, Cumberland. During Conrad's illness in 1910, Garnett looked after his literary interests; later, he did the same for D. H. Lawrence. Garnett was a keen book-collector and an authority on Alexandre Dumas, the Elder.

Henri GHÉON was the pseudonym of Henri-Léon Vangeon (1874–1944), poet, critic, and playwright. He published his first collection, *Chansons d'aube*, in 1897; his later work included *Algérie* (another collection of poems) and more than sixty plays. From 1901 to 1909, Vangeon practised medicine in Bray-sur-Seine, his native town. His intimate friendship with André Gide began in 1898; in 1900, they travelled together in Tunisia and Algeria; the two of them were among the founders of the *Nouvelle Revue Française* in 1908. His experience as a military doctor in the First World War turned Vangeon towards Christianity, and he later worked with Claudel.

Maisie GIBBON (née Daniels), a Londoner, married Perceval Gibbon in 1904, when she was 21. Conrad dedicated *Victory* to them both. The marriage was later dissolved.

Reginald Perceval GIBBON (1878–1926) was the son of a Welsh Congregational minister. After a spell in the merchant navy, Gibbon spent five years in southern Africa, was captured and escaped while reporting the Anglo-Boer war as a uniformed correspondent, and then worked for the *Natal Witness*, *Rand Daily Mail*, and *Rhodesian Times*. On his return to London in 1904, he was able to sell a series of South African stories to *Blackwood's*. Thereafter, Gibbon followed a double career writing fiction and journalism. As a foreign correspondent, he travelled

all over Eastern Europe; his novels include *Souls in Bondage* (1904) and *Margaret Harding* (1911). He published as Perceval, but to family and friends he was 'Reggie'.

Of all the literary friends of Conrad's later years, André-Paul-Guillaume GIDE (1869–1951) was the most distinguished and the most artistically remarkable. A born-again pagan and a recidivist puritan, his strengths lay both in intimate autobiography and in ironic fiction. Among his works are *Les Nourritures terrestres* (1897), *L'Immoraliste* (1902), *La Porte étroite* (1909), *Les Caves du Vatican* (1912), and *Les Faux-monnayeurs* (1926). He first met Conrad in July 1911 and dedicated *Voyage au Congo* (1928) to his memory.

Douglas GOLDRING (1887–1960) worked for Ford in his *English Review* days, later published Ford's poetry, and wrote a study of him, *The Last Pre-Raphaelite* (1948). During his long career, Goldring produced essays, memoirs, poems, and books of travel.

Robert Bontine Cunninghame GRAHAM (1852–1936), socialist and (according to some scholars) rightful King of Scotland, had worked and travelled widely in the Americas. He drew on his experiences in many volumes of tales, sketches, and essays and also in his histories of the Spanish conquest. From 1885 to 1892 he represented North-West Lanarkshire in Parliament; he spent four and a half weeks in gaol for his part in the Bloody Sunday demonstration of 1887. His enduring friendship with Conrad began in 1897.

Austin HARRISON (1873–1928), an essayist with a strong interest in German politics and culture, the son of the Positivist Frederic Harrison, took over the editorship of the *English Review* late in 1909, when Sir Alfred Mond dismissed Ford.

Tadaichi HIDAKA (c.1875–1955) was Professor of English and American Literature at Waseda University in Japan. In 1922 he visited Conrad at Oswalds. Hidaka published a bilingual edition of *Some Reminiscences and Amy Foster* in 1929, a volume on *The Background of English and American Literature* in 1933, and *Essays on English and American Literature* in 1937.

Laurence HOUSMAN (1865–1959), brother of the poet, was an illustrator, poet, and playwright. Among his works are *Rue* (1899), *An*

Englishwoman's Love Letters (anonymously, 1900), *The Chinese Lantern* (1908), *Victoria Regina* (1924), and illustrations to Christina Rossetti's *Goblin Market*.

Elsie HUEFFER (née Martindale, 1876–1949), married Ford in 1894. She wrote several novels and published her translations from de Maupassant in 1903.

Ford Madox HUEFFER: see FORD.

Aymeric-Eugène-Robert, Vicomte d'HUMIÈRES (1868–1915), an author and translator, active in the Théâtre des Arts. Well known to Wharton and James and close to Marcel Proust, he was to die in a hopeless charge on the German lines. Among the works he translated were Kipling's *Plain Tales from the Hills* and Lew Wallace's *Ben Hur*. His translation of *The Nigger* appeared in 1909 as a serial and 1910 as a book.

James Gibbons HUNEKER (1857–1921) wrote fiction and what he called 'impressionist' criticism of literature, art, and music, chiefly modern. He knew France and French literature, admired Polish culture, and had been a friend of Stephen Crane in New York. Huneker refused the credit for 'discovering' Conrad in the United States but wrote often and enthusiastically about him.

Henry JAMES (1843–1916): Conrad's friendship with the Master began with the presentation of *An Outcast* in 1896, reciprocated by a gift of *The Spoils of Poynton* in 1897. They met infrequently.

Louis-Joseph LABAT lived in Bayonne. In choosing for translation such authors as Conan Doyle and A. E. W. Mason, he showed a taste for detective and adventure stories.

John Edward LONG (1889–1940) became president of the Greater New York News Service.

Edward Verrall LUCAS (1868–1938) was a critic, journalist, children's story-teller, and surreal humorist who knew Conrad by way of Garnett. Lucas worked for Methuen for many years.

Wincenty LUTOSŁAWSKI (1863–1954) was a Polish philosopher and zealous nationalist. He wrote to Conrad while he was studying in London; later he taught in Cracow, Geneva, Lausanne, London, Paris, and Vilnius, where he held the chair of philosophy from 1919 to 1928. In his work, he attempted to combine Platonism with the belief that Poland is the Messiah among nations. His *The Origin and Growth of Plato's Logic* (1897), published in English, established the chronology of Plato's work. An unstable man, he suffered a number of nervous breakdowns.

William MAAS worked for the literary department of the *Daily Chronicle*. Later, he was a contributor to *Punch* and editor of the *Winner*.

Robert Dunbar MACKINTOSH (1865–1934) practised in Barnes, South West London. From 1909 to 1921, when they had a falling out, Conrad valued the company and the advice of this Scottish doctor, an amateur playwright and inventor described by his great-niece as 'an unpractical enthusiast and dreamer' (Jellard, p. 95).

As 'Archibald Marshall', Arthur Hammond MARSHALL (1866–1934) wrote a multitude of novels and critical essays. He was a partner in the short-lived publishing house of Alston Rivers and worked for a time on the *Daily Mail*.

David Storrar MELDRUM (1864–1940) was the literary adviser in Blackwood's London office; he became a partner in 1903 and retired in 1910. Among the first to recognize Conrad's talent, he published a novel himself in 1902.

Algernon METHUEN (originally Stedman, 1856–1924; baronetcy 1916) founded his company in 1889. Besides text-books, the source of the firm's prosperity, he published works by Kipling, Stevenson, and Maeterlinck; between 1906 and 1915 he brought out six Conrad titles.

Edward MOORE was Pinker's assistant until 1911.

Sir William Robertson NICOLL (1851–1923), founded the *Bookman* in 1886 and remained its editor; he also started the *British Weekly* and the *British Monthly*. A Scotsman with strong ties to the Nonconformist churches, Nicoll often wrote as 'Claudius Clear'; his was a powerful influence on late Victorian and Edwardian literary taste. He collabo-

rated with T. J. Wise on *Literary Anecdotes of the Nineteenth Century* (1895–1896).

James Brand PINKER (1863–1922), a Scot, was one of the first literary agents in London. Over the years his clients included Ford, James, Crane, Wells, Bennett, and D. H. Lawrence. He began acting for Conrad in 1900 and helped him through many financial crises, but a serious quarrel in 1910 suspended their relationship for several months and strained it for many more.

Carlo PLACCI (1861–1941), a literary critic, musicologist, and poet, lived in Florence. He wrote articles on Conrad for the *Corriere della Sera* and *Il Marzocco*. Violet Paget ('Vernon Lee') described him as 'a well known Italian polyglot & critic'.

Marguerite PORADOWSKA (née Gachet, 1848–1937) was the widow of Conrad's cousin, and thus his 'Aunt' – but also his good friend. Her novels of French, Belgian, and Polish life were well known in their day.

John QUINN (1870–1924), the son of Irish immigrants, came from Ohio. As a New York lawyer, he had a highly lucrative practice in commercial and financial law, particularly the law of tariffs. As a supporter of the arts, he won an exemption for artists from sales taxes and built up a great collection of modern painting and sculpture; he was the chief private buyer at the Armory show in 1913. He also amassed modern literary manuscripts; among the writers he collected on a large scale were Yeats, Pound, Eliot, Joyce, and Conrad. When Quinn auctioned off his Conradiana in 1923, several years after relations between patron and author had chilled, manuscripts and inscribed volumes bought for a total of $10,000 fetched $110,000.

Stephen REYNOLDS (1881–1919) was one of Edward Garnett's protégés. In 1906, moved and fascinated by the hard life of the Devon fisheries, Reynolds settled in Sidmouth, where he shared a cottage with the Woolleys, a fishing family. His books about what he saw and did include *A Poor Man's House* (1908) and *Alongshore* (1910). With Bob and Tom Woolley, he collaborated on *Seems So! A Working-Class View of Politics* (1911).

Agnes Mary RIDGEWAY (née Sanderson, 1875–1967) was Ted's second-oldest sister. The affectionate enmity between Conrad and 'Miss

Agnes' began around 1894, the time of his first visit to the boisterous household at Elstree. In 1908 she married the Rev. Neville Vibart Ridgeway, a master first at Elstree then at Tonbridge.

Arthur Llewelyn ROBERTS (1855–1919) was Secretary of the Royal Literary Fund, an institution that helps needy writers.

Henry Chalmers ROBERTS (1870–1940), a Texan, had been a junior diplomat and a war-correspondent for the *Daily News, Daily Mail*, and *Brooklyn Eagle* before he came to London in 1906; from then until 1932 he edited the English edition of the magazine known variously as *World's Work* and *World Today*. He became a director at Heinemann, the magazine's British publisher.

William ROTHENSTEIN (1872–1945; knighted 1931), was notable for his portrait graphics, paintings, and drawings. Max Beerbohm described him as a young phenomenon in 'Enoch Soames' (*Seven Men*): 'He wore spectacles that flashed more than any other pair ever seen. He was a wit. He was brimful of ideas... He knew everyone in Paris.'

Agnes SANDERSON: see RIDGEWAY.

Edward Lancelot ('Ted') SANDERSON (1867–1939) took passage in the *Torrens* in 1893; on that voyage, Conrad read him a draft of *Almayer's Folly*. Sanderson taught at Elstree, his family's preparatory school in Hertfordshire. After service in the Boer War he remained in Africa, first in Johannesburg then in Nairobi, where he served as Town Clerk; soon after his return, in 1910, he became Headmaster of Elstree.

Helen Mary SANDERSON (née Watson, c. 1874–1967) married Ted in 1898. She was a Scotswoman full of moral and intellectual vigour. As 'Janet Allardyce', she contributed sketches of East African life to *Scribner's Magazine*.

Geneviève SÉLIGMANN-LUI translated *Almayer's Folly* (1919) and Edward Gordon Craig's *The Art of the Theatre*.

The Abbé Joseph de SMET (1870–1933) was a Belgian priest and writer who became Inspector General of Catholic Education. By no means a traditionalist, he felt a great enthusiasm for the poetry of Emile

Verhaeren, of whom he published a study (Malines, 1909). After translating 'Typhoon', de Smet turned to *Nostromo*. His 1912 essay on Conrad in the *Mercure de France* was the first in French.

Yeats's friend Arthur SYMONS (1865–1945) wrote poetry, essays, and fiction. As a critic he showed broad tastes in literature, music, and painting, and spoke up for such then-neglected or misread figures as Baudelaire and Blake. In 1896, Symons took 'The Idiots', the first short story Conrad ever sold, for *The Savoy*. In 1925, Symons published *Notes on Joseph Conrad*.

An Anglo-Welsh poet and an ally of Robert Frost, Edward THOMAS (1878–1917) was killed in the First World War. He supported himself by a prodigious output of literary journalism and popular scholarship. Garnett's close friend, he often attended the Mont Blanc lunches; it was probably there that he met Conrad and Gibbon.

Agnes TOBIN (1864–1939) came from San Francisco. She knew Gide, Yeats (who called her the greatest American poet since Whitman), Alice Meynell, and many other literary people. Her own work included plays and translations from Petrarch. Conrad, whom she put in touch with John Quinn, praised 'her genius for friendship' in the dedication of *Under Western Eyes*.

Thomas Fisher UNWIN (1848–1935) published Conrad's first three books. Neither his business practices nor his adherence to the Liberal party endeared him to Conrad.

VANGEON: see GHÉON

Herbert George WELLS (1866–1946) began his friendship with Conrad with anonymous reviews of *Almayer's Folly* and *An Outcast*. They were good friends for over ten years, and Conrad liked the scientific romances such as *The Invisible Man* and *The Time Machine*, but their differing social, literary, and political ideas led to an estrangement.

EDITORIAL PROCEDURES

Hoping to balance the comfort of the reader against the requirements of the scholar, we have adopted the following conventions:

1. The texts stay faithful to Conrad's spelling, accentuation, and punctuation, but letters missing from within words are supplied in square brackets. Rather than use *sic*, we mark words that might be taken as misprints with an asterisk. Missing apostrophes are not restored.

2. Where absolutely necessary for the sense, missing pronouns, prepositions, and auxiliary verbs are also supplied in brackets. Gaps in the text, such as those caused by damage to the MS, appear thus: [...]. [?] marks a doubtful reading.

3. Again when sense dictates, full-stops are tacitly provided and quotation marks completed; words apparently repeated by accident have been deleted. A list of silent emendations will be found at the end of the volume.

4. Especially in pronouns, Conrad used capitals more profusely than other English writers of his time. We preserve his usage, but distinguishing between upper and lower case must often be a matter of judgment rather than certainty. The same is true of locating paragraph breaks.

5. For the letters in French we observe the same conventions, but use square brackets and asterisks more sparingly. Conrad's erratic accentuation we leave as it is, except in texts from *L. fr.*, where some presumed misprints or misreadings have been changed.

6. For the convenience of those who do not read the letters in sequence, information in footnotes may appear more than once.

7. Although he kept the surname Hueffer until 1919, Conrad's collaborator is called Ford Madox Ford throughout the edition. His first wife (who always kept the name) appears as Elsie Hueffer, and the couple as the Hueffers.

8. American readers should note that Conrad used the British system of abbreviating dates; thus 3.6 would mean 3 June, not 6 March.

9. In this and subsequent volumes the Nonesuch rather than the less reliable Bobbs-Merrill edition of the letters to Garnett provides the copy-text when no manuscript is available.

10. This edition collects all available letters, but only the more interesting telegrams; references to most others appear in the notes.

11. In the provenance headings, letters that have appeared only in microfilmed dissertations or as disjointed fragments in books or articles are described as unpublished. Letters appearing in fuller but still incomplete form are described as published in part.

12. The heading TS/MS denotes a typed letter in which passages other than the salutation or farewell are handwritten.

Variations in stationery often help to date Conrad's letters. At Someries, he used three varieties of printed stationery: for an illustration of type one letterhead, please see Volume 3, p. xlii.

Type one (24 October 1907 to 31 March 1908): watermark LONDON CONQUEROR; the left edge of the first E in SOMERIES is over the middle of the N in LUTON

Type two (4 March 1908 to [25? July 1908]): watermark J.S. & CO. ORIGINAL HARD SIZED; SOMERIES slightly farther to the right, but not as far as in type three

Type three ([28? July 1908] to 14 November 1908): watermark J.S. & CO. ORIGINAL HARD SIZED; the left edge of the E flush with the right edge of the N.

There were two Aldington letterheads:
Type one ([2 September 1909] to [13 or 20 January 1910]):

Type two (3 May 1910 to 18 June 1910): in the telegraphic address, ALDINGTON and HYTHE are joined with a bracket, and CONRAD is omitted; NR is omitted from the postal address.

There were two Capel House letterheads:
Type one (26 June 1910 to 29 December 1911):

TELEGRAMS:- } HAMSTREET.
STATION:-

CAPEL HOUSE,

ORLESTONE,

Nᴿ ASHFORD.

Type two: used from January 1912 onwards, this letterhead has no bracket on the left-hand side.

Until the spring of 1917, Capel House stationery had no watermark.

1908

To Elsie Hueffer

Text MS Yale; Unpublished

[letterhead: Someries]
1 Jan 1908

Dearest Señora.[1]

May this new year bring you health is our most ardent wish. I've been too dismal and morally unwholesome to come near you. It's absolutely a fact. I dared not.

I can't help feeling glad that we couldn't find anything for you in this neighbourhood. You have no idea of the soul corroding bleakness of earth and sky here when the east wind blows.[2] We had a fiendish 10 days of it. I am sure you would have been the worse for it.

Of course I've had gout. That is the refrain of my doleful existence. I should think the world must be tired of it—but I have no other time for my friends. It is played to the accompaniment of gnashing teeth and ends in a howling note.

Do ask Ford to let me know how Sandgate agreed with you.[3] A post-card is no great matter.

With love from us all.

Your most affectionate and
obedient servant
J. Conrad.

To David Meldrum

Text MS Duke; Blackburn 190

[letterhead: Someries]
1st Jan 1908

Dear Mr Meldrum.[4]

May every good attend You and Yours through all this coming year and for all years to come.

I haven't had the heart to write after our return from our disastrous

1 Elsie Hueffer (née Martindale, 1876–1949), married Ford in 1894. She wrote several novels and published her translations from Maupassant in 1903.

2 Someries stood on high ground near Luton, Bedfordshire.

3 She had gone to the seaside for her health, while Ford remained in London (Mizener, *The Saddest Story*, p. 131).

4 David Storrar Meldrum (1864–1940) was the literary adviser in Blackwood's London office; he became a partner in 1903 and retired in 1910. Among the first to recognize Conrad's talent, he published a novel himself in 1902.

trip abroad. Borys had two illnesses, both grave, one of them rh[e]umatic fever with pleuresy*. We went away for 8 weeks and had to stay no less than eight months away in hotels with doctors hovering around all the time.[1] It was a ghastly and ruinous time—it won't bear talking about.

Since we got back and moved (in September) into this new home I have had gout twice. From the last bout I've just got up to day. I would not begin a new Year in bed.

Don't think that my silence arose from forgetfulness. That could not be. No day passes for me without mental reference to the few good friends of whom you are one. We have been deeply touched at you and dear Mrs Meldrum remembering the boy. I can't tell you sufficiently how glad I am. The last book hasn't done so well as it looks on the surface.[2] Still Methuen professes himself very well satisfied.

Believe me always

with great regard and affection

J. Conrad.

To Marguerite Poradowska
Text MS Yale; Rapin 186; G. & S. 109

[letterhead: Someries]
1 Jan. 1908

Chere Margueritte*.[3]

Mille souhaits de bonheur de la part de nous tous.

Merci de Votre bonne lettre. Depuis notre retour j'ai été malade deux fois; toujours la goutte. Je viens de me lever aujourd'hui car je ne veux pas commencer la nouvelle année au lit.

Depuis le mois de Sept. nous sommes dans cette nouvelle maison— Elle est plus grande que le Pent et possède un vieux jardin entouré de murs. L'aspect du pays est tout à fait différent aussi. Nous sommes aussi loin de la mer qu'il est possible de l'être en Angleterre.

Borys est a l'école ou il travaille bien, même tres bien.[4] Du Samedi midi au Lundi matin nous l'avons chez nous. L'école est a 7 kilomètres d'ici a peu près. Jack a une légère bronchite en ce moment-ci. Il

[1] First in Montpellier, then in Geneva.
[2] Methuen had published *The Secret Agent* in September.
[3] Marguerite Poradowska (née Gachet, 1848–1937) was the widow of Conrad's cousin, and thus his 'Aunt' – but also his good friend. Her novels of French, Belgian, and Polish life were well known in their day.
[4] Borys would be ten on the 15th.

commence a marcher mais il ne parle presque pas.[1] Jessie souffre
beaucoup du genou.[2] Elle a du courage comme toujours. Moi je suis
fatigué et attristé. Le travail m'est très difficile et les affaires en general
ne marchent pas. Mon dernier livre a eu quelque succès—comme
toujours. On a même fait quelque peu de bruit autour; mais quand* a la
vente c'est toujours la vieille histoire. Je suis un de ceux qui ne se
vendent pas.[3] Et voilà la cinquantaine commencée![4] Enfin! Nous Vous
embrassons tous bien fort

<div style="text-align:center">Le Votre de tout son coeur
Conrad</div>

PS J'ai ecrit a cette chère pauvre Angela.[5] En voilà une autre qui a
besoin de tout son courage. J'ai eu une bonne lettre d'elle mais il parait
que ses yeux vont bien mal.

Translation

Dear Marguerite,
 Many good wishes for your happiness from us all.
 Thanks for your good letter. Since our return, I've been ill twice: gout,
as usual. I have just got up today, as I don't want to start the new year in
bed.
 We have been in this new house since September—It is larger than
the Pent and has an old garden surrounded by walls. The look of the
countryside is also quite different. We are as far from the sea as one can
be in England.
 Borys is at school, where he is working well, even very well. From
Saturday noon to Monday morning we have him at home. The school is
about seven kilometers from here. Jack has a touch of bronchitis at
present. He is starting to walk, but he hardly talks. Jessie suffers a good
deal from her knee. She is brave as ever. I myself am tired and dejected.
Working is very difficult for me, and my affairs in general do not go well.

[1] Jack (John Conrad) would be seventeen months the next day.
[2] An accident in 1904 had exacerbated a teenage injury. Despite various cures and
operations, the knee tormented Jessie Conrad for the rest of her life.
[3] A justifiable complaint until the success of *Chance* (1914).
[4] Conrad was born in December 1857.
[5] Aniela Zagórska, the widow of Conrad's cousin Karol; there are no known letters to her
between 25 December 1899 and 9 October 1914.

My last book has had some success—as usual. There was even a certain stir about it, but as for sales, it's the same old story. I am one of those who don't sell. And my fifties have begun! Still! We all embrace you heartily

<div align="right">Yours most affectionately</div>

<div align="right">Conrad</div>

PS I've written to poor dear Angela. That's someone else who needs all her courage. I had a good letter from her, but it seems that her eyes are troubling her.

To H. G. Wells

Text MS Illinois; Unpublished

<div align="right">[letterhead: Someries]</div>

<div align="right">1st Jan 1908</div>

Dear Wells.[1]

May all good attend you and yours.

The first instalment of your story in the PMM[2] opens the year brilliantly. How good You are in presenting the human interest of a story in terms of jesting. It is superexcellent that gift of yours. And how amusing you can be! I don't mean merely entertaining but amusing. Anybody almost may be entertaining in the way of statement—but how many writers have been amusing? I couldn't use the fingers of one hand in numbering them. Swift was that. I can think just now of no one else with that quality which in you is so pronounced. It is the vehicle of your thought as it were. *Time Machine* so deeply interesting had it not. It burst out—so to speak—later. The *First Men*—the *Sea Lady*—above all *Kipps* are alive, resplendent with it.[3] Others too of course; and almost all the short stories.

May you continue many, many years this work of making us think and feel while we are amused.

I've been gouty ever since Boxing day; but I got up to-day—so as to

[1] Herbert George Wells (1866–1946) began his friendship with Conrad with anonymous reviews of *Almayer's Folly* and *An Outcast*. They were good friends for over ten years, and Conrad liked the scientific romances such as *The Invisible Man* and *The Time Machine*, but their differing social, literary, and political ideas led to an estrangement.

[2] *The War in the Air* in the *Pall Mall Magazine*. Like 'The Duel', it began serialization in the January number. The serial soon modulated from suburban comedy set in a future full of mechanical wonders to visions of global carnage.

[3] *The Time Machine* came out in 1895, *The First Men in the Moon* in 1901, *The Sea Lady* in 1902, and *Kipps* in 1905.

begin the new year on my feet anyhow. A superstitious feeling nerved me for the effort.

<div style="text-align:center">Affectionately yours</div>

<div style="text-align:right">J. Conrad.</div>

PS A young man called Reynolds (Stephen)[1] has been here for a day or two. We talked—or rather I let him talk—of you. It was intelligent talk. You put your impress on the minds of the younger generation. An enviable achievement. That youth can write a bit too.

To J. B. Pinker

Text MS Berg; Unpublished

<div style="text-align:right">[letterhead: Someries]
Thursday. [2 January 1908][2]</div>

Dear Pinker[3]

I send you Razumov *51 to 70.*[4]

It has got to be what fate wills it but it won't be a mean thing. If you get the end by Monday I won't be a week late on the date I fixed for myself. Please have it run through the machine 1 copy only as it will have to be corrected considerably—perhaps.

I am in good working trim. R shall make two inst: of 7000 each. And he who reads the first shall want to read the second. I feel strongly in favour of *Fort: Rev:*[5] I should like the thing to attract attention.

Please send me £20 for rent made out to B. Cole Esq*re*.[6] I had two reminders. It was due on the 19*th*. I enclose an account which can be settled direct by You. Please send me also a cheque for *£1.10* and one for £3. extra this week.

[1] Reynolds (1881–1919) wrote about the Devonshire fishing-people with whom he had chosen to live.

[2] Marked as received in Pinker's office, January 1908. Conrad refers to the Parisian newspaper he requested on 30 December.

[3] James Brand Pinker (1863–1922), a Scot, was one of the first literary agents in London. Over the years his clients included Ford, James, Crane, Wells, Bennett, and D. H. Lawrence. He began acting for Conrad in 1900 and helped him through many financial crises.

[4] Begun by 4 December, the origin of *Under Western Eyes*, and still envisaged as a substantial short story. Keith Carabine gives a comprehensive account of its progress in the Chronology of the Cambridge *Under Western Eyes*, edited by Carabine and David Leon Higdon, forthcoming.

[5] The *Fortnightly Review* published Conrad's essay 'Autocracy and War' in 1905; it, too, attended to Russian politics.

[6] Agent for Sir Julius Wernher, owner of the Luton Hoo estate.

The *Chance* has not been wholly neglected.[1] Its the main thing. Thanks for your letter and good wishes. I suppose I will get the Petit Jour[n]al of the first tomorrow.[2] You are very good to let me trouble you with these trifles.

<div style="text-align: center">Yours</div>

<div style="text-align: right">Conrad.</div>

To John Galsworthy
Text MS Forbes; J-A, 2, 64 (in part)[3]

<div style="text-align: right">[letterhead: Someries]
6th Jan of the New Year
1908</div>

Dearest Jack[4]

May you be ever happy (I am writing to the Signora Ada separately[5]) may your shadow never grow less and your fame always increase.

As to me: the old story of which no doubt you are sick by this time. Gout. I am not like M^r Peter Magnus—I afford no entertainement* to my friends.[6] Gout since Boxing day to this time of writing. I never really shook off the fit of it I had 3 weeks before Your dinner.[7] And indeed I've known not a single moment of bodily ease since we got into this new house:—

"Et le misérable écrivait toujours!"[8]

He is writing now a story the title of which is *Razumov*. Isn't it expressive. I think that I am trying to capture the very soul of things Russian—Cosas de Russia. It is not an easy work but it may be rather good when it's done. It may also be worth a hundred £ if the good Pinker flies round with it actively enough to become crimson[9] . . . But there's no

1 Originally a short story: Conrad began to consider *Chance* as a novel in autumn 1905 (*Letters*, 3, pp. 280, 287), laid it aside first for *The Secret Agent*, then for *Under Western Eyes*, and finished it in 1912.

2 With its announcement of lucky numbers in the French national lottery.

3 As far as 'with Borys abroad', without reference to Galsworthy's loans.

4 John Galsworthy (1867–1933) met Conrad in the *Torrens* in 1893. His early work was tentative, but in 1932 he won a Nobel Prize (an honour denied his friend) for his fiction and his plays. Like the Forsytes, his family was well supplied with money, and he helped Conrad with many gifts and loans.

5 Galsworthy's wife, a musician and translator.

6 Mr Peter Magnus, a 'red-haired man with an inqusitive nose and blue spectacles', delights complaisant friends by signing his letters 'Afternoon': *Pickwick Papers*, 22.

7 In London, 10 December.

8 'And the wretch kept on writing' – just as Mâtho, the dying rebel in Flaubert's *Salammbô*, kept on walking.

9 Turning from a mild to a revolutionary colour?

heart in my jokes. Listen to the theme: The Student Razumov (a natural son of a Prince K——) gives up secretly to the police his fellow Student Haldin who seeks refuge in his rooms after com[m]itting a political crime (supposed to be the murder of de Plehve[1]). First movement in St Petersburg. (Haldin is hanged of course). [in margin] "done"
 2d in Geneva: The Student Razumov meeting abroad the mother and sister of Haldin falls in love with that last, marries her and after a time confesses to her the part he played in the arrest and death of her brother. [in margin] "to do"
 The psychological developments leading to Razumov's betrayal of Haldin, to his confession of the fact to his wife and to the death of these people (brought about mainly by the resemblance of their child to the late Haldin) form the real subject of the story.
 And perhaps no magazine will touch it. B'wood since the old man has retired do not care much to have my work.[2] I think of trying the Forty. Ah my dear You don't know what an inspiration-killing anxiety it is to think:—is it saleable? There's nothing more cruel than to be caught between one's impulse, one's art and that question which for me simply is a question of life and death. There are moments when the unholy fear sweeps my head clean of every thought. It is agonizing—no less. And—you know—that pressure grows from day to day instead of getting less.
 But I had to write it. I had to get away from *Chance* with which I was making no serious progress.
 Otherwise things are not well with me. The S[ecret] A[gent] may be pronounced by now an honourable failure. It brought me neither love nor promise of literary success. I own that I am cast down. I suppose I am a fool to have expected anything else. I suppose there is something in me that is unsympathetic to the general public—because the novels of Hardy, for instance, are generally tragic enough and gloomily written too—and yet they have sold in their time and are selling to the present day.[3]

1 Vyacheslav Konstantinovich, the harsh and fanatical Minister of the Interior, was killed outright on 15 July 1904 by a bomb hurled at his carriage by Egor Sazonov. De Plehve was particularly hateful to Poles, Jews, Lithuanians, and Finns, the victims of his policy of 'Russification'.
2 William Blackwood (1836–1912) published *Youth* and *Lord Jim* in book and serial forms. His relations with Conrad were strained by a financial disagreement in May 1902. Blackwood accepted two *Mirror of the Sea* essays for *Blackwood's Edinburgh Magazine*, but in April 1906 rejected 'The Brute' (Blackburn, p. 188).
3 Even though Hardy abandoned long fiction after writing *Jude*, sales of his earlier works had made him prosperous; the recent Macmillan Pocket Edition of his works added to

Foreignness I suppose.

All this is matter for anxious thought. Will the long novel[1] serialize? If it does not! I shouldn't wonder if P[inker] were not anxious about that too. He does not hurry me up but is very expectant. It must be confessed that the work of the last three months makes a miserable show—as to the quantity. And I have sat and sat days and days—It is an impossible existence. I am a vegetarian now. I eat very little too on purpose. The head is very clear just now but there are moments when I think against my will that I must give up. It's fatal for an imaginative man—this illomened* suggestion coming like that from outside as it were. I fight it down of course—while I can.

I have cast up my account at the beginning of my 50[th] year. Eleven novels. If each had averaged £1000 I would have now 5000 in hand. For casting up all I owe you; other debts, the balance against me with P (1572 to date) and the grant I had[2] together with all I have earned it works out at £650 p year in round numbers. Even if I have made a mistake of a 100 a year too little which is improbable (for however carelessly I counted I am not likely to have underestimated all I had by 1200 pounds st[erling]) this is not outrageously extravagant. And in this there's Jessie's illness, all of my own—(the year wasted when writing Nostromo when I had six fits of gout in eleven months)—and this last fatal year with Borys abroad.

That last was very bad—for pressed by necessity (when a child is ill one does not stop to count) I have had to use all the money remitted by Pinker—it was none too much—and have left a lot of bills unpaid in Kent.[3] I have managed to pick up some by this time (and that's not so bad as I also reduced my balance with P by just a hundred since last Aug[st] the 10[th]) with the greatest difficulty. But there is a residuum and naturally enough some of the people (not all) are dunning me pretty hard. I talked over things with P a week or so before Xmas. He confessed to me that he was pinched for money, in a sufficiently convincing manner. No doubt if the *SA* had showed a brisk sale or even if there had

this prosperity: Michael Millgate, *Thomas Hardy: A Biography* (New York: Random House, 1982), p. 457, n.

[1] *Chance.*

[2] £300 from the Royal Literary Fund, July 1902; £500 from the Royal Bounty, March 1905.

[3] Incurred while living at Pent Farm.

been more of *Chance* in hand he would have made an effort.† All I could arrange with him did not amount to much. He agreed that if I could find the money (£60) he would pay it off at the rate of £3 a month; not a very brilliant affair to propose to any one—nearly two years to pay off. After that I went home and got a bad foot. I haven't budged from here of course and have made no effort in any direction. For indeed where could I go? This miserable worry got on my nerves so that I throw all decency to the winds. I am too weary to resist as I ought to the idea of asking you whether you could advance me the sum on these conditions—and no others. To be paid off in 20 monthly instalments. Directly I hear from you in that sense I shall renew my verbal agreement with P though he told me distinctly enough that I can count on that. The truth is that I get my living expenses (other than the six pounds a week for Jessie) with considerable difficulty from him. Jess after she paid the gardener out of it and the household washing (some 30/- or more) does not find this a penny too much. But write too in another sense without compunction my dear good patient Jack. To have done so much for me materially and morally is no reason to do more. Your friendship has been a great support to me and that I am not likely to lose in any case. Little less or little more worry does not matter much in a sense.

Borys has a good report from school. A determined and intelligent worker. He never lost an hour which is not bad considering that we more than once sent him off on a monday lame and with a swollen wrist. Several afternoons he has been kept from play too. Imagine that he has most marks in Latin (!!!) next comes arithmetic and next . . . scripture!!! He also seems to have a sort of painstaking aptitude for drawing—but no gift in any sense I think. Still with a miserable dozen of lessons he can draw better now than I ever could after months and months of

†There is to begin the year with: 150 due for *Duel* in Eng[land]. 70 agreed for same in US. Then a vol of short stories ready for which 200 can be got in both countries[1] and also *Razumov* will be done in a few days—say 100 (serial rights here *and US*). It ought to bring *that* if it brings anything at all. So it's not so bad. But P is afraid I will lag with *Chance* and wants to keep hold of as much as he can to dole out for my living expenses. Moreover the volume could not appear much before June.

1 The British edition of *A Set of Six*, which included 'The Duel', came out in 1908; in the United States, where 'The Duel' had been published separately as *The Point of Honor* (1908), this collection did not appear until 1915.

teaching.[1] Anyway in the second half term he got 260 marks out of a possible 293. But his handwriting is simply abominable. Atrocious. And it used to be quite nice.

He has not a very lively time; he plays the part of the devoted son to me coming in several times a day to see whether he can do something for me—for I am very crippled and once anchored before the table can not budge very well. He stood the frost well but as the thaw came he got a swollen elbow. This rh[e]umatism still hangs on about him. Hackney[2] told us it was sure to. But he is more solid-looking and has a good colour.

I give slack rein to my paternal instincts but dear Jack if I didn't write to you about my children to whom could I write of them.

Jackolo also is quite ill these two days. Bronchitis and lots of fever. We hope it's nothing worse than teething. Eye teeth are generally troublesome. He is simply a charming invalid reasonable and quiet. Of course he is very exacting; has been hardly out of Jessies arms for the last 40 hours; but he opens his beak for medicine with touching readiness and has never even whined once. Teeth or not it's evident he feels very ill. To night as I write the fever seems less. And so the year begins.

Jess very game but that knee is getting worse that's clear. Otherwise she seems well enough. If she knew I was writing to you she would send her love. It was dear of you both to remember the children. Borys has become a Turnerite.[3] But the text being written by Lewis Hind inspires him with mistrust. He knows Hind from the old Winchelsea days.[4] Jackolo was extremely surprised at the horse. When are you coming back?

<div style="text-align:center">Yours ever</div>

<div style="text-align:right">J Conrad.</div>

[1] For samples of Conrad's drawings see Karl, *Three Lives*, between pp. 412 and 413.

[2] Clifford Hackney (1874–1956), friend and family doctor.

[3] Having seen Hind's edition of *Turner: Five Letters and a Postscript* (1907), with eight colour plates.

[4] When the Hueffers lived there: Conrad also did some reviewing for him while Hind (1862–1927) was editor of the *Academy*.

To Arthur Llewelyn Roberts

Text MS RLF; Unpublished

[letterhead: Someries]

6. Jan 1908

Llewellyn* Roberts Esq^{re}

Dear Sir.[1]

I am requested by my friend M^r Ford Maddox* Hueffer[2] to vouch for the facts stated in his application to the R. L. Fund.

I have been aware for some time past of his material difficulties caused by unexpected money losses and the long illness of his wife.[3] As to the first I don't think they have been brought about by any lack of common prudence in the management of his affairs. As to the second I know that from the nature of the case the expenses have been very heavy indeed and are likely to go on unfortunately for an indefinite time.

The merits of the applicant lie open to the enlightened and broad-minded competency of the Committee. His work:—verse, essays, fiction and criticism—a considerable performance in itself appears to hold too the promise of a still more noteworthy achievement. The certitude that with his rare talent and unimpeachable industry he can not fail to retrieve his position, if tided over the present difficulty, may be a further argument in his favour as a subject for the R. L. Fund's assistance.[4]

I am dear Sir

very faithfully yours

Joseph Conrad

[1] Arthur Llewelyn Roberts (1855–1919) was Secretary of the Royal Literary Fund, a charity that helps needy writers.

[2] For consistency's sake, he is known throughout this edition as Ford Madox Ford, the name taken in 1919.

[3] Elsie Hueffer's illness, tuberculosis of the kidney, was not properly diagnosed until May 1908 (Mizener, p. 137). What Mizener (p. 126) calls 'Ford's permanent financial difficulties' had been worsened by Pinker's failure to place *The 'Half Moon'* and a taste for London life.

[4] A note on the letter by one of the fund's officials reads: 'Hueffer was not awarded a grant as both his debts and his income were considerably higher than the average applicant['s].'

To J. B. Pinker

Text MS Berg; Unpublished

[letterhead: Someries]
Wednesday.
6pm. 7 Jan. 08

My dear Pinker.

I have just sent off 8 or 10 pp of Razumov. I have more in hand and shall start writing again about 9 o'clock till one in the morning. I am anxious to throw that story off my chest.

You may let any Editor know that C. would shorten it (in reason) for serial publication. But I think that L. W.* Courtney[1] might be approached on the ground of the story's essential seriousness—a contribution to and a reading of the Russian character. It is just the fiction for a review of the *Fort*^y's standing. In the States I've no doubt it will be appreciated and shall find a home easily. But perhaps You have other views for England.

Here is given the very essence of things Russian. Not the mere outward manners and customs but the Russian feeling and thought. You may safely say that. And, I think, the story is effective. It is also characteristic of the present time. Nothing of the sort had* been done in English. The subject has long haunted me. Now it must come out.

I have looked through the acc^t with an anxious eye. Anyway the debt at the present time is less than it was on <u>Augst 10</u>th, on our return from the ill fated journey abroad, by some £50.[2] And we have lived—and not only that: a lot of expenses which are not of a permanent sort have been met. The sixty You did let me have and certainly no less than another sixty connected with the moving operations. But we are fixed and You shall see that as time goes on I shall grow lighter on your hands. The old incubus[3] still hangs on but it grows less and less. Anyway to begin the year there is the payment for Duel—150. There shall be the vol of short stories. And in this connection I beg You to consider the advisability of publishing them as soon as the *Duel's* serial pub: permits.[4] I think my name should be shoved forward while we can. And at any rate there would be no room in one vol for three big machines like *Strong Man*[5] *the Duel* and *Razumov*. That last story in its sustained intensity would not be appropriate, either, for that collection. It shall

[1] William Leonard Courtney (1850–1928), prolific author, and editor of the *Fortnighly Review*.
[2] See *Letters*, 3, pp. 459–64. [3] The debt of over £1,500.
[4] *Pall Mall Magazine*, January–May 1908.
[5] 'Gaspar Ruiz'.

form the nucleus of another *vol*. It is altogether on another plane. The fact is my dear Pinker I haven't yet given my measure. I am not thinking of the writing—the style. It is something else that I am thinking of—what may be called "my powers". You know well that in fact nobody who was "aware" of my literary existence expected anything like the *Secret Agent*.[1] Well there is more—and different things too—in me yet. This is what I mean.

But coming back to what I was saying. There will be the Duel. The vol of Short Stories—for which no doubt you will get another *150* (in both countries) and the serial *Razumov* whom* we can surely put down for a hundred. Meantime *Chance* will be done. Do not take a gloomy view of my work on that book. It *is* going on. But a big conception can't be kept going like a shorter work. It matures as it goes. I am by no means stuck. And you shall see that as it progresses it shall come out faster and faster simply because it matures then quicker than it is written. You must have remarked this with all my work. I am always capable of an effort. I was tremendously unsettled last year and I assure you very unhappy and anxious. You have no idea how awfully I was shaken by the events abroad. Not only by what it was then—but also by what it meant for the future. It was a horrid nightmare.

I must ask you for some special assistance. My wife spent last year some £14.13 in dresses, renovation of coats and so on. She had it done by a simple sort of woman who is going to Canada this month and has asked for a settlement on the 18[th]. No doubt I ought have* paid this long ago from the money I had in France but I could not spare it. In respect of that sum you may deduct 10/- from each weekly cheque till it is made up. More she can't spare. When she has paid 17/- for washing and 3/- for cartage to and fro of the same and 10/- to the gardener which is the proportion she undertook to pay there is not much to spare.

Besides that I must ask you to give me *specially* two cheques of *12.10* and *2.10*. I ask because I must. Make out the first to Messrs: Lewis & Hyland[2]—the second to me. Don't count that into the cost of living. That we shall try to keep as low as possible but to worry about every coal scuttle and over every doctor's visit makes existence impossible. And I do now. I am wasting my nervous force which should go into the books. My gout must be watched—whatever Martin Maartens[3] may think—

[1] New both in subject and in tone. [2] Drapers patronized while at the Pent.

[3] Maarten Maartens was the pseudonym of the Dutch author, Jozua Marius Willem van der Poorten Schwartz (1858–1915). Perhaps Conrad was thinking of his novel *The Healers* (written and published in English, 1906), which addresses, among other issues of faith and doubt, the problem of psychosomatic illness.

but to count them with anguish converts a mere disease into a hellish time. I don't want to do anything for my personal gratification but there are certain things I must do. I must let people come to see me if they want to. I must get them here from the station and send them back again. It is expected. It is all very well to say "You need not do this or that" but life must be made worth having. If I can't let my boy be driven to and fro[m] the school once a week at the cost of 7/6 or if I can't go to the station to meet a friend or go out when I have been lame and shut up for days—then it is not worth having. And all this is not so very monstrous after all. There is an idea of my extravagance but I have made account of the 12 years of my writing counting everything my debt to you, the grant I had and all my other debts, together with all I have earned and it comes to £650 per year. How much of that went in doctors bills You know as well as anybody for it is you who stood by me: Wife. Myself. Child. On the other side there are eleven books—which at any rate nobody else could have written. When I've finished Razumov I want to take Borys to town for one afternoon at Maskelyne.[1] That is if I am not disabled. The baby has an awful bronchitis and high fever. And now I shall eat something and go back to Razumov.[2]

> Yours always
>
> J Conrad.

To John Galsworthy
Text MS Forbes; Unpublished

> [letterhead: Someries]
> 14 Jan. 1908

My dearest Jack.

　　Thank you for your dear letter. It is very much like you to object to repayment; but you should consider my feelings too. I must salve my conscience in my poor way. If You knew how I feel about it sometimes in the still watches of the night you would not grudge me that satisfaction.

　　I don't think P could be used that way. A most damnable development happened. I found him yesterday in a most extraordinary state of worry. As I told you I had the greatest difficulty in getting anything whatever—except Jessie's weekly cheque—out of him. Anyway it was difficult to mistake the man's distress—or to mistrust it either. I don't think it was put on. He was extremely embittered against a lot of people,

[1] John Nevil Maskeleyne (1839–1917), the celebrated conjuror.
[2] On the 9th, Conrad wired 'May I have what I requested by tomorrow' (Berg).

but less against me perhaps than at his other authors. In fact I could not help being sorry for him for this sort of emotion was the last thing one could think of in connection with the little man.

What precisely happened I don't know; but the fact is that he finds himself *a sec*[1]—for a time he says. I pass over the details of his frenzy.

He is far from refusing to do things for me only he says he does not know whether he will be able to satisfy my requirements (you know I have always lived on the book ahead) as they arise. Even now—as I write—as he has been unable to pay the coal acct/ which I sent him for settlement a fortnight ago—I sit shivering in the study trying to put a good face on the matter—and the whole Luton* is no doubt aware that the people at the Someries won't get any coal till they pay the old bill. That's why I had to rush to London yesterday, as I was living in blissful ignorance till the man refused—in a 'billet doux'—to send me any more. This sort of thing is impossible. I haven't the nerve for it. My spirits aren't high enough to see the fun of such incidents. Fortunately there is just enough to cook with and for Jackolo's fire in the Den: and I hope all will be well tomorrow. I've gone round the Horn in a cold ship's forecastle[2] but I've never realized before how inclement a time winter can be.

I don't tell you this to harrow your feelings. Mine aren't (as I am in fairly good writing trim) but as I told P—if as he says, he can't sleep o' nights—and I can't sleep—and Jessie can't sleep—that will not improve matters—it won't help me to a book anyhow.

I cast about for some relief and we examined the situation.

It amounts to this:

On Dec 26. I owed him roughly *1500* and there is (including Razumov which I am finishing now) 500 in sight *absolutely certain*. Out of that he has advanced some £50 since the balancing of the acct/. The object now is to relieve him from me for some 5–6 months. Says he: I'll guarantee to pay any person you like to name ⅓ total proceeds of *Chance* (from first moneys received) which we will put at say *900* (Nostr: was *1100*. Secret Ag. *1.300*). (We assume that I will finish *Chance* in 5–6 months.)

Meantime he will pay himself in that time—Inc Tax. 37 no doubt. Borys' schooling: say £15 now and 15 next term. Rent next quarter say 20. Also keep up payments monthly of 2 to Stacey (furniture)[3] and 3 for

[1] 'Run dry'.
[2] In the *Duke of Sutherland*, 1879.
[3] Messrs Norman & Stacey, who had furnished Someries.

the loan (which he doesn't know I asked *from you*) that's = 30 for the six months. In august then assuming *Chance* finished and sold for the 900 estimated he will find himself with the following moneys to the credit of my acct *600* for *Chance* and *230* out of the money already earned—say— which will reduce my indebt[ed]ness to him to 670. Then, he says, I shall be able to finance you as before.

That he wants this relief is evident to me since that means to have his position disclosed to a third party. What is in his mind too is to have his liability on Chance limited to one third, no matter how long I am in writing it. I have no reasonable doubt I can finish *Chance* by July—but then something unreasonable may happen to me. I don't allude to the ever present possibility of my demise. I shall fight that tooth and claw. I must leave 20 vols behind me and there are only 11 written—Chance will make the 12th and then only eight more—a trifle indeed—before I can drop the pen. Too much gout may happen to me. But we won't suppose that.

Of course P says that if I cannot arrange anything to ease him he will do what he can. We will struggle through together somehow he says. But I can't look at it like this. I am too tormented. By the time you read this I would have tried what can be done. If I fail well then I will have to worry through somehow.

I have told you all this to let you see why I think P impracticable in any arrangement where I am involved. And for goodness' sake let him pay you off in this ridiculous way which will take 20 months. You see that the position is not so desperate as all that. It is only infinitely worrying and damnably complicated, for I don't know any phil- ant[h]ropic banker since poor Watson failed.[1] How handy he would have been at this juncture, with his readiness to do anything for one a[t] 7%. Anything. He was a romantic figure and the world is nearly 3/4 of a million the poorer for his going.

Jackolo[2] had a rough time of it but is much better now. Only he must be kept indoors and that makes Jessie unhappy. That baby is very funny. He won't pick up words as other children do. You [have] got to teach him like a parrot. They taught him to say "hot pies" (I don't know why) and now he expresses most of his needs and sentiments by saying "hot pies" in a variety of inflexions. However there is a rumor about the house that he had been heard to say "more" off his own bat. He's been

[1] William Watson declared bankruptcy in February 1904, thereby obliging Conrad to pay off an overdraft of about £250.

[2] The Conrads' younger son, John Alexander.

taught too to say "all away", and he uses this to express his disapproval of things.

He's a dear little chap. Borys enters his 11th year tomorrow and my eleventh vol. shall be published this year too—the short stories—in Augst I imagine. It will contain *Duel Strong man, two Anarchist tales, The Brute, Il Conde.* Razumov shall be kept for nucleous* of the next collection. Feeling nervous and shaky after gout I took B with me to town yesterday. You may guess how I felt on leaving P. but anyhow I spent my last loose shillings in taking B to Maskel[e]yne. I want him to have a good impression of me when I am no more. Hang it all life must be made worth living in some way. Worrying over every cheque extracted from P is not a sufficiently fascinating object. Dear love to you both.

<div align="center">Ever your</div>

<div align="right">Conrad.</div>

I am made happy to hear of your writing so well. I wonder how? You must bring the MS with you.[1] Soon! Soon!

To J. B. Pinker

Text MS Berg; Unpublished

<div align="right">[Someries]
14. Jan 08</div>

My dear Pinker.

In reference to our conversation I understand that I may state the case mentioning for instance my indebt[e]dness to you to the person (a quite trustworthy one) whose name you shall know[2] *if the thing comes off* of which of course I am not certain. If it *does not* I don't suppose the name matters.

Am I right in understanding that you will engage yourself to pay over from the proceeds of *Chance* book and serial *one third* as soon as possible? That for negociation*.

———

Now as between ourselves only have I understood aright that from the money coming in independently of *Chance* you will allow me 1° the cheques I've asked specially for—*12.10. 14.13* and further cheques for

[1] On Galsworthy's return from southern France; he had been working on 'The Shadows', later called *Fraternity*.
[2] Galsworthy?

£7.10 in the name of Bavister for work done.[1] One for say *5* in the name
of Sharpe & Sons Chemists in London (part of it owing more than a
year) and such other cheques as will not amount in all to more than £100
(or as much less as possible) out of the 500 which are in sight at the
present moment (the hundred to include *weekly and all other cheques* paid
for me since the acct was balanced). 2° from the 400 thus left I
understand you will pay the sums we noted on a piece of paper while I
was in your office—as they come due in the course of the six months
beginning in Febr. '08.

—that is. Inc. Tax.? *Borys school.* — 16 or so in the last week of Jan^y,
and the same next term *Rent* when it comes due 20. Insurance. 22? and
monthly payments to Norman and Stacey (furniture) *2.0.5* another to me £*3*
say 30 for the six months.

Altogether as we reckoned in the six months 130 about.

As you say only nothing but riding—writing—can mend matters. I
propose to get some 260 *if I can* to carry me through the six
months—and chance it. But I think I'll finish the book by July. Anyhow
the advantage for you is that your liability on my account from proceeds
of *Chance* will be limited to 1/3 of the amount no matter how long I take
in writing that book.

I reckon your talents will get 900 for it that is 1/3=300—but I
stipulate that if it is 800 or a little more you will still pay 300. If it is only
700 you will pay 250 as a third. If we can get nothing but book rights
alone they will be on the scale of S. Agent that is 500 and out of that you
will pay 200. But I refuse to contemplate the sad extremity. On the other
hand all that you may get *over* 900 will go to the cr. of my account with
you, not falling under the rule of one third.

[1] Among the Luton Bavisters were a plumber and a cobbler.

in six months
300 to Conrad
130 extra payts
100 as above

530

as against in hand

500.
Chance

500

1000

this does not mean that I would keep on at the same rate all the year. I would do with 150 less the next 6 months.

If you were to do all this yourself you would still in the worst case (no serial) have 470 off your account (see margin).

However I think that you have a fixed impression that Conrad to "inability to work" too much gives way! It is not so. You have said: *You all* (literary men I suppose) *talk like that. Other people have to work whether they can or not.* I beg to point out that I am not a literary man. In 1890 coming out of the hospital after 6 months illness I managed for 4 months[1] the straw plait warehouse of Barr Mo[e]ring & C° introduced a new system altogether both as to book keeping and storage. I have now a letter from Simpson & Sons in Adelaide telling me that for years before I took command the Otago barely earned her insurance. The two years I had her[2] that ship paid 16% on her actual value. So I know what all sorts of work mean. It is extraordinary that people who understand that a carpenter can't make a box if somebody keeps on jogging his elbow will say that no jog of any sort shall matter to a mind. I have no charm, no flow of wit or of facetiousness or mere patter to fill in chinks with. I have only a mind a quite different gift from the gift of the gab. I have no literary tradition even which will help to spin phrases—the chewed up silly phrases. I am not a "Sedulous Ape".[3] I wish sometimes I were. Why none of the business men would *sit* as I do with nothing but an inkstand and a pen to make things of. They couldn't. Their health would

[1] August–November 1891. [2] Fourteen months in 1888 and 1889.

[3] Rightly or not, Conrad suspected Pinker of admiring Robert Louis Stevenson as a 'literary' author who was yet a commercial success. Stevenson confessed to his sedulous aping of dead writers in *Memories and Portraits*, Chapter 4.

give way. Mine, rotten as it is, has got to stand it. I have no amusement, no relaxation of any kind—none whatever. I haven't seen a play or listened to a piece of music it seems for years. Jack G's dinner and the day out with Borys yesterday is all I've had since last August. I hate to get away from my table. I've not willingly, on purpose, lost a single minute of my time. It really was hardly worth while to throw a six penny telegram at me. I don't say this as a reproach but as a simple reflection.

It occurs to me that if you were to write me a letter something like this: Dear C. I find it will be extremely difficult for me to finance you for the next 6 months but I engage myself to pay you in a lump sum 1/3 from proceeds of Chance whenever the MS is placed if you can make meantime some arrangement to ease the heavy pressure on me—something of that sort. I could show that letter and it would save a lot of explaining. Will you?

Please try meantime to get me the *14.13* I explained to you all about, for the good woman who is going to Canada. She ought to have it on the 18th.

Answer this as soon as you can.

<div style="text-align:right">Yours always</div>

<div style="text-align:right">J. Conrad</div>

To Marguerite Poradowska
Text MS Yale; Rapin 187; G. & S. 110

<div style="text-align:right">[letterhead: Someries]</div>
<div style="text-align:right">15 Jan 1908</div>

Tres chère Margueritte*.

Je vais Vous ambêter* bien fort avec ma petite com[m]ission mais il faut bien avoir la paix dans la maison.

Imaginez Vous que Jessie a achété un billet de la Pochette Nationale a Montpellier. C'est une loterie—Vous savez. Donc il y a eu un tirage le jour de l'an. Mais on a decouvert que la roue ne fonctionnait pas bien donc on a decidé d'avoir un autre tirage. Il a du avoir lieu le 8. Il m'est impossible de me procurer un numéro du Petit Journal le numero du 9 courant. J'avais promis a ma femme j'ai oublié. Pourrez Vous trouver moyen de savoir quel numéro a gagné le gros lot? Peut-être bien votre bonne tout simplement en s'informant a un bureau de tabac dans la rue de Passy[1] (on vendait les billets aux bureaux de tabac et là sans doute on aura une liste) obtiendra pour moi la paix domestique.

[1] Mme Poradowska's address, in a fashionable quarter of Paris.

J'ai eu une goutte atroce pour la Noel. Mieux en ce moment. Je suis très occupé avec un roman et une nouvelle (cette dernière Russe—la première fois que j'aborde le sujet). Du reste mes affaires vont assez mal—mais j'en ai l'habitude. Avez Vous vu une critique de mon dernier Roman dans la Nouvelle Revue?[1] Tout à coté se trouve la critique du roman de mon ami Galsworthy qui Vous a été presenté a Pent Farm[2]—Vous rappelez Vous? Comme c'est loin tout ça! Avez Vous reçu mon petit mot écrit le jour de l'an? Jessie et Boris Vous embrassent bien fort
Jean Alexandre va bien.

<div align="right">Tout à Vous</div>

<div align="right">Conrad.</div>

Translation

Very dear Marguerite,
 I am going to annoy you with my little errand, but I must have peace at home.
 Just think: Jessie bought a ticket in the 'Pochette Nationale' in Montpellier. You know—it's a lottery. There was a drawing on New Year's Day. But they found out that the wheel didn't work properly and decided to have another drawing. It must have taken place on the 8th. It's impossible for me to get the *Petit Journal* for the 9th of this month. I had promised my wife; I've forgotten. Could you somehow find out what number won first prize? Perhaps simply by asking at a tobacconist's in the rue de Passy (the tickets are sold at such shops, and they will surely have a list there) your maid will procure me some domestic peace.
 I had a dreadful attack of gout for Christmas. Better now. I am very busy with a novel and a long short story (this latter Russian—my first try at the subject). For the rest, my affairs are going badly—but I am used to that. Have you seen a review of my last novel in the *Nouvelle Revue*? Alongside it is a review of a novel by my friend Galsworthy, who was introduced to you at Pent Farm—do you remember? How distant

[1] A puzzle: T. de Wyzewa had discussed Galsworthy's latest novels in the *Revue des Deux Mondes* (15 December, pp. 897–920); Davray noticed *The Secret Agent* in the *Mercure de France* (16 January, p. 350); neither these journals nor the *Nouvelle Revue* examined *The Secret Agent* and Galsworthy side by side. (See also Rapin, p. 187, n. 9.)
[2] In April 1900?

all that seems! Have you had my note written on New Year's Day? Jessie and Borys hug you warmly.

John Alexander is well.

<div align="center">All yours,</div>

<div align="right">Conrad.</div>

To [?]
Text MS Temple; Maser

<div align="right">[letterhead: Someries]</div>
<div align="right">15 Jan '08</div>

Dear Sir[1]

I don't think an interview would be much to the advantage of either of us. There are two or three books which I want to write yet before my time runs out; and, frankly, I don't want any suggestions for that enterprise which is the only one that interests me.

<div align="center">Yours faithfully</div>

<div align="right">J. Conrad.</div>

To J. B. Pinker
Text MS Berg; Unpublished

<div align="right">[Someries]</div>
<div align="right">16 Jan. '08</div>

My dear Pinker.

Drop me a line whether you can let me have that Cheque for £14.13 I asked you for—for a specified purpose.

From the beginning of Jany I had so far £*12* in cheques and *10* in notes. Cheque for *1.13* also. Please besides the weekly £6 which you will be sending tomorrow send me also a cheque for £1.4 wages.

I feel every time I write as if I were begging. I don't like it. It grows impossible. Here out of this month['s] nominal money I have paid 4 months coals practically. This sort of thing won't do.

Of course I am going to try and arrange a loan as soon as possible. But as it cannot be presented as a business matter it all depends on friendly feelings which may or may not be strong enough.

Meantime why not start me fair for a trial. I can't pretend to pick up the overplus I spent from Aug. to Dec last. And anyhow there is included in it a lot of expenditure (including the 60 extra you did let me

[1] Unidentified.

have) which will not occur again. I've pointed it out to you in a former letter.[1]

Nobody can say I have a vice—gambling or drink to lead me astray. It may be that I don't *count* my money very well. Well let's try for a month like this:

The prop[ortion] of rent is about £6 p month (this year. It will be only 5 next year) and Borys['s] bare schooling (with books & other school furniture) another *4.10*. That makes *10.10* off every 50 p m. agreed. (I won't mention the income tax. We will see when they put on the screw.) Well if you will be generous and send me £*40* every month lump in notes we shall see what we can do. As it is I take money from my wife for this and that and then of course I must come to you for cheques. I hate it. And perhaps I do take too much. Perhaps I don't *count* strictly enough. When one does not *see* what one spends one is apt to spend too much. Though this is *not* an admission of extravagance.

In that way too you won't feel that I am likely to spring demands upon you. There could be no accounts send* into you as this last adventure.

I would ask you tho' to pay the £2. to Norman & Stacey monthly at least till I discover if I can manage that myself.

In that case (supposing my little arrangement does not come off) even if Chance takes 6 months more—*even if it does not serialize at all* you will have upwards of £500 to put to my credit when the MS is completed.

This estimate includes the hope that you will give me extra Cheques for *12.10. 14.13. 7.10. 5*=39.13 whenever possible or if possible.

But I shall try my damnedest to get that 40 a month from some good soul and so relieve you for 6 months. I am very anxious. Anyway provide in the way I say for a month beginning next week? Just try. For I can't and won't be begging. It's really impossible.

N.B. If I get the negotiation through I will return the proportion of the month.

Please let me know.

<div style="text-align:center">Yours</div>

<div style="text-align:right">Conrad.</div>

MS. going tomorrow morning.

[1] 7 January.

To J. B. Pinker

Text MS Berg; Unpublished

[letterhead: Someries]

Thursday. [23 January 1908][1]

Dear Pinker

I send here 27 pp. just over half of the *Black Mate*[2] and 3.700 is as near as I can judge. The work of the last 24 hours.

It's supposed to be funny.

Don't let them think its anything second hand—inferior stuff. For it isn't for what it is.

Have it typed meantime. I shall go on through the night and send balance by rail to-morrow unless I hear from you that it does not matter for 12 hours or so. Then it will go by post in the evening.

Yours

J. C.

Dont worry about Raz. being interrupted 2 days is nothing. And anyhow it's all in the next six months programme.

To J. B. Pinker

Text MS Berg; Unpublished

[letterhead: Someries]

Friday. 10.30 am [24 January 1908][3]

Dear Pinker

I had to give up last night. The gout was too severe.[4] So I send what I've done up to night at once by early train.

I think I shall be able to go on writing this afternoon. I shall be either very ill or very much better—think that last.

[1] All three letters about 'The Black Mate' were received in January 1908. As the first in the series, this one could not have been written on the 30th; on 2, 9, and 16 January, Conrad was working on 'Razumov'.

[2] Published in the *London Magazine*, April 1908, and posthumously in *Tales of Hearsay*. For the controversy about its origins – either an entry for a magazine competition in 1886 (and thus Conrad's first story) or a hasty improvisation on an idea by Jessie Conrad – see Karl, pp. 234–6 and Najder, *Chronicle*, pp. 228–9. In ' "The Black Mate": June–July 1886; January 1908', *The Conradian*, 13 (1988), 128–48, Keith Carabine offers persuasive evidence, external and internal, that the central anecdote could indeed have gone to *Tit-Bits* in 1886, the frame narration being added in 1908.

[3] Following immediately on the letter of the 23rd.

[4] Conrad's handwriting is exceptionally shaky.

If so, pages shall go by post to night but how many I don't like to say. Anyhow there is but little now to do to finish the *BM*.

Can't they[1] lay off till Mond[y]—I've been trying to be nice to them, you may say.

This is heart-breaking but you must work me as I am. I've done 35000 words last month but with me it isn't safe to conclude till stuff is all there.

Drop me line to say what You want done with R[azumov]. If you want me to prepare instalment for press I can do it by to morrow.

I would prefer R. anywhere else but the *L.M.* It *won't do* there—I feel it. It's better for us I think to give them as *suitable* stuff as possible.

Please write today whether everything is knocked on the head or whether you can save situation yet.

> Yours always
>
> Conrad.

pp 28–41 of B Mate enclosed
Type of B. Mate needs no revision

To H.-D. Davray
Text MS Texas; *L. fr.* 86

> [letterhead: Someries]
> 26 Jan 1908

Cher Davray.[2]

J'écrivais furieusement dans les intervalles d'une goutte atroce qui me tient depuis le Jour de l'An.

Merci de votre bonne lettre et de la carte. Oui, la vie sépare les hommes d'une façon cruelle. On se réjoint par la pensée quelque peu: et je suis heureux de savoir que vous me gardez toujours un amical souvenir.

Voilà bien 2 ou 3 ans déjà que M d'Humières travaille a cette traduction.[3] Je ne m'en plains pas: mais ma conviction que je ne suis pas très traduisable s'en augmente.

[1] The editors of the *London Magazine*, who must have been promised prompt and lively copy.

[2] Henry-Durand Davray (1873–1944) encouraged French and British writers to know each other better. He appeared regularly in the *Mercure de France* and edited its Collection of Foreign Authors. Among those he translated were Kipling, Meredith, Wells, and Conrad.

[3] Robert d'Humières asked leave to translate *The Nigger of the 'Narcissus'* in January 1905: *Letters*, 3, p. 212.

J'ai essayé de reproduire quelque peu le sentiment de l'époque Napoléonienne dans ma nouvelle *The Duel*. Lisez-là si vous en trouvez le temps. Cela me fera plaisir—grand plaisir. Mais n'oubliez pas que la chose est écrite pour les Anglais—au point de vue de l'effet a produire sur un lecteur anglais.

C'est toujours mon but. Voilà pourquoi je suis tellement un écrivain Anglais se prétant peu a la traduction. Un ecrivain *national* comme Kipling p. example* se traduit facilement.[1] Son interêt est *dans le sujet* l'interêt de mon oeuvre est *dans l'effet* qu'elle produit. Il parle de *ses compatriotes*. Moi j'écris *pour eux*. Donc lui peut tres bien interesser les etrangers—pour moi c'est bien plus difficile—peut être impossible.

Voilà un petit bout d'analyse a Votre usage. Quand je ne serai plus là si on parle de moi devant vous, Vous pourrez toujours dire "qu'au moins Conrad savait ce qu'il voulait faire."

Savoir ce que l'on veut faire est le fait d'un artiste.

Nos amitiés bien sincères a Mme Davray et a Vous cher ami.

<div align="right">Toujours le votre.</div>

<div align="right">J. Conrad.</div>

J'ai ecrit a Mme Poradowska l'autre jour.

Translation

Dear Davray,

I have been writing furiously in the intervals of atrocious gout which has had hold of me since New Year's Day.

Thanks for your good letter and card. Yes, life separates men in a cruel way. One pulls oneself together with one's thoughts, and I am glad to know you always have a friendly recollection of me.

M. d'Humières has already been working on this translation for two or three years. I don't complain about it; but I am strengthened in my conviction of being not very translatable.

I have tried to reproduce in a small way the feeling of the Napoleonic epoch in my story *The Duel*. Read it if you find the time. That will give me pleasure—great pleasure. But do not forget that it is written for the English—from the point of view of the effect it will have on an English reader.

[1] 'National' both in owing allegiance to a single country and in speaking as that country's voice. Kipling was another of d'Humières' interests.

That is always my object. That's why I am so much an English writer who lends himself so little to translation. A *national* writer like Kipling, for example, translates easily. His interest is in the *subject*: the interest of my work is in the *effect* it produces. He talks about *his compatriots*. I write *for them*. Thus he can interest foreigners very well—for me it's more difficult indeed—perhaps impossible.

There's a little bit of analysis for your use. When I am no longer around, if someone talks about me in your presence, you can always say that 'at least Conrad knew what he wanted to do'.

To know what one wants to do is the business of the artist.

Our very sincere regards to Mme Davray and to you, dear friend.

<div align="center">Always yours,</div>

<div align="right">J. Conrad.</div>

I wrote to Mme Poradowska the other day.

To Algernon Methuen
Text J-A, 2, 66

<div align="right">Someries.</div>

<div align="right">26 Jan., 1908.</div>

Dear Mr. Methuen,[1]

I was laid up with slight gout or I would have answered before.

It's difficult to find a general definition of the stories.[2] They are varied. No monotony is to be feared either in feeling or incident. There is the story of a South American Bandit. "The Strong Man,"[3] warlike in its feeling. There is "The Duel, A Military Story"—an attempt to realize the spirit of the Napoleonic Era. These two are long, 4 chaprs. each.

Two Anarchist stories, "The Anarchist" (dealing with an escape from a French penal settlement) and "The Informer" (discovery of a plot—in London) are slightly shorter, 3 & 2 chaprs. respectively. The two shortest: "The Brute: A Piece of Invective" (sea subject) and "Il Conde" (Story of an Adventure in Naples) complete the contents of the volume.

All the stories are stories of incident—action—not of analysis. All are

[1] Algernon Methuen (originally Stedman, 1856–1924; baronetcy 1916) founded his company in 1889. Besides text-books, the source of the firm's prosperity, he published works by Kipling, Stevenson, and Maeterlinck; between 1906 and 1915 he brought out six Conrad titles, most recently *The Secret Agent* (September 1907).
[2] *A Set of Six*, to be published 6 August. [3] 'Gaspar Ruiz'.

dramatic in a measure but by no means of a gloomy sort. All, but two, draw their significance from the love interest—though of course they are not love stories in the conventional meaning. They are not studies—they touch no problem. They are just stories in which I've tried my best to be *simply entertaining*.

I can't think of anything else I could say about them which could be of practical use to your travellers. For yourself I may mention that in that collection I aimed at a certain *virtuosity* of style for its "Master quality."

I failed in places and in others I've succeeded—I believe.[1]

To J. B. Pinker
Text MS Berg; Unpublished

[letterhead: Someries]
Monday. *2am* [27 January 1908][2]

Dear Pinker.

I couldn't begin to write till Sunday morning. I am going to leave off now at p 68—which makes 27 pp in this batch, as good a day's work as a man drenched with Colchicum and Salicilate[3] is capable of doing.

I am anxious you should have no worry with this story at least. Another 12 pp will see the end of it—say 9000 quite readable words in all.[4]

The last pp shall leave to-day (Mond) by the 5 o'clock post. But they shall be ready by 3 or thereabouts. If You want them absolutely to-day they may be got off by the 4 oclock train and be in your office before six but I won't do that unless you wire.

This batch will be sent off by rail by the man who takes Borys to school and you ought to have it about One pm.

Drop me a line to say how You are. Moore's note on Sat. said you were not well.[5]

Yours

J. Conrad.

[1] Jean-Aubry printed his texts without farewell and signature.
[2] The only Monday between the date of the first 'Black Mate' letter and the end of the month.
[3] A diuretic extract of autumn crocus used in the treatment of gout and a pain-killer cum febrifuge akin to aspirin.
[4] The MS of 'The Black Mate' ran to 98 pages (BL Ashley 2949).
[5] Therefore Edward Moore, Pinker's assistant, was handling correspondence.

To Edward Moore
Text MS Lohf; Unpublished

Someries.
Luton
Wednesday [29 January 1908][1]

Dear M[r] Moore[2]

The copy of the vol of short stories is all written and most of it is serially published, except 2 inst[s] of Duel and the story *Il Conde* the corrected proof of which for Cassell's Mag I sent you last evening.[3]

I have text of Duel (in slips) ready for the vol by me.

But I haven't got the others viz: *The Strong Man.* (Pall Mall) the *Anarchist & the Informer* (Harpers) *the Brute* (Dly Chronicle Xmas N[o] 1906) Have you in the office the typed copies of these four stories?

If not we will have to hunt for them as I have not a scrap.

The *Il Conde* I presume shall appear in Febr[y]'s Cassell's. Please secure the number.

I imagine that the *Black Mate* is *not* going into that vol. I would like to know what M[r] Pinker thinks about the matter?

Razumov certainly shall not go into that collection. I intend it for the nucleous* of another vol.

In reference to *Black Mate* please ask the Editor of London to send me proof *as early as possible*. That story is totaly unrevised as you know.

Yours faithfully
J. Conrad.

PS Are you in communication with M[r] Pinker?[4]

To J. B. Pinker
Text MS Berg; Unpublished

[Someries]
2 Febr. 1908.

Dear Pinker

I send the papers signed. The girl made a mistake as to the place where her signature should have been placed but that I hope may be set right by correcting the references.

The particulars of the policy are as on my instructions to Hinton Cole

[1] Received Thursday, 30 January. [2] Edward Moore was Pinker's assistant.
[3] 'The Duel' ran in the *Pall Mall Magazine* from January to May; 'Il Conde' appeared in the August *Cassell's Magazine*.
[4] On 3 February, Conrad asked Moore whether Pinker had returned (Telegram, Berg).

& Hill:[1] *the usual life policy at Lloyds for £500 for six months at the rate of 20/- per cent, made out in the name of James B Pinker*, with further instructions to forward same to Messrs: Darley & Cumberland[2] who will pay the premium (to be deducted from amount of loan as suggested by yourself).

I will send you some MS. to night but no need to type it till receipt of a few more batches. I don't like to send too many pp in one envelope—as accidents happen even to reg^d letters at times.

I went to see Masterman and John Burns.[3] The first may be useful in the affair of the pension later on. The second notified me his intention to come and see me here on his return from Bedford where he is going next week.

We leave here on the 15^th.

Yours ever

J Conrad

PS Pray send the docts to D & C as speedily as possible

To H.-D. Davray
Text MS Texas; *L.fr.* 88

[letterhead: Someries]
3 fev. 1908.

Tres cher ami.

Je suis infiniment touché de votre bonne lettre. Elle m'a fait du bien, infiniment du bien; mais en verité je n'ai jamais douté de Votre franche et bonne amitié. En dedans de moi meme j'en ai été tout fier. Vous êtes un ami génénereux*—de cela aussi je n'ai jamais douté.

Je suis très heureux de pouvoir Vous dire que je n'ai pas donné aucune autorisation a aucun traducteur. Un monsieur de Bayonne vient de m'écrire a ce sujet. Son nom est Louis Labat.[4] J'ai refusé.

[1] Insurance brokers, Tower Chambers, Finsbury Pavement.
[2] Solicitors, 36 John St, Bedford Row, Bloomsbury.
[3] John Elliot Burns (1858–1943), M.P. for Battersea since 1892, started his political career as a socialist and union organizer and was gaoled with Cunninghame Graham for figuring in the Bloody Sunday demonstration of 1887. In 1905, now in alliance with the Liberals, he became 'the first artisan to reach cabinet rank' as President of the Local Government Board. Charles Frederick Gurney Masterman (1873–1927), his under-secretary, published the influential *The Condition of England* in 1909; Masterman's enthusiasm for social reform and his belief in the political force of literature endeared him to Galsworthy and Stephen Reynolds.
[4] For what seems to be a reply to Labat, see the letter of 29 April.

Vous pensez bien que je vous aurais consulté. Mais si Vous voulez Vous charger du sort de me[s] oeuvres en France—tant mieux! tant mieux! J'accepte avec joie. Dans tous les cas ce sera Vous—ou personne. On m'a fait des propositions par l'entremise d'une maison d'agence littéraire; mais quand j'ai demandé des informations précises il c'est fait* un grand silence. Ceci a eu lieu en novembre je crois.

Ecrivez moi donc cette lettre officielle dont Vous parlez et je vous répondrais de même.

The *Secret Agent* n'est pas si long que ça. Voyons, pensez a Tolstoi. Mais plaisanterie a part, La *guerre des mondes* ou *Le Dormeur* sont des romans beaucoup plus longs, je pense.[1]

Nostromo est très long j'en conviens, mais il y a un tas des nouvelles dont on pourrait faire un choix.

Du reste mon cher quoique j'ai une grande confiance en Votre jugement, j'avoue que je ne vois pas comment mes écritures pourraient intéresser le public français. Je le désire tant que cela me paraît impossible.

J'y refléchis: Je ne dis rien de neuf; je n'aborde aucun problème; je ne suis ni fin, ni même très éloquent. J'ai quelques sentiment[s] des choses lointaines et un goût pour l'analyse des sentiments simples avec un tour de[s] phrases qui frappe—les Anglais. Notez bien que je ne dis pas *qui plaît*. Je crois que je ne plais a personne ici. Je m'impose a quelques uns. Ces reflexions ne sont pas gaies pour moi. Voilà ou j'en suis au bout des* douze volumes en la 50ème année de ma vie.[2] Quelques bonnes amitiés (comme la votre) me consolent de tout cela.

<div style="text-align:center">

Je vous serre la main bien
affectueusement.

J. Conrad

</div>

Translation

Very dear friend,
 I am infinitely touched by your good letter. It has done me enormous good: but in fact I never doubted your frank and good friendship. Deep

[1] Davray was Wells's friend and translator. In the original octavo editions, *The War of the Worlds* ran to 304 pages, *When the Sleeper Wakes* to 330, and *The Secret Agent* to 442.
[2] He had completed his 50th year in December; including *A Set of Six* and the collaborations with Ford, the count of volumes came to thirteen.

inside, I have been very proud of it. You are a generous friend—that too I have never doubted.

I am very happy to be able to tell you that I have given no authorization whatsoever to any translator. A man from Bayonne has just written to me on this subject. His name is Louis Labat. I refused.

You might have expected me to consult you. But if you wish to burden yourself with the fate of all my works in France—so much the better! so much the better! I accept with joy. In any event it will be you—or no one. Some propositions have come my way through a literary agency; but when I asked for precise information, there was a great silence. This happened in November, I believe.

Write me, then, this official letter that you mention and I will answer in the same way.

The *Secret Agent* is not that long. You're thinking of Tolstoy. But joking aside, *The War of the Worlds* or *The Sleeper* are much longer novels, I think.

Nostromo is very long, I agree, but there is a pile of stories to choose from.

Besides, my dear fellow, although I have great trust in your judgment, I confess that I do not see how my writings could interest the French public. I want that, much as it seems to me impossible.

I am thinking about it. I say nothing new; I attack no problems; I am neither very subtle nor very eloquent. I have some feeling for far-off things and a taste for the analysis of simple feelings with a turn of phrase which impresses—the English. Note well that I do not say which pleases. I believe that I please nobody here. I impose myself on a few. These are not cheerful reflections for me. That is where I am at the end of a dozen volumes in my fiftieth year. Some good friendships (like yours) console me for all that.

> I shake your hand very
> affectionately,
>
> J. Conrad

To J. B. Pinker
Text MS Berg; Unpublished

> [letterhead: Someries]
> Monday [3 or 24? February 1908][1]

My dear Pinker

Please let me have the statement of incme, I asked you for some time ago. The damn'd tax man has been here worrying me.

> Yours
>
> J Conrad.

[1] Received February 1908; Conrad was sick on the 10th and wrote another letter on the 17th.

To Norman Douglas
Text MS Colgate; Unpublished

[letterhead: Someries]
5 Febr o8

Dear Douglas.[1]
Just a line to tell you that you are expected in this house as soon as ever you can find time to come.[2] There are many trains—every hour almost—and you can always find a conveyance at the station—a 2 mile drive. We lunch at 1.30. And we can also put you up for the night if you will come to dinner. Drop a warning line in case of some unforeseen thing. Don't delay.

Yours

J. Conrad

Wife's kind regards

To Marguerite Poradowska
Text MS Yale; Rapin 188; G. & S. 111

[letterhead: Someries]
5 Fevrier 1908

Tres chère amie.
Merci de votre bonne longue lettre. Je me reproche amèrement mon negligence a Vous écrire; mais en vérité la vie est si difficile pour moi d'une façon et d'autre que le courage manque parfois de prendre la plume.
La maison que nous habitons aprésant* est bien plus grande que le Pent: et le pays est bien different. Mais nous sommes beaucoup plus près de Londres: 30 milles anglaises au lieu de soixante-six. Les trains express mettent 38 minutes entre Luton et la Station St Pancras. D'autres 45–50 minutes jusqu'a lh. 10m—mais il n'y en [a] que deux qui sont si lent que cela. Et il y a une trentaine des trains dans le[s] 24 heures en chaque sens. Donc Vous voyez que les communications avec la Ville sont faciles: et comme il y a un train a minuit vingt qui arrive a Luton a

[1] George Norman Douglas (1868–1952), traveller, polyglot, polymath, wit, and former diplomat, first met Conrad in 1905, on Capri. Douglas's oeuvre, ranging from 'The Herpetology of the Grand Duchy of Baden' (1891) to *Venus in the Kitchen* (1952), includes *South Wind* (1917) and *Old Calabria* (1915).
[2] Douglas had come to London in January, seeking legal custody of his two sons (Holloway, *Norman Douglas*, p. 161).

une heure du matin on peut, a la rigueur aller au theatre (par le 5.22 soir) et revenir coucher chez soi.

Mais pauvre Jessie n'est guère en état de faire des fugues comme cela. Se mouvoir pour la pauvre femme est toute une affaire. Moi aussi je me fais vieux. Helas. Il ne peut être question pour nous de voyage en France cette année ci. Les affaires de mon agent littéraire se sont gatées; et comme je lui dois beaucoup d'argent je m'attends a des soucis matériels assez serieux. Il faudra se tenir très tranquilles. Du reste Borys est a l'école a Luton et on ne peut pas interrompre ses études par des voyages. Quand* a le laisser ici nous ne pourrions pas le faire car sa santé demande encore une surveillance attentive. Une fièvre rhumatismale laisse des traces. Il vient a la maison chaque Samedi midi jusqu'a Lundi matin neuf heures. Et comme l'école est a 5 kilomètres de chez nous, Jessie se sent rassurée. Je suis heureux de Vous dire qu'il travaille très sérieusement. C'est un très brave garçon, très loyal, un peu pessimiste, d'une humeur un peu inégale mais avec un grand fond d'affection pour ses proches. Il adore Jean Alexandre—qui le lui rend bien a sa façon.

Pauvre petit—il a été bien malade en Suisse avec la coqueluche. Pendant trois mois il était comme un bébé mort, entre les affreuses quintes de toux. La moindre petite complication l'aurait enlévé. Aprésant* c'est un solide gaillard qui commence a marcher mais qui ne parle pas beaucoup encore. Il est beaucoup plus tapageur que son frère ainé ne l'a jamais été. Tout le monde lui trouve beaucoup de charme. Moi aussi je pense qu'il est très gentil. Il a des cheveux chatain clair—un peu cuivré, les yeux brun foncé et de cils très noirs avec des grandes joues roses. On le gâte beaucoup. C'est fatal. Tout le monde s'y met y compris papa.

Dites moi donc chère Marguerite qui est ce parent d'Angela qui habite Londres? Est-ce un Unrug—Angela est née Unrug ou Unruh—n'est-ce pas?[1] Et que fait-il en Angleterre?

Je crois que pour Mme Gâchet et sa fille habiter a Londres n'est pas une mauvaise idée.[2] J'ai été fort intéressé par tout ce que Vous me dites de Jean. Je pense souvent a ce jeune homme qui m'était si sympathique comme enfant.[3] Que fait-il precisement au Canada? A-t-il un objet bien

[1] Aniela Zagórska, née Unrug.
[2] Mme Poradowska's sister-in-law, née Maud Chamberlin, was English (Gee and Sturm, p. 11, n. 3); her children, now young adults, were Alice and Jean.
[3] As a child, Jean spoke a mixture of French and English; he was once heard to cry 'I want mon petit tant[e]!' (Rapin, p. 208).

defini en vue pour rester la-bàs? Je crois que Vous seriez heureuse de le savoir en Europe, plus près de Vous.

Je n'ose pas faire des projets pour l'avenir. Il se presente assez sombre en ce moment-ci. Mais il faudra venir nous voir chère Marguerite. Si je venais a Votre rencontre a Boulogne bien sur que la traversée (soixante dix minutes) ne Vous effrayera pas tant que cela. Pensez y pour l'été prochain quand le temps sera beau.

Je termine ici. Nous sommes a 3 1/2 kilometres de Luton et le facteur est là qui boit une tasse de thé dans la cuisine. Il est pressé cet homme. Donc en tout hâte love and kisses from Jessie—(qui est là) et de ma part aussi. Borys joue aujourd'hui dans un football match contre une école de Bedford.

<div align="right">Toujours à Vous de coeur

J Conrad.</div>

Translation

Very dear friend,

Thank you for your good, long letter. I bitterly regret my remissness in not writing to you, but life truly is so hard for me in one way and another that I sometimes lack the courage to take up a pen.

The house where we live now is much larger than the Pent, and the countryside is very different. But we are much closer to London: 30 miles instead of 66. The express trains between Luton and St Pancras take 38 minutes. Others from 45–50 minutes to an hour and 10 minutes—but only two are that slow. And there are about 30 trains in 24 hours in each direction. So you see that connections to town are good; and as there is a train at 20 past midnight which arrives in Luton at one in the morning, one can, at a stretch, go to the theatre (by the 5:22 p.m.) and come home to sleep.

But poor Jessie is hardly fit for escapades like that. Simply to move about is quite a business for the poor woman. I too am getting old.

Alas. There can be no question of our going to France this year. The affairs of my literary agent are in poor shape; and as I owe him a good deal of money, I expect some serious material worries. We must live very modestly. Moreover, Borys is at school in Luton, and we cannot interrupt his studies with a trip. As for leaving him here, we cannot do that either, for his health still requires careful watching. Rheumatic

fever leaves its marks. He comes home every Saturday noon and stays until Monday morning at nine. And since the school is only 5 kilometers from our house, Jessie feels easy about him. I am happy to tell you that he works very seriously. He is a fine fellow, very loyal, something of a pessimist, of somewhat uneven temper, but with a great store of affection for those near him. He adores John Alexander—who reciprocates in his way.

Poor child—he was very ill in Switzerland with whooping cough. For three months he was like a dead baby between frightful fits of coughing. The slightest complication would have carried him off. Now he is a strapping fellow who is beginning to walk, but doesn't yet talk. He is far more of a blusterer than his older brother ever was. Everyone finds him very charming. I think he is very nice too. He has light chestnut hair—slightly copper-coloured, dark-brown eyes and very black lashes, with big pink cheeks. We spoil him badly. It can't be helped. Everyone does it, and that includes papa.

Tell me, then, dear Marguerite, who is that relative of Angela's living in London? Is it an Unrug—Angela was born Unrug or Unruh, wasn't she? And what is he doing in England?

I don't think it's a bad idea for Mme Gachet and her daughter to live in London. I was very much interested in everything you tell me about Jean. I often think of this young man who was so agreeable to me as a child. What exactly is he doing in Canada? Does he have a particular reason for staying there? I am sure you would be glad to have him in Europe, nearer you.

I dare not make any plans for the future. It looks rather gloomy just now. But you must come to see us, dear Marguerite. If I met you in Boulogne, then the crossing (seventy minutes) would not frighten you so very much. Think about it for next summer when the weather is good.

I close here. We are 3 1/2 kilometers from Luton, and the postman is drinking a cup of tea in the kitchen. He is in a hurry. So, in all haste, love and kisses from Jessie—who is here, and from me, too. Borys is playing today in a football match against a Bedford school.

<div style="text-align:right">

Ever affectionately yours

J. Conrad.

</div>

To [?]
Text MS Rosenbach; Unpublished

[letterhead: Someries]
Feb 5th. 1908

Dear Sir.[1]

I send my signature with the greatest pleasure. It is always a great satisfaction to hear of my work being appreciated on your side.

I wonder whether you would care for the page of Lord Jim's MS which I am sending you.[2] Inserted in the Vol it would make of it a copy *unique* in the US. and that may please the recipient of Your gift.

In offering you this original page I am moved by no spirit of vanity—as if it were anything so very precious—but simply by the wish to express my regard for my readers in the United States.

Believe me sincerely yours
Jph. Conrad

To J. B. Pinker
Text MS Berg; Najder (1983) 337 (in part)[3]

[letterhead: Someries]
Thursday 12 [13?] Febr 1908[4]

My dear Pinker

I am sending you 10 pp of Razumov. I send only 10 pp because I've been laid up since last Friday till yesterday afternoon when I began to write again, and this is all I could do till this post time.

I wrote the short story for the London for no other reason but that I don't want to have Razumov mangled by fools; also to have a freer hand with that story. If I can't have a free hand—time—for elaborating my work and freedom from interference I would just as soon stop writing entirely. But I am quite willing to make a special effort now and then in view of the material position. Should you therefore happen to get an inquiry for something short, on very good terms, if you let me know I've a subject which I can make use of for say 10000 words' story.

If I don't do it at once it isn't from indolence. 13 vols since 1895 when my first book was published[5] are no sign of indolence—considering too that there are such vols as Lord Jim—the *Youth* collection, the Outcast—the Secret Agent—and considering too that at least 1/3 of the

[1] An American, evidently.
[2] The page, still accompanying the letter, is numbered 643; it belongs to Chapter 34.
[3] All but the first two paragraphs [4] Thursday was the 13th.
[5] See 3 February to Davray, n. 3.

time should be deducted for illness, depressing in itself and treated too usually by most depressing remedies.

I've been drenched with Colchicum since last October and I have enough of it. I have begun what I am told may be a radical cure with some new drugs. This last attack, the 5th since Oct. has been brought on by the medicine and I've felt very ill for 3 days. Now it is passing away apparently and I am going to persevere for another 40 days so as to eradicate all poison out of the system—if it can be done. I am telling you all this not because I think it interesting but because it has some bearing upon my future production.

I want to know whether You will pay Borys' school fees for the current term. They amount to £*16.18.9*. If I don't hear on Sat. I shall take it that it is impossible.

I referred to you some time ago a proposal from a firm of Literary Agents for the rights of trans: into French. I conclude you haven't heard from them. I want to be sure that you have not disposed of any rights because the *Mercure de France*[1] is inclined to negotiate in that respect for the whole of my work. I have also proposals for working in French and I don't feel too old to make a fresh start. In the general uncertainty of what is to happen to me the idea doesn't seem so very bizarre. Rather interesting in fact.

The furniture people are reminding me that the Jan inst 2.0.5 has not yet been paid. If they come here to take the things away I will have to finish Razumov in French—I am afraid—wherein I shall not have to fear the competition of A Bennet[t], that true parisian.[2]

<div align="center">Yours</div>

<div align="right">J Conrad.</div>

<div align="center">•</div>

[1] Represented by Davray.
[2] Arnold Bennett (1867–1931), another Pinker client, prolific, commercially successful, an admirer of the French Naturalists and a frequent visitor to Paris.

To Ada Galsworthy

Text MS Forbes; Unpublished

[letterhead: Someries]
Thursday
Feb^y 13 1908

Dearest Ada[1]

I have been too lame in all my limbs to tell you before how grieved we were by the horrible rh[e]umatism.

I've started a wonderful gout cure which began operations by half killing me. However this attack is passing away and I am going to persevere with the blessed drug for full 40 days. And *note*: it is supposed to be a sovereign cure for rh[e]umatism. If I survive you had better try. Let my life be of some use. It's a beautiful opportunity for You to be kind.

The new edition of the Island Ph:[2] arrived during the crisis of horrors and I tackled the preface with such mind as I had then. It is thoroughly good I think. Sterling good. In general I don't approve of prefaces as they often turn out superfluous or beside the mark. But Jack is a safe man. My love to him and congratulations on the event.

I see that the Fortnightly has put off again dear Jack's article.[3] It's intolerable that John Galsworthy should be treated so. You know—you may guess at any rate—how much I care for *The Disquisition*. But really I think that Jack ought to take it away from the stupid brute.[4] Perhaps he has thought of doing so already: In that case pray dear Ada ask him not to let any tenderness for me stand in the way. The thing is written—my gratification can not be increased by its publication. But it is insupportable for me to see dear Jack's dignity suffer (if such an ass can affect it) through his friendship for me.

The man, as you know, is literary editor of the *Dly Telph*. I am told that in the general review of the years' literature the *S.A.* is not even mentionned*. I can't pretend that I care a bit. I really don't. But when it comes to a distinguished piece of work like Jack's article being slighted

1 Ada Nemesis Galsworthy, born Ada Pearson (1864–1956), was adopted by Ernest Cooper, a Norwich doctor. As a teenager she studied the piano in Dresden; later, she wrote songs. Officially, she remained married to John Galsworthy's cousin Arthur until the end of 1904, when the death of John, Senior, eased the threat of family sanctions.

2 The second edition of her husband's *The Island Pharisees*, first published in 1904; this revised edition had a preface by the author.

3 'Joseph Conrad: A Disquisition' came out in the 1 April number. Pinker had handled the MS in October (*Letters*, 3, p. 502).

4 W. L. Courtney, editor of the *Fortnightly Review* since 1894. He had published 'Autocracy and War'.

because it deals with my work I am too infuriated for adequate expression. I will say no more.

<div align="center">Dear love to you both</div>

<div align="right">J. Conrad</div>

PS. There is a publisher who thinks of putting out a translation of something of Anatole France.[1] Hueffer advised Hist. Comique—I say *Pierre Blanche*—emphatically that. What do you think? I mean You and Jack—either collectively or separately.

To John Galsworthy

Text MS POSK; Danilewiczowa

<div align="right">[letterhead: Someries]
1908 Monday. 17 Febr</div>

Dearest Jack

I wrote to Ada last week and I don't know that I have anything special to say now. The fact is that I feel so confoundedly ill that I want to tell you of it. The gout is better; but there is something wrong with the leg. Looks like the extension of the varicose veins I've had already for the last 30 years of my life. It hurts damnably and if an inflam[m]ation sets in it may be dangerous. I am as weak as a cat anyhow. I haven't been outside the door for 13 days. I had no doctor this time. I am tired of having a doctor—and the mere thought of the bill by and by makes me shudder. It's an impossible existence—but I keep on writing—trying to catch the spectre, the flying shadow of peace. The great thing is not to break down but there are moments I feel as if my resolution not to break down were weakening. I've been holding out like this since end October. Not so bad.

B[orys] is improving in health. It is a great relief. And indeed he's a good little chap. I begin to feel a great confidence in him. An apprenticeship at say 18 to some great Rway is clearly the way for him. J. C. Tarver (the man of the book on Flaubert)[2] has been here for a night and talked to me of his youngest 1/2 brother who went through that training with satisfactory results. Jack flourishes and runs about comically with

[1] France (Anatole-François Thibault, 1844–1924) was a mutual enthusiasm, and Ada Galsworthy had considered translating him; the books cited here are *Histoire comique* (1903) and *Sur la pierre blanche* (1905).

[2] John Charles Tarver (1854–1926) lived close by; he wrote a study of the Emperor Tiberius and *Gustave Flaubert as Seen in His Works and Correspondence* (1895).

very great determination. Poor Jess I imagine worries about me, tho' I am really doing my best to put a good face on very ugly feelings.

Young Reynolds has been here also for a night. We talked of you—becomingly. He's excited at the thought of your Devon novel.[1] I am thinking mostly of the one now on the bench.[2] How are you getting on with your task? Ada alluded to a cold hanging over you, and all these influenza fears in the papers make me anxious.

I see G-B, poor fellow, is hit again.[3] The stars in their courses are fighting for the Censor of Plays—as it seems.

Half past ten. I am going to crawl into bed. I dread it. And I dread getting up. Not a good symptom that. Love.

<div align="center">Yours ever</div>

<div align="right">J Conrad.</div>

To J. B. Pinker

Text MS Berg; Unpublished

<div align="right">[letterhead: Someries]</div>

<div align="right">Monday. [17? February 1908][4]</div>

Dear Pinker.

The school bill is owing since the beginning of the term that is the 22$^{\text{d}}$ of Jan. Make out the cheque to me. £*16.18.9*.

I send a batch of Razumov. More will follow during the week. The end is in sight. I am getting it off as fast as I can.

I've received with a note from Moore the text of all the short stories to be included in the next *vol*. My idea is that the *Black Mate* should *not* be included.[5] I don't want to give up a line more than is necessary. The order of printing should be like this:

The Strong Man.	4 ch.
The Anarchist.	1 ch.
The Brute	1 ch.
An Informer.	1 ch.
The Duel.	4 ch.

[1] Stephen Reynolds had gone to live in Devonshire.

[2] Published as *Fraternity* a year later.

[3] Harley Granville-Barker (1877–1946), playwright, actor, director, and critic, fought constant battles with the Lord Chamberlain's office. At the unpublic hour of 11 a.m. on 28 January, a cast that included Galsworthy, Shaw, and Wells had given a 'public' reading at the Savoy Theatre of Granville-Barker's *Waste*, incorporating cuts made by the Examiner of Plays.

[4] Received in February and probably close in date to the query about school fees of the 12th or 13th.

[5] It was left out.

44 Letters of Joseph Conrad

A blank page between each story with $\frac{1}{2}$ title. On second thoughts we may keep the last story out as there will be 80000 without it.[1]

Here's the third *vol* to be published by Methuen[2] for which the advance is pretty poor. That much (£120) was to be paid for the Typhoon vol (some years ago) before I made up my mind to sell it outright for an additional *60 or 70*.

It is annoying to think that I owe *still* 3 novels. I never understood how the Secret Agent escaped the general agreement. Certainly when signing the special agreement for it I had no idea what I was doing. I was too busy thinking how to make that book—what it is: a distinguished piece of work. I don't think that the book has been made the most of. It has been passed off in the ruck. The others shall too no doubt be treated in the same way. Of course! But I am not satisfied. Far from it. 3 books is a large slice of Conrad's life. I am not a sausage machine that takes rotten scraps in at one end and turns out the marketable sausage at the other. Morally I feel bound to let M. have another novel after *Chance*. and that's all—and morally he has no right to expect more. There is the legal aspect of the case I know. But if I am to go to the devil I'll go in my own way—where he certainly will find neither profit nor honours. When one has got an *unique* aut[h]or one had better treat him in a special way. I am tired to play* second fiddle to Mr M's Williamsons[3]—and such like rot. He will find it'll pay him better ... but this is idle. I expect to be made *a feature* of his advertising. If I am not worth that I am not worth holding on to. The talk about special *selling* arrangements or capacities is just talk—you know. Other men sell as well, and I *know* where the best traveller in the trade is working now. It isn't with Methuen.

<div style="text-align:center">In haste yours</div>

<div style="text-align:right">J Conrad</div>

I am not in a position to dispute the enclosed bill. Neither have I the money to pay it. I've got 3/- in the house.

[1] At the bottom of the list, Conrad originally wrote 'Il Conde 1 ch.'; the story was kept, however. He gave a more accurate but still inflated tally on 5 March.

[2] The other two being *The Secret Agent* and *The Mirror of the Sea*.

[3] Mrs C. N. and A. N. Williamson, unstoppable writers; between 1906 and 1908, they published four titles with Methuen and five more with other houses. Thus they were among Pinker's more profitable clients.

To Baroness Janina de Brunnow
Text L. fr. 89; Najder 249

<div align="right">
Someries.

Luton. Beds.

19 fév. 1908.
</div>

Chere Madame,[1]

Rien qu'un petit mot pour le moment pour vous remercier de votre lettre et pour m'associer à votre douleur.[2] Et ce n'est pas seulement une façon de parler, chère Madame. A mesure que la vie s'écoule les souvenirs d'enfance deviennent plus précieux.

Il était vif, remuant, un peu étourdi avec beaucoup de charme et d'un esprit ouvert. De tous vos frères, mes compagnons de jeunesse, les seuls! (je n'en ai jamais eu d'autres)—c'était celui, il me semble qui ressemblait le plus à sa Mère. Et il n'est plus! Je me sens attristé jusqu'au fond de l'âme.

J'aurai l'honneur, chère Madame, et amie, de vous envoyer mon dernier ouvrage. Je suis fort touché de l'intérêt que vous daignez porter à mes livres: donc je me permettrai d'y joindre un volume plus ancien,[3]—esquisses de mer,—peut-être sans grand intérêt, mais à qui je tiens car il parle des choses déjà lointaines et des hommes simples que j'ai connus.

Veuillez avoir la bonté de présenter de ma part à Madame votre Mère mes hommages les plus respectueux. L'homme déjà grisonnant qui vous parle a gardé pour Elle un sentiment presque filial et une reconnaissance pour ses bontés que le temps n'a fait qu'accroitre. Et permettez-moi, Madame, au nom des précieux souvenirs que nous sont communs, de me dire

<div align="right">
votre très affectueux et très fidèle

serviteur.
</div>

Translation

Dear Madame,

For the moment, only a short note to thank you for your letter and to join you in your sorrow.

[1] Jeanne or Janina, Baronne de Brunnow (née Taube, 1854–1943), a friend from Conrad's boyhood in Cracow and a ward of his uncle Tadeusz Bobrowski.

[2] The death of her brother, Roman Taube (Najder, p. 249, n. 5).

[3] *The Mirror of the Sea* joining *The Secret Agent.*

And this is not only a manner of speaking, dear Madame. As life slips away, the memories of childhood become more precious.

He was vivacious, restless, a little heedless, with much charm and an open spirit. Of all your brothers, my companions in youth—the only ones! (I had no others)—it was he, it seems to me, who resembled your mother the most. And he is no more! I feel myself saddened to the bottom of my soul.

I have the honour, dear Madame and friend, of sending you my last work. I am strongly touched by the interest that you kindly bring to my books; thus I will permit myself to add an older volume—sea sketches—perhaps without great interest, but one of which I am fond, for it speaks of things already distant and of simple men whom I have known.

Please have the goodness to present my most respectful regards to your mother. The now greying man who speaks to you has kept for her an almost filial sentiment and a gratitude for her kindness that time has only increased. And permit me, Madame, in the name of the precious memories which are common to us, to sign myself

> your very affectionate and very
> faithful servant.

To Ford Madox Ford

Text MS Yale; Unpublished

[letterhead: Someries]
20 Feb 1908.

Dear Ford[1]

The other day I have been breaking a lance on your behalf against a man—not a fool.—You don't know him.[2] And I had occasion to say:

Yes. You write, I write, C. Graham writes, ten thousand of us write with more or less sincerity but all of us—even I in my hole—have some axe to grind—if only, like C Graham, the axe of indignation.[3] And of all the men that write to day it is only Hueffer who writes for love—for the sheer love of this world of vain appearances and mortal men. He is not

[1] In his novels and his memoirs, Ford Madox Ford (1873–1939) created some of the best English fiction of the twentieth century. He was also a poet and an inspired editor. At the time of his collaborations with Conrad, however, his list of publications was still short. For consistency's sake, he is called Ford throughout this edition, even though he did not change his surname from Hueffer until 1919.

[2] Tarver, Douglas, or Reynolds?

[3] R. B. Cunninghame Graham's crusading temperament surfaces in his work.

passionate. Passion is cheap—but that sort of impartial love is a rare and distinguished motive of expression.

I took up the H of the C[1] which was lying there and opening it at hazard I showed sentences here and there asking whether they could have been written from any other conceivable motive. There was, I said, a thick sort of [volume] in folio[2] downstairs, 4 other volumes, verse—all inspired by the same deep religion of the lover. And I also said that your note was as clear as a bell on a calm evening and that any prose read directly after yours produced the effect of thick mouthing. That any body could mention, in connection with you, that Virtuoso Cymballist* Stevenson[3] passed my comprehension. I pointed out that were it not for the tenderness and felicitous grace of thought Your prose was absolutely austere. The lyricism was all in the inspiration.

The man was surprised—but that affirmation can be demonstrated books in hand.

I tell you all this a propos of the III[d] Hist: Romance[4] because indeed if that book were not written for love then its existence cannot be accounted for. There is not a single false note, not a jar, hardly ever a pause. It is a great harmony. How fine—how very fine! It is in fact—the whole cycle—a most noble conception. Last night when I closed the proofs for the last time I asked myself whether this was not the Swan song of Historical Romance.

Well nigh a hundred years is a long time for any form of artistic expression to endure. It is well that it should end with this pathetic and marvellous dignity—and for my part I can only say that I am glad *d'avoir vu cela*—the last gesture of historical romance:[5] the hat cast upon the paving. Simply tremendous!

As to the story—in itself—I have nothing to say. We will leave that to the critics who being deaf and blind shall be thrusting their thick fingers into the nooks and crannies with mole-like industry, presently. I won't even think of it. C'est trop triste. But you may be sure that as You have loved much nothing will be forgiven to you.

Yours affectionately

J Conrad.

[1] *The Heart of the Country* (1906). [2] *The Cinque Ports* (1900). [3] Robert Louis.
[4] *The Fifth Queen Crowned*, the last of the Katharine Howard trilogy.
[5] Ford had already written another historical novel, *The 'Half Moon'*.

To John Galsworthy
Text MS POSK; J-A, 2, 67

[letterhead: Someries]
20 Febr o8

Dearest Jack.

Thanks for your letter.

I've had a doctor to see me and am glad to say there is nothing wrong with the veins. It was simply gout in the muscle. I feel a little better—but had a day without a line—no, two days. Which is awful. But I've picked up my work to day: 5 pages—which is not enough.

Let me know how you both are in Your whirl. I stagnate—tho' there has been J. C. Tarver, a friend called Douglas, and young Reynolds to see me, in quick succession. Mary Martindale[1] is coming for the week end. Ford's last Fifth Queen novel is amazing. The whole cycle is a noble conception—the Swan Song of Historical Romance—and frankly I am glad to have heard it.[2]

The first 2 vols: produced quite a little sensation amongst French lettrés. The Revue des Deux Mondes had a fine article in \underline{X}^{er} I think.[3] The SA is going to appear in book form in autumn by the *Mercure de France*.[4] And I have made arrangements to have *everything* translated on the basis of 20% of all profits for me.

And the water flows under the bridges. Its raining. But the glass is rising slowly. We may have some sunshine presently.

I don't think I can come to swell the deputation.[5] At any rate I don't feel I can—today. But I am better, and perhaps...

I hear the postman.

Love.

Ever Your

J Conrad.

[1] Elsie Hueffer's sister.
[2] Behind this ambiguous remark lies Conrad's own experience of writing historical fiction: *Romance* (in collaboration with Ford), and 'The Duel'; he also had as-yet-unrealized plans for a 'Mediterranean' novel about the Napoleonic wars.
[3] 15 December, pp. 897–920.
[4] Translated by Davray, published by Gallimard and the *Mercure* in 1912.
[5] After many delays, the Prime Minister had agreed to receive a deputation of writers opposed to theatrical censorship. Led by J. M. Barrie, they finally saw not Campbell-Bannerman but Herbert Gladstone, the Home Secretary.

To J. B. Pinker

Text MS Berg; Unpublished

[letterhead: Someries]
[late February 1908][1]

My dear Pinker.

Thanks. As to the matter of publicity I can tell you something which you will see at once. We can't compare B[lack]wood with M[ethuen]. B'wood Mag. is unique in its way. Nearly 300 000 words passed through that Magazine and took my name wherever the English language is read.[2] And the Conrad who wrote *Lord Jim* was not the Conrad of to-day, who has done Youth, Typhoon, Nostromo, Mirror of the Sea since.[3] B'woods paid me for the *book* £240 (including 40 from Gage Toronto[4] which they arranged for me). But only say 200. M[r] John Brown[5] told me 3 years ago that my sale did cover up the advance—and no more. The roy: was 20% I think,[6] certainly not higher. Well, on that basis if *M*. sold 5 times as many copies (I only wish he had) of S. A. already, then 200 × 5 = 1000. Simple facts and figures. But as a matter of fact *he* has done nothing of the kind—or at least I can't believe it till proof positive as above. And that will be a long time in coming.

The last I heard of *SA* in Dec I think was a report of 4.600 cop: of which 1.200 Col Ed. the three-penny thing.[7] And that's about the size of it. Therefore my remarks on publicity stand. Whatever *M* tries to do he will never do for me what the B'wood connection has done.

The only recent publicity I had was from Heinemann 3 reviews on day of publication[8] and enough stir made around the book (Typhoon) to impress Harvey[9] when he came over here. Pawling[10] took some trouble over it. So he did over the *Nigger*. But *M* is a mere shop anyhow. That's how it strikes me. He has 200 authors and doesn't care for one more than for another. But I've only one life to live. A man eminent in his way and

[1] Received in February and reiterating the arguments against Methuen sketched out on the 17th.

[2] *Blackwood's* was consciously an imperial publication; its penchant for essays and stories from overseas assured a wide circulation.

[3] 'Done' in the sense of *published*: of the three stories in *Youth*, only 'The End of the Tether' was finished after *Lord Jim*.

[4] W. J. Gage & Co. advanced only £30 (Blackburn, p. 114). [5] Of Blackwood's?

[6] One shilling per copy: 16 2/3%. [7] I.e. three pence a copy.

[8] The *Morning Post*, *Daily Chronicle*, *Daily News*, and *Daily Mail* all reviewed *Typhoon* on 22 April 1903.

[9] George Brinton McClellan Harvey (1864–1928), president of Harper & Brothers, editor of *Harper's Weekly* and the *North American Review*.

[10] Sydney Southgate Pawling (1862–1922), Heinemann's partner and one of Conrad's first admirers.

who had been concerned with the publication of books[1] (not a publisher) told me that the SA was quite worth a special effort of pushing. An effort which was *not* made. The fact is the good man is not in touch with the literary world. People will do things for my work if they are properly approached. A mere hint on my part was sufficient for the Ev. Standard to give me a pubon review of the SA.[2] But it isn't my business, tho' even I could do something from my hole if I tried.

I repeat that M won't get 4 novels out of me on some damned pretence or other—unless by Jove he does something for it except asking *me* to write instructions and a synopsis and a description for his travellers— for his famous travellers. And if I write a 65000 novel he will have to take it. I am not a draper to measure my stuff to the exact yard. If he won't then I'll have no difficulty to get another publisher for it. The next *vol* he gets will have to be taken as the 2d under the contract and in no other way. That will make him a pretty set of five vols if he cares to have it.

Under the Berne Convention *Al'ers Folly. Outcast. Tales. Nigger* have now no protection against free translation.[3] In negotiating with Davray and *Mercure de France* I had to take it into consideration. They could have translated these 4 without payment of any sort. Therefore I accepted the 20% as applying to *all* my work these vols included. It is quite on the cards that the earlier books may have the better success. Davray had the first 3 taken in hand at once so as not to be forestalled by any one else in case the SA (which will be the first to appear) should attract attention. The *Nigger* I am afraid has slipped through our hands by the fault of that humbug D'Humières.[4] But he is of course an honest man and we may get something for it yet.

<div align="center">Yours</div>

<div align="right">J Conrad.</div>

[1] Tarver? [2] 12 September 1907.

[3] The Berne Convention (1866) set up the International Union for the Protection of Literary and Artistic Works; the agreement was revised in 1896 and 1908.

[4] Who had been talking of translating it for the last three years.

To J. B. Pinker
Text MS Berg; Unpublished

[letterhead: Someries]
Friday [February 1908]¹

My dear Pinker.

Send me to day besides the £6 a cheque for £*1.14* one for *1.8*. Also one for £*5.10*.

Tell Moore not to send me the type of the enclosed pp till he gets some more on Monday.

Yours ever

J Conrad

To Norman Douglas
Text MS Berg; J-A, 2, 67

[letterhead: Someries]
29 Febr. 1908

My dear Douglass.²

This is *most excellent* from every point of view.

It is obvious to me that you have a distinguished future before you as a writer. And also some hard times before You get known. Think seriously of writing a novel. Write your fiction in the *tone* of this very excellent article³ if you like. Place it in S Italy if that will help.† Try to make it a novel *of analysis* on the basis of some strong situation. A man like You who has seen things and known many people has got only to descend within himself for material. And I promise you that everything I and two or three more can do shall be done to get the novel published with a proper flourish.

—This is a counsel of wisdom. A novel is the shortest way to a living.

Before all *imitate no one*!!

I send you the article back. Have You another copy?

†But don't make it a novel of Italian peasant life—not yet! Later on you may indulge. Place *European* personalities in Italian frame. European here means an international crowd.

¹ Received in February: Fridays were 7, 14 (the day of the gout attack), 21 (after the worst was over), and 28 (receipt on Saturday 29th was possible); 31 January would not match the movement of 'The Black Mate' MS, and thus the pages must belong to 'Razumov'.
² Quite possibly by accident, Conrad often used the original spelling of Douglas's name.
³ Revised to incorporate Conrad's suggestions, this essay about Ischia was published as 'The Island of Typhoëus' in the *English Review*, February 1909, pp. 398–419; fragments appear in various chapters of *Siren Land* (1911).

I send the article back because I want you to see what I have done to it. You'll see it is *just nothing*. It doesn't require anything. I took out a par or two at the beginning. You'll see yourself that it is purely a question of *literary* tact. The Caraccioli anecdote is very much known and as it stands makes a dissonance in the first rate beginning of Pagan and Xtian miracles. D'you see my idea?

The excellent episode of the "the head" I've tinkered a little—*Commemorative* was put in for clearness of reference to what stands above. *Resting on* makes a better image—more startling. *Concealed* (instead of swathed) after "otherwise" requires no justification—it's in the very sense of the phrase. "*To my horror etc etc*" detracted from the effect of the "country folk etc etc".[1]

The *merest* trifles as you see—and only done to show my great regard—my very high opinion of this very charming picturesque, interesting, sympathetic piece of work.

You will see a word added here and there up to p 4. On p 8 I took out one *But* at the beginning of a par. Afterwards nothing. And indeed why should one touch a thing so individual in style and so full of life. It would be presumption. The descriptions touched me deeply. The anecdotic episodes are indeed excellent. I wept—positively tears ran out of my eyes—over the chase of the hen. The whole thing is most harmonious in feeling, in vision, in expression. And harmony is the form of beauty.

I suggest with all deference the addition of a few words at the end.

You may not like a full close—but the ordinary reader expects it. And the ordinary reader also wants the nail hit on the head before his very eyes simply in order that he should *see* the nail. Later on you will realize the inconceivable stupidity of the common reader—the man who forks out the half-crown.

How would it be to end like this

.... but it needs neither learning nor acumen to see through yesterday's growth the beauty of the antique form.[2]

Something like that. Or *ancient form*. Think of some phrase in strict relation to the image of the amphora. *to do so* are _not_ good words to *end with* a piece of work which hath music to its delicate soul and much vigour in its expression.

One more remark: P. 19. I think you may with advantage take out the words *disrespect or* and also replace *disharmony* by *antagonism*—in the same period.[3]

[1] See pp. 398–9 of the magazine version. The head belongs to an Englishman who has had himself buried to the neck in sand for the good of his health.
[2] Douglas used this ending. [3] See p. 410.

Voilà. Now I want you to send me this piece back. I want to show it about (by post alas as I can't move yet) to some people who may be of use to you later on. Can you retype the first & 2ᵈ page. It would just make one page I think. Jessie would have done that for you but our machine is broken down at last.

> No time for civilities
> but always yours
> J Conrad.

To Norman Douglas
Text MS Colgate; Unpublished

[letterhead: Someries]
Tuesday [3 or 17 March? 1908][1]

Dear Douglas
So sorry I neglected to write you till now. A piece of silly forgetfulness on my part.
I conclude You will come to-morrow (Wednesday) for lunch? If not drop us a wire before noon.

> Yours
> J Conrad.

To H. G. Wells
Text MS Illinois; Unpublished

[letterhead: Someries]
4 Mch 1908

My dear Wells
Thanks ever so much for the book.[2] One would want a long and warm talk about it. To set down the several trains of thought suggested by your pages would take many pieces of paper like this. I must resist the temptation. But I hope that some day we shall meet yet.[3] I have been

[1] Stationery, Someries One: therefore from the time of Douglas's stay in England, January–April, and later than 5 February, when Conrad explained the location of Someries. Douglas wrote on the MS 'Wire Too cold today next Sunday if fine unless you write'. With maximum temperatures of 50°, 49°, and 46°, later Wednesdays in February were too warm to have deterred even a recent arrival from Capri, and thus the visit in question was not the one paid by 20 February. Chilly Wednesdays in March were the 4th (35°–41°) and the 18th (35°–43°), although neither date is easily reconciled with dated correspondence.

[2] Probably Wells's recent collection of essays, *New Worlds for Old*, which developed the ideas set out in *Anticipations* and *A Modern Utopia*.

[3] 'Yet' in the sense of *again*.

more or less ill ever since Nov. The work grows more difficult from day
to day and the faith ebbs out of one as one counts the sunsets and looks
at the beggarly tale of pages.

<div align="right">Yours affectionately</div>

<div align="right">Jph Conrad.</div>

To J. B. Pinker
Text MS Berg; Unpublished

<div align="right">[letterhead: Someries]</div>

<div align="right">5 March 08.</div>

Dear Pinker

I send back the McClure agreement, duly signed.[1]
What about the rest of the vol of Short Stories?

{ *Strong Man Informer. Anarchist, Brute*
{ *Il Conde* under the general title

<div align="center">A Romantic Tale: and some others.</div>

(or words to that effect) ought to make a very possible vol either with
McClure or Harpers—or anybody else. (60,000 pretty nearly.)

I suppose you have already thought out the matter—but I just
mention it and would be glad to know what you think of the chances.

You remember that McClures published the Typhoon vol—without
the Typhoon—under the title of *Falk*.[2] The Vol I propose would have
more matter than *Falk*. And if we only get another £50 for it it would be
that much to the good.

What do You think of publishing the Duel in the States under title *The
Point of Honour*.[3] or *An Affair of Honour* or simply *Honour: A Military Tale*.
Duel seems commonplace. But of course let McClure decide.

<div align="right">Yours always</div>

<div align="right">Conrad.</div>

[1] For book publication of 'The Duel' in the U.S.A., 1908.
[2] In 1903: the year before, Putnam's had published 'Typhoon' as a separate volume.
[3] Spelled in the American form, this was the title chosen.

To J. B. Pinker

Text MS Berg; Unpublished

[letterhead: Someries]
[early? March 1908]¹

Dear Pinker

Here are some further pp. More tomorrow and so on till the end, but You will excuse me from forcing[?] the day. It is a question of days not weeks anyhow. The story is worth the trouble.

Thanks for your wire home[?]. I had to go and dine with G[alsworthy]—I returned immediately to my work.

I suppose the receipt will be sent to you.

Yours

J Conrad

To J. B. Pinker

Text MS Berg; Unpublished

[letterhead: Someries]²
Wednesday. [11 March 1908]³

Dear Pinker.

I send you some 18 pp of MS. which they forgot to post yesterday. On Friday You will get the end of Chap III and as much of Chap IV (and last) as I can get ready between this and to morrow's post time.

Please send cheques with the acct of all these people; and send me one for £5.

Thanks for your letter of this morning. I don't wish to correct *The Duel* to any extent. I haven't the time. But I would like to see the proof for misprints. It need not cause undue delay. I would keep it only one day. But if McClure's object then let it go. The story is all right as it stands.

Raz. will be 43000 words.⁴ You may take this estimate as pretty correct should you have an inquiry. There is a good bit of type that you could show to an earnest inquirer. Meantime I keep it all by me.

¹ Received in March, written on Someries One stationery (watermarked LONDON CONQUEROR). The stationery and the account of 'Razumov' place this letter before those of [11] and 12 March.

² The first datable use of the new stationery, watermarked J. S. & CO. ORIGINAL HARD SIZED. The letter of the 12th is on a lower half-sheet of the same type.

³ The progress of 'Razumov' indicates the day before the next letter. Chap. IV would begin the second part. Conrad found the transition from St Petersburg to Geneva particularly vexing (Carabine and Higdon, *UWE*).

⁴ *An Outcast, Lord Jim, Nostromo*, and *The Secret Agent* also went through a stage of being seen as novellas: 'the form I like best (30–40000 words)': *Letters*, 2, p. 455.

If Duel goes well in the States Raz in vol form will be worth something more.

<div align="center">Yours in haste</div>

<div align="right">J. Conrad.</div>

To J. B. Pinker

Text MS Berg; Unpublished

<div align="right">Someries Luton</div>
<div align="right">12 March 1908</div>

Dear Pinker.

As you will notice the Febry payment has not been made to Stacey and the march one is due day after tomorrow. Pray have it put right.

I forward 9 pp of Raz to the end of Chap III. I wish to keep the beginning of last chapter by me till I add a few pages to it this evening and tomorrow morning.

Please let me know at once if the damnable tax people sent you the receipt?

I will ask you also to procure le *Petit Journal* to be sent to me *for a week* beginning with Saturday the 14 inst. Many apologies for bothering you with this commission.

<div align="center">Yours</div>

<div align="right">J Conrad.</div>

To H.-D. Davray

Text MS Texas; *L. fr.* 90

<div align="right">[letterhead: Someries]</div>
<div align="right">14 mars 1908.</div>

Cher ami.

Ne Vous imaginez pas que je veux Vous imposer un souci extraordinaire de mes écritures mais je pense que vous devez savoir les projets pour cette annee.

D'abord *le Duel* paraissant dans le Pall Mall Mag. sera publié en Mai (je crois) aux Etats Unis par McClure dans un petit volume avec—j'en ai peur—quelques illustrations du Pall Mall.[1] Cochonneries—hein? Je suis malade chaque fois que je les aperçois. C'est une idée a McClure

[1] As a book, *The Point of Honor* appeared in October, with illustrations by Dan Van Sayre Groesbeck; the *Pall Mall* serial was illustrated by W. Russell Flint (1880–1969), later celebrated for his graphics.

dont je suis très content car j'avoue une faiblesse pour cette petite machine ou j'ai tâché de mettre un peu de l'esprit militaire de l'époque. J'ai deux officiers de Napoléon parmi mes ancêtres. Mon grand oncle maternel et mon grand père Paternel.[1] Donc c'est une affaire de famille comme qui dirait. Du reste c'est le coté léger, le côté bravoure dont je voulais traiter.

Ici cette nouvelle paraîtra en vol en Sept[e] je pense chez *Methuen* avec cinq autres—sous le titre general *A Set of Six* et pour avertir les lecteurs de l'intention *artistique* du livre avec les sous-titres suivants:

(L'homme fort) A Romantic Tale	A Loveless Tale (L'anarchiste).
(Le Traître) A Cynical Tale	A Military Tale (Le Duel).
(La Brute) An Indignant Tale	A Traveller's Tale (Il Conde).[2]

Tout ça a été serialisé en Ang et aux E.U. depuis 1905. Les sous-titres ci-dessus donnent le *ton* de chaque conte.

Je suis en train de finir (je devrais même y travailler au lieu de venir vous embêter) un court roman (seulement il n'est pas romantique) a peu près de la longueur de l'Histoire Comique de France.[3] Cela s'appellera *Razumov* et sera Russe—très russe en verité. Absolutisme et Revolution—et les affres morales du susdit Razumov—étudiant tranquille—qui en meurt. Voilà tout. On pourrait en faire quelque chose en Français. Seulement la "grande passion" ne se montre qu'a la fin. Du reste—analyse, mais assez mouvementé tout de même—voilà le *ton* du roman.

Il faudra serialiser ça ici et aux E. U. cette année—mais si Vous voulez je vous enverrais un exemplaire machiné.

Chance le roman de mer (?) marche a pas de tortue en attendant la fin de Razumov.

[1] On his mother's side, Mikołaj (Nicholas) Bobrowski, born in 1792, Chevalier of the Légion d'Honneur, joined the Polish Army in 1811. His nephew Tadeusz recalled that 'he silently and unreservedly worshipped Napoleon' (Najder, *Familial Eyes*, p. 6). On his father's side, Teodor Korzeniowski: during the Napoleonic campaigns, he fought for the Duchy of Warsaw against the Austrians; he fought against the Russians in 1830–1 and was on his way to fight them again when he died in 1863. Both men held Poland's highest military decoration, the Military Cross.

[2] In *A Set of Six*, 'Gaspar Ruiz' ('The Strong Man') has no sub-title; 'The Duel' and 'The Brute' have the subtitles given here; 'The Informer' is 'An Ironic Tale'; 'An Anarchist', 'A Desperate Tale'; 'Il Conde', 'A Pathetic Tale.'

[3] About 45,000 words.

Remerciez Kozakiewicz de ma part avec beaucoup d'amitié pour le Conte Egyptien de Sienkiewicz.[1] Mes salutations très empressées a Madame Davray et amitiés de la part de ma femme. Poignée de main.

<div style="text-align:center">Tout à vous.</div>

<div style="text-align:center">J. Conrad.</div>

Je vous envoie la fin du *Duel* car ces gens là[2] ont coupé cela en cinq morceaux. C'est odieux. Le conte parait interminable.

Translation

Dear friend,

Don't think that I want to make my writings into a heavy burden for you, but I think you should know about the projects for this year.

First of all, the *Duel*, appearing in the *Pall Mall Mag*, will be published in the United States, in May I believe, by McClure in a little volume with—I am afraid—some illustrations from *Pall Mall*. Beastly, isn't it? I am sick every time I see them. It is McClure's idea which I am pleased about, because I admit to a weakness for this little contraption wherein I have tried to instill a little of the military spirit of the epoch. I have two of Napoleon's officers among my ancestors. My maternal great-uncle and my paternal grandfather. Thus it is a family affair, as one might say. Besides, I wanted to treat the light, the bravura side.

Here, this story will appear with five others in September, I think, with Methuen, under the general title: *A Set of Six*, and in order to alert the reader to the book's *artistic* intention, with the following sub-titles:
(The Strong Man) A Romantic Tale—A Loveless Tale (The Anarchist).

[1] Bronisław Kozakiewicz (1856–1912) translated from Polish into French, and had contemplated translating Conrad into Polish (*Letters*, 3, p. 117). With various collaborators, Kozakiewicz had made French translations of several historical novels by Henryk Sienkiewicz (1846–1916; Nobel Prize 1905) among them *Quo Vadis*, and *The Teutonic Knights*. The 'conte égyptien', however, may have been another Polish work translated by Kozakiewicz: Bolesław Prus's *Faraon*, published in French in 1905.
[2] The editors at the *Pall Mall*.

(The Traitor) A Cynical Tale—A Military Tale (The Duel).

(The Brute) An Indignant Tale—A Traveller's Tale (Il Conde).

All these have been serialized in England and the United States, from 1905 on. The sub-titles above give the *tone* of each tale.

I am in the midst of finishing (I should be working on it now instead of pestering you) a short novel (but not a romantic one) about the length of France's *Histoire Comique*. It will be called *Razumov* and will be Russian, very Russian in fact. Absolutism and Revolution—and the moral pangs of the above-mentioned Razumov—quiet student—who dies of them. That's it. One could do something with it in French. But the 'grand passion' shows itself only at the end. For the rest, analysis—but movement enough all the same—that's the *tone* of the novel.

It ought to be serialized here and in the United States this year—but if you wish I shall send you a typed copy.

Chance, the sea novel (?), moves along like a tortoise, awaiting the end of *Razumov*.

Thank Kozakiewicz for me warmly for Sienkiewicz's Egyptian tale.

My earnest greetings to Mme Davray and regards from my wife. Handshake.

<div align="center">Sincerely yours,</div>

<div align="right">J. Conrad</div>

I send you the end of the *Duel*, for these people have cut it into five pieces. It is odious. The tale seems interminable.

To J. B. Pinker

Text MS Berg; Unpublished

<div align="right">[letterhead: Someries]
17 Mch. 1908</div>

Dear Pinker.

The subtitles are to be on the side of the cover not on the back. But I will be sending the stories to Methuen tomorrow and shall explain exactly what I mean too. The thing was to make him accept the idea and this I see you have managed to do.

I have had a touch of influenza since last Sat.[1] I am up today and have been busy correcting a little the text of the stories for Methuen and also the typescript of Razumov. All that had to be done sometime. This evening I shall go on writing the last Chap. of that tale.

[1] The 14th.

I have received no newspaper up to this time—I mean no Petit Journal. I thought I would get last Saturday's N° by this morning's post.

<div align="center">Yours ever</div>

<div align="right">J Conrad.</div>

To J. B. Pinker
Text MS Berg; Unpublished

<div align="right">[letterhead: Someries]
Thursday. [19? March 1908]¹</div>

Dear Pinker.

I send you the agreements specified, about which you have been asking me in the past. They have been only mislaid—not burnt as I feared.

I am going on as fast as I can with the last part of *R*. It is the difficult part. More pages will be sent off to morrow and on Sat Moore may send me the type. By Monday I expect I shall be running free and fast with it. What there is of the type is practically ready corrected for the printer— or an editor.

Thinking of the Duel. My first idea for a title to that story was *The Masters of Europe. A Military Tale*. But I never put it forward. It was really too good for serial and a collection. But now since it is going to have a book to itself if you suggest it to the McClure agent here he may think it worthwhile to put it before the firm. I did hesitate to do so when I wrote to McClure the other day (asking for proofs and at the same time recommending highly young Reynolds). The fact is people are dense to any title which has a wider scope.

I have this morning sent the complete copy of text of the stories to Methuen with a page of full instructions for the typography and get up of the book. That is out of the way now. I don't suppose I will have any proofs till August. I don't want them till then. They take a lot of time and put me off most damnably. I don't want to correct I want to write.

<div align="center">Yours</div>

<div align="right">J. C.</div>

¹ Someries Two stationery, received in March: surviving letters from the 5th and 12th make these dates unlikely; on the 17th, Conrad intended to send Methuen's texts the following day.

To Norman Douglas
Text MS Texas; Unpublished

[letterhead: Someries]
Sunday night. [22 March 1908][1]

My Dear Douglas

Could you try to do something for me? It's not an easy job but it can be compassed I believe.

Voilà. I need to have all the back numbers of the *Petit Journal* for last week—from Monday last that is till, say, the next Thursday.[2]

If you know where the Monico Café is You will find there near the door a foreign newspaper seller who either will be equal to that piece of business himself or may put you in the way of finding a place where the affair could be undertaken. Of course if there is anything extra to pay for the back numbers please finance the whole transaction with proper generosity and send me the bill of costs.

A thousand apologies for asking Your help in that matter which has a certain importance. My usual man (Smith's bookstall)[3] failed me completely—played me false in fact. I don't write to the Monico man myself because I doubt very much if a letter would have any effect. A friend's zeal and devotion are required here. Of course if the thing's too complicated don't trouble.

We hope Archie was not too tired—or cold.[4] We were stupid not to give you a ring. We have been bewailing our imbecility ever since.

Yours always

J. Conrad.

PS Café Monico, Piccadilly Circus[5]

[1] On the 17th, Conrad was still expecting Pinker to find the Parisian newspapers; by 1 April, Douglas had succeeded. Since the ensuing 'Saturday night' letter must also have been written by 1 April, the only Sunday to allow enough time was the 22nd.
[2] For news of the lotteries? [3] On Luton station.
[4] Archie, Douglas's elder son, had recently turned nine. Perhaps his father had been late to meet him at St Pancras after a solo visit to Someries?
[5] There were two branches of the Café Monico near Piccadilly Circus: 46 Regent Street and 19 Shaftesbury Avenue.

To J. B. Pinker
Text MS Berg; Unpublished

[letterhead: Someries]
23 Mch '08

Dear Pinker

Please send my coal man the amount of his bill (enclosed). I promised him the money for Wednesday.

Razumov as it will be may turn out a good thing. A serial of 45000 (say) is easier to place than one of 90 000. As to book form it comes into my mind that Fisher Unwin (who is always writing to me)[1] may be induced to publish in book form on acct of the subject. I could write in by and bye a scene of 5,000 words which I've deliberately left out in view of the possible serial. Methuen should have no objection to make as the novel (?) is less than the stipulated length. P. M. Mag. people have cut the last inst: of Duel in two again. It's exasperating!

By the bye: Mrs Atherton wrote a novel entitled *Rezanov* some time ago[2]—very much the same sound. Only my title has a significance whereas her's* probably has not. My story deserves a better title than a man's name anyhow[3]—with a subtitle perhaps: *A story of the present time*—or something of that sort, but better. I will think of it as I take my daily walk.

Yours always

J Conrad

To Baroness Janina de Brunnow
Text L. fr. 93; Najder 250

Someries.
Luton. Beds.
24 mars 1908.

Chère Madame et amie,

Je vous remercie infiniment pour les intéressantes photographies. En vérité vos filles sont tout-à-fait charmantes. Cela se voit très bien. Vous m'avez fait le plus grand plaisir du monde. Votre bonne lettre est arrivée dans l'après-midi et j'ai passé la soirée dans le pays des souvenirs.

Oui. Le canapé était vert. Je me le rappelle bien.—et vous étiez une

[1] Surviving replies to Conrad's first publisher are few: nothing between 4 May 1904 and 17 May 1911.

[2] Gertrude Atherton (née Horn, 1857–1948), the American novelist, published *Rezanov*, a historical romance about Russian intrigues in California, in 1906.

[3] In Russian, *razum* means 'intellect', 'mind', or 'reason'.

toute petite personne avec des cheveux bouclés et d'une gentillesse exquise.[1]

Aussitot que le temps deviendra meilleur nous ferons venir le meilleur photographe de Luton pour prendre une série de photographies dans le jardin à votre intention. En ce moment je n'ai pas un portrait de moi pour vous envoyer toute de suite. Il vaudra mieux vous envoyer toute la bande. Nous sommes quatre. Notre ainé Borys a dix ans, le second Jack a 20 mois.

Les livres se sont fait attendre parce que je voulais vous envoyer les premières éditions. Hélas! Il m'a été impossible de me les procurer. Il y a des gens que me collectionnent. Du reste mes éditions ne sont pas bien grandes. L'élite me lit et aussi des gens tout-à-fait humbles. Un de mes amis me dit que dans les Librairies publiques et populaires on demande mes livres. La grande classe moyenne connait mon nom, mais pas mes livres. Les peintres aussi,—je veux dire les jeunes, les indépendants,[2]— aiment beaucoup ma prose. Dans le monde littéraire j'ai une position marquée. Je vois peu de monde cependant. Nous vivons fort retirés a 40–50 minutes par chemin de fer de Londres. Puis il y a bien 5 kilomètres de la station à notre porte.

Ai-je raison de croire que madame votre Mère est avec vous à Fribourg? Dans tous les cas, veuillez, chère Madame, lui transmettre mes hommages les plus respectueux et croyez moi toujours

votre très fidèle serviteur et ami.

Translation

Dear Madame and friend,

I am infinitely grateful to you for the interesting photographs. Truly, your daughters are altogether charming. One sees that very well. You have given me the greatest pleasure in the world. Your good letter arrived in the afternoon, and I passed the evening in the land of memories.

Yes. The sofa was green. I recall it well—and you were a very small person with curly hair and exquisite charm.

As soon as the weather improves, we shall have the best photographer

[1] After her father's death Janina Taube and her six brothers and sisters became the wards of Conrad's uncle and guardian, Tadeusz Bobrowski. In the early 1870s, Conrad and the Taubes lived together in Cracow.
[2] Will Rothenstein brought Conrad into this milieu.

in Luton come to take a series of photographs in the garden for your benefit. For now, I don't have a portrait of myself to send you right away. It would be better to send you the whole crew. There are four of us. Our elder son, Borys, is ten; the other, Jack, twenty months.

The books have been delayed because I wanted to send you first editions. Alas! I've not been able to obtain them. There are some people who collect me. Moreover, my editions are not very large. The elite reads me and also some altogether humble people. One of my friends tells me that at the most frequented bookshops my books are in demand. The great middle class knows my name, but not my books. The painters too—I mean the young ones, the independents—are very fond of my prose. In the literary world I have a definite standing. I see few people, however. We live a very retired life, 40–50 minutes by train from London. Then there are five whole kilometers from the station to our door.

Am I right in thinking that your mother is with you at Fribourg? In any case, please, dear Madame, convey to her my most respectful regards and believe me always

> your very faithful servant and
> friend.

To the Rev. S. R. S. Colquhoun [?]
Text MS Berg; Unpublished

[letterhead: Someries]
25 Mch 1908

Dear Sir.[1]

Here's the play.[2] I am surprised you should have a favourable recollection of that dismal failure. I remember of course and shudder at it yet.

But if you think it may fit in with your two plays the only stipulation I make is that the MS should not find its way into the waste-paper basket of the distinguished actress.[3] It is the only copy I have.

[1] 'The Rev. R. S. Colquhoun, St. John's, Sandymount' has been pencilled on the verso in another hand. One cannot, however, be sure that he was the recipient. Samuel Randal Sproule Colquhoun took his B.A. at Trinity College, Dublin, in 1906 and was ordained as a priest of the Church of Ireland in 1909; from 1908 to 1911, he was Curate of Kilmore, Co. Cavan. After several other appointments, he became the incumbent of St John's, Sandymount, a seaside suburb of Dublin, in 1930.

[2] *One Day More*, a dramatization of 'To-morrow' presented by the Stage Society, 25–27 June 1905.

[3] By 21 August, it was safely back at Someries. The 'distinguished actress' has not been identified.

The play has been translated into French and is going to be performed in Paris, I am advised, sometime this year.[1]
Wishing the best of luck to Your two one acts
I am
 Yours faithfully
 J. Conrad

PS When reading, the silly pencil marks are to be disregarded. I have the licence[2] and the separate parts in typescript.

To Arthur Hammond Marshall
Text MS Indiana; Unpublished

[letterhead: Someries]
25 Mch 08
My dear Sir[3]
The delay in acknowledging your book must not be scored down to indifference or even mere laziness. I read the book at once and deliberately have put off writing to you till after another reading.

I am no critic—but neither am I blind or deaf. Therefore I am perfectly aware of the beauty in general and of other beauties too of the book. It brings to mind irresistibly Maupassant's novel *Une Vie*.[4] It has many of its qualities—it has its great defect: the suggestion of fate working like a mechanism. It is dangerous to walk in the footsteps of Maupassant—even unwittingly.

As I've said I am no critic. You I believe write many criticisms but for the purposes of this letter you are just a mere author for me.[5] In that quality You can not be offended if I tell you that the critics remind me always of horse flies buzzing about a ploughing team. They buzz and sting even till blood comes but the furrow is drawn to the end. God forbid that I should buzz about your ears. You have done a piece of work

[1] A version by P.-H. Raymond-Duval opened at the Théâtre des Arts on 14 April 1909.
[2] From the Lord Chamberlain, giving permission for public performances; because the original production was 'private', it had not needed a licence. There is no mention of any play by Colquhoun in the register of applications (BL).
[3] As 'Archibald Marshall', Arthur Hammond Marshall (1866–1934) wrote a multitude of novels. Methuen published *Many Junes*, a story of marital discontent, in March. The ironic closing sentence reads: 'There's no such thing as a man being the sport of fate.'
[4] A novel published in 1883.
[5] Conrad knew him primarily for his editing and publishing activities; both as partner in Alston Rivers and as editor of the ill-fated *Daily Mail* literary supplement, Marshall had worked with Ford.

which has high qualities. Why it does not seem quite convincing to me would take a long time and many pieces of paper to tell—unless perhaps it may be said in one line: I am too dense. Yet I don't think I am too dense since I am alive to the very real charm of the book and I rejoice at the skill of presentation and the serene quality of the phrase. Indeed the art of fiction is *too difficult* as a successful french novelist once said.[1] Trop difficile! And that is the truth. Good luck to your pen.

<div align="right">Yours sincerely</div>

<div align="right">J. Conrad</div>

PS When are you coming? Can't you run down on some evening of the week have a good talk and get back to your work next morning. There are a good many trains.

To [?]
Text MS Duke; *Listy* 278; Original unpublished

<div align="right">[letterhead: Someries]</div>
<div align="right">25 Mch 1908</div>

Dear Sir.[2]

I have never written a single word upon the question which occupies your thoughts at present.

I am surprised at your complaint of want of material for forming a judgement. There is an immense stack of literature on the subject written by people more or less qualified to ventilate their views and opinions.

I am positively unable to understand what you mean by saying that socialism is Christianity. Socialism is an economical* system dealing with the management of property and Christianity is a religion. One is temporal—the other spiritual. Really the thing is unthinkable.

Thanks very much for Your kind reference to my writings. I regret very much that not being equipped for the consideration of economical* questions I can not be of any help to you. But let me warn you against bringing emotion instead of reason to your inquiry.

<div align="right">Yours faithfully</div>

<div align="right">J. Conrad.</div>

[1] Alphonse Daudet told Henry James 'Le roman est un art trop difficile' (Conrad to Jean-Aubry, 26 August 1920).
[2] Unidentified.

To H. G. Wells
Text MS Illinois; *Listy* 278; Original unpublished

[letterhead: Someries]
27 Mch 1908

My dear Wells

I am applying to the Royal Literary Fund, and I ask you to back me up by a letter "in support" as the regulations require.[1] Last year I made just £*420*—and how much I spent during the 8 months of Borys' two illnesses I don't like to say. Anyway it made P[inker] shut down on me—not altogether but sufficiently to put me in a hole. I can't be angry with the man. He wants to see some of his money back and at any rate while the trouble lasted he strained himself to furnish what was needed. I thought I could retrieve the situation in the last 4 months of the year—but from the beginning of October till middle Jan[y] I've had the doctor constantly in and out looking after my gout. For the last 10 weeks I have been better—in fact quite well, for me, but it's no use. I can't make up the leeway of the last 12 months.

This is the situation in a nutshell. You will know what to say.[2] And please my dear fellow write at once to Llewelyn Roberts the Secretary RLF *296 Vauxhall Bridge Road Westminster SW*. It is important that he should get all letters and documents in support before Tuesday next as the committee meets on the 8 Ap.[3] If this thing must be done the sooner it is over the better.

———————

Next year—as soon as we can get out of this house we will go and creep into some small hole somewhere even more out of sight and hearing than this one. I am awfully tired of it all.

Yours affectionately

J. Conrad.

[1] The Royal Literary Fund, which assists needy authors, had granted Conrad £300 in July 1902.

[2] Wells wrote to the fund on the 28th. His letter began: 'Conrad, that great artist, is hard up again' (RLF archives 2629).

[3] A Wednesday.

To Norman Douglas
Text MS Colgate; Unpublished

[letterhead: Someries]
Saturday night [28 March 1908][1]

My dear Douglas.

I am very sorry to hear you can't stand London. I understand this in a measure too. All I have to say is that you must come to see us as soon as possible.

We will talk over your plans of work—if you care to talk about them. If I were informed I could seize any chance that may present itself. Its weary slow work at best this trying to get a footing in the world of scribblers and publishers. Yet it can be done—with patience.[2]

I've been feeling seedy in a vague fashion since last Thursday. Thanks ever so much for arranging the papers for me. Nothing came yet but there is no hurry.

Enough for the present

Yours ever

J Conrad.

Come for the night. Send a warning.

To Norman Douglas
Text MS Colgate; Unpublished

[Someries]
[30 or 31 March 1908][3]

Tres Cher.

The papers began to come along this morning. You are a brick.

You must see us *more than once* before You go. Come any time.

Yours

Conrad

[1] The only Saturday between 22 March, when Conrad first asked for the *Petit Journal*, and 1 April, by which date copies had arrived.

[2] By 14 April Douglas had returned to Capri (Holloway, p. 161). Conrad went on trying to place his friend's work.

[3] The Monday or Tuesday after the letter of 'Saturday night' [28 March].

To Ford Madox Ford

Text Violet Hunt's copy, Cornell; Unpublished

[Someries]
31 March 1908

Dearest Ford.

Thanks for the book.[1] You know what I think of it in so far as I have been able to express it.[2] I did not do it well. There is a singular fascination about this last volume of the trilogy. I've been dropping into it ever since it came—and I am as far as ever from discovering a sufficiently precise formula of my admiration.

For that one must be a critic I suppose—whereas I have only a feeling for a book.

What do you think its fate will be? Have you had any important reviews as yet?

I am stuck dead with R[azumov]. Inventions dead. And yet the imagination works dans le vide.[3] Its a most cruel torture.

Yours ever

Conrad.

To Edward Garnett

Text G. 221

Someries
Luton
31 March 1908

Dear Edward,[4]

Thanks for your card of admission.[5] I have a morbid horror of the theatre. It grows. It has prevented me from seeing Jack's *Joy*.[6] I simply

[1] *The Fifth Queen Crowned*, the last part of the trilogy about Katharine Howard, published by Eveleigh Nash on 26 March.

[2] See the letter of 20 February.

[3] Cf. the image of snowbound Russia 'like a monstrous blank page awaiting the record of an inconceivable history' (*Under Western Eyes*, 1, 2, p. 33).

[4] Edward Garnett (1868–1937), a publisher's reader and critic, was the husband of Constance, the translator. They lived at the Cearne, a meeting-place for writers, artists, anarchists, socialists, and Russian refugees. Edward's encouragement of Conrad was typical of his generous attention to new writers.

[5] To the Stage Society's 'private' production of *The Breaking Point* at the Haymarket Theatre, 5 and 6 April. Although filled with misgivings about the quality of Garnett's play (*Letters*, 3, pp. 375–80), Conrad had joined the outcry over the Lord Chamberlain's denial of a licence.

[6] Performed in September 1907, another play Conrad had read in manuscript.

could not make up my mind to enter the place of abominations. It is not the horror of plays: it is the horror of acting.

Lately I haven't been ill. I have felt only very useless—and that's worse. I lose hold of my work too often not to grow demoralised. One reacts only up to a certain point. But it's no use talking of these things.

Jessie is very pleased to have been included in your invitation. The poor woman is getting more and more crippled. There is a good deal of pain too. For either of us it is not a smiling life.

Our love to you

Yours ever

J. Conrad

To J. B. Pinker

Text MS Berg; Unpublished

[letterhead: Someries]
31 march [1908][1]

My dear Pinker.

I have received ch. for rent for which thanks. The next quarter will be only £18.10.

I would have liked immensely to see James' play. There was neither time nor money for that indulgence.[2] How did it go. I am afraid it was not a great success or you would have mentionned* it in your note.

Please send me a cheque for 2.13.3.

I have had a rather bad 4 days last week. Not ill but unable to get on. I feel better now. I send you some pages—more will go by to morrow's post.

Davray thinks the mag *Je Sais Tout* will take the Duel.[3] I've sent him all the pages. He's very busy with Wells just now.[4]

Yours

J Conrad.

[1] Stationery and the reference to *Je Sais Tout* give the year.

[2] Because the try-outs for Henry James's *The High Bid* were held in Edinburgh. James was one of Pinker's clients.

[3] A translation appeared in the *Revue de Paris*, 15 October–15 November 1923. *Je Sais Tout*, 'Magazine encyclopédique illustré', was a Parisian monthly.

[4] In collaboration with Bruno Kozakiewicz, Davray was translating Wells's bicycling novel, *The Wheels of Chance*.

To H.-D. Davray

Text MS Texas; *L. fr.* 94

<div align="right">[letterhead: Someries]
1 Av. 1908.</div>

Cher Davray.

Pardonnez ce sale papier.[1] Je ne trouve pas d'autre feuille.

Ecoutez! Il ne faut jamais m'écrire *pour répondre*, seulement. J'ai tenu a Vous donner la* programme de l'année voilà tout. Ça me fait de la peine de savoir que vous m'écriviez au lieu de respirer l'air pur du dehors. Il ne faut pas Vous imaginer que j'ai des impatiences ou des ésperances. Je suis heureux de savoir qu'un jour on me lira en Français dans Vos belles traductions. Cela me suffit. S'il y a succès—tant mieux.

Vous dites que je produis avec abondance! Voyons mon très cher: 10 vols en treize ans cela n'a rien d'indécent. Voyez un peu Wells. Lui—il est fécond.

Le directeur de *Je Sais Tout* aime les illustrations? Je l'en felicite de tout mon coeur.[2]

<div align="right">Tout à vous

J Conrad</div>

Translation

Dear Davray,

Excuse this soiled paper. I can't find another sheet.

Listen! It is never necessary to write me simply in order *to reply*. I wanted to give you the programme for the entire year, that was all. It is painful to know that you were writing to me instead of breathing pure air outdoors. You do not have to fancy I am hopeful or impatient. I am happy to know that one day I will be read in French in your fine translations. That suffices. If successfully—so much the better.

You say that I produce abundantly! Come, my dear fellow: ten volumes in thirteen years; that's not indecent. Think of Wells. He—he is fecund.

The editor of *Je Sais Tout* likes the illustrations? I congratulate him on them with all my heart.

<div align="right">Sincerely yours,

J. Conrad</div>

[1] An apology for its lack of cleanliness rather than its lack of quality.

[2] Given Conrad's opinion of his illustrators, the congratulations must be ironic.

To Norman Douglas

Text MS Texas; Unpublished

[letterhead: Someries]

1st Ap. 08

Dear Douglas.

Lucas is absent from town just now and I want to begin my efforts by him.[1] Therefore there is some delay. But I will despatch your *MS* this week to try its luck.

You haven't told me how much I owe you for the N°s of the P[etit] J[ournal] for which many thanks. If not too great a bore would you order it for me for the *whole of April* (including today) from the good man at the Monico. Like a fool I've lost the wrapper and can't write to his place direct.

Pardon this idiotic worry I am giving You.

I feel unable to write a single line just now. Even this little note is an effort of thought and will. It's horrible. At such times I feel positively suicidal.

Yours always

J. Conrad.

Jessie's kind regards.

To H. G. Wells

Text MS Illinois; Unpublished

[letterhead: Someries]

Wednesday [1 April 1908?][2]

Dear Wells.

Thanks. I shall be there—. I've written to Barrie.

Ever yours

J. Conrad.

[1] Conrad knew Edward Verrall Lucas (1868–1938), critic, journalist, and humorist, by way of Garnett. For an explanation of Lucas's ability to help, see the letter of 27 April.

[2] The MS is marked 'April 1908' in another hand, but the type one stationery rarely appears after mid-March. The mention of J. M. Barrie and the thanks for Wells suggest the time of the Royal Literary Fund application – but might refer to the anti-censorship deputation of 27 February.

To J. B. Pinker
Text MS Berg; Unpublished

[letterhead: Someries]
2 Ap. 1908

Dear Pinker.

Please settle this bill for necessaries of various sorts. I must ask you also for a cheque £*1.15* to settle an account on which I cannot lay hands just now, and £2 for myself.

I am glad of H James' success especially as You say that it was obtained in his own way and by his own methods.[1]

You will ask Moore please for the type[2] on Sat: as usual. The thing is horribly difficult. You won't get more than 2000 words this week I fear. I hoped for better things.

Yours

J Conrad.

To J. B. Pinker
Text MS Berg; Unpublished

[letterhead: Someries]
[early? April 1908][3]

Dear Pinker.

I've posted you slips of Duel to the US. edition. I was appalled to see that they have been set up not from the serial text as on[e] of your letters had led me to think but from a *completely uncorrected* typed copy.

That sort of thing is not fair to me. McC should have had the P[all] M[all] M[agazine] slips to set up from. Or at any rate the type might have been corrected before being sent over; as there was the corrected typed copy from which the PM text was set up.

I had to do *all* the damnable grind over again—and instead of the few hours given up to misprints and final polishing I was at it all Friday & all Saturday on till 2 am on Sunday.

When I saw how it was I could have wept. It put me off cruelly from the current work. However I am thankful I did get the proof, by

1 Although *The High Bid* was moderately successful in Edinburgh, it only ran for five matinées when eventually staged in London.
2 Edward Moore, Pinker's assistant, for the latest batch of 'Razumov' in typescript.
3 Received in Pinker's office '4/08'; Conrad expressed an interest in the American proofs of 'The Duel' on 11 and 19 March.

insisting on it in a private letter to SS McC.[1] It would have been too awful.

Well, that's all over. *Don't* let Methuen come near me with the proofs of the Vol. End Aug[st] will be soon for that. I don't want interruptions.

Yours

J Conrad.

To Henry Mills Alden
Text MS Morgan; Unpublished

[letterhead: Someries]

10 Ap. 1908

The Editor Harper's Magazine

Dear Sir.[2]

Thanks for your letter. I'd[3] certainly try to get a story ready by June, for to appear in "Harper's" is always a pleasure;[4] but I am now struggling with the end of a long novel of Russian life and daren't turn my eyes another way. I find it a tougher job than I expected. In these circumstances the future course of my pen is uncertain.

Believe me

Sincerely yours

J. Conrad.

To J. B. Pinker
Text MS Berg; Unpublished

[letterhead: Someries]

15 Ap. 1908

Dear Pinker.

I had my spring touch of gout—extremely light, thanks I believe to the cure which I followed in Jan and Febr.—

I feel quite well again to day.

[1] Samuel Sidney McClure (1857–1949), publisher of *The Point of Honor*, the U.S. book form of 'The Duel'.

[2] A Vermonter, Henry Mills Alden (1836–1919) was appointed managing editor of *Harper's Weekly* in 1863, at the height of the Civil War. In 1908 he became editor of *Harper's Magazine*, a position he had held ever since.

[3] Changed from 'I'll'.

[4] *Harper's Magazine* had published 'An Anarchist' and 'The Informer' (August and December 1906); 'The Secret Sharer' appeared there in August and September 1910.

Please send me besides the weekly cheque another for wages etc to the amount of £6.

<div align="center">Yours ever</div>

<div align="right">J Conrad.</div>

To John Galsworthy
Text MS Forbes; Unpublished

<div align="right">[letterhead: Someries]
16 Ap. 08</div>

Dearest Jack.

I didn't write the news of the Vauxhall Bridge R^d Providence. I heard from it[1] to the tune of £200 on the Saturday[2] (this letter was delayed through getting mixed up with a circular) and intended to come and tell you about it in person. Jessie having manifested the desire to come to town too I did wire you the day before of our intention. This must be the mysterious wire of which you speak. We surmised you would be going before the rush of Easter traffic and Jessie wanted to see Ada and Mrs Sauter.[3] We ran up to your door, saw the shutters up and steered for 1 Holl[an]d Pk Ave. We had the luck to find Mrs Sauter at home with Rudo,[4] and inflicted ourselves upon her for a considerable time. Rudo and I talked boats—model sailing seems to be his hobby just now—and got on very well. He is an engaging boy and no mistake.

I am grieved at your report of Edward's play. As it happened I had occasion to see one or two ugly notices. The dread of something of that sort counted for nine tenths of my dislike for the Breaking Point. I feared and hated the idea of *that kind* of failure. Mere instinct on my part I suppose. I disliked that thing with all the warmth of my affection for Edward & I wished the Stage Society at the devil when I heard they were going to perform it. How much better it would have been for him to be left with a censured* play![5] I know he has not a grain of vulgar vanity in his character but an experience of that sort has its depressing effect. And that certainly was not desirable for Edward who is a grave and

[1] The Royal Literary Fund. Galsworthy had sent a letter of support on 29 March (RLF archives 2629).
[2] The 11th? [3] Galsworthy's sister Blanche Lilian (1864–1924).
[4] Her son, Rudolf (born 1895).
[5] Frank Vernon, the Stage Society's producer, wrote in 1924: 'It is not of course the office of the Censorship to quarrel with a play because it is not stage-worthy, but it was the affair of the agitators to have made their concentration on a play better worth their efforts than *The Breaking Point*' (*The Twentieth Century Theatre*, p. 111).

brooding spirit without any sort of elasticity whatever. It's a confounded business altogether.

Borys came home yesterday. Having at the beginning of the term announced casually his intention to be first in all the subjects he has done it and I suppose he is pleased with himself, but there are no discernable* signs. He went out at 7 this morning with his gun and came late for breakfast having bagged one rook (with a bullet). I don't suppose he will even look at a book for the next 3 weeks. My coal man has offered me a pony on loan for no consideration unless love and respect—and if I can borrow a saddle from the landlord of the Bell Inn on the same terms B shall have a happy holiday.

Jackolo is very well and very funny.[1] I have had a very slight touch of gout which passed off in 36 hours. But I haven't been working very well of late. Still there are 60 000 words since last Xmas which is not so bad for me. Razumov will grow into a short book before I am done with him. Whether anybody will read him (anybody of the public I mean) that's another question.

I have a good mind to send You the first 3 chap[s]—or rather to Ada; because you may not want to be bothered with another man's prose while you are deep in your own work.

I see Heinemann is behaving very decently to the *Island*, advertising it in his spring list. Its the first time that I see a fresh season's book so thoroughly put forward again.[2] It is a momentously good sign anyhow.

More power to your pen with the new novel.[3] My hopes are running high. Our very dear love to you both

Yours ever

J. Conrad

To H. G. Wells

Text MS Illinois; Unpublished

[letterhead: Someries]
16 Ap. 1908.

My dear Wells.

Just a word to tell you that the Literary Providence descended upon me to the tune of £200. Barrie must have worked hard.[4] Of course it is a

[1] John was now twenty months old.
[2] Heinemann published a revised edition of *The Island Pharisees* (1904) in February 1908.
[3] *Fraternity*, begun in July 1907.
[4] J. M. Barrie lobbied energetically on behalf of needy writers. His letter supporting Conrad's application is dated 23 March (RLF archives 2629).

relief—and yet! But You understand how I feel.

I see there is an article on You in the last Quarterly. I haven't seen it yet. Attack—I suppose?[1] I stick here writing that damned Russian tale with the fear in my heart that when its finished there will be no place for it serially anywhere.

Your balloons are really very first rate stuff. I think your illustrator is good too. I've had no luck with mine.[2]

Our dear love to you all

Yours

J Conrad

To Agnes Sanderson
Text MS Lubbock; Unpublished

[letterhead: Someries]
18 Ap. 1908

My dear Miss Agnes[3]

Of late you have been very much in our thoughts. You can not doubt that from a distance (and for this you must forgive us) we take the part of sincere friends in the event which is to assure your happiness.

Our congratulations. Jess wishes you a sunny day, like the day in which we were married.[4] It is a simple and symbolic wish born from the memory of a great light and a great serenity. May these[?] blessings attend you both through all your guarded and sustained days.[5]

Yours always with great regard
and affection

J. Conrad.

[1] A lively one, denouncing Wells as 'a revolutionary fanatic' yet 'the child of an age of *schwärmerei*': 'The Ideas of Mr. H. G. Wells', *Quarterly Review*, 208 (April 1908), pp. 472–90.

[2] See Conrad's complaint of 14 March. Many of the illustrations done by A. C. Michael for the serial and book forms of Wells's *The War in the Air* showed dirigibles in combat.

[3] Agnes Sanderson (1875–1967) was Ted's second-oldest sister. The affectionate enmity between Conrad and 'Miss Agnes' began around 1894, the time of his first visit to the boisterous household at Elstree.

[4] 24 March 1896.

[5] She was going to marry Neville Vibart Ridgeway, an assistant master at Tonbridge School and candidate for ordination. Previously, he had taught at Elstree.

To J. B. Pinker
Text MS Berg; Unpublished

[letterhead: Someries]
21st [April] 1908[1]
5 pm.

My dear Pinker

The letter with cheques for which thanks reached me only to day. It has been found in a circular delivered in Westminster.

On the R[azumov] question I don't like to be positive. You may reckon on my trying hard.

Yours

J. Conrad

To Cora Crane
Text MS Columbia; Unpublished

[letterhead: Someries]
27 Ap. 1908

My dear Cora[2]

I can not sufficiently thank You for the memento of poor Stephen. I had for him a very deep affection; hardly a day passes without my thoughts turning to that genius so soon lost to the world.[3] I am deeply grateful for the proof of Your continued friendship for us both.

Jessie will be writing to you soon. Borys sends his love.

Believe me my dear Cora always

your very affectionate friend and servant

J. Conrad.

To Norman Douglas
Text MS Texas; Unpublished

[letterhead: Someries]
27 Ap. '08

My dear Douglas

Just a word to say I was uncommonly glad to hear from you.

E. V. Lucas is quite taken up with your Ischia paper. We shall try

[1] Received in Pinker's office '4/08'.
[2] Cora Crane (née Howorth, 1865–1910) had travelled as Stephen's wife. A Jacksonville brothel-keeper, she wrote short stories and had been the first woman war-correspondent to see active service.
[3] Stephen had died in 1900, aged 28.

B'wood or the Cornhill. As to the book on Calabria¹ *Methuen* should be your publisher. You must know that Lucas besides being sub-editor of Punch is the literary adviser of Methuen & C°. Apart from that his influence in the literary world is considerable. Your work has a useful friend in him.

If you send me the *Sorrento* book (or some chapters of it)² I will go to work with it—showing it around—talking it over and so on. I don't see why Methuen should not take that work first (I mean before the Calabrian vol). Of course we would try to serialise parts of it if suitable. It would not however be a bad move if you can finish the thing soon to make yourself known with a book first of all. It would be too late for this springs publishing season, and the autumn one is not so good for a new writer. At any rate rest assured that if you write you will be printed. It won't be a gold mine, of course, especially at first but there is distinctly a future. I was sorry you flew off so suddenly.³ We have been nearly frozen up here. No more at present.

<div align="center">Yours</div>

<div align="right">J Conrad.</div>

PS My wife's kindest regards

To Louis Labat [?]
Text MS Indiana; Unpublished

<div align="right">[letterhead: Someries]
29 Ap 1908</div>

Cher Monsieur.⁴

J'ai cru Vous avoir dit qui je suis lié par un contrat en forme avec mon ami Henri Davray pour la traduction des tous mes ouvrages. Pardonnez moi de ne pas m'être expliqué clairement là-dessus.

Je suis touché de la bonne opinion que vous avez sur mon compte et que Vous exprimez si amicalement. Il y a loin, bien loin de *The Duel* a Barbey d'Aurevilly,⁵ écrivain qui j'admire infiniment, moi aussi: la

¹ An anticipation of *Old Calabria* (1915). ² The raw materials for *Siren Land* (1911).
³ Back to Italy.
⁴ The circumstances suggest him to be Louis-Joseph Labat, the 'Monsieur de Bayonne' who appears in the letter to Davray of 3 February. Labat had translated a short story by 'F. Anstey' (Thomas Anstey Guthrie) for the August 1907 issue of *L'Illustration*. His later translations, including books by Conan Doyle and A. E. W. Mason, show a taste for detective and adventure stories.
⁵ Jules-Amédée Barbey d'Aurevilly (1808–89), dandy, ultramontane Catholic, and creator of fantastic and macabre fiction. In 'The Duel', Conrad showed a similar interest

difference, a peu près, d'un verre d'eau de seltz eventée avec une coupe de champagne qui vient d'être versé.

> Croyez cher monsieur a mes
> sentiments très amicaux
> J. Conrad.

Translation

Dear Sir,

I thought I had told you that I am bound by a formal contract with my friend Henri Davray for the translation of all my works. Forgive me for not having explained myself on that point.

I am touched by the good opinion you have of me, expressed in such a friendly manner. It's a long way, a very long way, from *The Duel* to Barbey d'Aurevilly, a writer whom I too admire enormously—almost the difference between a glass of flat mineral water and a freshly-poured goblet of champagne.

> Please accept my most cordial
> greetings,
> J. Conrad.

To J. B. Pinker
Text MS Berg; Unpublished

> [letterhead: Someries]
> Sat night. [May 1908][1]

Dear Pinker

Thanks for everything. Please send me as soon as possible a note of the life policies—Nos, amounts office, etc, etc—quite exact for the purposes of filling the Inc. Tax return.

I am being specially harried for some obscure reason or other. It's positively indecent.

> Yours
> J. Conrad.

to Barbey's in the code of honour and the history of revolutionary France. Both men came from the petty aristocracy and Conrad in his youth frequented the kind of legitimist circles familiar to Barbey throughout his life.
[1] Received '5/08': possible dates would be 2, 16, 19, or 23 May.

To J. B. Pinker

Text MS Berg; Unpublished

[letterhead: Someries]
Wednesday. [13? May 1908][1]

Dear Pinker.

I can't let you have Razumov yet. That story must be worked out as it is worth it. Anyway You will have a volume very soon—or speaking strictly a serial story which for many reasons (subject, manageable length) will be easier to place than a long sea machine. When the time comes the now suppressed passages will be restored (a fortnight's work) for book form[2]—which perhaps Methuen will be willing to publish at 6/–. I will see to it that he gets a decent length for that.

I send some copy in a separate envelope for typing.

Broadway Mag. announce the arrival in England of somebody from their Edt*al* Dep*t*. and ask me to see him.[3] Shall I? Harpers ask for a short story to go into the Xmas N*o* but they want [it] in June.[4] Is that generally worth doing? I have a subject that would do I think, and I could perhaps write that directly R is finished.

The printer did send me the proofs of the *Set of Six*, but in pursuance of my resolve not to let my mind be distracted from Raz: I haven't looked at them—and I won't till you let me know that it is absolutely necessary.

In haste yours
J. Conrad

To J. B. Pinker

Text MS Berg; Unpublished

[letterhead: Someries]
Friday. [15? May 1908][5]

My dear Pinker.

I send these pages specially as I should like to receive them typed

1 Received '5/08': the contents, especially the query about proofs, indicate the middle of the month.
2 On the question of 'suppressed passages', see David Leon Higdon and Robert F. Sheard, 'Conrad's "Unkindest Cut": The Canceled Scenes in *Under Western Eyes*', *Conradiana*, 19 (1987), 167–81.
3 The *New Broadway Magazine* was a New York monthly, later known as *Hampton's Magazine*. The representative was probably Harris Merton Lyon: letter to Pinker of 2 March 1911.
4 See the letter of 10 April.
5 Received '5/08': the request for £1.5 suggests the week before the letter of [c. 19–21? May]. The more conciliatory tone vis-à-vis 'Razumov' does not rule out a date close to 'Wednesday' [15? May].

(with all the others of this week) on Monday[1]—if it can be done without undue trouble.

Send me extra cheques for *1.5. 1.10* (wages) and one for *2.14* to meet a bill.

Would you like to see the first 3 chap. of the novel? There will be six altogether. I am well inside the fifth. You may have some occasion to talk about it. Please tell me what (if anything) will be done with the vol of stories (less Duel) in the *USA*.

Jack writes he has done a lot to his novel.[2]

<div align="right">in haste Yours

J. Conrad</div>

To J. B. Pinker
Text MS Berg; Unpublished

<div align="right">[Someries]

[c. 19–21? May 1908][3]</div>

My dear Pinker.

By the general agreement with Davray filed in your office he has for* the exclusive right of translation of all my works. I explained I think the negociation* to you at the time. No offer can be accepted. I am bound in France.

You did not send me last week one of the cheques I asked for. It was the one for £*1.5*. Send it to me this week and another for *1.13*.

Tell me also whether you will settle Borys' school-term which is due. It is *16.3.4*. Early next week will do.

You will get more pages of MS to morrow. I note what you say in the matter of short stories in US. Your experience ought to decide; but I don't see how the publication of a small vol (The Duel) affects the publishing of a short stories vol.—I am working as hard as I can on the novel.[4] The necessity of correcting Methuen's proofs is an unpleasant surprise. I thought the *Set of Six* was to come out in Sept. or Oct. There's no hope now of writing a short story besides finishing the novel in June. However we shall see.

<div align="right">Yours

J. Conrad</div>

[1] Pinker's office opened on Saturdays.
[2] He had secluded himself in Devonshire to work on 'Shadows', later known as *Fraternity*.
[3] Received 'May 1908': approximately two weeks before the reminder about school fees in early June?
[4] The present letter indicates Conrad's progress; of a type used for the 'Razumov' MS, the sheet carries the cancelled page-number 483.

To John Galsworthy
Text MS Forbes; Marrot 223

[letterhead: Someries]
30 May 1908
evening

Dearest Jack

The book arrived by the first post. I thought it would be much longer. You must have made a severe selection surely.[1]

Lost Day, Fashion, Jack I had seen before. Of the others—but it is impossible to name any one of them before the other. Each goes right into one's vitals and the effect of the whole is overwhelming in its terrible quietness and in its accusing force.

In its parallel arrangement the book might be described as an appalling indictment of the middle classes—a sufficiently small and precise definition to serve a practical purpose. But in the introspective silence which came over me after I closed the volume and sat through a solitary afternoon I felt that this might be the Conscience of the Age overheard by John Galsworthy in its uneasy whisperings—and overheard worthily.

The "still small voice" of the impersonal conscience requires an interpreter—an exponent, it must view warmth and strength from the humanity and courage of a personal conscience inspiring a resolute mind. For the Age whatever its date has no mind. It has many minds looking in many directions.

Pursuing my solitary train of thought, with your book lying close at my elbow, I felt too that I would give all my volumes—the only thing of my own on earth—for the ownership of some of these pages so much your own. I wondered at such impartiality in the domain of pure sentiment, at the unfaltering mastery over expression in the service of such deep emotion. Your indignation itself remains undefaced by bitterness or arrogance. It looks at moral miseries with the eyes of compassion. And as, at the end of day, I heard footsteps and the voices that would be presently calling me away from the solitary communion with the spirit of the book my thoughts turned to the writer. At the end of that meditation born from the first impact of that humanity so deeply felt I was profoundly moved by the thought that the writer was worthy of the book.

Yours ever

J. Conrad.

[1] *A Commentary* was a freshly-published collection of Galsworthy's sketches for the *Nation*.

To Stephen Reynolds
Text MS Berg; Unpublished

[letterhead: Someries]
Wednesday. [May? 1908][1]

Dear Reynolds[2]

I was glad to hear of the vast range and the great success of Your activities.[3]

I haven't been very well, neither have I worked to much purpose. Send me the novel of which you speak so well. As to Your stuff in the Albany I shall instruct P. to send me the last number at once. I reckon I'll more or less spot your intentions.[4] What you say of them is interesting. I like to be told of Your inside purposes nevertheless for man is natural[l]y blind where his *semblable* is concerned.[5]

Ah. Yes. Anatole France. I did hear. They have translators for that work[6] who have got to look up words in a dictionary! Fact. And even with that they come upon phrases they can't understand. Simple phrases. I have been told of one instance at any rate, by Ford. I dare say I would have been of some use but indeed I have trouble enough with my own work, so that my obscurity serves me: because I could not have refused.

Send me Lane's exact address so that I may forward him the MS of *Mountain*.[7] I've just finished re-reading the whole. My impression— which You know of—is generally strengthened. The book stands looking into very well, very well indeed.

Yours

J. Conrad.

[1] The *Albany Review* serialized *A Poor Man's House* between May and August.

[2] Stephen Reynolds (1881–1919) was one of Edward Garnett's protégés. In 1906, moved and fascinated by the hard life of the Devon fisheries, Reynolds settled in Sidmouth, where he shared a cottage with the Woolleys, a fishing family. His books about what he saw and did include *A Poor Man's House* (1908) and *Alongshore* (1910). With Bob and Tom Woolley, he collaborated on *Seems So! A Working-Class View of Politics* (1911).

[3] As a fisherman as well as novelist and eye-witness.

[4] In the Preface, Reynolds expressed his 'firm belief that ... the educated man has more to learn of the poor man than to teach him'.

[5] 'Hypocrite lecteur, mon semblable, mon frère': the echo of Baudelaire's 'Au lecteur' links Conrad with Reynolds, and also Reynolds with Bob Woolley.

[6] Five Anatole France titles appeared in English between June and December 1908; the translators included Alfred Allinson, Winifred Stephens, and Lafcadio Hearn.

[7] *The Holy Mountain*, a satirical novel written before *A Poor Man's House* but not published by John Lane until September 1909.

To J. B. Pinker

Text MS Berg; Unpublished

[letterhead: Someries]
Tuesday. [2? June 1908][1]

Dear Pinker.

Please let me know whether you have perchance sent the cheque for the school fees *16.3.5* as the post office here is not to be trusted.

Last week I've done finally (except for the revise) with the short stories. Methuen's have accepted my suggestions as to the get up of the book.

Yours

J Conrad.

To John Galsworthy

Text MS Forbes; Unpublished

[letterhead: Someries]
10 June 08

Dearest Jack

I hope you do not think that when I write to you about your work I mind the style or select my words. I haven't said half of what I've felt while reading *A Commentary* just because I did not look for words. It is very difficult to speak about a book of such sincere and deep humanity. I am glad if you think I've read the book as you would wish it to be read; but rest assured that what I have said is mere nothing to what I've felt—mere frothy skimmings from the boiling pot; if that homely image does not offend your ears.

Yes!. Of course there is nothing in the way of you two dear people coming here on the 27 and making us happy thereby. The 27 by the by falls on a Saturday. You say *Friday* but it is Saturday you mean—don't you? It's a good day as Borys will be at home. Come by the 12:15 from Pancras—to lunch, and stay on till a really cool, late train. We are counting the days. Jessie, with her love, thanks Ada for her letter. She has not been very well.

I am living and writing anxiously as usual. Jackolo is a jolly little ruffian. Poor B stutters painfully on some days and on others not at all. Something will have to be done with his nose and throat—perhaps

[1] Received '6/08': on the 10th, the revises were 'just finished'; 2 and 9 are possible, but the former is more likely. Publication would be on 6 August.

during the holidays, in London under Tebb's[1] advice. We'll see. I didn't
send the MS[2] because P thought he might want to show it any day and
there's only one copy. You shall see it when you come back. I've just
finished final proofs of the Stories. Did I tell you that the general title is
to be *A Set of Six?*

Au revoir—soon. Our dear love.

<div style="text-align:center">Yours ever</div>

<div style="text-align:right">J. Conrad.</div>

To Norman Douglas

Text MS Texas; Unpublished

<div style="text-align:right">[letterhead: Someries]</div>
<div style="text-align:right">16 June '08</div>

My dear Douglass*

It looks as if one of my letters had not reached you when You wrote for
last* received here a couple of days ago.

I send you Reg Smith's[3] letter to Lucas. I always felt *that* would be the
difficulty. All magazines now are short and snippy and even the more
serious "Reviews" go in for a lot of short articles. The world is silly. At any
rate you can see that your book commands appreciation because you
understand that R Smith's letter being written to Lucas is perfectly sincere.
R. S. is not extravagantly intelligent but just an average reader. He is the
only partner in the firm of Smith Elder publishers—a house of much stand-
ing and fame. It is at any rate useful to have impressed him favourably.

I keep the MS to have a try in another quarter. Meantime write Your
book in the tone of that sketch[4] as much as possible.

Sorry for all these delays. Very! I wish I had an overwhelming
influence in the world of ink.

No more at present except to congratulate you on the real end of your
bitter trouble.[5] We are glad to hear the boys are well. My wife's kind
regards.

<div style="text-align:center">Yours ever</div>

<div style="text-align:right">J. Conrad</div>

[1] Albert Tebb (c. 1864–1943), a London physician who attended the Conrads, the
Hueffers, and the Rothensteins among other families in the worlds of literature and
painting.

[2] The opening chapters of 'Razumov'.

[3] The principal of Smith, Elder & Co., Reginald John Smith (1857–1916) had also been
editor of the *Cornhill Magazine* since 1897.

[4] Of Ischia, 'The Island of Typhoëus'.

[5] The successful battle in Chancery for custody of his sons, Robin and Archie.

To Baroness Janina de Brunnow
Text Copy, Yale; Najder 251

Someries. Luton. Beds.
20 juin 1908

Chere Madame,
Enfin je puis vous envoyer les photographies promises il y a long-temps. Elles sont bien villaines et je regrette infiniment de ne pas pouvoir vous offrir quelque chose de mieux en échange de vos sympathiques et pittoresques snap-shots.

J'espère que vous allez bien, chère Madame, ainsi que Monsieur votre mari[1] et vos charmantes filles. Veuillez présenter mes respectueux hommages à Madame votre Mère.

Croyez-moi toujours

votre très dévoué serviteur et ami
J. Conrad.

Translation

Dear Madame,
At last I can send you the photographs promised a long while ago. They are quite wretched, and I am infinitely sorry to be unable to send you better ones in exchange for your vivid and attractive snapshots.

I trust you are well, dear Madame, and also your husband and charming daughters. Please give my respectful regards to your mother.

Believe me always

Your very devoted servant and friend
J. Conrad.

[1] A Russian diplomat and soldier who had retired to his estates near Grodno.

To Ernest Dawson
Text MS Yale; J-A, 2, 69

Someries. Luton
25 June '08

My dear Ernest.[1]

I am touched and a little appalled at the effort your letter must have cost you in your state of mysterious weakness. Pray don't do it again but just two words and your initials on a post-card shall be looked for from time to time to report progress. We are much concerned at your news.

I have been in a state resembling yours, some time after my Congo experience. It was not the convalescence from the fever. The convalescence was over for a year, and I was apparently as well as ever when that sort of weakness stole over me. I couldn't move *my fingers* (not hand, *fingers*) without sending the pulse up an incredible number of beats. I lay on my back in dismal lodgings and expected to go out like a burnt out candle any moment. That was nerves, and it was a six months job.[2] But you being looked after ought to do this variety turn in 3 months at the outside.

Jessie is delighted with your charming offering—and still more with your thought of her. You don't know what a great store that girl sets on your and Your brother's friendship.[3] She's awfully crippled. It's heart breaking for me simply.

The "western-style" painting looks most fascinating in its proper place—that is on the wall above Jessie's writing table.

Her kindest regards to Miss Gambrill[4] in which I join. She will be writing to you in a day or two. Dear old Jack![5] We are so sorry he is being constantly kept on the rack. I haven't read Noble's book. I know the man tho'.[6] No more at present.

Yours ever,

J Conrad.

[1] Captain, later Major Ernest Dawson, brother of A. J., was introduced to Conrad by Henley and Wells. Dawson contributed reminiscences and stories of Burma and Australia to *Blackwood's*; he served in Burma as a magistrate and an officer in the Rangoon Volunteer Rifles.

[2] In October and November 1890, while in the Congo, Conrad was gravely ill with dysentery and malaria. Between returning from Africa and shipping in the *Torrens* – from late January to mid November 1891 – he lived at 17 Gillingham St, Pimlico. He spent a month of that time in hospital and nearly a month recuperating in Switzerland, but for the entire period he was fatigued, low in spirit, and subject to frequent bouts of pain.

[3] Ernest's brother Alec John (1872–1951), a novelist and traveller. [4] Unidentified.

[5] Unlikely to be Galsworthy, who was not a mutual acquaintance. Dawson's brother, perhaps?

[6] Conrad had corresponded with Edward Noble, another sailor beginning to write fiction, in 1895. In the spring of 1908, Noble published *The Grain Carriers*, a sea novel.

This is a bracing place, 500 ft up. I don't think of the sea now. No one cares about it really, or I would have had as much success here as Loti in France.[1] Borys after trying twice to leave this world (last year) is fairly well now, and at a little prep school in Luton. He will be pleased to hear when he comes home on Saturday that you remember him as a friend.

To R. B. Cunninghame Graham

Text MS Dartmouth; Watts 172

[letterhead: Someries]
Wednesday. [July? 1908][2]

Très cher et excellent ami.[3]

The *Dark night* was received yesterday and the *Wonderful Life* of the wonderful saint came this morning.[4] I am very much touched by you giving me these two books. I hope that by the force and depth of my appreciation I am worthy of the gift.

Your short and to me so delightful visit has done me an infinity of good. Do not forget that we are to see You once more before You leave for the north.[5] And many thanks from us both for the book for Jackolito—tho' arriving in the morning and being delivered to him in his bed it was a cause of a great and rebellious uproar when the time came to leave it for the bath.

Tout a vous

J. Conrad

[1] Pierre Loti was the pseudonym of Louis-Marie-Julien Viaud (1850–1923), a French naval officer. He had great critical and popular success with novels of the sea and of 'exotic' life such as *Pêcheur d'Islande* (1886), *Madame Chrysanthème* (1887), and *Les Désenchantées* (1906). Among those who saw a connection between Loti's work and Conrad's was Henry James (Blackburn, p. 200).

[2] Watts makes a persuasive case for a date in July or August 1908; the stationery is of a kind not normally used after the end of July. Perhaps the book for Jack was intended for his birthday, 2 August.

[3] Robert Bontine Cunninghame Graham (1852–1936), socialist and (according to some scholars) rightful King of Scotland, had worked and travelled widely in the Americas. He drew on his experiences in many volumes of tales, sketches, and essays and also in his histories of the Spanish conquest. From 1885 to 1892 he represented North-West Lanarkshire in Parliament; he spent four and a half weeks in goal for his part in the Bloody Sunday demonstration of 1887. His enduring friendship with Conrad began in 1897.

[4] Gabriela Cunninghame Graham's translation from St John of the Cross, *The Dark Night of the Soul*, and her biography of St Teresa of Avila. In July, Robert Cunninghame Graham sent copies of the translation, a posthumous publication, to several friends (Watts, 173).

[5] He was home in Scotland by mid September.

To J. B. Pinker

Text MS Berg; Unpublished

[letterhead: Someries]
4th July '08

Dear Pinker.

Please settle the enclosed direct. I will be writing to you with more MS next week.

Yours

J. C.

They forgot to post the envelopes on Sat and on Sund as well.[1]

To John Galsworthy

Text MS Forbes; Unpublished

[letterhead: Someries]
Saturday [4 July? 1908][2]

Dearest Jack.

I'll be dumb as directed, but You will send me the first two section[s] of Your MS to begin with.[3] I will return them say in 24 hours and ask for more. I won't have any mental rest now till I have seen.

Pink sent me the wrong cheque, which I enclose here. You have mine probably.

I won't send you my MS just yet. It is too messy altogether and even in justice to myself I ought to have it retyped before anyone sees it.

The lark with Ada and You has made a new man of me.

Our dear love to you both

Yours ever

J Conrad

[1] 27 and 28 June.
[2] Written soon after the visit to Someries planned for 27 June (see letter of 10 June)? The Galsworthys had come back from Devon around 20 June, and the stationery is of the kind used from March to late July.
[3] On 18 July, Galsworthy told Constance Garnett that he still had five chapters of his novel to write (*Letters from John Galsworthy*, p. 166); nevertheless, Galsworthy was eager to show what he had done – a total of 36 chapters.

To J. B. Pinker

Text MS Berg; Unpublished

[Someries]
Tuesday. [14? July 1908]¹

Dear Pinker.

Please have these four pages of type retyped and the few leaves of MS typed and send them back to me at once. I am finishing a chapter with some difficulty.

Send me please a cheque for £10. You will observe that I haven't asked you for any money (except one or two old bills that turned up) other than the weekly cheque for some time. It's impossible to keep going on £6 a week. What we want is a small cottage and if it were possible I would get out of this next week. Send me also a cheque for £1.3.6 and for £1.5 for wages.

It occurs to me that if I had a short-hand writer and type-writer down here for a couple of weeks soon, she could take down a story and *at the same time* begin typing a clean copy of *Razumov*. The present type is so interlined that I don't like to show it even to you. I would, say, dictate to her 1000 words of story first thing in the morning which she would type before lunch. In the afternoon she could give some 3 hours to typing a clean copy of Razumov. This would save a little money.

But I must first have my story arranged in my head and get nearer the end with Razumov.

Yours

J. C.

¹ Although the sequence is clear, dating of this and the other July letters must be tentative. Those to Pinker were received in his office '7/08'; those to Galsworthy and Reynolds belong to this month by virtue of their contexts, their stationery, or both. The reference in the letter of [11 August] to three weeks of 'depressing drugs' gives the firmest evidence that Conrad fell ill around 21 July; this event gives a point of reference for the others. If the visit to London was made on the 16th, the first letter, which must have led Pinker to threaten a month's notice, was probably sent on the 14th rather than the 7th.

To J. B. Pinker

Text MS Berg; Unpublished

[letterhead: Talbot House,
Arundel Street, Strand, London
W.C.][1]
[16? July 1908][2]

My dear P.

You must not treat me as a journeyman joiner. Am I to understand that if the book is not finished by say 10–15 then You will drop me on the 15[th] of Aug[t]. I don't inquire whether it is You *can't* or *won't*. From the practical point of view it amounts to the same thing. Hall Caine takes two years to write his books.[3] J. C. may be allowed some time. If your idea is that my stuff is unsaleable then all I can say is that I haven't made it so. If I must starve or beg I won't do it *here*. That's all I have to say really. Consider whether it would be good policy (from a practical point of view) to drive me away. This is nothing but a *statement of the case*. Don't take it in any other spirit. I have no vice to prevent me working and I am willing as soon as practicable to get away into a most economical hole imaginable and write there night and day. I can't believe that my reputation has gone to pieces suddenly.

Yours

J. C.

To John Galsworthy

Text MS Forbes; Unpublished

[letterhead: Someries]
Thursday. [16? July 1908][4]
10.30 pm

Dearest Jack

I found Jessie crazy with tooth ache which had lasted all day, and transported—it's the only word for it—with admiration of the 15 chapters she, it appears, has read before posting the MS to you. She

[1] Pinker's office stationery; Conrad wrote in pencil.
[2] Assuming that the '10.30 pm' letter to Galsworthy was written on the same day.
[3] Two years in other words, to turn out shoddy novels. Thomas Henry Hall Caine (1853–1931), author of *The Scapegoat* (1891) and *The Christian* (1897), was Conrad's perennial example of the writer as pretentious but inartistic popular success.
[4] Someries letterhead two and praise for the MS give the general period; a note in Galsworthy's hand reads: 'on part of Fraternity, I think'. The opening sentence suggests 1) that Conrad had just returned from a day away from home and 2) that Galsworthy knew of this excursion, circumstances which point to the day of their meeting in London.

cried "wonderful"—which she has never done for anything of mine. But I am not jealous, since I share, I won't say her opinion, but her *feeling*.

Without exaggeration it's no mean achievement for an imaginative work to produce such an effect on a person in bodily suffering and mental strain. I've never seen anything like this. She absolutely glowed as she tried to talk about it; and I, quite impressed and silenced, could only pat her on the back.

It appears she had begun a letter to Ada and tore it up as inadequate. I saw the pieces in my waste-paper basket. It was certainly somewhat incoherent.

I may say that to day has been revealed to me the power of literature—and perhaps something more than that, something more mysterious—the indefinable quality of a writer which is not so much in the style as in the conception, or, more remotely in the spirit of a writer's imaginative power. Anyway I have been so moved by this artless tribute that I can't refrain from telling you of it before I sleep.

<div align="center">Love to you both</div>

<div align="right">J. Conrad.</div>

To John Galsworthy

Text MS Forbes; Unpublished

<div align="right">[letterhead: Someries]
Thursday. [23? July 1908][1]</div>

Dearest Jack

I wish you would ask P. to answer my note I left in his office the day I saw you. He has not done so and from his communication which brought me to London the only thing I gather is that if he has not got the book by the 10 aug. he will have nothing more to do with me. I've been ill the last two days—a sort of liver upset. My brain is in such a muddle that I can't think of anything very clearly. I am trying as hard as I can not to go to pieces.

I admit I've botched everything by coming into this house but even that is a folly which can be explained in a way. However the point is to remedy it. I am sure you are right in saying that it would be better to get out with some loss of rent. I would go to-morrow. But yet I must have the means to look for something. And as far as I see P won't (or can't) finance that business. Yet this seems the only way for him to see his money back in any other manner than that of my demise. I will creep

[1] A week after the visit to London and two days after the ensuing illness began.

into a hole for the next 3 years—if I can only manage it. As I told you I am willing to let my expenditure be regulated—say up to £500 and another £100 for Borys. There is a very good school (with laboratories and workshops) kept by English *Benedictine* Fathers in Ramsgate[1] and the above amount would be ample for the boy. And if anything can be saved on both so much the better for P. These are the maxima providing he settles me clear. But to drop me entirely because Raz. is not up to date will of course finish me in a way and do him no good.

I can't just now write to him—especially as he does not seem inclined to answer a simple question. Ask him please whether he will pay the current quarter's rent? It was due a month ago[2] but I didn't ask him thinking that the book would be more advanced. I must know. It seems to me he won't. And all this does not make the writing any easier. There are moments when I feel myself going crazy. It is a silly and disgusting agony—and so fatal to my powers!

That I run him up to £900[3] is not quite correct. From the acct before me I see I had £479 in the six months—but from that the charges for comm[ission] interest and insurance should be deduced *£109.10*. It also happened in this half-year that a grossly over assessed income tax had to be paid—£50 under threat of immediate proceedings.[4] This leaves £320 in round figures of personal expenditures much too much I admit, of course—but it is only fair that it should be stated to you since he took You into his confidence.

Please forgive this—but I really can't either see him or write to him just now.

<div align="center">Yours ever</div>

<div align="right">J Conrad.</div>

[1] St Augustine's. [2] Due 19 June. [3] I.e. ran up his total indebtedness.
[4] In his recent application to the Royal Literary Fund, Conrad had declared his income as follows: 'Last year £427. The average since 1895 I can't state exactly but it is under that amount. The last 3 years about 600' (RLF archives, 2629).

To John Galsworthy
Text MS Forbes; J-A, 2, 71

[letterhead: Someries]
Saturday night [25? July 1908][1]

Dearest Jack

I won't return the MS till Monday morning's post.

In H. James' Little Tour in France[2] (which I will send to Ada to take west with her for leisurely reading) there occurs a simple sentence which came forcibly to my mind. He has been looking at some picture in a provincial gallery—and he says: All this is painted in a manner to bring tears into one's eyes. I don't quote literally[3]—(the book is downstairs where it is dark and I feel too fagged out doing nothing to move from my chair)—but that's just it! It brings tears into one's eyes literally by the way it is done. After finishing my reading I sat perfectly still I don't know for how long as a pilgrim may sit after a long and breathless ascent, on a commanding summit in view of the promised land.

There is in such a prospect after the sustained excitement of the road the reaction of serene wonder and the gift of much meditation. Various thoughts passed through my head. And they were many, too. But they were not disturbing; for I was thinking in the mood of quiet assurance, of blessed certitude. On the high emotional altitude where your art had irresistibly placed me my heartbeats were indeed quickened but my heart was at peace with itself. There was no discord in my thoughts, tho' some I admit had a questioning accent. I won't trouble You with them all. I did ask myself several things one of them being whether we have not here a writer in direct descent and the great tradition of the English art of novel-writing—I mean the highest tradition.

As I have asked myself that question in perfect sincerity you will understand easily that this one resuming in its magnitude the whole interplay of mental impulses and hesitations in the face of emotional surrender must remain unanswered. Sufficient that it came, not as a mere jingle of words lent as a dignified and austere witness to the power of your pages—that your work so much of its time in its inception,

[1] Someries letterhead two. Written before the end of the month, when the Galsworthys left for Cornwall. Jean-Aubry puts the letter in August but might have confused it with the one of [23 August], which he assigns to the 'end of July' (J-A, 2, p. 70).

[2] *A Little Tour in France* (1885) had reappeared in 1907.

[3] In Chapter 25, James marvels at the features of a kitchen scene by Gerard Dou – a greasy napkin, raw vegetables, a copper cauldron: 'The way these things are painted bring tears to the eyes.' The gallery was in Montpellier, a place well known to Conrad.

conception and treatment seems to carry a great national art one step forward on the historical road of self-expression.

After saying that much I must leave you. All discussion would seem idle. There it is! looking very, very big indeed—and all the pages and pages I could write about it wouldn't, in comparison, be worth more than a book of cigarette papers.

Moreover I haven't slept for 3 nights and have eaten nothing to speak of for the last two days and have written not a page for a week. And it is late too. So I will go to bed and lie there staring at nothing—a greatly refreshing occupation.

All the same I would like a ½ hour talk (but not with the pen) with you about your wonderful Shadows.[1] Not that the book requires it—but still . . .

Our dear love to you both

<div align="center">Your</div>

<div align="center">J. C.</div>

To Stephen Reynolds
Text MS Berg; Unpublished

<div align="right">[Someries]
Sunday. [26? July 1908][2]</div>

Dear Reynolds

You are too young to give way to the hopeless mood, known, I should say, to all writers at one time or another. I regret that you should know it already. It is not a good symptom to have at 26 or even 28 (I don't know your age exactly)[3] with, say, 4 volumes written and one published.[4] I imagine, I fancy I've observed, that you think a little too much of what you have done. The merits of our achievement (I am speaking of *artists*) should not be dwelt upon mentally too much. Contemplated with persistence, they cease to be inspiring. The best would be if they could be forgotten completely for long stretches of time and only now and then recalled. For to reject utterly the help of proper pride would be foolish. Remember that a man is never 'done' till he drops; and an artist should be a man and a half. All the others may be anything in the way of a fraction up to 9 tenths and be still adequate for their work. For the rest you may take it from me that you are not meteoric—neither so brilliant

[1] Called *Fraternity* when published in February 1909.
[2] The final sentence sets the medical scene; two days later, the 'liver attack' had become 'gouty dyspepsia'.
[3] Reynolds was 27. [4] A guide-book, *Devizes and Roundabout* (1906).

nor so short lived. Much could be written on the subject of a writer's hopeless mood but it's a beastly morbid subject. And don't think I am callous. I quite understand that your suffering is tremendously real and your difficulty in arranging your life quite serious enough.

Sorry for the McClure episode. Beastly—wasn't it? And so useless— eh? I assure you and I believe I've told you before that no man has been the better for any connection with McClure.[1] I mean no man of *any value* or any man with a soul slightly better than a chicken's. But on that subject it is unnecessary to enlarge.

The MS and the book shall be leaving Jessie in a day or two at the latest.

I have been worried into a liver attack by things too contemptibly silly (and yet galling enough) to be written about.

<div style="text-align:center">Yours ever</div>

<div style="text-align:right">J. Conrad</div>

To J. B. Pinker

Text MS Berg; Unpublished

<div style="text-align:right">[letterhead: Someries][2]
Tuesday. [28? July 1908][3]</div>

Dear Pinker.

I could not answer your last letter at once as I've been in bed with (I am told) an attack of gouty dyspepsia. Whatever it was it was a very nasty thing and pulled me down in an astonishing manner.

I am back at the table this morning and I pray for no interruption now. Ed. Garnett is coming this evening to have a look at the MS of *Raz[umov]* as the subject interests him greatly.[4] I have arranged with him for a couple of decent reviews of the vol of short stories[5]—that is he will see to it that the right men get the book for review.

Please send the rent £18 cheque to me.

I learn from Fisher Unwin that the *Duel* is appearing in the *Forum*. He

[1] S. S. McClure, publisher of books and magazines, including *McClure's*.
[2] The first use of letterhead three, in which SOMERIES appears slightly farther to the right.
[3] Clearly the end of the sequence.
[4] As well as proselytizing for Russian literature, Constance and Edward Garnett took an eager interest in projects for Russian revolution; numbering many conspiratorial exiles among their friends, they would not have looked on the dissident community in Geneva as harshly as Conrad did in his novel.
[5] *A Set of Six.*

thinks it's a novel and asks for book rights. *Forum* is an Am: magazine—
is it not? What about the McClure small book publication?[1]

Believe me I am very sensible to all You say in this friendly way. I
wish I had two brains and four hands to write with.

Yours

J Conrad.

To Ford Madox Ford
Text MS Berg; Unpublished

[letterhead: Someries]
Friday night. [31 July or 7
August? 1908][2]

My dear Ford.

I've just finished the book[3] which reached me this morning from
N.C.[4]

It comes off magnificently. What delights me most is this: that there
you have *expressed yourself.* You have indeed done it. And it is perhaps the
feeling that you were doing so which has given to the book that
extraordinary serenity of diction and tone. It may indeed have been
written by M^r Apollo himself;[5] for one has a queer sensation of reading
something impeccable and absolutely above criticism. One leaves off
with the impression of having had a memorable experience. Something
not startling but unique. Oh yes. You have done it. No doubt is possible.
And if you experience perchance that feeling of intimate secret gratifi-
cation which visits sometimes an artist, then you may take it from me
that in this case the moment of "ivresse divine"[6] is sufficiently justified.
As to picking holes in the stuff of such living texture (which, I suppose
could be done) it would be an impious occupation simply, and unworthy
of une âme bien née.[7] We'll leave that to the journalists, my dear boy. I
say nothing more. I have been ill in body and am too diseased in mind to
say anything about myself. I don't think I can come down to you.[8]
Everything is very bad here. Give my love to Elsie

Yours ever

J. C

[1] *Forum*, a Philadelphia magazine, ran *The Point of Honor* as a serial from July to October,
whereupon McClure published it as a book.
[2] Between the appearance of new stationery and the letter of [11 August].
[3] The proofs of *Mr. Apollo*, to be published 20 August.
[4] Somebody at Methuen's, now publisher for them both?
[5] The god, now returned to a charmless world.
[6] 'Divine rapture'. [7] 'An unspoiled soul'.
[8] The Hueffers were staying in Aldington, Kent.

To J. B. Pinker

Text MS Berg; Unpublished

[Someries]
[August 1908]¹

Dear Pinker

Send me two cheques of £1.5 each for wages.

I am writing as hard as I can but my worry on the account of being stuck here where I ought not to be is awful. We ought to creep away somewhere at once but yet one must find the hole.

Yours

J Conrad.

To Arthur Symons

Text Copies, Princeton and Read; J-A, 2, 72; Hunter (1985, 3)²

Someries
Monday.
[3, 10, or 17 August 1908]³

My Dear Sir,⁴

Thanks for communicating to me your study of my work⁵—this "rejected address"⁶ to the public on behalf of my art. I can be nothing but grateful for the warm, living sincerity of your impression and of your analysis. You may imagine with what curiosity I went on from page to page.

You say things which touch me deeply. Reading certain passages I

¹ Received '8/08'.

² Although Symons himself made the Read texts, Jean-Aubry proves the most faithful transcriber whenever the three copies of letters to Symons can be collated with a surviving holograph (e.g. 29 August 1908 and 7 February 1911). Thus Jean-Aubry provides the copy-text for letters without MS; farewell and signature, however, must always come from the other copies.

³ Dated 1907 in Symons's *Notes on Joseph Conrad*, but August 1908 in all three transcriptions. Contents and the style of greeting place this letter before those of 21 and 29 August; on 4 November, Conrad told Rothenstein that the article had arrived in July.

⁴ Yeats's friend Arthur Symons (1865–1945) wrote poetry, essays, and fiction. As a critic he showed broad tastes in literature, music, and painting, and spoke up for such then-neglected or misread figures as Baudelaire and Blake. In 1896, Symons took 'The Idiots', the first short story Conrad ever sold, for *The Savoy*. In 1925, Symons published *Notes on Joseph Conrad*.

⁵ Probably the ancestor of 'Joseph Conrad', *Forum*, 53 (May 1915), 579–92, an essay that mentions no work later than *The Secret Agent*.

⁶ The *Quarterly* had turned this essay down (letter to Rothenstein, 4 November 1908). The allusion is to the parodic poems in *Rejected Addresses* (1812), by James and Horace Smith.

feel that 14 years of honest work are not gone for nothing. A big slice of life that, which thanks to you I may say, is not altogether lost. There has been in all that time not 10 minutes of amateurishness. That is the truth. For the rest I may say that there are certain passages which have surprised me. I did not know that I had "a heart of darkness" and an "unlawful" soul. Mr. Kur[t]z had, and I have not treated him with the easy nonchalance of an amateur. Believe me, no man paid more for his lines than I have. By that I possess an inalienable right to the use of all my epithets. I did not know that I delighted in cruelty and that the shedding of blood was my obsession.[1]

The fact is that I am really a much simpler person. Death is a fact, and violent death is a fact too. In the simplicity of my heart, I tried to realize these facts when they came in. Do you really think that old Flaubert gloated over the deathbed of Emma, or the death march of Matho, or the last moments of Félicie?[2] And for the other things you say, things splendid and laudatory, particularizing and generalizing your generous appreciation, I will simply say, I don't know. I've never asked myself, or looked into myself or thought of myself. There was no time in these years to turn my head away from the table. There are whole days when I did not know whether the sun shone or not. And, after all, the books are there! Also a sense of disillusioned weariness. You may be sure that the Editor who rejected your article has never known such faithful service nor yet what it costs one.[3] But the writing of novels, as a charming lady who disturbed me cruelly on a certain afternoon said, "is such a delightful occupation."[4]

Delightful or not, I have always approached my task in the spirit of love for mankind. And I've rather taken it seriously, an attitude I should say[5] impossible for the Editor of a serious Review, perhaps of an august Quarterly.[6]

1 In the *Forum* article, Symons wrote of Conrad: 'Like a spider in his web, he throws out tentacles into the darkness ... At the centre of his web sits an elemental sarcasm discussing human affairs with a calm and cynical ferocity ... Behind that sarcasm crouches some ghastly influence, outside humanity some powerful devil, invisible, poisonous, irresistible, spawning evil for his delight' (p. 579). In *The Secret Agent*, Symons detects 'that destroying element, "red in tooth and claw", which turns the wheel on which the world is broken' (p. 592).
2 In *Madame Bovary, Salammbô*, and 'Un Coeur simple'; the name of the poor servant in the last (one of the *Trois contes*) is really Félicité.
3 Princeton and Read: 'cost me'.
4 This Person from Porlock, a general's daughter, appears in Chapter 5 of *A Personal Record* (pp. 97–105).
5 Princeton and Read: 'should think'.
6 The editor in question was G. W. Prothero of the *Quarterly*.

It seems almost indecent to thank you. But I stand outside and feel grateful to you for the recognition of the work, not the man. Once the last page is written the man does not count. He is nowhere. F. Cooper is a rare artist. He has been one of my masters.[1] He is my constant companion. That dismal "bajazzo" with his debased jargon of niggers and "mean" whites smirches whatever he touches.[2] He's a "mean white" himself, about the meanest that ever stole the gift of words from a nodding god.

Là-dessus une poignée de main bien attendrie.[3]

Yours

J. Conrad.

To J. B. Pinker
Text MS Berg; Unpublished

[letterhead: Someries]
Tuesday. [11 August 1908][4]

Dear Pinker.

Will you please settle this little bill for repairs of typewriter. My wife wants to type the two clean copies of Razumov herself if you will send me a packet of typing paper and a couple of sheets of carbon paper. She will begin at once so that by the time the novel is done the copies will be ready at less cost than typing generally amounts to. Meantime I will be sending you the MS for the first type,[5] unless she finds she can manage that too. But what with her cooking and sewing she may not have the time to do it all.

I have been filled with depressing drugs, all the last 3 weeks to get the beastly gout out of my stomach. It was just like an attack of indigestion, only one felt more ill all over as it were. And the mental agony for the loss of time was worse than anything. I would like a little change for all of us. There is a country inn in Kent where we could get a couple of rooms and live on the weekly cheques for a fortnight or so, if you would find the money for the railway fare, there and back. I have the horrors

[1] James Fenimore Cooper was one of Conrad's first literary passions: *Letters*, 2, p. 467. See also 'Tales of the Sea' in *Notes on Life and Letters*, pp. 53–7.

[2] The *Forum* article identifies no such literary villain; in German, 'bajazzo' means 'a white-faced clown': Thomas Mann wrote a story of that name in 1897.

[3] 'On that, a very affectionate handshake'.

[4] *A Set of Six* appeared on the 6th; by the 15th, he had seen at least one review.

[5] In other words, Conrad sent the original longhand draft to be typed commercially; after he had revised the resulting 'first type', Jessie Conrad would make clean copies.

here. As I have told Galsworthy I would get away into some small hole at once if it were possible. There is also another consideration which makes me desirous to go down to Kent. In that neighbourhood there are several cottages advertised and my wife could have a look at them at a small cost for fares—whereas from here we can't afford the journeys. There is one house near Walmer[1] advertised at £25. It may do. And we could hear of something also on the spot, perhaps, under £30, that being the outside limit.[2]

The *Set of six* is out and looks tolerably well as to the get up. I have no cuttings; but two people wrote to me saying they have seen some good reviews, especially in the Dly News.[3] Could you send me that one? It isn't for the glory of the thing, you understand; and anyhow criticism as done in the daily press is of not much use to one; but all the same it is sometimes possible to get a hint of what pleases the general public and I am adaptable enough to profit by it. Anyway if you come upon anything worth looking at in the way of notices send it on to me. If you are making a collection of your author's notices I will send them back to you without fail.

You will get more MS tomorrow as I am not sending all the pages I have by me. One must look over the night work always.

Yours

J Conrad.

PS. Jack's novel is simply admirable—and it may *ring the bell* too I believe. H[ueffer] sent me the proofs of *M^r Apollo*. It's far and away the best thing he has ever done; and apart from being essentially a *good* piece of work with a peculiar originality in it, it is extremely readable. I prophesy a very fine reception for it—perhaps a fine sale too.[4] Could you procure me a N*°* of the Forum? I don't know that paper at all. I hear that Il Conde is in the summer N° of Cas[s]ell's.[5]

[1] About six miles from Dover and two from Deal.
[2] £30 had been the annual rent of Pent Farm.
[3] For Conrad's reaction to this review, see the letter to Garnett of 21 August.
[4] Pinker also had the task, not an easy one, of representing Ford.
[5] *Cassell's Magazine*, 46 (August 1908), 243–53.

To John Galsworthy
Text MS Forbes; Unpublished

[letterhead: Someries]
15 Aug 1908

Dearest Jack.

I was glad to get your letter. I send you my belated many happy returns of the day. You begin your 41 year[1] with a noble book. What I have read of it haunts me—not with any special cadence here and there but more triumphantly—as a whole, like a remembered harmony. And so you are at grips with your last chapter! I wondered. One had got to trust you now; but I hope that for that piece of vibrating humanity you have composed one of those finales that have a prolongation into silence. That's clumsily said but you will guess what I mean. Moreover all that's superfluous. One can't help trusting you; the compelling power of your great gift has come out and may not be questioned now. Yes. W L Courtney is satisfactory.[2] He has managed to convey sufficiently the dreary nature of my philosophy, the brutality of my *pose* and the inhumanity of my heart. All this is as it should be. The poor man cries aloud for pity and sorrow and its very clear that I will never be able to soothe him by the offering of a book bedewed with tears and wreathed in sighs.[3] His moral superiority is assured. No my dear Jack. I don't believe a word of that article. If there is a *poseur* anywhere in this connection it isn't me. But heavens! I must be mad to go on like this about nothing.—Give my love to dear Ada and ask her to forgive me for not answering her precious letter. I sat to do it but something came over me—perhaps in the words of W.L.C. "the unyielding tyranny of circumstance" or something equally mysterious. I am getting accustomed to such visitors, of late. I am glad she liked the Little Tour. Enough for the present.

Our dear love

J. Conrad.

[1] Conrad habitually regarded birthdays as the beginning rather than end of a year. Galsworthy had reached his 41st birthday the day before.

[2] Reviewing *A Set of Six, Daily Telegraph*, 12 August (reprinted in Sherry, *Critical Heritage*, pp. 213–17), William Leonard Courtney (1850–1928), editor of the *Fortnightly Review* and a regular reviewer for the *Telegraph*, accused modern literature of a want of human sympathy (*ibid.*, p. 213). In this review, Courtney refers to Galsworthy's enthusiasm for Conrad.

[3] In 'Gaspar Ruiz', for example, 'Mr. Conrad tells his story not as though he were particularly enlisted on the side of his hero, not even wishing us to be very interested but merely as one who draws up the veil of an unknown corner of life, and bids us watch the blind happenings of destiny.' Courtney places Conrad, along with Kipling, in the 'modern school of violence which ... appears to be the most popular mode or pose among our writers of today.'

To Ada Galsworthy

Text MS Forbes; J-A, 2, 74

[letterhead: Someries]

18th Aug 1908

Dearest Ada.

I am so glad you had a good, several good words for the Conde. Truth is I am rather proud of that little trick. It took me ten days—you know; and it's the very last thing I wrote with something approaching an easy mind—comparatively speaking. I did it immediately after finishing the shorter (serialised) version of the *Sec Ag'*.[1] Those times won't come back again. No—I am not very well; and the worst of it is that it's getting visible. Yesterday Borys walked in about noon and sat down in my room with his cap in his hand as an old friend might have done. Then suddenly: Come along dada—I'll take You round the fields. As I was sitting before a blank page I got up meekly to follow him and heard more about farming in an hour and a half than I ever heard in my life—good, positive, dead certain information. There's nothing of a dilettante or hobbyist about him. All work is interesting to him as *work*; and his capacity to take things in, without any special show of "going for them", strolling about as it were, is perfectly amazing. And all the time perfectly consistent, never bored, never idle: always himself. He takes some knowing but really he's a most worthy character. But enough of him.

I am glad you like James' little tour. I am keeping the Jeanne d'Arc till you return to town, unless you want me to send it out west to you. Upon the whole I think that it is disappointing. One asks oneself why on earth A[natole] F[rance] wanted to touch that subject at all, and if he had to touch why in that way precisely.[2]—You may well believe that *the* novel is never for a day out of my thoughts. Please remember us warmly to Mrs. Sauter and the Reynolds. We are so glad to hear that the children are well.[3] Our dear love to you both

Yours ever affectionately

J. Conrad.

[1] The MS of 'Il Conde' is dated 4 December 1906.

[2] A surprisingly respectful way for such a sceptic? The two volumes of France's *Vie de Jeanne d'Arc* were new that year.

[3] Rudolf Sauter, Owen and Veronica Reynolds, the Galsworthys' nephews and niece.

To William Rothenstein
Text MS Harvard; Unpublished

<div align="right">Someries. Luton.

19 Aug. '08</div>

Dearest Will.[1]

I've been so glad to hear from you. Your letters have for me the great quality of comfort. You always do say something that puts heart into me. The words of a man who is so completely an artist, not only in temperament and in genius but in the very soul, have a special significance, an absolute value apart from the preciousness of the friendship of which you have given me so many proofs. And all this, Your friendship, your amazing mind that seems to understand everything on the merest hint and the confidence inspired by the uncompromising nature of your artistic judgment, all this forms the greatest part of the moral support I receive from the outside world.

I am 'enormously' (as poor Flaubert would have said)[2] pleased with what you tell me of M[r] Booth.[3] Of course his name has been familiar to me as the author of Life & Labour an undertaking whose very idea must have been prompted by a large human sympathy. As shipowner the name of his firm has been known to me much longer in the honourable references of my fellow seamen. For firms of shipowners have their "name" just as the ships they own—a name of good, indifferent or bad report.

Yes! Yes! We must see each other soon. Things are not well with me but we'll manage it. Meantime with love from Jess & Borys I am always

<div align="right">yours with great affection

J Conrad.</div>

(Pardon these sheets of MS paper. I can't find anything else in the drawer)

[1] William Rothenstein (1872–1945; knighted 1931), notable for his portrait graphics, paintings, and drawings. Max Beerbohm described him as a young phenomenon in 'Enoch Soames' (*Seven Men*): 'He wore spectacles that flashed more than any other pair ever seen. He was a wit. He was brimful of ideas ... He knew everyone in Paris.'

[2] This is not a word that figures often in Flaubert's fiction, his correspondence, or his conversation as recorded in the Goncourts' *Journals.*

[3] The Rt Hon. Charles Booth (1840–1916), Privy Councillor and FRS, wrote the vast and influential survey *Life and Labour of the People in London* (17 vols., 1891–1903). Besides assembling statistics and writing on social questions, he was chairman of two great Liverpool houses, Alfred Booth & Co. and the Booth Steamship Co. In 1896, Constance Garnett asked Booth to help find Conrad a command. Booth expressed his enthusiasm about Conrad as a writer but not about his prospects as a captain (Garnett, *Letters from Conrad*, pp. xxi–xxii). Rothenstein was at work on a portrait of Booth.

To J. B. Pinker

Text MS Berg; Unpublished

[Someries]
Wednesday [19 or 26 August
1908][1]

My dear Pinker.

Thanks very much for the cheques.

I can't complain, certainly, of the reception of the *Set*. I even confess to astonishment at the notice taken of a mere vol of short stories.

Everything is said, affirmed and denied the author* being both black and white not to mention several other colours.[2] Whereas the truth, the simple truth is that author is just an artist: the stimulator of imagination apart from whatever effect the subject itself can have. The subject being slight and as it were not controversial in the Il Conde[3] all the critics who mention the story extol its art.[4] Whereas as a matter of fact its art is no lesser or greater than the art of the other tales.

All this is curious to me. We shall have much more clacking over Razumov and after that *Chance*[5] will come with its old effect—analysis applied to the life at sea.[6]

Yours always

J. Conrad.

To Edward Garnett

Text MS Free; J-A, 2, 74; G. 221

[Someries]
21 Aug. morning
1908

Dearest Edward.

I write instantly to tell you of the great, great pleasure your note brought to me to begin the day with.

Your classification of the tales is eminently satisfactory to me. I feel it

[1] Received '8/08': as of 12 August, only three reviews (*Scotsman*, *Daily News*, *Daily Telegraph*) had appeared; the later Wednesdays in August are therefore more likely.

[2] A protest against biographically-inclined reviews? Robert Lynd, for example, began his review for the *Daily News*: 'Mr. Conrad, as everybody knows, is a Pole, who writes English by choice, as it were, rather than by nature.'

[3] As opposed to the political or historical stories such as 'The Informer' or 'Gaspar Ruiz'?

[4] 'Il Conde' ... 'artistically considered, is the best of the set': *TLS*, 13 August, p. 261. Many reviewers, however, agreed with the *Observer* (16 August) that every story was 'a consummate work of art'.

[5] At the end of 1907, Conrad had interrupted *Chance* to dash off – as he then expected – 'Razumov'.

[6] In other words, a return to the mode of *Lord Jim*?

is perfectly right. I am delighted to see you put the *Conde* 3d; and as to the *Informer* (for which I have been complimented and lauded from the US[1] and from France) I put it in to make up the vol to requisite thickness— not from a desire to please all the world and his wife. I could not call the vol *The Duel* because R. Marsh, novelist, had protested against the title (when appearing serially in Pall Mall Mag.) as having been already used by him.[2] Finally I concluded to arrange the tales chronologically and thus Gaspar Ruiz had to come first—dating from Jany 1905.[3] As at that time I was also writing the middle papers of the Mirror of the Sea you will admit that the child of your literary adoption has some versatility. Eh?

W. L. Courtney in a long article calls the *Duel* tedious and *Gaspar Ruiz* a masterpiece; and myself a heartless wretch with a pose of brutality like the rest of the moderns. Still, always according to WLC, there are two masterpieces and a half in the vol—*G Ruiz* being one of them, *An Anarch*: the other and the *Brute* the doubtful one.[4]

Your acceptance of *The Duel* is balm to my soul. My first intention was to call that story *The Masters of Europe* but I rejected it as pretentious. Anyway I did conscientiously try to put in as much of Napoleonic feeling as the subject could hold. This has been missed by all the reviewers, every single one being made blind by the mere tale. I confess to you that I rested my trust on your judgment and would have been horribly cut up if you had condemned the story. It has been waved away by more than one editor I believe—and the P.M.M. (which favours me generally as witness *Typhoon*, *G. Ruiz*) accepted it with some hesitation I am told. A complimentary phrase to the address of the P M M would be a reward of moral courage and some insight.

Yes dear. I'll like and respect all you have to say. The *Times'* review seemed to me insignificant.[5] But there is a fellow in the *Dly News* who calls me—God only knows on what provocation—a man without country and language.[6] It is like abusing a tongue-tied man. For what

[1] Where it had appeared in *Harper's Magazine*.
[2] Richard Marsh and Conrad shared a publisher, but not much else. Methuen brought out *A Duel* in 1904, one of the 30 volumes that Marsh produced between 1901 and 1905.
[3] First mentioned (as 'Benavides') October 1904; by 4 January 1905, two-thirds had been written (*Letters*, 3, pp. 171, 200).
[4] In his *Daily Telegraph* review, Courtney asserts that of the six stories 'two, or, perhaps, three . . . are masterpieces'; 'The Duel' he calls 'tedious through its unnecessary length'.
[5] The *TLS* review (13 August, p. 261) praised Conrad for overcoming 'that confusion between a short story and a novel from which he suffered sometimes in the past'.
[6] Robert Lynd's review appeared on 10 August; Sherry reprints it in *Critical Heritage*, pp. 210–12. The offending sentences read: 'Mr. Conrad, without either country or

can one say. The statement is simple and brutal; and any answer would involve too many feelings of one's inner life, stir too much secret bitterness and complex loyalty to be even attempted with any hope of being understood. I thought that a man who has written the *Nigger*, *Typhoon*, *The End of the Tether*, *Youth*, was safe from that sort of thing. But apparently not. If I had made money by dealing in diamond shares like my neighbour here Sir Julius Wernher, of Hamburg,[1] I would be a baronet of the U K and provided both with a language and a country. Still I suppose the man is simply an ass; and even the tribute he pays to your wife's unforgettable achievement[2] fails to mollify me, for this once. For he goes on shoving me with incredibly folly on to Turgeniev à propos of *G. Ruiz*, comparing it with *The Lear of the Steppes* do you understand?—The Lear!!! that infernal magazine fake with *The Lear of the Steppes*!!![3] It is enough to make one wonder whether the man understands the words he writes—whether he has sense and judgment enough to come in when it rains? Has ever the Shade of a great artist been more amazingly, more gratuitously insulted? Who's that fellow Lynn?[4] Couldn't someone speak to him quietly and suggest he should go behind a counter and weigh out margarine by the sixpennyworth? I can understand Anderson Graham to whom I am such an offensive fraud that he can't even see me scratch the side of my nose without exasperation at the indecency of the thing.[5] That's a genuine temperamental expression, frank and honourable enough in its way tho'

language, may be thought to have found a new patriotism for himself in the sea. His vision of men, however, is the vision of a cosmopolitan, of a homeless person. Had he but written in Polish his stories would have assuredly been translated into English and into the other languages of Europe; and the works of Joseph Conrad translated from the Polish would, I am certain, have been a more precious possession on English shelves than the works of Joseph Conrad in the original English, desirable as these are.'

[1] Someries stood on the land of Sir Julius Charles Wernher (1850–1912), the German-born speculator who had made a fortune in South Africa.

[2] Lynd asks 'What greater contribution has been made during the past twenty years than Mrs. Constance Garnett's translations of the novels of Turgénieff?'

[3] Although the invocation of Turgenev's story might at first seem complimentary, Lynd uses the comparison to diminish Conrad who 'is not, when all is said, a tragic writer'.

[4] Robert Lynd (1879–1949), a journalist from the North of Ireland: later he became literary editor of the *New Chronicle* and the 'John O'London' who gave his name to the weekly assortment of bookish gossip.

[5] Anderson Graham's unsigned review for *Country Life*, 15 August, pp. 234–5, reappears in *Critical Heritage*, pp. 217–19. Graham patronises his victim throughout: 'Mr. Conrad possesses many of the attributes of the artist, and nothing could be more disappointing than his misuse, for example of the term ironic.' Of the ending of 'Gaspar Ruiz' he writes: 'This, surely, is not very great art; it is not much greater than that of the sensational reporter who gathers together thousands of readers for the rag that will print his account of the last dying struggles of some wretched criminal hanged for murder.'

certainly a little funny. He jumps on me with both feet[1] in the *Country Life* "book of the week". But the Dly News article is beyond everything the gloomiest pessimism as to the good feeling and common decency of daily criticism could imagine.

Thanks once more for your dear little note and for the forthcoming review.[2] Remember me to your wife and David[3] when You write. Love from us all.

<div style="text-align: right">Yours ever
J. Conrad.</div>

PS No. The house was unsuitable. We are trying for something Ashford way, towards Aldington and Smeeth.

To Arthur Symons
Text MS NYPL; Unpublished

<div style="text-align: right">[letterhead: Someries]
21 Augst 1908</div>

Dear Mr Symons.

I am ashamed of the bedraggled condition of this the only copy of the play[4] now in existence.

It would be a happy coincidence if you, who were the first to serialize my beginner's prose in to the light of the larger day,[5] should help cette petite chose là[6] towards the footlights.

<div style="text-align: right">Very sincerely yours
J. Conrad.</div>

P.S. I am not responsible for the *pencil* erasures and additions. I neither approve nor disapprove them.

[1] The phrase recurs in *A Personal Record*, Chapter 6, p. 106.
[2] See the letter of 28 August.
[3] Constance and Edward's son, the novelist-to-be. [4] *One Day More*.
[5] 'The Idiots' came out in a single issue of *The Savoy*, October 1896.
[6] 'That trifle'.

To John Galsworthy
Text MS Forbes; J-A, 2, 70

Someries
Luton
Sunday night [23 August 1908][1]

My dearest Jack

Let us shake hands on that *last chapter*. I am sure that Your misgivings have no reason to be—yet it it is unavoidable and perhaps even right that they should be.

For my part I am awaiting the promised MS without misgivings. I only wish I were one hundre[d]th part as certain of my own work.

I am awfully done up and want a change. If we could take a cottage somewhere in Kent for 3–4 weeks it would be nice. At the same time we could look out for something permanent down that way. Of course that would not mean stopping writing—quite the contrary. It's here that the pen is clogged. I have a positive horror of this place, and wake up each morning with a dread of the day before me.

Courtney did not discompose me much. What does it all matter? There is an ass who tells me in Dly News on god knows what provocation that I am a man "without country and language." It is like abusing some poor tongue-tied wretch. For, what can one say? The statement is gross and palpable and the answer that could be made would be incomprehensible to nine tenths of the hearers who would not have imagination enough to believe that a complex sentiment can be true. I wonder in what language the Nigger, Youth or the Mirror *could* have been written? But the fellow must be an imbecile anyhow since he goes on falling into raptures over Gaspar Ruiz and comparing that wretched magazine fake with the Lear of the Steppes!!! It's incredible isn't it? Idiocy can no farther go! Still a kick from a donkey hurts as much as from a nobler animal and is in a way more humiliating.

I don't know why I am telling You all this. My heart has been like a stone and my hand wore lead all day—and I don't know why I should inflict this mood on You. It's indecent. And yet to hold one's tongue is too difficult, at times. To turn out a volume in 10 months is difficult, too[2]—what do you think? The above Dly News genius exclaims that my novels would have been much better if translated by Mrs Garnett. That's an idea. Shall I send her the clean type of Razumov? But why

[1] After the note from Garnett on the 20th or 21st, but before going to Aldington on the 29th.

[2] Conrad had been working on 'Razumov' for about nine months.

complicate life to that extent? She ought to write them; and then the harmless reviewer could begin something like this: "M^r Joseph Conrad's latest novel written by Mrs Garnett is a real acquisition for our literature, not like the others previously published which on the whole were rather noxious if amazing phenomena etc etc".

A propos of masterpieces (the article seems rather common nowadays) Edward thinks the *Duel* is one. That means that it is worth just three and six (3/6). For observe: The volume is priced at six shillings (6/-) and I can't really let the five other stories go at less than sixpence (6^d) a piece. It wouldn't be business.

Seriously, I am glad Edward likes the thing. I had him rather in my eye and would have been cut up if he had failed me there. He puts that first, the *Anarch* second *Il Conde* third. A concensus* of noble minds (Ada's and Edward's) exalts this trifle, to my unspeakable satisfaction. *Gaspar* comes last in his list. As to the *Informer*—il crache dessus[1]—he won't have him at any price.

So, writing to you I have written myself into courage to go to bed at last. And now I am really going. Love to Ada.

Yours ever

J. C.

To Edward Garnett

Text MS Yale; J-A, 2, 82; G. 225

[Someries]
28 Aug '08

Dearest Edward.

I have the *Nation* and I must thank you for the article.[2] No doubt to put one's tongue into both cheeks at once is an immoral trick and I suspect that it is on that ground that you and W. L. Courtney (bow) meet in the condemnation of the *Informer*.[3]

I don't defend him—it. But let me ask is my earnestness of no account? Is that a Slavonic trait? And I am earnest, terribly earnest.[4]

[1] 'He spits on him'.
[2] 'The Genius of Mr. Conrad', 22 August, pp. 746–8; reprinted in *Critical Heritage*, pp. 221–3. Garnett's review is unsigned.
[3] Courtney judges the tale 'comparatively speaking, a failure, for we do not quite understand from the last few sentences what he is driving at'. Garnett complains of the characters' 'not acting true to type, but being plausibly brought together for the purpose of the story'.
[4] The *TLS* reviewer calls Conrad's stories 'characteristically English by virtue of the humour that plays all about them'; in rebuttal, Garnett argues that his friend's humour

Carlyle bending over the history of Frederick called the Great was a mere trifle, a volatile butterfly, in comparison.[1] For that good man had only to translate himself out of bad German into the English we know whereas I had to work like a coalminer in his pit quarrying all my English sentences out of a black night.

For that reason, I suppose, I read in a study (still unpublished) of Conrad,[2] that I gloat over scenes of cruelty and am obsessed by visions of spilt blood.

At any rate I think I have always written with dignity, with more dignity than the above-alluded-to butterfly ever could command. And that not certainly from lack of conviction which often takes that outward form. The fact is that I have approached things human in a spirit of piety foreign to those lovers of humanity who would like to make of life a sort of Cook's Personally Conducted Tour[3]—from the craddle* to the grave. I have never debased that quasi-religious sentiment by tears and groans and sighs, I have neither grinned nor gnashed my teeth. In a word I have behaved myself decently—which, except in the gross conventional sense is not so easy as it looks. Therefore there are [those] who reproach me with the pose of brutality with the lack of all heart delicacy, sympathy—sentiment—idealism. There is even one abandonned* creature, who says I am a neo-platonist.[4] What on earth is that?

However as long as *You* are there my memory will be safe. That's what I thought while reading your review. The quotation is most skilfully selected since it is effective per se not depending on the remote context and giving a good, almost too good, idea of the story.[5]

We are going for a week or so to Aldington—rooms in a farmhouse not very far from the Hueffers.[6] I shall probably take a long spell of heavy

'is essentially Slav in its ironic acceptance of the pathetic futility of human nature, and quite un-English in its refinement'.

[1] A tireless author pursuing a tireless subject, Thomas Carlyle spent fourteen years working on his six-volume *History of Frederick the Great* and paced every one of his hero's battlefields.

[2] Presumably the one by Arthur Symons.

[3] Those who used the services of Thomas Cook and Sons had no fear of rude surprises by the unforeseen.

[4] Untraced: In the *Star* (15 August), James Douglas placed Conrad with Hardy as 'philosophic story-tellers'.

[5] The extract comes from pp. 146–8 of 'An Anarchist', describing Paul's drunken antics in a café and his arrest for 'assault, seditious crimes, and anarchist propaganda'.

[6] Elsie Hueffer had been living at Hurst Cottage, Aldington since the autumn of 1907; more often than not, Ford stayed in London.

pulling at the novel without a name.[1] I have it all in my head and yet when it comes to writing I simply can't find the words. I have been like that before 10 years ago[2] but now it is a more serious portent. I am just a bit scared—but don't mention it to anybody. I wish I could believe in an intelligent, benevolent Supreme Being to whom I could leave the task of paying my debts—such debts as the one I owe you for instance. And perhaps there is one. I don't know but it is clear that unless there be a God to repay you in some heavenly coin I shall die in your debt. Love from us all

<div style="text-align:center">Yours</div>

<div style="text-align:right">J. Conrad.</div>

To Arthur Symons
Text MS Lohf; J-A, 2, 83; Hunter (1985, 3)

<div style="text-align:right">[Someries]
29 Aug 1908</div>

Dear Mr. Symons.

I doubt whether I have expressed sufficiently that sort of special pleasure the recognition of my work by a man like you was certain to give me. That feeling partaking of shyness and delight is difficult to express. And the characteristic generosity of the recognition has almost frightened me. Meditating the trouble You have taken over my pages I feel remorseful also—as though I had cheated You—not your intelligence that would be impossible, but your benevolence and perhaps Your hopes a little—just a little. A reader like you puts so much of his own high quality into a work he is reading directly the writer has been lucky enough to awaken his sympathy! I am afraid that You have given without counting—and yet I would be glad to believe that I deserve this profusion; for indeed what you give is eminently worth holding.

One thing that I am certain of, is that I have approached the object of my task, things human, in a spirit of piety. The earth is a temple where there is going on a mystery play childish and poignant, ridiculous and awful enough, in all conscience.[3] Once in I've tried to behave decently. I have not degraded the quasi-religious sentiment by tears and groans; and if I have been amused or indignant I've neither grinned nor gnashed my teeth. In other words I've tried to write with dignity, not out of

1 'Razumov' had come to seem an inadequate name. The first occurrence of *Under Western Eyes* as a title comes in the letter of [12? January 1910].

2 See, for instance, the unhappy letter to Garnett of 29 March [1898] (*Letters*, 2, pp. 49–50).

3 Much in this passage recalls the Preface to *The Nigger of the 'Narcissus'* (1897).

regard for myself but for the sake of the spectacle, the play with an obscure beginning and an unfathomable *denoûment*.

I don't think that this has been noticed. It is your penitent beating the floor with his forehead and the extatic* worshipper at the rails that are obvious to the public eye. The man standing quietly in the shadow of the pillar if noticed at all runs the risk of being suspected of sinister designs. Thus I've been called a heartless wretch a man without ideals and a poseur of brutality.[1] But I will confess to you under seal of secrecy that I *don't believe* I am such as I appear to mediocre minds.

But enough. You have, unexpected, like a burglar, forced the lock of the safe where I keep my stock of megalomania. So I don't apologise for these worthless outpourings. It's your fault clearly, but you shall be no longer punished. As I wrote to a friend lately[2] I have been quarrying my English out of a black night, working like a coalminer in his pit. For fourteen years now I have been living as if in a cave without echoes. If you come shouting gloriously at the mouth of the same You can't really expect from me to pretend I am not there.

I am profoundly touched by your letter but that I am sure you understand already.

<div align="center">Yours</div>

<div align="right">J. Conrad</div>

PS We are going off to day to stay near Ford Madox Hueffer in Aldington n[r] Hythe. Kent. Hogben House. Should you hear anything of the play[3] a letter will find me there for the next fortnight. I will be struggling desperately with a novel now already overdue.

To John Galsworthy

Text MS Forbes; J-A, 2, 76

<div align="right">[Aldington]
Wednesday night
[2–3 September 1908][4]</div>

Dearest Jack.

From one point of view I've nothing but admiration for the ending of

[1] As in Courtney's review for the *Telegraph*. [2] To Garnett the day before.

[3] The letter of [4 September] shows that Mrs Pat Campbell had looked at the script; she had recently acted in Hugo von Hofmannsthal's *Elektra*, translated by Symons.

[4] After the letter of [23 August], when Conrad had not seen the ending of 'Shadows'/ *Fraternity*; also after meeting in 'a most inconsiderate thunderstorm'. There were no such storms before Wednesday the 26th, but there were on 28 and 30 August, and 2 September. [2 September, PS on the 3rd] is the last possible dating to accommodate the sequence of undated letters about Galsworthy's novel written before the dated letter of 19 September.

Shadows. Its naturalness is appalling. Of course it can be attacked, but its quality comes out in the fact that the objections fade away as soon as one tries to formulate them to oneself. I will not touch on [a]esthetic value of these last pages. That can not be questioned. The beauty of certain passages glows and sighs at one. The question if one could stand up before the sheer merit of expression would be rooted deep under the fair surface.[1]

Having said that much I could go on writing several pages of pretty-pretty talk to you and it would not be insincere either. But life is too short for that—not yours, but mine I mean to say. And there is another consideration as well. It would not be worthy of you—and, well, of me too.

The social background of the story is too big for the personages in front and perhaps a little too remote.[2] If the story had been the story of the loves of Martin and Thyme[3] it would have been impossible to make those objections—or at any rate very difficult to make them. As it is the background is connected with the action not by the developments of the action itself but more or less by analysis. That I think is a defect. But that observation, I am ready to admit may spring not from the truth of things but from some defect of my understanding which causes me to be blind to subtler connections existing both in your mind and in your work. I may have missed many delicate indications. A book like this demands many auditions. It is anything but simple. Its suggestions are multiple—(in which by the bye it does not resemble the work of Turgeniev whom the idle paragraphist proclaims your chosen master[4]) and run in and out of each other.

Yes! It is a complicated book. It is possible to view it in innumerable ways for it excites imagination at every step. But before all it is the book of a moralist.

For that is my dear Jack what You are—a humanitarian moralist. You are revealing yourself as a moralist in all the greatness of your talent.

This fact which you can not help and which may lead you yet to become the Idol of the Public—if I may so express myself—arises as the

[1] Jean-Aubry's added commas after 'question' and 'expression' make the sentence clearer.

[2] *Fraternity* contrasts the well-to-do inhabitants of Campden Hill (Galsworthy's own territory) with their 'shadows' down, in every sense, in Notting Vale.

[3] Martin Stone, a young doctor, and Thyme Dallison, an art student; both are more vigorous than their elders.

[4] Galsworthy himself called Turgenev and Maupassant the first authors to give him 'real aesthetic excitement' (Marrot, p. 136).

greatest danger in the way of your art. It may prevent the concentration of effort in one single direction—because your art will always be trying to assert itself against the impulse of your moral feelings. This may lead to a certain uncertainty of intention which may conceivably lead further to a vain harrowing of our feelings—tho' I don't believe that it will ever lead you into the gratuitous atrocity of, say, *Ivan Illyitch* or the monstrous stupidity of such a thing as the Kreu[t]zer Sonata,[1] for instance; where an obvious degenerate not worth looking at twice, totally unfitted not only for married life but for any sort of life is presented as a sympathetic victim of some sort of sacred truth that is supposed to live within him.

No. I am not afraid of that aberration for you. It is unthinkable.

Then—You may ask me—why talk about it at all? Well, I have a subtlety of my own—and You may well believe that it is not for the fun of displaying it that I am writing these pages. A moralist must present us with a gospel—he must give counsel not to our reason or sentiment but to our very soul. Do you feel in yourself the stature for that task? That you must meditate over with great seriousness—because my dear Jack, because it is in You to be a great novelist.

It is impossible to read a book like that without asking oneself—what then? Are we to be Sanitists,[2] or write cheques or are we to let casual girls embrace our knees till our, what shall I call it?—refined desire is completely satisfied, our humanity at the same time not being imperative enough and not elementary enough I may say to knock her mercifully on the head afterwards? Or is this—I won't say tale—is this vision of life and things so admirably imagined, so felicitously and poetically presented, is it a mere declaration not of the vanity of things (that would be a too optimistic view) but of the utter futility of existence?—Pessimism can no further go.

This is the danger of the moralist who has not a faith however crude, distorted or extravagant to present to his audience.

And don't think that I am an exceptional reader. There will be thousands who will feel a sort of uneasiness. It will to them dwarf the greatness of the book. I am talking of simple people. The other kind will no doubt discover varied interpretations not one of which will be worth having.

All the incertitude and all the danger arise from the predominance of

[1] *The Death of Ivan Ilyitch* appeared in 1884, *The Kreutzer Sonata* in 1890. In 1902, Constance Garnett published an English translation, *The Death of Ivan Ilyitch and Other Stories*.

[2] A nickname given to Martin Stone, who works 'at putting everything to the test of Health' (Chapter 14).

Hilary. For the view can be taken that the book is a study of temperament. What is Hilary? He cannot be a type.[1] He is a man of forty. A man of forty unless he is a pathological case must have a formed character, that sort of knowledge of his own weakness which (the knowledge I mean) is a sort of strength and also some sense of moral independence and perhaps—surely it is not too much to ask—a certain power of resistance. But H has no individuality as above defined, he is refined into a special monster. I don't think my dearest Jack that in the glow of inspired composition (I am speaking with the utmost serious- ness, I am under the charm of it) you have realized the harrowing atrocity of his conduct.[2] You have refined and spiritualized that poor wretch into a remote resemblance to those lunatics—there are such—who try to cut of[f] locks of women's hair in the crowds. He is a degenerate who is completely satisfied with the last scene with the girl and therefore with incredible villainy and a total absence of moral sense will act as you make him act. The strain on the reader is tremendous and the whole thing borders on the intolerable. The talk of the men drinking coffee in the club—their supposed advice to him—is a positive relief—a whiff of fresh air by comparison.

What I say above is the only explanation that can stand in good psychology and nature of men. Morbid psychology be it always understood, which is a perfectly legitimate subject for an artist's genius. But not for a moralist. You my dear Jack seeing the evil the great and insensate evil of the class convention bred through generations into the bone of society ask us to believe that the mainspring, the motive of that most base abandonment (all that is *masterly* in execution) is the feeling of class—and therein You—as happens to moralists—betray the very truth of things. For considering the atrocious character of his conduct the motive is incredible. It is *not* the motive whatever your art may make us believe at first. If it had that strength the strength to annihilate the man's pity and conscience it would have been so great so immense in its power as to have stopped him long before—*effectually* stopped him— which it had not done. Ergo: it was not strong enough then. In commonest humanity it can not be strong enough at the end. One would behave with more compassion to an insect. Therefore it is some other

[1] In *John Galsworthy: A Biography* (pp. 159–60), Catherine Dupré notes the resemblances between Hilary Dallison and his creator: both independently wealthy authors in their early forties, both concerned by the misfortunes of other people, and both unsure of what to do about them.

[2] Having lavished help on a poor artist's model, Hilary realizes that his unconscious motives were not as noble as his conscious ones and summarily backs away from her.

motive—or the desire is weakened, nonexistent because of the last scene. A pathological case of spiritual sensationalism.

I felt bound to say all that. The night passes over my head but my mental absorption in your work abides with me. One more point I must touch for we are craftsmen as well as seers, labouring in the flesh as well as in the spirit.

The end by the disposition of episodes resembles too much the termination of Hilary's biography as it were. And that dwarfs it somehow in its intention—reduces it too much to the point of view of the study of a temperament. To mask that aspect which in my soul and conscience I believe hurtful to the effect of the book I venture to lay before you a suggestion, and beg you to consider it impartially.

It amounts to nothing more radical than a transposition. My idea is like this: After the last scene of Hilary with the girl stop short and put in the whole block of Hughes' return home to break the continuity the "all Hilary" feeling. Then pick up Hilary again (perhaps even so far as the point where he returns home and talks with his wife?) and so on ending with the word *Brother* as it stands now.[1] I don't know if I express myself clearly. The night is over (I am a slow writer) and I feel tired but you will have seized my idea—for what it is worth.

Note.[2] There is the difficulty in the girl saying she *has seen* Hughes. But the end will be attained (to explain her coming) if she says that Hughes has come out of prison. Anyway that can be managed somehow.

—It was like having seen you two in a dream a fugitive, evanescent impression of Ada and Jack looking extremely well and animated. A good impression; but we could have done with something more. Did you get wet at all or a little or very much. It was a most inconsiderate thunderstorm.

Drop me a line before you leave London. Our dear love

Your

J Conrad.

PS (morning) I've slept four hours and have been walking one hour thinking and interrogating myself. My feeling is the same. I won't read over what I have written. I am perfectly satisfied as to my honesty and I do not wish to look at the confused expression of that honesty. Moreover

[1] Although Galsworthy made various revisions, he chose not 'to break the continuity' with the return of Hughs (spelled without an 'e') from Wormwood Scrubs. An extra paragraph follows the exclamation '"Brothers!"'.
[2] This note is on the same MS page as the paragraph before.

one may be honest and foolish. But folly if it only be really honest is bound to contain a grain of wisdom. And you cannot be angry with me if I am concerned with something that is in you, something greater than the book itself. It is also possible that I am blind, deaf and lame, that I can neither see you clearly, nor hear you distinc[t]ly nor follow You closely. And if so nothing that I say or leave unsaid matters in the least.

To John Galsworthy
Text MS Forbes; J-A, 2, 80

[Aldington]
Friday. [4 September 1908][1]

Dearest Jack.

Here I am once more. I have laid aside my MS (a beggarly six pages) for a last word which in effect is no other than the preceeding* words.

I don't know what you have made of my 16 pp[2] sent off yesterday with the Type of *Shadows*. One thing must have been obvious to you and that is that I have been deeply moved by the book. If I could believe that there is work in me which could move you as deeply I would be less at variance with life.

It all can be reduced to saying that for me Hilary is not a sufficiently big and human figure to stand in the forefront of the great Question the enormous interrogation point which for me symbolises the book. You have robbed him not only of his flesh (by a careful analysis) but also of his bones. With all the space he occupies he is conceived—or carried out in a minor key throughout. He is almost angelic—and if the downfall of an angel, happening accidentally upon the affairs of this earth, is a foregone conclusion it is not a sight to move men either to repentance or to reflexion. That a pure spirit (pure: that is inhuman) thrown amongst impure conditions will end in some base betrayal of himself may be taken as pretty certain—but it is not this thesis you wanted to illustrate. The man you set up is an incapable—impotent. Of the two incapables that come to one's mind—the loquacious and the nervous—Rudin and Nejdanov[3] that can not be said in the absolute sense. They were both necessary—to society and even to the state—at any rate to the community. They had at least *some* intention. But in Hilary there is nothing to

[1] Two days after [2–3 September]. [2] The 'Wednesday night' letter.
[3] Rudin in Turgenev's novel of that name (1856) and Nezhdanov in *Virgin Soil* (1877) are idealists as unsatisfied with the world as the world is with them.

be discovered. One asks oneself what that infortunate* creature was afraid of losing. He is shown as having nothing in his possession. (I don't speak here of the "captaincy of his soul"[1] which is a highfaluting way of suggesting a bagman's aspiration)—but he has no hold on anything in the world. This, under the tenderness of your presentation, notwithstanding the art you lavish upon him (and because no doubt of your most amazing insight) becomes apparent very soon. It is complete decadence exposed as never before perhaps.[2] But that is not your object—either as moralist or as novelist—is it? It's another evil you are aiming at—or I have missed the theme of the book, which I don't think I have done.

All the way along you show him as absolutely betraying his class in the whole course of his inner life, of his intimate relations—in thoughts, in half speeches, in his silences. Why? For what object? (except as a secret gratification) is not disclosed to us. He is so. There is nothing positive about him. He is perfectly faithless. He is so from the beginning. He ends by betraying by an unparalleled atrocity of this same impotence not the girl herself but the hope—the supreme hope—he himself had put into her heart. This is perfectly devilish (and the devil is a sort of 'pure' spirit too—only I understand he has some pride which makes him fit in a way to walk this imperfect earth) and is I take it an ultimate instance of the evil of class—the moral evil of the class feeling. But by that time we can no longer believe in the instance. We feel—or I feel—that class is just the mask of impotence, and your attack misses its mark.

No my dear Jack. A pure spirit such as Your wonderful Hilary (he *is* wonderful) ends always by sitting down in the mud—for indeed what does it matter to a pure spirit where he sits?—and he will sit snivelling too, in nine cases out of the ten, because pure spirits have no use for simple human dignity which is made up of good and evil faced openly, grasped with full knowledge. But then don't you see what happens to Hilary does not matter. And *that* not only in this book but looking into the future seems to me to be the danger lying in wait for your art. If the thesis of the book is as I understand it you should have presented to us a man really belonging to the class and with a noble instinct trying to assert his manhood against the heart-withering, brain-muddling convention—and then—had you so willed—knocked him down. For

[1] Echoing the last line of W. E. Henley's 'Invictus': 'I am the captain of my soul'.
[2] According to this idea of decadence, familiar in the works of Nietzsche, individual or social energy is not so much perverted as exhausted, kept going only by an ineffectual pity.

obviously the time for the Bible in the bedroom of small country inns to be replaced by Mr Stones Great Book[1] has not come yet. But enough. At last enough!

I have been telling you things dearest Jack which you won't hear from anyone—either from critics or from littérateurs. This is talk between you and me brother. Not that I suppose for a moment You care if I shouted it from housetops but because words can pass between you and me which are not for everybody's hearing. Beware of *Sheltonism*[2] You understand me? I love Shelton with an exceeding love—but beware of him—I mean of that side of him which is purely and exclusively Sheltonian. No—don't abandon Shelton; he's your creation, your embodied conscience you[r] wistful spirit going about on the earth. Hold him. Stick to him—but don't let him write your novels. And if that would be like excising some part of your very being—well you will suffer no doubt—but You can't pay too high a price for the greatness of inspiration for that voice which is in you.

Our dear love to you both

Yours ever

J Conrad.

PS—Just heard from Mrs P. Campbell.[3] Can't find actor to play Harry therefore can't perform play.[4]

To John Galsworthy
Text MS Forbes; J-A, 2, 85

[Aldington]
Sunday. [6–12 September 1908][5]

Dearest Jack

I sit rebuked with your letter before me. It is the fate of all men, who count, to be misunderstood, and of writers most of all. But it is not an ignoble fate and you do well not to be angry. I can't take back anything I've said; and I would not do it if I could. Let it all stand between You

[1] In *Fraternity*, the philosopher Sylvanus Stone is writing a Book of Universal Brotherhood.

[2] Richard Shelton, the chief figure in Galsworthy's *The Island Pharisees* (1904), is constantly appalled by social injustice.

[3] Mrs Patrick Campbell (Beatrice Stella Tanner, 1865–1940), famous for her performances in plays by Shakespeare, Ibsen, and her good friend Shaw.

[4] *One Day More*: Harry is Captain Hagberd's son.

[5] Written between a Sunday and the following Saturday, after [2–3] and [4 September], before 19 September. Jean-Aubry leaves out the final PS, written on 'Saturday' [12 September]; its contents match those of the dated letter to Reynolds.

and me as a visible sign of my almost fierce affection for your work—that highest expression of your personality—of my jealous concern, and therefore unreasonable concern, for its fate amongst the minds of men. I should not like it to be touched by the most remote shadow of doubt and thus I do see danger where probably the danger does not exist. It's clear I haven't read the book sufficiently—I felt that as I wrote, and a written word has a certain brutality which is softened in the living speech between man and man. I wish we had talked!

No dearest Jack, Hilary is *never* bad—neither first nor last. Hilary is simply wonderful whichever way one looks at him. He is not bad. He is good, I repeat—in a wonderful manner altogether unique and your very own. What perhaps could make him better would be some slight inconsistency of speech or action—a few lines—just for once; or rather what would make him altogether admirable as an artistic achievement would be some slight inconsistency in your *conception* of him—a thing that would not (that need not) be expressed at all but somehow *felt*. You know, that sort of inconsistency that one is aware of in Bazarov in the inflexible Bazarov himself[1]—say, somewhere, a hint of "firmness".

I am afraid I am growing stupid, but I trust in your long familiarity with the falterings of my mind. You will guess what I would say. That thing I am wishing for in my dumb way would give him more "relief"—in the plastic sense.

And since you take what I say in good part I will take the liberty (if it *is* a liberty) to call your attention once more to my suggestion about the re-arrangement of the end. Hilary gets in front of the larger tragedy—of the great suggestive background. By bringing forward the other ruined man[2] the unlucky biographical effect is destroyed at once. The end becomes more spacious—I mean more visibly so. Have you time and inclination for the experiment? I think it would be worth making from an artistic point of view. The *absolute* value of the book nothing that you can do or leave undone can now affect. It is there—quite triumphant—profoundly moving. I prophesy an impressive success. Love to you both. Jessie says Ada may well be a proud woman.

<div align="center">Ever yours</div>

<div align="right">J. Conrad.</div>

Note. I discover to my great dismay that this letter written immediately on reception of yours has remained hiding within my writing pad to this

[1] The nihilist in Turgenev's *Fathers and Sons* (1869).
[2] Hughs, the drunkard gaoled for assaulting his wife.

day. I am ashamed of its inadequacy but I send it on all the same, for it is the spontaneous utterance of my remorse and of my obstinacy. At this moment I could write at greater length and even with more fulness but I daresay that you—as a moderate man—will think that "enough is as good as a feast."

Thursday.

PPS I have read and reread every word giving due weight to every shade of your meaning and I still think that the idealising for moral purposes of a man capable of such a spiritual crime is too Tolstoyan to be approved by a plain man without tears and sensibility like myself.

J. C.

(Saturday)

We are fairly well. There is a chance of a 4 roomed cottage in Aldon and if we can secure it we shall pile in there as soon as possible.

To Stephen Reynolds

Text MS Berg; Unpublished

12 Sept. '08'
Aldington, Nr Hythe
Kent

Dear Reynolds.

Call me a brute and think no more about it. I've been in my mood of dumb worry and when it's like that—well!

It's not over yet. So I just say with love from us all that we are thinking of shifting berth to this village—for various reasons. The difficulty is to find a 4 roomed cottage or something of that sort where we could pile in and thank our stars it's no worse.

Too* day dawned a chance of something likely. But in any case we will be going to Someries about the 20th for some 3 weeks or perhaps six.[1]

Believe me—us—always yours
J. Conrad.

PS I was touched by your letter about the review in Dly News. It was a beastly thing and what's worse a silly one. I am glad you felt it for me.

[1] They did not leave Someries until March 1909.

To J. B. Pinker
Text MS Berg; Unpublished

Church Street
Aldington
nr Hythe Kent.
18 Sep$^{t\cdot}$ [1908][1]

My dear Pinker.

As the time approaches for my return to Someries I beg you to categorically answer the following questions.

Are you willing things being as they are to pay the next term for Borys—beginning this 21st?

Will you find the rent for the quarter due £18 (*not* fifteen) punctually on the 29th when I intend to give notice. It is absolutely necessary for my peace of mind and for both our sakes that I should get out of that place as soon as possible. I've made a fatal move and it's no use persisting in a mistake. Gals: who has been to see me here[2] approves my idea. Will you pay the bill for coals something about £10, so that I can get in some as soon as I arrive, there being only a day's supply in the house. (That I will ask you to hand me as I go through on Monday[3] when I intend to call upon you.)

Will you give me the usual cheques for wages amounting together to £2.8.

If you are not disposed to do that then my writing career must come to an end for I can't pursue it under a hedge. I am stating this simply as a fact not with any other purpose. Sometimes you think my letters menacing, sometimes crawling, as when while writing from Switzerland I felt only inexpressibly distressed at the thought of the strain I was putting on You[4]—not through my fault either.

If you will do what I ask above I'll tell you what my plans are. Galsworthy told me (on the day he lunched with you) "P complains that you don't stick to any specified amount. Name a certain sum and stick to it, whatever it is."

Well, the only way I see is for us to get into a largish cottage or part of a farmhouse the *outside* rent being £30. (I would make it lower but so much of my time being spent indoors there is a necessity for some space.) In a place of that kind conveniently situated we have calculated

[1] The plans for the *English Review* establish the year.
[2] Some time after the 12th, when Conrad finished his mislaid letter to Galsworthy.
[3] The 21st.
[4] In the spring and summer of 1907, while Conrad revised and expanded *The Secret Agent* and Borys lay desperately ill.

that we can live on a pound a day everything included—or say £360. That is wages and everything pertaining to housekeeping. The rent being say *30* (I have now the option of two places in and near Aldington at that price) that makes *390*. For clothing and incidental expenses etc etc *£110*. For Borys £100. (or less perhaps but that is not very likely).

The most important thing is to come to that footing *at once*. To put it off till this or that book is finished will neither help me on nor yet the book. On the contrary. As for Someries I must give 6 months notice. Jack thinks that it will be better to bear the loss. Obviously I can't live there for another half year. Either of the places above mentioned could be made ready for us by end of October.

If you will help to clear me out of that damned Luton place I promise to contribute towards it by a series of papers for the English Review,[1] without the slightest check to my other work. Hueffer suggested them to me and offered to take me down from dictation.[2] I've done the first of which you will receive a proof in a few days for securing copyright in Am. The first N° of the *E. R* will be out on Nov. 25[th]. Another 3 papers will be ready by Dec[er].

These are to be intimate personal autobiographical things under the general title (for book form perhaps) of the Life and the Art. They will tell in a measure my own story and as it were the story of my books—they will be concerned with Polish life and life at sea, intimate thought and sensations. Are you open to begin negotiations* in *US* with reviews like Atlan[ic] Monthly. Scribner—or some *newspaper syndicate* for a series of say six with more if desired.[3] But it must be treated as a very special thing and made much of. I believe there is a good deal of curiosity as to my personality in the *US* and, if I am to believe several competent opinions, in this country as well.

The Eng. Review is certain for four numbers. These are things which I could not dictate to anyone but a friend—and such a friend is Hueffer who consents to hold the pen for me—a proof of friendship and an act of

[1] The new and remarkable magazine, to be edited by Ford, who announced that it had 'the definite design of giving imaginative literature a chance in England' (Mizener, p. 154). The 'series of papers' became *A Personal Record*.

[2] As he had done for parts of *The Mirror of the Sea*. In 1936, Ford sent George T. Keating a vivid but patently inaccurate account of forcing Conrad to dictate his memoirs (Ludwig, *Letters of Ford Madox Ford*, pp. 267–8). Evidence that Ford took *some* dictation comes in the letter to him of [12 October].

[3] Aside from one instalment printed in a limited edition to secure copyright (*Some Reminiscences*, New York: Paul R. Reynolds, 1908), *A Personal Record* did not appear in the United States until book publication in 1912.

great kindness. He says that if the Review goes on[1] he will have another four papers after an interval of a couple of months but practically he has promised his assistance for the 12 or whatever number is necessary. As I've said one and a half are ready. If you fall in with my views I shall go on with them and they will help to move me into some tiny hole. £60 from the Review are certain.

I should like to see the letter you will write to America.

The appearance of these papers will by no means hinder the serializing of Razumov. Their writing under the conditions made by me by H. won't delay the novel by a single day.

Please answer me by yes or no to all my questions so that I may know how to act on Monday when our rooms in this cottage have to be given up. If you want to see me I will call on you on Monday—on my way back that is if it is worth our while to go back to S. at all.

To go on as I am is impossible. But to go on surely *is* worth while. Jack told me on the same occasion that you believed in me. I told him that I was only too willing to believe this but that the only man who has spoken of *failure*, who had uttered the very word was you.—This is reminiscence without the slightest bitterness. I feel any amount of stuff in me and am only too anxious to bury myself for 3 years on end and get it out.

I will post *MS* on Sunday morning or bring it myself on Monday.

Yours always

J. C.

PS If you answer me on Sat I shall get your letter on Sunday.[2] You may imagine my state of uncertainty and how hard it is to keep my mind fixed on my task.—I forgot to say that as You were not in town I borrowed £5 from my friend Hope[3] which must be repaid at once. They cover travelling expenses and house hunting as well.

[1] Ford was recruiting a group of contributors that included Hardy, James, and Wells, but the magazine's finances were and continued to be unstable.

[2] Pinker worked on Saturdays; rural post offices delivered on Sundays.

[3] George Fountaine Weare Hope (1854–1930), one of the first friends Conrad made in England; Hope lived in Essex and worked in the City.

To John Galsworthy
Text MS Forbes; Unpublished

[Aldington]
19 Sept. '08

Dearest Jack

Whatever set me off wrongheadedly on my critical remarks you do well—I repeat—not to be angry. My vehemence of expression was nothing else but the natural outcome—the 'other' aspect—of my admiring enthusiasm.

I am delighted and excited by what you tell me of the reconstruction. I *do* want to see what You have done.

Coming to the immediate question: that of the title—

The Voice? It may be mere prejudice but I feel a strong distaste for that kind of title—there is a whole crowd of unestimable works: The Jungle —The Circle, The Column[1] the—devil knows what—which seem to form a damnable category of more or less pretentious emptiness. I don't like the idea of you joining that style of nomenclature. Neither did I like *The Shadows*; but supposing that your mind was made up I held my peace.

In regard to your view of M^r Stone don't forget that ironically as he is treated he is after all a heroic conception. He is a heroic figure by the force of his tremendous and inspired earnestness—My dear boy he is wholly *tremendous*. Whatever he is he is more than a voice alone.

The Voice is not too solemn! It is *not enough*. It seems almost an impossible task to find an adequate title. If it is to be the *Voice* then it must be qualified in some way. I have been thinking for many hours. Nothing worthy of the book occurs to me. My mind is a desert ringing with M^r Stone's voice the voice of a great faith also of a great love.[2]—There is too the public to consider. A writer like you must make himself accessible for the sake of *that* which he is working for. No decidedly I am gone stupid as Jackolo now and then, 'goes naughty'. But mine is a hopeless case I fear.

Our dear love.

J. C.

We are going back on the 21^st. Cottage found—the thing now is to get into it.

[1] Upton Sinclair, *The Jungle* (1906); Katherine Cecil Thurston, *The Circle* (1903); Charles Marriott, *The Column* (1906).

[2] Sylvanus Stone, with his final cry of ' "Brothers!" ' and his Book of Universal Brotherhood did indeed give the cue for *Fraternity*, the final title.

To H. G. Wells

Text MS Illinois; *Listy* 282; Original unpublished

[letterhead: Someries]

25 Sept 1908

Dear H. G.

The similarity of initials with those of the efficient Manager of the BOS estancia[1] is not an effect of my impudence. I was greatly astonished at your discovery. It must have been done at one of those rare moments when I am not thinking of you. As to the blessed Ruiz I give him up to your scorn—I was certainly not thinking of *you* when I wrote *him*. I know I shall get several additional centuries of Purgatory for that tale—that is if the Recording Angel of man's deeds knows what he is about, and it would be impious to doubt that.

As to the great news about yourself: I am torn in two in the stuff of my judgment for who could deny your influence on the thought of the generation most worth influencing that is the generation that numbers 18 to 20 summers at this date.[2] I have seen and heard enough of it to know it well. You get hold of them by your gentleness, your persuasiveness by your extraordinary accessibility—and that utter absence of superior pose joined to the warmth of conviction which can be felt. No one *can* be more honest intellectually—and the very young—the workers of our more distant hopes—perceive this at once. And as your grip on every side of the question is very firm—a thing too they require—they repay your high qualities by a sort of mental devotion. It is an enviable fate.

On the other hand there is your mastery of the art—that side of your writer's genius which contains an infinite possibility. And indeed I need not suffer from divided judgment. For your art—whatever you do—will contain your convictions where they would be seen perhaps in a more perfect light. Your work, like all work that counts must have its connection with the laborious past and its bearing on the future—that future on which you have willed (and perhaps succeeded) to put the impress of your personality; which you will not see but in which Your voice will be heard—till in the ever-increasing distance even that trace of our short day shall be lost.[3] Yet when all the questions are settled, reopened and settled again the story of Mr Lewisham's contact with

[1] In 'An Anarchist', which Wells had read in *A Set of Six*, the manager is Harry Gee.

[2] Wells was still popular among the younger Fabians but had quarrelled with their seniors.

[3] A fitting comment to the author of *The Time Machine*.

Love[1] will have an unchanged significance both as an artist's vision and as a life's record. It will never grow archaic or lose its meaning as a mere statement of view may appear to the greater enlightenment of our distant descendants. Thus, upon the whole, I am glad to hear of your intention.[2] So it seems to me that you have selected the greater, the more difficult part.

We have been in Aldington for a few days; and I think we shall come there again for a permanency. It is a fact I am not happy here. I am sorry to say that poor Jessie's knee has been troubling her horribly. The doctor has seen it today and he told me: this looks very bad. He has ordered her to bed for a few days—a great trial to her. What other trials there may be in the future I don't know. Anyhow I have the greatest difficulty in keeping my mind down to the task—what with one thing or another. One does not grow younger either—which in itself is no great matter—only when one becomes aware of it, it is far from pleasant.

I could not manage to get down to Sandgate.[3] Everything gets so difficult nowadays—and I heard you were extremely busy with a new book—a new novel.[4] I am still in the 60 thou: of mine and nothing seems done. Ford persuaded me to some reminiscences for the *E.R.* (may its fate be ever propitious![5]) A megalomaniac's stuff but easy to spin out comparatively speaking.

And so with love from us to you all and in the hope of reestablishing contact (in military phrase[6])

Yours ever

J. Conrad.

To William Rothenstein

Text MS Harvard; Unpublished

Someries
Friday late night
[25 September] 1908[7]

Dearest Will.

I ought to have written before. Indeed I dont know how to thank you for your very dear very precious letter. It would be worth while for an

[1] In *Love and Mr. Lewisham* (1900).
[2] Wells was at work on *First and Last Things*, a major statement of his philosophy.
[3] Wells's home in Sandgate is about ten miles from Aldington. [4] *Tono-Bungay.*
[5] Wells was among the writers who launched the *English Review*; originally he agreed to do half the editing (Mizener, p. 154).
[6] Wells had a passion for toy soldiers.
[7] The news about Jessie Conrad's knee gives the day and the month.

artist to work for you alone. Nothing misses your brotherly and miraculous eyes—and of the faults you do not speak.

I won't write a long screed. A sort of cramp comes into my hand to day every 10 minutes or so. I hope it's not the writer's cramp. That would be indeed le comble![1]

Dear Alice[2] and you will be sorry to hear that there is, I fear, something very serious the matter with poor Jess' operated knee. She has suffered cruelly for a week and I had the doctor to-day.

The good man was very impressed and told me confidentially that the outlook is distinc[t]ly bad. He sent her to bed for a few days. We shall see. He fears a general diseased condition setting in—and to that of course there would be only one remedy.[3] This *en confidence*.

Oh! but it is a weary world.

The stories[4] had a very good reception generally. Quite a little event. As to selling that's another matter. I am no end proud of the Brute hitting Booth plumb center*. Its no small testimony after all to the truth of my intuitions—for I know nothing of shipowners.[5] Absolutely nothing. Love from us all to all your house.

<div align="center">Ever yours</div>

<div align="right">J. C.</div>

To Norman Douglas
Text MS Texas; J-A, 2, 86

<div align="right">Someries
Luton
29 Sept 1908</div>

Dear Douglas

Just a word to say that your Isle of T. is accepted by the Editor of the *English Review*. The life of that publication will begin on the 25 *Nov* with its December N⁰. Your paper will appear in the third issue—that is in Febr^y 1909. It was impossible to arrange it better as in the first issue W. H. Hudson writes on *Stonehenge*, in the 2^d issue Cunninghame Graham on *Andorra* and you in the 3d on *The Isle of Typhoeus*.[6]

Hueffer the Editor (and my "intime") asks you most heartily to call

[1] 'The limit'.
[2] Rothenstein's wife (1867–1951): as an actress, her stage name had been Alice Kingsley.
[3] Amputation. [4] *A Set of Six*.
[5] 'The Brute' tells the story of the *Apse Family*, an unruly vessel named for its owners; Charles Booth headed his family's steamship company.
[6] There was a ration, in other words, of one essay about place per issue.

on him in a friendly way at *84 Holland Park Avenue* as soon as ever you arrive in London.

They have enough capital to go on for 4 issues. Then if the thing shapes well it will be continued—and may become a permanent outlet for Your work. If the public does not respond to the new monthly magazine devoted to Art, Letters, and Ideas—the publication will end with the 4th issue.

When are you coming over?—Send *me* the Sorrento book and I shall see to it that E. V. Lucas has it without delay.

> Yours affectionately
>
> J Conrad.

PS Please advise me whether perchance the *Isle* is placed somewhere else.[1] Jess is far from well. She sends her kindest regards. I am nearly done up but keep on going still.

To Ford Madox Ford
Text Violet Hunt's copy, Cornell; Unpublished

> [Someries]
> Tuesday [29 September or 6
> October 1908][2]

Dear Ford.

Yes! I share your opinion. Mlle Roxane isn't ... Not quite. But *La Lecon bien apprise* is really quite. ... And what's the matter with *Les Etrennes de Mlle Doucine?*[3] I don't like it most, but I think it most suitable owing to its humourous and sentimental characteristics. I recommend it strongly as perfectly fit for general reading and even "seasonable"[4] (The December number). And it is beautifully done, anyway.

The 2 short pieces have not much quality.

It is nice of you to have sent me the proofs and asked my advice.

Mes remerciments for attending so quickly to the little play.[5] It would be a real God-send if by any chance? ... I daren't say more for fear of spoiling the luck.

Soyez tranquille in regard to the 2nd instalment of Reminiscences. The trouble is, what to keep out. If I fall unconsciously into mere *radotage*,[6]

1 It appeared in the *Review* at the promised time.
2 By 8 October, the second part of the reminiscences was done.
3 Ford chose the last of these Anatole France stories for the December issue of the *Review*.
4 'Les étrennes' are New Year's presents. 5 *One Day More* again? 6 Drivel.

you'll tell me of it as frankly as the Seigneur Gil-Blas spoke to the Archbishop of Segovia—or was it Salamanca?[1] Jessie is but little better. She sends her love.

Yours ever,

J. C.

To John Galsworthy
Text MS Forbes; Unpublished

[Someries]
Tuesday. [29 September or 6
October 1908][2]

Dearest Jack

Miss Hallowes[3] has arrived here and I must try to make use of her as much as I can for the next fortnight. So I won't come to town. I will sit still and dictate if I find anything in my head for that purpose.

As to going to Kent or anywhere else I don't know. I am too weary and disgusted with everything to wish for that or anything else. Jessie has got up but the knee is very evidently in a bad way. Since the beginning of this year I've written roughly 75 000 words (of which about 65 of Raz) including in that nearly 8 thou for the Eng. Review. But P thinks it is not enough evidently. He won't think of moving me from here till he has got a vol in hand and then says he "we will talk about it". Promises nothing and tries in addition to pick a German quarrel (querelle d'Allemand[4] as the French saying goes) with me on a charge (God only knows how arrived at) that I am going about trying to get people to help me as against him. "I give you your liberty" he says magniloquently—giving me something which is not his to give. I am utterly sick of it all. There is some work in me but I can't do it to any purpose under these conditions. Every day I stick here makes it worse for me. I've given notice here of course, but as I can't tell the man with

[1] In *Gil Blas* (VII, Chapter 4), the picaresque novel by Alain-René Lesage (1668–1747), the hero gives an imprudently frank opinion of the latest homily by his master, the Archbishop of Granada, thereby losing his job.

[2] Miss Hallowes arrived on Tuesday the 29th and stayed until 17 October. A dating on 6 October could account for what may, however, be only a casual discrepancy: the figure of 65,000 words for 'Razumov' here and 62,000 in the letter of 30 September. The tally for the reminiscences, however, suggests the earlier date.

[3] Lilian Mary Hallowes (1870–1950) did her first work for Conrad in 1904; with substantial interruptions, she remained his secretary and 'typewriter' for the rest of his life.

[4] 'A groundless quarrel'.

the cottage in Aldon anything definite he can't proceed with the work of making it habitable. He wanted to let it to me at 8/- per week but as it is not fit to live in he proposed I should bear 1/2 cost of the work and pay in augmented rent. That would make it about £30 for the first year and perhaps 24 for the next. A reasonable proposal quite. He has just sent me the estimates but I can't answer him. And really I don't know whether I care or not—much.

All this is too bad. Here is the doctor coming and – – – – but no. No more of this.

The Set of Six had a quite remarkable reception for a vol of short stories.

No dearest Jack—I can't write about anything.

Ford was here for weekend. I hope the ER will be a success

Our dear love to you both

<div style="text-align:center">Yours ever</div>

<div style="text-align:right">J Conrad.</div>

To J. B. Pinker

Text MS Berg; Unpublished

<div style="text-align:right">[Someries]
30 Sept. 1908</div>

Dear Pinker

Send me a cheque for 18/6—made out to *J. Cumberland & Sons* to cover my fire insce and Servants ins: premiums now overdue. Also a cheque for *£2.14* for wages which I have not received yet. Borys' schooling will do next week.

Miss Hallowes began with me yesterday (Tuesday). She is typing a clean copy of *Raz* which amounts in all to at least 62 thou words.[1] I will dictate to her either my Remces which are (I see by a shoal of notices) being made a feature[2]—or a short story. Or even if I feel in the mood the novel itself. Anyway her wages which will amount to say 25/- per week

[1] This 'clean copy' constitutes the first 313 pp. of the TS (Free). It breaks off immediately after the re-introduction of Razumov into the Geneva narrative. The remainder of the TS consists of unpaginated batches, varying in length from 12 to 51 pp., lettered A to T. Pinker's office arranged for the typing of these batches; Conrad called them 'intermediate' because he intended to rework them while continuing with the MS (Carabine and Higdon, *UWE*).

[2] For example, according to the *Nation* (26 September, p. 908), the *English Review* promised 'to make a bold bid for permanence'; 'the first instalment of Mr. Joseph Conrad's "Autobiography"' would contain 'interesting details of the Polish revolution'.

will not be wasted. That is what she used to have in 1904–5 though of course would work for nothing if I only let her.

The weather is so beautiful this morning that I feel that you running down here would be no hardship. Could n't You come to lunch to-morrow and give me an afternoon say till the five-ten train. I have something to talk about—as the theatrical people have been after me ever since last December.[1] Disregarding them may be perhaps throwing away a good opportunity. I have written this year 80 000 words (including Black Mate[2] and first inst: of Reminiscences) not so bad for me. And yet I feel that I could have blocked out two acts also without encroaching on the other work. It is worth considering.

<div align="right">Yours</div>

<div align="right">J Conrad.</div>

To Stephen Reynolds
Text MS Berg; J-A, 2, 84

<div align="right">Someries</div>

<div align="right">Sat evening. [October? 1908][3]</div>

Dear Reynolds.

There are books one seems to have read before, and books one doesn't want to read, books that one reads with annoyance, pleasure, exasperation or wonder; but this, your PM's H[4] is a book for which one seems to have waited all the time, without knowing it exactly; not a revelation, but the satisfaction of an intimate need of which one becomes aware after it has been satisfied at last. I am not a critic, as You know, nor a man to utter pretty, beautiful, or deep things about a book. I keep no store of pregnant phrases. The usual civilities I could write to a young author, I dare say if I tried very hard, but since I don't mean to insult you this is not to be thought of. I will tell you instead what has happened. I walked into my room, came up to the table you know, took up your book and opened it at the first page of the text (not of the preface). When I came to myself with a queer sense of unutterable fatigue I was still standing, and I had reached page 62—not glancing

[1] For a new, full-length play rather than the short and already-performed *One Day More*.

[2] The letter of [29 September or 6 October] omits 'The Black Mate' from the tally. The omission may be accidental, but it does stoke up the controversy about how much of this story was actually written in 1908 (see the letter of [23 January], n. 2).

[3] *A Poor Man's House* appeared in this month: Saturdays were the 3rd, 10th, 17th, 24th, and 31st.

[4] *A Poor Man's House*, Reynolds' first major book, describes the life of Devonshire fishermen and their families.

through, mind you, but giving each phrase, each word, each image its full value as I went.

Compact, harmonious, without a single—I won't say false—but uncertain note, true in aim, sentiment and expression, precise and imaginative, never precious, but containing here and there an absolutely priceless phrase—that is what I think of your piece of prose. It is, no doubt also a good action because the aim is worthy and the sentiment is human—if a little didactic. Searching my heart with some care I feel convinced that any difference there may be between us must be merely verbal. If I didn't think you true I would want you to be.

If I were sufficiently saintly or patriarchal enough I would give my solemn blessing to those pages where your great talent first speaks to the world in a cause altogether just and in an admirable manner. But I am neither a saint nor a patriarch—I am not even a good man. And a blessing is a serious thing. Unless the hand is worthy evil may ensue. So I hold my hand but I rejoice with you in the accomplished beginning. The thing now is to keep thy torch burning bright—and to hold it high.

Love from us all

yours

J Conrad.

To J. B. Pinker
Text MS Berg; Unpublished

[Someries]
Sunday night. [4 October 1908][1]

Dear Pinker

I send you the first papers, all 7.500 words of the Reminiscences.

The second is nearly ready.

Go in for the Yanks with it. I suppose you will find it necessary to have it typed clean from this scored proof. Anyhow the text now is ready for printing.

Please let me know what is your idea in dealing with it in the States?

Pray send me more typing paper to complete the clean 2 copies of Razumov as far as it is ready. I am writing on steadily and more I can't say.

Yours

J Conrad.

1 Received '10/08'; by the 8th Conrad had finished the second instalment of his memoirs.

To Harriet Mary Capes

Text MS Yale; Unpublished

[Someries]
Tuesday [6 October 1908][1]

Dear Miss Capes.[2]

Indeed you must come for the night. And we do hope you will kindly arrange to stay on Saturday long enough to see Borys who comes from school for the week end. There is an excellent train at 5²⁰pm which will take you to Pancras[3] in 40 minutes early enough to reach any part of London without undue fatigue.

Jessie finds herself relieved by the rest and the lotions of the doctor here. Should the improvement not last there will be nothing for it but a visit to a surgeon in London—with all that may ensue. But God forbid!

With our dear love

your most obedient friend and
servant

J. Conrad

Till Friday then at 12.59 on Luton station.

To E. V. Lucas

Text MS Buffalo; J-A, 2, 89

Someries, Luton.
6 Oct. 1908.

My Very Dear Lucas.[4]

I have tasted, sipped and consumed the delectable nectar prepared surely with the milk of human kindness and spiced with Your wit.[5] And if at bottom one may discern some honest bitterness it is surely right since we are no Olympians but mere mortals—for whom that gentle feast has been prepared.

This is delightful; and what's even more delightful is this that one feels that what You have said You have said excellently well but You have

[1] Date from postmark.
[2] Harriet Mary Capes (1849–1936), who lived in Winchester, wrote inspirational stories for children. A great admirer of Conrad's works, she 'selected and arranged' *Wisdom and Beauty from Conrad* (1915); he dedicated *A Set of Six* to her.
[3] St Pancras, terminus of the Midland Railway.
[4] Edward Verrall Lucas (1868–1938) was a critic, journalist, children's story-teller, and surreal humorist who knew Conrad by way of Garnett. Lucas worked for Methuen for many years.
[5] Conrad's tone suggests that the vintage to hand was *Over Bemerton's*, published by Methuen on 1 October, a bookish novel.

not said all you have to say. There will be more from you for our profit and
pleasure. I put the nature of my anticipation in that way because You—
at least—will understand me when I say that there is nothing more
profitable in the world for a man's soul than certain pleasures. A good
book is a good action. It has more than the force of good example. And if
the moralist will say that it has less merit—let him. Indeed we are not
writing for the salvation of our own souls. "A man should not be tame"
says the Spanish proverb and I would say: An author is not a monk. Yet a
man who puts forth the secret of his imagination to the world accom-
plishes as it were a religious rite. In all the pages that come from your pen
I discover my dear Lucas that spirit of piety towards things human, to
which I myself (even so) dare to lay claim (because certain of my inten-
tion) in the first instalment of some fragmentary reminiscences that are
to appear in the English Review.[1] But at the sight of your lines the phrase,
already used, slips under the pen as a tribute to an evident truth.

I am worried rather more than usual on account of my poor wife's
knee, which is developing alarming symptoms. She asks me to send her
love to Mrs Lucas—(who I hope remembers Conrad—he of the
hansoms)—and her greetings to you. And from us both love to Audrey
the undying flame of our first-born.[2]

<div style="text-align:right">Ever Yours</div>

<div style="text-align:right">J. Conrad.</div>

To J. B. Pinker
Text MS Berg; J-A, 2, 87

<div style="text-align:right">[Someries]</div>

<div style="text-align:right">Wednesday. [7] Oct. 1908.[3]</div>

Dear Pinker.

Thanks for the quick dispatch you have given to my request for more
paper. I am anxious to have all *Raz^v* up to date typed clear and out of the
house. I corrected as Miss Hallow[e]s typed thus making it absolutely
ready for pub: in serial form.[4] You will receive the two copies very
soon—as they are much better in Your care than here.

[1] In the last paragraph of Part One, Conrad writes: 'An imaginative and exact rendering
of authentic memories may serve worthily that spirit of piety towards all things human
which sanctions the conceptions of a writer of tales, and the emotions of a man reviewing
his own experience' (*Personal Record*, p. 25).

[2] Audrey was born in 1899, a year after Borys.

[3] Conrad had asked for more paper on the 4th.

[4] Serial rights were not yet sold. The novel eventually appeared in the *English Review* and
the *North American Review* (December 1910–October 1911).

I am anxious in other ways as to the Rem*ᶜᵉˢ*. To make Polish life enter English literature is no small ambition—to begin with. But I think it can be done. To reveal a very particular state of society, bring forward individuals with very special traditions and touch in a personal way upon such events for instance as the liberation of the serfs[1] (which in the number of people affected and in the general humanitarian significance is a greater fact of universal interest than the abolition of Negro Slavery[2]) is a big enterprise. And yet it presents itself easily just because of the intimate nature of the task, and of the 2 vols of my uncle's Memoirs which I have by me,[3] to refresh my recollections and settle my ideas. I can safely say that I feel equal to the work.

A mere casual suggestion has grown into a very absorbing plan. Every one thinks well of it, the latest favourable opinion coming to me in your letter received this morning. My literary reputation which seems more clearly defined with every published vol (I am struck by the general tone of the reviews of the *Set*) has already enough substance to weigh favourably in the scale for the success of a *personal* book. This seems the psychological moment—and the appearance of a new Review is a good determining factor. My friendship for the editor (which is known) is a sufficient motive. It is a generally lucky concourse of circumstances. It may be, so to speak, *the* chance of a lifetime—coming neither too soon nor yet too late: for, my acceptance as an English writer is an accomplished fact—and the writer himself is not "used up", either in regard to his own mind or in the public estimation of his work.

This is my feeling at the present juncture. I think that in England a certain amount of attention is assured for the serial appearance. In regard to the U. States I note what You say with some concern. I don't want these forthcoming pages bound, as they are, to be unique in their character, to be thrown away. I regret your remark that "the time is short". It is really no one's fault. But I ask myself whether it would be not worth while to secure the technical pub*ᵒⁿ* to save copyright in U S? Is that practicable? The first ins*ᵗ* being protected you would have more

[1] A topic that Conrad did not pursue.
[2] Whatever the relative degrees of cruelty and suffering under the two systems of slavery, the various emancipations in the Russian empire freed far more people – about one third of the entire population – than the 1863 and subsequent emancipations in the United States.
[3] The memoirs of Tadeusz Bobrowski (1829–94) were published in 1900; Conrad drew extensively on his uncle's accounts of provincial, political, and family life while writing *A Personal Record*. Bobrowski dwelled at length on the liberation of the serfs. See further, Jean M. Szczypien, '*A Personal Record* and the Bobrowski Memoirs', *The Conradian*, 9 (1984), 81–9.

time for the necessary negociations* bearing upon the appearance of the whole.[1] What do you think of the suggestion? *Please let me know.*

The part of this letter bearing on the plan scope and intention of the *Recs.* is open for your use in the negociations* you may enter into with editors and pub*ers* in U S. You may say also that in the course of development the inner story of most of my books will come out also—a sort of literary confession as to the sources as well as to the aims. I have been even thinking of a title something like: "The Art and the Life", or

> The Pages and the Years
> Reminiscences

As to England nothing presses for book form. In regard to serial*s* here, there is the *Esh Rev:* for the first 4 inst[alments]. If the *Rev:* should fail no doubt another place will be found to continue in. In this connection as you ask me what the length of the next inst: will be I may say that for myself (and Ford approves) I contemplate an av*ge* length of 4,000. The first *inst.* is nearly 8—but it was advantageous to make the beginning full—and anyhow I wanted to give good measure. In Nov it may be divided into 2 portions if they like.[2] But it would be a pity as it has been planned as a whole.

Lastly I can tell you that with that subject I am confident to meet your requirements whatever they may be (in reason) as to length and speed of production. It must all be dictated and then revised. *No other* method will do.[3] But with that, comparative speed is possible. On the other hand I must not devote myself exclusively to it either at once or even when *Raz* is finished. *Chance* must be taken up and pushed on (as before contemplated) in my usual manner of production. In such conditions I think I can guarantee (*if needed*) 1.500 to 2000 words of Remin*ces* per week—that is if some really important advantage for us both should depend on it.

<div align="right">Yours

J Conrad.</div>

[1] To preserve copyright, a tiny edition of Chapter 1 did appear in New York, but the book as a whole was not serialised in the U.S.

[2] It was not so divided. Only the fifth and seventh chapters are significantly shorter than the others.

[3] See p. 125, n. 2. Neither Ford nor Miss Hallowes was always there to take dictation.

To Norman Douglas
Text MS Texas; Unpublished

8 Oct 1908
Someries
Luton
Beds

My dear Douglas.

I have the complete text of *The Isle* in my possession. Some small alterations (mostly the transposing of a couple of pars) suggested by Hueffer I will see to.

You must be careful not to cause a devil of a complication by selling *The Isle* to some American Mag having a circulation in this country.

That parts of it are incorporated in your Sorrento book matters not in the least. On the contrary if we could manage to serialise a chapter or two as *articles* in some magne or other before the book appears it would bring grist to your mill.

I would prefer that You should send me the Sorrento Book *complete*. I will then communicate at once with Lucas and we shall see what Methuen is ready to offer for it. It will not be much I warn you—still it may do for a start.[1]

If the Review keeps going after the first 4 numbers Hueffer may ask you for an article on John de Procida.[2] The short passage in *The Isle* interested us all very much.

Excuse this hurried and obscure scrawl. Wife's kindest regards

Yours always

J. Conrad

To J. B. Pinker
Text MS Berg; Unpublished

[Someries]
8th Oct. o8

My dear Pinker.

It is time to settle this acct/ for B[orys]. Will you please do it in the course of next week.

[1] Dent published *Siren Land* in 1911.

[2] A doctor in the great medical school of Salerno, but also an instigator of the massacre known as the Sicilian Vespers (1282). Conrad may well have known Verdi's opera on that patriotic subject. In *Siren Land*, Giovanni appears in the chapter called 'The Headland of Minerva'.

I've finished the 2ᵈ paper of R[eminiscen]ces and also finished
superintending correct typing of Raz.

Yours always

J Conrad.

To H.-D. Davray
Text MS Texas; *L. fr.* 95

9 oct 1908.
Someries
Luton.

Cher Ami.

J'ai demandé a Methuen de vous envoyer (au Mercure) le volᵉ des
contes *Set of Six.*

Croyez-vous pouvoir faire paraître quelque petite traduction
bientôt?[1] Le temps passe et il me semble que je ne rajeunis pas.

Un ami a moi fonde une revue mensuelle *English Review.* Je vais leur
donner quelques pages des reminiscences melées—les deux vies[2] pour
ainsi dire. Wells fera paraître son roman sérieux[3] la-dedans. Enfin c'est
une Revue expérimentale comme qui dirait. Nous avons prié R de
Gourmont d'ecrire quelque chose.[4] Le Prince Anatole donne un conte
qui ne sera pas profané par un traducteur—au moins![5]

Allez Vous bien? Nous nous rappellons au bon souvenir de Mme
Davray.

Tout à Vous

J. Conrad.

Translation

Dear Friend,

I have asked Methuen to send you (care of the *Mercure*) the volume of
tales, *A Set of Six.*

[1] The *Mercure de France* did not publish any translations from *A Set of Six.*
[2] In Poland and in England? On land and at sea? As sailor and as writer?
[3] *Tono-Bungay*: in retrospect, Wells called it 'a real full-length novel at last': *An Experiment
in Autobiography* (Gollancz, 1934), p. 639.
[4] Rémy de Gourmont (1858–1915), poet, novelist, playwright, and advocate of Sym-
bolism; he did not contribute to the *English Review* during Ford's editorship.
[5] The *Review* printed Anatole France's 'Les Etrennes de Mlle. de Doucine' in the original
language.

Do you think you can get out some of it in translation soon? Time passes and I don't seem to grow any younger.

A friend of mine is starting a monthly review, *English Review*. I am going to give him some pages, miscellaneous reminiscences—the two lives, so to speak. Wells will publish his serious novel there. It's an experimental review, one might say. We have asked R. de Gourmont to write something. Prince Anatole bestows a tale which—at least!—will not be profaned by a translator.

Are you well? Remember us to Mme Davray.

Sincerely yours,

J. Conrad.

To Ford Madox Ford

Text Violet Hunt's copy, Cornell; Unpublished

[Someries]
10th October 1908

Dearest Ford[1]

Voilà. The thing[2] ran itself into 6000 words I fear. I am sorry for that stress under which you suffer. For goodness sake, don't over do it.

If I may be allowed to give my opinion I think that a 2nd story from "Anatole" is a mistake. The subject is not good—really it isn't—and as it is with H[enry] J[ames] and myself going on you must guard against stereotyping the Review.[3] The story is a charming and philosophical *polisson[n]erie*[4] but who here will see the charm and the philosophy—I want to know? Reste la *polisson[n]erie*. It is hardly worth while.

Does the A[natole] F[rance] next book consist of the proofs you've let me see? And what on earth is one to write about it?[5]

Jess has never thought of going to Aldington. Indeed she isn't fit.—though she is better. But the pain continues desperately at night which as you know is a distinctly bad sign.

I do long to see you. I am losing my grip on everything again.

Love from us both

Yours ever

J. Conrad.

[1] According to a note on the copy, Elsie Hueffer translated this text from French.
[2] The second instalment of the memoirs.
[3] James's 'The Jolly Corner' appeared in the first number of the *English Review*, 'The Velvet Glove' in the fourth; Conrad's reminiscences were a regular feature. Anatole France, on the other hand, had only the one story in the first four months.
[4] 'Bawdy story': one of the pseudo-mediaeval *Contes de Jacques Tournebroche*?
[5] Conrad reviewed *L'Ile des pingouins* for the first number of the *English Review* (pp. 188–90); the review is reprinted in *Notes on Life and Letters*.

To J. B. Pinker

Text MS Berg; Unpublished

[Someries]
Saturday evening [10? October
1908][1]

Dear Pinker.

Thanks for your letter explaining the situation as to US copght so clearly. I quite see now and am sorry for it. I know full well that you will do your best under the circumstances.

Thanks also for letter with enclosure received this morning. In re German translation I confess I do not desire it at all.[2] I tell you this frankly and with equal frankness I recognise that as things stand I have no right to object to anything of that nature. Only I ask myself if the offer is good enough. I remember that in *1898–1899* I had in various instalments from a good woman in Vienna something like 150 m[ar]ks for the translation rights of some stories out of Tales of Unrest.[3] (*Serial pubon only*) Is 300 mks at the present time a sufficient advance on the terms of that old transaction?

Of the name you mention I know nothing whatever.

Anyway I am ready to sign any agreement in that matter you may think advisable to enter into.

Yours

J Conrad

PS I lunched with H. James on Friday. He was very lively and interesting. I was glad to see him looking so well.

PPS (Sunday morning). Wife found old notebook where I see that translations of tales brought only 90 mks. Therefore I suppose 300 for SA[4] is about as much as can be hoped for.

[1] Received '10/08': Conrad asked about copyrights on the 7th; Pinker usually answered by return of post.

[2] In 1903, Conrad told Pinker 'As to the Germans make the best terms you can for as to me I had never anything worth mentioning from there' (*Letters*, 3, p. 11).

[3] Nothing is known of this transaction. An offer to translate *An Outcast* had arrived in 1898 (*Letters*, 2, p. 84).

[4] There was no published German translation of *The Secret Agent* until 1926.

To J. B. Pinker
Text MS Berg; Unpublished

[Someries]
Monday [12 October 1908][1]

Dear Pinker

I send you the Nº II of R. for *U.S.*[2] It is longish. There's no help for it. I have made *all* the corrections so that it may be printed straight off without authors proof.

I send another copy to Ford.

Yours

J. Conrad

To Ford Madox Ford
Text Violet Hunt's copy, Cornell; Unpublished

Someries
Monday evg. late
[12 October 1908][3]

Dearest Ford.

I forgot to say in my letter joined to M.S. that the 2nd Instalment is complete without the few words which you were good enough to let me dictate to you when last here.

I made a fresh start and I am afraid I have produced something intolerably bad.

How to guard myself against the most deplorable prosiness is my difficulty—the thing itself, my haunting fear, and the necessity of writing my despair.

Yours ever,

J. C.

[1] Received '10/08': between finishing Chapter 2 on the 8th and promising a swift completion of Chapter 3 on the 13th.
[2] *Some Reminiscences* rather than 'Razumov'.
[3] Towards the end of the same day as the letter to Pinker; the state of *Some Reminiscences* provides the clue.

To J. B. Pinker

Text MS Berg; Unpublished

[Someries]
13 Oct '08

Dear Pinker.

The IV. V. VI of *Raz* will follow tomorrow evening's post.

———————

It's a good sample anyway. Please send Miss *L. Hallowes* cheque for 3 weeks £3.15. She is leaving on Sat[y] I think but she will come back in a fortnight's time for another week to do more Rem[ces] a paper or two anyhow. You will get the N° 3 of R. by next week—early, I hope. It ought to facilitate matters in *US* as the N° 3 won't be pub[d] here till 25[th] Jan[y] '09.

Putnam's have pub[d] a big mangled slab of *Mirror of the Sea* in their Oct[er] N° under the title *Rulers of East & West*.[1] They sent me a copy of their Mag[e].

Is it done with Your knowledge and consent?

I see by the ad: *Duel* has appeared.[2] Are McClure's going to let me have some copies?

Yours

J Conrad.

PS Before sending out the carbon copy of *Raz* — the few corrections will have to be copied from the Type copy.

Raz[v] wont do for title and I can't waste my time thinking it over. Something may suggest itself suddenly.

To J. B. Pinker

Text MS Berg; Unpublished

[Someries]
14 Oct[er] [1908][3]

My dear Pinker.

Herewith Raz typed clean IV. V. VI and some of the VIIth. I am sending you MS again as Miss Hallowes will be too busy with my dic[tati]on to do any more just now.

She is going on Sat.

Yours ever

J Conrad.

———

[1] *Putnam's Monthly*, 5, pp. 19–23. [2] In the U.S., as *The Point of Honor*.
[3] Miss Hallowes' tasks give the year.

To Ford Madox Ford
Text Violet Hunt's copy, Cornell; Unpublished

<div align="right">Someries
15 Oct. 1908</div>

Dearest Ford

Do come and bring your secretary. Miss H. is going away on Saturday and the room will be vacant for Miss Thomas.[1] We are overjoyed at the good news of Elsie's cough I especially as having heard it more—was much concerned.

I trust the book will be of use. The *finishing* at Ten (*or* began about one—did it not?). The bird-cage *might* have been *outside* only in *one* place and that is the quarter-gallery. But that's Adm'als quarter. No inferior officer could have had access.[2]

<div align="center">Yours ever</div>

<div align="right">J. C.</div>

Bring your own paper, as ours is rubbish.

To J. B. Pinker
Text MS Berg; Unpublished

<div align="right">[Someries]
Wednesday [21 or 28] Oct '08.[3]</div>

Dear Pinker.

Thanks very much for the cheques.

I withdraw the unparliamentary expression. I do my work as well as it can be done and have no pretension to teach others.

I send you a letter received this morning. If You think the request ought to be met in that way I could no doubt get out a paper (say nautical)[4] when Miss Hallowes comes back—besides making ready the Nº4 of *Rems*. Only unless there is some distinct advantage in taking some trouble for that Mag I confess to You I had rather not; because I grudge every hour away from *Raz*.

In haste

<div align="center">Yours ever</div>

<div align="right">J Conrad.</div>

[1] For Ford's grand editorial visit to Someries, see Conrad's letter to Ford of 23 October 1923 (J-A, 2, p. 323) and Jessie Conrad, *Joseph Conrad as I Knew Him*, p. 57. Miss Thomas was secretary to the *Review*.

[2] Improvements to Ford's historical novel, *The 'Half Moon'*, finished in 1907 but only published in 1909. It tells the story of Henry Hudson's voyages.

[3] After Miss Hallowes' departure on the 17th.

[4] No such paper is known from this period.

To Marguerite Poradowska
Text MS Yale; Rapin 190; G. & S. 113

3 Nov^{re} 1908
Someries
Luton

Chère et bonne Tante.

Je viens de recevoir Votre carte et je vais écrire par le courrier de ce soir a Mlle Alice Gâchet[1] la priant de venir passer la journée avec nous cette semaine-ci. Vous parlez de mon succés. En vérité il ne vaut pas quatre sous. Il y a eu naturellement des articles dans les journaux. A ce point de vue là je compte. C'est evident. Mais pour sûr je n'ai pas besoin de leur louanges, et du moment que le grand public ne veut pas de moi tout m'est egal. Voilà 15 ans que j'écris et a mon age il m'est permis d'en être un peu las. Du reste tout ça ne vaut pas la peine d'en parler.

Pauvre Jessie peut a peine se trainer.—Ce genou va mal décidement. Il faudra j'en ai peur finir par une amputation un de ces jours-ci. Vous pensez que cette perspective n'ajoute rien a la gaîté (?) de notre vie retirée.

Borys est assez bien. Il a été fort ebranlé par les deux maladies de l'année dernière. Cependant il se tient assez bien, il travaille avec succès et partage les jeux de ses camarades. Jean Alexandre se porte a merveille. Il est bien gentil en verité avec un caractère emporté—à la polonaise Vous savez—et une jolie petite intelligence. Jessie Vous enverra présentement 3 petites photographies de famille que valent mieux que le groupe que l'on a pris dernièrement.

Je me demande ce que ces pauvres gens deviendront quand je ne serais plus là? Ni famille ni argent, ni même des connaissances. J'ai mal mené ma vie. Je n'ai pas su—car certainement je l'ai voulu. Et puis peut être il n'était pas possible de faire autrement.

Jessie vient de m'apporter le[s] photos pour Vous. Le[s] voilà. Elle Vous prie de croire a sa profonde affection et Vous embrasse bien fort. Borys parle bien souvent de Vous. Avec tous ses defauts c'est un bien brave homme que ce garçon. J'ai beaucoup de confiance en lui.

Votre toujours aimant et devoué
Conrad.

[1] Mme Poradowska's niece.

Translation

Dear, good Aunt,

I have just received your card, and I am going to write by the evening post to Mlle Alice Gachet, asking her to spend the day with us this week.

You speak of my success. It really is not worth tuppence. There have of course been articles in the newspapers. In that respect, I do matter. That's clear. But I certainly don't need their praise, and if at present the public at large does not want me, it makes little difference. I have been writing for fifteen years, and at my age I may be permitted to be a little weary. However, none of this is worth discussing.

Poor Jessie can hardly drag herself around. That knee is doing very badly. I am afraid it may be necessary to end up with an amputation, one of these days. You can imagine that this prospect adds nothing to the cheerfulness of our secluded life.

Borys is quite well. He was badly unsettled by two illnesses last year. However, he is getting on very well; he works successfully and takes part in his schoolmates' games. John Alexander is in fine fettle. He is really very nice, with an impulsive character—in the Polish style, you know—and an amiable little mind. Jessie will soon send you three small family photographs which are better than the group taken recently.

I wonder what will become of these poor creatures when I am no longer here. Neither family, nor money, nor even any acquaintances. I have led my life poorly. I didn't know any other way—for I have certainly wished I did. And besides, perhaps it wasn't possible to do otherwise.

Jessie has just brought me the photos for you. Here they are! She assures you of her deep affection and embraces you warmly. Borys speaks quite often of you. With all his faults, the lad is a very fine fellow. I have great confidence in him.

Your ever loving and devoted,

Conrad.

To H. G. Wells

Text MS Illinois; *Listy* 287; Original unpublished

3ᵈ Nov. 1908.
Someries
Luton

Dear H. G.

I think that I have already told you a propos of the *War in the Air* how tremendously interesting you can be. That was after reading only five inst*ᵗˢ*.[1]

And you are tremendously interesting to the very end, quite apart from being extremely amusing all the way through. The end is striking and the most convincing of all. One feels profoundly that the end can be just that. What imagination! And you can give it a living body too. The whole had an extraordinary force and picturesqueness and a distinct grandeur of aspect, the sense of the fate of multitudes even more impressive than in the *Sleeper*.[2]

I am now eager for the novel that is to come out in the *E. Review*. I saw just 3 pages. Ford has been exclaiming over it with a very sincere accent indeed. He thinks it is in its bearings and associations more *universal* than Kipps.[3] I tell you I *am* eager.

Ford has persuaded me to give some personal stuff for the R. His arguments have been too strong for my doubts and reluctances. But I was thinking of doing something of that kind for the boys, yet fearing that I would never do it from mere horror of writing, and this seemed an unique opportunity to pull myself together for an effort in that direction. But I fear it is a silly enterprise besides (what with the stirring up of all these dead) being a somewhat ghoulish one. I explain to you so that you should not suspect me of incipient softening of the brain. Our love to you all

Yours ever

J. Conrad.

[1] Conrad refers to the serial in the letters of 1 January and 16 April.
[2] *When the Sleeper Wakes* (1899), another tale of the future.
[3] *Kipps* appeared in 1905. Wells himself regarded *Tono-Bungay* as his most ambitious novel: David C. Smith, *H. G. Wells* (New Haven: Yale University Press, 1986), p. 203.

To William Rothenstein
Text MS Harvard; Unpublished

4 Nov 1908
Someries
Luton

Dearest Will.

I have stupidly sent you the wrong letter of which I am advised today by the man who received the one meant for you.

There was nothing specially interesting in it. I was telling you that I had been working without pleasure and profit and what is more not working fast enough. But that's an old story and there's no need to say anything more. It explained only why I haven't been able to come and see you. The book which I thought to finish in July is not done yet.

Poor Jess is getting gradually more and more crippled. We dread the disease of the joint setting in; in which case there would be nothing left for it but amputation, I suppose. A cheerful prospect. But don't mention it to people as we are not yet reduced to that extremity.

I believe you know the Prothero who is editor of the Quarterly? I think I've met him once in your house.[1] If I am correct do please mention to him, when You see him (or write to him) that I am infinitely grateful for *first* having the idea of publishing an article on my work in the Q. and *next* (even more so) for refusing to publish such an article offered him by poor Symons.[2] (I suppose you've heard that Symons has gone hopelessly mad, in Italy, as I've been told). The poor fellow sent me the article with a letter complaining of P's refusal; a letter which struck me then (July) as making too much of it altogether. An unbalanced sort of letter. As to the article it was wildly laudatory and I was simply appalled by it. I wrote as delicately as I could and he took my letter in very good part[3]—but all the same hastened to send it on for acceptance to the *XIX Century*. However I imagine it won't see the light either there or anywhere else.[4]

I hope you are all flourishing. Are you pleased with your year's work and especially with the Booth portrait?[5] Our chicks are fairly well tho' poor B had a feverish cold and doesn't look very robust.

I am writing some reminiscent stuff for the new monthly which

[1] Conrad dined with George Walter Prothero (1848–1922), historian and editor of the *Quarterly Review*, on 16 October 1904 (*Letters*, 3, p. 171).

[2] Prothero found it 'indecent, over-praising, hysterical, not fault-finding, calculated to do Conrad harm by praising him' (Beckson, *Symons*, p. 252).

[3] See Conrad's letter of [3, 10, or 17 August]. [4] It remained in darkness until 1915.

[5] Of the Rt Hon. Charles Booth, shipowner and writer on social questions.

Hueffer is editing, the English Review. The first N° is due on the 25 of this month.

This is all my news. Our dear love to dear Alice yourself and the precious kiddies

Ever yours

Conrad.

To [?]
Text MS Weber; Unpublished

[letterhead: Someries]

14 Nov 1908

Dear Sir.[1]

I hope you will not take it ill if I decline to compete with M[r] H. Caine.[2]

If I ever take the public into my confidence in the matter of earnings, prizes and so on, it will have to be in my own time and without referring to anyone else's experiences.

Yours faithfully

J. Conrad

To John Galsworthy
Text MS Forbes; Unpublished

[Someries]

20[th] Nov 08

Dearest Jack

The India book is most interesting. Nevinson is a dear.[3] What is happening now there only shows that nations as well as men may find themselves in a bitterly false position. Of course I am aware that there are many people in this country who do not think that there is anything false about the position; but I imagine that Nevinson feels it deeply.

[1] Unidentified.

[2] The unknown editor had compounded the tactlessness of his inquiries by mentioning Hall Caine, Conrad's favourite example of undeserved success.

[3] Henry Woodd Nevinson (1856–1941) wrote for all the Liberal newspapers and magazines. Many of his books explored political issues at home and abroad. *The New Spirit in India* (Harper & Brothers, 1908) found India to be alive with a new spirit of self-reliance that the British administration should encourage. Conrad would have agreed with the contention (p. 320) that the worst possible fate for India would be a takeover by the Russians. With its traveller's account of political tumult, Nevinson's *The Dawn in Russia* (Harper, 1906) could be a source for *Under Western Eyes*: Paul Kirschner, 'Revolution, Feminism, and Conrad's Western "I"', *The Conradian*, 10 (1985), 4–25.

I return the Jeanne d'Arc[1] with many thanks. I've found it very disappointing.

I have been cursing Frohman[2] at odd moments. I am exasperated at the matinée business. It would have been better if it had been practicable, to get somebody to try the play in the provinces first. Still I can't help believing that 'greatness will out' in spite of all the Frohmans in the world.

I was sorely tempted to ask You for the last four chapters of *Shadows*[3] (it's the title *I* like best after all); but I feared that my curiosity (?) might displease you. Yet I think you will know that it is not curiosity—it's a very deep and even anxious interest. Anyway if you don't think that this interest is misplaced send them to me if you have the MS by you. Should the idea be repugnant no notice is to be taken of this petition. Love from us both to Ada and Yourself.

<div style="text-align:center">Yours ever</div>

<div style="text-align:right">J. Conrad.</div>

To J. B. Pinker
Text MS Berg; Unpublished

<div style="text-align:right">Someries</div>
<div style="text-align:right">20 Nov o8</div>

Dear Pinker

We have incurred since last Whitsuntide[4] a bill for £4.17 for various farm produce, which has been presented, and I must ask you to send me a cheque for that amount in the name of *Benjamin Cole Esq^{re}*.

Herewith the photograph of which I spoke. If you don't like it throw it on the fire, but I think it is more characteristic of me than the horrible faked portrait over your office-mantelpiece.

I am getting on better with R.[5] since the little break in London.

<div style="text-align:center">Yours always</div>

<div style="text-align:right">J. Conrad.</div>

[1] The new life by Anatole France.
[2] Charles Frohman (1860–1915), the Anglo-American theatrical manager, had arranged six matinées of *Strife* at the Duke of York's Theatre, London, for the following March. Galsworthy's new play was successful enough at these matinées to move to an evening run.
[3] In their revised form. [4] In 1908, Whit Monday fell on 8 June.
[5] Probably 'Razumov'.

To J. B. Pinker

Text MS Berg; Unpublished

[Someries]
[24 or 25 November 1908?][1]

My dear Pinker.

I send you some more Raz. a *clean* copy to join the batch you have in your possession.

Tomorrow I shall send you 2 to 3 thou words more of *interlined* type to be *clean copied* (with carbon set) for the set. I find that I can (for the present at any rate) save sending you the *pen MS* for intermediate typing. My wife finds time to do that.[2] Therefore whenever you get interlined type you may take it that it is ready for final copy (and carbon). But should you get *pen MS* then please have one typed copy only made and sent back for my corrections.

Yours

J Conrad

To J. B. Pinker

Text MS Berg; Unpublished

[Someries]
25[th] Nov 08

Dear Pinker

Thanks for cheque which came to hand yesterday. I must ask you to settle the enclosed bill.

I am sending you some 2000 of Raz*[ov]* for clean typed copy. More will be ready to morrow. I am also doing the 4th paper of Remin*[ces]*. The reception of the Point of Honour* in the States seems remarkably good,[3] and generally my name is well to the front over there.

I don't think that the vol of Reminis*[es]* need be more than 80000.[4] I will think of something to round it off at that length—and then by and bye we shall let out a 2[d] vol. Don't you think so?—If you settle anything about it in the States let me know. Unless there is an offer for a series I

1 This may be 'the letter posted tonight' (meaning 'last night' or 'in time for today's last post'?) cited in the letter of 'Wednesday evening' [25? November]: this dating, however, makes a conjectural link with another tentative date.

2 Miss Hallowes had either just left again or was about to leave.

3 Albeit sometimes patronising: the *New York Times* Book Review (24 October, p. 624) found it 'an hour's agreeable reading'.

4 *Some Reminiscences* ran to little more than half that length.

think that after this last paper[1] (the 4th) I will concentrate myself on Raz'v's last pages. I must do a lot of thinking.

Jack is still retouching his novel. Will you kindly send him the corrected copy (*not* carbon) of my novel as he says he's anxious to see what it is like.

To day appears the Eng^sh Review Good luck to it.

Yours

J. Conrad.

To J. B. Pinker
Text MS Berg; Unpublished

[Someries]
Wednesday evening
[25? November 1908][2]

Dear Pinker.

I send you some pages for *clean* copy to add to final MS in your poscession.*

As I have explained in the letter posted tonight I shall avoid troubling with intermediate typing as long as my wife can do it for me here.

This little lot completes 100.000 since say 24 Dec^er last—rather over than under.[3] That is not so bad for me—considering 2 heavy gout attacks in Jan & Mch. It is as good as when I first began to write, quite.

I am sorry to say I am in for influenza as it seems. I am off to bed now to get doctored. It may be only a cold.

Yours ever

J Conrad.

[1] Of those Ford had originally commissioned.
[2] Received '11/08': the 'influenza' may have been a prelude to the attack of gout.
[3] At the last count (30 September), the total for the year was 80,000; the new figure, however, apparently includes the 20 pages of 'Razumov' written at the end of 1907. In October and November, Conrad had written the second and third instalments of the reminiscences (c. 13,000 words), some of the fourth, and an uncertain quantity of 'Razumov'.

To J. B. Pinker
Text MS Berg; Unpublished

[Someries]
Thursday. [26 November 1908][1]

Dear Pinker.

Please post the cheque direct as we want the fuel, and have the kindness to notify me in your weekly letter.

I hoped to have the Rem*es* paper ready by Monday. I am doubtful now, as gout in the big toe came on at night. But it has not prevented me working to day and if the pain gets no worse there will be no delay.

Send me a packet of typing paper please.

Yours ever

J. Conrad

To John Galsworthy
Text MS Forbes; J-A, 2, 90

Someries.
30 Nov '08

Dearest Jack.

I am ever so glad you find Raz interesting. Your criticism as to the II[d] part[2] is the very echo of my own worrying thought. And yet...

You see, it is all part of the general crookedness of my existence. You will not be surprised to hear that the doing of the I[st] part has been very difficult. What you see is the residue of very many pages now destroyed, but by no means wasted from an unmaterial point of view. But good work takes time; to invent an action, a march for the story which could have dispensed with part II[d] as it stands was a matter of meditation, of trying and re-trying for goodness knows how long. This I could not afford to do. I went on the obvious lines and on these lines I developed my narrative to give it some sort of verisimilitude. In other words I offered to sell my soul for half a crown—and now I have neither the soul nor the coin—for the novel is not finished yet. A fool's bargain—no great matter when one is young but at my age such passages embitter and discour[a]ge one beyond expression. I have no heart to think of compressing anything, for I have no illusion as to the quality of the stuff. The thing is "bad-in-itself". It should not be there at all.

I have no doubt as to the success of Shadows. Besides containing all

[1] Received '11/08': subsequent letters date the onslaught of gout.
[2] Not the whole of this part as published (Carabine and Higdon, *UWE*).

the excellences of your best work it has another, a new, not easily defined, element of beauty—it has a greater ardour, a more masterful moulding of the material—and with that the larger suggestiveness of a poem. My anxiety to see the MS was not anxiety in a 'temporal' sense, if I may so express myself.

I am just over a heavy fit of gout—or perhaps not so heavy as acute. It began on Wednesday and is now ended all but the lameness which may hang on for weeks or be gone tomorrow.

Jessie, who is as usual sends her dear love. Borys looks better and Jack is very well. This morning I said to him: show me your fists—when all of a sudden with the word "punch!" he hauled off and hit me in the jaw straight from the shoulder. I was never so surprised in my life. Borys on the point of going off to school was inexpressibly delighted. "Won't he know how to fight by and by!" Such, my dear boy, are the delights of paternity.[1]

Dear love to Ada and You

Ever yours

J Conrad.

To J. B. Pinker

Text MS Berg; Unpublished

[Someries]
Thursday ev[g] [3 December
1908][2]

Dear Pinker

Only a word to tell You that the attack of gout was worse than I expected. I sent Miss Hallowes away last Mond.[3] She is coming back to morrow tho' and I hope to start work at once.

I hear by a letter from the States that McClure's have made over their publishing business to Doubleday.[4] Is that a fact—and am I in any way affected by it?

Yours ever

J Conrad.

[1] The Galsworthys had no children.

[2] Received '12/08': the activities of Miss Hallowes and the persistence of gout identify the date.

[3] Probably the 23rd rather than the 30th.

[4] In November 1908, to save his crusading magazine from hungry tycoons, S. S. McClure sold his book-publishing company to Frank N. Doubleday for $100,000 less than it was worth: Peter Lyon, *Success Story: The Life and Times of S. S. McClure* (New York: Scribner's, 1963), p. 322.

To John Galsworthy

Text MS Forbes; Unpublished

[Someries]
Saturday ev^g [5 December 1908][1]

Dearest Jack

I haven't the books where a good motto can be found;[2] and then to find one is mostly a matter of luck as you well know. Still I have looked in such books as I have, without success. I don't seem to be a very lucky person.

I've had a slight relapse. It was slight and I don't complain. I feel myself falling behind gradually. Can't be helped.

Both Jessie and I are very much struck with the Fisher of Men.[3] The other day Miss Capes was here—a great admirer of yours. She told us that in Winchester *A Commentary* had produced a very serious impression in the 3 worlds: Clerical scholastic and military.[4] That is as it should be.

Our love to you both.

Ever yours
J. Conrad.

To Ford Madox Ford

Text Violet Hunt's copy, Cornell; Unpublished

[Someries]
Monday [7 December 1908][5]

My dear Ford

I've finished the No. 4 for you and P. is typing now a copy for the States. I've instructed him to forward my MS to you directly he's done with it. Can you send me the cheque for £18? I hate to mention it but I am literally *sans le sou.* I haven't the wherewithal to go to the dentist with. Sober truth.

Ecoutez: Ella D'Arcy[6] wrote me about some short story of hers which she thinks is good. I took the liberty to tell her if she sent it to you direct,

1 The appearance of Galsworthy's story gives the general period; by the following weekend, 'the entertainment' supplied by gout had 'been over several days'.

2 For a never-accomplished republication of *Jocelyn*: see the letter of 18 December.

3 'A Fisher of Men' appeared in the first number of the *English Review* and was collected in *A Motley* (1910).

4 In a city dominated by a garrison, a cathedral, and a public school, the 'very serious impression' made by Galsworthy's assembly of socially-conscious sketches from the Liberal *Nation* may have been closer to dismay than admiration.

5 The contents match those of the letter to Pinker of this date.

6 The author of a short novel and two collections of short stories, Ella D'Arcy came from the Channel Islands. She had been a contributor to the *Yellow Book*.

it would be read sympathetically.[1] Rien de plus. At the same time I warned her that as far as I, in my quality of the Editor's *"intime"* was aware, the four numbers were made up already; thus leaving you an open door for the rejection of the story. I hope I haven't presumed!

I hope also that my remarks as to the No. did not offend. As to the English text of Anatole France in my goutty* half crazy state it was simply *impossible* for me to look at it.

I rather expected Reynolds to turn up here. Is he still with you?[2] Greet him from us both and from *both* boys, because Jackson[3] mentions him constantly.

How are you? How do you feel? Postman waits.

Our dear love.

Ever yours

J. Conrad.

To J. B. Pinker

Text MS Berg; Unpublished

[Someries]
Monday. [7 December 1908][4]

Dear Pinker.

I send you sixteen pages of Remces N° IV. The other eleven are typed already but must be revised, which will be done to night. Please let them start making one copy for the States (if you want it) and when that is done send my own type to Ford, at once.

I send you the two bills. I had to had to have books, at least I thought so. But I dare say I can do without them. At any rate I've stopped Mudie[5] some time ago.

I will keep Miss Hallowes at Razov till her week's up and then send her away. Gout hangs about me yet but I can work all right.

Sorry to hear what you tell me of America. Would not this be an opportunity to get the McClure books back?[6]

But you know best.

Yours always

J. Conrad.

[1] Ford published D'Arcy's story 'Agatha Blount' in June 1909.
[2] For a brief period, Ford championed Stephen Reynolds and gave him work (Mizener, p. 164).
[3] John Conrad.
[4] Received '12/08': Miss Hallowes stayed from the 4th to the 10th.
[5] His subscription to Mudie's Circulating Library.
[6] Various McClure companies had published *Lord Jim*, *Falk*, *Youth*, *The Point of Honor*, *Romance*, and *The Inheritors* in the US; McClure also owned North American rights to *The Rescue*, whose completion Conrad had been promising for the last ten years.

To J. B. Pinker

Text MS Berg; Unpublished

[Someries]

Wednesday. [9 December 1908][1]

My dear Pinker

Here's the last of the N° 4. I would take it as very kind of you if you can manage to have my copy posted to Hueffer to morrow (Thursday) evening. *There is a special reason.*[2]

I will send Miss Hallowes away to morrow. My wife will do the preliminary typing of Raz's last part and if she's unable I will ask you. I am horribly anxious about that end. Jack thinks well of the story.

This is the end of Reminis*es* for the present. The Review, counting one paper with another has, say, 32 000 words; I hold some 8000 which got written in the course of composition but which I keep back from serialisation altogether but which count for book form.[3] Here we have half a vol. I will do no more especially as you are not calling for america. Of course the thing is very far from conventional in its composition. It does not much resemble other people's reminis*ces*. Oh dear no!

Won't Harper's even nibble?[4]

Thanks for your letter and the settled bills. I hate to ask you—as you ought to know.

Post time.

Yours alway[s]

J. Conrad

Have you got the snapshot portrait? Discovering I had none left I took it away from our faithful maid Nelly.[5] If you don't like it send it back.

[1] Received '12/08': the fair copying of *Some Reminiscences*, Chapter Four, gives the appropriate Wednesday.

[2] See the letter to Ford of the 17th for some indication of what was troubling Conrad.

[3] The withheld material may have become 'Prince Roman', the historical narrative worked over in September and October 1910, published in 1911, and reprinted in *Tales of Hearsay*.

[4] Harper & Brothers did publish *A Personal Record*, but not until 1912.

[5] Nellie Lyons: she had been in service with the family since 1898: see the letter of [15 December 1909].

To J. B. Pinker
Text MS Berg; Unpublished

[Someries]
Friday. [11 December 1908][1]

My dear Pinker

I have your letter. I forgot stupidly the Harpers circulate in this country.[2] Thanks.

3. Blessington Rd. Lee. SE. is Miss *L. Hallowes'* address. Please send her direct £*2.10* which pays for a fortnight, three days due last time and about ten now.

I've just received 6 vols from H James of his Colld edition.[3] It is extremely nice. I am greatly pleased at him giving it to me.

Pray keep the snapshot since you approve of it. The next prints may not be so good as something has happened to the plate. Can't make out what from the letter. I am going on being cheered by concensus* of favourable opinion.

Yours ever

J. Conrad.

PS Could you send me ½ dozen writing pads like this paper in size and ruling[4] but perhaps of slightly better quality. Can't get them here.

To Elsie Hueffer
Text MS Berg; Unpublished

Someries
Luton.
12 Dec 1908

Illustrissima Señora.

Since I am honoured by Your permission to offer You my works I am sending you this American edition of the *Duel* not because it is beautiful (oh dear no!) but to complete your collection.

There is a collector of my books in New Zealand who writes to me for information sometimes—but his collection is not of inscribed copies. No one in this wide world will be able to show that (when I am gone and the

[1] Received '12/08': Miss Hallowes had just left and Henry James's volumes had just arrived.

[2] Thus neither *Harper's Weekly* nor the *Magazine* could acquire the serial rights for *Some Reminiscences*; they already belonged to the *English Review*.

[3] The New York Edition, which James prepared as the definitive text of his work to date.

[4] Ruled MS paper, without watermark and measuring 10 inches by 8.

thin trickle of vols ceases) but You. And I have it much at heart that Your set should be as complete as friendship can make it.

This envoi would require no acknowledgment—only I must beg you to give me the present address of Mr Marwood.[1] I have here 3 vols which he was good enough to lend me in Octer and it is about time I sent them back.

Alas! Even if we have been otherwise ready for the move a horrid lingering fit of gout would have prevented us. Everything is knocked into a cocked hat by it anyhow. I haven't been able to go to Ramsgte to look at Borys' future school.[2] I was even too low spirited to write. I don't know when we will move. I can't think of anything or decide on any point. I suppose You will be leaving early next year for the South of France? We envy you.

Jess sends her love and I am as ever (You don't doubt it)

Your affectionate friend and
obedient servant

J. Conrad.

To Henry James

Text MS Harvard; J-A, 2, 91

12 Dec 1908
Someries
Luton Beds.

Très cher Maître,[3]

They have arrived—the six of them;[4] I have felt them all in turn and all at one time as it were, and to celebrate the event I have given myself a holiday for the morning, not to read any one of them—I could not settle to that—but to commune with them all, and gloat over the promise of the prefaces.[5] But of these last I have read one already, the preface to the *American*, the first of your long novels I ever read—in '91. It is quite a

[1] Arthur Pierson (or Peirson) Marwood (1868–1916), the scholar and country gentleman whose fortunes were elaborately and often painfully enmeshed with those of the Hueffers.

[2] St Augustine's, the Benedictine school mentioned on [23? July], or the Anglican St Lawrence College?

[3] Conrad's friendship with the Master began with the presentation of *An Outcast* in 1896, reciprocated by a gift of *The Spoils of Poynton* in 1897.

[4] *Roderick Hudson, The American, The Portrait of a Lady* (2 vols.), and *The Princess Casamassima* (2 vols.): the copies probably came from the British issue of the New York Edition; this issue, an 'Edition de Luxe', had begun to appear on 29 September.

[5] Written expressly for the New York Edition.

thrill to be taken thus into your confidence; a strong emotion it is a privilege to be made to feel—a cinquante ans! Afterward I could not resist the temptation of reading the beautiful and touching last ten pages of the story. There is in them a perfection of tone which calmed me; and I sat for a long while with the closed volume in my hand going over the preface in my mind and thinking—that's how it began, that's how it was done!

I thank you for the gift, I thank you before all for the opportunity to breathe in the assurance of your good will the fortifying atmosphere of Your serene achievement.

> Yours most affectionately and
> gratefully
>
> Joseph Conrad.

To Edward Garnett
Text G. 227

> Someries
> Luton
> Sunday 12 [12 or 13?] Dec '08[1]

Dearest Edward,

I have been in hopes of seeing you at the M.B.[2] week after week. Then gout came and I find that even the next Tuesday must be given up; the foot is too swollen yet, tho' the entertainment has been over now for several days.

Pray let me know all there is to tell of David.[3] We have been anxious ever since I learned your fears and told Jessie of them. To ask you for news, since goodness only knows when I may see you, is the only object of this. Or almost the only object. I want also to know where he is now. The generous McClure has sent me 4 copies of the *Duel* in (small) book-form; and whether he has read the story or not I want to send him an inscribed copy on the strength of our old acquaintance.

Do you see the Editor as of yore? He seems very busy. The E.R. looks noble and I hear from all sides that the first No. has gone off very well,

[1] The Bobbs-Merrill edition dates this letter '15 Nʳ '08'; the Nonesuch '12 Dec '08'. Even if the Nonesuch text were not generally more accurate, references to gout and the success of the *English Review* would put the earlier date out of the question. 12 December, however, was a Saturday.
[2] The Mont Blanc restaurant, where Garnett presided once a week over informal luncheons.
[3] The Garnetts feared their son had tuberculosis.

remarkably so. Is that a fact? I would like to know, for I am anxious for Ford to make a success.

Tarver (the "Flaubert" Tarver)[1] who is now in Chile writes me that *Nostromo* has met with no end of appreciation on the seaboard where the scene is laid,[2] and from people in the know. That's something, tho' I admit it doesn't amount to much.

Our love to you

Ever yours

J. Conrad

Do drop us a few lines.

To Marguerite Poradowska

Text MS Yale; Rapin 191; G. & S. 114

[Someries]
13 Dec. 1908

Chère et très aimée Marguerite.

Je suis profondement touché par Votre affection qui veille toujours. Il m'est infiniment doux de savoir que j'occupe un peu Votre pensée. C'est vrai!—de toute la famille je n'ai plus que Vous.

Que signifie un salon Russo-Polonais? Les choses, les sentiments changent sans doute—mais moi je n'ai pas changé.[3] Enfin. Tout de même c'est curieux.

Raychman—c'est un nom Allemand et même un peu Juif—eh? Que m'écrira cette dame?[4] Que voudra-t-elle savoir? Si Vous saviez comme je me méfie des 'interviews'.—Ecoutez. Vous l'avez vue. Vous êtes a même de juger si la chose vaut la peine. Après tout j'ai peut-être quelque chose a dire. Decidez Vous même—voulez Vous?

Je viens d'avoir une abominable attaque de goutte. Pauvre Jessie souffre de son genou beaucoup cet hiver-ci. Les enfants vont bien. Borys etudie avec perseverance et même avec facilité. Ces deux se rencontrent rarement.[5] Le petit est encore charmant. Nous nous sommes pris de

[1] John Charles Tarver, author of *Gustave Flaubert As Seen in His Works and Correspondence* (1895).

[2] I.e. on the Pacific coast between Mexico and Chile. Conrad remarked that 'Costaguana is meant for a S. Am^{can} state in general' (*Letters*, 3, p. 175).

[3] In his refusal to mix with Russians.

[4] On the 27th, Davray wrote to Mme Poradowska, agreeing to meet a M. and Mme Baychman 'au sujet de notre cher Conrad' (Rapin, p. 211). The correct spelling remains unknown.

[5] Because Borys was away at school.

beaucoup d'amitié pour Alice.[1] Nous vous embrassons tous.

<div style="text-align:center">A Vous de coeur</div>

<div style="text-align:right">J Conrad.</div>

Translation

Dear and much loved Marguerite,

I am profoundly touched by your unflagging affection. To know that I am a little in your thoughts is exceedingly sweet to me. Truly—of all the family I have only you left.

What does a Russian-Polish salon mean? Things, feelings change no doubt—but I have not changed. Well. Still, it's unusual.

Raychman—a German name and even a little Jewish, eh? What will that lady write to me? What will she want to know? If you knew how I distrust interviews.—Listen. You have seen her. You can judge whether the affair is worth the trouble. After all, I do perhaps have something to say. Decide yourself—will you?

I have just had a dreadful attack of gout. Poor Jessie is suffering a good deal with her knee this winter. The children are getting on well. Borys studies with perseverance and even with ease. Those two rarely meet. The little one is still charming. We feel a great friendship for Alice.

We all embrace you.

<div style="text-align:right">Yours affectionately,</div>

<div style="text-align:right">J Conrad.</div>

To Edward Garnett
Text G. 228

<div style="text-align:right">[Someries]</div>

<div style="text-align:right">16 Dec '08</div>

Dearest Edward,

It is an *immense* relief.[2] You don't know how that thing has been lying on us. You see we had the same experience with Borys only some 20 months ago.

Yes! You speak words of wisdom as to the E.R. That is the way. I've

[1] Alice Gachet's visit must have gone ahead.
[2] David was not consumptive after all.

said already something to the same effect; but I don't want to appear as if I wished to meddle; the more so that I can't pretend to any experience—tho' I may have some 'sense'—of affairs.

Since your letter the year-end doesn't seem so gloomy. I'll be sending the little vol. to David in a day or two as I want to write him a short note too.

Our dear love to you

Yours ever

J. Conrad

To Ford Madox Ford

Text MS BL Ashley 2923; Unpublished

[Someries]

17 xer [December] '08

Dearest Ford.

I have almost lost the hope of seeing you this year here. My foot is very swollen yet and I have still less hope of being able to come and see you in town.

I can't somehow get rid of the idea that I have been in some way indiscreet—I can hardly say offensive—vis à vis de Vous. I have said something to that effect in a letter to you which has remained unanswered.[1] Perhaps you thought it was not worth answering, the supposition being too silly. If so—good. And indeed it is incredible that you should suspect me of an offensive intention on the ground of some remarks which are not and could not have been of any consequence. And considering our friendship and the confidence You gave me in that particular matter even the charge of mere impertinence could not stand. It was an expression of very great interest which was *not* critical in its intention. But enough of that. I dare say you think I am mad—and truly sometimes I think so myself.

Please my dear boy give me a moment of attention:—

In order to regularise my position with Pinker to whom I am bound by a strict agreement as to *all* the proceeds of my work I am going to answer his query as to my contribution to the Review as follows.

—That this is a special arrangement between you and me. That without your encouragement and assistance and without the opportunity presented by the R. I would never have written these papers. That I wished (had I been able) to give them to you but that You have

[1] The letter of [7 December]?

offered me *verbally* a participation in the R.[1] and that it is on *that* condition that our relations as Editor to contributor are based. The details of it do not concern him. But in view of the agreement giving him a lien on the proceeds on my work I propose that he should debit my account with a sum not exceeding £100 as against the 4 papers supplied to the R, for which you paid me £80.

The above is a fair statement of the transaction and of how I understood our conversation. The actual cash which passed between us I look upon as a friendly advance on your part, since You know my pressing necessities. And indeed you did know them! There is no need to disclose that for in reality no one has the right to question you upon it, the basis of our connection being as stated above.

In my state of absolute dependence on Pinker I must be very cautious for, should he refuse making even the present absolutely insufficient advances where would I be? It's a perfect agony. I don't think that this is anything he can object to, for, after all, the whole thing is a voluntary service—a generosity on your part even to the point of you taking me down from dictation. It is as if you had *lent* me the money against your own verbal promise of participation if we both live and the E. R. goes on successfully. Under these circumstances, I judge, that to let P debit my acct/ with £100 is a perfectly fair treatment.

Please preserve this letter of which I have no copy, and just drop me a word.

Elsie acknowledging my offering of the Am. Edition of *Duel* (to keep her collection complete) tells me that she is coming to London for the holidays and mentions a reception (on the Sunday) to be held in her honour—in Holl[d] Pk Av[e2] I presume. I propose if I can put on a boot to come to it—if I can spare the shillings for my fare, bien entendu.

<div align="right">Love from us all. Ever Yours
J. Conrad</div>

PS Of course in regard to anything said in the body of this letter I declare that there was no negociation* of any sort between us, that I did not ask for any terms, that all you said as to what may happen in the future was simply the proof of your friendship, alone and no business understanding of which there *was not and could not be* question between us

[1] Participation in Ford's plans for profit-sharing and, perhaps, in editorial decisions. See n. 1 on p. 168 for the tangled financial arrangements.

[2] The headquarters of the *Review* at 84 Holland Park Avenue: Ford occupied rooms there over a fishmonger and poulterer's. Elsie Hueffer avoided the place as much as she could.

in that matter. It was a conversation creating no claim (except upon my feelings) and in no way amounting to any sort of promise whatever. The £80 which I received from You *pay completely and in full* for my contribution to the E. R. If I mention at all your generous purpose (to which I hold you not at all) it is only to bring it out clearly before Pinker that the transaction was quite special and unique arising from your unwearied readiness to help me in my difficulties and can not fall morally under the terms of my agreement with him. As to the material aspect of the case as it touches him and in order that the literal terms of the agreement should be observed I will authorise him to debit my acct in the sum of £100 (or some such arrangement) to make it up for the money passing directly from you to me.

It occurred to me that I had better state all this at length (which I do immediately after finishing the letter) so that should my conduct be questioned my view distinctly affirming that I have no claim and am only under obligation to you remains clearly recorded.

<div style="text-align: right">Joseph Conrad.
17 Dec 1908</div>

To J. B. Pinker
Text MS Berg; Unpublished

<div style="text-align: right">[Someries]
17 Dec 1908</div>

My dear Pinker

This is a special matter on which I was about to write you. If it had not been for the hatching out of the R and the insistence together with actual help from Hueffer these papers (whose existence is obviously advantageous) would never have come into being. I would have liked to *give* them to him as I am under more than one obligation to the man. It was anyway an old affair (as you know) between him and me.[1]

He has offered me verbally a participation in his Review on conditions which I own, in detail, are not very clear to me. Roughly speaking the proprietorship is divided into 5 parts. Duckworth gets 2/5ths and the remaining 3/5ths are to be divided between four participants whose names I don't think I am at liberty to disclose. The man who has

[1] Quite apart from any money still outstanding, Conrad owed Ford a debt of gratitude for his help in the early part of 1904; Conrad had dictated some of *The Mirror of the Sea* pieces to him, and Ford even took a hand in their composition (*Letters*, 2, pp. 120, 167).

furnished the money for the start (I know not the amount) will only take 5% and no more.[1]

What it all amounts to I really can't say. The main consideration between H and me is the participation. And after all more unlikely things have happened than the success of a literary Review. At any rate it [is] a transaction of friendship and not of business, the seeds of which (the transaction) have been sown more than 3 years ago as you may remember. The participation is practically a gift and the affair could not have been negociated* by any one in the way of ordinary business.

It is a purely personal matter which I could not have carried out with any other man but Hueffer. You must look at it in that way to see its true bearing. However I have no doubt that you can see it. Hueffer might have done excellently well without any contribution from me. He saw my extreme necessities and volunteered to take pen in hand for my dictation and then made the offer as above. I did not as you may guess press him for details. It is a remote chance.

My view is this: if the *E.R* goes on after 4 numbers and I, apart from a moderate but *certain* fixed fee (per page or thousand) receive a share of profits for my contributions you are to have the commission upon the whole and *all* the money is to pass through your hands, Hueffer's generosity (for it's nothing else after all) falling thus under our agreement. (On what ground I accept that generosity is my affair exclusively.) So much *for the future* of which you may have your opinion hopeful or not—and no doubt it is not very different from mine. But at any rate it is (remote as it may be) a chance, helpful to us both, obtained by me on purely personal grounds. *For the present* I propose that You should debit my account as against these four initiatory papers in a sum no less in any case than £80 and <u>com</u>[2] but which I suggest should be arrived at by adding 33% to whatever amount you can obtain for these papers serially in the U.S.A. I make this precise suggestion in view of your opinion that the price of serialisation in the *US* is depreciated by the previous publication here. I put this depreciation at one third and thus I

[1] Gerald Duckworth published the *Review*, into which Marwood and Ford had each put £500, Ford's share coming mostly from his German relations. The publisher and the two backers were to take one fifth each of any profits. The remaining two fifths were in theory to be shared among the contributors. In practice, the profit-sharing consisted of paying everyone else at a rate per page determined by Ford's estimate both of quality and the writer's need, while assuming that Wells and Galsworthy could afford to wait for their portion of the entirely hypothetical proceeds. See Mizener, pp. 160–3 and p. 551, n. 16.

[2] Pinker normally took a 10% commission.

arrive at the supposed serial rights in Engd had you gone with the papers into the open market.— — — —

All my contributions in the R. will be available in the States, as I understand no attempt to circulate on the other side will be made at all no matter what prosperity may attend it here. And of course there will be the book. E. Garnett writes me (after seeing proofs and of course he knows my plan of this particular work) that the pubon being skilfully engineered there is money in it.

My friend Hope was here a fortnight ago and I asked him to make inquiries in the City about insuring the termination of Razumov. Years and years ago I used to know one of the partners in the firm whose letter I forward[1]—the one who signs. I had some correspondence with them and gave them particulars of *title of work, my state of health, the office where I am insured* and generally all they wanted to know. I also explained the nature of the insurable interest you have in the book. I forward their last letter to you now, as you see, accepting the risk and giving the rate for six months. But no doubt it could be done for 3 months as well though for the specific purpose three weeks perhaps would be sufficient. As you see however they offer a sort of policy which makes it a rather good business in my humble judgment. For observe that more than the object we would seek is attained as far as I can see. The policy covers obviously the termination of the book since as long as I live I will write; but also if I understand the letter it does more; as it appears to be a policy for so many months. Thus after the book is finished say in 4 weeks[2] my life remains covered still for £1000 for the remainder of the time and so far the forwarding of the next book whether *Memoirs* or *Chance* is covered too. I never, I may safely say, felt less like dying than I do at the present time but pray my dear Pinker consider the matter and let me know what you think on Monday.[3] I must add that I have warned them of my health even saying that I just got over my usual winter fit of gout. The doctor here will give a certificate that I am better than the same time last year.

Yours ever

J. Conrad

p.t.o.

PS I don't send You anything because my wife had no time these last days to type and I shall want to look it over of course. But I am rather

[1] Conrad's dealings with the Standard Life Insurance Co. went back at least as far as 1900 (*Letters*, 2, p. 307).
[2] It was finished on 22 January 1910. [3] The 21st.

anxious to go ahead. Looking over will have to wait. The end is in sight. Please send me the wages cheque £2.*10*.

To John Galsworthy

Text MS Forbes; Unpublished

[Someries]
18 Dec 1908

Dearest Jack

I have nothing particular to say; but sitting here under the lamp after blackening a few sheets of MS paper and loth to go to bed yet, I take a moment to tell you that I had an unexpected pleasure of receiving a letter from Borys's Schoolmaster[1] praising the boy exceedingly from every point of view (a quite unexpected testimony) saying how very sorry he is at losing him and assuring me that the boy is sure to do well anywhere. It looks a most genuine tribute—and indeed I don't see why it should be otherwise. For the last two terms he has been with them the only boarder, which at 15 gs per term is not a very profitable business surely. Jessie has called there (second time this year) and was quite astonished at the almost affectionate footing he's gained in the household. It was perfectly evident—she says. And the best of it is that they are quite commonplace people! House himself seems to be a very good schoolmaster all his boys taking very good places in the big schools when they leave him.

With whom could I share my satisfaction but with Ada and you—and so you get this letter where paternal weakness stands revealed.

Every book I opened of late I've been on the lookout for the motto for *Jocelyn*. In vain! But anyhow I suppose it would be too late by now. When is that vol: coming out?[2]

Are you going to be in town for the holidays? I may try to get down to see Elsie Hueffer who I believe is coming up with the children for a few days. But I have no mind for gaieties anyway. Besides my foot is swollen yet and I hate parading in the capital in a gout-boot. And then I've no great heart to leave Jessie. On the other hand I long for a look in at 14 Addison R*d* and if I only can give a good shove to the book within the next seven days I'll feel more perky. The end is just, just below the horizon and my nervousness increases. How will it turn out? The

[1] William House, of St Gregory's School, Luton. Borys remembered his habit of conducting the morning's hymn-singing with a cane (*My Father*, p. 72).

[2] Nothing came of the plan to republish Galsworthy's early novel (1898).

unsatisfactory part is that I who could always sleep am beginning to know what a bad night is like.

We've been wondering how Ada and you stand the weather of this year end. No colds we hope. Our dear love

Ever yours

J. Conrad

PS I send back at last! this book belonging to you. I have another one yet—but I can't spy it out on the disorderly shelves.

To Elsie Hueffer

Text MS Yale; Unpublished

[Someries]
18 Dec 1908

Dearest Elsie.

Thanks for Your very charming and very friendly letter which is much more than I deserve but not the less valued for that. Au contraire.

If I can ram my foot into a shoe I shall try to come Vous saluer at the reception. As to Jess, travelling (I mean the mere vibration) makes any sort of journey a small torture to her now, and she gets more and more sensitive as to her crippled state especially where there are many strangers.

I know that you too must not overfatigue Yourself—but couldn't you just pousser une pointe as far as here to see us if only for a day? We have been congratulating ourselves on the news of your journey to the South being given up. It puts a different complexion on the future. We will try to reach Aldington in Febr early.

May I give here an affectionate greeting to M^r Marwood. You know how much I think of him. Au revoir in more or less short time.

Our love

Your affectionate friend and
servant

J. Conrad

To Stephen Reynolds
Text MS Berg; Unpublished

[Someries]
18 Dec 1908

My dear Stephen.

I was glad to get your letter with all its news. I can understand Your feeling as to the effect of your book perfectly well.[1]

It's damnably regrettable that You have heard something about my wife which prevented your coming to see us. I suppose it was something about her suffering a lot from her knee. But your holding off was not likely to make it better—and You know that whether there is anybody with us or not she will keep moving about her household and maternal duties. In fact this sort of talk which got about (not as to her knee which is bad enough but of her having to be spared occasions for exertion and so on) does her no good as she has a dread of being looked upon as a cripple. We both hoped to see you; but as I thought you may be busy in one direction or other I did not write to urge you to a visit.

It is only the fear of being indiscreet that prevented us asking you for Xmas. But only the other day we were saying how nice it would have been to have you with us. To which Borys made the remark "No such luck I suppose". Well we don't ask in so many words now, since You are at present with older and, surely, more valuable friends. We only say that the door stands open wide enough to let in the Holy Mountain[2] too. Comprenez-Vous? And it would be appropriate for you to arrive here all in readiness for the day when your Ass' Editorial duties begin.[3] Drop us a line to fix the day of arrival either before, during or directly after the holidays.

Raz. is not finished yet. I can't turn out a novel with the polish on in eleven months—you know. But the end is just peeping above the horizon and the moral support of your superb assurance would come handy. *NB* That does *not* mean that I want to read you fragments of the last part. Oh dear no! I would see you died* first. I am generally ashamed rather of my work now. A lovely state of mind to be in—and helpful—and inspiring—je ne vous dis que ça!

Borys is a good chap. Keen at his work and steady at play. I have unexpectedly got a most glowing communication from his schoolmaster

[1] Reynolds was pleased with the reviews of *A Poor Man's House*: Harold Wright, ed., *Letters of Stephen Reynolds* (Richmond: Hogarth Press, 1923), p. 114.
[2] Reynolds's satirical novel, which came out in 1909.
[3] Reynolds lasted a month as assistant editor of the *English Review* (Wright, p. 114).

in testimony of the boy's general worthiness. I tell you of this because I am pleased. I hope that you all who honour me with your regard will not let him feel too much alone in the world when I am gone.

All our love to you

Yours

J Conrad.

Remember me in real friendly terms to Bob.[1]

To David Garnett
Text MS EAG; G. 229

22 Dec 1908
Someries
Luton.

My dear David.[2]

Your father (who is an older friend of mine than yourself but only by some ten months or so[3]) tells me you have read already the story.[4] But still I send you the little volume as I want you to have something of mine, from myself, in memory of the days when we both were considerably younger—and less wise.

As the years go on you will remember those days better. For me they have a very special value on which I will not enlarge at present. You were a child then, and I but an infant—a literary infant—whose first steps were—like your own—watched over by your mother and father, though I don't mean to say with the same anxious interest. That's a bond between us, surely. I think that in those days under the roof of the Cearne[5] we were very good friends—you and I.

It pleases me to think that on some far distant day, when you are as grizzled as I am now, you may, in a pause of serious occupations, take down this little book from the shelf and glancing through it give a kind smile to my memory.[6]

May the coming year bring you success in everything you undertake.

Your sincere friend

J. Conrad.

[1] Bob Woolley, Reynolds's friend and fellow fisherman; in *A Poor Man's House*, he figures as Tony Widger.
[2] David Garnett (1892–1981), the future author of *Lady into Fox* (1923) and many other novels, was the son of Constance and Edward.
[3] Conrad first met Edward late in 1894. [4] 'The Duel'.
[5] The Garnetts' secluded country house.
[6] An echo of Yeats's 'When you are old and grey and full of sleep' or Ronsard's 'Quand vous serez bien vieille'?

To Sidney Colvin
Text MS Indiana; J-A, 2, 92

Someries
Luton
28 Dec. 1908

My dear Colvin.[1]

For your very welcome letter and Mrs Colvin's most kind message[2]—thanks.

You are very indulgent to my—let us call it—psychology. I've buried myself, and yet I don't want to be buried in the least. It is not indolence. Neither is it misanthropy for if there is any mistrust it is not of mankind but of myself. I wouldn't go so far as to call it lunacy. It isn't all that. What it is I could perhaps explain, but it would be sinful to waste paper and ink on such a subject; and as long as your charity prevents you casting stones I am content to remain gratefully unexplained.

I am glad you think well of the Set of Six. I've spent over these stories more time than they are worth; but this is true I fear of all my work. The vol has been generally well received—better, in a sense, than The Secret Agent, whose reception has been defined by Mr Belloc (I think) as "uncertain". The appearance of that word in a distinctly friendly notice of my work (in the Mor[nin]g Post)[3] donne a penser.[4] Perhaps that is the very word of the riddle. Man, work, everything is just "uncertain" before the world. And there too may lie the concise explanation of my hermit-like ways which are not really in my character. But enough of that.

The winged rumour is correct. We are coming back to Kent sometime before the springtide sets in. A very small (and poky) cottage has been got ready for us in the village of Aldington, within a stone's throw from the church where I believe Erasmus preached in his time, whether

[1] Sidney Colvin (1845–1927; knighted 1911) became a good friend to Conrad, as he had been to Stevenson. Colvin had been Slade Professor of Fine Arts at Cambridge and director of the Fitzwilliam Museum, and was now Keeper of Prints and Drawings at the British Museum; among his literary works were editions of Stevenson's letters and biographies of Landor and Keats.

[2] Frances Colvin (née Fetherstonhaugh, 1839–1924) was an essayist and the friend of many other writers.

[3] An unsigned review of *A Set of Six*, 20 August: 'All his best work ... is in his volumes of short stories and in "Lord Jim", which is after all but a short story that has broken bounds ... The idea of growth or movement that is not purely physical seems to disturb his work.' In contrast to novels such as *The Secret Agent*, each story of *A Set of Six* is 'a masterpiece', written 'in a style that can only be called inevitable'.

[4] 'Makes me think'.

in praise of folly or not I don't know.[1] And by the by, his note too, in a world full of great noises, was considered as "uncertain". N'est-ce-pas? The matter of the Reminiscences has been the subject of much hesitation and not a few heart searchings.[2] The defect you point out is manifest to myself and as a matter of fact has been considered. Yes. There it is. And in a sense it expresses a reluctance to start that kind of work at all. That sort of discursiveness gives an air of detachment—interprets really a sincere attitude—I am not a personage for an orderly biography either auto or otherwise. It did cost an effort to begin—I assure you. Now there will, in the end, be a book and, who knows, from the rambling discourse a personality of sorts will yet emerge. Meantime this defect saves the pangs of my shyness—if you like to call it that. I explain, because of all people in the world I don't want you to think me either stupid or wilfully perverse. I don't mind being thought somewhat foolish—an adept in folly I mean.

I am finishing a confoundedly difficult novel. But how long that bone will be sticking in my gizzard I can't tell. Meantime it keeps me in agonies within the four walls and renders me unbearable to wife and children. What with the gout (ten days) and the novel I have been in an atrocious temper. Your letter made me feel human this morning the first time for I don't know how long. Once more—thanks! And pray give our kind regards to Mrs Colvin. I am sorry the weather turned thus miserably horrid spoiling Your holiday.

Always Yours most sincerely

J. Conrad

To J. B. Pinker
Text MS Berg; Unpublished

[Someries]
29 Dec 1908

My dear Pinker

I am perfectly aware of the importance of the matter you mention; and I was under the impression that the age *was* admitted.[3] That

[1] Desiderius Erasmus (1467–1536), the great Dutch humanist, kept his sceptical good temper amid the din of reformation and reaction. He spent several years in England and wrote the *Encomium moriae* (*Praise of Folly*) as a compliment to Sir Thomas More.

[2] This paragraph anticipates the 'Familiar Preface' written in the summer of 1911; see, e.g., the defence of 'discursiveness' on p. xxii. Perhaps Colvin was the unnamed sceptic whose opinions are quoted there.

[3] Duly verified and taken into account.

impression resulted from the conversations with Watson[1] (through whom my first policy was taken out) and also with the Secretary of the Standard Life. I have a recollection of being assured that the age *was* admitted. I did not ask for visual evidence but I remember distinctly being told "that was all right". I had no reason to doubt it having produced to Watson the documents proving my age sufficiently.

There are three of them corroborating each other. Imprimis my father's passport (1869) delivered under the signature of the provincial governor Prince Galitzin to the *"nobleman Korzeniowski travelling with his son Conrad aged 10 years"*.[2]

I mention this first as it is in two languages Russian and German and most easily put in, in a translation, and should be sufficient, such passports being very precise in their details—at any rate in Russia.

The principal document however is the certificate of my baptism performed upon a child of 2 1/2 years, born on the *21st Nov 57* old style—*3d of Dec 57* New Style, signed by the officiating priest and stamped in the Consistory of the Diocese as the true copy of the entry in the register. This is in polish* and can no doubt be translated in some authoritative way if needed.

The third document (corroborative) is the admission to the citizenship of the town of Cracow of the orphan C.K. signed by the Burgomaster. It is dated 1871 and of course recites my age.

It should be pointed out to the Standard office that the above papers being produced to back up my verbal declaration were accepted as sufficient to establish my age by the Board of Trade for my examination as Master in the Merchant Service and by the Home Office in the matter of my naturalisation.[3]

Finally the N° for July (I think) 1889 of the *Senatorial Gazette* (Russian official paper)[4] containing my name as being released from allegiance as Russian subject by Imperial Decree states my age to be 31.

The possession of all these documents should be sufficient to establish my age. They have been all communicated to old W. Watson (in '96 or '97) as agent for the Standard Life and I was told then that it was *"all right"*.

[1] Until his failure in 1904, William Watson was Conrad's banker and also handled Conrad's many requests for insurance.
[2] Prince Golitsyn, Governor of Chernikhov, confirmed the permit to leave Russian-occupied Poland in January 1868, when Conrad was indeed ten (Najder, *Chronicle*, p. 24 and p. 503, n. 67).
[3] In 1886.
[4] *Sanktpeterburgskiia Senatskiia Viedomosti*, 20 June 1889, p. 1.

The above papers, with some others are now under Your care having been deposited with you in two sealed envelopes 3 years ago I think.

If you are going to move in the matter I had better come up and point them out to you. I certainly think it is important to have the age admitted. I thought it was done years ago. I am *almost* certain of having seen a policy thus endorsed; but it may have been a lapsed one.

Wouldn't it be worth while to make inquiry of the Standard Life? I don't think they have any doubts.

Yours always

J. Conrad.

1909

To H.-D. Davray

Text MS Texas; *L. fr.* 96

2 Jan. 1909.
Someries.
Luton.

Cher Davray.

Ma femme a avoué avec honte et douleur qu'elle a oublié de Vous envoyer nos souhaits de la nouvelle année. Il faut lui pardonner car elle a été surchargée de besogne de toute espèce sans parler du mauvais accès de goutte qui m'a pris juste avant Noël. Elle a du faire la garde-malade en même temps.

Merci mon cher de Vos bonnes paroles. J'espère que Vous ne doutez pas de nos sentiments a votre égard. Je regrette de ne pas Vous avoir vu pendant votre visite a Londres dont Hueffer m'a parlé. C'est un très brave garçon et un homme de talent.

Je n'espère ni gloire ni fortune. Je n'ai pas le temps d'attendre. Je doute même si M d'Humières reussira a finir la traduction du *Nigger* avant ma mort.[1] Assurement je ne lui en veux pas. Je suis en paix avec tout le monde.

Nos meilleurs souhaits de la nouvelle année.

Tout a vous

J. Conrad

Translation

Dear Davray.

My wife has confessed, shamefaced and sad, that she forgot to send you our wishes for the new year. You must forgive her, for she has been overburdened with chores of every sort, not to mention the bad attack of gout which struck me just before Christmas. She has had to be a nurse as well.

Thank you, my dear man, for your kind words. I hope you do not doubt our feelings towards you. I am sorry not to have seen you during

[1] Robert d'Humières had first proposed the translation in January 1905 (*Letters*, 3, p. 212).

your visit to London, which Hueffer told me about. He is a very fine fellow and a man of talent.

I hope for neither glory nor fortune. I haven't the time to wait. I even doubt if M. d'Humières will manage to finish translating the *Nigger* before I die. I certainly hold no grudge against him for that. I am at peace with everyone.

Our best wishes for the new year.

Sincerely yours,

J. Conrad

To J. B. Pinker

Text MS Berg; Unpublished

[Someries]
Tuesday. [5? January 1909][1]

My dear Pinker.

Thanks for your letter in the matter of age. I am glad that my recollection was right.

Reynolds told me of your boy joining you Yesterday.[2] I congratulate you warmly on an event which must be a source of very great gratification to you; for I remember how a couple of years ago you were pleased to see his inclination pointing that way. On this auspicious occasion let me express my most sincere wishes of success both for yourself and for him. Life has its good moments, and this is such a one for you surely; I hope that working in [an] association so satisfactory to your affection You will both find many of them in your way.

——I've been preaching a little to R. The man has a distinct value and I feel that he ought to concentrate his young powers upon production, production and again production. That was my text—and I suppose You understand what I had in my mind. His artistic energy ought to be kept concentrated upon the only work which will in the years to come give him satisfaction without alloy. Let him write and not scatter himself upon all sorts of enterprises—distinctly inferior to what his literary gift can do.[3] As I know from him that he has a great liking

[1] Received '1/09': probably on the Tuesday closest to 29 December, when a previous letter pursued 'the matter of age' for insurance purposes.

[2] Military service aside, Eric worked for his father until J. B.'s death in 1922 and then became Conrad's agent himself. His career ended with a jail sentence for embezzlement.

[3] These enterprises would include his brief stint at the *English Review*, his miscellaneous contributions to newspapers and, perhaps, his time in the fishing-boats.

and regard for you a hint in that direction from you may do good. It would be a pity if he were to turn into a mere workman of letters.

Yours ever

J. Conrad

To J. B. Pinker

Text MS Berg; Unpublished

[Someries]

[early January 1909][1]

Dear Pinker

Eric did give up a most distinguished last year[2]—and in all this you seem the more blessed if I may use that word.

Please send me <u>one</u> typed copy of these pages (up to N° 700 in MS.[3])—and would you have the kindness to buy a copy of the *Nigger* for Reynolds and send it to me here for inscription.

Yours in haste

J. C

To Ralph W. Ashcroft

Text MS Lubbock; Rude (1988)

Someries

Luton

7 Jan. 1909

Dear Sir[4]

Thanks for your interesting communication. One can only wish success to M^r Clemens.[5]

For myself I am if You like of the literary world but I am not in it. I have no acquaintances (only a few friends) my name would carry no

[1] Received '1/09': close to [5? January], if the reference to Eric is any guide.

[2] At school.

[3] 700 is the last page of TS Batch A: Conrad had taken eleven weeks to write what became fifteen typed pages (Carabine and Higdon, *UWE*).

[4] Ralph Ashcroft, a Liverpudlian (1875–1947), was Samuel Langhorne Clemens's business adviser, travelling companion, and secretary. Ashcroft created the Mark Twain Company to make the most of his elderly employer's name, but a series of financial and personal misapprehensions led in April to a parting of the ways.

[5] For many years Clemens had campaigned against literary piracy, which had been checked but not eliminated by the International Copyright Act of 1891. Ashcroft had come to England on a double mission: to ask a long list of writers (including Kipling, Meredith, Andrew Lang, and Rider Haggard) for their support of copyright reform, and to ask Sir Thomas Lipton, the tea merchant, for his help with the Plasmon Milk Products Company, one of Clemens's disastrous investments.

weight or influence; and my ignorance of the subject being absolute I feel I would be wasting your short time inexcusably if I were to ask you to come here for a talk. I could not even offer an opinion as to any action here having a chance of success at present.

Whatever may be the scheme for a new U S Copyright Law to which Mr Clemens is lending the authority of his great and popular name it would be presumption in me to offer a comment, as an ignorant person in the matter of details and as not being a citizen of the country interested. The names of the many able men in this country competently interested in the question you know, no doubt, better than I do.

<div align="right">Believe me faithfully yours</div>

<div align="right">J. Conrad</div>

To Agnes Tobin
Text MS Newberry; Unpublished

<div align="right">Someries</div>
<div align="right">Luton</div>
<div align="right">Beds.</div>
<div align="right">9 Jan 1909.</div>

Dear Miss Tobin.[1]

Pardon my long delay. The fact is I've been ill and am far from well yet. I am afraid I simply could not come, even if it were certain that my visit would do no harm to the poor patient.[2]

I've had the cruel news first from Mr Henry James some time ago. It was a terribly painful shock. We had exchanged several letters of late and I just missed seeing him before his departure for Italy[3] by a mere misunderstanding which I regretted very much. It is as You say a tragic catastrophe. The pity of it is present to me from day to day, I assure You. May I ask you to express to Mrs Symons my deep sorrow and my

[1] Agnes Tobin (1864–1939) came from San Francisco. She knew Yeats (who called her the greatest American poet since Whitman), Alice Meynell, and many other literary people. Her own work included plays and translations from Petrarch. Conrad, whom she put in touch with the great collector John Quinn, praised 'her genius for friendship' in the dedication of *Under Western Eyes*.

[2] The previous autumn, Arthur Symons had suffered 'a thunderbolt from hell', a severe mental breakdown in Italy, which resulted among other humiliations in his being thrown manacled into a Ferrarese dungeon. Currently he was a patient in a private asylum in East London where he could be visited by Rhoda, his wife, and by Agnes Tobin, who had travelled from California to be near him (Beckson, *Arthur Symons*, pp. 254–73).

[3] James made his last visit to Italy in the summer of 1907.

genuine sympathy for her in her terrible affliction. It is difficult to find words to fit one's very sincere feeling for such a cruel misfortune.

Believe me, dear Miss Tobin,

> Your very faithful and obedient servant
>
> J. Conrad

To Ford Madox Ford

Text Violet Hunt's copy, Cornell; Unpublished

> [Someries]
> Monday [11 or 18 January 1909?][1]

Dearest Ford,

I return the MS of the Countess. There is no reason whatever why it should be published. It has no historical interest whatever and no quality of any kind.

I've been very bad with all sorts of flesh-ills. It was impossible to come to you for that and other reasons.

I will send on Douglas's thing[2] to-morrow.

How are you? How is Elsie?

> Yours ever
>
> J. Conrad.

To J. B. Pinker

Text MS Berg; Unpublished

> [Someries]
> Thursday.
> 14 Jan '09

Dear Pinker.

Thanks for the type.

I'll send a good lot more MS by Sunday's post.

Please send me cheques (2) for wages of £*1.5* each and also one for £*1.1* to settle a bill. Three in all. *Please note* that if You get a proposal for

[1] The only possible dates if the MS under consideration was the Countess Rossetti Agrosti's report, published in the February *Review* (1, 600–4), of an aristocratic relief expedition to the earthquake-smashed city of Messina. The expedition was in Sicily from 31 December to 6 January. Under normal circumstances, mail from southern Italy took about three days; by the 25th, the *Review* would have been on its way to the subscribers.

[2] Perhaps 'Sirens', published in the May issue.

Reminiscences in *US* the same will have to be set up over there from the proof sheets I have here, and *not* from the *typed copy* in your (or the editor's) possession. I would send the Proofs to you, now, only I haven't got the 4th paper as yet.

Thanks for the book received the other day.

Doubleday & C° have sent me a copy of their magazine—I believe. I see,[1] they are advertising me as one of their authors.[2] So I presume I am "transferred" to them with your concurrence

<div style="text-align: right">Yours always</div>

<div style="text-align: right">J. Conrad.</div>

To Ada Galsworthy
Text MS Forbes; J-A, 2, 93

<div style="text-align: right">[Someries]</div>

<div style="text-align: right">17 Jan '09</div>

Dearest Ada

It might have been a serious affair this passage with the wild 'bus. A sort of shudder remains from reading Jack's letter with its pooh-poohing reference. I always feel (when I am there) that the bit of Strand in front of Char + Station is about as near Eternity as any spot on Earth. Well, since you've escaped there's nothing more to say—except a serious warning not to do it again.[3]

The news Jack sends me is just what I wanted to hear—except of course the news of his cold. I suppose he will be off to M[an]ch[est]er to morrow.[4] His letter does not read as if You were going with him—but of course with the man's negligent epistolary style one never knows. I think his novels are decidedly better in that respect. Decidedly. What's your opinion? Strictly entre-nous be it understood.

As he omits to say how the Riviera profited *you* we can only hope that you have made a provision of sunshine to carry you through the dreary months—or the months which would have been dreary but for the promise of two plays and a book![5] I applaud with all my heart the

[1] Changed from 'I say'.
[2] Acquired by the purchase of McClure, Phillips; the association with Doubleday was greatly to benefit Conrad.
[3] For the details of Ada Galsworthy's collected behaviour when two horses panicked at Charing Cross, see Marrot, p. 225.
[4] For rehearsals of *The Silver Box* and *Strife*, the former a revival, the latter a try-out for the London run.
[5] *Fraternity*, scheduled for publication in February.

conjunction of all these events. I feel somehow that it will work for good. Do you intend to see the Maner first performance?

But it's Strife! Strife. We mustn't talk about it. Yet with that and the book in the full occupation of my thoughts I feel a premonition of a great, triumphant taking possession of the land. After this confession— silence.

In answer to Jack's distinct question I can only say that I've written 110 000 words[1] in the last 12 months. But of course Raz. is not finished yet. It isn't very far off tho'—unless—unless a batch gets torn up suddenly in some moment of imperative inspiration. And that too may happen. Meantime I am scheming how to get away from this place to the little hole in Aldington which has been made ready for us rather nicely Ford says. We haven't seen it since it has been done up. It is the house on the opposite side of the road next to the cottage in which you saw our desolate tribe last Septer. Just at the foot of the hill—you know.

CBQ[2] vanquished the gout in due course but I am chary of giving it (the drug) too much free play. I suspect it makes me imbecile for a time—and that's too high a price to pay for life itself—let alone mere freedom from pain. And moreover it would be a fool's bargain anyway for write I must to stave off remorse, despair etc etc—often things less fanciful too, with, amongst them, a suspicion that will come on now and then that "all this is no good" do what I may.

Excuse this discordant strain; but the fact is that I've just received the accts of all my publishers from which I perceive that all my immortal works (13 in all) have brought me last year something under five pounds in royalties.[3] That sort of thing quenches that *Joie de Vivre* which should burn like a flame in an author's breast and in the manner of an explosive engine drive his pen onward at 30 pages an hour.

Jessie does not let anything quench her flame, bless her. The kids have been fairly well this holiday-time. B remains for another term at the school here.

A[n] Xmas pudding goes by next post—in proof of Jessie's unquench-

1 Changed from '120 000 words'.
2 A proprietary medicine also known as Post's Tablets. 'Analysis made in 1908 showed that each tablet contained 1½ grains of Potassium Iodide, a small quantity of Salicylate, a vegetable Extract and Magnesia, also a small quantity of Alkaloid which was not identified', W. Harrison Martindale and W. Wynn Westcott, *The Extra Pharmacopoeia* (Lewis, 14th edn, 1910), p. 742.
3 Although Heinemann's statements for *Typhoon* and *The Nigger* and Blackwood's for *Youth* and *Lord Jim* had not yet arrived, they could not have added much to the total.

able flame partly—but mostly as the artless symbol of her affection. If You are both in Man. it will keep till your return of course. She didn't chase you with it down to the very Mediterranean only from fear of the Douane I believe. But You didn't really think You were to escape this year—did you? Pardon this silly letter it's all this CBQ you know. I trust in your fortitude. I know *you* will be able to stand it; and I leave to Your discretion such passages as may be selected for showing to Jack—always bearing in mind the greater frailness of the masculine intellect and the state of exasperation the rehearsals are certain to provoke. I'll appear promptly in Febry to hear and be heard without any moderation whatever. Meantime I restrain my runaway pen on the very edge of the paper as you see. And that also is a proof of my affection. Our dear love.

<div style="text-align:right">Always yours de coeur</div>

<div style="text-align:right">J. Conrad.</div>

To J. B. Pinker
Text MS Berg; Unpublished

<div style="text-align:right">[Someries]</div>
<div style="text-align:right">18 Jan '09</div>

Dear Pinker.

I send you some pp of which please have only *one* copy made. There is no hurry as I am too busy writing to bother about revising just now.

The enclosed bills pray settle directly—as done before. I hate having to send them—as always.

From the received acc/[t] I see that B[lack]wood and Heineman[n] have not sent their statements. I can't forbear a groan at the miserable result of royalties from US. Have you Harper's statement of *S Agent* sales? One would like to have some idea—but after all as the publishers are not controlled their statements aren't worth much. All the same I haven't any doubt that my time will come yet. It will.

<div style="text-align:right">Yours ever</div>

<div style="text-align:right">J. Conrad</div>

PS In order that you may not think the last statement of the letter a meaningless boastful cry I will say that I base my conviction on the axiom that "force never fails"[1]—and force (not brutality) is the only attribute which *no reviewer or critic* has ever denied to my work. Not one. On the contrary *every* critic has felt its presence. It is there. I count on it.

[1] An axiom in mechanics.

Charm, subtlety, sentiment do go to waste sometimes. Force (not the parade of force but the genuine power of it) never fails.

To J. B. Pinker

Text MS Berg; Unpublished

Someries Luton
Thursday 21 Jan '09

Dear Pinker.

Thank you for the detailed statement, for which I did not really mean to trouble you, but was glad to see anyhow.

Cole my landlord has been dunning me for the rent due on the Dec*er* quarter. £15. to M*r Joseph Cole*.

I send you some 1800 words for rough type. There is no hurry for it. I want the MS out of my way. Now every page tells, the amount done being over *75000* words.[1] I am frightfully anxious and absurdly overstrained.

What do You say to abandoning the *Nigger* to H[einemann] & C*o* for as big a set-off against the *Rescue* debt as your diplomacy could secure.[2] I throw out the suggestion for what it is worth; and if treating in that direction a stipulation could be made that H should fall in (as regards *Typhoon* & *Nigger*) with any scheme later on to publish a collected edition.[3] The balance of the debt then could perhaps be taken into consideration while arranging the payment in advance of roy: for the one or two vols of Reminiscences, which I would rather like H to publish if terms can be arranged. I put those points for your consideration.

You may say: Why open a discussion at all? It's a matter which unless we pick it up must lie where it is indefinitely. That's true. But apart from every other consideration, my view is that if we can *liberate* the *Rescue* in that way we do really secure some advantage. We get back a novel all but *three parts written* to follow say *Chance*. If you think that I can't finish the R you judge me wrongly. I can. I will be even glad to go back to the Malay seas presently.

In this connection can you get hold of the Rescue Typescript 2*d* copy

[1] Of 'Razumov'.

[2] Heinemann had bought the book rights to the perennially-delayed *The Rescue* in 1898; the proposal here is to waive royalties on *The Nigger* – which by now was bringing in very little.

[3] A collected edition – eventually published by Heinemann – would follow the example of Hardy and James.

which is in McClure's hands.[1] The horrid fact is that my typed copy which I left with Hueffer two years ago (for safety) is not forthcoming.[2] What they have done with it God only knows. Of course Ford says he never had it—but he is mistaken. It is somewhere in his drawers but as they broke up one or two homes since it has got mislaid.

Yours ever

J Conrad.

To J. B. Pinker
Text MS Berg; Unpublished

[Someries]
Tuesday.
26 Jan [1909][3]

Dear Pinker.

I really can't stand this anxiety any longer and I must ask you whether you will arrange to enable me to remove from the Someries at once. It is too absurd to continue in this expensive place and since you intend to help me out of it why not do it at once. The cottage in Kent is ready for us since Dec. It will cost for the first year £30—to cover the alterations they have made—and after that the rent will be 8/- per week. Don't wait till the very last words of the book are written and let me cut that expense going on here, which makes it impossible for me to keep within the limit of £600.[4] You may say that this is not your affair but I fancy that it would be good business to give me the best chance possible—since we are working together.

Once over there by sending me £7 a week You will have no bills forwarded to you for settlement—no cheques for coals, wages etc etc. That amount=£364 per year will cover everything except the rent which, the first year, will amount to 7.10 a quarter and the next year to £5. Altogether for first Year—counting from March next *£394.* The other *206* I would draw as required for B.[5] and my own incidental expences.*

I have given notice here and will have to go by March anyhow. But I want to get away at once say the 15^th of next month. The move need not

[1] McClure held the serial rights.
[2] Ford may have worked on the partially-completed novel (Mizener, p. 81, and *Letters*, 3, p. 194).
[3] The question of houses gives the year.
[4] The limit on expenses Pinker had set in August 1907: *Letters*, 3, p. 464.
[5] For Borys's schooling.

interfere with my writing on the contrary it will help it. You have always said that when the book is done you will advance £80. Well advance it now and also £50 for the move and you will be doing twice as much, as it were, for me than if You put it off. The above amount I must have—nothing less will do—that is if you do anything at all.

If you do that I am willing at the end of the year (if you say the word) to apply for the pension on Civ[il] list which has been offered to me through J. G.[1] But let us see first how things look at the end of the year. You will have by then some <u>240</u> thoud words more or less, and we shall see what they bring. If you think the position too unsatisfactory I will apply and the pension will ease you considerably for they would hardly give me *less than* 250.

I will call on you this afternoon about 3.30 or four.

<div align="center">Yours</div>

<div align="right">J. C.</div>

I want to talk over Pawlings beastly attitude.[2]

To Stephen Reynolds

Text MS Berg; Unpublished

<div align="right">[Someries]
30 Jan '09</div>

Dear Reynolds.

I've had an awful time but at any rate we are going away from here. I've secured the means for that move with conditions that leave me still in a hole—but the main object is secured.

My nerves are gone to pieces; otherwise everything here is as usual. How did you get on?

In the midst of my sordid (and befogged) worries I spared a thought now and then for the burly form of *one* who pervades the West Country nursing the dreams of great deeds and cruel books for the discomfiture of the harried bourgeois.

We all send our love

<div align="center">Yours J. Conrad.</div>

[1] The reading of the initials is tentative, but 'J. G.' for John Galsworthy would be true to his involvement in the campaign. Unlike the grant Conrad had received in 1905, a pension would be a regular source of income; the Civil List was the Prime Minister's discretionary fund.

[2] S. S. Pawling, Heinemann's partner, must not have taken kindly to the offer of forgone royalties on Conrad's books.

To Norman Douglas
Text MS Texas; Unpublished

[Someries]
Tuesday.
2^d Febr. 09

Dear Douglas

Like a damned fool I am* I've forgotten to write to Ford of your visit to morrow.

My only excuse is that I was writing MS up to the very moment the postman came—and getting it ready for post the other matter went clean out of my head. However there is no harm done as Hueffer expected to see you early in the week anyhow.

In the matter of coming ever* to write in the country,[1] I have consulted my wife on the scruples which Your manner imperfectly concealed from my eye. She is indignant at the mere idea of the good Mrs Garrett poisoning You with half-cooked flesh. She tells me that I may let you know from her, that out of regard for your feelings You shall be charged the actual cost of your "vittles" whenever your stay at the cottage *exceeds one week.*

You will get no other concession so I advise you to close with the offer.

So if ever the spirit moves You to have a spell in the country for work or rest, board with us you must. You will be allowed to pay Mrs Garrett for your room and Jessie will see to it that it is properly fitted out with sheets and pillows etc etc from our own store. Her kindest regard.

Yours

J. Conrad

To Norman Douglas
Text MS Indiana; Unpublished

Aldington
Kent
22 Febry
'09

My dear Douglas

My wife had the letter anent the MS. I will be ready for it next week. Meantime we have a small petition to present: Can you without any inconvenience meet Borys at S^t Pancras at 10.20 next Saturday and go

[1] In Aldington, where the Conrads were to move on the 14th.

across with him to Char[ing] + to catch the 11AM for Smeeth.—It can be done in a taxi easily enough.

We want to have him for a couple of days at the 1/2 term.

But *don't* let this put you out in the least. He can manage alone or some other arrangement can be made.

I am thinking that You could perhaps come along for the weekend by the same opportunity and bring the MS.

Kindest regards

Yours ever

J Conrad

To Norman Douglas
Text MS Texas; Unpublished

[Aldington]
Wednesday. [24 February 1909][1]

Dear Douglas

Ever so many thanks. Jessie (who is very busy just now) directs me to tell you to come along without compunction.

So we shall expect you with the boy by the train arriving 12.58 at Smeeth. I will have the fly-motor waiting for You.[2]

Should something prevent you coming on at the last moment *don't* give the MS to the boy. He would feel the responsibility too much. Better trust reg^d post.

Au revoir then.

Yours

J. C.

The train for Smeeth leaves Char + at 11 o'clock so you will have not much time between the stations.

Borys will be coming by the *9.37 train from* Luton. I am not certain to five minutes when it arrives at Pancras. It may be 10.15.

You are a dear good fellow to take the bother of it all so kindly.

[1] On Monday, 22 February, Conrad asked Douglas to escort Borys across London 'next Saturday', the 27th.

[2] The cottage was about two miles from the station and reached by taxi-cab.

To Robert d'Humières
Text MS Vaugelas; Guérin

Aldington Forehead.
Nr Hythe
Kent.
2 Mch 1909.

Cher Monsieur.[1]

Dans mon contrat avec Davray[2] j'ai éxcepté formellement *The Nigger of the Narcissus*. Il me semble souverainement injuste que Vous fussiez privé de l'avantage matériel de la publication dans la Revue,[3] si, comme vous le croyez, il y a une chance de ce coté là. Vers la fin du 1910 sera une bonne date pour la publication en volume du *Nigger*. Car enfin Davray a 8–10 volumes a traduire et a publier coup sur coup si tel est son projet pour me créer un public de lecteurs. Du reste comme evidem[m]ent il ne suit pas l'ordre chronologique (puisque le *Secret Agent* sera le premier à paraître[4]) je pense que vous pourrez vous entendre facilement avec lui.

Pour ma part j'aimerai bien voir ce bon Nègre habillé dans le couverture du *Mercure de France* comme le reste de la petite famille. Je sais que Vous avez le droit de choisir tel éditeur qu'il vous plaira; seulement si Vous pouviez Vous arranger avec Davray cela me faira* plaisir et sera peut-être avantageux pour le livre lui-même qui est assez exceptionel en soi; et même dans mon oeuvre a un caractère spécial. Avec les autres, le public (si public il y a) l'avalera sans doute sans s'apercevoir de la différence.

Je pense que décidement il faut donner a la Revue l'opportunité de se faire l'honneur d'accepter votre traduction d'un ouvrage qui, il y a dix ans de cela, a trouvé un courageux protecteur dans feu Henley, alors directeur de la *New Review*.[5] Mais feu Henley n'avait peur de rien une fois sa conviction faite. Il accepta l'ouvrage pour sa revue sur la foi des 3 premiers chapitres—et même sans m'écrire un seul mot. Il m'a fait dire par un ami commun que "*si le reste était comme l'échantillon c'était affaire*

[1] Aymeric-Eugène-Robert, Vicomte d'Humières (1868–1915), an author and translator, active in the Théâtre des Arts. Well known to Wharton and James and close to Marcel Proust, he was to die in a hopeless charge on the German lines. Among the works he translated were Kipling's *Plain Tales from the Hills* and Lew Wallace's *Ben Hur*. His translation of *The Nigger* appeared in 1909 as a serial and 1910 as a book.

[2] For a French translation of Conrad's works.

[3] The *Revue de Paris*, which was considering d'Humières' translation.

[4] Davray had already published 'Karain' in the *Mercure*.

[5] William Ernest Henley (1849–1903), poet and editor, had an eye for promising newcomers, among them H. G. Wells. Henley had, however, turned down *Almayer's Folly* (*Letters*, 1, p. 211).

conclue".[1] La dessus je suis resté collé sur ma chaise, pour ainsi dire, pendant 4 mois. J'écris fort lentement et j'avais peur, vous concevez, que Henley n'oublia. Mais cet homme n'oubliait rien. Il m'écrivit sur une carte postale "*C'est même mieux que l'échantillon*"—et j'en fus quitte pour une semaine au lit après.[2] Mais les temps heroïques sont passés!

Je regrette cher monsieur de ne pas pouvoir me rendre a Paris exprès pour faire Votre connaissance.[3] Ce n'est pas l'envie qui me manque croyez le bien. Mais je ne perds pas l'espoir d'avoir le plaisir un jour de vous serrer la main. En attendant cher monsieur et confrère croyez moi toujours le votre

<div style="text-align:center">très cordialement</div>

<div style="text-align:right">J. Conrad.</div>

Translation

Dear Sir,

In my contract with Davray, I specifically excepted *The Nigger of the 'Narcissus'*. It seems to me supremely unfair that you should be deprived of the material advantage of publication in the Review if, as you believe, there's a chance in that quarter. A good date for the publication of the *Nigger* as a volume will be towards the end of 1910. After all, Davray has nine or ten volumes to translate and to publish one after another, if that's his plan for creating me a readership. Besides, since he's not, it seems, following the chronological order (as the *Secret Agent* will be the first to appear), I think you'll easily come to an understanding with him.

For my part, I would like very much to see the worthy *Nigger*, like the rest of the little family, wearing the clothes of the *Mercure de France*. I know you have the right to choose whatever publisher you please; but if you can settle with Davray, it will please me and, perhaps, be of advantage to the book itself, which is unusual by nature; even among

[1] S. S. Pawling passed on the good news; Henley had seen no more than 64 pages (*Letters*, 1, p. 320). Conrad liked his comment well enough to quote it in his Author's Note to *The Nigger* in the Heinemann Collected Edition (p. x).

[2] Conrad heard from Henley in late November 1896 and finished the book in mid-January (*Letters*, 1, pp. 319–20, 330–2). Translation was taking far longer than composition.

[3] Conrad had hoped to meet him in 1905, when d'Humières first proposed a translation.

my own works it has a distinctive character. The public (if there is one) will consume it with the others, no doubt not noticing the difference.

I think that the Review should definitely be given the chance to grace itself with your translation of a work which, ten years ago, found a courageous protector in the late Henley, then editor of the *New Review*. But, once his mind was made up, the late Henley feared nothing. He took the work for his magazine on the strength of the first three chapters—not even writing to me about it. Through a mutual friend, he told me that 'if the rest was like the sample, the deal was done'. Thereupon I was glued to my chair, so to speak, for four months. I write very slowly and, as you can imagine, was afraid that Henley would forget. But that man forgot nothing. He wrote to me on a post-card 'It's even better than the sample'—and I paid for it after with a week in bed. But the heroic age is past.

I am sorry, my dear Sir, that I can't come to Paris expressly to make your acquaintance. I would like to come, believe me. But I don't despair of having the pleasure of shaking your hand one day. Meanwhile, dear Sir and colleague, I am always yours

Very cordially,

J. Conrad.

To Norman Douglas
Text MS Texas; Unpublished

Saturday 6th March
1909
Aldington
Kent

Confidential

Dear Douglas.

Your letter this moment to hand. Your plan of cutting out 2 books out* of the material you have I highly approve.

The immediate concern however is to deal with the situation as created by the new attitude of the ER.

—I understand from M[arw]ood that he has extracted from the MS you gave him a page here and a page there and made up an article which he has asked your permission by urgent letter to put into type at once for N° VI.[1] See what comes of your unguarded permission (against which I

[1] The article in question, 'Sirens', appeared in the May number of the *English Review*.

protested to you at the time) to meddle with your work. I am no end annoyed. They are not in a position to make you an offer for the whole MS as a four-number-serial. That's clear from that very proposal to extract an article from the whole MS into which they seem to be hurrying you. I don't know what you answered. I hope you have refused point blank. I wish I knew. Damn!

However I will assume that you have consented. In that case my advice is to take the following line at the interview on Wednesday evening. Say:—

"You can't make me an offer for serial publication. Very well. You only want to publish that article. But consider that I by consenting to it am ruining my chances of having the whole or part of the MS serialised elsewhere. I can't go to B[lack]wood for instance with a[n] MS the guts of which have been torn out in that manner. Therefore I must have £25 for that article You have selected out of the pages which I have sub-mitted to your consideration as a whole. Moreover you must agree to publish (out of that material) two more papers at say £20 each."[1]

That will make £65 in all, not so bad considering the whole position and the possibility in that case of having the (shortened according to your new plan) book published for the next Xmas season. But you may try for more. For instce 30 for the selected first pages and 25 for each of the two others. Try to get anything between 60 and 90. See?

You must stipulate further:—

"If you fall in with my reasonable proposition I want a foot note to the title (whatever it may be) of each article stating that it is a chapter out of Mr Douglas' forthcoming volume on the Peninsula of Sorrento under the title *Syren Land*. I on my side engage myself not to publish anything serially *in Engd* while I am appearing in the *ER*. In effect I give you the exclusive right to publish *serially* in England as much or as little as you like of *Syrenland* (in 3 articles) for the sum of—providing that the publication is over by the month of October so that the book may come out in good time for the Xmas trade.[2] That's my attitude in justice to myself and from the necessities of my position. If you can't fall in with it then I must ask you to return my MS and cancel the proof." (that is: proof of the M'wood selected article if you have permitted.) You ought also to stipulate for payment on publication and all such details. Also

[1] The punctuation in Conrad's 'advice' has been simplified: as he often did when prompting his friends, Conrad put quotation marks before every MS line of dialogue.

[2] Chapters 1, 2, 4, 11, and 12 of *Siren Land*, which came out in 1911, include material already published in the *Review*.

enquire what they can do with the U States rights so as not to lose copyright on the articles. The book itself will be safe enough; and you must busy yourself at once negotiating with publishers. But that's another story.

Talk to them as above and take no less than £60 in any case. At least that's my feeling about it.

I repeat that I highly approve your idea of having *two* books under different titles. One made up more or less of the stuff in possession of the ER, the other out of the materials you have ready.[1] You need not say anything to them about it unless you *must* have some of their chapters back for carrying out your new scheme.

That's all I think. Write me fully after Wednesday's dinner. Our love
 Yours

 J Conrad.

To John Galsworthy
Text MS POSK; Danilewiczowa

 [Aldington]
 Saturday
 6[th] March '09
Dearest Jack.

I am miserably seedy—a horrid cold with a slight temperature. I send the stall back at once[2] but when it will reach you goodness only knows. We are still snowed up and the post comes and goes when it can in a most erratic fashion. Jessie says she *must* see the play. So perhaps a little later on You will give me two seats. I am afraid I won't be fit to go abroad on Tuesday and so I daren't keep this stall and ask for another. Promise to let me know of the reception at once. Won't you. I had the greatest difficulty to finish my paper for the *ER*.[3] It's done at last! Very silly. I am sick of everything I write.

A fine book[4] dearest boy! I've read it several times. There's a brea[d]th, an ease in it which gives one a quite new view of John Galsworthy. The humanity of it is infinitely deeper than in the *Man of Property* or the C[ountry] H[ouse]. M[r] Stone is an amazing creation, a memorable figure—and the whole a great performance. The end seems

[1] Some went into *Old Calabria* (1915) and some into *Summer Islands* (1931).
[2] A ticket for the first London performance of *Strife*: a matinée at the Duke of York's Theatre on 9 March.
[3] The short fifth chapter of *A Personal Record*. [4] *Fraternity*, published 23 February.

to me *just right* factually, emotionally psychologically.[1] Just right. What sort of press—how much have they understood?[2] I feel dam' bad. No more. Our dear love.

<div align="center">Your[s] ever</div>

<div align="right">J. C.</div>

To Stephen Reynolds
Text MS Berg; Unpublished

<div align="right">Forehead Aldington
11 pm. 6th Mch '09</div>

Dear Man Stephen.

Just done a paper for the ER vth N^o and at once start abject apologies for not congratulating You before on promotion in the fleet.[3]

Also the 2^d letter including brazen-puff-sample to hand. The stories shall be read[4]—but dear I've been a month off my own tale and the wolves are howling all around the "Cottage in the Snow." So be patient with me for a few days. I must make a start before I look at anything.

Glad Bob better. Tell him so with a handshake from me. Your fishing letter was warm living suffering flesh stuff. The criticism of N[5] in the same by no means stupid. But why that stab. "Et tu Brute!"[6] Let me veil my face and fall with decency.

But all that's mere trifling. What is good is to hear that you are better in health and therefore looking up in spirit. Write! Write. Write. This is one time to haul on Your nets with all your might and make your way home (understand?—*home*!) on the *rising tide*.

Feel awfully tired and mentally snowed up, with cold sawdust in my head, poison in my entrails, a ton of lead on my heart.

Am impatient to see the mountain-top peep above the horizon of publicity.[7] M[ar]wood's been here talking nicely about you. So long. Our dear love.

<div align="center">Yours</div>

<div align="right">J. Conrad</div>

[1] Cf. Conrad's remarks on the ending in MS [2–3 September 1908].

[2] According to Galsworthy's notebook, the novel 'met with a curious reception, both highly appreciative or snubby, according to the temper of the journals reviewing' (Marrot, pp. 236–7).

[3] Becoming Bob Woolley's mate.

[4] On 30 March, Reynolds told Garnett: 'My short stories refuse absolutely to sell' (Wright, *Letters from Stephen Reynolds*, p. 120).

[5] *Nostromo?*

[6] According to some traditions, Julius Caesar believed Brutus to be his illegitimate son; Conrad saw himself as Reynolds's literary father.

[7] Reynolds's satire *The Holy Mountain* was to appear later in the year.

To J. B. Pinker
Text MS Berg; Unpublished

[Aldington]
Sunday evening [7 March 1909][1]

Dear Pinker.

My wife just tells me that I could not have sent you our new address. She also says she has spoken to me about it before. I don't remember. I haven't had my head off the paper for a moment since my table has been set up here in this new abode. I have the impression of writing you a line on the 14th, at the last moment just before leaving the old house. Perhaps the girl simply neglected to give it to the postman, the routine of the household being broken by that time.

Anyway my apologies. Here it is:

Forehead

Aldington

Kent

I left Someries feeling ill and with a swollen foot, in a motorcar belonging to a friend of Gibbon[2]—or else I could not have moved.

Please send me the rough type-copy which is with you yet corresponding to pp 763–791 of MS which of course you have also. I am not coming up for Jack's play having a beastly cold. I am not going to take chances. You will probably be there. It will be a friendly act on your part to drop me a postcard—just a word—how it went. Jack won't do it, I fear.

I will send you some copy in a day or two. The end *is* the devil. Jack knows something of it too. And by the by, he has got a book success—hasn't he? A real one?

We have been snowed up to the keyhole for 3 days.

Yours always

J. Conrad

[1] Received '3/09': snow blanketed Kent early in the month.
[2] By Jessie Conrad's account (*Joseph Conrad and His Circle*, p. 134): 'Joseph Conrad had been a little gouty, sufficiently so to make me grateful to a dear friend, Dr. Mackintosh, who came with Perceval Gibbon and his wife to fetch him to stay with them while I conducted the move.' Conrad insisted that the furniture be kept in place until the medical escort departed.

To Norman Douglas
Text MS Texas; Unpublished

Aldington
Kent.
8 Mch 1909

Dear Douglas
Voilà.
The school is indubitably enjoying an excellent reputation. I don't
know what you will think of the terms. Probably too high. On the other
hand I doubt whether you'll find anything much cheaper quickly—or at
all.
There is one suggestion that can be made. You could perhaps entrust
Bobby[1] to the Houses (Borys' schoolmaster). It is Luton its true but on
the other hand The Downs is a good healthy part; and the people are
really decent. At the same time they are not likely to *form* the boy too
much. Just a commonplace kindly couple. Some of the day boys are as
young as 6 1/2. The question is whether they would take a boarder so
young? I imagine it would be a matter of £60 or maybe less.
Anyway its a hint of something not brilliant it is true but needs must
when the devil drives. A pis-aller distinctly. I don't present it as
anything else.

Yours in haste
J. Conrad

PS If you decide to have a look at Seabrook[2] its understood you come
here for the night. N'est-ce pas?

To Ford Madox Ford
Text Violet Hunt's copy, Cornell; Unpublished

Aldington Forehead
Kent
9th March 1909

Dear Ford.
Thanks for your wire. Jessie is extremely sensible at you *never* (she
affirms) forgetting her in your communications.
I've a horrid cold. I suppose at this moment you are sitting looking at

[1] 'Robin' (Robert Sholto), Douglas's younger son, would be seven in July; his father
wanted to return to Italy.
[2] Seabrook Lodge, a nearby private school.

"Strife." M'wood imparted to me horrid news of "*The Vth Queen*".[1] He made me rather wretched but may be he exaggerated his account of utter disorganization of the production.

No good talking I suppose—but you are a prodigal of your toil and your talent. Yet one would like to see your largesse used respectfully. The world does not know the inner history of these things. That's the worst of it. And the ignorant judgement remains on record—*Vous le savez bien.*

Once more, merci.

Our dear love

Yours

J. C.

To H.-D. Davray
Text MS Texas; *L. fr.* 97

Aldington
Nr Hythe. Kent.
10 Mch 1909

Mon cher ami.

Nous etions fort peinés d'apprendre que Vous êtes souffrant. C'est un affreux hiver celui de l'an neuf. Nous avons tous soufferts* plus ou moins, excepté les enfants, heureusement.

Vous me donnez des bonnes nouvelles et je suis heureux d'apprendre que le Secret Agent supporte bien toutes ces lectures consécutives. C'est bien gentil à Vous d'avoir eu la pensée de me dira cela.

Je suis en train de finir mon roman dont les personnages sont Russes et la scène e[s]t a Genève.

C'est ecrit au point de vue Anglais bien entendu, mais avec sympathie, du moins je l'espère.

Nous voilà revenus a Kent de nouveau, non loin de Wells et Henry James.[2] C'est un tout petit cottage sans charme ni beauté—mais enfin.

Rappelez nous bien cordialement a Madame Davray. Nous esperons vous voir chez nous cette année. Songez-y.

A vous bien affectueusement

J. Conrad

[1] An inept dramatization, by another hand, of *The Fifth Queen Crowned*: see Mizener, p. 184.
[2] Wells lived ten and James fifteen miles away; the journey took 30 minutes by train for the former, 40 for the latter.

Translation

My dear friend,
 We were most distressed to learn that you are unwell. The winter of
'09 has been frightful. We have all suffered more or less except, luckily,
the children.
 You give me good news, and I am happy to learn that *The Secret Agent*
stands up well to consecutive readings. It is indeed kind of you to have
thought of telling me that.
 I am in the midst of finishing my novel; the characters are Russian,
and Geneva is the scene.
 It is written from the English point of view, of course, but with
sympathy; at least I hope so.
 We have returned to Kent again, not far from Wells and Henry
James. It is a little cottage without charm or beauty—but there it is.
 Remember us cordially to Mme Davray. We hope to see you at our
house this year. Think about it.

<div align="right">Very affectionately yours,

J. Conrad</div>

To J. B. Pinker
Text MS Berg; Unpublished

<div align="right">[Aldington]
Thursday. [11 or 18 March
1909][1]</div>

My dear Pinker.
 Don't send me the type of these pages till I ask for it; and this request
will apply to all the batches of *MS* which I am going to send you as fast
as I can get them ready for typing.
 Thanks for your letter and inquiries. Yes. I think I will like the place
well enough. At any rate one does not feel that it is unsuitable.
 I intend to bring my wife up to London on Monday to see *Strife*.[2] This
extravagance simply must be perpetrated. I can't shut myself off not
only from my friends but from their work as well.

[1] Received '3/09': between the postponed and the actual excursion to see Gals-
worthy's play.
[2] Letters to Ada Galsworthy and Dr Mackintosh show that the Conrads saw *Strife* on a
Wednesday – the 17th or, more probably, the 24th. Either they changed their plans
or the Conrads meant to stay in town.

I am fairly well—at any rate from the working point of view.

Yours always

J. Conrad

NB Just a mention: I wouldn't hawk too much the Remces in America. A time may come later.

To Stephen Reynolds
Text MS Berg; Unpublished

Aldington Forehead
Kent.
Friday. [12 or 19 March 1909?][1]

Dear Stephen.

I say emphatically Good boy!

Things don't go well with me. That's not to be expected. All the same I've read Your two short stories. Very good both. Very good indeed. But I am not going to think out a string of complimentary phrases for your benefit. You are a big person to understand what *very good* means.

Thanks for your letters. They are ever welcome—and your presence here would be still more so. But I myself can not write letters. I can't write anything. Moreover you don't like my handwriting. You've said so twice—which is definitive—and also dam' convenient for me. Take care of your liver, nerves and the rest of your machinery. I prophesy some noises (of falling brickbats and cheers) about the Holy Mountain and are* very impatient for the row to begin. There is but little I have to live for but I want that little quick.

Our love to you

Ever yours

J. Conrad.

[1] Before *The Holy Mountain* began in the April issue of the *Review*, which was published in late March. On the 6th Conrad promised to read some short stories.

To Norman Douglas

Text MS Texas; Unpublished

Aldington Kent.
Late on Sunday. [14 March
1909]¹

Tibi soli²

Dear Douglas.

We had a notion You might turn up today. Your letter arrived only by this mornings post. It's obvious that for purposes of extended publication the *E[nglish] R[eview]* is of no use. You must abandon the idea. But it is obvious too that there is an opening for some of you're* papers if they keep going. I would definitely object to the rape of the Syrens.³ Hueffer tells me that he *will* take your Tiberius article.⁴ But of course that is not official. When you hear stipulate your price. For the rest don't let them take hold of you too much. I hear something of H & M[arwood] helping you in the publication of the book. Remember that Lucas (Methuen's reader) has declared his readiness to recommend Your Vol to his house. The fact is that H. loves to manage people. No doubt he helps too but his assistance has an obverse side.

I wish you could run down here for the night. There are things it takes too long to write and which look too brutal in writing.

Main thing: terminate the book (under the new scheme) *make it ready*. for showing around.

Re school for Bobby.

Mͬ W. House and his spouse are quite decent undistinguished people. Address:—Sᵗ Gregory's School The Downs. Luton. It would be advisable to see personally in that direction if Seabrook is out of question and nothing else offers.

Say you are coming on my suggestion. Have a good look round. Discuss fully, every point.

And come here at any time or without warning.

Jess sends her affectionate regards.

Yours

J. Conrad.

¹ Between the letters of 8 and [19 March]. ² 'For thee alone'.
³ The essay published in the *English Review* as 'Sirens', later the first chapter of *Siren Land*.
⁴ A rewritten version of one of the *Three Monographs* (1906), it appeared in the August number as 'Tiberius'.

To Norman Douglas
Text MS Texas; J-A, 2, 90

[Aldington]
Friday. [19 March 1909][1]

My dear Douglas.

One has got to be careful what one says before you. But I haven't the heart to scold being really awfully pleased with your romantic gift of sauerkraut and Frankfort sausages. Ever so many thanks, but pray let me know whether the choucroûte is to be boiled and if so how, exactly, and for how long. Its so excellent per se that I would eat it as it is only I don't want (as a family man) to run any deadly risks.

The stupid Garrett woman disclosed the presence of your pipe only last night. Jessie is, this moment, making up the parcel and instructs me to say that if it had been left in our house you would not have waited so long for it. I should think not! It would have followed you by the very next post. The leaving behind of a pipe is not an incident to be treated lightly. There's unhappiness in it, and profanity, and a deep moral disturbance which no rightly-thinking person can contemplate with indifference. Now Jessie *is* a rightly-thinking person.

I close this hastily to go into the parcel.

Our affectionate regards

Yours

J. Conrad.

Let us know what's decided as to the little chap—and generally what's happening to you in every way. I hope you have not missed this as much as you would have done your pillow.

[1] Douglas scrawled '20' on the MS, giving the day but not the month of his reply. A stay at Mrs Garrett's cottage in Aldington before 20 February would have been too soon after the Conrads' arrival. Because Douglas was in Italy during their previous time in Aldington, Jean-Aubry's ascription to 1908 must be wrong. On [14 March] Conrad encouraged a visit; by the 19th, the fate of 'the little chap' was decided: a prep school in Yorkshire.

To John Edward Long
Text MS Yale; Unpublished

Aldington Forehead
Kent.
20 Mch 1909.

Dear Sir.[1]

I've been overtaken by influenza almost directly on arrival here, which made me unable to attend to anything. Now I find I cannot obtain the book which I wished to send you, the 2d Ed being for the present out of print.

Therefore I send you my copy of the American Ed of the *Secret Agent* begging your acceptance of it since you have been good enough to express a liking for my work.

With kind regards believe me

yours faithfully

J. Conrad.

To Ada Galsworthy
Text MS Forbes; Unpublished

Aldington Forehead
Kent.
Thursday [25? March 1909][2]

Dearest Ada

I write—as I generally do—in both our names to thank you for the two hours under your roof yesterday, two very delightful hours.

I was so excited in the theatre[3] (I don't exaggerate) that I could not speak to Jack—or rather could not *say* anything to him. It was after the first act when the powerful impression of the opening combined with the anticipation of what was to come positively oppressed me. I don't understand much of the theatre; my own imagination is so tyrannical that the stage can never attain for me to the necessary force of illusion. But surely there *is* greatness in that play! The felicity, the force and the tenderness of the imagination are combined together with—I fear not say*—inspired justness, expressing the right human feeling in this

1 Tentatively identified as the John Edward Long (1889–1940) who later became president of the Greater New York News Service.
2 The Conrads had seen *Strife* 'yesterday' – either the 17th or the 24th. The later date is more likely, given the tone and content of the next letter to John Galsworthy, 29 March, and the letter to Pinker [1? April].
3 After its brief but triumphant run at the Duke of York's, *Strife* had transferred to the Haymarket.

dramatic form. This deep humanity of the conception rises superior in its inherent nobility (for which I love the play beyond anything Jack has ever done) above all the miserable artifices of the actor's craft. But here I must stop. You don't want my views on acting in general and on Barkerism in particular.[1] They are (my views) not popular certainly and just as certainly of very little importance; for the importance of a view depends exactly on its popularity. But I am willing to admit the play was acted as well as it could be done. Yes they were all good—and no one too good. What one felt about them was that they were intensely loyal to the work fate had overwhelmed them with. And so far they shall be blessed. The classical simplicity of the theme, the heroic quality of the action emerged quand même.

———————

Could you my dear Ada give me the number of a man called Sydney Brooks in Addison Rd.[2] Jessie seems to think that you can. He waylaid me yesterday at your very gate and said mysterious things which have surprised me.

 Postman at door. Our dear love and great thanks

 Yours ever

 J Conrad.

To R. D. Mackintosh
Text MS Colgate; Unpublished

 [Aldington]
 Friday. [26? March 1909][3]

My dear D[r] Mackintosh.[4]

 Your good and so informing letter arrived yesterday and from that I date the beginning of the cure. The "admonition" reached me this morning and in time to begin the treatment after breakfast. It seems to me wonderful that I should be worth all this trouble and forethought on your part. I can only say that we are both deeply touched by the

[1] The playwright and director Harley Granville-Barker (1877–1946), who did so much to reform the British stage, favoured a subdued style of acting, alternately introspective and ironic – a far cry from the grand romantic tradition.
[2] He lived at number 80, contributed political articles to the *Fortnightly*, and worked with or for Harper & Brothers. For what he said, see the letter of [1? April].
[3] The day after the letter to Ada Galsworthy.
[4] Robert Dunbar Mackintosh (1865–1934) practised in Barnes, South West London. From 1909 to 1921, when they had a falling out, Conrad valued the company and the advice of this Scottish doctor, an amateur playwright and inventor described by his great-niece as 'an unpractical enthusiast and dreamer' (Jellard, p. 95).

earnestness of your friendly initiative in coming to the rescue of a discouraged man. And the fact is that he is so no longer.

No gout in the joints is felt at present. But day before yesterday we went to Galsworthy's play. In the theatre I felt that peculiar nervousness I know so well—a sort of shock and gasp it is—and by the time we got home my back was full of "small-shot" feeling and now eczema has broken out from neck to tail—but not so very severe as I have it known* to be. Spirits: tolerably good. Work: 8 pages this morning. Confidence: unlimited. In these conditions the treatment begins!

And now for the sight of the good physician. As a motorist you have the map of the fair County of Kent. From London to Ashford all is plain sailing. At about 3–4 miles beyond Ashford on the high road to Folkestone you will come to four cross roads. Take the turn to the right indicated by the sign *To Smeeth Station*. From that point I send you the detail of the road (*not* to scale) down to our very door. This about 3 to 3 1/2 miles.

And now for a fine Sunday! Come early to lunch in our cage where alas we could not find you a perch for the night. But if you don't mind sleeping in another cottage (across the road) you shall be made tolerably comfortable in the camping out style. Our own Salvator too,[1] of course. Don't let—as far as you can oppose—that raiding Yankee McClure waste his brain and nervous force too much. S is too good for such barren fooling. *Much* too good.[2]

I have been thinking daily of the new metal[3] and wishing it all possible success. But I don't know exactly what *has* been done. I've only heard of a contract for rollers. Is that so? Wife's kindest regards and thanks.

<div align="center">Yours gratefully</div>

<div align="right">J. Conrad.</div>

[1] A nickname for their mutual friend, the writer Perceval Gibbon. Gibbon dedicated *Salvator*, a novel published in 1908, to Ford Madox Ford.

[2] Between May 1909 and April 1910, *McClure's Magazine*, whose editor was Willa Cather, published three stories and two articles by Gibbon. Eventually McClure hired him as a chief staff writer.

[3] A new alloy? The reference to 'rollers' suggests a hardened steel used in making metal strip. Mackintosh had an interest in a foundry – and Conrad was an engineer manqué.

To John Galsworthy
Text MS Forbes; J-A, 2, 96

[Aldington]
29 Mch 1909.

Dearest Jack.

What comes out uppermost is the intellectual honesty of your play. That quality nay—that great and rare virtue shines tenfold when set out in the artistic simplicity of your method. There is none of that subtleness akin to decay in your conception of human problems. We have there human beings in their littleness and their heroism presented to us in a work of art with no didactic purpose but with a moral intention.

Probably You care but little for this fruit of my meditations; but I have been trying to understand, to penetrate the secret of the play's power and guage* the depth of its appeal. For this calm work of sifting the effects I had to descend to the underside of my direct feelings which, You do not doubt, were deeply engaged. I have tasted in that theatre moments of profound, unquestionable satisfaction. To get at its sources I had so to speak to part from your personality which holds so much of my life-stock of affection. I think I succeeded in getting sufficiently far away only of course to come back to it with the conviction that you are a good servant to the state.

If your personality is to loom large in the mental and emotional history of your time—as I believe it must—the notion of a play dealing with the dramatically intimate side of the country's domestic political life suggests itself to complete a trilogy of which the first two expressions are *The Silver Box* and *Strife*. Thus the three great divisions of the social aspect of our days would be indicated.[1] That party-parliamentarism contains in its qualities and imperfections a drama of conscience capable of being expressed by poignant and interesting action, I have no doubt. The intellectual honesty the great and simple method are yours. Then why not try? To strike a blow at the tragi-comic charlatanism inherent in the conduct of human affairs is a task worthy of your gift. I hope you don't think I am meddling. I am not accustomed to keep anything back from you.

Ever Yours

J Conrad.

[1] By adding parliament to industry and law as the third troubled institution: *Strife* anatomizes a strike, and *The Silver Box* asserts that justice favours the wealthy. *Justice*, Galsworthy's next completed play, is about the penal system, but *The Patrician*, his next novel, concerns political ambition.

PS Our love to you both. Jessie after coming a bit to herself, thinks that
the tea at Mrs Roberts' cottage is too lavish for the situation. The supply
of milk she says would be the first to go. There should have been a *milk
tin* to scrape hard with a spoon. She knows what she's talking about.[1]
But don't think the woman's soul is lost in trifles. She got hold of
everything and responded to everything almost too much.

To Norman Douglas
Text MS Texas; Unpublished

Aldington
29 Mch 1909

My dear Douglas
 Your letter came by this evening's post and I have written and sent off
instanter a note to Lucas saying that you were now in England with a
finished book on the Sorrento peninsula—the Syren-Land and that you
wanted to call on him in acknowledgement of the interest he took in your
MS. I stated also that you wished to offer your MS of the book to
Methuen. Just that and no more—so that if he wants to talk to you about
it he has an opening. Finally I've given him your address. I hurried on
because with Easter approaching the Lucas'es* may go out of town any
day almost to a little place they have near Edenbridge.
 My heartiest congratulations on the happy end of your first long
work. May luck attend it. Jessie joins me in these sentiments. We are
glad to hear the boy is located satisfactorily. The final arrang' with *ER* is
all right.
 When are you coming down here. No ceremony pray. We ought to
have a talk directly You have seen Lucas or should he put you off till
after Easter then before as soon as ever you feel you like to come to us.
Our affectionate regard[s].
 Yours
 J Conrad.

[1] Having grown up in a struggling family, she would understand the plight of Annie
Roberts, the sick and impoverished wife of the strike-leader in Galsworthy's play.

To E. V. Lucas
Text MS Wellington; Knowles

Aldington Forehead
N^r Hythe. Kent.
29 March 1909

My dear Lucas.

I am addressing you again on the subject of my friend Norman Douglas whose work you may remember you've judged favourably.

His book on the Sorrento Peninsula under the title *Syren-Land* is now ready. He is in London with it; and he wishes to call on you in acknowledgement of the kind interest you took in placing his work.

He is an interesting personality to know with wide experience and culture. I encouraged him to write—as I told you before—when we got acquainted in Capri. I would take it as a personal kindness if you would drop him a note telling him at what hour and day he may call on you. His intention is to offer his MS to M^r Methuen. It is jolly good—a distinguished and interesting piece of work.

We are established here—back in Kent as you see. Someries was too big a house. Now we have part of a cottage, near the church at the very foot of the hill. If ever You come that way try to remember the above details.

Things are very soso with us but the children are well.

In haste yours very cordially
J Conrad.

Douglas address is 9. Coptic Street. WC

To J. B. Pinker
Text MS Berg; Unpublished

Aldington
N^r Hythe. Kent.
Thursday. [1? April 1909][1]

Dear Pinker

I've been to see Strife on the day I told you.[2] It is first rate anyway and no end of things can be said of it.

[1] Received '4/09': a Thursday before 15 April and probably soon after the visit to London.
[2] Actually on a Wednesday rather than a Monday: evidently Conrad was steering clear of Pinker's office.

I see by the press cuttings which now and then turn up from the States that there is a reprint—quite lately—of *Nostromo*.[1]

As I stood at Galsworthy's gate paying the cab (my wife had gone in) S. Brooks rushed across the road and engaged me in conversation. He wanted my address—as if to visit me—and made some remark on the desire of Harpers to publish my work.[2] I reflected upon it all and a day or two ago I wrote from here a letter stating that I was not aware of my relations with H & Brothers being in the least interrupted except in so far that *The Point of Honour* was published by McClure. And then I added that I would personally be very glad if *H* proposed to consider the serial and book rights of the novel I was finishing now. That is all I said.

My play of To Morrow is in rehearsal at the Theatre for Arts in Paris.[3] I hear the cast is very hopeful. I let the translator have my share of the rights as in any case it was a trifle. The advantage of a little publicity will come in well just now as Davray advises me that the *Secret Agent* is translated and to be offered to the *Temps*. first. d'Humières writes to say that the *Nigger* is being considered by the *Revue de Paris* with a fair chance of being accepted, as serial for end of this year.

I tell you these things without attaching undue importance to what may come of them. Kindest regards

Yours ever

J Conrad.

Here's one of the cuttings—that's the sort of thing.

To Norman Douglas

Text MS Colgate; Unpublished

[Aldington]
6 Ap. 1909

Dear Douglas

What do you say to coming over here and staying with us for a few days after you return from Yorkshire? There is the room at Garretts freshly papered—ready.

You may write a little. We will talk a little. B will walk with you if You care for his company or leave you alone if you prefer it.[4] The weather seems settled fine.

[1] Of the original Harper & Brothers edition.
[2] See also the letter of [6 January 1910].
[3] Translated by P.-H. Raymond-Duval, it opened on 14 April.
[4] Borys was coming home for the Easter holidays.

Jessie was going to write herself but was too late for post today and now I've sent her to bed. She [sends] her most friendly regards.

Yours ever

J Conrad

To R. D. Mackintosh
Text MS Colgate; *Listy* 288; Original unpublished

Aldington. Nr Hythe
Kent
Easter Sunday. [11 April] 1909

Dear Dr Mackintosh.

Ease for the suffering mankind follows in your footsteps or to be modern rolls after your car. The greatest success attended the application of the lotion through last night (at frequent intervals). To-day I am just aware I have a skin—and no more. The dread is removed from my mind; I had a real refreshing sleep in the afternoon, and I am writing this at the usual hour of torment—10 pm—in greater bodily comfort than I have known for the last 20 days.

My wife has just left the room recommending me earnestly not to fail to express to you her gratitude.

We are looking forward with great delight to seeing you next Sunday with our Salvator and dear Mrs Gibbon—or I should say we have been looking thus forward till about six pm today. At that hour Hueffer turned up in a car just for a moment and told us confusedly of a new arrangement by which you are to come on Saturday to stay the night at Hueffer's cottage and dine with us at six (why at six I don't know) if it is not *inconvenient* to us. The word *inconvenient* in connection with a visit from you *does not exist for us*. Of that you may be certain as long as there is a roof over our heads to receive you under "and a piece of bread to put before you with a pinch of salt"—as the Ukrainian peasant woman at whose breast I have been suckled would have expressed it. But in the course of that interview Ford uttered an unlucky phrase which left me no option but to say that till I heard from you I could take no account of what he had told me. I won't enlarge on cause and effect just now but on the first fitting occasion I will explain fully to you; meantime I beg you not to put an unfavourable interpretation on this perfectly open confidence; and to believe that as far as You are concerned any day, any hour in which you come to see us will ever be considered fortunate. But I had really to make a stand against that mania for managing the

universe, worse even in form than in substance. I think that when You know everything You will approve me. My attitude is perfectly consistent with a firm friendship now of so many years' standing. Please then drop me a few words. Our love to the Gibbons big and little. With grateful regards from my wife I am dear Mackintosh, let me say, affectionately

<div style="text-align:center">Yours</div>

<div style="text-align:right">J. Conrad.</div>

To Stephen Reynolds
Text MS Berg; Unpublished

<div style="text-align:right">[Aldington]
14 Ap 09
Midnight</div>

Dear Reynolds

Thanks for your good letters. I am glad to hear of you as if you were my son or younger brother. But as to writing myself c'est un[e] autre affaire. I am hard at it now but—but never never can I get on fast enough. I am pen and ink ridden. Its a nightmare.

I suppose there is no chance of seeing you here moderately soon. Apart from the sentimental satisfaction there are things (good many of them) that are easier talked over than written about. So I will only tell you that the 1st inst of the novel[1] is brilliantly effective.

As to the proper booming of this that and the other book—the wisdom of the serpent is a good thing in its way but at your tender age the innocence of the dove is more becoming.[2] *NB* That's a joke.

Generally I am pleased at the tone of your last letter. You seem to derive healthy enjoyment from the small and the great things of existence—the astonishment of "frights" and the hommages of Sydney* Lee.[3] That's how it should be. You have made a first rate start but don't be astonished (like a naïve "fright") should some of the angels turn into devils by and bye and try to gore you. Keep yourself to yourself; be careful what you say to people you are not sure of—I mean in the most innocent matters.

But away with the wisdom-cap. Go on and prosper. We are all

[1] *The Holy Mountain.*

[2] 'Behold, I send you forth as sheep in the midst of wolves: be ye therefore wise as serpents, and harmless as doves' (Matthew 10.16).

[3] Editor-in-chief of the *Dictionary of National Biography*, royal biographer, and author of many Shakespearean studies (1859–1926).

talking and thinking of you frequently, including just now the *two* boys.
A friendly hail to Bob.

<div align="center">Yours ever</div>

<div align="right">J. Conrad.</div>

To J. B. Pinker
Text MS Berg; Unpublished

<div align="right">Aldington.</div>

<div align="right">Hythe Kent.</div>

<div align="right">15 Ap. 1909</div>

Dear Pinker.

After some reflexion[1] I think I'll see Col Harvey when he comes over
here[2] which I suppose will be soon.

I've been accustomed to have my books waited for—beginning with
Henley who took the Nigger on the view of the first 4 chap. My books
deserve it—and the change of attitude which I seem to feel in the air is
not pleasant to me. However they will have their day.

I think I will talk to him of my Remces (so called) of which you don't
seem to think much. Nevertheless they will be a quite unique thing in
their way and as they can be taken up at any time, I think there's no
harm in sounding him. What I want You to tell me is your opinion of
Harpers' standing—of their stability too. One hears all sorts of rumours
which may be mere bosh. I've been receiving a good many letters from
US of late. Huneker sent me his book only the other day.[3] If Harper (or
Harvey) were to turn out unsatisfactory I could get in touch with other
people I think. Of course I would make no move without consulting you.

I am undergoing a systematic treatment by a doctor who has
volunteered for the task and has been already twice down* in his car to
have a look at me. Even that imbecile Dutchman, what's his name,
could not find an interested motive there.[4] It was time that something
were done gout affecting my head too frequently of late. The improved
health would mean easier, quicker work—and that's all I care for, for
neither of pain nor death I am afraid.[5] We shall see—but I know you

[1] 'Changed from 'reflection'.
[2] George Brinton McClellan Harvey (1864–1928), president of Harper & Brothers;
his colonelcy was bestowed by the Governor of New Jersey.
[3] See the next letter.
[4] *The Healers* (1906), by Maarten Maartens (Jozua Marius Willem van der Poorten
Schwartz), is a fictional anatomy of medicine.
[5] Possibly an echo of the patriotic students in Mickiewicz's *Dziady* (*Forefathers' Eve*),
Part III.

will like to hear that so far the thing promises well. I abhorr* quackery, but when a man of scientific attainments assures me that there are 9 chances in ten of getting rid of that horrible clog on my faculties or on my free exercise of them I am anxious enough to let him prove his assertion—and feel cheered up too as to the mere prospect.

<div style="text-align: center;">Yours ever</div>

<div style="text-align: right;">J Conrad.</div>

To J. G. Huneker

Text MS Dartmouth; Schwab

<div style="text-align: right;">Aldington</div>

<div style="text-align: right;">N^r Hythe. Kent.</div>

<div style="text-align: right;">16 Ap. 1909</div>

My dear Sir[1]

I am extremely gratified by the arrival of your book of Supermen.[2] I will not conceal from you that I take it in the sense most flattering to myself. After this confession You can not doubt the sincerity of my gratitude.

I am not spoiled by too much recognition of this (or any other) sort. But, apart from that, your pages can give nothing but pleasure to a man who loves *la littérature critique* (not literary criticism). According to my habit when a fascinating book comes in my way (a sort of angel's visit) I've read it at once, wilfully and of malice prepense neglecting my daily task to entertain the rare visitor.

I am not given to analyse my pleasures. You must take my delight for granted—and what's more delightful than to find one's own half-formed thoughts expressed with force, conviction and charm in an unexpected and authoritative book coming to one from over the seas? The warmth of feeling underlying the impartiality of your judgement wins the sympathy of a humble craftsman who certainly had never lacked piety towards the illustrious dead.

[1] James Gibbons Huneker (1857–1921) wrote fiction and what he called 'impressionist' criticism of literature, art, and music, chiefly modern. He knew France and French literature, admired Polish culture, and had been a friend of Stephen Crane in New York. Huneker refused the credit for 'discovering' Conrad in the United States (Schwab, p. 223) but wrote often and enthusiastically about him.

[2] In sending Conrad *Egoists: A Book of Supermen* (New York: Scribner's, 1909), Huneker ranked him with the writers he discussed, among them Ibsen, Nietzsche, Stendhal, Flaubert, Baudelaire, France, Huysmans, and Barrès. Neither in his political nor in his literary opinions was Huneker an egalitarian.

I too began my communion with Flaubert by Salammbo.[1] I might have seen him—but in 1879 I was somewhere at sea, *au diable bouilli*— Kerguelen Land[2], I think, or thereabouts. It was another life which I remember with misty tenderness, as a transmigrated soul might be supposed by a miracle, to remember its previous envelope.

This is but a short word of thanks for a lasting acquisition; yet the same kindness which prompted your action will enable you to extend Your indulgence to a very impotent letter-writer. Besides, just now, a sort of horror of pen and ink, a mistrust of the written phrase sits on me like a cold nightmare. It's a passing phase but it doesn't make life easier while it last[s].

And on this confidence I end with a cordial handshake and renewed thanks.

<div style="text-align:right">

Believe me gratefully yours

J. Conrad

</div>

To Edward Garnett
Text MS Indiana; G. 230

<div style="text-align:right">

Aldington

Hythe Kent

17 April 1909

</div>

Dearest Edward

Thanks for the play[3] which reached me today and, as you may imagine, was read at once.

It is magnificently suggestive—to begin with—in a general way; in its psychology, I mean. Though I detest the stage I have a theatrical imagination—that's why perhaps I detest the stage—that is the actors who mostly poor souls, have no imagination. And my theatrical imagination has been profoundly satisfied by the certainty of the effects—all the effects—of the atmosphere and of the passions; that sort of contentement* the middle plays of Ibsen[4] give one. Never a moment

[1] Huneker calls *Salammbô* 'an opera in words' (p. 120); for its presence in Conrad's work, see the letter to d'Humières, 23 December.

[2] In 1879, outward bound for Sydney in the *Duke of Sutherland* and 'diabolically tossed about' in the roaring forties, Conrad could have sailed near Kerguelen Island (49° S, 68° E), known to the whalers who had recently abandoned it as Desolation. Flaubert died in 1880, the year after Huneker believed he had glimpsed him in Paris.

[3] *The Feud*, derived from the Icelandic sagas.

[4] Such as *The Pillars of the Community* (1877), *A Doll's House* (1879), and *Ghosts* (1881)? Some earlier plays, including *The Vikings at Helgeland* (1858), had dramatized the Norse past.

of doubt in acting the thing to oneself as the eye follows the lines—a great testimony to the poetical truth and force of the work.

At the end one wishes there were more of it. This my dear Edward I mean as criticism; but you will remember that this criticism may proceed from some defect of my theatrical imagination; which I *know* I have, without being certain of its soundness or of its completeness, however. It is as if the subject had been treated too summarily. A sort of artistic uneasiness remains, very faint indeed and yet too persistent (I've been living exclusively with the play for the last 8 hours) not to be mentioned from me to you. I have been asking myself: What is it? One seems to feel that you held your hand—yet on re-reading that impression vanishes. There is an exactness, a clearness which leave nothing to lay hold of. No! decidedly the defect is in me. The more one examines the mechanism and the expression the more the conviction grows upon one that a family drama of the "gentry" in 13th Century Iceland could not have been rendered with more precision or sentiment and truthfulness of detail.

I congratulate you upon your luck in the matter of your interpreters. Did you "produce" yourself?[1] I'll try to drop in at the Mont Blanc on some not too distant Tuesday[2] for a real talk with you. Meantime don't think me an insensible fool, an irresponsive ass. I have responded indeed and feel very happy in the play—but every one has a devil in him, you know. Mine makes me so ambitious for those who have any affection that in the end my affection won't be worth having. But enough of that. It was very dear and charitable of you to think of sending me a copy. Our best love to you all. Jessie begs to be specially remembered to your wife for whom you know she always had an instinctive admiration.

<div style="text-align:center">Ever yours</div>

<div style="text-align:right">J. Conrad.</div>

[1] The play had just been staged by Annie Horniman and Iden Payne at the Gaiety Theatre, Manchester, an important venue for enterprising new plays.
[2] For one of the literary lunches held every week at the restaurant in Gerrard Street.

To Ford Madox Ford

Text MS Berg; Najder (1970)

[Aldington]
Wednesday evening. [28 April or
5 May 1909][1]

My dear Ford.

The number of the ER received today strikes so far the highest note both as to *Letters* and *Ideas*. The paragraphs of Critical Attitude dealing with the general political situation surpass my expectations and that apart from the fact that I was really on the look-out for something quite different.[2] I congratulate you with very great delight in being able to do so. Now I hope that with the appearance of this tip-top number the phase of coalescing with McC[lure] and the phase of making the *Spectator* crawl[3] which were indeed mere talk but talk which upset and discouraged me utterly are over. Why I should have been treated to it while still sore as sore can be from the unsuccessful issue of your play[4] (not as a theatrical coup manqué—that's nothing—but from the reckless wasting of Your substance) devil only knows. It added immensely to the soreness the more so that (I own it now) full of unhappy forebodings as to the result, I did hold my tongue. I was afraid of being waved away from some superior attitude and indeed it would have hurt me too much to turn out right in the end. Any coalition with McC apart from an occasional buying of some Taft article—and by the by in that transaction the good man with characteristic levity nearly left you in a hole[5]—could

1 By themselves, the comments on the latest *Review* are not specific enough to identify it as the April issue, received in late March, or the May issue, received in late April. External evidence, however, suggests the later date: i) the account of what Conrad termed on 30 April 'the execution of Marwood'; ii) Ford's letter to Elsie of 8 May: 'I have had a long letter from Conrad pointing out the evil of my ways' (Mizener, p. 184); iii) an allusion in the letter of [4 August] to a half-crazed letter of apology from Ford 'about beginning of May'.

2 The May issue includes poems by T. Sturge Moore, Dollie Radford, and Verhaeren, essays by Douglas, Hudson, Percy Wyndham Lewis, and Perceval Gibbon, short stories by Gertrude Bone and Dostoevsky, several political articles, an instalment of Reynolds's *The Holy Mountain*, the sixth instalment of Conrad's reminiscences, and (ironically in the light of this letter) the second half of 'The Nature of a Crime', the final collaboration, uneven in every sense, between Conrad and Ford. The 'Critical Attitude' section, pp. 355–64, a regular feature, offers Ford's views on the fate of small nations (Poland not least among them), the British obsession with national degeneracy, and the state of agriculture.

3 By threatening a libel suit: *Spectator*, 102, pp. 451–2, 495, 537.

4 The stage version of *The Fifth Queen Crowned*.

5 In the April number, the *Review* carried an apology for not printing an article on his election by President Taft; instead, this article was promised for June and his article on the Panama Canal in May. Only the Canal article appeared.

only mean the debasing of those ideals which, on your own declaration, were to guide your editorship of the Review. Even the rumour of such a thing, in London, would be like a hint of failure. The ER. may have to stop but it mustn't fail. Moreover between you and me I know and *you* know that McC. is nothing but a sort of *farceur* and a *faiseur*[1] as well, and that no human being worthy of the name has been the better morally or even materially for any connection with him. Did he perchance offer you to buy up the ER including the Editor, lock stock and barrel including the shop downstairs and the tube station, transplant the whole show to the US, whip creation, break things etc etc *pantoufle?*[2] I shouldn't wonder and I hope that all he got from you was a soothing smile. It is inconceivable to me that you should take such a prestigious person seriously. Then why give me this stuff which makes me furious and unhappy, simply because it is not worthy of you. And then that vapouring about making the *Spectator* crawl. Why? Wherefore? There's not a shadow of an attack upon the *ER*. If Robert[3] backs you up in that notion then he isn't the man I take him for. Success itself considering what the ER is supposed to stand for would be discreditable under the circumstances. It seems to me dear Ford that you have round you people who care not for telling you the truth in the dislike of a probable rebuff. But I am under too many obligations to you to shrink before that small danger. The press has received you decently. That's the truth. More decently than I expected. If you start out crushing people you will discover that they don't "crush" so easily as all that. Take my word for it that the *Spec* won't crawl. And talk of that sort when it gets about will raise a crop of animosities, a very fine crop. And all for what? For nothing at all. Nothing! Less than nothing. Whereas if you detach your mind from these fanciful undertakings the fair fame of an honourable attempt—at least—lies open to you, if not of an honourable and dignified success.

This is not all. Last Monday on her way from the station your wife called here. She informed me that all your differences were happily settled and warned me against the plots and intrigues (vulgo lies) of

1 'A ... humbug and a charlatan'. Willa Cather said of McClure: 'He's lost more money on Joseph Conrad than any editor alive!' Elizabeth Sergeant, *Willa Cather: A Memoir* (Lincoln: University of Nebraska Press, 1963), p. 40.
2 Either 'like a jackass' or 'in an appallingly casual manner'; while the offer to 'whip creation' would fit British (or Polish) expectations of Yankee bravado, McClure came from the North of Ireland.
3 Robert Garnett, Edward's brother, had the challenging task of directing Ford's legal and financial affairs.

certain people. I confess I was literally shocked by the nature of her communication the more so that she implied that those dark untruths had, in your opinion, already affe[c]ted my attitude towards you. Against that I oppose an unqualified denial; and as this denial expresses the exact truth I warn you that I demand to be believed without any reservations or doubts whatever. I had heard nothing about you or Elsie except what passes current in ordinary conversation.[1] We, that is Jessie and I had been aware for a week or so that there was some tension the nature of which of course was not our affair and was barely a subject of one or two remarks between us. For the rest I told Elsie with every consideration which is due to her in my house that I could not believe these people[2] were as black as they appeared to her. She seemed to take but little heed of my protest. Later on she proposed that you should come down and stay *with us* for a week. You know that no one is made more welcome under our roof. Let ten years of perfect confidence and intimacy be witnesses to it. But I said at once: no. That can not be. If you are reconciled so completely Ford's place when he is in Aldington is in the cottage.

What is the end of such a proposal, what object, what purpose can be served by re-creating an equivocal situation? By such juggling with the realities of life an atmosphere of plots and accusations and suspicions is created.[3] I can't breathe in situations that are not clear. I abhor them. They are neither in my nature nor in my tradition, nor in my experience. I am not fine enough for them. We are a pair of silly innocents.

I need not tell you that we parted with Elsie on perfectly friendly terms and there is no earthly reason why they should not continue. That I am upset is beside the mark. I havent eaten or slept properly nor yet written a line ever since. This evening the people in question have called. The man when we were alone said he felt bound to inform me that he had just dispatched a letter to you breaking-off your intimate relations. He told me he was very unhappy and in truth he looked ill. As he is of good birth and upbringing and has always seemed to me a gallant-homme I can't give him up for a ruffian as long as he remains in this neighbourhood which I imagine won't be for long. He was your friend not mine and I have never sought his acquaintance. His devotion

[1] Although his chronology is problematic, Mizener (pp. 180–4) gives an extensive account of the charges of literary, financial, and sexual mismanagement involving various combinations of Hueffers and Marwoods. The most alarming charge was Elsie Hueffer's – that on several occasions Marwood had propositioned her.
[2] The Marwoods, who were living nearby.
[3] Ford had thus brought to Aldington a whiff of 'Razumov' (Carabine and Higdon, *UWE*).

to you was notorious—a matter of public knowledge. What advantage
he sought, what ends he had in view when he trotted about after you
like a faithful dog, God only knows. You too perhaps. In this case if it is
any satisfaction to you you have done some crushing. I won't believe
it's altogether without cause but it strikes me my dear Ford that of late
you have been visiting what might have been faults of tact, or even
grave failures of discretion in men who *were* your *admiring* friends with
an Olympian severity. A man who not often takes* liberties ventures to
ask you now whether it is worth while. Unless words are wind, facts are
mist, the confidence you've given me a mere caprice of fancy, and
unless an absolute loyalty of thought and act on my part contra
mundum gives no privelege* I have the right to warn you that you will
find yourself at forty[1] with only the wrecks of friendships at your feet.
You have always sought to do good to people—that I believe—but
don't fail in the other kind of generosity. I've had four most unhappy
days but I am afraid you will dismiss it all with a wave of the hand.
And indeed I don't know why I should be wretched except from sheer
affection.

<div style="text-align: center">Yours always,</div>

<div style="text-align: right">J Conrad.</div>

To John Galsworthy
Text MS Forbes; J-A, 2, 96[2]

<div style="text-align: right">Aldington, N^r Hythe
Kent.
30 Ap. 1909</div>

Dear Jack.

We feared you would be rushed towards the last.[3] Our disappoint-
ment of course was great but your loss is small. I have been beastly
seedy—in fact quite ill—as ill as a man out of bed and knocking about
aimlessly can be. It's awful—awful. Good D^r Mackintosh was twice
down here—watching his case. It may be I am feeling the spring winds
only. But if the spring winds are to affect me in that way then I had
better resign from all my dignities and offices[4] and get myself buried
without pomp and pageant of any kind.

Its a fact I was too nerveless to answer your good letter at once. You

[1] In four years' time. [2] Omitting the paragraphs about Marwood.
[3] Revising *The Eldest Son* and therefore unable to come down to Kent?
[4] Like King Lear?

may guess from that how the work progresses. There is really no day without a page[1]—but what is that! A drop in the ocean.

We have fallen here into a most abominable upset the execution of Marwood by Ford and Elsie.[2] I have seen a man guillotined* 30 years ago[3] but it hasn't made me feel half as sick as the present operation. For weeks poor Marwood looked as if after a severe illness. My view of *M* is that he is a gallant-homme in the fullest sense—absolutely incapable of any black treachery. We couldn't keep the horrid affair off us anyhow—what with E coming with horrible details and revelations (I told her plainly I could not believe what she said—and she only smiled) which it was impossible to silence and the poor *M's* whom one *had* to listen to out of common humanity. A beastly affair to be mixed up with even in the role of mere spectators-auditors.

I have been and am still thoroughly upset.

Thanks my dear Jack for your efforts on my behalf.[4] I really feel as if I were cumbering the earth with my existence doing no good to any one, exhausting the patience of Gods and men—and a sort of intolerable scandal to myself.

Yes. I saw the Frohman declaration and was greatly edified thereby.[5] I haven't heard anything from France as to *Tomorrow*[6] and, truth to say, I had forgotten all about it I shall go on with Chance directly this novel is done and at the same time shall write enough to complete a vol: of Reminiscences. Pink. can't do anything with them in the States and gave me to understand that he does not think much of them. I have lived long enough to hear that. However I differ from him on that matter. Anyhow they permitted me to pay B's schooling and some other things. But I don't know whether any more instalments will be needed for the *ER*.

[1] Just as Apelles, the painter, let no day pass without a line: Pliny, *Natural History*, II, xxxv.36.

[2] Conrad apparently thought that the Hueffers fabricated the allegations against Marwood in order to oust him from the *English Review*. Although Ford was in the process of squeezing Marwood out, the charges of sexual misconduct, justified or not, were caused more by the tension between the Hueffers than by collusion and were connected to Ford's growing involvement with Violet Hunt.

[3] In Marseilles or the French Antilles, between 1874 and 1878.

[4] In the quest for a Civil List pension.

[5] Charles Frohman, the Anglo-American impresario, had announced his intention of turning the Duke of York's Theatre into a repertory house for new plays. His principal dramatists were to be Granville-Barker, Barrie, Shaw, and Galsworthy (*The Times*, 22 April, p. 10).

[6] As to the run of the French dramatisation.

Yes. I do believe that in the end out of these Rem: a not altogether contemptible personality will emerge.

I am glad to hear of the comi-tragic play. A jolly good title.[1]

Our dear love to you both

Ever yours

J. Conrad

Do remember us warmly to Mrs Sauter if she is still with you and give my best wishes to the boy for his school "Career". You know we saw Mrs Sauter and Rud° just for a minute in the vestibule of the Theatre.[2] He struck me as very big and nice with a most sympathetic glance of any boy I ever knew.

To Stephen Reynolds

Text MS Berg; Unpublished

·, [Aldington]
Monday. [Spring 1909?][3]

My dear R.

Yours just received. I've heard nothing except, some time ago, some expression of real good will towards you from Marwood.[4]

There's nothing more common in life than misunderstandings in the plainest matters.—And since you've mentionned* the man's name I'll confess to you that your contemptuous manner towards M'ood has shocked both Jessie and myself. For we two being plain people could not see any reason for it. And even Douglas expressed some surprise at it.

On the action you say You've taken I express of course no opinion. But I cannot help fearing that it will fail in its main object. I believe there is still a chance of a sale but I imagine that any sort of complication would be fatal to it. It seems to me that a little more patience on your part would have served Your turn better. But it's the *merest impression* as I really *have no idea* of what is going on. I have no communi-

[1] Jean-Aubry suggests *The Pigeon*, but Galsworthy began that piece in February 1911 (Marrot, p. 310); among Galsworthy's plays-in-progress were the comic *The Winter Garden* and the allegorical *The Little Dream* (Dupré, p. 168).

[2] Galsworthy's sister Blanche Lilian Sauter and her son Rudolf, who was almost fourteen, at a performance of *Strife*.

[3] A very tentative placing: this may be the letter initiating a break with Reynolds that lasted until the overture of 31 July.

[4] Earlier in the year, Reynolds had worked briefly for the *English Review*.

cation with the quarter in question[1] and I am rather anxious to keep out
of it as much as possible.

<div align="center">

Yours ever

J Conrad.

</div>

To Chalmers Roberts

Text TS Berg[2]; Unpublished

<div align="right">

[Aldington]
May 1st. 1909

</div>

H. C. Roberts Esq.
Editor of "The World's Work".
c/o W. Heineman[n] Esq.

Dear Mr. Roberts,[3]

I received your second letter just as I was leaving for home. In the first
place, please accept my apologies if I was in any way hasty during our
short discussion at the Savoy yesterday morning. I feel very much
aggrieved in this matter, but I do not in any way associate you with my
wrongs, as I recognise, of course, that you are not an independent agent.

I have read your letters, which summarize what you said to me
yesterday, but the whole matter is, after all, very simple. Your people
have held over for more than a month the conclusion of the agreement
with Little Brown and Company, under the pretext that I owed them
money.[4] From the very first, Mr. Pinker's books were open to their
inspection. From the very first, here I was within a hundred yards of
your office, even when Mr. Everett[5] was with you, ready to answer any
questions, ready to show my own ledger and tell you, on my word of
honour, or on the strength of my bank-book, exactly what money I have

[1] Ford? [2] A carbon-copy.
[3] Henry Chalmers Roberts (1870–1940), a Texan, had been a junior diplomat and a
war-correspondent for the *Daily News*, *Daily Mail*, and *Brooklyn Eagle* before he came
to London in 1906; from then until 1932 he edited the English edition of the
magazine known variously as *World's Work* and *World Today*. He became a director at
Heinemann, the magazine's British publisher.
[4] The nature of the frustrated agreement with the Boston house of Little, Brown is not
known: one possibility would be an attempted reprint of 'London River', originally
published in the December 1904 issue of *World Today*. The reason for the frustration
can nevertheless be inferred. The American publisher of *World's Work* was Frank N.
Doubleday; one of the authors he acquired when he took over McClure, Phillips was
Conrad, who still had not delivered *The Rescue*, eleven years after receiving an
advance.
[5] Samuel A. Everitt, a recent Yale graduate who worked for Doubleday.

received from McClure's. Mr. Pinker *did* put the exact figure before you which you now accept. From the point of view of your people, however, Mr. Pinker was evidently a person not to be trusted, nor did it ever occur to them to even refer to me. They got hold of some muddle-headed accounts, kept, apparently by the most incompetent firm who ever presumed to call themselves publishers, and on the strength of these have put me to immense inconvenience and loss, sooner than believe that either Mr. Pinker or myself could be relied upon to furnish you with accurate information. I notice that in your second letter you admit that your people must have had some other reason for keeping this matter open so long. Well, I shall wait and see whether that is so. If, however, as seems to be the case, I have been put to this serious inconvenience simply for the reason that your people were afraid to trust Mr. Pinker's word or mine, after Mr. Pinker had offered his books for Mr. Everett's inspection, all I can say is that my own feelings with regard to your firm will continue as they are at present,—inexpressible, in polite phraseology—and I shall be thankful of the opportunity which the close union between us English authors affords me, of warning all my friends against negotiations with a firm who conduct their business in such a manner. To you and your people, perhaps, it may seem that I take somewhat seriously the fact of this month's delay. As a matter of fact, it has been an exceedingly inconvenient and serious matter for me. As soon as the arrangement was come to, Little Browns had promised me their remittance, and directly I received word that your people and Little Browns had agreed, I entered into engagements to keep which I have had to, for the first time in my life, borrow money. I have been kept in a state of continual worry, and have lost financially, through the incomprehensible behaviour of your firm, and if they have no further explanations to offer than those suggested in your letter, I shall always consider their treatment of me inconsiderate and inexcusable.

I am sending a copy of this letter to your firm in New York.

<div align="center">Sincerely yours,</div>

To Norman Douglas
Text MS Texas; Unpublished

[Aldington]
Tuesday. [4 May? 1909][1]

Dear Douglas.

That horrible oppression is the effect of the English spring. It's no good to be too much alone when you feel like that. But I don't know whether coming down here will be any good. I am not a comforting person. But just walk in whenever You like. Do! There will be no one here—and you may as well brood in the fields as in the streets. Ah! Don't I know it well this horrid state that comes over one worse than any nightmare. Awful!

The tea arrived. Why? oh why will you spoil us! But all the same it is nice. Jessie sends her most friendly regards and tells me to let you know that since you *will* have it the cost of the stuff will be covered by 3/-. B went to school yesterday alone. We have a note today telling us that his taxi broke down twixt Char + and Pancras but that he managed to catch his train by seizing a hansom. Is very proud of himself. *M*'d is gone to London on the matter of sale.[2] If it comes off it will be good for us poor devils for there will be really some money behind. *Lyons* (eating house keeper)[3] is the man who hankers after it. But consider this as strictly conf*al* please.

Yours

J Conrad.

To R. D. Mackintosh
Text MS Colgate; Unpublished

Aldington N*r* Hythe
Kent.

5 May 1909

My dear Mackintosh.

You have an infinite patience quite beyond any thanks one could give. The tonic arrived this afternoon and I had my first dose this moment.

[1] On the MS, Douglas noted the date of reply, '10 May'; Marwood's activities give the year.

[2] Of the *English Review*.

[3] Already famous for his gigantic Corner House on Coventry Street, Joseph Lyons expressed a passing interest in the *Review* (Mizener, p. 186). Before going into the restaurant business, Lyons (knighted 1911, died 1917), had been a professional painter.

The "metal" question[1] has been very much in my thoughts ever since you were here last. Was the Yank up to some tricks? Trying to get out of his contract maybe? They are fellows of infinite resource, but what Percival[2] told me looked mainly like an inexcusable neglect, levity—I don't know how to call it—of the inventor. The carelessness of old men is sometimes amazing. Upon the whole your letter on the subject cheered me up; and I am awaiting now further news of this memorable episode in the life of the Doctor and the Buccaneer.

I wrote yesterday to P. G. about his Afrikander memories.[3] I didn't quite tell him how good they are for fear he should think I was gushing. But really, in that short production, look at the poetic vision, the existence of simple language, the breadth and force of the effects. It's no mean talent that can put such quality into a magazine article. And the creative faculty is in him too. Volumes of painstaking statement on the contact of black & white races couldn't give us a better psychological knowledge than this description of the Kaffirs going home at the end of the day.[4] Suggestiveness—the mark of a real artist in words (not a mere rhetorician) informs his pages. A remarkable talent. Shall we say a great talent? Well—yes. I believe so. The question is: what will he do with it? Will his grasp of life prove as universal as his power of expression? Sometimes I think so. But I don't think him quite safe yet. There are so many what I may call be-littling influences, waiting upon the life of a literary man—upon the life of *any* man—upon the life of a doctor, of a statesman, of a priest, of a teacher, of a saint. To keep firm hold of reality and yet deal with it in a lofty idealising spirit is so difficult! So difficult. And yet truth, expressive, effective truth, the combination of beauty and honesty of outlook can only be conquered by that almost impossible feat.

Pardon this flight. I don't often let myself go; but I believe you will understand me. And the occasion of it. P. G. himself is interesting to us both—as a friend. That's perhaps a sufficient excuse. I need not say that his *success* in a purely popular sense is for me a certainty, sooner or later.

I will drop You a line by Friday's evening post.[5]

Yours gratefully

J. Conrad.

[1] See the letter of [26? March]. [2] Perceval Gibbon.
[3] Gibbon had lived in South Africa from 1898 to 1903. 'Afrikander Memories' appeared in the May *English Review* (pp. 266–78).
[4] Gibbon describes African workers heading back to their 'location'. Once in sight of home 'The mob of them parted into groups: a certain gravity and responsibility governed them, and their voices sank, and one heard the tones of intimacy and familiarity ... It seemed as if the dawn that sent them back to their labour in the town joined them all in a conspiracy to wear a conventional face before the white man, to cut a slight and futile figure, to wear a mask' (p. 266).
[5] Two days hence.

To J. B. Pinker
Text MS Berg; Unpublished

[Aldington]
5 May. 1909.

My dear Pinker.

In the matter of the Nelson 7d edition of Romance[1] if you think it advisable I have no objection and I don't think Hueffer can have any. I suppose You are in communication with him.

I have heard from Jack a few days ago. He tells me that in the matter of the Civil List pension all the principal signatures have been obtained. Everybody, he says, has been *most* cordial etc etc. The representation or petition whatever it is called, to the prime minister[2] will go in in a week or two. There is every chance, I am assured, of its being successful. At the same time the Income-tax people whom I've been trying to keep off in the hope of this thing going through quickly notify me that no delay beyond the 12th inst. can be granted me.

Under the last arrangement note which you made me sign as part of another transaction there is a sum of £40 over and *above the provision for the weekly* cheques on which I consider myself as entitled to draw. I wished to leave it untouched—but at this juncture I must ask you whether you will let me make use of it to satisfy the claim (it amounts to £*33*) for the tax which claim they tell me is a final one. Under the distribution and ap[p]ortioning of the £600 made by you and subscribed to by me[3] I believe I may ask for the amount as above without breaking the arrangement. However I assert nothing. I only ask you to give me your answer at once. I would offer (without foregoing my right to such a balance of the £600 as may be left under our arrangement) to pay you back out of the first instalment of the expected grant—but the grant is not a certainty; it is only a *strong* probability.[4] But if it does come off (as Jack believes it will) I will be extremely willing to do that.

—Please send me, as you have been kind enough to do once before, some writing pads of British Linen Bank paper.[5]—I see the new edon of *Tales of Unrest* is being favourably noticed in more than one paper; and strangely

[1] A sevenpenny edition, in the Nelson's Library series, of the collaboration with Ford.
[2] Herbert Henry Asquith, Prime Minister from 1908 to 1915.
[3] The annual allowance agreed upon in 1907.
[4] Conrad was granted a pension of £100 a year in August 1910.
[5] The stationery Conrad preferred for his MSS.

enough in Country Life.[1] Has A. Graham repented—or did it creep in through oversight?

Yours always

J. Conrad

In another envelope, I am sending a batch of copy.

To [?]
Text MS Syracuse; Szczypien

Aldington. Nr Hythe
Kent.
6 May 1909

Dear Sir.[2]

To make up for the delay in answering your request I am enclosing here a page of my MS.

It belongs to my Reminiscences, and this part of the text has appeared in the N° vii of the *English Review*.[3] The scrawl of my work is by no means beautiful but at any rate it's my *intimate* handwriting.

Yours faithfully

J. Conrad.

To J. B. Pinker
Text MS Berg; Unpublished

[Aldington]
Friday. [7? May 1909][4]

Dear Pinker

Thanks very much for the cheque received today together with one writing pad.

[1] Understandably, Conrad had forgotten neither Anderson Graham's patronizing comments on *A Set of Six* (*Country Life*, 15 August 1908) nor the anonymous and bone-headed review of *The Secret Agent* (21 September 1907). The latest review observed that although technically simpler, *Tales of Unrest* (now appearing in the Adelphi Library) had as much 'vigour, imagination and poetry' as *A Set of Six*; moreover, 'Mr. Conrad's books come so rarely from the press that his many admirers will welcome an opportunity of renewing acquaintance with one of his less-known volumes' (1 May, Supplement, p. lxxx).

[2] Unidentified.

[3] The seventh (June) number would appear towards the end of May.

[4] Received '5/09': written on the 7th if Pinker had given a swift reply to the requests of the 5th.

No, decidedly, I mus'nt* interrupt my work for a short story. And generally I must go on finishing the commenced books Chance—Rescue etc. It's the long novels that *tell*.

<div align="center">Yours</div>

<div align="right">J. C.</div>

To Harriet Mary Capes
Text MS Yale; Unpublished

<div align="right">Aldington N^r Hythe</div>
<div align="right">Kent.</div>
<div align="right">13 may 1909</div>

My dear Miss Capes

It was an immense pleasure to get your good truly friendly letter.

We are settled. That we are very contented I would not like to say. Still this place must serve for a time.

Dear Jess is very crippled. I hesitate to affirm that her state is worse but it is certainly no better. It's a great anxiety to me. Her cheerfulness under the circumstances is perfectly touching. I will say no more. Except myself there is no one in the world I believe who has understood her so well as You. And she is infinitely proud of Your friendship.

The children are well. We had B for the Easter holidays to our great comfort; and now we miss him very much.

I am so delighted to hear that my Rems in the English Review find favour in your eyes. They are indeed written for friends—and only friends will discover how unreservedly frank I am in these confidences. I lay my temperament quite bare before the world in the assurance that the world at large will never perceive the whole extent of my sincerity. And it's just as well, perhaps, that it should not.

At present I can not obtain a copy of *Nostromo* in England. So I am informed by Harpers. A new edition has appeared in the U. S. lately and I am going to ask them for a copy.

Jessie will be writing to you very soon. I end here; it is late. I feel very tired after a day of unsuccessful toil; but I wouldn't put off any longer my answer to your dear letter. Believe me always

<div align="right">your affectionate and grateful
friend</div>

<div align="right">J. Conrad.</div>

PS The fate of the E. Review hangs in the balance as it has been hanging for the last 4 months;[1] and that is the only reason why Hueffer has refrained from writing to Mr Bernard Capes[2] asking for a contribution. Else it would have been done long before for he has talked to us often of his wish to publish something from that distinguished pen.

The position is such that only a sale to some plutocrat ambitious of that sort of prestige can save the Review from extinction. There is such a *nouveau riche* about[3] and he is nibbling, but. . . . The above in *strict* confidence.

J. C.

To J. B. Pinker

Text MS Berg; Unpublished

[Aldington]
Thursday. [13? May 1909][4]

Dear Pinker.

I've signed the agreement with Nelson and am sending it to H[ueffer] by this post.

Would you pay for me the subon of the Navy Records[5] now in arrears. If not I will just have to drop my membership—no great matter after all. It's £1.1 per year. But I must ask you also to settle with Romeike & Curtis,[6] a guinea for cuttings. I can do without them.

Yours always

J Conrad

To Norman Douglas

Text MS Texas; *Listy* 294; Original unpublished

[Aldington]
18 May 1909

My dear Douglas.

I am in a state of despair. The wretched tax gatherers after lulling with the prospect of granting a delay till end of year suddenly came

1 Ford was engaged in what he called 'very ticklish negotiations' (Mizener, p. 182).
2 Her brother (1854–1918), formerly editor of *Theatre*, specialized in historical romances and macabre tales.
3 Either Joe Lyons or Ford's brother-in-law David Soskice, about whom Conrad was consistently unpleasant. For Soskice, see pp. 253, 266.
4 Marked on verso as received '5/09'; '4/09' on recto cannot be right as on 5 May the contract for the new edition of *Romance* had not been signed. A dating on 6 May would fall too soon after the previous letter.
5 *Publications of the Navy Records Society.*
6 Romeike and Curtice, Ltd, the press-cutting agency.

down with a notice of payment with[in] seven days. £34 and of course all
I had and could raise in a hurry had to go to them. The borrowed money
I was going to send you went too. What can you expect of a man with a
knife at his throat! And to put a finishing touch F[ord] seems to have
gone bankrupt—and so my power to earn a few pence independently of
Pinker seems gone. But I will soon unearth somewhere some more cash.
It is a miserable existence. I have been off my chump with worry for the
last fortnight. It's too awful. It crushes my spirit and my imagination—
and my energy.

I will write to Lucas begging him to expedite the reception of your
book or, any rate, some sort of answer. For the MS I will see what would
be best. I will I think ask Courtney.[1] But even the little self-confidence I
had has left me and I daren't promise a successful issue for any of the
attempts. I can only assure you that they will be made.

I will write soon. Kindest regards from Jessie

Ever yours

J Conrad.

To J. G. Huneker
Text MS Dartmouth; Schwab

Aldington. Nr Hythe
Kent.
18 May 1909

My dear Sir.

Pardon this scrawl on a piece of my MS paper.

I did not know you were one of my reviewers in the U S.[2] I have seen
very few criticisms from your side; and the few I've seen were not
calculated to stimulate my curiosity as to the others. One of them I
remember referred to my long story The End of the Tether as "a sordid
tale of an Insurance fraud". By the natural ordering of events in this
valley of Tears (and gnashing teeth) that particular notice *had* infailli-
bly* to reach me. But your criticism where you overwhelm me with the
mantle of Flaubert never came under my eye.[3] Thanks for your
intention—but it is an ominous garment to put on a man's shoulders.

[1] W. L. Courtney (1850–1928), editor of the *Fortnightly Review* since 1894.
[2] Schwab (p. 223) cites Huneker's general praise of Conrad in the April 1905 issue of
Metropolitan Magazine. No signed reviews of specific books are known prior to this
letter.
[3] In his reply, Huneker repeats the compliment: 'you are the English (and the Polish)
Flaubert': see *Twenty Letters to Joseph Conrad*.

Yet there is one point in which I resemble that great man; it is in the
desperate, heart breaking toil and effort of the writing, the days of
wrestling as with a dumb devil for every line of my creation. And poor
Flaubert had no wife and children, he had neither himself nor others to
feed on the vain words which survive him for your delight and mine.
Death had for him no terrors either in this world or in the next.
 Mais laissons cela!.

So I may comfort myself in the dark hours (they come oftener as the
years go by) with the thought of a band of the Faithful—you and
many(?) others in the astounding New York City! It is really great news.
Please accept for Yourself and give from me to such choice spirits as
would care to know the assurance that I am indeed comforted. It is the
sober truth. To live (artistically) one needs the feeling that one is
believed in. But of this too I will say no more.

 I must go back to my MS on a page (just like this one) bearing the
N° 890 of the novel I have been at for the last 16 months. And the end is
not yet! And that also does not bear thinking about.

<div align="center">Bien à Vous</div>

<div align="right">J. Conrad.</div>

It is really friendly of you to propose sending me a vol of your stories.[1] I
am very curious. Laissez moi voir ça. But please do not forget to write
Your name and mine on the fly leaf.

To Ford Madox Ford

Text TS/MS Berg; Najder (1970)

<div align="right">Aldington Forehead
Hythe, Kent.
May 20th 1909</div>

Dear Hueffer

 What means your letter? It's the first I hear of you having anything to
do with this affair. I really don't understand what is (behind what meets
the eye) to make you fly out so indignantly. Surely you might have
dropped me a line on a p.c. *Dear Conrad I want you to see a Miss C[ather]* etc
etc. and of course I would have seen her. Instead of which reproaches for
not having guessed at things of which I had no knowledge whatever, are

[1] Huneker had published two volumes of stories, *Melomaniacs* (1902) and *Visionaries*
(1905).

heaped upon me.[1] Frankly I don't like it. It looks queer. The last line of your angry letter says that you give the *matter up. Are you aware* that you have never given me the slightest hint of there being any "matter" at all? *Are you aware* that it is *the first* I hear of Miss C being a particular friend of yours. You mentioned her casually once months ago, if I remember rightly. I didn't even remember the name.[2] The truth is that S.S. edits the Mag. himself; I know it because I have it under his hand—his talk, his actions, his correspondence prove that up to the hilt.[3]

But all this is not the question. The question is—what do you mean? What the devil do you mean? Come my dear chap, you know very well that I knew nothing, *nothing whatever* of your relations, of your friendship, of your regard for Miss C—I didn't even remember the lady's name. Elsie writes to me in the early morning a note asking whether I would see an American lady, apparently her acquaintance, literary editor of McClure's and who wants a story from me.[4] I reply that: *I have no story for McClure, that this is not the way to do serious business—that the thing looks like an intrusion.* I write frankly what I think, being as you know a man who *can't afford* to be disturbed by casual visitors. Then I get your letter like a bolt from the blue throwing at my head a lot of things of which I had no previous inkling—which you never even hinted to me before—as a basis for reproaches! Telling me my attitude is *too bad*!!

This looks like a pretty *coup de chien?*[5] Stop this nonsense with me Ford. It's ugly. I won't have it.

I tell you what is *too bad.* It is to send my letter written with perfect openness to your wife to a third party. And by Jove you good people haven't lost any time over it either. You caught the post all along most neatly. But, since my letters are to be sent about, I consider myself at liberty to forward the copy of all the correspondence: *Elsie's first note*[6]—

[1] As managing editor, Willa Cather had come to England looking for new contributions for *McClure's Magazine.* Ford reasoned that helping her would predispose McClure towards investing in the *Review* – a possibility that Conrad, who detested the man, wanted to avoid at all costs.

[2] Willa Cather (1873–1947) had published a volume of poetry (*April Twilight*, 1903) and a collection of short stories (*The Troll Garden*, 1905), but her first novels, *Alexander's Bridge* and *O Pioneers!*, did not appear until 1912 and 1913.

[3] For a cooler account of the relationship between Cather and McClure, see Sharon O'Brien, *Willa Cather: The Emerging Voice* (New York: OUP, 1987), pp. 270–1, 288–93. McClure probably wrote to Conrad in person because he had known him long before hiring Cather in 1906.

[4] On Elsie Hueffer's position, see Mizener, p. 157.

[5] 'Squall': the question mark is in the TS.

[6] A copy of this note (TS Berg) reads: 'Dear Conrad, Miss Cather—the literary editor for McClure['s] Magazine—now over here for a short time—intends descending on

your extraordinary letter, the material parts of <u>this</u> letter and Elsie's note received this morning to Miss Cather C/o McClure in New York—with my explanation of the episode. As she has my note to Elsie she may as well have the lot.

What's sauce for the goose is sauce for the gander and I will do it unless you are pleased to take back your most unfair letter of reproaches without any reserves whatever.

Enclosed copy of the material parts of Elsie's first note starting this mysterious game.

I am very much hurt by the contents and the tone of your communication. I don't think this transaction clear. It's an attack delivered from the dark; and the sending to Miss Cather of my note written hastily and intended only for Elsie's eyes an outrageous proceeding at variance with your professions of trying to render me a service (without my knowledge) with McClure.

I will be content to leave the case to the judgement of all fair-minded men.

<div align="center">Yours</div>

<div align="right">J. Conrad</div>

PS[1] Look here my dear Ford—this sort of thing I *won't* stand if you had a million dollars in each hand. The proper thing for Miss C was to ask for an interview. She did not because she did not want it. She was clearly coming casually. I am not to be treated like that. Unless I hear from you within the week I will clear up this matter—of which I have my own opinion not to be put on paper here but very much at your service if you will come and talk with me. Your wire as to proofs just received. They will be sent back first thing tomorrow. Am I to be paid for this article.[2] I don't urge it. I simply want to know.

each of us tomorrow. She apparently wants to get a story out of you, and Heaven only knows what out of me. She is arriving at Smeeth 10.45 in the morning and leaving in the afternoon. Will you let me know when you would rather see her? Ford arrived very late on Sunday, etc, etc, Elsie M.'

[1] The PS is handwritten.
[2] The seventh instalment of the reminiscences, for the June number.

To Robert d'Humières
Text MS Vaugelas; Guérin

22.May[?][1] 1909
Aldington. Nr Hythe
Kent.

Cher Monsieur.

Merci des bonnes nouvelles Vous me donnez.[2] J'ignorais l'existence
du "Correspondant" mais le nom de M. E. Lamy[3] naturellement m'est
connu.

Et la petite pièce?[4]

Pardonnez cette courte note. Je suis pour le moment fort occupé.

Croyez moi toujours le votre
J Conrad.

Translation

Dear Sir,

Thank you for the good news you give me. I was unaware of the
Correspondant's existence, but of course I know Monsieur E. Lamy's
name.

And the short piece?

Forgive this brief note. I am very busy at present.

Always yours,

J Conrad.

To John Galsworthy
Text MS Forbes; J-A, 2, 97

[Aldington]
5 June 1909

Dearest Jack

I was glad to hear from you.

I have been in bed all last week and am just beginning to pull myself
together. The good Mac came down twice flying in his car with

[1] The month is hard to read.
[2] *Le Correspondant* had taken the translated *Nigger*; the serial was to begin on 25 August.
[3] Etienne Lamy (1845–1919), a fervent Catholic but also a republican, was an
influential member of the Chamber of Deputies. He edited *Le Correspondant* from 1904
to 1910.
[4] It is not known what else d'Humières intended to translate.

1 Conrad at Someries, 1909

2 Stephen Reynolds

3 Aldington Church, whose bells Conrad heard in his sickness

THE UNKNOWN FACTOR

BY PERCEVAL GIBBON

AUTHOR OF "VROUW GROBELAAR AND HER LEADING CASES," ETC.

ILLUSTRATIONS BY WALTER JACK DUNCAN

4 Heading for one of Gibbon's stories of Russian terrorism: *McClure's Magazine*, April 1908

THE ALL-NIGHTMARE.

"STILL IT CRIED 'SLEEP NO MORE!' TO ALL THE HOUSE."—*Macbeth*, Act II., Scene 2.

5 *Punch* on the Liberal budget, 28 July 1909

√12/09

Dear Pinker .
I am sending by same post
the corrected type . Quite
a good enough story
For titles I suggest

{ The Secret Self.
or { The other Self

An episode from the sea .

It could be also The Secret Sharer
but that may be too enigmatic.

Pray select for me .

Yours hastily Conrad .

6 Letter to Pinker [c. 18 December 1909]

THE STEWARD BROUGHT IN A TRAY AND GLASSES

7 W. J. Aylward illustration for 'The Secret Sharer', *Harper's Magazine*, September
1910

9 John Quinn's bookplate, designed by J. B. Yeats

10 Edmund Oliver, owner of Capel House, with Cadet Borys Conrad and his father,
September 1911

medicines, bandages, lotions etc etc. cheering me up and putting heart into Jessie who has been quite extraordinarily worried by this bout of gout. Well it was pretty bad the horrible depression worst of all. It is rather awful to lie helpless and think of the passing days, of the lost time. But the most cruel trial is afterwards, when I crawl out of bed to sit before the table, take up the pen—and have to fling it away in sheer despair of ever writing a line. And I've had thirteen years of it, if not more. Anyway all my writing life. I think that in this light the fourteen vols (up to date) are something of an achievement. But it's a poor consolation—

> The way was long, the wind was cold
> The minstrel was infernal old;
> His harp, his sole remaining joy,
> Was stolen by an organ boy—[1]

That's how I feel.

I like immensely your verse in the last ER. The Second piece for choice but as a matter of fact I like best the one I am reading at the time.[2]

Yes, yes. Let us have a long talk. Nothing shall be allowed to interfere with that, if I know it. I have been fed up on that connection of late till my gorge rises at the thought of it.

I suppose you were in Berlin on dramatic affairs?[3]

How is dear Ada? You don't say; and after the bad winter she had one is anxious to know how this rather phantastic spring weather had affected her.

Au revoir then with our dear love to you both

Yours ever

J. Conrad

PS On the 13th *Sunday* Mackintosh is coming to inspect me; so any day but that one for your dear longed-for visit.

[1] Parodying the start of Sir Walter Scott's *The Lay of the Last Minstrel*: 'The way was long, the wind was cold, / The Minstrel was infirm and old; / ...The harp, his sole remaining joy, / Was carried by an orphan boy'.

[2] Four Galsworthy poems appeared in the June number (2, 411–13); the second is 'Rose and Yew'.

[3] Galsworthy went to Cologne later that year for the German première of *Strife*.

To Harriet Mary Capes
Text MS Yale; Unpublished

Aldington
N^r Hythe
Kent
8 June 1909.

My dear Miss Capes

I don't know whether Jessie has told you I have had a dreary bout of gout; in bed a week and now hobbling with difficulty as lame in my mind as in my feet.

Certainly, I will be delighted to know M^r Melrose.[1] It is indeed difficult to arrange on conventional lines. How would it be if I just simply called on him the first time I am in London to begin the acquaintance?

Two men having the honour and privilege of your friendship may approach each other without the usual ceremonies. But I am afraid he won't find [me] either very interesting or very amusing.

I am very glad you are going to Switzerland with a congenial companion. But we must see each other before this year turns to rain and sleet and murk.

Always Your most affectionate
friend and servant
J. Conrad

To R. B. Cunninghame Graham
Text MS Dartmouth; Watts 173

Aldington
N^r Hythe
Kent.
8 June 1909.

Très cher ami.

It is really good of You to have sent *Faith*.[2] Your magic never grows less; each of your prefaces is a gem[3] and my enthusiasm is roused always to the highest pitch by your amazing prose. I have already read (the book arrived but two hours ago) *The Idealist* and *The Saint*. Admirable in

[1] Probably Andrew Melrose, the publisher, who started his Favourite Series of novels in 1908; in 1915, he brought out Miss Capes's *Wisdom and Beauty from Conrad*.
[2] Duckworth had published this collection of essays, sketches, and tales in March.
[3] In the tradition of Cervantes, Graham took special pride in his prefaces.

conception and feeling are these two sketches.[1] Strange that I should have pitched on these two at first. I suppose the titles seduced me. This afternoon I shall sit down with the book and forget my miseries in the delight of your art so strong and human. I envy it to you with affection.

<div style="text-align:center">Ever Yours</div>

<div style="text-align:right">J. Conrad</div>

To Harriet Mary Capes
Text Yale; Unpublished

<div style="text-align:right">[Aldington]
Sunday evening [13 June 1909][2]</div>

My dear Miss Capes.

I could not find a moment to send you a line as first of all I had Galsworthy here and then a writer called Gibbon and they took up all my time.

I am glad to hear your brother[3] had the idea to send something to the *ER*.

Of course I am sure that You kept my confidence absolutely. It would never enter my head to doubt that.

I don't know what is going on at the Review. It has been kept going so long by a sort of miracle. I am afraid the payment they will offer will be miserable—and that's the only thing that worries me, and very likely is worrying poor Hueffer at this very moment.

I haven't either seen him or heard from him for ages.

Please give your brother a fellow-craftsman's warm greeting and believe me

<div style="text-align:center">always your[s] most
affectionately</div>

<div style="text-align:right">J Conrad</div>

Jessie's dear love.

[1] Both portray anarchists who are fierce in word yet inoffensive in deed.
[2] The envelope is postmarked 14 June, a Monday.
[3] Bernard: see the letter of 13 May, PS.

To J. B. Pinker
Text MS Berg; Unpublished

[Aldington]
Sunday evening [13 June 1909][1]

My dear Pinker.

Thanks for the page received yesterday by the afternoon post.

Re Douglas. You are wrong in ascribing to me an enthusiastic attitude otherwise than from a literary point of view. At any rate the Spectator which can not be charged with being enthusiastic in its tone compares *D.* to J. A. Symon[d]s.[2] I would not establish such a comparison myself, since *D* is much more virile, much more classical much less [a]esthetic than J. A. S, not to mention his philosophical liberalism (which could not have been pleasing to the Spectator) whereas J. A. S had no convictions except on matters of art. But the fact remains that J. A. S. was one of the most distinguished and erudite prose writers in the 19[th] century and that the comparison has been made by a paper whose critical attitude is cautious and pondered to the point of coldness.

I advised *D* more than a year ago to go to you in order to place the few articles he had then by him. When he returned from Italy with the book practically finished I thought that it would be better for him to make himself known a little before putting his affairs in Your hands. He's not a youngster and can't be treated like one. I did not wish to expose him to the experience of being told that nothing could be done with his "*stuff*"—or some thing of the kind. I addressed myself to Lucas because I trusted his literary sense and counted on his assistance from sheer love of letters; but as far as I know it was and is still D's intention to call on you on his return from Italy. It's obviously necessary for him. I will be writing to him in a day or two and [will] say that I've seen You and that you are disposed to take some trouble about his work both here and in the US—where he is not altogether unknown.

For myself I can not be of much use to a beginner. The horrible illness which has swallowed up at least a full third of my writing life has kept me from making useful acquaintances or even living on the fringe of the world. Only a couple of days ago I had to refuse an invitation to meet

[1] Received '6/09': visits from Galsworthy and the Gibbons furnish the precise date.
[2] Like Douglas, John Addington Symonds (1840–1893) loved Italy: his work included *The Renaissance in Italy* in five parts, 1875–1886, and *Sketches in Italy and Greece* (1874). The *Spectator* discussed 'Sirens' on 8 May.

Alfred Lyttleton[1] who wishes to know me. I am not well enough now—but if I were I could not afford the time.

Jack was here on Saturday looking well. He could tell me nothing as yet of the affair you know of[2] but in the natural course of events it must be decided soon. He assured me only that I had many friends. Gibbon with his wife left this afternoon after a long call. Complains of not being able to write a word on account of the move into the country hanging over his head.[3]

<div style="text-align: right">Yours ever</div>

<div style="text-align: right">J. Conrad.</div>

To E. V. Lucas
Text MS Berg; J-A, 2, 98

<div style="text-align: right">Aldington</div>

<div style="text-align: right">Hythe Kent</div>

<div style="text-align: right">14 June 1909</div>

My dear Lucas.

I write to your ex-address though I know from Galsworthy that You are already in the country. I dare say this unimportant letter will find you all right.

Could you give me an idea what are the prospects of my friend Douglas' book, *now* with Mr Methuen for consideration. Douglas is now in Italy and I haven't heard from him for some time; but I know how anxious he was about his fate when leaving England.

I have heard of the *Spectator* having given a laudatory par: or so to his paper on the *Sirens* in the 6th (I think) number of the E. Review. If that is so (I haven't myself seen the *Specor*) then I am very glad for Douglas and highly flattered at having my judgement backed by the calm and pondered authority of the *Spectator*.

In this connection let me mention (for I don't know what you may have heard) that I have been in no sense associated with the *ER* except that I wished Hueffer well in his venture. I showed him the Douglas MS I had by me which to say the least of it was being as kind to the Review as to Douglas. And of course there are my own contributions which obviously I could not have placed elsewhere—not because they are

[1] The Rt Hon. Alfred Lyttleton was Liberal-Unionist M.P. for Leamington, 1895–1906, and Balfour's Colonial Secretary, 1903–1905. A lawyer and among the most famous of amateur cricketers, he owned a country house in Wittersham, Kent, near Arthur Symons's cottage.

[2] The Civil List pension. [3] They were moving to Kent.

improper but for other reasons one of them being that editors are not falling over each other in their eagerness to get at my stuff—oh dear no! This is absolutely the whole extent of my connection.

If you don't like long letters I apologise for the dimensions of this one with the greater confidence because I am conscious of not being a great sinner in that respect—I mean not an habitual sinner.

Please remember me to Mrs Lucas.

<div style="text-align: right">Yours cordially</div>

<div style="text-align: right">J. Conrad</div>

PS On reflection I'll address this c/o Methuen.

To Norman Douglas
Text MS Texas; J-A, 2, 99

<div style="text-align: right">[Aldington]</div>

<div style="text-align: right">18 June '09</div>

My dear good Douglas

I've been ill—in bed and out of bed for the last month. Not a word written!

But I have managed to get off a pressing note to Lucas asking him to prod Methuen. No answer as yet.

Galsworthy writes me that he is most anxious to make your acquaintance should you be in London in the latter half of this year. He was here for lunch and we talked of you a good bit. He is a good man to know from more than one point of view.

The Spect*or* gave your *Sirens* articles a good notice—in fact a quite remarkable one for the cold cautious paper it is. People have noticed it too as far as I can judge from the rumours reaching me. Pinker was here and asked me to tell You that he is ready to take a good deal of trouble with your work should you wish to give him the opportunity. That's a pretty good sign. The man scents a profitable author.

I entreat you earnestly to try and throw your impressions of Messina[1] into the *form of a story*. Do try my dear fellow. I believe you would get both money and kudos that way. Where as an article or a small book would bring very little. The public here hardly remembers the earthquake now. Yet in the guise of fiction You would be read and probably

[1] Douglas had left Capri for a little less than two weeks to inspect the terrible devastation left by the earthquake of 1908 in Messina and Reggio di Calabria. He described what he saw in 'Land of Chaos', *Cornhill Magazine*, September 1910, and turned this article into a chapter of *Old Calabria* (1915).

appreciated. You need not make it a conventional novel or story. Just try to invent some action and hang a picturesque rendering of your impressions upon it.

If you can do it at all please try.

I say no more just now. This fit of gout has literally ruined me by stopping my work at a critical moment.

Yours ever

J Conrad

Jessie sends her kindest regards. I shall write again soon.

To J. B. Pinker
Text MS Berg; Unpublished

[Aldington]
Monday. [21 June 1909][1]

Dear Pinker

I enclose here Lucas' letter about Douglas' MS. I expect now every post to hear from that last. He will of course refuse the Methuen proposal.[2] I don't think he could entertain it even if he wished to do so. He will no doubt ask my advice and I shall certainly tell him that rather than accept such terms or even give the book for nothing it is better to throw his pen definitely away and starve, if he must, without the kind assistance of publishers.

That I can tell him—the question is what further counsel I can give him supposing he desires it. He has been in personal communication with *Reg. Smith* about the two papers already published in the Cornhill, and he may be inclined to try in that direction.[3] He had also the intention some six months ago or so to call on *B'wood* in the course of his visit to Scotland; but I dissuaded him or rather persuaded him to put it off.[4] He has also my letter (he must have got it about the time he heard from Methuen) in which I tell him that You are willing to take his work in hand.

I know you mean what you say but I also know that a little ready reputation is a great help to an agent in handling a new author. The *Spectator* article is but a slender outfit I am thinking; but still if you tell

1 Received '6/09': accompanying Lucas's letter to Conrad of 20 June.
2 Methuen would only undertake the book with a subsidy from Douglas.
3 As well as editing the *Cornhill*, Reginald Smith headed Smith, Elder.
4 William Blackwood's nephew George was now in charge of the publishing house and *Blackwood's Edinburgh Magazine*; Conrad had no liking for the new man.

me that you really think it worth your while to undertake Douglas I shall (without waiting to hear from him) write a short note urging him to have the MS of the Siren Land transferred at once to you.

I ask you so definitely in case you should have some definite plan for bringing him forward. Because if it is only a question of sending the MS round he may just as well do it himself; and at the same time I, through my acquaintance with Garnett, Meldrum, Seccombe & Chapman[1] (men who have a certain regard for my literary judgment), can insure him a fairly quick reading in four publishing houses anyhow. Heinemann I would not like to approach after seeing Pawling's letter to you but Galsworthy (who thinks highly of *D*) would see to that if I asked him, which I would have no hesitation in doing. As a matter of fact those two are to meet some time in July or August by Jack's desire. It's a matter of initial policy to be followed by a man who ultimately is bound to be one of your authors, and I state the question to you frankly.

———————

The Income tax people are worrying me for a return and I must ask you for a note of earnings during the 3 past years, to make the aforesaid return. Will you also please forward the Nos of the policies as I regret to say I have mislaid the slip you sent me last year. I must hurry up so as to lodge all my claims to abatement in good time.

I am quite myself again physically and mentally.

Yours always

J. Conrad

This in answer to a par: in my letter to him disclaiming all connection other than a contributor's with the E.R.[2]

J. C.

[1] Edward Garnett worked for Duckworth and David Meldrum for Blackwood. Thomas Seccombe (1866–1923) lectured in English at East London (later Queen Mary) College; he had been assistant editor of the *DNB* from 1891 to 1901 and had written *The Bookman History of English Literature*. After leaving London University, he held chairs at Sandhurst and at Queen's University, Ontario. Chapman's identity is uncertain; among the possibilities are R. W. (1881–1960), the future editor of Austen, Boswell, and Johnson, and William Arthur (1849–1917), head of Admiralty records since 1899 and the author of poems and plays.

[2] PS written on the back of Lucas's letter. Lucas complimented Conrad on his reminiscences but went on: 'the periodical as a whole does not seem quite to be well-loaded or well-aimed ... & it has been generally too foreign for its title'.

To E. V. Lucas
Text MS Yale; J-A, 2, 100

<div align="right">

Aldington N^r Hythe

Kent

23 June 09
</div>

My dear Lucas.

Thanks for your letter. Douglas won't be able to accept Methuen's proposal for the best of all reasons—because he can't afford it; and indeed one couldn't advise him in that sense even if he had the money.

I fully share your opinion of the ER. My reminiscences have come to an end now[1] and of course the fate of the *ER* is very uncertain I hear. So I don't suppose I'll ever appear in its pages any more.

Since you have mentioned my reminis^{ces} I am emboldened to ask your advice as to continuing them. I don't suppose I could serialise them anywhere but I am thinking of a volume (or even two short vols of say 65,000 words each) for later on with an interval of a couple of years. I know that the form is unconventional but it is not so casual as it seems. It has been thought out. I hope still that from that unmethodical narrative a personality can be made to emerge in a sufficiently interesting manner. My case (as before the public) being not only exceptional but even unique I felt I could not proceed in cold blood on the usual lines of an autobiography. However before going on I would value exceedingly your opinion (if you will give it to me) as to the discretion of doing it at all.

It saddens me to hear that You too are subject to these moments of cruel blankness when one's writing life seems to come to an end. I live in the constant dread of these visitations. They have been too frequent of late. One sets one's teeth and hangs on to hope with a desperate grip. That's my experience. And somehow the mind survives these temporary extinctions. But how long these resurrections will go on who can tell?

<div align="right">

Yours always

J Conrad.
</div>

[1] For Conrad's deeply unhappy explanation, see the letter of 13 July.

To Arthur Symons

Text MS Virginia; Hunter (1985, 3)

Aldington
N^r Hythe
Kent
24 June 1909

My dear M^r Symons.

It was very delightful to hear of your improved health under your own hand; and I thank You very much for Your friendly thought of writing to me.

While you were improving I have not been getting on at all. At present I am lame in knee and ankle and tho' I can just hobble from one room to another travelling is out of question for me just at present. But I too am improving (if very, very slowly) and I do hope we will manage to meet before end July.[1]

The lines commend themselves to me very much.[2] That sort of thing used to make me extremely indignant but now that age has dimmed all my fires I look upon such outbreaks of ineptitude and folly with a more equable philosophy. After all that everlasting pilot doesn't count. Let him be. It is but a vain and sorry noise, and you may perhaps know the Turkish proverb: It's difficult to keep dogs out of graveyards.

Well, a bientôt, if all goes well with me, and meantime I am

cordially yours

J. Conrad

To J. B. Pinker

Text MS Berg; Unpublished

[Aldington]
Thursday evening. [24 June
1909][3]

My dear Pinker.

Thanks for the statement and for your letter.

I thought I could do no better considering its extremely friendly tone than send it on at once (backed by a few words from me) to Douglas. As

[1] Although Symons still lived in the private asylum, his physical and mental health had improved remarkably. He was now able to make excursions to plays, lunches, and galleries, often in the company of Agnes Tobin. To illustrate the recovery, Beckson (p. 268) cites a letter Symons wrote on 12 June.

[2] Symons destroyed many of the poems from this period (Beckson, p. 266), but see also the letter of 3 July.

[3] Received '6/09': after [21 June], when Conrad asked Pinker to write to Douglas.

I managed to catch the morning post he ought to get it on Sunday for certain. Unless indeed he should be absent from Capri on a journey in Calabria which I do not think likely, as I had a note from Reggio lately.[1]

He is a ticklish personality—embittered sceptical and a little capricious—and without any knowledge of the conditions of literary life and work; but your letter so much to the point ought to steady him.

He found an extraordinary state of affairs in the districts affected by the earthquake; the distracted population, the philanthropists, and a lot of queer adventurers mixed up with them trying to exploit the situation to their own advantage. He asked my advice as to writing an article or even a short book. My advice (which I think confidently you will approve) was to throw all his stock of observations into the form of a story, not necessarily on conventional lines but anyhow a story—action of sorts.

The difficult part will be to make him write a novel. I think I'll be able to start him and also to keep him straight. But of that later.

<div style="text-align: right">Yours ever</div>

<div style="text-align: right">J Conrad.</div>

To Bliss Carman

Text MS Queen's; Unpublished[2]

<div style="text-align: right">Aldington</div>

<div style="text-align: right">N^r Hythe</div>

<div style="text-align: right">Kent.</div>

<div style="text-align: right">29 June 1909</div>

My dear Sir.[3]

I am made happy by the friendly words of your unexpected letter.

Need I say I would be glad of serving under your Editorship? Unluckily I am not ready at the moment for my bit of service. I am one of those writers who have nothing in the drawer of the writing table. Just now I am wrestling with a long novel, long delayed by a very unsatisfactory state of health. It's nothing new to me; pretty nearly half my writing life has been wasted in such struggles.

[1] To say that he was returning to Capri? Reggio is in Calabria.

[2] Located by Dr J. H. Stape.

[3] The Canadian poet William Bliss Carman (1861–1929) came from New Brunswick. After moving to the U.S., he wrote for the *New York Independent, Current Literature*, and the *Atlantic Monthly*. Among his collections of verse were *Sappho* (1902) and *Songs from Vagabondia* (with Richard Hovey, 1894); collections of essays included *Kinship of Nature* (1904) and *The Poetry of Life* (1905). Carman wrote to Conrad as editor of the *Gentleman's Journal*.

However directly I see a glimmer of daylight ahead I shall turn to doing something for the Gentleman's Journal[1]—probably an auto-biographical sea-paper.

There's one or two inside me some where which want to be written—but that's the sort of thing the usual magazine is rather shy of allowing inside its covers. Your appreciative reference to that kind of my work has touched me deeply.

Thanks very much for the pleasure of your letter. An old and completely captivated reader of your verse and your prose feels very proud at Your recognition of his own efforts.

Believe me cordially

Yours

J. Conrad

To J. B. Pinker
Text MS Berg; Unpublished

[Aldington]
Wednesday. [30 June or 7 July
1909][2]

My dear Pinker

I haven't the slightest wish to see the American Editor. I am not really in a fit state to receive casual visitors. I grudge the time to my friends; indeed I do.[3]

I had a short note from Douglas. He has apparently the MS in his possession and he tells me he is not very anxious to try either B'wood or Smith. That is all. What he will do goodness only knows. He is so damnably erratic in his purposes that it is useless to speculate on that.

[1] In 1910, succumbing to the spirit of the age after only a year's existence, it became the *Man's Book*. For Carman's request, see also the letter to Harper & Brothers, 31 October.

[2] There is no date of receipt. The answer to Douglas summarized here may have been the 'pretty strong letter' of the week beginning 5 July (mentioned to Pinker on 19 July); in any case the date must be after 24 June, when Conrad forwarded Pinker's letter to Douglas. The earlier date makes the letter of 2 July a softening of what Conrad has already said; the later date makes this letter the prelude to a stronger statement.

[3] Conrad did, however, want to see Pinker (perhaps over an offer from the unidentified American editor) as two telegrams (Berg) dated 1 July 1909 demonstrate. The first was sent at 12:41 p.m.: 'Can you manage to come here talk over matter of some importance tomorrow if possible by eleven train am'; the second went out at 5:35 p.m.: 'Sorry inconveniencing you but fullest consultation on main point and details imperative so perhaps you consent come by 3.8 returning 8.18 as unfortunately no spare room.'

Anyway he has your letter to me with a most earnest advice on my part
to put his affairs in your hands at *once*.

The last line of his letter is: What about Lane?——

I don't even know what that means exactly. I've never talked to him
of Lane[1] tho' I think Reynolds did. My answer was: That your chance of
placing *MS* in the quarter you think of was *at least* as good as his
(Douglas's) chance with Lane and that your chance of obtaining decent
terms was infinitely greater than anything *he* could hope to get at the
very best from Lane or for that matter from any other publisher.

I could say no more. Could I? A wilful man will have his way. It is
quite on the cards that I may receive his MS before long. And I would be
heartily glad to hear it.

<div style="text-align:center">Always Yours</div>

<div style="text-align:right">J. Conrad[2]</div>

To Lewis Saul Benjamin

Text MS Temple; Unpublished

<div style="text-align:right">Aldington
N^r Hythe
Kent.
2 July 1909</div>

Dear Sir[3]

You may have the use of the pars specified in your letter of the 30th
June for your sea-anthology with* which I wish all possible success.

<div style="text-align:center">Yours faithfully</div>

<div style="text-align:right">J. Conrad</div>

[1] John Lane (1854–1925), Reynolds's publisher, founder of the *Yellow Book* and co-founder of the Bodley Head.

[2] A note in another hand reads '23 pages of MS enclosed'.

[3] Mention of a 'sea-anthology' identifies the recipient as Lewis Saul Benjamin (1874–1932). He and his wife, Helen Mira Benjamin, took the appropriate pseudonyms 'H. and L. Melville' to edit *Full Fathom Five*, published in April 1910; the selection includes one excerpt from 'Youth' and three from *The Nigger*. 'Lewis Melville' wrote the lives and edited the letters of many authors, among them Lady Mary Wortley Montagu, Smollett, Sterne, Beckford, and Cobbett. His two-volume biography of Thackeray appeared in 1899.

To Norman Douglas

Text MS Colgate; Unpublished

[Aldington]
2 July '09

Dear Douglas.

My conviction is that after all *P* is the best move and *may* give the quickest result—or else I would not have sent you his letter; but you must of course follow Your feeling in the matter.

I haven't heard from Ford for a month or more. The 8 n° did come out. You are not in it; but I hear that No 9 is a certainty and that you are to appear in it.[1] Negotiations for sale are going on.

As usual I am sick at heart and sick in mind. Jess sends her kindest regards

Yours ever

J. Conrad

To Arthur Symons

Text Copies, Princeton and Read; Hunter (1985, 3)[2]

[Aldington]
3 July 1909

My dear Mr. Symons,

I thank you very tenderly for the book of your highly prized prose and the stanzas of verse in your handwriting so friendly in intention, so exquisite in form.[3] The sympathetic looking *mince* volume[4] with the autograph page pasted in will be one of my chief possessions. No more till we meet.

Yours with very great regard,

J. Conrad.

[1] 'Tiberius' came out in the August number.
[2] Copy text, Read (Symons's own transcription).
[3] Symons sent Conrad *London: A Book of Aspects* (1909) and an MS of 'The Fires of Youth'; poem and book are now in the Castle collection at Bryn Mawr.
[4] 'Slim volume'.

To Perceval Gibbon

Text MS Berg; *Listy* 298; Original unpublished

[Aldington]

Sunday night [4 or 11 July 1909][1]

Dear Gibbon[2]

Ever so many thanks for the strawberries—the most Excellent fruit—which we sat to devour last evening with immense appreciation. It is part of the eternal irony of things that Elsie Hueffer should have turned up attended by her Maid of Honour to partake. There are evils for which there is no remedy.

Totally unconnected with her I have had various reports of Ford's doings. His furies, his agonies, his visits to various people of distinguished quality and his general carryings on like a spoilt kid—together with a report of the male and female devotions attending upon his mental and moral convulsions.[3] To hear of the Review is like looking into a kaleidoscope. However the last pattern of its fate spells into a definite statement that a sale has been effected by the agency of Soskice, to some people (not named) on conditions not stated except that F retains the editorship.[4] Voilà. This news seems authentic enough; has been telephoned to M'ood in Yorkshire and by him communicated to me in a note of six lines received here last Friday. I hope it will hold.

Will it be convenient for Maisie[5] if I came for a night—after Wednesday next? Perhaps she will fix the day she prefers, either at end this week or the whole of the next. Anyway don't let me disturb your domestic peace or the flow of your inspiration. Our dear love to you all

Yours,

J. Conrad

[1] News of the *Review* gives the period, strawberries the season, and a proposed visit to the Gibbons the likely dates. Conrad returned from the visit on the 17th.

[2] Reginald Perceval Gibbon (1878–1926) was the son of a Welsh Congregational minister. After a spell in the merchant navy, Gibbon spent five years in southern Africa, was captured and escaped while reporting the Anglo-Boer war as a uniformed correspondent, and then worked for the *Natal Witness*, *Rand Daily Mail*, and *Rhodesian Times*. On his return to London in 1904, he was able to sell a series of South African stories to *Blackwood's*. Thereafter, Gibbon followed a double career writing fiction and journalism. As a foreign correspondent, he travelled all over Eastern Europe; his novels include *Souls in Bondage* (1904) and *Margaret Harding* (1911). He published as Perceval, but to family and friends he was 'Reggie'.

[3] The full frenzy of his affair with Violet Hunt did not keep Ford away from his protégée Gertrud Schlablowsky; meanwhile Elsie Hueffer remained in Aldington with her daughters.

[4] David Soskice, Ford's brother-in-law, was trying to put together a group of backers in the Liberal interest. By an interim arrangement concluded on 16 May, Soskice took over as business manager (Mizener, pp. 187–8, 554, nn. 34–5).

[5] Mrs Gibbon.

To John Galsworthy
Text MS Forbes; J-A, 2, 100[1]

Aldington. N[r] Hythe
Kent.
13 July 1909

Dearest Jack.

I was prevented from giving an instalment of my R'ces to the June N°
of the ER[2] on which I counted to pay for B's schooling. I recovered
mentally so slowly that it was simply impossible to write anything—not
even a letter. I made desperate efforts to do something but could not
finish two pages—not two pages!—in time. So I had to give it up; a very
awful failure to live with.[3] It almost unnerved me utterly.

Meantime, fearing something of that sort, I had offered the *Rems*
which have already appeared here to Col Harvey (Harpers) for serial
publication in the N. Am[an] Review or his other two publications for £80
which was not much to ask. I had previously various communications
from his henchmen (Brooks amongst others) protesting of his
(Harvey's) great admiration for my work and of his wish to be my _only_
pub[er] in the States. Would you believe that to that proposal—which
after all was a matter of business—I _haven't even had a reply_.[4] It's five
weeks ago. Not a word! I can't tell you how bad I feel at this treatment. I
can't even imagine a reason of it*; for it seemed to me that an offer from
J Conrad, deserved at least to be civilly declined. But it seems not.

This being so and there being no news so far as to the pension I
thought You could meantime help me out there. This term comes to £17.
The man does not worry me[5]—on the contrary. But it is a very small
school and I don't think he's making his fortune.

I had a letter from Bliss Carman the other day. He edits now the
Gentleman['s] Journal (in N York) and ask[s] me for a story. I would
do one for him but I must stick to my novel. I can only do that just now. I
am not equal to extra writing at present. But I will send him something
presently, and I suppose he will pay me decently. Anyway even if I
wrote now I could not do it in time for my purpose.

Our dear love

Yours

J. Conrad.

[1] Without the paragraph about school fees and the final sentence.
[2] The last of the reminiscences appeared in the June issue; it was the July issue,
published late the previous month, that lacked the continuation.
[3] Despite some exceedingly close calls, he had never missed a deadline before.
[4] Conrad wrote to Harper & Brothers again on 21 July: see the letters of 17 and 31 October.
[5] 'Does not pursue me'.

To John Galsworthy

Text MS Forbes; Unpublished

[Aldington]

Sat evening [17 July 1909][1]

Dearest Jack.

I've been away since Thursday on a visit to P. Gibbon at Wrotham[2] and have just returned not much refreshed. But I must sometimes see somebody.

Ever so many thanks for the cheque which I found waiting for me.

B won a cup for the 100 yrds to his immense gratification and also a prize for the football kick. House wrote me expressing the most complete satisfaction at the way the boy worked this term.

C. Graham is coming tomorrow for the day. I hear that the *ER* is sold to a friend (Englishman) of that horrible Jew Soskice (Ford's brother in law).[3] F is to be kept as editor at £300[4]—I am told (by M'wood); but the payment is to be made in shares. So the transaction is not too brilliant.

Our dear love to you both

Yours ever

J Conrad.

I will send the play[5] back on Monday morning. You ought to get it in the evening.

To John Galsworthy

Text MS Forbes; J-A, 2, 95

[Aldington]

Sunday [18 July 1909][6]

Dearest Jack

This is extremely fine and an exhibition of mastery in dealing with psychology and situation gave me unalloyed delight.

At the end of each act I got up and walked for a while in a sort of exultation over the sheer art of the thing. To criticize the psychology if I had the wish to do so, I would feel myself racially incompetent.

[1] The letter to Garnett, 19 July, gives the date of the weekend spent on Galsworthy's play.
[2] In Kent, about 35 miles from Aldington. [3] See the letter of [4 August].
[4] The amount could easily be read as '£360'.
[5] *The Eldest Son*: written February and March 1909, revised at various times and first performed in November 1912.
[6] The evaluation of *The Eldest Son* gives the Sunday.

The simplicity of all the characters is from a theatrical point of view admirable. Everything every individual is as clear as a bell. Given the millieu* there is never the slightest jolt on one's convictions—not a single false note! And the action is intensely interesting all the time![1] Intensely.

Two remarks I'll make one on psychology the other of stage "business." First:—Studdenham in the last scene seems to me too Olympian just a bit. (and incidentally the word (*plaything*) seems (with all deference) to smack a little of the stage "rustic." Why shouldn't he say "When you got tired of my girl you forfeited your right" or "*the girl*".)[2]

I've been made slightly uneasy there.

The point of stage business is this:

When Sir William feels hot (while his wife sits shivering) you make him speak to *her*. It's too pointed (though it's a stroke of genius to establish their difference even in the physical effect of the situation). It's too pointed. Some idiot in the audience is sure to laugh at it and start some other donkeys. Now to my mind no risk of that should be run. I think that letting Lady C shiver (through the scene as it were) Sir William might just put a handkerchief to his forehead and mutter "they make *infernal fires here*" or something of the sort. The intelligent will perceive the trait, the asses will miss it probably, but the opening for an inept guffaw will [not] be given.[3]

It's late dearest Jack. C. Graham was here all day. He is immensely pleased at the prospect of meeting you at lunch somewhere very soon. Elsie Hueffer came in the evening. This is the first free moment I have today to write and I am writing after a second reading.

Our dear love to you both.

Ever yours

J. Conrad.

[1] The son of Sir William Cheshire, a country squire, has impregnated his mother's maid, Freda Studdenham, frustrating his parents' expectations of a good match.
[2] In Act Three of the published text, Studdenham says: 'If the young gentleman has tired of her in three months ... she's not for him!': *The Eldest Son* (New York: Scribner's, 1912), p. 73.
[3] Galsworthy took the suggestion. Wiping his forehead, Sir William says: 'Infernal fires they make up here!' (p. 72).

To Maisie Gibbon
Text MS Berg; Unpublished

Aldington
Sunday night [18 July 1909]¹

My dear Maisie.²

I would not have let a post go out without trying to tell you how profoundly touched I have been by your more than perfect kindness, only on arriving home 1/2 an hour late I found Galsworthy's new play awaiting me since Friday morning with the request that it should be returned on Monday. There were also two unexpected letters to answer; bothersome things if ever there were, of which I'll have to tell you both at some length when we are within voice distance again.

A propos of that event Jessie told me that writing to you she proposed to engage the rooms for a fortnight certain. The letter being gone I had no resource but to call her "a pernicious idiot"; whereupon she called me a "woolly dunderhead" and a "stupid British subject".

This promising beginning was followed by a vivacious conversation; the outcome of it is that I am to tell you that this skimping of time is only *her* peculiar method "to be on the safe side". There has never been a question but that we mean to stay 3 weeks at least near you, if not a month. Nothing whatever that we can see is likely to curtail our stay. You may safely tell the poor old woman that we take the rooms for 3 weeks no less—and hang Jessie's method of prudence. That woman Jessie is full of wiles and (there! She has boxed my ears. She's been looking over my shoulder)

I've driven her off and now shall proceed in peace:—

I've had to describe your house and relate minutely all the words and actions of the children.³ We talked of you far into the night. This morning at eight (just before post time) a wire was delivered from Cunninghame Graham and I had just the time to bolt across the fields and meet him at the station. He stayed till 4. Directly he left E. Hueffer turned up (in the very white dress you have seen her wearing on that afternoon⁴). There was a long rigmarole, too long to put down here fully.

¹ Galsworthy's play and the press of visitors give the date.
² Maisie Gibbon (née Daniels), a Londoner, married 'Reggie' Gibbon in 1904, when she was 21. Conrad dedicated *Victory* to them both.
³ They had two daughters.
⁴ Had the Gibbons been there when she made the disturbing appearance described in the letter of [28 April or 5 May]?

In short they are on the eve of starting a squabble over their girls.[1] She stayed a long time.

This is the first free moment I have for writing to you. And a pretty use I've made of it! I ought to have told you how really grateful I am for your friendship but I haven't left myself any space. Perceval's strength and your graciousness and the sincerity of both your natures which only a half hearted and half-witted being could fail to see, compose an atmosphere for your home full of charm and security.—

Since you have seen the Author's Club correspondence I send for yours *and* P's perusal the enclosed abject letter. I propose to answer that: *I consider the incident as forgotten and that I prefer to trust to some other opportunity of meeting Shackleton.*[2] I would like Perceval's opinion on that answer. Always, dear Maisie,

> your affectionate friend and
> servant
>
> J. Conrad

To Edward Garnett
Text MS Indiana; G. 232

> Aldington. Hythe
> Kent.
> 19 July '09

Dearest Edward.

It is a fact I had a most damnable go of gout which absolutely prevented me from getting the 8th instt of Rems ready in time. But it was neither more nor less serious than other attacks of the kind for the last 15 years. I suppose one of them will finally do for me. All the same I was vexed by that silly editorial note.[3] There was no earthly reason for any note and if he had to do it, *indisposition* was a quite strong enough word for all practical, editorial purposes.

Thanks my dear Edward for your inquiry. How is it with you? I haven't either the time or the pluck to travel up to town. Rumour of the ER having been sold has reached me lately.

[1] At the end of one of his forays to Aldington, Ford had asked Elsie Hueffer for a divorce (Mizener, p. 188). Their daughters were Katharine and Christina.

[2] Sir Ernest Henry Shackleton (1874–1922), the Antarctic explorer: he commanded the expedition of 1908–09, which came within 97 miles of the South Pole.

[3] This statement appeared on p. 824 of the *Review*'s July issue: 'We regret that owing to the serious illness of Mr. Joseph Conrad we are compelled to postpone the publication of the next instalment of his Reminiscences.'

Did you review anywhere Masefield's latest book?[1] If so I should like
to see what *You* had to say of it.

Jack's in London and has sent me his new play *The Eldest Son*. First
rate—quite. However You either have seen it or shall see it soon and a
good lot might be said about it.

Our dear love to you. Remember us affectionately to your wife. I hear
David is preparing his exam[2]—the best of luck to him!

<div style="text-align:center">Ever yours</div>

<div style="text-align:right">J. Conrad</div>

To Perceval Gibbon
Text MS Berg; Unpublished

<div style="text-align:right">Aldington, N^r Hythe
Kent
19 July 1909</div>

My dear Perceval.

I hope the day will never come when You will curse the moment you
set eyes on me. I really don't want to worry you indefinitely with my
affairs but your suggestion for clearing the financial position between P
and myself was so clever, business-clever—that I can't pretend even to
putting it aside. And as the situation as it is puts a sort of nightmare
strain on me I frankly ask you to test the feasibility of the scheme as soon
as you can without (of course) interfering with your occupations.

Whether it will give me a better position materially or not I don't
know. But it will be a mental and moral relief which certainly will ease
my working-strain and in so far at least is certain to affect me for the
better materially.

As we stand now I pay yearly (or am indebted by Pinker in the
amounts) £63 for insurance premiums—and about £100 for interest on
the floating debt.

I would much rather pay the £100 for premiums of the speculative
insurance under the scheme you have suggested as appearing to you
feasible, on purely business lines.

Something of the sort I did think of but more in the way of friendly

[1] John Masefield (1878–1967), the future Poet Laureate, sometimes came to Garnett's
Mont Blanc lunches. His new book was *Multitude and Solitude*. Despite his experiences
at sea, Masefield did not endear himself to Conrad: see Sherry, *Critical Heritage*,
pp. 141–2.

[2] The University of London matriculation, for which he was cramming at the London
Tutorial College.

service or of a publisher's spec.[1] But I did not see my way to ask anybody and as to approaching anyone connected with books and publishing I dared not make that more for fear of giving away Pinker's position[2]—you understand what I mean?

And truly I did not look upon the thing as having much chance till you showed it in the light of a purely insurance speculation quite legitimate and as far as I can see quite safe for the investor. Can you then take a cast of the lead and see what sort of bottom you will bring up.

The financial terms stand as follows.

I am in need of £2250 in hard cash for which I offer 3 policies of the Standard life totalling *£1600* and a fresh policy of say *£1800* to be taken out with one yearly premium paid in advance out of the loan.

The understanding being that the loan is to be used for paying off old liabilities.

My age is *52*

Of course this is a mere sketch of the transaction; the actual terms can be only fixed on the basis of actuarial tables.

Ever so many thanks

Ever Yours

J. Conrad

Love to Wife and Chicks.

To J. B. Pinker
Text MS Berg; Unpublished

[Aldington]
19 July 1909

Dear Pinker

I received on Sat. a note from Douglas to whom I had written a pretty strong letter the week before.

I enclose it here and beg you to destroy both D's letter and this note.

I need not tell you I am glad. My aim was to save him from getting in with certain people whom I will not specify with more precision. He came here[3] (encouraged to write *by me*) in utter ignorance of literary conditions, very touchy and very depressed, and generally liable to fall under influences which would have done him no good. If you would

[1] He had been fascinated by the fund-raising ability of insurance policies since at least 1885 (*Letters*, 1, pp. 14–15).
[2] Of having Conrad heavily in his debt. [3] To England, from Italy.

drop him a few friendly encouraging lines on receipt of his MS I would take it as a kindness on Your part to me. He's not conceited by any means. I want to *give him* a little conceit so as to keep his nose to the grindstone. He has any amount of really good stuff in him and he *will* work once he understands that there is some chance for him to earn a little money.

Is it true about McClure?[1]

Ever yours

J. Conrad.

I've been two days with Gibbon. Jack sent me his new play to read: *The Eldest Son.* First rate—quite. Perhaps you had better keep that secret for a time as I don't know whether he wants the news to leak out.

To R. D. Mackintosh

Text MS Jellard; Jellard

Aldington. N[r] Hythe
Kent.
25 July 1909

Dear D[r] Mackintosh.

Don't think you have been out of our minds. That would be impossible.

Now as to your great enterprise: I sleep, I eat, I don't work as much as I ought to, but the feeling of hopelessness is passing away. I take 6 tablets of Solurol[?][2] every day. The skin trouble which followed the attack of gout (as I expected) never attained to the virulence of the previous visitation. It ran its usual course as to the extent of surface affected and so on but feebly. It is as if the poison in the system were becoming languid.

I ran over to see the Salvators for a day and stayed two days. On the 6[th] of August we are going to Trosley[3] in force for three weeks. The news that you are coming down there during our sojourn has made us happy.

[1] McClure was in London, trying to win support for a peace movement to be led by J. P. Morgan and Elihu Root.

[2] 'Nucleotin/phosphoric acid', an extract from animal glands, chiefly the thymus, capable of dissolving uric acid and therefore indicated for gout: Martindale and Westcott, *Extra Pharmacopoeia* (14th ed., 1910), p. 831.

[3] The Gibbons ('the Salvators') had moved to Trottiscliffe, between East Malling and Wrotham. The village's name is usually pronounced–rather than written–'Trosley' (information from Mr. P. L. Harden, formerly of Maidstone).

We shall have a late talk or two. I am looking forward very much to our meeting.

Wife sends kindest regards.

Yours affectionately

J. Conrad

PS since the subject will be taboo over there I should like to know (if I may) how the metal affair progresses, before we meet.

To John Galsworthy
Text The Times, 13 August 1909, p. 4

Aldington, Kent
26 July 1909

My dear Galsworthy,[1]

—I have just received your letter.

You know my feelings as to the Censorship of Plays.[2] I have always looked upon it with indignation. It is an outrage upon the dignity and honesty of the calling. But whether a dramatic author is ever deterred from producing good work by the existence of the Censorship I cannot say. I am certain that he may be shamefully hindered, and that such a situation is intolerable; a disgrace to the tone, to the character of this country's civilization.

Ever yours,

J. Conrad

To John Galsworthy
Text MS Forbes; Unpublished

[Aldington]
30 July '09

Dearest Jack.

I suppose the formal "censorship" letter I wrote you 2 days ago was what you wanted.

I am at work but still not as I should be.

[1] Conrad wrote this letter for Galsworthy to submit to the Joint Committee of Lords and Commons on Censorship of Plays. When Galsworthy appeared before the committee on 12 August, he presented letters from James, Wells, Bennett, and Maurice Hewlett as well as the present text. The censor's most recent victims were two Shaw plays, *Blanco Posnet* and *Press Cuttings*.

[2] Cf. the attack on the censorship written for the *Daily Mail* in October 1907 (*Letters*, 3, pp. 493–5).

B arrived for his holidays bringing with him the cup for the 100 yards race a set of stamps for the best kick at the football and a very good report. Your namesake has grown very thin lately but his activity remains unimpaired. The only person he stands in awe of a little is his brother—but that I fear will wear off in a day or two.

We are going away for 3 weeks on Friday next, to *Trosley, West Malling Kent*. It is a village where P. Gibbon has taken a house lately. I want change, for this hole here is growing more odious to me every day; and Jessie deserves a little respite from cooking.

I'll try to run up to London from there—only one hour by rail.— Our best love to dear Ada and Yourself

Ever Yours

J. Conrad

To Ford Madox Ford
Text MS BL Ashley A470; J-A, 2, 101

[Aldington]
31 July 1909.

Dear Hueffer.

If you think I have discredited you and the Review—why then it must be even so. And as far as the Editor of the *ER* is concerned we will let it go at that—with the proviso that I don't want to hear anything more about it.

But as writing to a man with a fine sense of form and a complete understanding, for years, of the way in which my literary intentions work themselves out I wish to protest against the words—*Ragged condition.*

It is so little *ragged* to my feeling, and in point of literary fact, that in the book (if the book ever appears) the *whole* of the contribution to the *ER* as it stands now without the addition of a single word shall form the Part First.[1]

It expresses perfectly my purpose of treating the literary life and the sea-life on parallel lines with a running reference to my early years. It treats of the inception of my first book and of my first contact (psychologically and de facto) with the sea. It begins practically with the first words of appreciation of my writing I ever heard and ends with the first words ever addressed to me personally in the English tongue.[2]

[1] He wrote no more of it. [2] 'Look out there' and 'shove off – push hard'.

And actually the very phrase ending the 7ᵗʰ instalment is to my mind an excellent terminal,[1] a perfect pause carrying out the spirit of the work.

All this is not got up ad hoc. I have exposed this view in a letter written to certain publishers in America a fortnight ago.[2]

It is another instalment which would make the thing ragged. It would have to begin another period and another phase. On a dispassionate view I see it so clearly that nothing on earth would induce me to spoil the thing as it now stands by an irrelevant instalment. I will say no more except to add that my contributions were for a *person* not for an *editor*. The ER I hear is no longer your property and there is I believe another circumstance which for purely personal reason[s] (exceptionally personal I mean) make[s] me unwilling to contribute anything more to the *ER*.[3] This reason has of course nothing to do with You you understand. It is not a critical reason. A pure matter of feeling. If I have discredited the R, well I must bear the disgrace.

<div align="right">Yours</div>

<div align="right">J. Conrad</div>

To Stephen Reynolds
Text MS Berg; Unpublished

<div align="right">[Aldington]</div>
<div align="right">31 July 09[4]</div>

My dear Reynolds.

I am sorry to hear you are not writing—as you ought to be but are wasting the precious days in reviewing and such like. But the news you give of your health causes us a more serious concern.

I am *not* the man to keep either white or black books. You know on what point our correspondence got suspended. I wrote to you frankly on a matter of good feeling.[5] You answered me by a sort of lecture— and I remained silent on a disagreeable impression.

<div align="right">Yours</div>

<div align="right">J. Conrad</div>

[1] 'The Red Ensign, the symbolic, protecting warm bit of bunting flung wide upon the seas, and destined for so many years to be the only roof over my head.'
[2] The missing letter to Harper & Brothers of 21 July.
[3] Although he was a refugee, Soskice could not be forgiven his Russian origins.
[4] '09' is a hard reading, but the affinity with the letter of 7 August confirms it.
[5] See the letter tentatively dated [Spring 1909] p. 225.

To J. B. Pinker
Text MS Berg; Unpublished

[Aldington]
Wednesday. [4 August 1909]¹

Private & Conf[identi]al
Dear Pinker.

It's hardly necessary, I imagine, to tell you that it is the first I hear of the important piece of news you give me in your letter just to hand.² What I heard was that he sold the *copyright* of *everything* appearing in the Review to Col. Harvey. An absurdity I took no notice of.

The last rumour about myself reaching *my* knowledge (some 5 weeks ago) was that F[ord] H[ueffer] was going about saying he has "called Conrad out". The basis of it is a letter I received from him about beginning of May containing 1° An apology which I did not demand. 2° a sort of hint of a challenge being possible. Why? God only knows. 3° A statement that he was on the eve of com[m]itting suicide. 4° An invitation in the most pressing terms to come and stay with him at his flat that very night.

I showed this strange document to two sensible men and that's all. I have also told the story leading up to it to Jack Galsworthy and P. Gibbon.

I've heard also, since, that I am made responsible for the failure of a negotiation with McClure for the sale of the ER which was he affirms nearly concluded for £2000.—The ground for that phantasy seems to be the fact that I refused to see Miss Cather here. He tried to ram that visit down my throat and charged me with ingratitude for all his efforts to serve me. I told him in effect to go to the devil and warned him that if I heard any more of that nonsense I would take steps to make it perfectly clear that his interference (whatever it was) in my affairs is an unauthorised and impertinent assumption on his part, completely without my knowledge and highly distasteful to me.

That shut him up as far as I am concerned; but of course no one can stop him telling all these stories. His conduct is *impossible*. All this will end badly. He's a megalomaniac who imagines he is managing the universe and that everybody treats him with the blackest ingratitude. A fierce and exasperated vanity is hidden under his calm manner which

¹ Received 'August': Ford's behaviour gives the year. The question about Douglas's MS and the reference to Elsie Hueffer's being 'here' (i.e. Aldington) point to the 4th, before the Conrads had left for Trottiscliffe.
² Presumably another rumour about Ford's dealings with the *English Review*. The rest of the paragraph was added in the margin.

misleads people. Writing to you *in confidence* I do not hesitate to say that there are cases, not quite as bad, under medical treatment.[1] This is not a joke. I have suffered too much mental worry and moral discomfort to joke upon the matter.

Mrs Hueffer was here the day before yesterday. She upset my wife and spoiled my day for me completely. But I can't go into that part of the story which anyhow would not interest you.

In short he has quarrelled with every decent friend he had; has nearly made mischief between me and some of my best friends, and is, from all accounts, having a most miserable time himself—because he has his lucid intervals. Generally he's behaving like a spoilt kid—and not a nice kid either. I am told that Violet Hunt is mothering him just now and that a Russian Jew refugee (his brother-in-law)[2] has found some unknown person to buy the Review—or something of the kind. At any rate it is to go on apparently with him for Editor. I haven't seen him for quite two months and had only two wires from him in that time, which I answered negatively.

<div align="center">Yours ever</div>

<div align="right">J. Conrad</div>

PS Thank you for writing to Douglas. I conclude you have his *MS*.[3] By the bye; I don't intend to take notice of the news you send me, to Hueffer. At first I thought of asking him peremptorily to contradict that tale. But I am unwilling to open a correspondence with him unless you wish me to.

[1] Mizener writes of Ford at this period: 'There is little doubt that he was mentally a wreck' (p. 192).

[2] In 1881, David Vladimir Soskice, a doctoral candidate in law at the University of Kiev, witnessed a pogrom that moved him to join a revolutionary group; he was imprisoned several times and took refuge in England in 1893. There he married Ford's sister Juliet Hueffer. Twice between 1906 and 1909 he returned to Russia as St Petersburg correspondent for the *Tribune*; as correspondent for the *Manchester Guardian* he had also lived in Geneva, another point of contact with the geography of *Under Western Eyes*. Both Ford and Conrad were intolerant of his politics, his Russian background, and his Jewishness. Carabine (*UWE*) points out the significance of Soskice's article about the fantastic double dealings of Yevno Azeff, Tsarist spy and agent provocateur, who was involved in the killing of de Plehve: *English Review*, March 1909, 816–32.

[3] *Siren Land*.

To John Galsworthy
Text MS Forbes; Unpublished

6 Aug[st] 1909.
after tomorrow
Trosley
West Malling Kent

Dearest Jack

We do ardently hope that the cure will do Ada all possible good.[1] But was this treatment undertaken because of any special and recent visitation of the disease? You did not contemplate anything of that kind when you were here.

As You say—it'll be interesting to see what will come of the Censorship Commission. Shaw's evidence was somewhat imbecile—in the classical meaning of the word. I've just read through G. Barker's which is quite another thing.[2]

We shall be back end Aug. Poor Jessie is very crippled. There is no doubt that knee is getting worse. I am watching it with concern and dread.

For the rest I am recovering my tone and feel the power of work returning to me. I intend to work in Trosley as hard as I can; Jessie will get a rest, Borys will go for walks with Gibbon, and Jackolo, I suppose will carry on as usual. The other day he poured a jugful of water into a ten pound bag of flour. The mess was truly awe-inspiring—not to speak of the expense. Later on we found him swimming his shoes in Borys' sponge-bath. He remarked they made lovely boats. Afterwards we lost him altogether for ever so long. Finally he was discovered under Nellie's bed.[3] Being poked at with sticks he only laughed and finally we had to move the bed to get hold of him.

Such are our main diversions.—

With our best wishes for the success of the cure and dear love to you both

Ever yours

J Conrad.

[1] The Galsworthys had gone to Ilkley, Yorkshire, where she was treated for rheumatism (Dupré, p. 165).

[2] Shaw tried to present a 55-page pamphlet. When the Parliamentary Committee balked at accepting it, he wrote a facetious letter to *The Times* (2 August, p. 6) announcing that the pamphlet would soon become a rarity. Granville-Barker argued that the censorship had checked the growth of original drama (*The Times*, 6 August, p. 7).

[3] Nellie Lyons, their maid.

To Stephen Reynolds
Text MS Berg; Unpublished

[Aldington]
7th Aug 1909

Dear Reynolds.

When you have knocked about a little longer you'll discover that impressions *do* wear out, wear off—at any rate with people who are not mere bundle[s] of nerves. It's deeper things, sentiments, judgements that remain. I trust we shall meet as friendly as ever, notwithstanding my outspokenness when my feelings were touched. I never supposed you *wished* to lecture me in this special case tho' I don't see why You should not if occasion offered. I kept quiet for a while; but in that I followed only the traditional wisdom of mankind.

I hope you will send Jessie a copy of your book,[1] and in the very same spirit of good will and friendliness as when you formed the intention. Nothing will please me more.

You are right. Things will be what they must be without life and work. These things are "written" if not exactly on our foreheads for the fools to scoff at, then deep down somewhere on the bed-rock of our nature. All the same one may be anxious and form wishes—and speak idle words.

We are going away for three weeks or so. Starting in a couple of hours in fact, and I write this with an infamous pen everything being packed and put away. I'll drop you a line soon—nothing much for I haven't much heart for any sort of correspondence.

All our loves to you

Yours

J. Conrad

[1] *The Holy Mountain* was to appear in book form in September.

To J. B. Pinker
Text MS Berg; Unpublished

Trosley.
West Malling
Kent.
Monday. [9 August 1909][1]

Dear Pinker.

I send you on Cumberland's reminding letter[2] which only reached me last Saturday late.

Please send me the typed pages here to the *address as above* we shall stay here 3 weeks. Gibbon has given me access to his Russian notes[3] which is just what I wanted to give me the tone of the last part. He would like to see the novel from the beginning and if it isn't too much trouble I would be glad if you would send the clean Copy by registered post.

Yours always

J Conrad

PS You *have* received Douglas' MS. haven't you? Your letter before last does not say so definitely. Many thanks for the pads received safely last Friday.

To H.-D. Davray
Text MS Yale; *L. fr.* 98

27 Août [1909][4]
Aldington
N^r Hythe, Kent

Cher ami.

Oui. J'ai reçu Votre lettre; ma reponse j'ai laissé sur la table au moment de notre départ pour un bout des vacances. La bonne femme jure par tous les dieux qu'elle l'a mise a la poste. Enfin.

Je vous remercie tres cher de vos efforts pour me presenter au public Français. Votre succès avec le *Temps* me cause une vraie satisfaction. Mais deux ans c'est bien long.[5] Ce n'est pas que je suis impatient, mais enfin quand on a passé la cinquantaine! . . .

[1] Received '8/09': probably the first Monday in Trottiscliffe.
[2] Charles Henry Cumberland, of Darley and Cumberland, was a Bloomsbury solicitor; Robert Garnett was one of his partners.
[3] Gibbon had been to St Petersburg on an assignment for the *Standard*.
[4] The only August in Aldington.
[5] *Le Temps* began publishing Davray's translation of *The Secret Agent* in 1910.

Pour[r]ai-je voir le type-script? J'avoue de bruler d'envie de connaitre le texte Français. Je sais les merveilles que vous avez fait avec la prose de Wells.[1] Faites moi ce petit grand plaisir. Voulez vous?
Votre bourgade a l'air tout a fait charmant[e].
Nos amitiés bien sincères a Mme Davray

<div align="right">Le votre très affectueusement

J Conrad.</div>

Translation

Dear friend,

Yes, I have had your letter; I left my reply on the table just when we were leaving for a short holiday. My good wife swears by all the gods that she posted it. So much for that.

I thank you, dear fellow, for your efforts to introduce me to the French public. Your success with the *Temps* gives me real satisfaction. But two years is a long time. I am not impatient, but after all when one has entered one's fifties! . . .

May I see the typescript? I must admit that I'm longing to acquaint myself with the French text. I know the marvels that you have done with Wells's prose. Grant me this great little pleasure. Will you?

Your village has an altogether charming atmosphere.

Our sincere regards to Mme Davray.

<div align="right">Very affectionately yours,

J. Conrad.</div>

[1] In translations of, for example, *The Island of Dr Moreau* (1901), *When the Sleeper Wakes* (1905), and *A Modern Utopia* (1907).

To J. B. Pinker

Text MS Berg; Unpublished

[letterhead: Aldington]¹

Thursday. [2 September 1909]²

Dear Pinker.

Please send weekly letter *here*.

I've heard (at 3ᵈ hand it is true) that someone wishing to purchase the vol of *Youth* could not obtain it as *out of print* and was informed that it was *not* to be reprinted.³ It sounds unlikely. Could you find out if perchance it is true.

Yours

J Conrad.

To John Galsworthy

Text MS Forbes; Unpublished

7 Sep. 1909.

Aldington

Dearest Jack

We've been home since the 24ᵗʰ I think and have expected to hear from you. But I suppose you are now in Devonshire. However I am sending this note (pardon this scrap of paper) to London.

Our stay in Trosley was not a great success. Jackolo had a sort of mild heat-stroke—a couple of days' fever. Of course we had to have a doctor. As the place generally did not seem to suit him we cut our visit short by a whole week and have all felt better since our return to the windy, bracing Aldington.

I havent done very well this last month. In Trosley I could not write. Here the house is impossible. But what must be must be. The locality is all right; but in these rooms I can't have that absolute quiet, complete silence, without which it seems that now I cannot work to any serious purpose.⁴ There is a charming farmhouse to let within a mile or so—but its no use thinking about it. If I could only write at night when

¹ The first use of an Aldington letterhead. In MS, Conrad has deleted his name and added S[outh] E[eastern] R[ailway] after SMEETH.

² Received '9/09': the closest September Thursday to the return from Trottiscliffe.

³ In 1913, George Blackwood proposed a shilling edition (Blackburn, pp. 193–5).

⁴ The squealing of stuck pigs in his landlord's slaughterhouse was particularly distressing (Borys Conrad, *My Father*, p. 60).

everybody is asleep I would not care. I've tried all last week. It's no go. The time of all night sittings is gone for me. Of course I can *sit*—but there's nothing to show for it.

I promise not to worry you any more about the matter but I must ask you this one time more whether the pension matter—do you think—has been solved one way or another. There may have been some public announcement of the grants in the papers; but I don't see the papers regularly; I might have missed it. Could you find out for me, not that I expect success but to get rid of the suspense.

Do let us know how Ada's health is. It's a fatal year for that sort of complaint.[1]

Our dear love

<div align="center">Ever yours</div>

<div align="right">J. Conrad</div>

PS I hear Ford is enraged with me for not giving him more of my Rem[iniscence]s. He says I made a fool of him. Don't see how that can be. A Russian has got hold of the *ER*[2] and I can not contribute any more.

To Perceval Gibbon

Text MS Berg; Unpublished

<div align="right">[Aldington]
Saturday [11 or 18 September?
1909][3]</div>

Dear Perceval.

Your remark that "surely there must be a time of the day when I *don't* write Razumov" has cut me to the quick. You must accustom yourself to show the most extended mercy to my sins as correspondent. There is *no* moment in the day when I don't hate the sight of pen and ink. And this hate at times overcomes all my other more worthy feelings such as those of love, friendship politeness and even decency.

Their Serene Excellencies our Wives being in active correspondence I contented myself by participating in spirit, with the alternatives of hope

[1] The soggy weather had its predictable effect on sufferers from rheumatism.

[2] Under the interim agreement, Soskice was still business manager.

[3] The Saturday before Captain Marris sailed. The *Prinzessin Amalia* does not appear in the relevant records, but the *Prinzessin Alice* (Norddeutscher Lloyd) left Southampton for India, the Straits Settlements, and China on Tuesday, 14 September; on the 21st, the Dutch *Koningin Wilhelmina* left for Batavia.

and fear borne with becoming stoicism. Their SS. EE's having failed in bringing about a meeting I disguised my sorrow in silence. I wish you distinc[t]ly to understand that the silence was mournful. But the swearing directed at old Raz was vivid as the lightning of hurricanes. Enough!

Joking apart my dear fellow I felt a good bit cut up, tho' I understand quite the force of circumstances. Better luck next time—And let it be soon! And for the rest may the disappointment which I feel be compensated by the knowledge of a successful spurt of work in your blessed workshop.

Mine has turned out nothing to boast of. Still the buzz and hum and sweating goes on—for next to nothing.

I quite understand your very lucid exposé of the financial considerations.[1] I always felt that such would be the difficulty. I am not disappointed. As I've said this is a case for a friendly millionaire (an animal introuvable in my world) to interfere for the easing of the stress. Failing this I must pound along till death does ensue. I am quite ready to pound on night and day if I only could.

You know Marris—the man of the East who wrote the letter I read to you?[2] Well he is going back to his Malay princess wife and his kid, right away. I have asked him to come on Monday here for the day. On Tuesday he joins the Prinzess Amalia in S'hampton for the Straits. If you had that motorbike I would ask you to dash down here for a 3 cornered yarn. Eh?

Love to the Lady Maisie and the two small princesses—may their shadows lengthen every day!

<div align="center">Ever yours</div>

<div align="right">J. Conrad</div>

PS Thanks for details as to P. the nourisher of geniuses.[3] Ford has been telling other people that he makes 1000 a year. (one thousand) I shall run up for lunch with Galsworthy on Tuesday returning same day.

[1] In the insurance scheme mooted on 19 July?
[2] Carl Murrell Marris (born 1875) had written to Conrad on 18 July (MS Yale) wondering if they might meet. Captain Marris, a resident of Penang and other places in the Straits Settlements for 21 years, was visiting England in the hope of a cure for partial paralysis (*Joseph Conrad and His Circle*, p. 137). The meeting stirred up Conrad's memories of the Malay Archipelago. In gratitude, Conrad dedicated *'Twixt Land and Sea* to him.
[3] Pinker was Gibbon's agent too.

To Stephen Reynolds
Text MS Berg; Unpublished

[Aldington]

Friday. [September? 1909]¹

Dear Stephen

Jessie will be writing to you presently to morrow, I think, but I am acting independently after reading and dipping into and re-dipping into your blue volume.² Fact is I've just banged it down this minute—and I shan't look into it now for some weeks.

You are all right—that's clear, rather more clear to me than it was before. It is (apart from more substantial qualities) a very fine charge à fond, in cavalry-man's language. And that means dash, brilliancy, courage—and good riding. I use this image because the language for talking about books has grown abominably stale to my senses; it—not to put (in the words of the immortal Snagsby) too fine a point on it³—stinks in my nostrils.

So much about the book in *se* its outward spirit, its open declaration. Now for its inside, its art, the indissolubly joined intention and expression.

As to that, one's appreciation can be only expressed critically. Anything else can be only verbiage. From that point of view it seems to me that the tempo of the whole is too fast. An effect of skimming is perceptible. I have to defend myself from the absurd notion that the whole thing has been dashed off in an hour and a half.⁴ Swiftness is a great qualility*; but remember my dear boy that twenty lightning blows produce not so great an effect than a deliberately delivered stab—and for all the rapidity displayed they take more time. There is more than one kind of swiftness. Your effect is not enhanced because all Your blows (with a most admirable exactitude) land on the nose of your subject. The skill (or the instinct for straight hitting) is wonderful. The reader is amused—but when the tale is told he is not silenced, as he should be, into some emotional state or other. No. He mutters: Dam' clever that!

You will get both praise and abuse. I am giving you the truth which is in me. I don't suppose you will take it for disparagement. I show my

¹ *The Holy Mountain* appeared, in blue boards, during the week of September 14.
² A novel satirising religious posturing and small-town ways.
³ A favourite phrase of the modest Mr Snagsby, a lawyer's stationer in Dickens's *Bleak House*.
⁴ In stark contrast to Conrad's work in progress.

regard, my high regard in the best way I know. If you could get a clear idea how I hate writing you would understand what these few pages mean for me. These pages which you are at liberty to toss aside with the remark that I obviously don't understand what the book is. But as a matter of fact I have said to myself:—do not let us forget that this is *Satyre*! Well—even with that in my mind I must let my words stand.

Well—enough for this time. I am no end glad to hear of the amount of work done. On the motorboat subject I feel like you absolutely.[1] What must be must be. I conclude your health has been tolerable. Mine has been good as far as gout goes but I *can't* simply can't concentrate myself on my work for more than an hour at a time and that with positive pain. Afterwards comes despair. What between pain and despair it takes me a day to write 4 pages. But I don't even average that. It's a great trouble. Don't talk about it at large please. It may improve—it must! Meantime let it be entre nous.

(to be continued soon)

Ever Yours

J Conrad.

To J. B. Pinker
Text MS Berg; Unpublished

[Aldington]
Tuesday [5 October 1909][2]

My dear Pinker

I beg You most earnestly to exert your diplomacy to induce those people (whoever they are) to accept the book which is now all but done.[3] Surely my reputation may count for something in such a transaction. I am not likely to put in anything improper or otherwise unprintable. My view is that even if you had to give in somewhat on the terms it would be

[1] The Sidmouth fishermen had refused a benefactor's offer of a motorboat. Reynolds was determined to get one anyway and show its value (Reynolds to J. F. Drew, 3 September, Wright, p. 125).

[2] Received '10/09'. On 5 October, Conrad sent Pinker two telegrams (Berg). At 11:44 a.m. he wired: 'Impossible this week Will you write'; at 3:40 p.m. he wired: 'Four fifths ready except shortening for serial purposes which can be done as required and a matter of three weeks writing fully tonight.' This must be the promised letter.

[3] An American magazine had asked Pinker if Conrad had a serial novel ready. According to Keith Carabine's chronology, Conrad had sent in 1,013 pages of what became a 1,351 page MS, finished in January.

worth doing still. As I said in the wire the delivery of the end would be [a] matter of three weeks. The preparation for serial form will not take me more than 3 days being merely excision of analysis and some shortening of conversations. I am not hinting at anything outrageous. Lord Jim was only half written when the printing as a serial commenced.[1] With the End of the Tether it was worse, as, practically, all the MS was burnt on the very day the first instalment appeared.[2]

Try to work on this suggestion putting aside (for both our sakes) every feeling of annoyance with me because I am not ready yet. I assure you that in these 20 months there has* not been 14 working ones. But that I really believe is all over thanks to Mac[k]intosh. Last October coming as a visitor he became concerned at my state but said nothing then. Then in Febr^y last coming to move me in his car from Someries he thought my general state so much worse that he spoke to Gibbon very seriously. He declared at the same time that he would be glad if I allowed him to take me in hand for a radical cure. He seems to have done it; but meantime I have had an awful time during May, June, and July, what between disease, drugs and worry I wonder I did not go out of my mind. But it is certain that I feel now as far as bodily health is concerned as I haven't felt for years at this time of the year. The next 12 months shall see some work done—I hope.

I will say no more just now as I wish to catch the post.

<div style="text-align:right">Yours always</div>

<div style="text-align:right">J Conrad.</div>

To J. B. Pinker

Text MS Berg; J-A, 2, 102

<div style="text-align:right">[letterhead: Aldington]</div>
<div style="text-align:right">Monday. [11 October 1909][3]</div>

My dear Pinker

Thanks for your letter of Wednesday. I completely agree with your view of the transaction. Better show the whole book. Henley took the Narcissus on the strength of 3 chapters—but he was Henley—a man not

[1] When the serial began in the October 1899 *Blackwood's*, Conrad had written not much more than 20,000 words: about half the story as he then envisaged it – and about one eighth of its final length.

[2] The lamp indeed exploded on 23 June 1902, just as the July number of *Blackwood's* came out. For the extent of the damage, see *Letters*, 2, pp. 413, 428–31.

[3] Received '10/09': before the note about insurance of the 17th and probably after the letter of the 5th. A note in another hand reads '*30 pp. M.S. sent*': this would mean ff. 1,014–45 of 'Razumov'; the typed copy of these pages is dated 16 October.

a cheese-monger or something nearly equivalent; and the New Review is now an embodied phase in the history of English letters.[1]

As to the kind people who inquire whether I have given up writing, you may tell them that in the last 20 months C has written nearly 160 thousand words—each one of which has some meaning—and under such mental and physical conditions as would have made 9 out of ten of them break down time after time. This is not, I admit, what the situation requires—but we shall feed it up with "production" presently.—Never fear.

I shall write to the Ins*ce* Agents for the policy a month if possible 3 if not.[2] Mac[k]intosh will give me the necessary attestation of usual health.

The history of my contribution to the Daily Mail is this: Reply prepaid wire asking me if I would write 1200 wds on Waratah case. My reply yes twelve guineas. A wire accepting terms. I wrote the column that night *after* I felt I could do no more then with the novel.[3] Nothing was laid aside for it. And if it had been I would not have cared—not a damn. I sent on the cheque to the boy's schoolmaster and anyhow it's not enough to cover the quarter. I want £5.12.8 more. You might send it to me. The pension business seems fallen through this year tho' Gosse[4] wrote to Jack in Sept*er* that it was receiving the best consideration. I was fool enough to reckon on it to a certain extent.

I shall sit pretty well night and day now till end Raz. It's not so much of a figure of speech as you think. I am not like F[*ord*] M[*adox*] H[*ueffer*] who can dash off 4000 words in 2 hours or there abouts. Who are the people and is the offer good. Surely it is not necessary to keep me in the dark. A magazine is not a secret society.

Salvator[5] might have told you I had a visit from a man out of the Malay Seas. It was like the raising of a lot of dead—dead to me, because most of them live out there and even read my books and wonder who

1 See the letter of 2 March.
2 The policy would insure the novel's completion against sickness or death.
3 Conrad's article 'The Silence of the Sea' appeared on 18 September in the *Daily Mail*, the newspaper that had published his 'Overdue', 'Missing', and 'Stranded' five years before. The fate of the S.S. *Waratah*, overdue on the short voyage from Durban to Cape Town since 27 July, was much discussed in the press. For text and commentary see Paul Kirschner, 'Conrad: An Uncollected Article', *Notes and Queries*, 213 (1968), 292–4.
4 Edmund Gosse (1849–1928), the literary historian, biographer, and auto-biographer, had already helped Conrad with his grants from the Royal Literary Fund in 1902 and the Civil List in 1905.
5 Perceval Gibbon.

[the] devil has been around taking notes. My visitor told me that Joshua Lingard made the guess; it must have been the fellow who was mate in the *Vidar* with Craig.[1] That's me right enough. And the best of it is that all these men of 22 years ago feel kindly to the chronicler of their lives and adventures. They shall have some more of the stories they like.[2] Well I must stop

<div align="center">Yours</div>

<div align="right">J Conrad.</div>

To Harper & Brothers
Text MS Colgate; *Listy* 300; Original unpublished

<div align="right">[letterhead: Aldington]
17 oct 1909.</div>

Gentlemen.

I wrote you in July last a letter containing a distinct proposal[3] couched in such friendly terms as an author of high literary standing would use when addressing a publishing firm which has published three of his books in succession.[4]

Such a letter, as a matter of mere business and also, I won't say, courtesy, but common decency should have been answered at once in one way or another . I don't know how to qualify, even to myself, the fact that it has remained unacknowledged up to date. I am willing to take it as an unbusiness-like oversight. But in order to do away with all doubt I have the honour to lay now before you a formal request for an answer which is *my due* by every rule of civilized intercourse.

Be good enough to understand distinctly that I no longer care in what sense your answer is worded, nor yet whether you even publish or not another line of my writing; but from a regard for the dignity of English Letters in which I occupy a recognised position, I will not let pass what looks like a deliberate slight without calling upon You for such an

[1] Joshua Lingard (c. 1857–1920), Jim's brother, was an officer on the King of Siam's yacht when Conrad knew him in Singapore (letter to W. G. St Clair, 31 March 1917). At that time, Conrad was first mate of the *Vidar*, Captain James Craig, master. For the Lingard family in Conrad's fiction, see Norman Sherry, *Conrad's Eastern World*.

[2] Two months later, he wrote 'The Secret Sharer'. 'Freya of the Seven Isles', written in 1910, grew from one of Captain Marris's anecdotes.

[3] He wrote on the 21st, but see also the letter to Galsworthy of 13 July.

[4] *Nostromo* in London and New York, *The Mirror of the Sea* and *The Secret Agent* in New York.

expression of regret as the least spark of good feeling may prompt You to offer. Failing which I shall leave the merits of the case, with perfect confidence, to the appreciation of all cultured and fair-minded men in the New World and the Old.

Meantime, Gentlemen, I remain, with all the consideration to which you are entitled,

Yours obed^{tly}

J. Conrad.

Messrs: Harper & Brothers
New York.

To J. B. Pinker
Text MS Berg; Unpublished

[Aldington]
Sunday [17 October 1909][1]

Dear Pinker.

Macintoshe's* letter of *usual health* will reach them to morrow. The premium will have to be deducted from next year's allow^{ce}. I ask you to make it so because I have yet Norman & Stacey on my back[2] and some other things which won't be there next year. I instructed H[ill] & C[oles] to make the policy out in your name.

Yours

J. C.

[1] Written on a letter dated 16 October 1909 from the insurance agents Hinton Hill & Coles, Ltd.
[2] For final payments on furniture for Someries.

To John Galsworthy

Text MS Forbes; Unpublished

[Aldington]

Tuesday. [19 October 1909]¹

Dearest Jack.

P advised me a week ago that some Am: Mag is nibbling at a long serial from me if I could get the thing ready in 3 weeks. I am now desperately trying but I feel it is not to be done. However I am sitting night and day and shall sit on till the end whatever the end is.

I snatch a ½ hour before going to bed to tell you I was extremely glad to get your letter. Apart from that there is not much to say; and indeed I feel too tired by a clear 14 hours of writing to be able to put it into decent phrases if there *was* anything to say. It's delightful to hear you have the 4 act play finished.² Send it on—do! And when you drop a line again don't forget to say how is Ada.*

Yes my dear Jack. Let me hear from you as often as you can. I want that to keep me up. No voices reach me here and even if they did yours, as you know, is a special one.

It seems there should be a lot to tell you always. And behold I feel too stupid to speak. But there is always the weather! We have been drowned with four days' rain here. To day there was some sun and Jessie trundled me out in the governess car³ for an hour or so. Got out and walked a couple of miles by the wheel. This is the only way I can have a walk with her. On the high road, in Smeeth a man called Holland who has been all over Africa⁴ and has now bought a house within 2 miles of us wanted to drag us in to tea. He's a nice fellow specially nice—but I felt much more ready for a decoction of hemlock than a brew of tea.

I'll try to get Borys here for the 1/2 term—a couple of days. It will do *me* good and him no harm. Jackolo declares he is going to be a farmer and evidently thinking sheep stealing an agricultural operation proposes to set himself up by "taking away Hooker's ba-lambs."⁵ That

¹ Galsworthy finished 'the rough' of a four-act play c. 29 September (Marrot, p. 249), and Conrad committed himself to a speedy end to his novel early in October. Although at least two weeks after Pinker relayed the magazine's offer, 19 October fits the description of a fine Tuesday after four wet days better than the three Tuesdays preceding.

² *Justice.* ³ A small, easily-driven cart which could be hauled by a single pony.

⁴ The Hon. Michael James Holland (1870–1956).

⁵ They belonged to Edwin Hooker of Pattison and Bank House farms.

fellow will make his way yet. I am only sorry I won't be there to see it for it's bound to be an exciting career to watch.

Our very dear love to you both

Ever your

J. Conrad

To Robert d'Humières
Text MS Vaugelas; Guérin

[letterhead: Aldington]
29 Oct 1909.

Cher Monsieur.

Je vous remercie de Votre bonne et amicale lettre contenant le cheque pour frcs *832.50*[1] dont Vous voudrez bien considerer ceci comme un reçu en forme.

Quand* aux coupures pratiquées dans le texte voici ce que j'en pense: je pense que d'avoir fait accepter le bon Nègre par le Correspondant est déjà un joli succès. Et certes j'en veux donner tout le crédit possible a M Lamy[2] mais j'en conçois la plus vive admiration pour le talent de M. Robert d'Humières. Je me dis: il a du y mettre du sien, beaucoup du sien pour faire passer ce cable par le trou de cette aiguille. Et puis cher monsieur et collaborateur (car le *Negre* en français e[s]t bien notre oeuvre commune) un public qui vous montre le poing est en cela-même respectacle*. Auriez vous préferé d'être lu par des douairières completement paralysées et quasi-mortes. Je serais surpris de Vous l'entendre dire. Quand* a moi je partage Votre indignation mais c'est surtout au sujet de *Votre* travail mutilé que je m'indigne. Mais voilà. La revue en s'excusant nous dit en effet:—"Que voulez vous? Il faut vivre"—et la reponse classique: "Je n'en vois pas la necessité"[3] serait mal venue puisque le cheque est là.

Vous m'avez fait longuement sourire par Votre allusion aux massacres du Septembre.[4] Quelques illusions qu'un écrivain se fasse sur la puissance de son oeuvre l'idée ne me serait jamais venue que l'histoire de James Wait fût capable d'évoquer les images de la Terreur dans les

[1] About £33 in the currency of the day: payment for the serialised *Nigger*.
[2] The editor.
[3] Originally a reply to the plea 'Il faut que je vive': Voltaire, *Alzire*, Discours préliminaire; the plea is echoed by a poor satirist in Rousseau's *Emile*, Chapter 3.
[4] The slaughter of royalists, real or alleged, in the streets and prisons of Paris, September 1792.

âmes timorées des lecteurs du Correspondant.[1] Ce serait a proprement parler un miracle d'art. Mais je veux bien y croire et j'en conçois quelque orgueuil quoique a fond et par nature je ne suis guère revolutionnaire. J'aime même assez les douairières, que, du reste, je ne pratique pas et dont je me fais une conception plutôt idéale.

Vous me faisez* le plus grand plaisir en m'envoyant les épreuves du livre et je vous remercie de cette bonne intention. Je me permets de joindre a cette lettre un exemplaire de la préface que j'ai écrit* dans le temps pour le Négre. Henley la fit paraître dans la New Review a la fin, comme note de l'auteur; mais elle n'a pas été imprimée autrement car comme vous le savez le roman fût publié en volume sans préface.[2] Qu'en pensez vous pour l'édition française? Mais mon objet en vous envoyant ceci est de completer en quelque sorte l'exemplaire du Nègre que vous avez, sans doute, par la possession de cette pièce qui appartient a l'histoire de cet ouvrage.

<div align="right">

A Vous bien cordialement

J. Conrad

</div>

Nous ne pourrons pas venir dans le midi cette année. Merci de votre invitation de vous voir chez vous. Je regrette bien vivement de ne pouvoir pas l'accepter. Disons que c'est partie remise—car il faut toujours garder l'ésperance

Translation

Dear Sir,

Thank you for your kind and friendly letter containing the cheque for 832.50 francs: please consider this as a formal receipt.

As to the cuts in the text, this is what I think: having the *Nigger* accepted by the *Correspondant* is already quite a coup. Indeed I'd like to give all possible credit to M. Lamy, but what's most admirable is the talent of Monsieur Robert d'Humières. As I tell myself: you have had to apply yourself, a great part of yourself, to get this cable through the eye of this needle. Besides, dear Sir and collaborator (for the French *Nigger*

[1] Alarmed not so much by Wait as by Donkin and his levelling talk?

[2] Conrad had the Preface reprinted as a pamphlet in 1902, but its first appearance between boards was in the 1914 Doubleday, Page 'Deep Sea' edition.

is really our joint effort), a public that shakes its fists at you is a public worth respecting. Would you rather have been read by dowagers, completely paralysed and virtually dead? I'd be surprised to hear you say so. I share your indignation, but I'm indignant above all about *your* mutilated work. But there you are. In making excuses for itself, the magazine as good as says: 'What do you expect? One has to live'—and the classic retort: 'I don't see the necessity' would be open to censure because the cheque has come.

Your allusion to the September massacres made me smile for a long time. Whatever the illusions that a writer might have about the power of his work, it would never have occurred to me that the story of James Wait might be capable of evoking images of the Terror in the timorous souls of the *Correspondant*'s readers. Properly speaking, it would be an artistic miracle. But I would like to believe it, and it makes me rather proud although at bottom, and by nature, I am hardly a revolutionary. I am even fond of dowagers, a group, anyway, that I don't frequent and of which I have formed a somewhat idealised picture.

In sending me the proofs of the book, you do me the greatest of pleasures, and I thank you for this kind thought. I venture to enclose with this letter a copy of the preface that I wrote at the time for *The Nigger*. Henley published it in the *New Review* at the end of the serial, as an author's note; but it has not otherwise been printed, for as you know the book was issued without a preface. What do you think of it for the French edition? But my purpose in sending it to you is to complete, after a fashion, your copy of *The Nigger*, with this piece which belongs to the work's history.

<div align="center">Very cordially yours,</div>

<div align="right">J. Conrad</div>

We can't come to the South of France this year. Thank you for the invitation to visit. I am acutely sorry to have to turn it down. Let's call this a pleasure deferred—since one should always hope.

To Harper & Brothers

Text MS Colgate; Unpublished

[letterhead: Aldington]
Oct 31 1909.

Messrs: Harper & Brothers
New York

Dear Sir.

I am very sorry to hear of Col. Harvey's serious accident.[1] Will you have the kindness to transmit to your President the expression of my sincere concern and my heartiest wishes for his complete recovery.

In acknowledging your cable message to the fullest extent and in the same spirit in which it was sent, I consider the incident as completely closed both personally and as to its subject matter. It is only to mark the better my sense of the frankness of your proceeding that I consent, in deference to your request, to re-open that last.

My letter, then, of the 21[st] July (for which I hold a registration receipt) contained the following points:—

1[st]. Stating that I was attending *personally* to the disposal of my Reminiscences (and not through my agent *or any other person whatever*).

2[d]. Expressing the hope that when ready for publication the book would have the advantage in the U.S. of your distinguished imprint.[2]

3[d]. With a view to the above, inquiring whether you would be disposed to use serially in any one of your periodical publications the portion which had appeared on this side in the English Review (about 35000 words) for the sum of eighty pounds sterling payable on acceptance; that portion forming a complete whole in itself, telling the story of the inception of my first book and of my first contact with the sea.

4[th]. On account of certain circumstances, asking you for the favour of a specific answer at your *earliest convenience.*—

(one of the circumstances, and the principal, was, that M[r] Bliss Carman having asked me for a contribution to the Gent: Mag: just about that time,[3] I wished, in case of Your declining, to offer him the use of that material.)

An informal PS to the above letter touched upon the probable time of publishing in vol: form (70–80 thou: words); suggested title (The Leaves & The Years: A Personal Record by J.C.); explained the peculiarity of the form I contemplate (the recording *together* of the literary life and the

[1] He had been in a car crash but was now on the mend. [2] As it did, in 1912.
[3] See the letters to Galsworthy, 13 July, and Pinker [15 December].

sea life, etc, etc); expressed the confident hope that the novelty of form, in such an intimate piece of writing, would not be found unacceptable by the American public.

I am, dear Sirs,

faithfully yours

J. Conrad.

To John Galsworthy
Text MS Forbes; Unpublished

10th Nov. 09
Aldington
N^r Hythe, Kent

Dearest Jack.

I send you these two magazines as you may be interested in the prison articles.[1] When done with consign them to the dust-bin.

Poor Nellie[2] has been on the point of death. She is now in the Folkestone hospital where she has been removed under D^r Hackney's supervision[3] after a week of illness here. It came on suddenly giving a great shock to Jessie and to me. It appears now she has been ill for a long time without saying anything about it. She kept on till she literally dropped, while talking to Jessie after helping her to bathe Jack. Its a wonder she is alive now tho' of course she's not out of danger yet.

Jessie was concerned about her for some time past, but there was nothing to be got out of the girl but "I am all right" till as I've said she dropped as if shot. I picked her up and was horrified at her lightness. Hackney whom we called in discovered an advanced stage of stomach ulceration and was struck with amazement. She must have been months getting into that state. Her greatest trouble was "causing all this upset" to us both, while, as she told Jessie last Sunday in the hospital in a voice hardly above a breath, "the book must be finished."

It has not helped it on certainly. What's worse I who never, or hardly ever, catch a cold, did get one somehow, of a feverish kind too, last week. It has been an awful hindrance. No luck. Moreover there is no denying the fact that I am not capable of keeping up a great spurt. I can sit as

[1] Galsworthy's campaign for a mitigation of solitary confinement took him to Dartmoor, Pentonville, Chelmsford, and Lewes prisons, led to an interview with the Home Secretary, and is reflected in *Justice*.
[2] Nellie Lyons, the maid.
[3] Clifford Hackney (1874–1956), a doctor from Hythe, had attended the Conrad family at the Pent.

long as ever but the results are not what they used to be—nor anything like it. But its obvious that my gout is being eliminated. The tone of my mind is better than it has been for years—and the old power may come back yet. Mac[k]intosh is very confident that it will. So be it. Meantime I am driving on.

When shall we have the happiness of seeing you both here? There are various things I would fain tell you of but I'll put them off till then. Borys came for 1/2 term and got a sore throat so we keep him for a day or two more. That throat is a great trouble. Otherwise the boy is very sound they tell me. The other kid flourishes greatly.

Marwood was here the other day and indulged in school boy reminiscences related to you.[1] He also told me the subject of your story in *ER* which I have not seen,[2] being no longer on the free list.

Our dear love to you both. Jessie has too much to do just now to write herself, Nellie's absence making a difference as the kid is a handful, but she begs Ada not to fail to come and see our cage before we escape from it. It's simply awful.

<div align="center">Ever yours</div>

<div align="right">J Conrad.</div>

To Robert d'Humières
Text MS Vaugelas; Guérin

<div align="right">Vendredi 11 [?] Nov 09[3]
Aldington
N[r] Hythe
Kent</div>

Tres cher Monsieur

Je viens de lire les épreuves[4] et j'en suis emerveillé.

Que puis-je dire si non merci. Cet* étonnant de fidelité et de vigueur. Jamais je n'aurais cru qu'on pouvait rendre avec cette exactitude et cette force, dans une autre langue, les effets que j'ai visés* en écrivant. Cher monsieur vous avez reussi au-delà de mes éspérances et je vous en suis infiniment reconnaissant.

Je me suis permis de faire quelque[s] petites corrections; et c'est a

[1] Marwood had gone to Clifton, and Galsworthy to Harrow.

[2] 'The Neighbours', in the November issue, a story of murderously mismatched spouses and atavistic behaviour in a remote village. Conrad approved when he read it in *A Motley* (letter of 18 June 1910).

[3] The date is smudged, and the handwriting throughout unusually hard to read. The 11th was a Thursday.

[4] Of the translated *Nigger* in book form.

cause de cela que je vous renvoie les epreuves cette fois ci afin que vous puissiez en juger et decider. Ce sont du reste des retouches tout à fait insignifiantes au fond. Mais moi j'ai la triste manie des corrections. Je voudrai ardem[m]ent pouvoir retoucher tous mes livres.

Je suis tout a fait de votre avis quand* a cette preface. Je l'ai envoyée simplement pour Vous seul. Mais si vous ecrivez jamais un article cela pourra servir, peut être. Heine—oui jusqu'a un certain point, et dans ce que vous dites il y a beaucoup de vrai. Seulement Heine ecrivait dans les deux langues[1]—tandis que moi je n'ai jamais eu qu'une seule langue d'ecrivain tout comme si j'etais né anglais.

Enfin merci de tout mon coeur. J'ai eu là un rare plaisir. Je finis ce gribouillage car il se fait tard. Votre bonne lettre, ces epreuves, tout ça m'a reconforté un peu et même beaucoup. J'ai besoin de ça quelquefois.

Croyez moi bien a vous.

J Conrad.

Merci pour le 4 Nos de la Revue.[2] En effet il y a des coupures—mais je comprends tout a présent.

Translation

Very dear Sir,

I have just read the proofs, and I am astonished.

What can I say but thank you? The vigour and the fidelity are marvellous. I'd never have believed that one could render with such energy and precision, and in another language, the effects I had in mind while writing. Dear sir, you have succeeded beyond my hopes, and I am infinitely obliged to you.

I've allowed myself to make a few small corrections; that is why I am now sending you back the proofs for you to judge and decide. Besides, they are touchings up, fundamentally insignificant. But I have a

[1] Heinrich Heine (1797–1856) spent the last 25 years of his life in Paris; although continuing to write mainly in German, he became perfectly bilingual. The affinity that d'Humières had evidently suggested between Conrad and Heine is illuminating: both writers were exiles and ironists, both took up the theme of cultural dislocation, and both felt drawn to the figure of the double. Conrad's father translated some of Heine's poetry into Polish.

[2] *Le Correspondant*, with the serial of *The Nigger*.

regrettable mania for corrections. I very much want to touch up all my books.

I agree with you entirely about the preface. I sent it for your eyes only. But it could perhaps be helpful if you ever write an article. Heine—yes, up to a point—and there's a lot of truth in what you say. Yet Heine wrote in both languages, while I have only ever written in one, just as if I had been born an Englishman.

So thank you, with all my heart. I have had a rare pleasure. I finish this scribble because it's getting late. Your kind letter and the proofs have cheered me up a little, even a lot. I need that sometimes.

<div align="center">All yours,</div>

<div align="right">J Conrad.</div>

Thanks for the four numbers of the magazine. There are indeed cuts—but now I understand everything.

To John Galsworthy
Text MS Forbes; J-A, 2, 105

<div align="right">[Aldington]
Monday night. [15 November
1909][1]</div>

Dearest Jack.

Poor Ada is having a horribly rough time this year.[2] And the weather keeping as atrocious as it can be too!

The French proofs of the *Nigger* coming in for correction complicate matters. It means a lot of margin writing. And how can I let it pass? Apart from my affections I have nothing in the world but my books. On the other hand Mac[kintosh] writes with some authority and some right too demanding from me not to endanger and perhaps destroy his good work by putting on too heavy a strain. However I walk a couple of hours and sit for no more than 10- to 11 hours. I think that's strain enough for a man who knows that when this bout is over there can be no lying back (unless in illness) and that this sort of thing must be kept up, and moreover that even if kept up it won't be good enough anyhow. Sufficient moral tenacity is all I pray for, not to save me from taking to drink because I couldn't even if I wanted to, but from the temptation to throw away the oar. And I have known some good men do that too,

[1] The day of the newspaper story: see p. 289, n. 3.
[2] She was still tormented by rheumatism.

saying: It's no use. Then was my turn come to keep the boat head to sea for fourteen solid hours. Yes. Moi qui Vous parle have done that thing just thirty years ago—all but.[1] I wish sometimes I had remained at sea which had I honestly stuck to it would no doubt be rolling now over my head.

Poor Nellie still hangs between life and death. The danger now is of her sinking from sheer weakness. At best it means months in the hospital and then we shall have to look for a convalescent home.

I think dearest Jack that it would be better not to add importunity to -er- mendicancy. Those people are very busy.[2] After they have given everybody the "right to work" and strung up all the horrid Lords to lanterns up and down Pall Mall and Piccadilly and all around Buckingham Palace the writing of novels shall no doubt become (like maternity) a "municipal function" with an eight hour day and a living wage; and then perhaps I shall be offered the chance along with the crowd of becoming a government employé—the worthy fate and the only refuge of all sorts of failures under the new dispensation which dawns over our heads. But let it come. Have you seen that case to day of a poor miserable man with a baby dead practically of starvation and a sick wife being *summoned for the poor rate*!!![3] It appears he couldn't speak in court for

[1] As he recalled in 'Youth'. When the *Palestine* went down in March 1882, Conrad and three other sailors spent 23 hours in an open boat (Karl, *Three Lives*, pp. 211–12).

[2] As the letter of the 22nd makes clear, Conrad has in mind the Liberal government (which Galsworthy supported) and its Labour allies. The latter group pressed for legislation guaranteeing employment ('the right to work') and limiting the working day to eight hours. The Liberal administration itself was in the midst of a constitutional battle with the House of Lords. In order to pay for new social programmes (including old age pensions and school meals) and the usual increase in naval estimates, the latest budget's fiscal measures included a raise in income tax to $8\frac{1}{3}$% and a surtax on income over £5,000. The Lords' threat to veto the budget (as they indeed did on 30 November) provoked a fusillade of anti-aristocratic remarks such as Lloyd George's complaint at Newcastle in October that 'a fully-equipped duke costs as much to keep up as two Dreadnoughts'.

[3] A local tax levied on householders: the percentage of valuation demanded varied from parish to parish. This report from Willesden Magistrates' Court appeared in the *Standard* of 15 November, p. 12:

'A man who was summoned for non payment of poor rates handed in the following letter from his wife:

Poor rates! Why there can be none poorer than we are, and if you take my husband away I don't know what will become of me and the children. If you know what we had gone through you would have pity on us.

A few months ago my baby, aged eight months, died of starvation, and at night the parish undertaker called for the body and placed it in his handbag, in which was another body.

I have another baby now, and that is dying for want of proper nourishment.

tears and handed over a letter written by his wife. Have you seen it? It's terrible. Summoned for his *poor rate!* That's how officialism works, and indeed must work. That little case gives one furiously to think—it opens vistas both comic and appalling. Do dearest Jack come over as soon as you can and bring us good news of Ada—our dear love to her. I really can't come to town—and yet I would give anything for a talk with you. Razumov *will* be something when it's done. I haven't the heart to spoil him. Well no more

<div align="center">Ever your</div>

<div align="right">J Conrad.</div>

To William Rothenstein
Text MS Harvard; J-A, 2, 103

<div align="right">Aldington
N^r Hythe
Kent.
15 Nov '09.</div>

Dear old Will.

Yes. I want to and I shall before long. The last year and a half has been like hell from which I have just emerged thanks to a good volunteer doctor who took me in hand I believe only just in time. But twenty months have gone already over a novel and now I *must* finish it—or I am totally undone. I daren't budge from the desk. Moreover the first of my books in French transon is about to appear. It's the *Nigger*; and I have proofs sent me for correction which means a lot of writing on the margins. How could I resist the chance of putting something of my real self into the translator's prose? And with that I am still shaky a bit and subject to sudden accesses of mental exhaustion.

If I did not write to you so long it's only because there was nothing to write—nothing that you as a friend would have been glad to hear. As to my affection I'm sure You've never doubted it any more than I could doubt yours. The thought of your friendship has often comforted me.

The fourteenth year of my writing life draws to an end and when I look at the result I am appalled. I speak from a worldly point of view, but then we live in the world and its weights and measures impose themselves upon our judgement—yes, even upon our feelings. One

The woman's statements were declared to be perfectly true, and in nominally sentencing her husband to one day's imprisonment the magistrates commended the case to the missionary.'

needn't be particularly vile and base to suffer a little from that truth. And there is just 14 published volumes. Not a great tale. But you know as well as anybody that of these years a full third must be taken off for illness alone—not speaking of other pieces of bad luck. So I don't think I've been indolent or even unduly slow, taking into consideration the nature of my work. I mention this so that some day you should, at need defend my memory; for I am pretty certain of coming in for some hard sayings—unless indeed no one ever says anything—which is quite possible too.

Love from us both to your dear wife and all the chicks. Why John must be over nine now.[1] I do really want to see you all—and, like Ant[a]eus the earth,[2] touch some warm friendship to regain a little strength and hope.

<div style="text-align:center">Ever Yours</div>

<div style="text-align:right">J Conrad.</div>

To John Galsworthy
Text MS Forbes; Unpublished

<div style="text-align:right">[Aldington]
19 Nov 1909.</div>

Dearest Jack.

Thanks for the volume[3] which looks very well. I think the idea good. Of course I have a sentimental weakness for the original editions both of the novel and of the tales and shall stick to them for my re-readings.

I am well and working better. If I only could hope to keep up, the future would wear another aspect!

When can we expect you here. And how is dear Ada.

Our best love

<div style="text-align:center">Your</div>

<div style="text-align:right">J. Conrad</div>

[1] John, the future director of the Tate Gallery, would be nine the following July.
[2] The titanic Antaeus took strength from Gaia, Mother Earth; when Herakles snatched him aloft, he died.
[3] Duckworth had just published Galsworthy's novel *Villa Rubein* (1900) and the collection of short stories *A Man of Devon* (1901) in a 'second and revised edition', *Villa Rubein and Other Stories*.

To John Galsworthy
Text MS Forbes; Unpublished

[letterhead: Aldington]

27 Nov '09

Dearest Jack

Our best wishes for dear Ada's complete recovery follow you to Devonshire. I watch the glass; it keeps up so far; but I fear that the weather will break up first to the westward. Here we have it rather raw but at any rate dry. Yesterday there was no sun till late in the day when it set over the marsh[1] very red with extraordinary effects of light.

I was not alluding seriously to the Lords—and the Commons. The two charitable benefactors of humanity L George & W Churchill[2] inspire in me no more respect than the other lot—but I think that their adversaries are at least as sincere. As to suffering humanity I feel certain that since it has the vote[3] (if very little else), something (as little as possible) will be done for it. But that suffering should at least be respected. And what arouses my scorn is the unreality nay the hypocrisy of the whole thing (either conscious or unconscious), the dread of grappling with the real issue, which lies quite elsewhere. But there is much to be said on all that—too much![4]

I am writing—reasonably; trying not to think of anything else. The French proofs of N of the N are finished. Not so bad! But the book won't be published this year after all. So here is another hope gone. Harpers refuse (after being slanged in a letter for their silence and having apologised by cable) to use the Rems. Everything melts like snow in the hand. Our dear love

Yours

J. Conrad.

[1] Romney Marsh, visible from the higher ground of Aldington.

[2] David Lloyd George, Chancellor of the Exchequer, and Winston Leonard Spencer Churchill, President of the Board of Trade, aggressively promoted the Liberal social agenda inside the Commons and out. Both men denounced the Conservative opposition with gusto.

[3] In its British and Irish varieties, about 30% of it did. Women's suffrage and reform of the electoral laws that also prevented many men from voting were, of course, fiercely contested issues.

[4] Conrad was now at work on Part IV of *Under Western Eyes*, which resumes Mikulin's question 'Where to?'

To Stephen Reynolds
Text MS Berg; Unpublished

[letterhead: Aldington]
27 Nov '09

Dear old Stephen.

Yes. I am sort of a dumb brute—and there's no more to be said—unless that kindness to such is enjoined either by the Bible or by Shakespeare—I ain't sure which.

No I am not writing a serial for McC[lure]. Pray, as you love me, let me know how that rumour originated. Is that inf[ernal] Ford still going about raving.

Like the tone of your letter. Somehow see in it Stephen the Strong man (nothing of Sandow[1]). That does not prevent me being very sorry to hear of difficulties in the way of book-writing. Damn! But don't mistake my preaching on the matter. I have enough confidence in you to believe firmly in your making your way anyhow. That opinion I haven't concealed from anyone and I wish you to adopt it strongly.

The title of forthcoming vol[2] is really good. Beastly to have to wait for it so long. My benediction extends to everything you do—never doubt that.

But what the devil has Lane to do with your writing books—novels.[3] Do you mean he's unwilling to publish? Am I to understand that such a tolerably acute person as yourself had delivered himself into his hands to the extent of not being able to negociate* with another publisher?

Fishing news very interesting. Wish I had anything half as honestly valuable to tell you. Give my regards to Bob.

We are fairly well. I am working at last! At last! After something like a year of futile agony. It may be I am permanently better—and it may be only a foxy day—you know what I mean.[4]

You are much in our thoughts and in our affections.

Yours

J. Conrad.

[1] Eugene Sandow (1867–1925), the German-American strongman and promoter of 'natural' cures.

[2] *Alongshore*, published in October 1910.

[3] Lane published Reynolds's fiction only to gain the rights to his reports of fishing life: Roy Hattersley, Introduction to *A Poor Man's House* (Oxford University Press, 1982), p. viii.

[4] Besides meaning 'strong smelling' (here, 'having the scent of success'?), 'foxy' (according to Partridge's *Dictionary of Slang and Unconventional English*) was the army nickname for anyone called Reynolds.

To J. B. Pinker
Text MS Berg; Unpublished

[letterhead: Aldington]
Friday. [10 December 1909][1]

Dear Pinker.

This is a short story of say 8 thou. which could be reduced to 6 if necessary. Pray have these 64 pages typed and sent back to me say on Sat—as I have Sunday post. The last 15 pp will be sent by to-night's mail if I can get them ready by six o clock. If not then you won't get them till monday. With them I'll send you title and letter explaining why the thing came to be written. No time now

Yours

J. Conrad.

To John Galsworthy
Text MS Forbes; Unpublished

[Aldington]
Friday [10 December 1909][2]

Dearest Jack.

We are so glad Ada is better—but you are coming back in very stormy conditions.

I am awaiting anxiously the promised play[3] which is to be the precursor of your visit. I have been working rather well of late. I took off last week to write a short story. *Raz* is really nearing the end. The French *Nigger* has been made to look like an original work—almost. And no gout so far! I am aware of a marked mental improvement. Only 2 years of no worse health would put me nearly right with the world. But I daren't hope—and yet I am unwilling to despair.

I am very glad of Your warm commendation[?] of S. Reynolds. That good fellow is worth encouraging and I know that you are one of the very very few men for whom he has a[n] intellectual, moral and artistic respect. He's only 28 and if his health does not give out we may yet have some comfort from that baby. For under many defects of form, there is in him a very sound substance; a lot of service for the ideas you and I have

[1] Received '12/09': the work in progress must therefore be 'The Secret Sharer'; it was finished by the time Conrad wrote to Galsworthy on the 14th and had taken ten days.
[2] Galsworthy came down to Aldington the following Friday (see the letters of 14, [15], and 22 December). By 'last week', Conrad must mean the week just ending. The 'stormy conditions' were mild but blustery.
[3] *Justice.*

always shared as the basis of the emotional life, with only superficial differences.

Give our dear love to Ada. May we hope to see her here? One hesitates to say much because of the really awful character of the journey out and home on the same day. There is a house going here which we may yet secure.—I shall try because I *must* move if I am really to take the greatest advantage from my improved health.

Au revoir

Your

J. Conrad

To John Galsworthy
Text MS Forbes; Unpublished

[Aldington]
Saturday night. [11? December
1909][1]

Dearest Jack.

I hear definitely from d'Humières that the Mercure won't publish the Nigger this year. I had still hopes of it bringing in enough this year to pay Borys' school. So my dear fellow I must take advantage of your offer—since I haven't managed to even finish the novel; which would have allowed me to squeeze the amount out of Pinker. The amount is £18—and I have had a reminder from House by this morning's post.

If that poor girl had not been ill I could have found half of that or at least 10—but I've had to pay the hospital. She is back now after a wonderful recovery—a wonderful example they tell me of what injection feeding[2] can do when no nourishment whatever can be retained in the stomach.

I've been writing all day to day and feel horribly stiff and discouraged

Yours ever

J. Conrad.

[1] Nellie Lyons's recovery gives the approximate period; the letter of 14 December acknowledges what may be the loan requested here.
[2] Intravenous feeding.

To John Galsworthy

Text MS Forbes; Unpublished

[Aldington]
14 Dec 1909

My dearest Jack

Thanks. I would be much more ashamed if I had not tried my damnedest to provide. It was the third bad year—but the next what with the improvement in my health and something from France coming in things perhaps'll take a turn. If I could only really depend on 300 working days! Working as I do now I could write 6–8 stories in 150 days to provide the amount Pinker advances yearly; and in the other 150 advance or perhaps finish either Chance or Rescue. Thus this Razumov which I'll deliver in Jany would go entirely to reduce that heavy debt to P. And then one could look forward with some confidence.

I've just finished the short story—12000 words in 10 days.[1] Not so bad. I had to lay aside Razumov for a bit tho' I didn't think it would take 10 days. No great harm done tho! Doing something easy has given me confidence.

We are expecting a wire from you. Don't let anything short of social revolution prevent you on Friday.

Our love

Ever yours

J Conrad.

To Stephen Reynolds

Text MS Berg; Unpublished

[Aldington]
14 Dec 1909[2]

My dear Stephen.

Quite all right. Pardon any delay in sending the Ms back.[3] It's quite worthy of you. Excuse my saying more just now.

I sympathise and feel with you to the fullest extent.[4] But You must stand up to it. Life is still before you. Your talent is undeniable—and

[1] In '"The Secret Sharer": A Note on the Dates of Its Composition', *Conradiana*, 19 (1987), 209–13, Keith Carabine draws attention to the circumstances of its writing: Conrad began this soul-searching story on or just after his birthday.

[2] '1909' is a debatable scrawl, but mention of the *Thistlemoor* assures the year.

[3] *Alongshore?*

[4] On 30 December, Reynolds wrote to Pinker: 'now I'm damn'd utterly with the worst attack of head, sleeplessness and hump that I've had for years – simply can't work – and can't afford to get to sea and be better' (Wright, p. 128).

something more than that too. Try to believe what I say—and perhaps the trust, I have the right to demand, in my sincerity may help you to regain a firmer belief in yourself.

Jack's opinion of your article, as written to me, contains the word admirable. And I don't shy at it tho' I have perhaps the right to reserve that word for things which I am confident shall come from You yet. But Jack is as sincere as myself. You may rest assured of that.

Yes. I was struck by the *Thistlemoor* affair. I imagined it a calumny—simply.[1] The D[aily] M[ail] asked you for the article on my suggestion as I knew they wanted something of the sort.[2] They evidently jumped at the hint. Good.

Our collective love. We must have a sight of each other soon.

<div style="text-align:center">Yours</div>

<div style="text-align:right">J Conrad.</div>

To J. B. Pinker

Text MS Berg; Unpublished

<div style="text-align:right">[letterhead: Aldington]
Wednesday. [15 December
1909][3]</div>

Dear Pinker.

I've dispatched the end of the story by rail this morning, being anxious to have it typed and returned for correction so as to close this episode at once and return wholly to the other work. I am going on with it even now.

The idea originated from a letter by Bashford of the *D. Mail*[4] asking me for sketches or articles of 1200 words at £5 a piece. At the time (a fortnight ago) we had the faithful maid Nellie (who has been with us for nearly eleven years) lying dangerously ill in Folkestone Hospital, but getting then* better. So I had before me the prospect of an account from there at a guinea a week at least. I thought at once I would take an evening off and do something for B. But you know how that sort of thing is distasteful to me. Anyway I started looking for a subject and this one

[1] On the night of 2 December in a severe gale, the *Thistlemoor*, a collier outward bound from Cardiff, was wrecked off the North Devon coast with heavy loss of life. A coroner's jury found fault with the coastguard for not keeping an adequate lookout (*The Times*, 8 December, p. 12).

[2] The literary editor had probably asked Conrad to write the article: see the next letter. Reynolds's piece, 'The Coastguard', appeared on the 16th.

[3] The day after Conrad told Galsworthy he had finished the story.

[4] Lindsay Bashford (1881–1921) was the literary editor.

turned up, which could have been made use of in the form of an anecdote, but I hadn't the heart to throw it away. The story you have is the result of that reluctance. We may call it 10 000 words;[1] it is a very characteristic Conrad, and I don't think the change has done me much harm or even very seriously delayed the other matter. For your guidance in handling I must mention that I had lately a letter from Alden (Harper Mag) asking me for a contribution to their 60th anniversary N°.[2] I had a curious little passage with Harper a month ago or more which ended in a cabled apology from them. (Too long to tell here—leave that till we meet). I think they'll want to be nice to me just at present. If you conclude to approach them let me know and I'll drop a note to Alden. Also I have had a friendly letter from Bliss Carman (in Sept[er]) who seems to be editing a paper called *Gentleman's Journal* asking me for a *man's story* or generally for a contribution. No price mentioned. If the *Gent: Jour:* is good enough then the story is certainly so too. I would write to him too, if necessary.

I did not communicate with you before hand trusting that the story being done under these circumstances you will provide for the Hospital bill which is six guineas. And I would also ask for another £5 as I have to get things for the boy who changes schools.[3] But please understand that the first is the only *material* requirement. And even in that respect I make *no demand* whatever and have not planned all this on purpose. I can still do the hateful things for Bashford in 'my own time' as it were. I would be glad to think that the story (written in 8 days[4]) has provided (under your skiful handling) for a few weeks of our agreement. I am now feeling as well as I have not felt since the Lord Jim days—which were the last good ones. It seems that Mac has done the trick. He has been down here twice watching my case of which he is proud, as well he may [be] if this is permanent. He believes it is. And if that's so then things are changed indeed. I propose next year to write six short stories to begin with— which may nearly secure my 'keep'—and then to push on either Resc. or Chance. So that Raz. may go entirely towards diminishing my indebt- [ed]ness.[5]

[1] It is closer to 15.
[2] Henry Mills Alden gave the story its American publication in the August and September 1910 numbers of *Harper's Magazine*.
[3] Borys stayed on at St Gregory's.
[4] When comparing this figure with the ten days reported to Galsworthy and Gibbon, we should remember that a day less on 'The Secret Sharer' would be a day more on 'Razumov'.
[5] As of 9 February 1910, the debt, secured by four mortgages, had become £2,702-19-9 (Withers, Benson, Birkett, and Davies to Pinker, TS Berg).

In that last respect I must confess now to you that one or two things stood in the way. Since we exchanged these letters the proofs of the Nigger in French came in for my revision. I've made it a French work now. And it could not be done without time and labour. But when you think that this was my only chance to do anything you will judge me leniently. I simply could not throw it away. The book will be published by the *Mercure* early next year. I am glad also to have to tell you that the *Temps* has accepted the Secret A. for serial some time in *1910* and immediately after the book form will follow I understand. So there is a prospect of something coming in from France to help through next year under the agreement with Davray which you have on file in your office. In November I had a feverish cold—I who never have a disabling cold. Its bad luck. It did away with a whole week—or nearly. But then in any other year it would have turned into gout and knocked me over for a month perhaps. I was not anxious to tell you at the time, but Galsworthy knew of my anxiety. And by the way he's coming down here on Friday with a new play called *Justice*.—Thanks very much for the books received to-day. Kindest regards

<div align="right">Yours

J. Conrad</div>

PS What do you think for title of the story *The Second Self. An episode from the Sea.*

To William Rothenstein

Text MS Harvard; J-A, 2, 104

<div align="right">[letterhead: Aldington]

17 Dec 1909</div>

Dearest Will

Don't you think that if I could possibly spare the time I wouldn't rather take a day and come and see you and yours to whom my heart goes out many times a week? Here I've been 2 years writing a novel which is not yet finished. Two years! Of which surely one half has been illness complicated by a terrible moral stress. Imagine yourself painting with the Devil jogging your elbow *all the time*. But you who are one of the most intelligent men I know, or know of, and a stylist also (because you are—I've been looking at Your Goya[1] only the other day) you will know what a torture that sort of thing is when the effort and hindrance are

[1] A study published in 1900.

mental. It is to make you realise how really unfit I am for what I call the casual intercourse of mankind. And the truth also is, my dear Will, that we live here now in such conditions—crowded into four tiny rooms in half of a cottage, that I really don't like to receive strangers even the most admiring and the best disposed. You must not charge me with littleness of mind; we must take the world as it is; and indeed there is some concern for the dignity of letters in my reluctance.

I speak to you here as to a second self[1] and thus I cannot conceive you taking it ill. Perhaps I am unreasonable. But to-day in the second week of my 52[nd] year, a failure from the worldly point of view and knowing well that there can be no change—that this must go on usque ad finem[2]—I may perhaps be allowed a little unreason.—Well, no more just now. I will only mention that I haven't seen you for more than a year, Galsworthy for nine months, that I have been in town for about six hours in march last and not since. Voilà. And if you think that I am indulging in a capricious savagery of disposition you are mistaken. Our dear love to you all

<div style="text-align:center">Yours ever</div>

<div style="text-align:right">J. Conrad.</div>

To J. B. Pinker
Text MS Berg; Unpublished

<div style="text-align:right">[Aldington]
[c. 18 December 1909][3]</div>

Dear Pinker.

I am sending by same post the corrected type. *Quite* a good enough story For titles I suggest

<div style="text-align:center">or { The Secret Self
{ The other Self</div>

<div style="text-align:center">An episode from the sea</div>

It could be also *The Secret Sharer* but that may be *too*[4] enigmatic.

Pray select for me.

<div style="text-align:center">Yours as always</div>

<div style="text-align:right">J Conrad.</div>

[1] Cf. the following letter.
[2] Following the dream and again following the dream, as Stein counsels in *Lord Jim*, Chapter 20, and faithful to the motto of Conrad's uncle, Tadeusz Bobrowski (Najder, *Polish Background*, p. 155).
[3] The last of the MS went off on the 15th; typing up, returning the story to Conrad, and correcting the TS would have taken at least two days.
[4] Or 'too' with a rule beneath: see Plate 6.

To Perceval Gibbon
Text MS Berg; Unpublished

[Aldington]

19 Dec. [1909][1]

Dear Gibbon,

Many thanks for the fowls of the air which shall taste all the sweeter for coming from you and as if spiced by the excitement of the romantic provenance at which You hint.

Oh yes! Don't I know it! I lunched last with McClure 5 years ago or so, and I feel still hungry whenever I think of it.

Likewise I know the vagaries of the infernal typists employed by the great P. What *is* that story? And what is being done to the Lady of the Hatpins?[2] I imagined You exclusively busy with that chronicle. Yes. Raz. wants 20000[3] words more. Then with proper shortening carried all through the body of it (say five lines (on average) in every page) it will come out as 150,000 words novel, reading yet swiftly enough. You may smile at this hope as an author's self delusion—but I've a certain practice in that matter.

I've given P. a 10 000 or perhaps 12 000 words story done in 10 days which is a great speed for me. A good specimen of Conrad. Therefore in two years I stand thus

to date MS pages of Raz 1228 — 130 000

Black Mate	10
Story as above	12
Rems	35

187 000

That's what I've written since last Xmas. Say 24 months of actual time. But *you* know what my health was end last year and begin[n]ing of this. Yes my dear boy, practically from July last year till Aug*st* this I've been either actually laid up or recovering, or sickening for gout. Hard fact. That is either disabled utterly or hindered. Add to this a crushing load of anxiety. Shall we take 8 months off for all that? I don't think it's too much. Do you? That leaves 16 months. 11630 per month. And that's good work for a slow writer.

Is it—or is it not?

And I get yesterday a letter from P. telling me he hopes to have

[1] The year 'Razumov' was nearly finished.

[2] In Gibbon's story 'Between the Lights', *McClure's Magazine*, 33 (1909), 419–25, a woman travelling in East Africa foils a robber with her hatpins.

[3] By Carabine's reckoning, Conrad wrote about 15,000 words more.

manuscript sent regularly. That I've given him nothing to sell for two years and threatening to stop short if he don't* get end of R. in a fortnight. If he does that I shall fling the MS of Raz in the fire—and see how he likes that. He positively writes as if [I] had done nothing. You imagine how charming it is to be following the psychology of Mr Razumov under these conditions. It's like working in hell. Love to you all.

<div align="center">Yours</div>

<div align="right">J Conrad.</div>

To J. B. Pinker
Text MS Berg; Unpublished

<div align="right">[letterhead: Aldington]
20 Dec 1909.</div>

Dear Pinker.

Had you answered simply I can't or I won't do what you ask for there would have been nothing to be said. But in a manner which is nothing short of contemptuous you seem to be holding out a bribe—next week forsooth!—as though it were a bone to a dog to make him get up on his hind legs.

I wrote you frankly as to all I've done. Now I beg to point out that in the last $23\frac{1}{2}$ months I've written 187,000 words (of which 130,000 in round numbers of Razumov—but I am a novelist who writes sometimes long novels—Outcast—Lord Jim. Nostromo—) In the course of these $23\frac{1}{2}$ months as two *honourable* professional men[1] can testify, from July last year to August of this I've had five severe attacks of gout—which means that actually I was either utterly disabled or sickening for it or recovering from it. Thats twelve months: but as I often worked when far from fit—yes with temp at over 100°—when most men would be utterly unable to do anything—yes and creative work too—let us deduct only 8 months; which would leave 16 months of effective health and works out at the average of 11630 w. per month. Out of the total there were 40000 words[2] which you told me: "*I can do nothing with that*" with an air as if it were dirt which it isn't, you know. But never mind that. And all that time there wasn't a day when I got up without thinking of you and went to bed without thinking of my work in relation to you.

Raz. wants 15–20 thou words more and shall get it as fast as I can write them. You have the story. Sell it. I myself could get a 50 for it by

[1] Mackintosh and Hackney. [2] The reminiscences.

the expenditure of a couple of postage stamps. I wrote it for the very purpose of easing the strain. This is all I have to say on my side.

Now I beg you to inform me plainly if with that story in your hands you really mean (as your letter seems to foreshadow) to slam the door on me when I am nearly through for the sake of an odd week. It is necessary for me to know—not of course that it will affect the termination of the story one way or another. Three men[1] have seen it to date and they shall see the end in any case, before I am many days older. Please let me know, to govern my action by. Also kindly tell me please whether you intend to approach Harpers as I must write to them on another matter and wish to allude to their request.

<div style="text-align:center">Yours
J. Conrad.</div>

PS I didn't write of my health in a conventional way nor yet to fish for anything. I alluded to it because it has a direct bearing on the situation. All I know is that Raz. when handled may cover two fifths or perhaps more of my indebt[ed]ness and that for next year a scheme of work may be arranged which would bring quick returns for the immediate needs and would allow at the same time a long novel to be kept going. I've now all *Chance* in my head as a Malay sea tale.[2] That's what health is good for. I am not a confounded hypoc[h]ondriac in search of sympathy.

To John Galsworthy
Text MS Forbes; Baines 359 (in part)

<div style="text-align:right">[letterhead: Aldington]
22 Dec 1909</div>

Dearest Jack

Jessie is sending back the N⁰ of the Fortnightly. Your paper on the Drama[3] has pleased me so much in the form and has appealed strongly to my convictions which it clarifies and expresses. I read it the evening you left—and that's the last tolerable moment of life I had ever since, I may say.

You remember perhaps what I told you about the story I wrote and sent to P—in connection especially with the occasion it was written for.

[1] The most likely men would include Galsworthy, Garnett, Gibbon, Mackintosh, and Marwood.
[2] A better description of the also unfinished *Rescue*.
[3] 'Some Platitudes Concerning Drama', *Fortnightly Review*, 92 (1909), 1,004–10.

It originated in a proposal of Blatchford (Dly Mail)[1] to write some article. I thought that if I had to take a day off I may just as well take 7 days or so and do something which would bring in a little money. I sent that story to London just writing to P that I had an acct/ for hospital hanging over me and suggesting that as the story was worth say £60 he should send me at least six; that of course I had *no* idea or pretension to *demand* it. That I left it to him to say yes or no. At the same time it being the first letter I wrote him for months I mentionned* that it looked as if a permanent improvement had taken place in my health etc etc—improvement of prospects anyhow for the next year.

On Saturday morning[2] I got the enclosed.

I answered him, imprimis: that if he had answered I *can't* or even I *won't* simply, there would have been nothing more to be said; but I resented the general tone and especially the proceeding of holding up that offer as if it were a bone to a dog to make him stand on his hind legs.

(and I think I had the right to resent it, as I could not have a plain refusal which would have been the assertion of strict right or of plain impossibility. You write like that to a loafer who wants spurring. It's casting a distinct aspersion)

Then I went on stating that: in the last 23 1/2 months I have written 187000 words of which 130000 of the novel. But then I was a novelist who sometimes wrote long novels e.g. Outcast. Lord Jim. Nostromo. Of that time as two honourable professional men could testify 8m must be taken off for illness at least. (I've often worked with temp. over 100° or at any rate *sat* at it). That left 16 working months and gave an average of 11.630 words p. month. That, further, out of the total there were 40000 words of which he told me himself: *I can do nothing with that*—with an air as if it were dirt which it wasn't, as he knew.

(as a matter of fact I nearly placed it myself and the only difficulty was the want of Copyright. The terms Harpers offer me for book form are unusually good. He might have done something if he had taken some trouble)

The above, I said, were the facts on my side. *Razv* wanted 15–20 thou. more and was going to get that as fast as I could write them. He had the story. Let him sell it. I wrote it on purpose to ease the strain.

And at last I asked him whether he really, <u>with the story in his possession</u> meant to slam the door on me (for the sake of an odd week or

[1] Conrad meant Lindsay Bashford: Robert Blatchford (1851–1943) edited the *Clarion*, also a jingoistic paper but a socialist one.
[2] The 18th, the day after Galsworthy's visit.

two), now when I was nearly through! I wanted to know, whether his letter foreshadowed *that*. Let him say yes or no.

———————

I have been nearly out of my mind ever since. If he says *yes*, that was what he meant I wonder if I can restrain myself from throwing the MS in the fire. It's outrageous. Does he think I am the sort of man who wouldn't finish the story in a week if he could? Do you? Why? For what reason. Is it my habit to lie about drunk for days instead of working? I reckon he knows well enough I don't. It's a contemptuous playing with my worry. If he had said—No. I will stick to the lot—I wouldn't have been hurt. But this gratuit[o]us ignoring of my sincerity in spirit and also in fact is almost more than I can bear. I who can hardly bear to look at the kids, who without You could not have the boy at school even—*I* wouldn't finish the book in a week if I could—unless a bribe of six pounds is dangled before me!—I sit 12 hours at the table, sleep six, and worry the rest of [the] time, feeling the age creeping on and looking at those I love. For two years I havent seen a picture heard a note of music, hadn't a moment of ease in human intercourse.—not really.—And he talks of *regular supplies of manuscript* to a man who in these conditions (taking all the time together ill or well) sends him MS at the rate of 7.600 words a month; and he actually writes as if I were a swindler from whom nothing can be got unless he's pinched. Is it a swindle to write a long novel? He had better get some of his clerks to write stuff which he can sell. But 16 months for a long novel nearly done and some 57000 words of other work is not so bad—even for a man with his mind at ease, with his spirits kept up by prosperity, with his inspiration buoyed by hope. There's nothing of that for me! I don't complain dear Jack. I only state it as an argument—for when people appraise me later on with severity I wish you to be able to say:—I knew him—he was not so bad. By Jove all the moral tortures are not in prison-life. I assure you I feel sometimes as if I could drop everything and beat at the door—you understand. The thing is that, so far, I don't. But I feel now that if he stops the miserable pound a day I *must* throw the MS in the fire.—And indeed why not. It's nothing—it's a mere swindle—it's no good to me. The man would be a fool because that book finished would pay full half I think of my indebt[ed]ness to him. Next year even if the health is only so-so a fourth more would be paid off, after providing that pound a day and something besides, for me. But all this is vain talk. I am at the present moment unable to write a line. One must secure a certain detachment which is

beyond me. I can hardly sit still. If it wasn't for dear Jess—well I don't know.

<div align="center">Ever yours</div>

<div align="right">J Conrad.</div>

To R. D. Mackintosh
Text MS Jellard; Jellard

<div align="right">22 Dec 1909
Aldington
Kent.</div>

Dear Benefactor.

Your name is never pronounced in this household but accompanied by praises and benedictions. It looks more and more as if the gout were bankrupt utterly. The beast has defaulted twice—and there is no sign of the December instalment which is now much overdue.

I hope I am not provoking the Fates by crowing thus. Well, but it is you alone who have carried me through this year by the hope you have given and the confidence you have inspired.

The only thing which lags a bit yet is the brain. It isn't steady. I don't wish to overstrain it or put to hazard in any way the success of your good work. But I am now at the last chapters of that interminable novel and if you think you can help me to more *continuous* working, I would be grateful. You mentioned something last Oct. and even promised a prescription but nothing has come so far.

Pray accept our best wishes for Christmas and the new year. And believe in our affectionate gratitude

<div align="center">Yours always</div>

<div align="right">J. Conrad</div>

To J. B. Pinker
Text MS Berg; Unpublished

<div align="right">[Aldington]
Wednesday. [22 December
1909][1]</div>

Dear P.

It's all a matter of money. I have the same intense dislike for all these American humbugs in the publishing line. If McClure should take it

[1] Received '12/09': just before Christmas, evidently.

there would be a chance of serial: in Eng*ᵈ*. On the other hand Harpers, I suppose, pay the price for both countries.[1]

You must decide. Only you will please let me know after the holidays because I want to write to H. this year and I must mention something. It's a fact that they have asked me for something. I am certainly not anxious to appear in McClure Mag. I am too English and even too European a writer for my prose to fit in with the dreary crude stuff he prints.

<div align="center">Yours</div>

<div align="right">J Conrad.</div>

I won't send any MS this week as this Xmas traffic is sure to delay it; but will post on Monday.

To H.-D. Davray

Text MS Texas; *L. fr.* 98

<div align="right">[letterhead: Aldington]
23ᵈ Dec. 1909</div>

Cher Ami.

Ma femme a expedié la carte de Noël mais moi j'écris a la Revue[2] car je ne suis pas sur de l'adresse. Une forte poignée de main et mes meilleurs souhaits pour la santé et la prospérité de l'année prochaine et des longues années a venir.

J'ai écrit deux fois depuis le mois d'août. Je ne sais [ce] qu'est devenue la première lettre que j'ai laissée sur ma table au moment de partir en visite pour une semaine chez un ami. J'ai répondu tout de suite a votre carte postale. Mais je me demande si l'adresse était correcte. Il y a des jours ou je suis idiot, completement.

D'Humières a eu l'amitié de me laisser voir les épreuves du Nègre. Sa traduction m'a fait plaisir. Un jour quand vous avez le temps peut-être voudrez Vous me dire à quelle date le Mercure compte publier le volume.

L'année 1910 comptera dans mon existence. Vous ne pouvez pas Vous imaginer combien je suis ému a l'idée d'être lu en Français par les Français.

<div align="center">Croyez-moi toujours à vous bien
affectueusement</div>

<div align="right">J. Conrad</div>

[1] Because their *Magazine* circulated on both sides of the Atlantic.
[2] The *Mercure de France*.

PS—Avez vous vu mes articles autobiographiques (est-ce bien l'orthographe) dans la feu[e] English Review?[1] J'ai l'idée d'en écrire encore 30 000 mots et cela fera un volume. Croyez vous que cela vaut la peine?

Translation

Dear Friend,

My wife has sent a Christmas card, but I am writing to the *Mercure*, for I am not sure of the address. A firm handshake, and my best wishes for your health and prosperity next year and for long years to come.

Since August, I have written twice. I don't know what has become of the first letter, which I left on my table just as I was setting off on a week's visit to a friend's house. I answered your post-card immediately. But I wonder if the address was correct. There are days when I am a complete idiot.

D'Humières kindly let me see the proofs of the *Nigger*. His translation pleased me. One day, when you have the time, perhaps you will tell me when the *Mercure* plans to publish the volume.

The year 1910 will be a notable one for me. You cannot imagine how moved I am by the idea of being read in French, by the French.

<div style="text-align:right">Believe me always very
affectionately yours,
J. Conrad</div>

PS Have you seen my autobiographical (is the spelling right?) article in the deceased *English Review*? I have the notion of writing 30,000 words more, and that will make a volume. Do you think it worth the trouble?

To Norman Douglas
Text MS Texas; J-A, 2, 105[2]

<div style="text-align:right">[letterhead: Aldington]
23^d Dec 1909</div>

Dear Douglas.

I don't know what you think of me. You can be no more disgusted than I am. I simply couldn't write to you—tho' God knows—I wanted

[1] Deceased only as far as Conrad was concerned.
[2] Leaving out all but two sentences of the second paragraph.

to very badly. There is nothing to say. We have barely existed. As for myself all I can say [is] that I wonder at it.

Marwoods bought a small farm and are settled down. The very echoes of the great upheaval have died out. Hueffer goes about lying exuberantly about everything and everybody. His wife is apparently going to sue him for restitution of conj^al rights and then proceed further. But there is some plot under that and at any time they may get reconciled and turn together upon some one or other. However we are out of all that and see very little of her. In fact "everything is over but the stink" as they say after fireworks.

The novel hangs on the last 12000 words but there's neither inspiration nor hope in my work. It's mere hard labour for life—with this difference that the life-convict is at any rate out of harm's way—and may consider the account with his conscience closed; and this is not the case with me. I envy the serene fate and the comparative honesty of the gentlemen in grey who live in Dartmoor.[1] I do, really. I am not half as decent or half as useful.

Health is better. My wife is as usual. The kids too. And nothing is any good! It's a horrible feeling and I can't shake it off for more than a day or two at a time.

All the same don't give me up, in your thoughts, entirely. In the light of a "tormented spirit" I am not to be altogether despised. What are you doing? Are you ever coming back.[2] Our best wishes

Yours ever

J Conrad.

To Robert d'Humières
Text MS Vaugelas; Guérin

Aldington, N^r Hythe
Kent.
23 Dec. '09

Cher Monsieur.

Merci de votre lettre reçue ce matin. Mes Reminis^es ne paraîtront pas en volume avant un an au moins. Les avez-vous lus? J'ai là la Revue.

Il y a eu un temps ou je savais des pages entières de Mme Bovary par coeur. Mais si Mme Bovary est un chef d'oeuvre, Salammbo frise le

[1] Long-term convicts. In his work, Conrad was preparing himself for Razumov's confession and punishment.
[2] Douglas was now on his way to Tunisia.

miracle. Je me rap[p]elle bien, quand j'écrivais le *N of the N* Salammbo était mon livre de matin. En avalant mon café j'en lisais une page ou deux au hasard—et il n'y a presque pas de page la dedans qui ne soit merveilleuse. Et il n'y a pas a dire: l'influence de l'infiniment grand sur l'infiniment petit peut se voir. Dans mon traitement des marins il y a un pale reflet de la grande maîtrise de Flaubert dans son traitement des Mercenaires. Peut-être ce n'est qu'une illusion flatteuse. Mais je sais bien que j'étais sous l'influence de ce livre unique.

Pourriez Vous me dire Cher Monsieur quand le Mercure compte publier le livre?

Encore une fois—merci de tout mon coeur. Mes meilleurs souhaits pour la nouvelle année.

Votre tout devoué

J. Conrad

Translation

Dear Sir,

Thanks for your letter received this morning. My Reminiscences will not come out as a book for at least a year. Have you read them? I have the *Review* on hand.

At one time I knew entire pages of *Madame Bovary* by heart. But if *Madame Bovary* is a masterpiece, *Salammbô* is close to a miracle. I well remember that when I was writing the *N of the N*, *Salammbô* was my morning book. While taking my coffee, I would read a page or two at random—and there is hardly a page that isn't marvellous. And it's perfectly obvious: one can see the influence of the immeasurably great on the immeasurably small. In my treatment of the sailors, there's a pale reflection of Flaubert's masterly treatment of the mercenaries. Perhaps that's merely a flattering illusion. But I well know that I was under the influence of that unique book.

Could you tell me, dear Sir, when the *Mercure* intends to publish the book?

Again thanks with all my heart. My best wishes for the new year.

Your devoted

J. Conrad

To Perceval Gibbon
Text MS Berg; Unpublished

[Aldington]
Wednesday. [29 December
1909?]¹

Dear old boy.

I am immensely touched by your good letter. You don't realize how much of the old salt there is in me. Haven't you ever heard a hard shell-back when out of temper wish "the bloody old hooker" to sink.²

Your letter is wise in every way. I was exasperated beyond endurance by a side-episode in this affair which I'll tell you all about when we meet. At the time I really felt as if I could snatch all that pile of pages and fling it in the fire—and writing to you I let myself go. Yes. I'll use a little *very gentle* pressure on P. when it is done. I don't hate him.

I am really glad you think that I have worked fairly well. As to the book if it only brings in 1.200 it will be *a* great step in advance. Then I calculate that next year 6 short stories will keep me for at least 6 months at £30 per month and leave perhaps something over to help the next six months during which I may finish *Chance* at the rate of 9.000 per month. If that comes off P. is all but paid off! What luck. Only I haven't got any luck.

——— ·· ———

Strangely enough we had foreseen something of that sort. Jessie (who talks of you as if you were a younger brother very admirable and brilliant but of the sort that causes anxiety) said to me with a care-worn air: "I wish Reggie wouldn't. There will be trouble some day". I derided her fears—and lo and behold there was trouble. Your account of it is simply impayable³ as the french say. Most amusing. What a subject for a funny short story! With that touch of grimness which lurks in your humour you could make something quite first rate of it. Ain't I cold-blooded with that suggestion. Poor Maisie must have been considerably worried by all those agonising developments. Your superintendent *lives* in your account. Your creative vein is very strong. I am going to slave like anything. Raz wants 15–20[000] words and that will make 150—altogether. But to give him a chance of serialising I'll take the guts out artistically. It'll take me three days extra. And then I shall

¹ The condition of 'Razumov' and the new year greetings place this letter at the very beginning of 1910 or, more probably, at the end of the old year.
² 'Hooker': in the early nineteenth century a two-masted fishing-boat, but later any sailing ship (Partridge, *Dictionary of Slang and Unconventional English*).
³ The 'priceless' story in question is unknown.

come to see you whooping and singing savage warsongs with an eagle's feather in my hair and Pinker's scalp at my waist. Amen!

Our best loving wishes to all your wigwam o man mighty in the hunt and wise in council! May you raise the hair of a large public on your next year's war-path and may peace and happiness dwell by your fireside—ever and ever.

<div style="text-align: center">Yours</div>

<div style="text-align: right">J. Conrad.</div>

To David Meldrum
Text MS Duke; Blackburn 190

<div style="text-align: right">[letterhead: Aldington]
31st Dec '09</div>

My dear M^r Meldrum.

It was a great pleasure to see your hand-writing. In any case I would have written to day;[1] so do not look upon this letter as an answer. You may be certain that in this household neither You nor yours can be forgotten. Our best wishes for next year go out to you as sincere as any the many friends you have known how to conquer can form.

Please remember always that if it [is] a long time since I've seen you I haven't seen much of anybody else. There can be no question here of coldness or neglect—it's simply the course of life and necessity. But enough of that. I don't think you suspect me.

In the course of the last 12 months I have seen Galsworthy twice—and that illustrates clearly the rigour of my solitude. Another intimate[2] I have seen oftener but I am not likely to see anything of him in the future. He's aggrieved—not I. But that is not worth talking about. Still after eleven years of intimacy one feels the breach.

My health has wonderfully improved in the last six months, thanks to a doctor who has volunteered to take me in hand. He's a friend of P. Gibbon—a B'wood "young man"[3] and a very good fellow as I found out on an acquaintance now over a year old. That excellent doctor came to see me last year with G, moved thereto by admiration (!) for my work. Obviously writing novels is not such a waste of time as some severe utilitarians think. Here I am, then, with renewed hopes. They are just

[1] In tribute no doubt to Meldrum's Scottish origins, Conrad usually wrote to him on New Year's Eve.
[2] Ford.
[3] Blackwood had published some of Gibbon's South African stories, first in serial, then in book.

now temporarily obscured, because strangely enough, your good letter found us all more or less overcome by influenza. My wife made the best show. I am still, figuratively speaking, on my hands and knees. Indeed I feel so stupid that I doubt whether I am expressing myself intelligibly. You must forgive all the shortcomings of this epistle for I could not let the year end without making myself heard to You—even if I have nothing worth saying to utter.

With affectionate greetings from wife and myself to all Your household believe me

always Yours

J. Conrad

To Stephen Reynolds
Text MS Berg; Unpublished

[Kent?]
Thursday [1909 or 1910][1]

In haste!
Dear Stephen.

Political article first rate as to form and of course quite sound in my judgement.[2]

The sketch perfectly interesting. Very good indeed. There's nothing wrong with the French.[3]

Thanks for letting me have a look.

Yours

JC

[1] The stationery (watermark ORIGINAL ROCKLEIGH MILL with dolphins and anchor) was used several times in the period, e.g. 26 January 1909 and 23 May 1910; see also n. 3. Alternatively, this note may be about the 'story' mentioned in the letter of 14 February 1911.

[2] The political articles written with the Woolley brothers and collected in *Seems So! A Working-Class View of Politics* (1911) appeared in at least nine different newspapers and magazines during 1909 and 1910.

[3] In October 1910, two sketches with French dialogue were collected in *Alongshore*: 'Two Fishers Abroad' and 'A Herring Haul in a French Steam-Drifter'. The latter, which carries the date '1909–10' also appeared in the May 1910 number of *Blackwood's*.

1910

To J. B. Pinker

Text MS Berg; Unpublished

[Aldington]
Thursday. [6 January 1910]¹

My dear Pinker.

We have all had influenza and as a matter of fact every house I believe between Hythe and Ashford has had it. This explains why I failed to thank you for your good wishes and send you mine. For the same reason I haven't written yet to Harpers; but I am doing so by this post.²

What is to prevent you arranging with them the pub. of a Volume of tales early this year? The fancy pub. of *Duel* in that silly little form—with silly illustrations,³ need not stand in the way. You have now the Black Mate and the Other Self to make up a vol of 70–80 thou words. But what I propose would be this: Hold back the *Informer* for some future collection and give six stories arranged thus: *G. Ruiz. The Brute. An Anarchist. The other Self. Il Conte.* Black Mate.* and call the vol. *Alternate Stories* by J. C. meaning 3 sea, and 3 land stories alternately arranged.⁴ The whole will just make 70 thou. words I think. Please let me know your opinion.

I will dispatch to you on Monday what will be the penultimate batch of Raz. MS. I havent done anything for nearly a week. I simply could not think and absolutely felt too listless to hold the pen.

Yours

J Conrad.

¹ Received 'Jan 1910': before the letter of 'Monday' [10 January] sent with the MS promised here; 6 January is more probable than 31 December, given the references to unsent new year greetings and the timing of a possible volume from Harper's.

² On 1 January, Sydney Brooks wrote to Colonel Harvey urging Harper & Brothers to put Conrad on an annual income, thus saving him from bankruptcy: 'Ford Madox Hueffer was in here yesterday & telling me that Joseph Conrad is in a great state over his relations with Harper Bros. You will remember that when you were over here you asked me to let Conrad know you would take all the things he had on the stocks & that for the future you would be glad to act as his sole publisher in the United States. I did so & got a letter from Conrad wanting to know if you would sign a regular contract.' On 19 January, Harvey replied that Conrad did not bring in enough to justify putting him on a salary. (Formerly MSS Sutton, sale catalogue 2,493: not sold to Indiana.)

³ *The Point of Honor* (McClure, 1908), illustrated by Dan Van Sayre Groesbeck.

⁴ A note on the MS in another hand proposes a different list of contents: 'The Duel about 32000/The Secret Sharer 15000 words/Gestures 8,500 words/The Inland Sea about 12000 words (appeared in Tribune)'. 'Gestures' was another name for 'The Informer'; part of the original 'The Inland Sea' appeared in the *Tribune* as 'The Sea of Adventure', reprinted in *The Mirror of the Sea* as 'The "Tremolino"'.

To J. B. Pinker

Text MS Berg; Unpublished

[letterhead: Aldington]
Monday. [10 January 1910]¹

Dear Pinker.

I send this small batch unregistered. If it hadn't been for this confounded epidemic which had got amongst us the thing would be done.

Re your letter as the vol of short stories. If you think that you can get more money later on for them then of course its good policy to keep back the book. But otherwise I don't see the point. I am not a beginner on my promotion. The public which I have gained in the US will buy the short stories vol, whether a long novel precedes its publication or not. If the silence has been long I don't see the use to prolong it unless to serve some material end which you have in view or a settled policy to which you wish to adhere for a definite reason of your own. But otherwise I don't see how the publication of a vol of short stories can affect adversely a man of my standing. But you'll understand that I am not impatient to see myself in print! The stuff being there the only question is the question of money. That's all I feel about it. One more remark I'll make: it may very well be that by the time Raz. comes out in *book form* there will be enough of short stories for another vol. And wouldn't they then stand in each other's way? I have 5 subjects which I shall tackle at once—or at least was thinking of tackling at once one after another.

No more of this. You'll do what you think fit

Yours

J. Conrad.

To J. B. Pinker

Text MS Berg; Unpublished

[letterhead: Aldington]
Wednesday. [12 January 1910]²

My dear Pinker.

Thanks for your explanation. I did not mean to take up your time. I have no *personal* feeling whatever in the matter and not the least

¹ Received 'January 1910' with '20 pages' of MS. As Carabine shows, these pages would have become Batch R of the TS, which is dated 15 January; professional typing could not have taken more than a few days.

² Received 'January 1910': another stage in the correspondence about U.S. publication of the stories? Too calm a letter for a day as late as the 19th?

intention to interfere in your management. Will you send me some writing paper—I've got so used to it—and the people in Ashford would want a fortnight to get it for me.

What do you think of the tittle* to give the book. Would *Under Western Eyes* do at all—or something of the kind? A title pertains to the publishing part of the business. I would not venture to ask your advice if I did not feel that strongly.

<div style="text-align:center">Yours sincerely</div>
<div style="text-align:right">J. Conrad.</div>

<div style="text-align:center">t[urn] o[ver] p[lease]</div>

I have just received the enclosed. *Monds bought the E R.*[1] It may be useful later on to place an article or a story—provding the pub:on in the US could be arranged as well.

Would you when writing to America, in the usual course of business, ask Harpers to send me a copy or two of the *2d edition of Nostromo* for my collection. I wrote to Alden[2] re story saying that I asked you to send it to him and that it was done as a contribution to the 60th anniversary No of their magazine—which is sufficiently true as I had them rather in my eye. But of course I don't care where it appears, really.

To J. B. Pinker
Text MS Texas; Unpublished

<div style="text-align:right">[letterhead: Aldington]
Thursday. [13 or 20 January
1910][3]</div>

Dear Pinker.

I shall probably come myself on Monday with the last pages. I haven't been in town except once for a few hours since March last. I keep all the MS by me till then. I want to talk over with you the plan of further work. I feel quite well now—but its extraordinary how a quite insignificant touch of flue* knocks a man over for days. Everybody in the house had it except the dog, I think. My wife isn't herself yet.

[1] Sir Alfred Moritz Mond, MP (1868–1930), the Liberal industrialist, had bought the *English Review* at Ford's urging (Mizener, p. 195). Conrad evidently found Mond more acceptable than David Soskice.

[2] Henry Mills Alden, editor of *Harper's Magazine*.

[3] A date on either side of the 19th is possible: the 20th if the present text postpones the dash to London anticipated in the letter of [19? January]; the 13th if the Monday visit promised here is on the 17th, in which case the letter of [19? January] explains why Conrad did not show up. The mention of illness favours the earlier date.

The title *Under Western Eyes* was meant for the novel—not for the short stories as I fear I have given you the false impression of. Will it do for *that*? However we'll talk of this on Mond. In haste

<div style="text-align:center">Yours</div>

<div style="text-align:right">J. Conrad</div>

To J. B. Pinker

Text MS Berg; Unpublished

<div style="text-align:right">[letterhead: Aldington]
Wend* 2 pm. [19? January
1910][1]</div>

Dear Pinker.

Colvin[2] turned up on Sunday for the whole day and when he left I could only crawl to bed. Herewith the pages up to 1300. Twelve more ought to do it—or perhaps a few more. If I finish in good time to night I shall catch the 10.30 to morrow from here. But if not then next day.

<div style="text-align:center">Regards yours</div>

<div style="text-align:right">J. C.</div>

To J. B. Pinker

Text Telegrams, Berg; Unpublished

<div style="text-align:right">Hythe
26 Jan 10 1.38 p.m.[3]</div>

Pinker Bookishly London

Book finished this morning too late to catch train have you carbon copy as batch of 2000 words apparently missing here please wire

<div style="text-align:right">Conrad</div>

[1] Received 'January 1910': a note, not in Conrad's hand, reads 'Ms enclosed'; this would be Batch S, ff. 1266–1300. Batch R went off on the 10th; Conrad reached f.1351, the original ending, on the 22nd. This letter, then, belongs either to the 12th or the 19th. The earlier date, favoured by Carabine on textual grounds, has Conrad writing 35ff. between the 10th and the 12th; the later, favoured here on grounds of congruence with other letters, has him writing 50ff. between the 19th and the 22nd – in either case a rate astonishing in terms of Conrad's usual speed, but reminiscent of the pace at which he finished *Nostromo* and *Lord Jim*.

[2] The scholar, Sidney Colvin.

[3] Time, date, and place supplied by the post office. These telegrams show that although the MS is inscribed 'End 22 January 1910', the author did not consider himself done. Carabine argues that Conrad worked until the 26th on the 25 ff. revision of the final chapter, which is at the Rosenbach.

Aldington

26 Jan 10 5.5 p.m.

Pinker Bookishly London

Sorry have troubled you the part found with you tomorrow[1]

To John Galsworthy

Text MS Forbes; Unpublished

[Aldington]

Thursday evening [mid March ?

1910][2]

Dearest Jack

I have stood up today for several minutes, the first time in six weeks. But both feet and one hand are still bandaged.[3]

I feel all crumpled up beyond all hope being* ever smoothed out again—but of course it will come. I find the writing of this, the greatest mental strain imaginable. A wretched state to be in.

I have seen all the cuttings dear Ada has sent us. No single criticism is worthy of the play.[4] Archer is perhaps the best but even he is somewhat dense.[5] I understand you have had a great number of private communications. Anyway the effect produced is very great—is not so?

I have received a copy of the *Nigger* in French. It seems the book has been published ten days ago.[6] D'Humières also sent me a cheque for 375 frcs[7] on acct of royalties which just pays Borys' term at the Luton school. I don't think he will return there after the holidays. It's impossible. But I can't think so far ahead. You can't imagine my state of mental weakness. Of course I can't do anything in the way of revising Raz. yet.

[1] When in London, he quarrelled with Pinker: see the letter of 23 May. On the 30th, Conrad collapsed. On 3 February, Jessie Conrad wired Pinker: 'Conrad alarmingly ill since Sunday doctor will confirm'; on the 6th, she wrote: 'Conrad very seriously ill. The doctor says it is a complete nervous breakdown and that it has been coming on for months. He forbids anyone to see him or any mention of business ... It is a terribly anxious time and I dare not leave him for a moment' (telegram and MS Berg). Although Dr Hackney's confirmation (3 February, MS Berg) predicted that he would 'not be anything like well for another ten days', Conrad's illness lasted many weeks: for Jessie Conrad's account see *Joseph Conrad and His Circle*, pp. 140–8. See also Keith Carabine, 'Conrad, Pinker, and *Under Western Eyes: A Novel*', *The Conradian*, 10 (1985), 144–53.

[2] About six weeks after the initial collapse: the 10th, 17th, or 24th?

[3] They were severely inflamed with gout.

[4] On 21 February, *Justice* had opened triumphantly at the Duke of York's.

[5] Marrot (pp. 256–7) quotes part of the review in the *Nation* by William Archer (1856–1924), the playwright, translator, and influential critic.

[6] By the *Mercure de France*. [7] The equivalent of £15.

Hackney[1] says it will pass very quickly by and bye. Meantime the days pass—it's maddening to think how quickly.

I don't know what to say to you my dearest Jack. Without you I would have perished materially and morally too. I daren't ask what has been done by Robert.[2] Indeed I am not fit to hear it that or anything else.

Love and thanks to Ada

Yours ever

J. Conrad

To John Galsworthy
Text MS Forbes; Unpublished

[Aldington]
31 m[ar]ch 1910.[3]

Dearest Jack

My last[4] relapse had taken the form of gout in the abdominal muscles—an experience which I shall not forget if I live to a hundred. The last symptoms disappeared five days ago. But both feet remain swollen (tho' not particularly painful) and till that subsides I can't be fairly said to be out of the wood. Still there is a marked turn for the better. They are treating me now exclusively with sour milk and thymionic* acid[5] all the more usual remedies having been used up in the course of these fatal ten weeks during which You have kept us all out of the ditch. I am still extremely limp both mentally and physically; but I shall to morrow try to go on with the revision of MS and discover how far I am capable of sustained mental effort. I am afraid it will not be a very brilliant result. I am growing desperate with the pain and weariness and the worry of this fatal stoppage of work.

I had a letter from R Garnett of which no doubt You know the

1 Clifford Hackney, the doctor from Hythe.
2 Robert Garnett was now acting on Conrad's behalf on literary as well as legal matters: see the letter of [7 April].
3 An alternative reading of Conrad's pained handwriting would be '3 M[a]rch', but the passage of a 'fatal ten weeks' would take the date to the end of the month – and even a week or so beyond.
4 'Latest'.
5 Thyminic acid was another name for Solurol, a treatment for gout: see also n. 2 to the letter of 25 July 1909. Enthusiasm for the 'Lactic Acid Bacilli' cure, taken as yoghurt, kefir, or milk curdled by special tablets, dated from the translation of Ilya Mechnikov's *The Prolongation of Life* in 1907. *The Extra Pharmacopoeia* (14th ed., pp. 44–57) recommended sour milk for dyspepsia, colitis, eczema, neurasthenia, and loss of appetite.

contents. Of course the first thing is to get the MS ready for pubon and perhaps soon the creative power will return—or wake up.

I can't write more just now. My heart is too full and my head too muddled.

My dearest love to you both

Yours ever

J. Conrad.

Send me the vol of Justice. I am anxious to see it.

To Robert Garnett
Text MS Bryn Mawr; Unpublished

[Aldington]
Thursday. [7 April 1910][1]

My dear Garnett[2]

I send you this batch trusting to your kindness to have it put in hand at some good typing office. Another lot will follow in a few days but I cant yet work even at this sort of thing for longer than one hour at a time.

I hear with great joy that Edward intends to come down here to see me.

My thanks and most cordial regards from us both

Yours

J Conrad

To Robert Garnett
Text MS Free; Rude (1982)

[Aldington]
[14? April 1910][3]

Dear Garnett

Thanks for your kind letter. This batch is rather slender but the next early next week shall be bigger. A request I must make that if you feel

[1] Date-stamped as received on Friday, 8 April. The initials 'D[arley] C[umberland]' on the stamp show that the recipient was Robert rather than Edward Garnett.
[2] Robert Singleton Garnett (1866–1932), Edward's elder brother, was senior partner in the law firm of Darley, Cumberland. As a consequence both of the breach with Pinker and of the illness, Garnett was handling Conrad's literary interests; later, he did the same for D. H. Lawrence. Garnett was a keen book-collector and an authority on Alexandre Dumas, the Elder.
[3] Received in Garnett's office on 15 April.

inclined to look at the stuff at all you will use the shortened copy such as I mean it to appear serially.[1]

<div align="center">Yours cordially</div>

<div align="right">J Conrad.</div>

To H.-D. Davray
Text MS Texas; *L. fr.* 99

<div align="right">[letterhead: Aldington][2]</div>

<div align="right">3 mai. 1910</div>

Cher Ami.

Je viens de recevoir le No du *Temps* qui, je suis sûr, vient de vous. Merci. Cela m'a fait plaisir de me voir en feuilleton.[3] Et j'ai bien besoin d'avoir mon moral remonté. Je suis tombé malade fin janvier. Ça n'avait l'air de rien tout d'abord; et voilà que j'en ai eu pour 3 mois de lit! Une attaque de goutte, litteralement, depuis la nuque jusqu-aux talons.

Il parait que j'ai manqué d'en mourir; mais comme cela n'est pas arrivé n'en parlons plus. Je puis me dire guéri sauf que je ne marche pas encore très bien. Je me traine d'une chambre à l'autre avec l'aide d'une canne, c'est qui est assez triste; mais voilà huit jours que je me suis remis au travail et je m'en tire passablement.

C'est égal! C'etait une vraie maladie de luxe. Trois mois sur le dos, quatre mois sans rien faire. Un tiers de l'année parti, perdu!

Il faut pardonner a ma femme de ne pas Vous avoir écrit. Elle m'a soigné toute seule jour et nuit. Enfin.

Je vous écris a la Revue car tout est en desordre ici et je ne peux pas trouver votre carte de Noël qui porte votre addresse.

Le bon Nègre e[s]t tout-a-fait bien en jaune.[4] Je ne vous demande pas des nouvelles de la vente car je sens bien que c'est un livre impossible. L'Agent Secret va paraître en Suédois prochainement.[5]

Deux jours avant ma maladie j'avais fini un roman qui traite des* quelques Russes a Gèneve et un peu a Petersburg. Pinker est en train de le placer. C'est un roman plutôt psychologique mais très simple.

Aprésent je vais me remettre a la mer pour quelque temps. Rien de

[1] For the shortening of *Under Western Eyes*, see Higdon and Sheard, 'Conrad's "Unkindest Cut"'.
[2] The début of letterhead two.
[3] Davray's translation of *The Secret Agent* was just beginning in serial.
[4] The classic colour for a French novel.
[5] *Provokatören*, translated by G[ustaf] A[dolf] J[anson] and published in Stockholm

technique. Experience dramatisée en quelques contes de 7 a 10 mille mots.

Je m'associe a ma femme qui envoie mille amitiés a Mme Davray ainsi qu'a vous. Il faudra absolument venir nous voir la prochaine fois que vous venez en Angleterre. Croyez moi toujours

tout à vous

J. Conrad.

Translation

Dear Friend,

I have just received the number of the *Temps*, which comes from you, I'm sure. Thank you. It's pleasing to see myself in a serial.

And I certainly need a boost to my morale. I fell ill at the end of January. At first it seemed like nothing very much; and now I've spent three months in bed! An attack of gout literally from head to toe.

Apparently I nearly died of it; but as I didn't, let's say no more about it. I may call myself healed, except that I still don't walk very well. I drag myself from one room to another with the aid of a stick—a sorry state of affairs!—but I have been back at work for eight days, and I'm coming out of it fairly well.

Never mind! It was truly a first-class illness. Three months on my back, four months doing nothing. A third of the year gone by—lost!

My wife must be forgiven for not writing to you. She looked after me day and night, all by herself. So you see...

I am writing to you at the *Mercure* because everything is upside-down here, and I can't find your Christmas card with your address.

The good *Nigger* looks very fine in yellow. I don't ask for news of sales, because I know very well that it's an impossible book. *The Secret Agent* is coming out soon in Swedish.

Two days before my illness, I had finished a novel which deals with some Russians in Geneva and, to an extent, in St Petersburg. Pinker is in the process of placing it. It's something of a psychological novel, but very straightforward.

Now I'm off to recuperate by the sea. No technique. Dramatized experience in stories of seven to ten thousand words.

I join my wife in sending many greetings to Madame Davray as well

as to you. You absolutely must come to see us the next time you come to
England. Believe me always

<div align="center">Yours sincerely,</div>

<div align="right">J. Conrad.</div>

To Arthur Symons

Text MS Virginia; Hunter (1985, 3)

<div align="right">[letterhead: Aldington]
6th May 1910</div>

Dear Mr Symons.

I am inexpressibly glad to hear you are back in your world in the
freedom of wind and sea and the beautifully furnished space visible from
your charming perch of Wittersham.[1]

This letter must be short. I have been in bed 3 months; just got up;
just fit to crawl from one room to another; been out for short drive the
other day. The first long drive will be to look you up if permitted. But the
time for that is not yet.

We dare not ask your wife and yourself to come over—not just yet at
any rate. We have been pigging it in 4 rooms in a cottage looking out
meantime for a farmhouse to fall empty in this part of Kent. Our *intérieur*
is not fit to be seen at present my illness having had a generally upsetting
character.

Pardon this scrawl. I am writing in bed. Your appreciation is precious
to me. We shall soon meet, that's certain. Believe me

<div align="center">yours most cordially,</div>

<div align="right">J. Conrad</div>

[1] Symons came home to Island Cottage on 7 April of sound but diminished mind
(Beckson, pp. 271–2). Wittersham stands on high ground, the other side of Romney
Marsh from Aldington and about twelve miles away.

To Laurence Housman

Text MS Bryn Mawr; Unpublished

[letterhead: Aldington]
11 [14?] May 1910[1]

Dear M^r Housman.[2]

You will see that the delay arises solely from our change of address. This being Saturday another 24 hours must be lost, Ad majorem Dei gloriam,[3] before the infinitesimal support of my signature reaches Your hands.

With the greatest sympathy for the object I cannot share the beautiful optimism of the memorial.[4] Justice and moderation have never yet recommended a cause to the heads of parliamentary absolutism. One could expect more on these grounds from the servants of a simple autocrat, I imagine. I would augur better from the step, with which I associate myself unreservedly, had we been able to frame our request in the lurid language of menaces. But that unfortunately is impossible. We are too few for that, and truth to say of no particular weight in this literature-loving but not very discriminating community.

After 30 years attentive watching of the old-established and the only genuine Parliamentary Institutions[5] it seems to me that the shortest road to success for women's suffrage would be in its being made a party question on any ground under heaven except that of justice. But this is mere theory and most unwillingly held at that. Nothing would please me more than to find myself utterly wrong in the light of facts.

Believe me, dear M^r Housman,

very sincerely Yours

J. Conrad.

[1] Written on a Saturday, but the 11th was a Wednesday.

[2] Laurence Housman (1865–1959), brother of the poet, was an illustrator, poet, and playwright. Among his works are *Rue* (1899), *An Englishwoman's Love Letters* (anonymously, 1900), *The Chinese Lantern* (1908), *Victoria Regina* (1934), and illustrations to Christina Rossetti's *Goblin Market*.

[3] 'To the greater glory of God' (the Jesuit motto), London had no Sunday deliveries.

[4] The memorial was directed to the Prime Minister, urging him to back the Women's Suffrage Bill. The promoters of this bill, drafted by a committee of sympathisers from all parties, hoped to extricate the cause of women's right to vote from the snarls of party politics. Conrad was among the forty-three scholars and writers who signed the memorial (*The Times*, 15 June).

[5] Conrad came to England for the first time in 1878 and became a British subject in 1886.

To John Galsworthy

Text MS Forbes; J-A, 2, 107

[Aldington]
17 May. '10

Dearest Jack

I finished the revise of Raz. on the night of Wednesday last[1]—say a week ago. For the next 24 hours I lay supine but not so broken up as I feared. Then I had to write a letter to good Robert—as a matter of fact I had to write two letters. The second went off yesterday. Between whiles I went to bed and gasped. I did not even attempt to write to you. I thought that Garnett would let you know that the book was out of my hands at last, and that the stage of negociation* has been reached. He has been most friendly and wonderfully kind, volunteering to read over and correct the clean final copy. With three superimposed revisions there were a good many phrases without grammar and even without sense to be found in the rough typed copy. And I dreaded the task of wading through all that shallow, sticky stuff again.

I am but a wretched convalescent as yet, after all. Two painful ankles and one painful wrist (the left luckily) keep me in a state of uneasy irritation. I just can hobble along for a few yards. My voice too has not come back properly. At times I am hardly audible. But that don't matter much except that Jackolo imitates my extinct tones, while scolding his favourite Teddy-bear, to perfection. The other day, I understand, he gave to some yokels an exhibition of my limping which astonished them not a little. All this is done in the innocence of his heart. He goes through these performances with the utmost gravity. He's much like the other in his devotion to birds, flowers and engines. Borys is going to try for the Ox & Camb preliminary.[2] He went back to Luton for another term a week ago. While here he gave me much of his time, very tactful with his fractious father and really of great assistance in the arranging of MS. He put in order for me 600 pp all unnumbered and considerably shuffled working very methodically and with a quiet perseverance for an hour or so every morning. With one hand only one cannot do that sort of thing easily (and in bed at that) so I was really glad to have him to help. Going off at the railway station he said to Jessie "I really think I've done some good to Dada." He certainly comforted me not a little. He seemed well and looked strong enough.

[1] The 11th.

[2] Passing this examination would make him eligible for several kinds of secondary schooling.

I am thus coming back to the world. Yet that isn't exactly it. It's very much like coming out of one little hell into another. Don't think that I am ungrateful to gods and men (and of all men to you) by saying this. One can't help that feeling. I am glad enough to have changed one hell for another—for I do not feel either helpless or hopeless. On the contrary there is a sort of confidence—but indeed it may be only the sign of an incipient softening of the brain! However I am glad enough to feel it on any terms. Anything's better than black depression, which may be the sign of religious mania.

About this same brain: it is not equal to prolonged effort. I am writing this in 10 minute snatches. That's the limit at present. Nevertheless I am going to begin to morrow a short story—if the devil's in it. It's to be comical in a nautical setting and its subject is (or *are*) potatoes. Title: A Smile of Fortune.[1] May it be a good omen! Only, I don't quite believe in omens.

As to P[inker] I am trying (R. Garnett plenipotentiary) to obtain a promise of 3 pounds per thousand words—on delivery of MS, since he won't have it otherwise. I don't quarrel with him for that and would have nothing to say against it if I could be only certain of regular output. I dare say I can (if no knock down blow occurs) squeeze some 100 000 w per year out of myself. Of course it would be like working in chains—but never mind that.

Further I stipulate that when a work is finished he will make me an advance on it bringing up the amount to five pound[s] per thousand in all.

But the principal preliminary condition is that he should pay a 150 on delivery of Raz: I must have that. There is the tax man, a few other things, Borys' school and so on. And besides we have secured a house. I can't stay on in this (comparatively expensive) hole. It has become odious to me after this illness. I need that amount of change.

It's a farmhouse[2] with biggish rooms and 1 1/2 acres of orchard standing in the fields and surrounded by 750 acres of unpreserved woods[3] where I am at liberty to roam. 5 miles from Ashford and only a mile from Ham Street Station which has the same service as Smeeth only travellers must change in Ashford. It's a very attractive place and

[1] Inspired by Conrad's emotional and financial speculations in Mauritius, 1888, this story fulfills the intention, outlined to Davray on the 3rd, of writing 'Experience dramatisée'.

[2] Capel House, the Conrads' home from 1910 to 1919.

[3] Woods free of gamekeepers and gamekeeping.

cheap at £45.[1] It may be folly to take it—but it's either that or a breakdown; for my nerves are just on the balance. I require perfect silence for my work—and I can get that there. And as a fact the days of 20 pounds a year farmhouses are over. This is as cheap as almost any place we have tried for this last year and a half.

I won't write any more just now. I wanted you to know that I am getting hold again. I trust dear Jack you have saved me for better things. The post is ready to go.

Our dear love to you both

Yours ever

J. Conrad.

To Sir Hugh Clifford

Text MS Clifford; J-A, 2, 109; Hunter (1985, 2)

[letterhead: Aldington]
19 May '10

My Dear Clifford.[2]

This being eminently a case for Christian charity I won't make this letter long. Indeed I am not very fit for writing much as yet. Your letter to my wife has comforted me immensely.

I am too lame (in both feet) to come and see you in London.[3] I am also somewhat shaky all over. It seems I have been very ill. At the time I did not believe it, but now I begin to think that I must have been. And what's more I begin to see that the horrible nervous tension of the last two years[4] (of which even my wife knows nothing) had to end in something of the sort.

Perhaps it was the only way of relief?

I am ashamed to show my face to you even from a distance—in writing. Yet I shall be brazen to the extent of asking whether you will come and see me here when you have time. I don't want to bore you with

[1] It was much more substantial than Pent Farm, which had rented for £30 a year.

[2] Sir Hugh Charles Clifford (1866–1941; knighted 1909), a colonial administrator, was serving as British Resident in Pahang, Malaya, when he wrote one of the earliest general appreciations of Conrad's work. Later, he was appointed to the governorships of Labuan and North Borneo, the Gold Coast, Nigeria, Ceylon, and the Straits Settlements. He published many volumes of stories and sketches, collaborated on a Malay dictionary, and produced a Malay translation of the colonial penal code.

[3] Clifford was on home leave from his appointment as Colonial Secretary of Ceylon, a post he held from 1907 to 1912.

[4] The period of writing *Under Western Eyes*.

the story of my life since we last set eyes on each other[1]—but a few words may be said which will partly explain away the ugly appearances.

Shortly before my illness an Island-skipper[2] came to see me. A soft-eyed black-bearded man married to a Patani[3] girl of good family, with a house in Penang, on the beach and a small plantation of rubber trees. He came here to see his people in Durham. He wrote to me "I am like a crow in a strange country—may I come to see you?" We talked of You and your books for hours.

Jessie sends her kindest regards and I am as I have ever been

Yours most affectionately

J. Conrad

To John Galsworthy
Text MS Forbes; Unpublished

[letterhead: Aldington]
Friday [20 May? 1910][4]

Dearest Jack

Thanks for your unwearied services. I took the schooling for this term into acct/ while formulating my request to P—or rather Robert. But as I don't know how far they will be met and how long it may take you have relieved my mind considerably.

I am far from well to-day. Nerves. That must be got over. I had to lay the story aside for a day as after a little time a sort of queerness *would* come over me. All this is temporary—and not new. I used to disregard it but just at present prudence is necessary.

So sorry to hear you feel stale. I imagine You must have been at it too close and too long. Love to dear Ada

Ever yours

J. Conrad.

[1] A long time, perhaps. The most recent surviving letter dates from 1903.
[2] Captain Marris.
[3] From Pattani, a Malay-speaking area in southern Thailand.
[4] After the letter of the 17th, when 'A Smile of Fortune' is first mentioned. Another letter dates from the 27th, but 3 or 10 June would be possible. Robert Garnett's role as go-between specifies the period and the story.

To William Rothenstein
Text MS Harvard; WR 159

[letterhead: Aldington]
20 May. '10

Dearest Will.

I can just, just hobble over 50 yards or so of smooth ground but am too tottery and generally shaky to venture on the pavements of Babylon. Also one wrist is dead lame.

The mind is not much better. Can't concentrate for more than 1/2 hour at a time. How to write long or short stories under this disability I don't know. But they must be written and shall be. It'll be, no doubt, very delightful.

I can't go and see Your Pictures.[1] It's exasperating. I am keeping a tight hand on myself for fear my nerves go to pieces. I suppose I *have* been as ill as they tell me. At the time I was rather sceptical; now I begin to believe it.

To get away from this hole here is my ardent wish. We have found a home in the woods within 4 1/2 miles. It is picturesque and roomy. I *must* have space and silence—silence! I shall get that last there if anywhere outside the grave—which has no space.

You must come and see and approve, as soon as we get in. I mean you two—for your approbation without your dear wife's would be worth nearly nothing.

Our dear love to all your house

Ever yours

J. Conrad.

[1] At the annual show of the New English Art Club.

To Warrington Dawson
Text MS Duke; Randall 129

[letterhead: Aldington]
21 May 1910

My dear Sir[1]

Les amis des nos amis etc but as a matter of fact I had your name laid up in a cell of my brain for some time now. It is (I mean my brain) a rather crazy structure with rusty-hinged doors and dark corners—and all dusty with ashes of good intentions. Thus I haven't as yet obtained either of your novels.[2]

Let us meet without any more delay than may suit your convenience. Only you must understand the situation. You find here a man who has just got out of bed after a long illness: an attack of gout, literally from neck to ankles. You'll find him lame, grincheux[3] and stupid—more than usual. And you must come to see him. He can't come to You in London. Like figures in a bad novel l'animal ne tient pas debout[4]—at any rate not yet.

But this is not the worst. We have been living here in part of a cottage where we piled in a year ago with the idea of making it a centre for house hunting in this part of Kent—farm-house hunting. That sort of game is scarce; but we brought down a charming specimen only last week after no end of wearisome stalking.[5] That's very well, but meantime (we can't enter till June) we have no bedroom to offer You and you must be prepared for a most primitive reception. Something like the rude and unaffected hospitality of cave-men—with this difference only that the meat shall be cooked.

None but les intimes have been allowed to come near us here. Will

[1] Francis Warrington Dawson (1878–1962) came from Charleston, S. C.; his father was a newspaper publisher, and his mother, who followed her son to Paris when he made it his headquarters, belonged to a family of faded plantation-owners. Throughout his life Dawson wrote prolifically: fiction, essays, newspaper stories. He covered strikes, wars, peace conferences, the French Senate and the Chamber of Deputies. 'Furthermore', to quote Randall, 'he had a special taste and talent for conversing with the great and near-great' (p. 4). In 1909, while on safari in East Africa with Theodore Roosevelt, Dawson met Conrad's old friends the Sandersons. When Dawson came to England in May 1910, intending to report the funeral of Edward VII, he carried an introduction to Conrad.
[2] *The Scar* (1906) and *The Scourge* (1908), intentionally 'realistic' novels of Virginia life.
[3] 'Grumpy'.
[4] In traditional biology, as much as in fiction, uprightness marks the human from the bestial. Many commentators have noticed the significance of Kurtz's *crawling* towards the jungle.
[5] Dawson must have alluded to his own exploits after game.

you have the courage to join their ranks, to undertake a horrid railway journey of 2 hours (11 to 12.58) and the horrors of the return trip by the 8.20 up. Will you? The hardships of the caravan track are as nothing to the enterprise I am inviting you to. I have been frank; but if, in the pride of youth and recklessness (perhaps) of your disposition, you won't take the warning, why then—we shall be *very glad* to see you. Name your day (except Tuesday next[1]) and I'll try to meet the train or shall send a dependable native. We shall have an afternoon together; and if I quarrel with you after the manner of une vieille ganache[2] more than is becoming (as between two brother-craftsmen) you can always report me to dear old Ted[3] who no doubt will do justice by shooting me next time he comes home on leave. Voilà! Meantime believe me

<div style="text-align:center">very Sincerely yours</div>

<div style="text-align:right">J. Conrad</div>

Pardon this variegated scrawl; I am writing on the knee.

To J. B. Pinker
Text MS Berg; Unpublished

<div style="text-align:right">Aldington
Kent
23 May 1910.</div>

Dear Sir

From some word dropped by P Gibbon the other day I gather that a letter from you has remained unanswered.

This, I believe, can refer only to the Swedish proposal.[4] I was not at the time in a state to write to any one. As my wife has been nursing me single-handed night and day through a very anxious time (besides attending to heaps of correspondence in reference to my illness) I am certain you won't require a very elaborate apology for her oversight. But she regrets it and I beg to assure you that no discourtesy was intended.

As it can't have escaped your recollection that the last time we met[5] you told me that I "did not speak English" to you I have asked Robert Garnett to be my mouth-piece—at any rate till my speech improves sufficiently to be acceptable. I have asked him to telephone to you re reference to house-agents. I am under notice to quit here on June 24;

[1] The 24th. [2] 'An old fogey'.
[3] Sanderson – the once and future schoolmaster.
[4] For a translation of *The Secret Agent*. [5] When Conrad delivered *Under Western Eyes*.

and I really could *not* do any literary work sitting in a field with my family and furniture about me.

<div align="center">Yours faithfully</div>

<div align="right">J. Conrad.</div>

PS I venture to mention the above as I presume this is a matter not exclusively touching me but also of some interest to you.

To John Galsworthy
Text MS POSK; Danilewiczowa

<div align="right">[Aldington]
27 May 1910</div>

Dearest Jack

You must forgive me. I feel horrid to think how I intrude endlessly on your peace and your work. Being still rather helpless makes me nervous. Every molehill is a mountain.

I had a slight touch—a sort of faint relapse or a check in the slow improvement—a few days ago. It disturbed me profoundly—but its over. I hobble about again. Head clear enough and not so empty either if I only had a chance to concentrate myself. The new story moves on halting a little. I long for a clear run for my work. You understand. No gouty obstacles—a clear 12 months. I've never had that in all my writing life.

Our dear love.

<div align="center">Yours penitently</div>

<div align="right">J. Conrad.</div>

To John Galsworthy
Text MS Forbes; J-A, 2, 107; Randall 130

<div align="right">[Aldington]
Tuesday. [31 May 1910][1]</div>

Dearest Jack

Thanks for your letter. I am trying to work as fast as I can without knocking my feeble brain silly.

I'll report to you soon how I am *really* getting on. All that went before is mere trial run so to speak. I have been also interrupted. Hugh Clifford

[1] The Tuesday after Dawson's visit: evidently he had been to Aldington on the 28th, the only Saturday between Conrad's invitation (21 May) and his reply (4 June) to a letter of thanks.

return[ed] from Ceylon turned up last Friday. On Sat. a young American writer who has been with Roosevelt in S. Africa arrived for the day. The greatest news is that Mrs. Ted Sanderson has discovered in herself a talent for writing and that the Ex-President has been so struck that he placed three of her E[ast] A[frican] sketches with Scribners Mag.[1]

They seem very well and happy over there.[2]

Same young man brought a formal message from the only Teddy. He would have invited himself to come and see me, only too busy with official festivities.[3] Very safe bunkum that.

Many many thanks my dear best Jack. Our dear love to Ada. How is she? This weather is not very good.

<div style="text-align:center">Ever yours</div>

<div style="text-align:right">J. Conrad</div>

To Warrington Dawson
Text MS Duke; Randall 131

<div style="text-align:right">[letterhead: Aldington]
4 June 1910.</div>

My dear Sir

Thanks for all you say. I've ordered the Secret Agent—which, by the by, has begun to appear in French as feuilleton of the Temps.[4]

Let me in my turn remind you of the promise you have given me of sending me one of Your books. Les bons comptes font les bons amis.[5]

Give my love to the boy who has read *Youth* and expressed so artistically his reasons for liking my prose. I can send him no less than that. Before he acquires a boy of his own I shall be no longer here—on this earth of fine sights, honest endeavours and kindly hearts. But I like to think that my memory may be kept green by the youngest of the generations now existing.

Marwood was here yesterday and wishes to be remembered to you. We talked of you a good bit. You have awakened his sympathy and interest.

[1] Helen Sanderson wrote them as 'Janet Allardyce': see the letter of [16 or 23? October].

[2] Since 1904, Ted Sanderson had been Town Clerk of Nairobi, Kenya (then known as British East Africa).

[3] Ex-President Roosevelt, now touring England, was making speeches on a heroic scale.

[4] The serial, or 'feuilleton', began on 31 May.

[5] 'Good reckonings make good friends'.

I don't speak of myself; on that you must form your own judgement. Let me only say that I hope our acquaintance shall not be allowed to die out wherever you are—in the New World or the Old.

<div style="text-align:right">Yours cordially

J. Conrad.</div>

To H.-D. Davray
Text MS Texas; *L. fr.* 101

<div style="text-align:right">[letterhead: Aldington]

9 Juin '10</div>

Cher Davray.

Je viens de recevoir votre bonne lettre. Oui, certainement si Vous me le permettez je vais faire signe en marge s'il y a lieu.[1] N'oubliez pas cher traducteur et ami que malgré la saveur spéciale que l'on trouve dans ma prose ici, je suis un écrivain idiomatique en anglais. De sorte qu'en Vous servant de l'idiome français vous rendrez ma pensée même mieux qu'en suivant la valeur exacte des mots.

Puisque vous en parlez Vous même je vous dirais franchement qu'un peu d'argent me fera plaisir. Comme Vous le savez j'ai des habitudes luxueuses en matière de maladie qui me mettent[?] a sec periodiquement. C'est un triste vice cela.

J'espère que vous trouverez le temps, a votre prochaine visite ici, pour venir nous voir.

La dessus je finis ce gribouillage.

Mes devoirs a Madame.

<div style="text-align:center">Bien à vous</div>

<div style="text-align:right">J. Conrad</div>

Translation

Dear Davray,

I've just had your kind letter. Yes, certainly, if you permit it and if need be room, I shall mark up the margin. Don't forget, dear friend and translator, notwithstanding the special flavour that people here find in my prose, I write idiomatic English. Thus, by using French idioms you

[1] As it appeared in serial form, Conrad was perhaps going to mark up Davray's translation of *The Secret Agent* with an eye to book publication.

will render my thoughts even better than you would by following the precise meaning of each word.

Since you yourself speak of it, I'll tell you frankly that a little money would bring me pleasure. As you know, I have luxurious habits as far as sickness goes, and these habits leave me periodically high and dry. What a sorry failing.

I hope that on your next visit over here, you'll find the time to come and see us.

Whereupon, I end this scribble.

My regards to Madame Davray

<div style="text-align:center">Sincerely yours,</div>

<div style="text-align:right">J. Conrad</div>

To John Galsworthy
Text MS Forbes; J-A, 2, 110

<div style="text-align:right">[letterhead: Aldington]
18 June '10</div>

Dearest Jack.

I received the volume[1] the day before yesterday and laid it aside till this afternoon. So much of the delay is due to my deliberate desire to await a composed state of mind. The rest is Heinemann's fault. I tell you this because the inscription, I notice, is dated on the seventh.

I read A Portrait with greatly awakened curiosity and some emotion.[2] It is a very fine offering; a study, almost an analysis, which yet rises to be a creation. There is harmony in it, a balance, as in that commemorated life. Thus he is fortunate to the end! From my glimpses of him—three I think altogether—I believe that he would have liked these pages, the serene, twilight feeling of that prose enshrining his memory.

I suppose that I am now the only human being in these Isles who thinks Meyerbeer a great composer;[3] and I am an alien at that and not to be wholly trusted. I remember well you telling me of Your father's liking for Turgueniev. It seemed always a very mysterious thing till you enlightened me. Yes, it must have been that—the common worship of beauty.

[1] *A Motley*, the newly-published collection of stories and sketches.

[2] It is a portrait of the artist's father as an old man. John Galsworthy, Senior, died in 1904 at the age of 87.

[3] Like Conrad, the old gentleman admired Meyerbeer 'whom he insisted ... on considering a great composer' (p. 8). The operas of Giacomo Meyerbeer (Jakob Liebmann Meyer Beer, 1791–1864) were particularly popular in France; they included *Robert le Diable* (1831), *Les Huguenots* (1836), and *L'Africaine* (1865).

Those pages set apart I think that, without doubt, *The Neighbours* is the clou of that gallery. Roughly speaking it's all gold, without the slightest alloy. The total absence of grimness is miraculous[1]—it makes for perfection. And the finest descriptive passage of the book is there too—the moonlight night. I lingered over it in sheer delight. But I've done that over more than one page.

Next to that I place *Once More* and then the *Fisher of Men* as a unique presentment of despotic temperament expressing itself in fanaticism of evangelical kind. *A Prisoner* stands in a category by itself in the mastery of expression and depth of feeling. The *Miller of Dee* is terrific when quickly thought over. The *Lime Tree* as a prose-poem has no flaw that I could see and I've read it several times. It captivates. *The Choice* with its amazing and tragic prayer gets home to one with the sheer humanity of it. It is not only for the sake of old times that one welcomes the two "Ferrand" stories.[2] They *are* good; parables worthy of the Book of Pharisees. Quite! I like Compensation best. I don't know why. Perhaps only because it is new to me. The other of course is larger—more significant and before all more tender.

But why *A Reversion to Type* was ever written by you I can not understand! Anyone might have written it. Why, I myself could have written it—not so well—but still I could have written it. You will please take this as the strongest expression of blame I can lay my hands on at the moment. It's hard to believe that it is by the same man who has written *A Consummation*.[3] That is immense! After reading the first page I got up and opened the window to give my grin room to expand freely. But when I came to the part where the "man of genius" introduces the "critic" the grin exploded and displaced some tiles on the roof. It's perfectly delectable. Every word tells. The turn of the phrasing when looked at from the inside is irresistibly comic. O! it is a pungent piece. And ain't it beastly sarcastic too! It's precious!

Now as to the whole. There is a unity in the collection, the effect of mastery which never falters now and of a steady vision. That's on the surface. Deeper in there is the quality of your inspiration that in every subject, in every mood is always true to the worship of beauty with words ever ready, ever worthy to express that creed.

[1] In a story of madness and murder.

[2] 'Courage' and 'Compensation': Ferrand, a philosophical vagabond, narrates them both.

[3] The ironic history of a writer led astray by bad advice from a critic and a friend who is 'a man of genius'.

I haven't yet finished my story. It's no use worrying. What can't be can't be and there's an end of it. I am not able to walk any distance yet. For the move Jessie sends me off to the Gibbons in Trosley. It's a short rway journey and I shall be able then to sit all the time with my feet up. I go on the 23 and return to the new house on the 26. Jessie takes possession on the 24[th]. God knows how it will turn out. I hope Ada and you may find time soon to come and see us there—yes, while the days are warm and long. I am frightened of London yet.

Clifford (Sir Hugh) back from Ceylon is very anxious to make your acquaintance. Did I tell you he was here to see me? Marwood comes every Thursday afternoon. What is vexing is that my voice very often fails me suddenly. Did you know that Sanderson is coming home? His wife is I believe already here. I had a letter from Mrs Sanderson la mère.[1]

Jessie keeps badly but keeps going. What is hard on her is that poor Nellie Lyons got very ill again and has been away a month already. Looking after Jack tires Jessie awfully.

Our dear love to you both

<div style="text-align:center">Ever yours</div>

<div style="text-align:right">J. Conrad.</div>

To John Galsworthy
Text MS Forbes; J-A, 2, 111

<div style="text-align:right">[letterhead: Capel House]
Kent[2]
26 June 1910.</div>

Dearest Jack.

On returning from the Gibbons yesterday afternoon I found your letter. When giving it to me Jessie woman-like shed a few tears. It's good to have somebody to cry for one a little on fitting occasions. For myself I shall keep the lid down on the well of my emotions. It's a question whether I even could lift it off. The hot spring boils somewhere deep within. There's no doubt of that; but if uncovered nothing would come out but a little vapour—a thin mist of words which would appear to me contemptible and to you probably superfluous. No man would be what you are to me for the sake of mere spoken thanks.

[1] Katherine Sanderson encouraged Conrad in his earliest days as a writer; he dedicated *The Mirror of the Sea* to her.

[2] MS addition. The Conrads had a supply of Capel House stationery ready for their arrival.

On leaving Ashford all alone on my first outing since the illness I felt all of a shake and utterly lost without Jessie. Of course notwithstanding our good resolutions neither Gibbon nor I did a line of work while I was in Trosley. He rushed me about on his side-car moto[r]-bike storming up hills and flying down vales as if the devil were after him. I don't know whether that is particularly good for the nerves but on return from these excursions I felt ventilated as though I were a bag of muslin, frightfully hungry and almost too sleepy to eat. No other harm seems to have been done.

At the very moment of leaving Aldington last Tuesday[1] I had a letter from Bashford which I enclose here.[2] I need not tell you that it was totally unexpected. But here was this thing thrown at my head! Wonderful! After hurriedly reflecting upon this miracle I answered as noted; and now I am in possession of another letter offering 5 gs per column and cheering me on to have a try. No formal agreement of any sort and liberty for either party to terminate the arrangement at any time.

I am very tempted. My view is that nothing unfair to Pinker will be done if I accept.[3] I shall take one day of the week (or its equivalent in snatches) for that article. If I find I can't do it in the time I shall throw the thing up. Voilà! At the same time I must consider him entitled to his commission on everything I earn, for that, I believe, is the "custom of the trade". What do you think?

I am writing to Bashford accepting provisionally and asking him to send me a couple of books in the course of this week. Should P. object I shall simply leave off after an article or two.

Our best love to dear Ada and yourself. How is she? You don't say anything of her health so we trust it is tolerable.

<div align="center">Ever yours</div>

<div align="right">J. Conrad.</div>

[1] The 21st: Conrad's visit to the Gibbons began and ended sooner than originally planned.
[2] 'Please read' added in the margin. Bashford had asked Conrad to review books for the *Daily Mail*.
[3] In order to reduce his debt, Conrad had to write more novels; reviewing would not delay their production.

Letters of Joseph Conrad

To Stephen Reynolds
Text MS Berg; Unpublished

[letterhead: Capel House]
Kent
26 June 1910

Dear Stephen.

I *ought* to have written. I beat my breast and you must make the best of that ceremony of contrition. I have been beastly ill and it seems I was not far from dying. If so I may tell you that the border country seems to have no special terrors for the traveller himself however unkindly and gruesome it may appear to the watchers.

I am still not myself. Physically the inability to walk much remains. Mentally I am also in a sort of tottering state. Not so much empty-headed as just unable to keep up any sort of mental pace. Intellectually giddy, so to speak. And that is not exactly gay. But I am not depressed. And that is cheering.

Altogether your news pleases me. I am, on no very explainable grounds, glad to hear you have changed publishers. I have no reason to think McMillans* to be better than other publishers as far as common decency goes. They are obscene birds[1] one and all. Yet I am glad. I would not reckon too much on their admiration tho'. I have had handfuls of almost fulsome letters from that brood, which as far as any friendliness goes were worth just nothing.

But there's nothing to spoil my enjoyment of the good news of the motorboat.[2] My compliments, felicitations and generally three cheers for her and one more. The very next time you come East you must push as far as this and we shall have an interminable yarn for as you may think I shall have a ruck of questions to ask about both your avocations. The doddery old *Spectator* seems to be honouring you with his special predilection.[3] It's the fashion to abuse that publication but I've always had a soft spot for it. And lo and behold! that blind and unaccountable trust stands justified in an unexpected manner. Give Stratchey*[4] a kiss from me the very first time you and he go "on the burst" together. I am almost moved to tears.

[1] Like Virgil's owls, 'obscena volucres' (*Aeneid*, 12, 876).
[2] The *Puffin*, launched at Dartmouth in May, was now in service.
[3] The *Spectator* (11 June, 960–1) devoted four whole columns to praising Reynolds's objections to socialism as outlined in a contribution to the left-leaning *New Age*.
[4] John St Loe Strachey (1860–1927) was editor and proprietor of the *Spectator*; his most recent book was *Problems and Perils of Socialism* (1908).

Anyway lets have a sight of you as soon as possible.

Love from all

<div align="center">Yours</div>

<div align="right">J. Conrad.</div>

To H.-D. Davray

Text MS Texas; *L. fr.* 102

<div align="right">[letterhead: Capel House]
27 Juin 1910</div>

Tres cher ami.

Merci bien pour votre lettre et l'argent. Je suis fort faché d'apprendre que vous avez eu une bronchite en même temps que la grippe. Moi je me remets tout doucement, trop doucement!

Tous les N*os* du Temps me sont arrivés. C'est fort intéressant de me voir en français. Votre traduction mon cher Davray m'a fait beaucoup de plaisir—mais beaucoup! C'est fidèle, c'est vivant, j'en suis emerveillé.

Je n'ai pas encore comparé les textes. A t'on fait des coupures au Temps? Je ne m'en suis pas aperçu mais s'il y en a vous les rétablirez sans doute.

Vous me dites des choses qui me mettent du coeur au ventre. Mais quoiqu'il advienne au point de vue matériel vous pouvez être certain de ma reconnaissance.

Veuillez faire mes amitiés a Madame votre femme et croyez-moi mon cher Davray toujours

<div align="right">à vous bien affectueusement
J. Conrad.</div>

Translation

Very dear friend,

Thank you very much for your letter and the money. I was most upset to hear that you had had bronchitis and the 'flu simultaneously. For my part, I'm recovering slowly, very slowly!

All the numbers of the *Temps* have reached me. It's most interesting to see myself in French. My dear Davray, your translation pleases me very much—very much indeed! It's faithful, it's lively, I am astonished.

I haven't compared the texts yet. Did the *Temps* make any cuts? I haven't noticed any, but if there are, you will put them back no doubt.

You tell me things that buck me up. Whatever may happen, you can be sure of my gratitude.

Please give my regards to your wife, and believe me, my dear Davray, always

 Yours most affectionately,

 J. Conrad

To Laurence Housman

Text MS Bryn Mawr; Unpublished

 [letterhead: Capel House]
 27 June 1910.

Dear Mr Housman.

I send my name herewith by return of post your letter having reached me only today, there being no Sunday delivery here. I want the women to have the vote and generally their own way in anything and everything under heaven. It will please them and certainly it won't hurt me. My main concern however is with the welfare of *One* woman who as far as I can contrive it has her own way in everything she cares for. There are also two boys who, inferior animals as they are, must be fed too out of the same inkstand. Being a naturally slow-witted person troubled moreover with unnecessary literary scruples and hampered by frequent illness it takes me all my time to attend properly to these unromantic duties.

 Yours faithfully

 J. Conrad.

To E. L. Sanderson

Text MS Yale; Unpublished

 [letterhead: Capel House]
 27 June 1910.

My dear Ted.[1]

Warrington Dawson brought me a rather confused and uncertain account of your wife being in England—and then sent me an equally

[1] Edward Lancelot ('Ted') Sanderson (1867–1939) took passages in the *Torrens* in 1893; on that voyage, Conrad read him a draft of *Almayer's Folly*. Sanderson taught at Elstree, his family's preparatory school in Hertfordshire. After service in the Boer War he remained in Africa, first in Johannesburg then in Nairobi, where he served as Town Clerk; soon after his return, in 1910, he became Headmaster of Elstree.

doubtful sort of intelligence of you too coming home. Therefore I held my hand from writing till your dear Mother's letter gave us definite news of your arrival to-day.

I am still under the fresh impression of all W D had to tell me about you dear People. But I ask now no questions—except the *one*: When are you coming to see us?—And give you no news except just to tell you that I am like one arisen from the dead after a three months' illness which all but carried me off. Dawson saw me yet in the invalid stage and I am not quite myself to this day; or I would try to look you up at once somewhere. The truth however is that I am not quite fit for a railway journey. My appearance however is not ghastly by any means.

We tried to be as nice to Dawson as we could under adverse circumstances. He's certainly an engaging and interesting personality, and I think he understood how friendly we felt towards him for your sake and for his own as well.

Write me dear Ted directly you find a moment to spare. Meantime our dear love to you all

Ever yours

J. Conrad.

To Norman Douglas
Text MS Texas; J-A, 2, 113

[letterhead: Capel House]
28 June 1910

My dear Douglas

I am a pig for not having written before—but then I don't care. I've lost all self-respect and have abandonned* myself to a debauch of illness and laziness and—but the list would be too long.

Seriously—you may imagine what it was to have 4 months taken out of one's life. I am all of a shake yet; I feel like a man returned from hell and look upon the very world of the living with dread.

If it had not been for Galsworthy I don't know what I would have done. He has seen to everything. Enfin. Now I am trying to pick up the dropped thread—with rather nerveless fingers as yet.

This is only a preliminary letter; only to tell you how glad I am that you are writing a book—your second. Tell me: what has been done with the first—The Syren Land? I seem to remember last year only like a

dream. What do you intend to [do] with the second?[1] Tell me all about yourself. Meantime our dear love.

<div style="text-align:right">Ever yours</div>

<div style="text-align:right">J. Conrad.</div>

To E. L. Sanderson
Text MS Yale; Unpublished

<div style="text-align:right">[letterhead: Capel House]</div>

<div style="text-align:right">1st July '10</div>

Dearest Ted.

Yes—we can put you up in a sort of camp-fashion. Name an early day, for as you imagine we are impatient to see you.

You'll have to change in Ashford—at least by most trains. If you can catch the 11 am from Char + you will be in time for lunch. I'll meet you in Ham Street.

No use trying to talk on paper since we are to have the happiness to see you soon.

Remember me please to all the population of Elstree. Our dear love to you and your boy.[2]

<div style="text-align:right">Ever yours</div>

<div style="text-align:right">J. Conrad</div>

To John Galsworthy
Text MS Forbes; Unpublished

<div style="text-align:right">[Capel House]</div>

<div style="text-align:right">Wednesday. [13 July 1910][3]</div>

Dearest Jack

C Graham was here on Sunday and told me he saw you both at a theatre in London.

We are fairly settled. I have written two papers for the Dy Mail. The second one only yesterday. I find it possible—about 1 1/2 days. Utter bosh of course but that doesn't make it any easier. They begin—so Bashford wires—on Sat next.

I have 70 pp of the short story written *and typed*. Jessie does that. 3 or 4

[1] Now that he had finished *Siren Land* (1911), Douglas had started on *Fountains in the Sand* (1912), the fruit of his experiences in Tunisia (Holloway, p. 192).

[2] Ian: Conrad was much taken with him (*Letters*, 3, pp. 507–8).

[3] The day after completing the second *Daily Mail* review: see the other letters of the 13th for details.

more shall end it.[1] I've also worked a little at Chance. I should have done more but that's not possible yet. Outwardly I am told I look well. And physically I feel well—only the feet are still somewhat lame. Mentally I am not empty—the trouble is that after an hour or so I grow confused. But that's improving since I can by an effort of will get over that queer sensation and continue at work in six cases, say, out of ten.

Jessie looks fairly well and of course keeps on going; but I am not easy in my mind. There are pain spots and swollen veins in the *left* arm which in a person with a defective heart makes one anxious. She thinks it's nervous and I only wish I could think so too. But its very difficult to discuss that kind of anxiety. Ah! well. M^r House writes that he stopped Borys' swimming baths because of the cough the boy [has] had now for three weeks. I don't like that either. The boy's letters however are cheerful and he means to have a good try at that exam: he asks me only not to be too sanguine about it. I wrote him that if he does his best it will be good enough for me in any case.

Jack is a handful. He's a perfect pagan without any sort of conscience that I can see. Perhaps it's because he hasn't been baptised yet. C. Graham was fascinated—but he doesn't see so much of the diablito[2] as I do.

Hugh Clifford announces his visit for the 25^th. Gibbon who is almost awed by certain things in *Motley* rushes over sometimes on his fiendish cycle. Marwood on the other hand tramps eleven miles every Thursday drinks a cup of tea and tramps back again. I take—thanks to you—deep breaths of fresh air and feel myself coming back to life again. Poor Nellie is in the Char + hospital[3] and the case looks bad rather I am afraid. We live in hopes of seeing you both here some day—before very long. Hayward's car could take you home[4] from Ashford in a quarter of an hour.

Our dearest love to you both.

Ever yours

J. Conrad.

[1] The MS (Berg) of 'A Smile of Fortune' runs to 140 pages. [2] 'Little devil'.
[3] The Charing Cross Hospital in London.
[4] To Capel House, that is. Charles Hayward & Son, 32 New St, Ashford, operated the 'Onward' cycle and steam-motor works.

To R. B. Cunninghame Graham
Text MS Dartmouth; J-A, 2, 113; Watts 174

[letterhead: Capel House]
13 July 1910.

Très cher ami.

It is most kind of you. The cigarettes arrived yesterday evening but I was finishing an article for the *Dly Mail* (I am supposed to have a column every Saturday) and put off my thanks till this morning when, behold, Jackolito's boïna[1] was duly delivered. He is immensely fascinated by it and I see him in it outside my window devastating the flower-bed. He's a little devil but the red cap suits him exceedingly and charms his mother very much. That really good woman (tho' she doesn't want a vote[2]) is delighted with the cabue[3] cloth. You are spoiling us no end. And it is so exceedingly nice to be spoiled by you that I have no heart to protest. Le gentil menage[4] was extremely gratified at having met you. You see, to so many young men you are not only a great stylist but also a great romantic figure. No man of genuine talent, (and Gibbon is that) can remain unmoved by what you write and indifferent to what you say.

Don't forget the visit in the autumn. We won't talk of dates. A word from you to say you are coming is always most welcome here. And as the days will be well shortened by then you ought really let us put you up for the night. Enfin—Vous ferez ce qui Vous conviendra le mieux.

Well—so long—as they say in Australia.[5]

Yours affectionately

J. Conrad.

Pray remember us and give our duty to your mother.[6] We were so glad to hear she was well.

[1] The Basque beret.
[2] Graham insisted on women's right to vote and their legal and economic freedom: see, e.g. *New Age*, n.s. 3 (11 July 1908), p. 207
[3] Sisal [4] The Gibbons. [5] Conrad had made five voyages there.
[6] The Hon. A. E. Bontine (1828–1925): a resident of London, she took a lively interest in politics and the arts.

To Edward Thomas
Text MS Berg; Unpublished

Capel House
Orlestone
Telegrams: Conrad. Ham Street Station. Nr Ashford Kent
Hamstreet. S.E.R. 1¼m from house by road Wednesday.
(must change in Ashford 9 times out of 10) 13 July '10.

My dear Thomas.[1]
This is indeed most friendly of you. I don't know how I ever had the courage to hint the matter to Perceval.[2] It was the courage of a cornered rat I suppose for I had accepted the proposal and then got mightily frightened for no very lofty reasons. I take your consent as a brotherly act since there can be no doubt that we are brothers in letters.

This gives me a sense of security. I have done already two papers and each time I felt as I sat down to it that the feat was utterly impossible. They are, I may say, the products of despair and, as was to be expected from that condition, unspeakably fatuous. However Bashford wires me he is going to begin the column next Saturday and I suppose with the first paper—or perhaps with the Second. That First purports to be the review of a book on hypnotism[3] (of all things in the world!) and is so perfectly imbecile that even I, myself, am shocked by it. The Second seems to be concerned with a book entitled *Existence after Death: Implied by Science* by a person named Hunt who is some sort of obscure idiot.[4] The paper is mere low clowning. But of course, my dear fellow, should I call you to the rescue you need not descend to these dishonourable depths, and I shall have the credit of your virtue.

I barred novels almost entirely. They send me batches of books—one more silly than another—and I select the one that seems the most hopeless, on principle. For thus I feel less strange to the task. The tone I adopt is of the familiar "we are all fellow-mortals here" kind. I am trying for cold raillery and can achieve nothing but the vulgar tongue in

[1] An Anglo-Welsh poet and an ally of Robert Frost, Edward Thomas (1878–1917) was killed in the First World War. He supported himself by a prodigious output of literary journalism and popular scholarship. Garnett's close friend, he often attended the Mont Blanc lunches; it was probably there that he met Conrad and Gibbon.
[2] At a pinch, the *Daily Mail* reviewing could be done by Thomas, earning him some much-needed money, and reassuring Conrad.
[3] It has vanished.
[4] The author was Jasper B. Hunt. The review came out on the 16th and also appears in *Notes on Life and Letters* as 'The Life Beyond'.

the cheek. My trick is to begin irrelevantly, then to give something out of the book and say "if you want to know more you must read it—for my part I can only offer a few reflexions" and then, after those so-called reflexions to end on some false note or other.[1] This will do for the present. Later, say after 3 months, some other trick'll have to be found.

Well, thanks once more! Do not forget your promise to come with your boy end August. Wife's kind regards

<div align="right">Yours cordially</div>

<div align="right">J. Conrad.</div>

PS I may be sending you a book soon—if only for fun and to see how the dark plot works. It shall be of course by post and with every regard to the question of time.

How does one wire to you? Is Petersfield your station? How far is your house from station? Can one get a fly there? Might be useful for me to know these things in case of some desperate complication.

To Norman Douglas

Text MS Texas; Unpublished

<div align="right">[Capel House]</div>

<div align="right">27 July '10</div>

Dear old fellow

I haven't yet seen your letter to my wife but am sorry no end to hear you cannot sleep. That *is* bad. I don't like to think of you open eyed in the night.

I sent you a wire this morning for the iron should be struck while it seems hot. My idea is to just open the negotiation and then let you conclude unless you instruct me the contrary. For God's sake don't throw their inquiry away.[2] It means more than appears on the surface. How it came about the enclosed letter will explain to You.

I sent (about a fortnight ago) 3 of your papers to Austin Harrison (son of the old Positivist Pope[3]) the present editor of the *ER*, with a rather emphatic letter. As to that part of the business I had only a postcard of acknowledgement and thanks. But you see what's happened. I've no doubt that he will take the copy but how much of it I can't say.

[1] Conrad rounded off the Hunt review with a lengthy quotation from the master of the occult Sar Péladan (*Notes*, p. 70).

[2] An inquiry from Dent's: see below and the letter of 31 July.

[3] Frederic Harrison (1831–1923), a professor of law, president of the English Positivist Society (1880–1905), author of many books on literature, history, politics, and philosophy.

The *Headland of Minerva* & the *Caves of the S.* I just cut in half. The *Upland of Sorrento* (shorter) I sent whole.[1] I did this to give your prose a better chance for they are everlastingly cramped for room in that Review. Of course I *didn't* touch the text. It's possible you'll hear direct from AH to whom I've sent your address.

A. H. is worth being civil to as he represents the Mond interest in the world of letters. The Monds bought the ER. (I mean the German Jew[2] who has been made a Birthday Baronet[3] this year). They are "the money" of the Philosophical Radical lot. Lady Mond bosses the ER.[4] You had better come over and fascinate her and so make both our fortunes.

I understand (heard it yesterday) that the Review—(Lady Mond?) took my novel *Under Western Eyes* for a serial. A. H. has not written to me yet. J. M. Dent & Sons is a big house. They are sure to produce the book well. Otherwise you must be cautious with them I believe. But no great harm can happen. The main thing is to get published with some éclat.

<div style="text-align:center">Yours ever</div>

<div style="text-align:right">J. Conrad.</div>

To [?]
Text MS Bryn Mawr; Unpublished

<div style="text-align:right">[letterhead: Capel House]
29 July 1910</div>

Dear Sir.[5]

Thanks for your reminder. I have been very ill indeed and have hardly yet picked up the dropped threads. Undoubtedly I am in sympathy with the spirit of your proposal. I am still very lame and somewhat shaky, and rather inclined to shirk a railway journey.

Would you give me a more precise idea of what our collaboration should be? I would then consider whether it is within my capacity to do my part of such a sketch. They are 30 minutes' plays—are they not? My ignorance of stage matters is denser than a London fog—tho' I did once

[1] The *English Review* took 'Uplands of Sorrento' and 'The Caves of Siren Land'.

[2] Actually born near Widnes, Lancashire.

[3] A heritable honour announced, in this case, on the king's birthday.

[4] The greatest interest of Lady Violet Mond (née Goetze; D.B.E. 1920) was in children's health and welfare; she remained for many years an enthusiastic Liberal. Her husband played an active part in managing his magazine.

[5] Unidentified but not without distinguishing features: not only an aspiring dramatist, but a former sailor, perhaps of Conrad's generation.

write a one-act play which was performed by the Stage Society.[1] How to get a dramatic (either pathetic or comical) situation into 30 minutes of which a full half must be given to the songs? *That* seems to me to be the question. It must, I apprehend, be the crucial moment of some very simple position. Or it may be made a purely picturesque animated picture of say—"getting under way" (or "weigh") and I have some notion of how that could be arranged.[2] But in that case I would have my doubts as to the simplicity of the mise-en-scène of which you speak. The representation of a ship's forecastle-head trois-quarts to the audience would have to be contrived somehow—as near to truth as possible.

I won't say more just now, not till I hear from you again. Should we then see our way to a try you would perhaps allow me to ask you down here for an afternoon's talk.

I should think M^r H. Finck[3] would be the man to do justice to these weird suggestive tunes of our young days. That wistful capstan song "Along the Banks of Sacramento" should not be forgotten with its sub-chorus, a great shout "Hurrah! Santa-Anna!"[4] Most effective!

<div align="center">Yours faithfully</div>

<div align="right">J. Conrad.</div>

To Austin Harrison
Text MS Rosenbach; Unpublished

<div align="right">[letterhead: Capel House]
31^st July '10</div>

Dear Mr Harrison.[5]

Douglas would appreciate a line from you. His address is Villa Daphne. Capri.

[1] *One Day More.*

[2] 'The getting of your anchor was a noisy operation on board a merchant ship of yesterday – an inspiring, joyous noise': *The Mirror of the Sea*, 6, p. 21.

[3] Henry T. Finck (1854–1926), music critic from the U.S., wrote books on Wagner, Chopin, and Grieg, published many collections of songs, and advised on *Success in Music and How It Is Won* (1910).

[4] In the grand oral tradition, Conrad runs two songs together here: 'The Banks of the Sacramento' and the capstan shanty known as 'Santa Anna' or 'The Plains of Mexico'. In the original American version, the latter celebrates the Mexican general Santa Ana's defeat at Monterey: 'General Taylor gained the day, / *Hooray, Santa Anna! / And Santa Anna ran away, / Along the plains of Mexico!*' In some British versions, the other general wins: Frank Shay, *American Sea-Songs and Chanteys* (New York: Norton, 1948), pp. 79, 82–3.

[5] Austin Harrison (1873–1928), an essayist with a strong interest in German politics and culture, took over the editorship of the *English Review* late in 1909, when Sir Alfred Mond dismissed Ford. On 11 January 1910 (MS Berg) Harrison wrote to Conrad expressing his admiration and asking for contributions to the now solvent *Review*.

I am glad my novel stands the test of an informed judgement. Very good of you to mention your opinion. May I ask You to give instructions for a double set of slips to be forwarded to me when the time comes? The book publication will be from the text as established in the *English Review*.[1]

Allow me to express my very deep sense of Your spontaneous action as regards Dent's house. I've had a letter from them which I forwarded to Italy on the same day.

Believe me

Very faithfully yours

J. Conrad.

To John Galsworthy
Text MS Forbes; Unpublished

[letterhead: Capel House]
5 Aug. 1910.

Dearest Jack.

I am sorry to be a source of unending bother to you. Yes it is meet that for purposes of business P & I should correspond directly. I shall refrain from telling him how disgusted I am at his bargain with the *ER*. Ten years ago I had the same amount paid me by B'wood for serialising *Lord Jim*.[2] I have every reason to believe that had I negotiated personally I could have got Harpers to take the novel in satisfaction of an old agreement for £1100 which would have left the English book-rights to Methuen:[3] another 250 I believe. As it is I feel that P will fail in serialising in the *US* and thus the book won't bring in more than 800[4] *at best*. A material difference. He ought to have attended to the proper placing of the novel instead of bothering about the miserable 20% on my DMail articles which can bring him no more than £50 anyhow, supposing I continued for a year.

As it is materially impossible to *prove* that these contributions are not

[1] Conrad's normal practice was to regard the serial publication as yet another working draft.

[2] Blackwood paid Conrad £300 for the serial rights and a £200 advance on the book (Blackburn, p. 105, and *Letters*, 2, p. 274). Conrad received £200 as the second and final payment for *Under Western Eyes* (*English Review* to Pinker, 23 December 1910, TS Berg); the size of the first payment remains unknown.

[3] Harper & Brothers would be able to buy serial rights for both sides of the Atlantic as well as book rights for the U.S.

[4] Changed from '700'.

in the way of my other work I shall furnish 2 or 3 more and then tell Bashford that it isn't worth my while to go on with them.

I've 14 000 words of a long short-story ready. Another 6 will finish it.[1] The next one will be really short say 7000. and the next again longer—over 10 000. I can't write to measure tho' I know that it is to my disadvantage.[2]

I wonder what are your impressions of our rulers and masters. Grey bungled the Servian business in accordance with the best Liberal traditions.[3] Morley *is* interesting—but A isn't.[4] I shall certainly not read Blunt on Ripon.[5] It must be wonderful stuff. What made you? Harpers have my story in the Aug^st. n°.[6] Of course they split it in two. Beastly shame. In the same N° Nevinson has a story[7]—and Lord it *is* bad. The whole N° is so inept that I feel sick to see myself there. Love to dear Ada

Ever yours

J. Conrad.

[1] 'A Smile of Fortune' came close to 25,000 words.
[2] Because, when asking for a story, editors often specified the length.
[3] Sir Edward Grey (1862–1933) was Foreign Secretary from 1905 to 1916. When the British ambassador to Serbia left his post at the beginning of July, he was not replaced for a month; the delay gave rise to rumours of tension between the two countries. The real tension, however, was between Serbia on one hand and the Austro-Hungarian empire (backed by Germany) on the other.
[4] 'A' presumably stands for Herbert Henry Asquith (1852–1928), Prime Minister from 1908 to 1916. John, Viscount Morley (1838–1923), biographer of Cobden and Gladstone, formerly editor of the *Pall Mall Gazette* and the *Fortnightly Review*, historian, literary critic, and proponent of adult education, was the intellectual guardian of traditional Liberalism. In the autumn of 1910, he went from Secretary of State for India to Lord Privy Seal.
[5] As Viceroy from 1880–1884 George Frederick Samuel Robinson, Marquess of Ripon (1827–1909), a solid Liberal, worked to enable Indian participation in government. His frustrated efforts received sympathetic treatment in *India under Ripon* by the poet and champion of colonial independence Wilfrid Scawen Blunt (1840–1922).
[6] 'The Secret Sharer' ran in the August and September numbers: 121 (1910), 349–59 and 530–41.
[7] H. W. Nevinson's 'Sitting at a Play', pp. 464–72.

To J. B. Pinker

Text MS Berg; Unpublished

[Capel House]
[early August? 1910][1]

note

Herewith pp 1 to 39 roughly 9000, first half of story, ready for *clean* copy. Great part of other half is already written but as since receiving a letter from M[r] Galsworthy conveying your views on the subject I've broken my connection with *Dly Mail* (one more paper is to be pub[d] yet[2]) I must request you to forward me against the enclosed MS £20 = half the agreed advance on short stories.

The next one: *Character*.[3] will be comparatively short—7000 or less. The next after that longer again: *The Reef*.[4] I propose to call the series—or volume *Tales of Experience*. *The Secret Sharer* I look upon as the first of that set.

I think that Harpers should have been made to pay more for a 2-numbers story. May I ask if there is any prospect of the novel being placed in US. serially. I am anxious on that point.

With every consideration

Yours

J. C.

J. B. Pinker Esq[r]

[1] Received 'Aug 1910': references to the first half of 'A Smile of Fortune' and the *Daily Mail* 'connection' make a placing between the letters to Galsworthy of 5 and [15?] August likely, but mention of the last *Daily Mail* article also makes a date at the very end of July conceivable.

[2] The final piece to appear was the review of George Bourne's *The Ascending Effort*, 30 July. The *Mail*, however, still had the fugitive paper on hypnotism (letter to Thomas, 13 July), which Bashford must at some point have killed.

[3] Possibly the ancestor of 'The Partner'.

[4] Probably the ancestor of 'The Planter of Malata'.

To David Bone

Text MS Sprott; Knowles (1986)

[letterhead: Capel House]

10 Aug. 1910

Dear Sir.[1]

Your gift is none the less welcome because I've read your book a few weeks ago.[2] E. Garnett, Duckworth's literary adviser sent it to me shortly after publication. I am sincerely glad to hear that your volume has had a good reception from the press.

Strangely enough the day before your book arrived Gibbon was here and showed me your letter to him. If I may be allowed to put in a word let me entreat You not to "leave the ship." Never "leave the ship"—least of all for literature. Gibbon certainly did leave.[3] But apart from a remarkable journalistic gift the man is a born story-teller. He was bound to make his way. I left because I was no longer fit for the life[4]—otherwise I can assure you I would have never published a line. There is also the instance of F. Bullen, but, believe me, that is nothing to go by. Whatever qualities You may possess you haven't that which has made Mr Bullen's success.[5]

The above does not mean that you shouldn't write; I am only anxious that you should not leave the sea before making very sure of your footing ashore.

With apologies for thrusting on You unasked advice and with thanks for remembering me I am

Yours cordially

J. Conrad.

[1] A Scotsman, David William Bone (1874–1959; knighted 1946) began his career in sailing-ships. In 1899 he joined the Anchor Line, whose senior commander he eventually became. He was captain of the *Tuscania* when Conrad made his voyage to the United States in 1923. Conrad also knew his brothers, Muirhead and James Bone.

[2] Bone had sent Conrad a copy of his first novel, *The Brassbounder*, a fictional version of his apprenticeship. For Conrad's candid opinion, see the paragraph on Garnett's tastes in the letter to Galsworthy of 27 October.

[3] Before turning to journalism, Perceval Gibbon spent his late teens in British, French, and American ships.

[4] Here Conrad plays down his desire to become a professional author, and the shortage of good berths, but in any case weakening sight and recurrent bouts of malaria would have made it hard to remain at sea.

[5] Taking Conrad's advice, David Bone pursued a double career. On the other hand, Frank Thomas Bullen (1857–1915), who had been an errand-boy, and then worked his way from able seaman to first mate, became a professional, writing *The Cruise of the 'Cachalot'* and many other books about the sea, fictional and otherwise.

To H.-D. Davray
Text L. fr. 103

10 Août 1910.
Capel House.

Cher Ami,
 Le texte[1] du *Temps* n'est pas complet, comme du reste vous vous en êtes aperçu sans doute. Je n'ai pas d'observation à faire. Votre traduction, mon cher Davray, me plait beaucoup.
 Je suis fort occupé en ce moment pour les premiers chapitres d'un roman de mer dont on m'offre un bon prix en Amérique.[2]
Bien à vous.

Translation

Dear Friend,
 The *Temps* text is not complete, as you have no doubt noticed. I have no comments. Your translation, my dear Davray, pleases me very much.
 I am very busy at present with the first chapters of a sea-novel for which I am being offered a good sum in America.
Sincerely yours.

To Geneviève Séligmann-Lui
Text MS Yale; *L. fr.* 103

10 Aout. 1910.
Capel House
Nr Ashford Kent.

Chère Mademoiselle Séligman[n]-Lui.[3]
 Merci pour le cahier. La traduction est tout-à-fait remarquable.
 Je vous suis très reconnaissant pour les choses aimables que Vous avez la bonté de me dire. Mais, a parler franchement, le volume de Tales

[1] Of *The Secret Agent* as translated by Davray.
[2] *Chance*: see the letter of 17 August and the accompanying telegrams.
[3] Geneviève-Séligmann-Lui translated *Almayer's Folly* (1919) and Edward Gordon Craig's *The Art of the Theatre*.

of Unrest est celui de toute mon oeuvre que j'aime le moins. Je m'y vois "derivatif"[1] plus que de raison. Enfin!

Je vous assure que je prefère The Idiots dans votre traduction[2] à l'original. Je serais heureux de savoir que The Lagoon (le dernier conte du vol:) sera traduit par vous. C'est mon favori de cette collection.

Veuillez accepter mes hommages
réspectueux.
J. Conrad.

Translation

Dear Mademoiselle Séligmann-Lui,

Thank you for the manuscript. The translation is quite remarkable.

I am very grateful to you for the kind things you are good enough to tell me. But to speak frankly, *Tales of Unrest* I like least of all my work. I see myself there as more than reasonably derivative. Enough said!

I assure you that I prefer your translation of 'The Idiots' to the original. I should be glad to know that you were translating 'The Lagoon', the last story in the book. Of this collection it's my favourite.

Yours most respectfully,
J. Conrad

To John Galsworthy
Text MS Forbes; Unpublished

[Capel House]
Monday. [15? August 1910][3]

Dearest Jack.

This is the letter received to day. Can you tell me in which form the acknowledgement is to be written? Is [it] to be addressed to the P.M. himself or his secretary? I don't even know whether English Cabinet Ministers are addressed as Excellency or not.

[1] From Maupassant?

[2] Of 'The Idiots': published in *Grande Revue*, 25 September 1912, 324–47.

[3] The first Monday after 9 August, when Conrad received a Civil List pension of £100 and W. B. Yeats of £150; these awards were not made public until the following year (*The Times*, 7 July 1911, p. 9).

To all the infinite obligation[s] I owe you this one now is to be added.[1] The load lies lightly on my shoulders because of my trust and affection for you. But it is difficult to say anything adequate.

I've sent P. the first half (9000 w.) of the long short story asking him to let me have ½ of agreed advance. I had to do that as on reflection I have already terminated my connection with the *Dly Mail*.

In haste

Yours ever

J. C.

To J. B. Pinker

Text MS Berg; Unpublished

[letterhead: Capel House]
Thursday 17 Aug. 1910

Sir.

I intend now in any case to go on with Chance after the story in hand is finished[2] but I am prepared to use my best endeavours to furnish copy for serialisation in the N[ew] Y[ork] H[erald] on following conditions:

The novel to be no more than 80 thou. words.

To begin at *earliest* on last Saturday of September.

To run six months at the rate of 13.400 words per month = 3350 words per week.

If above conditions are agreed to by N. Y. H. I will send you on Sept 1st copy to the value of five instalments—(17–18 thou. words) for which you will pay me at once at the rate agreed (in terms of Mr Galworthy's letter to me) of £4 per thou.

The copy thereafter—(typed pen-corrected copy which the N. Y. H. must accept) shall be sent to you weekly to be paid for at the end of every month at the agreed rate.

Like this, with seven or eight instalments ready before the printing begins I shall feel fairly safe.

I should like You to promise that in case I were compelled for a time

[1] Galsworthy had campaigned for the grant, lobbying the government and collecting letters of support.

[2] Two telegrams (Berg) show that Pinker had asked about the condition of *Chance* without at first saying which paper had requested a serial. 'Have you clean copy of the eighty [?] pages Chance in view of offer may need slight alterations shall write fully but generally if 8000 words per month sufficient and total length 65 thousand may go ahead reply' (15 August). 'Please tell what paper and what date first instalment would appear and I shall write you tonight post' (17 August). Late in 1907, Conrad had set *Chance* aside to work on 'Razumov'.

to have recourse to dictation you would on my demand send me a
competent person for as many days as necessary. The expense to be
deducted from the next payment due to me against delivered MS. I
understand also that when the last of the MS is delivered you will pay
me at once the sum of £100 as agreed for every completed novel; and that
you will get for me the full set of Heralds.

In this way I reckon my share of the proceeds = £460—and yours
with book rights (Methuen—Harpers (?)) which I estimate at five
hundred shall amount to £840. I am willing to put myself under some
stress for such a result. But I beg you will give your consideration to the
suggestion on the enclosed paper.

Yours obed^{ly}

J Conrad.

The suggestion is to utilise *Rescue* for N. Y. H serial if it can be arranged
with Heinemann they having the book in England—to which I appre-
hend Messrs: Methuen can make no objection as that book was
contracted to Heinemann long before my connection with them.[1]

In that case I propose that for the portion now written (say 50 000
words) you should pay me at the rate of £3 only. For the additional
30 000 words at the agreed rate of £4. But probably I would cut out
some of the old copy and write a little more new—say then 40 thou of
each.

Thus I would get 120 for old & 160 for new say £280. But on
consideration of the book rights being already paid for by H[2]—I would
forego the agreed £100 on delivery of complete novel all but £20 to make
a round 300 for my share. You will then have the 500 balance of serial
price & the Am. book rights if these are free.[3]

Of that last point I am not sure—but even without it, it would be the
best way to utilise the Rescue which otherwise would have no value as I
will be a party to nothing which should deprive Heinemann of his rights
in the book—whatever they might have done (or left undone) to forfeit
them.

H. if properly approached can have no objection to serialisation. I
may, if you like, approach them myself.

At all events pray send me the MS to look at.

[1] Probably in February 1898.
[2] Conrad owed Heinemann's £360 (S. S. Pawling to Pinker, 28 March and 16 April
1914, MS Berg); the original advance had been £180, but Heinemann's had bought
out serial rights from McClure.
[3] As successor to McClure, Doubleday would have North American book rights.

I could get free of Rescue in 3 months and then start on *Chance* which I suppose could be handled to advantage as a finished work.

With *R.* you could start the N. Y. H pubon at their own date and their own rate of 4000 a week.

All this perhaps is worth considering.[1]

To J. B. Pinker
Text TS Berg; Unpublished

[letterhead: Capel House]
August 20th 1910

Sir.

It was within my recollection that Heinemann had refused the money and would be satisfied only by the delivery of the book. Perhaps you remember the conversation we had on the subject now nearly two years ago. However if they have changed their mind there's nothing more to be said. Permit me however to enter my protest here against your view that our agreement engages my past so far back as the "Rescue." All that stuff was written before we even heard of each other.[2] No assertion that you keep your engagements was necessary. There could be no doubt of that. I made the stipulation, which you decline, in view of the offered bargain which (in conjunction with the proceeds of Razumov) gave me the prospect of reducing in a few months my indebt[ed]ness to you to the neighbourhood of a thousand.[3] I thought that an additional engagement to write at a certain rate, within definite limits of time, was worth that much. I have done at least three serials under such conditions[4] and I know what it costs me. I don't see the necessity of endangering my newly recovered health for nothing. As you have thought [it] necessary to hint gratuitously that I am trying to get further advances on work delivered, I beg you to take notice that I shall write "Chance" when it suits me, exactly, and at my own pace.

Yours obedly

J. Conrad.

[1] On 18 August, Conrad wired 'Thanks yes we shall do it Writing fully' (Berg). More clearly than the next letter, the letter of 3 September shows that Pinker must have accepted at least part of the 'suggestion'.
[2] Conrad began 'The Rescuer' (as it was then called) in April 1896 (*Letters*, 1, pp. 268–73). Pinker first approached Conrad in August 1899 and became his agent in September 1900. Thereafter, references to the long-delayed novel often occur in the correspondence.
[3] A reduction from over £2,700. [4] *Lord Jim, Nostromo,* and *The Secret Agent.*

To John Galsworthy
Text MS Forbes; J-A, 2, 114[1]

[Capel House]
27 Aug. '10

Dearest Jack

I've got out of the habit of using the pen my last story (now in its 22[d] thousand of words) being all written in pencil for Jessie's typing. Another couple of thousand which I *must* do by next Monday[2] will end it. This will mean over 20 thou. words in two months because I did not really start till July. June's work was mere fooling—not on purpose of course. I was still too limp to grasp the subject and most of the pages written then have been cancelled in type-script. It was strangely nerveless bosh.

Of course I will do the Rescue. To tell you the truth I've forgotten that stuff. I've a hazy recollection of something highly inflated and verbose. But no doubt I can match it well enough out of the rubbish floating in my softened brain. Only I would like to know that Heinemann is a consenting party. There's a deadly feud between P & H and some trouble *may* arise. I don't know what—but I know that if it comes it'll be very beastly. The book is H's absolutely—and, if I never finished it, the fragment, as it stands, were I to die to morrow, would be worth 500 to him—unless it's an illusion of my overweening vanity.

My only objection to the *Rescue* would be that it does not advance me very much towards parting with P. whereas *Chance* would have been a long step.[3] But on the other hand, as you say, the enterprise looks much easier.

In a day or so when I send him the end of the *Smile of Fortune* (a good short serial—there is a market for that and I hope he won't part with it for seven pence) I shall ask him to forward me the typed copy of *Rescue*. It will take me a week to read and think myself into a proper frame of mind.

I've a swollen elbow (no pain) two sore ankles, my voice comes and goes in a very entertaining manner. But I certainly can write in this place. That is quite all right. Jessie, as ever, keeps up her end but she is very, very lame and begins to feel it—I can see that. Poor B has failed in his exam; and goes about with a long face rather. From a certain point of view it'll do him good; he was getting too cocky. As I don't want to let

[1] Omitting the two sentences beginning 'Only I would like' from the second paragraph.
[2] The 29th. [3] Taking Conrad more swiftly towards financial independence.

him go into a new school with the impression of that failure on him he shall go back to Luton for another term. House wrote assuring me that the boy did work well and steadily notwithstanding a very bothersome cold which lasted over six weeks. He has just stopped coughing and I am so glad not to hear that sound that I am not so much cast down as I thought I would be. Jackolo very slender and vivacious looks like a sprite and behaves like one. Our dearest love to you both.

<div style="text-align: center;">Yours ever</div>

<div style="text-align: right;">J Conrad.</div>

To William Rothenstein

Text MS Harvard; Unpublished

<div style="text-align: right;">Capel House
Monday. [late Summer or Autumn? 1910][1]</div>

Dear Will.

You are a very dear, a very good and a very indulgent friend. I will be ready to come up on any day you may suggest; but if you are going to give a whole day to my unworthy head why not give it to me here—where Jessie too would be so glad to see you? You could even in your generosity consent to spend the night under this "lowly roof". Qu'en dites Vous? But I don't wish to be importunate and won't do more than throw out this hint.

My left wrist is still swollen and the corresponding ankle pains me a good deal; but I can stand and even walk on my hind legs after a fashion. Moreover these things appear to be on the mend.

We await a line on a pc from you giving us your decision.

With our love

<div style="text-align: center;">Ever Yours</div>

<div style="text-align: right;">Joseph Conrad.</div>

[1] Placed by the state of Conrad's health.

To E. L. Sanderson

Text MS Yale; J-A, 2, 115

[letterhead: Capel House]

2 Sept. 1910.

Dearest Ted.

I was silent, while expecting you, simply because I was pushing on with a long short-story which I have just finished. When working under pressure I simply *can't* write letters. Jessie truly might have dropped you a line; but she too was extremely busy; and, as I say, we expected every moment to hear from you. Don't miss me dear old boy—whoever else you miss. You and yours are always in my thoughts.

We trust that when you come it will be with Your wife. I've been immensely interested by Dawson's account of her literary work. We would feel very unhappy if we could not see her this time. Just name a day and come to Ashford; I'll be there to meet you with a car for the last 5 miles of the journey into this sylvan wilderness.

I am glad to hear you are thinking of the navy for your dear boy.[1] Is it his own idea? Of course he's doing well. It was enough to look at him to see that he is of the sort that "does well".

Yes. This place is all right. I can work here. We are surrounded by woods and the soil is clay but the house is sympathetic—which Someries was not.

I am just beginning to pick up the threads of existence after the horrible nightmare of my long illness: seven months I may say of my declining life wiped off at one fell swoop. I am not quite myself yet.

Nothing could cheer me up more than to hear that You and your family are well and happy—may the Gods never grow jealous!

Remember us most affectionately to your dear wife. This letter doesn't seem worth reading much but I feel somewhat collapsed after finishing my first piece of work this year. So no more. With love

Yours ever

J. Conrad.

Jack's address is now:

Wingstone

Manaton

Devon.[2]

[1] Ian Sanderson.

[2] Sanderson had stayed in closer touch with Conrad than he had with Galsworthy.

To J. B. Pinker
Text MS Berg; Unpublished

[letterhead: Capel House]
3 Sept 1910.

Dear Sir.

I beg to acknowledge the receipt of £40 against MS *Smile of Fortune*. If I wired yesterday asking for acknowledgement of receipt it is only because a stranger took the envelope to the Rwy Station and I was uneasy as to its safe arrival.

I am beginning another story[1] which I hope may not take me more than 10 days to finish. But I wish to say that should the negociations* as to *Rescue* for the N. Y. H. be successful I would lay it aside and proceed with that novel at once. Should you think advisable you will perhaps forward me the typed copy in your possession (*insured*—as there is no other copy in existence). It will take me about a week to read and think myself into a proper frame of mind to proceed. It's an old work and I have forgotten much of it.

Yours faithfully[?]

J. Conrad.

To John Galsworthy
Text MS Forbes; J-A, 2, 118

[letterhead: Capel House]
8 Sep '10

My dearest Jack

I am really grieved at P worrying you with this fatuous business. Gordon Bennett[2] made a long stay in Ceylon late last year and Hugh Clifford (Col: Sec^y[3]) fired into him the whole, I believe, of my prose. He must have in addition preached not a little to that American citizen—but of that he does not boast. I shall at a fitting opportunity explain the matter to him. He, good fellow, has been patting himself on the back ever since he heard of the offer from the N.Y. Herald. If P had not flung away *Under Western Eyes* those people would have taken it. To make use

[1] 'Prince Roman', quarried out of materials for *A Personal Record*.
[2] James Gordon Bennett (1841–1918) inherited the *New York Herald* from his father and set up its first international edition. He financed various expeditions (including Stanley's in search of Livingstone) and, a keen yachtsman himself, established prizes for international sailing and flying races.
[3] Of Ceylon: Bennett had gone there on his steam yacht, the *Lysistrata*.

of *Chance* for this opportunity is now impossible. I wouldn't risk it.[1] I have dismissed all thought of it out of my head.

I had the other day a letter from Ted Sanderson, from Scotland, promising me his visit for some distant and vague date, and asking for your address. I've sent it to him.

I feel awfully tired to-night my dear Jack—and there's but little to show for it. It has been a bad day. Mrs Lyttleton[2] has announced her visit for to-morrow.—Pourquoi faire Mon Dieu! She has a cottage within 12 miles from here but that's hardly a reason.

Our dear love to you both

Ever yours

J. Conrad.

To John Galsworthy
Text MS Forbes; Unpublished

[letterhead: Capel House]
25. Sept '10

Dearest Jack.

I finished yesterday the second short story about 10000.[3] Well this makes all but 50 000 words since June[4]—half a volume. Not so bad as far as production is concerned. And that I have been able to do so much I owe to you. But what don't I owe to you! If you were not what You are the thought would crush me.

I hope you understand that I did not refuse to work for the N. Y. Herald especially, because of any cussedness. I was really afraid to bind myself to an undertaking which a fit of gout could have knocked into a cocked hat at any time. I must reckon with that horrid possibility. I shall go to work on Chance now. Clifford is coming for a day sometime in October. I don't know how thick he is with Bennet[t]; but if the mixture

[1] Risk falling behind with the serial or risk spoiling what he intended to be a major novel?

[2] Edith Lyttleton (née Butler, died 1948) belonged to the 'Souls', a coterie of aristocratic imperialists. A playwright, she campaigned for a national theatre; later she involved herself in psychical research. One of the Lyttletons' country places was in Wittersham, Kent.

[3] 'Prince Roman': see the letter of 1 October. A note (Berg) on Capel House stationery, 25 September 1910, reads: 'With Mr J Conrad's Comp^ts 8–9 thousand words'. On this note, Pinker instructed his assistant to 'Send the cheque that is already agreed'.

[4] If this total is at all accurate, Conrad must have worked on *Chance*; the two stories came to about 35,000 words and the reviews for the *Daily Mail* only a few thousand more. See the letter of 12 October for another word count.

appears sufficiently consistent I shall ask him to intervene so as to make it possible to have the offer renewed in say six months' time.[1]

I don't feel quite so well—but that's a passing thing. Jessie had an inflam[m]ation of glands in the throat—rather severe. So I had a doctor because with a heart like hers one is apt to wonder what such things mean. He has reassured me in that respect. She's run down simply. But as to the leg there is trouble. He told me plainly that the only safe course is amputation. He says that imprimis the state of the limb causes a constant nervous strain on the whole system on account of the pain and of sleeplessness caused by the pain. Secondly its by no means certain that there is not a disease of the bone. Thirdly the other leg (of which the knee joint is also somewhat damaged) is doing all the work, as all the weight of the body is always on it. And that is not safe. He told me that as far as one may be certain of anything she's quite fit now to stand the operation but that in a year or two it may not be so; and then he feared she would become an absolute cripple for the rest of her life. In his view the operation presents no difficulties. Any surgeon can perform it. It can be done here, at home; and in six weeks he says she will be able to walk with an artificial limb—and in his own words be a new woman. Poor Jessie is not only willing but almost eager, the only person she is thinking of in this connection being myself. However there's time to think the whole matter over. But something will have to be done! B. went to Luton for another term, in a chastened spirit; and Jack has a free hand now in bossing the whole show, which he does with immense energy. This place seems to suit him. I fear it'll take me a fortnight to get on terms with Chance. Just now I feel flat and sceptical. What I am most afraid of is of becoming an old bore, in my writing. And the less I believe in it the more difficult the task becomes. I wish I could find a subject that would appeal to everybody. But, alas, the gate of the sentimental ground where such finds are made is closed to me. Our dearest love to you both.

<div style="text-align:center">Ever yours</div>

<div style="text-align:right">J. Conrad.</div>

[1] In view of his help, the dedication of *Chance* to Clifford was particularly apt.

To Warrington Dawson
Text MS Duke; Randall 132

[letterhead: Capel House]
27 Sept 1910.

My dear Dawson.

I didn't dare to look at your book[1] till I finished a rather long thing which I was writing. It is really complimentary; I am shy of reading a man whom I credit with *power* while busy with my own prose. I have not been disappointed. Yes, certainly. There is *power* to begin with, and a great charm of style, a soberness of presentation which appeals to me extremely, l'oeil artiste as to details, with a large conception of the whole. In short, mon cher, beaucoup de talent. Talent, I mean, of the sort that is on the way of becoming *exceptional*. Voilà. That is, concisely stated, my impression corrected by some conscientious meditation; for as You may imagine I am not writing this after one reading only.

The first was rather rapid on account of the intrinsic interest of the story which caries one on finely. A great quality that! The second was au point de vue du métier.[2] You know what I mean. All this holds together excellently and all the figures stand square in surroundings which are rendered completely. The tragic atmosphere (because it *is* that) does not oppress one—these are human affairs and one feels them to be in life not on a stage. My congratulations—and my thanks for very real pleasure combined indeed with instruction; because as you may imagine all this—so removed from the ordinary convention—is quite new to me.

I had two letters from Sanderson who is now in Scotland. I hope to see him here in October. I am on the eve of tackling a long novel without a purpose but which I hope shall show some artistic sense. But it will be a devil of a job. Do believe my dear fellow in my thorough appreciation of your friendly letters if I don't answer them as quickly as decency would demand. And whatever you do don't forget us when you come over.[3]

My wife sends her kind regards. She enjoyed the book immensely. Marwood wishes to be remembered to you. He was very captivated by your novel which we have been talking over together only the other day.

Tout à Vous

J. Conrad

[1] *The Scar* (London, 1906; Boston, 1910), a novel in which Dawson said he wanted to show 'the hardships and fortitude in a remote corner of Southern country a quarter of a century after the war had ended and wounds were supposed to be healed' (Randall, p. 19).
[2] 'From a professional viewpoint'.
[3] He lived in Paris.

To Marguerite Poradowska

Text MS Yale; Rapin 192; G. & S. 115

[letterhead: Capel House]
27 Sept 1910

Ma chère Margueritte*.

Je viens de finir une nouvelle et un conte;[1] il fallait se mettre a écrire tout de suite, au sortir de ma maladie qui, comme vous le savez peut-être, a duré bien quatre mois. Le travail m'a été penible au point que la tâche du jour achevée je n'etais pas en état de tenir la plume, ni même de penser d'une façon soutenue. Il faut me pardonner mon long silence. C'est n'est pas l'affection qui manque. Croyez bien que vous êtes toujours présente a ma mémoire—toujours.

Sans aucun doute Jean a du talent.[2] Vous l'appréciez justement. Ma lettre a sa mère était fort courte; c'était pour ne pas la faire attendre. J'ai dit ma première impression aussitot après avoir lu le manuscrit.[3] Après tout chère Margueritte* c'est a Vous de prononcer sur la question que se pose: faut-il encourager ce talent? Vous le connaissez mieux que qui que ce soit (je n'excepte pas sa mère) vous l'aimez, vous le comprenez; il vous aime, il vous écoutera. Quand* a moi je ne conseillairais* jamais la carrière des lettres a personne. Du reste il est jeune encore. Il faudra voir. S'il a la vocation il écrira envers et contre tous. Il ne restera alors qu'a le guider en son dévelopement littéraire. Et pour cela, avec votre jugement si sûr et l'affection qui Vous unit, il n'y a que Vous!

Oui chère amie. Deménager après 18 ans c'est dur! Et ce logis de Passy[4] vous encadrait si bien! Enfin. Quand* a nous nous avons eu a deménager aussi, le 22 Juin. Cette maison-ci nous plaît. Elle est entourées des bois a 7 k d'Ashford et a 15 k de Pent Farm ou Vous êtes venue nous voir. C'est toujours le même pays de Kent que nous aimons tant.

Jessie souffre pas mal de la jambe. On parle d'une autre operation. Elle y est resignée. Les deux garçons vont bien. Borys va changer d'école l'année prochaine. J'aimerais bien de lui donner un trimestre ou deux en France pour apprendre la langue. C'est le seul moyen. Quand* a moi je me retablis tout doucement—trop doucement! Mais au bout du compte

[1] 'A Smile of Fortune' and 'Prince Roman': the generic distinction was harder for Conrad to make in English because of the association of *novella* with popular fiction.

[2] Mme Poradowska's nephew, Jean Gachet de la Fournière.

[3] Conrad originally wrote 'manuscript'.

[4] 84 rue de Passy, in a fashionable quarter of Paris.

j'ai repris le travail—et c'est le principal. Nous vous embrassons bien
fort.

<div align="right">

Toujours le votre de coeur

Conrad.

</div>

Translation

My dear Marguerite,

I have just finished a long short story and a short one. I had to sit hard
at work immediately after my illness which, as you perhaps know, lasted
quite four months. Work has been so hard for me that with the day's task
done I could not hold a pen, could not even think connectedly. You must
excuse my long silence. It is not that I lack affection. Please believe that
you are always present in my thoughts—always.

Without any doubt, Jean has talent. You judge him rightly. My letter
to his mother was very brief; I didn't want to keep her waiting. I wrote
my immediate impression right after reading the manuscript. After all,
dear Marguerite, it is up to you to pronounce on the question this poses:
should his talent be encouraged? You know him better than anyone else
(I do not exclude his mother). You love him, you understand him; he
loves you, he will listen to you. As for myself, I would never recommend
a literary career to anyone. Besides, he is still young. We shall have to
see. If he has the calling, he will write despite all opposition. Then it will
remain only to guide him in his literary development. And for that, with
your solid judgment and the affection binding you, you are the one!

Yes, dear friend, moving after eighteen years is hard. And the
quarters at Passy suited you so well. Still. As for us, we too have had to
move, on June the 22nd. We like this house. It is surrounded by woods,
and is seven kilometers from Ashford, fifteen kilometers from Pent
Farm, where you came to see us. It is still the same Kentish countryside
we love so much.

Jessie suffers a good deal with her leg. There's talk of another
operation. She is resigned to it. The two boys are doing well. Borys will
change schools next year. I should certainly like to give him a term or
two in France to learn the language. It is the only way. As to myself, I
am recovering slowly—too slowly. But after all, I have gone back to
work—that is the important thing. We embrace you warmly.

<div align="right">

Ever affectionately yours,

Conrad

</div>

To J. B. Pinker
Text MS Berg[1]; Unpublished

[Capel House]
29 Sep[t]. [1910]

This was received this morning.[2] As I don't know what agreement—if any—has been entered upon I can't answer this letter. I am referring M[r] Harrison to you.

Would the N. Y. H take the novel if it were withdrawn from the *ER*? on the ground of delay for instance. 2 August for publication does not strike me as a good date.

To Austin Harrison
Text MS Yale; Unpublished

[letterhead: Capel House]
30 Sept 1910

Dear Mr. Harrison.

Thanks for your letter. I think you had better settle the instalments as it best suits you. I beg only for the favour of early proofs, in duplicate.

Yours faithfully

J. Conrad.

To J. B. Pinker
Text MS Berg; Unpublished

[letterhead: Capel House]
1[st] Oct. '10

Dear Sir.

I quite see the point as the N. Y. H. is sent to Russia and its attitude is friendly to that country.[3]

[1] On the back of a letter from Austin Harrison dated 28 September 1910.

[2] Harrison told him that Wells's *New Machiavelli* would extend into the November issue of the *English Review*, thus postponing the start of *Under Western Eyes*. Conrad could decide where to make the breaks for serial publication or leave the job to the *Review*. Finally, 'as a great favour', Harrison asked if publication as a book could be delayed until 2 August 1911, because the last instalment would probably appear in the August issue. The serial actually ran into the October issue, and the book appeared on 5 October.

[3] In Bennett's own words: 'My attitude on foreign affairs is often called changeable ... It is simply this: If a nation is friendly to this country [the U.S.] I wish the *Herald* to be friendly to that nation, but if a nation shows an unfriendly policy I wish the paper to adopt an unfriendly tone.' Quoted by Robert W. Desmond, *The Information Process* (Iowa City: University of Iowa Press, 1978), p. 350, n. 2. Having been expelled from polite New York society for urinating into either his fiancée's parents' fireplace or their grand piano, Gordon Bennett controlled his newspaper from Paris.

I trust you will be able to conclude with the N. A. R but its a very small review—I mean in point of size.[1]

My objection to the Augst date was on the ground that *Under Western Eyes* is not exactly "holiday reading" sort of stuff. But unless the book came out during the London season the date of pubon does not matter much.

I beg to acknowledge with thanks cheque for £40—for Prince Roman.[2]

<div align="right">Yours obedly</div>

<div align="right">J. Conrad</div>

PS I've discovered a clean typed copy of *Chance* at which I shall work now steadily. Would it be inconvenient to send me the clean type-copy of Prince Roman for 24 hours at the outside. I just want to read it over once.

To E. L. Sanderson
Text MS Yale; Unpublished

<div align="right">[Capel House]</div>

<div align="right">Wednesday. [October 1910?][3]</div>

Dearest Ted.

We are "ever so glad" as Jack would say.

There's a train from W[inchel]sea 12.49 arriving *Hamstreet* 1.15—what you may call a decent 'lunch-train'. It will enable you to depart leisurely, with gravity and decorum, and I shall meet you—or at any rate you shall be met—there with the shabbiest pony-trap in the U. K. In this plutocratic age of meretricious glitter and luxury this is a distinction—in a way. Our love

<div align="right">Yours ever</div>

<div align="right">J. Conrad.</div>

[1] The size of each issue rather than the considerable size of its circulation. The *North American Review* had previously published 'Henry James' (January 1905) and 'Autocracy and War' (July 1905). The serial of *Under Western Eyes* began in December 1910.

[2] Published in the *Oxford and Cambridge Review* (October 1911), reprinted in *Tales of Hearsay*. See also the letter of [9 December 1908].

[3] Written during the early years at Capel House, as the instructions for travel show. The Sandersons went there in October (letter to Galsworthy, 27 October), but this note may refer to a visit in 1911 or 1912. It must precede the letter of [16 or 23? October] if the month and year are right.

To Stephen Reynolds
Text MS Berg; Unpublished

[letterhead: Capel House]
12 Oct 1910.

Dear Reynolds

I must thank you for the B'wood where your 'Puffin' was really interesting.[1] The "Open Window" is a very small matter but I was glad to see SS in print at last.[2] It *is* a good bit. The rest of the letter-press is astonishingly poor. Which is the drawing you like? The one I do is The Lark.[3]

I am pleased that Alongshore is coming out.[4] I've been waiting for it and I feel very confident as to its value. But you must forgive me if I don't say so Coram Gentibus[5]—it's simply because I am not in a state to say anything. I have had a beastly bad time of it mentally for the last fortnight. I've written 50 000 w since first week in July—two stories.[6] I finished the second on the 4[th] of Oct.[7] and haven't been able to put together a sentence ever since. I've overdone it. And now I worry so about my poor head that I am quite unable to pull myself together. A rotten state of distraction. But do send the book along; I'll be delighted and proud to have it from you. And I hope commercial success won't pass you by on the other side of the road. But it's a capricious goddess you know.

Won't you come and look us up?—at the *first* opportunity I mean. We can put you up here. The only decent train from London is 11 am Char +. A postcard will fetch me to station to meet you. We must have a talk: not that I have much to say but I should like very much to hear about your work and your plans.

Jess sends her love

Your[s] always

J. Conrad.

[1] Reynolds wrote the story of the *Puffin*, the motor-boat given to the sceptical fishermen of Sidmouth, for *Blackwood's*, 188 (October 1910), 478–90.
[2] The *Open Window* was an early 'little magazine' with illustrations. Its first issue, October 1910, included Reynolds's story 'Silly Saltie'.
[3] Claude Shepperson's dry-point of a shepherd watching a lark.
[4] *Alongshore*, a collection of sketches and stories about life on the Devon coast, was published in October.
[5] In public. [6] Cf. the letter of 25 September.
[7] A revision of 'Prince Roman'? He had asked for the typescript on 1 October.

To Helen Sanderson
Text MS Yale; J-A, 2, 116

[letterhead: Capel House]
Sunday. [16 or 23 October?
1910][1]

My dear Helen.[2]

All these sketches have the quality without which neither beauty nor, I am afraid, truth are effective, that is they are interesting in themselves.[3] Thus one may say safely that you have the root of the matter. Yes. It is there. I've spent all yesterday with your pages and so the impression being made and even assimilated I've slept on it. La nuit porte conseil[4]—as you know.

As to what sort of *conseil* that's another matter. I am not very fit to give advice. That is an especial talent. The few remarks that I offer are not valuable in themselves; they can be only worth something in the way of stimulus for self-examination. You have an individuality which *can* express itself. There's no doubt of that. So a seed in the ground expresses itself, manifests itself, in plant and flower. What is necessary is cultivation.

I understand now perfectly what you meant when you said that your subjects presented themselves to you in a very short form. You must let your gift of expression expand freely so as to touch what may seem irrelevant to the matter in hand. The apparently irrelevant is often illuminative. You must never be afraid of remote connections; you must let your mind range widely about your subject. This is the more necessary because your vision is very direct, very clear. Your expression too is very direct and certainly not obscure; but it is not always sufficiently precise.

[1] Jean-Aubry prints the date as 'Sunday, Sept.', but the month is not in the MS. The PS, which refers to a long separation, places this letter between the visit paid some time in October and the Sandersons' expected departure for Africa on 12 November. A Sunday close to 27 October, when Conrad told Galsworthy of his critical activities, seems the most likely.

[2] Helen Mary Sanderson (née Watson, 1875–1967) married Ted in 1898. She was a Scotswoman full of moral and intellectual vigour. As 'Janet Allardyce', she contributed sketches of East African life to *Scribner's Magazine*.

[3] Two pieces appeared in *Scribner's*, 'African Sketches and Impressions', 48 (1910), 627–32, and 'More African Sketches', 51 (1912), 103–10. Theodore Roosevelt had helped place them (Randall, pp. 27–8). The other sketches under scrutiny here are not known to have been published.

[4] From a French translation of the Menander Fragments.

You must try to say things fully; but do not imagine that I would lead you into verbosity. It is not more words that I recommend but—alas!— more toil.

I find it rather difficult to explain what is in my mind. Generally I would say that your prose, full of merit as it is, wants "stringing up". If we could have an hour together with the pages before us I could make my meaning clear enough. I say this with confidence because as a matter of fact our ways of thinking and of looking at things are not dissimilar. However I have taken the liberty to take the last page of the Spirit of the Land and make use of it to illustrate what I would be at in my dumb way. But for goodness sake don't suspect [me] of setting up a model for your writing. You have and you must keep your own way of saying what you have got to say.

The extract from the diary interested me very much as being a short story. And it is good. The general effect however is too harsh. I have asked myself—why? I think that the fault lies in the want of atmosphere. We see these people in a flash and, as it were, in vacuo. It needs a little more detail. For instance we don't know how the poor little woman came to marry Owen. His attitude towards his wife is indicated but you don't say anything of her attitude towards him. A little of that sort of detail is necessary to humanise the story. As it is it seems written only to show up Miss Anstruther; and that's all right. I am with you there. But a short story should before all be a human episode.

There is too little of the *Moving Tides* to form an opinion on; but the charm of the pages before me is undeniable. I am very curious to see what you will make of this beginning. I like *Safe Home* immensely. Of the Scribner papers I put the *Spirit of the Land* first and *On Leave* next. But the *Gramophones* is an excellent sketch too. I could talk about them all with you for a couple of hours with great pleasure for myself if not with profit for you. I am a poor critic—and what's worse I may be a misleading one. You see I've nothing but my instinct to guide me and no great facility in expressing my point of view. So pray don't put too much trust in what I say.

Jessie has been reading the sketches with extreme delight. She sends her dear love. I've been interrupted by a visitor; that's why this letter was not finished sooner. Believe [me] always your affectionate friend and servant

J. Conrad.

ffffffffffff

It's Monday now—and as I have managed to miss this evening's post this letter can't go till tomorrow. I shall write to Ted in a day or two. It seems awful to think we shan't see you both now for years![1]

I hope you won't suspect me of the intention of teaching you. You have your own style, your own expression. The alterations on that page are merely illustrative of my saying that your prose wants a little "bracing up". For instance A is a simple re-arrangement, the picture of the "lilies starring etc etc" being completed before the effect of surprise is mentioned. In B and D I have erased a few words which detract from the *actuality* of the impression. This is a purely descriptive passage, in which any suggestion of action is detrimental. It weakens the effect. At C I've added the word *wonder*, because wonder is one of the conditions of the childhood of the world. Greater precision, you see, and at the same time a larger statement helpful for the main idea of the page.

E. In the sentence crossed out there was an implied change of mood, from vision to dreaming. In a passage built up of visual impressions it was out of place—it seemed to me. The tone must be preserved, always.

F. "Something truly pagan" is too vague. That's what I meant when I said (in the letter) that your expression tho' direct was sometimes not precise enough. In letters suggestiveness itself—a great quality—must be obtained by precise expression. I feel with you that there is "Something truly pagan in the mystery etc etc etc"—but the sentence in itself means nothing. To awaken a responsive feeling something exact must be said. What is paganism? The pagan piety was an emotion evoked by the wonder, charm and fear of the visible world. I think that in this instance you meant the suggestion of fear, dread, "in the mystery of the deserts etc etc". I may be wrong. My sentence certainly is not good in itself but as an example it will serve. In writing and especially in descriptive writing one must guard oneself against the à peu près—the horrid danger of the "near enough".

G. I rearranged this passage. I think the construction is better thus. In descriptive writing one must either evoke images or make statements. The words "strange presence" are neither image nor statement. *Power* instead of *presence* is I think all right. *Compelling* I don't like very much. In view of what follows *fatal* might do.

Lower down I change *shores* for *birthright*. Less precise certainly but a more suggestive word.

It would have been so much nicer, easier, to have you here and

[1] Jean-Aubry omits this paragraph. The Sandersons expected to return to Nairobi. For the change in their plans see the letter of 17 November.

discuss all these instances. I trust you won't think me a horrid pedantic person—a conceited scribbler. You must give me credit for the best intention and accept my remarks in a spirit of affectionate *camaraderie* in which they are offered.

To E. L. Sanderson
Text MS Yale; Unpublished

[letterhead: Capel House]

[October 1910][1]

Here's something for you to read on board my dear Ted. I am ashamed to think the book[2] had not been sent to you before.

I have written at length to Helen; and I can only hope that in my anxiety to show my great and fraternal interest in her talent I have not given offence. Things black on white look so unnecessarily emphatic. We ought to have had a talk. Our dear love to you both

Ever your

J Conrad.

To Norman Douglas
Text MS Texas; Unpublished

[Capel House]

Thursday [20? October 1910][3]

Dear Douglas.

Of course come along[4]—you can *always* come. It makes us unhappy to think of you sitting alone. Pray understand that this *is* your country house.

Good luck to you with Dent. My heart is set hard against Smith.[5]
Au revoir then on Sat. Come to lunch if you can.

Yours

J. C.

[1] Probably within a few days of the letter to Mrs Sanderson.

[2] *A Set of Six?* Methuen had sent copies of *The Secret Agent* and *The Mirror of the Sea* in 1907 (*Letters*, 3, p. 508).

[3] Negotiations with the two publishers give the period. The Conrads expected a visit from Douglas on Saturday, the 22nd.

[4] Douglas spent October and November in London (Holloway, pp. 180–1).

[5] Reginald Smith, of Smith, Elder; Douglas had hoped to place *Siren Land* with him.

To Norman Douglas
Text MS Texas; Unpublished

[letterhead: Capel House]
Saturday. [22? October 1910][1]

My dear Douglas.

This is damnable; but what is one to do? Those fellows have money, time and everything else on their side.

My considered opinion on the *situation* is that this offer is either to be accepted or rejected: it is really unseemly for you to submit to further haggling on the part of Smith. It is better to submit to the Conditions. These negotiations have lasted too long, and Smith Eld[er] have stood too long in your way.

My opinion on *what to do* is to drop them right away and take up Dent.[2] The book will do just as well with one firm as with another. Dent at any rate is in earnest and offers a definite sum of money. He has approached you first and he is certain to try and make a commercial success with the book if only to back up his own opinion. Whereas Smith seems to make a favour of it and may not take any special trouble about it—as long as they get their expenses back. I would say to Dent: "All right. Give me 30 on publication and you shall have the refusal of my next book". This matter must be settled now—next week. You'll feel happier and you'll be able to turn your mind to future work—to *production* instead of tinkering. See?

This is my feeling.

Either title is good. When are you coming here? We expected you today or tomorrow. Anyway come soon. I think that you ought to try B[lack]wood *immediately* with one of the Oases.[3]

Our love

yours

J. Conrad.

[1] The contents give the month. Douglas wrote '26' on the MS, noting the date of his reply.
[2] Joseph Mallaby Dent (1849–1926) accepted *Siren Land*; later he became Conrad's publisher too.
[3] The descriptions of Tunisia that became *Fountains in the Sand*.

To Norman Douglas

Text MS Texas; Unpublished

[letterhead: Capel House]
24 Oct. [1910][1]

Dear Douglas.

Yes. In god's name let Dent catch hold for anything over £30, and the clause as to 10 years' copyright may be sacrificed.

I have read the story.[2] It's marvellous in a way but we must talk it over. As soon as you have settled finally the pub^on of Syren Land you must come down here. You are a good fellow to worry about garbanzas* beans. I was so far from thinking of them that I couldn't understand at first what you were writing about.

That snap was really good. What a pity it can't be used. Give my greetings to poor Jerome[3] when you write.

I do long to hear of the Syren Land being placed definitely somewhere. Conclude dear boy Conclude; and then try B'wood instanter with an oasis or two *not* mentioning however that there is a book of them.

Jessie's kind regards.

Yours

J. C.

To John Galsworthy

Text MS Forbes; J-A, 2, 119[4]

[letterhead: Capel House]
27 Oct 1910.

Dearest Jack.

I've been very anyhow; strange fits of giddiness in the morning; and absolutely unable to write even a letter. Better now.

Nothing done to Chance. Started a story in despair but it is too bad for anything and I don't think I'll let it go out.[5] In fact I am certain I won't. Neither have I been reading anything. It was an awful time which, I hope, is coming to an end. I haven't caught hold yet but I begin to feel as if I might in a day or two.

This is my news—very much as usual as you see. We were so glad to hear that Ada is free from rheumatism this autumn. I was wondering. I hope it's for good, but a mere respite is worth something. *Ted* was here

[1] Dent's offer supplies the year.
[2] Unidentified. [3] A scholarly ex-barrister living on Capri.
[4] Without the paragraph about Garnett.
[5] 'The Partner'? Conrad worked on this story in November.

for a day, likewise Mrs Ted. He told me he saw you in Harrow.[1] He
expects a visit from you in East Africa. You know it's a beastly
rheumaticky place, and, strangely enough, worst in the *dry* season.[2] He
told me several anecdotes. Mrs Ted writes. Descriptive sketches. Not
being able to write myself just now I've been in a devil of a temper and
looking at everything written with a jaundiced eye.

I perceive you have been moving briskly about this distracted realm;
but as it was in the interests of Justice I won't lecture you on these new
gad-about habits. Nothing however can excuse motor-car collisions.[3]
It's all very well to say that a miss is as good as a mile but it's a nerve
shaking experience. Did Ada feel it at all afterwards? Some years ago we
had an accident of the sort, in a modest way. We ran merely into a
baker's cart on a slant and took it backwards into the hedge. The road
was covered with bread. After the first scare it was rather funny (the
baker's man was a stutterer) but I couldn't sleep for three nights
afterwards.

What are the immediate prospects of the *Eldest Son*? Are there any?[4]
I've been tracking down the theatrical column of the Dly Tel: without
coming upon a sign. Why? The news of the *dream play* is a surprise.[5]
Can't I be given a sight of it?

I am very, very curious.

Is it possible that our Edward, the maliciously benevolent Edward, is
growing cantankerous?[6] I haven't seen him since April last when I was
in bed still. I wouldn't throw a doubt on his judgement but I understand
that he has been lately crying up two books of which one (a sea-book) is
the most suburban thing (I mean spiritually) I've ever read. The other
is a South American novel both portly and strangely disorderly—if I
may so express it.[7] But I had better say nothing more since I've written

[1] Where they had gone to school. [2] Cancelled: 'How thin and stooping he is!'
[3] On 14 September, the Galsworthys' car had 'met another motor end-on' (Marrot, p. 305).
[4] It was not produced until 1912.
[5] *The Little Dream* was to open on 15 April 1911.
[6] Edward Garnett had read the MS of Galsworthy's latest novel and did not like what he saw. Marrot (pp. 288–305) prints his judgment and the intensive correspondence that ensued. Garnett found *The Patrician* 'weak, hazy, and *deficient* in *certainty and tradition*. You are neither *critic* nor *realist* here.' He complained in particular that Galsworthy's portrayal of the aristocracy 'produces the *effect of guess-work* – done from outside' (Marrot, p. 289).
[7] See 'Two Powerful Novels', Garnett's unsigned review of David Bone's *The Brassbounder* and A. F. Wedgwood's *The Shadow of a Titan, Nation*, 16 July, pp. 570–2. Garnett places these first novels in a category of fiction 'which is at once realistic and romantic ... Mr. Conrad is the most brilliant, Mr. Cunninghame Graham the most

once a sea book and also a portly S. American novel. This deplorable coincidence seals my lips.

I was thinking that your novel must be nearly finished; I had no idea that you were so far on as the final revision. What is the title? I have an idea dear Jack that any comment on your work can be nothing by now but (in the words of the Pole in the Lear of the Steppes) "perfectly superfluous chatter".[1] I wouldn't chatter—you know. This is as far as I may venture to hint since I haven't lately sent you any of my work to see. But in truth it wasn't worth looking at, being neither particularly amusing nor in any way inspiring. All my notions of arrrt! have fallen off me like a worn out robe. Improving, instructing I can not be; rebellious I never was. Scandalous I daren't. Improper?—that's no longer fashionable; moreover I am afraid of Mudie.[2] The Williamsons have already written all the motoring novels.[3] Aviation is a too lofty subject....

Life's very difficult.

Joking apart I feel painfully out of touch with men and things. I mean mentally of course. Otherwise I may say I have been rather invaded. The other day A[ustin] Harrison came along in a Spyker 30–40 car with Frank Harris (once owner of the Saturday).[4] They patronised me immensely. It was funny but not very amusing. Harrison objected[5] to the title of my novel; but he was so solemn[6] about it that this rare visitor pity entered my heart and I let him be. I said: Have you considered the gravity of such a step as changing the title? Don't you know that I intend the book to be printed from the text as established in the Review? He surrendered gravely, then, with a sort of deference at which I felt remorseful, because—you know—because I didn't care whether he

delicate, member of this school of writers'. All these authors 'study civilisation in the light of half-civilisation'. Garnett praises *The Shadow*, set partly in 'Bolumbia', for its 'unusual power of imagination' and *The Brassbounder* for its vividness and its merits as 'a carefully planned and closely modelled work of art'.

[1] Kvitzinsky, the manager, in Turgenev's *A Lear of the Steppes*, Chapter 9.

[2] Mudie's Lending Library (founded 1842) and Mudie's bookshops were zealous their refusal to carry 'questionable' fiction; H. G. Wells was a frequent victim of their prudishness. In December 1909, the Circulating Libraries Association had instructed publishers to submit new novels for inspection as least one week before publication.

[3] C. N. and A. M. Williamson; the novel replete with motoring adventures (gloriously parodied in *The Wind in the Willows*) had replaced the bicycling novel of the nineties.

[4] Frank Harris (1854–1931), an American, former editor of two reviews, the *Fortnightly* and the *Saturday*, now a contributor to the *English Review*, notorious as a sexual predator and a theorist about Shakespeare.

[5] Originally: 'I tried to snub the Harrison child who objected'.

[6] Originally: 'fatuously solemn'.

printed the novel forwards or backwards with a title or without. He meditated a long time, then gently, not to give me too rude a shock, he said: I am afraid that novel won't be very popular. And we nodded at each [other] with immense seriousness.

Dear old Miss Capes is here. She's over sixty and hopes to meet you once at least before she dies.[1] Jessie has been practically unable to walk for a week. A doctor's coming on Sunday. Well—enough of this "superfluous chatter". Our dear love to you both

Ever Yours

J. Conrad.

To Stephen Reynolds
Text MS Berg; Unpublished

[letterhead: Capel House]
27 Oct 1910

Dear Reynolds.

The critics are mostly fools anyway.[2] You write twenty times better than I ever did and to compare the work of a strong individuality like yours with that of any other man proves not so much lack of discrimination as poverty of ideas. However we must suffer fools—gladly if we can—but we must suffer them.

It's first rate! I expected a good deal but nothing quite so fine as that. There isn't a single page which doesn't toe the mark. It's a magnificent transcript of a very fine reality. I won't mention special passages—I'll leave that to, say, Scott-James[3]—because I accept and absorb the thing as a whole, with all the charm of its actuality and its insistent force like the sea on the beach.

No end sorry not to see you this time. I have no interests whatever in London and you having much to do I would either take up too much of your time or not have enough of you. We must await some other opportunity for a talk.

I am convinced that you know how to take care of yourself (I don't mean the mere mortal envelope) in every way. But onlookers are proverbially able to see more aspects of the game. And if we were talking now, under the very strong impression of your latest achievement, I

[1] Born in 1849, eight years before Conrad, Miss Capes lived until 1936.
[2] They had gone to work on *Alongshore*.
[3] Rolfe Arnold Scott-James (1878–1959) was literary editor of the *Daily News*; later he edited the *London Mercury* and the *Spectator*, and wrote many books on literary subjects.

would take up the position that I don't see how you can go further, do better—and even greater—in that direction. I would say: don't specialize (it's so easy!)—I don't mean in the subject but in the form. The great question for me now, when I look forward, is how you are to go further—do greater? Which is the way? I think the way is to be found by giving rein and spurring your imagination. At moments I am haunted by a lofty (but elusive I own) shape of a great seaboard novel[1] by you with the whole of our civilisation, social & political for a background and with all your ideas and feelings presented to the populace, living, palpitating in a dramatic form. For that you'll have to invent—to come out of yourself in a measure. But all great men have been inventors.

This suggestion'll appear to you crude—but any mere suggestion must be that. The first conception of every great enterprise is a raw thing to get hold of. It's about time for a great creative prose work to come out, a fine ringing imaginative utterance drowning the thin, petty babble of fiction. A great *island* novel with all its life in the setting of the sea and the men nearest to the sea in the foreground—Eh?—the foreground of a really inspiring tale. England, the predestined ground of such comedy-drama may yet produce it; and I can't honour you more, in my own eyes at least, than by confessing the thought that you might be the man. But these I dare say, are mere reveries.

Yours affectionately

J. Conrad.

To J. B. Pinker

Text MS Berg; Unpublished

[letterhead: Capel House]
Monday. [November 1910][2]

My answer is an emphatic No! for reasons with which I don't trouble you but which are sufficient in my view. A friend staying here[3] is to take this to London and he wants to catch his train.

I'll write to Mr G[ordon] B[ennett] (from whom I heard about 10 days ago) and a copy of my letter will be sent to you.

J. C.

[1] A British *Nostromo?*
[2] Received 'Nov. 1910': without the correspondence with Gordon Bennett, a precise dating is impossible; Mondays in November were 7, 14, 21, and 28.
[3] Gibbon (who came on the 20th) or Douglas?

To John Galsworthy
Text MS Forbes; J-A, 2, 121

[letterhead: Capel House]
1[s]t Nov. 1910.

Dearest Jack.

I send back *The Windlestraw*[1] by return of post. In this sort of apologue you are simply incomparable. I revel in your grave, earnest slyness going deeper and deeper, leaving no nook unexplored and always managing somehow to achieve some bit of fine and beautiful expression. The direct, almost naive, preciseness of meditation fits a mind capable of taking a serious departure from a newspaper par:[2] Through that trait your "certain writer" is a perfect creation. His Truth-Conscience is as fair a shape as one ever need wish for a dream-vision. But why it should be scared away so swiftly by the most fatuous thing on earth—a journalistic phrase—I don't know, tho' I feel that it must have been so. For one can not gainsay the force of a public utterance.

That *chose introuvable*[3] the public finds us out in many shapes. We can't find it we can't avoid it.

Almost with everything you write I feel like that pool which the Angel came down to stir.[4] I become troubled. I have no healing qualities—in fact I am of no use in this world—but not being yet quite stagnant water I feel moved to talk back to the Angel.

As an exposure of that contemptible mode of thinking which for want of better invention I must call "newspaper cant" nothing could be better, nothing more effective; but with you, both the mastery of Your process and your almost passionate impartiality, prevent you from stopping short where the commoner sort of honesty would think it had done enough. To leave our brother, for the sake of perfectly impartial irony, at the mercy of every wind that blows, is to expose him to an

[1] This is the fable of a playwright who decides he is answerable to no one – neither to the public, which he finds an impossible abstraction, nor to himself; thus he becomes a windlestraw, a stalk of dry grass blown by the winds.

[2] The playwright, waking from an allegorical dream featuring his conscience, buys a newspaper with a leading article that begins '"There are certain playwrights taking themselves very seriously; might we suggest to them that they are in danger of becoming ridiculous?"': *The Inn of Tranquillity* (New York: Scribner's, 1912), p. 234.

[3] Conrad might have had both senses of *introuvable* in mind: 'undiscoverable' and, ironically here, 'matchless'.

[4] Bethesda: John 5.4: 'For an angel went down at a certain season into the pool, and troubled the water; whosoever then first after the troubling of the water stepped in was made whole of whatsoever disease he had.'

unworthy world only too ready to pour its scorn and its compassion on the head of "that kind of person".

A public is not to be found in a class, caste, clique or type. The public is (or are?) individuals. Le *public introuvable* is only *introuvable* simply because it is all humanity. And no artist can give it what it wants because humanity doesn't know what it wants. But it will swallow anything. It will swallow Hall Caine and John Galsworthy, Victor Hugo and Martin Tupper.[1] It is an ostrich, a clown, a giant, a bottomless sack. It is sublime. It has apparently no eyes and no entrails, like a slug, and yet it can weep and suffer. It has swallowed Christianity, Buddhism, Mahomedanism, and the Gospel of Mrs Eddy.[2] And it is perfectly capable from the height of its secular stability to look down upon the artist as a mere windlestraw!

As to your "certain writer's" feeling of elation[3]—I don't know. Perhaps. Perhaps an uplifting puff of inspiration may be a fine thing whichever way it drives. But we know what becomes of straws blown by the winds, they settle in dark corners and find their end there in obscurity and decay. Our dear love to Ada and you

Ever yours

J. Conrad.

PS Upon the whole I don't know if I can trust my discretion. I may get excited to "superfluous chatter" about the MS of which (or is it of the chatter?) you are sick.[4] In any case I would give it days and you know that I must write myself or perish. When is the book coming out? I wouldn't like to have to wait very long. Indeed I wouldn't.

Am taking Jessie tomorrow to Sandgate[5] for an X rays examination. There's some new mischief certainly. The strain of my illness did it probably. She never had the machine off for 3 weeks solid. And then the additional exertions. All this told on the joint which now looks monstrous.

[1] The sublime and the ridiculous, but all popular: Thomas Henry Hall Caine, the Manxman whom Conrad always considered the most appalling of novelists; Victor Hugo (1802–85), some of whose poems, plays, and novels were translated into Polish by Conrad's father; and Martin Farquhar Tupper (1810–89), whose ever-swelling *Proverbial Philosophy* (1838–76) instructed an audience in the millions.
[2] Christian Science.
[3] The piece ends: 'And with a feeling of elation, as of a straw blown on every wind, he arose' (p. 235).
[4] Galsworthy was revising *The Patrician*. [5] About eleven miles away.

To Norman Douglas
Text MS Texas; Unpublished

[Capel House]
Friday Mid*ght* [4 November
1910][1]

My dear Douglas

I was away for a day and found your letter (with some others) on returning home this evening.

This is business. There is nothing much to congratulate you on for the life at best is bound to be toilsome and disappointing—but still I think that when once the start is made You will be able to make a living and, as it were, wait for the future which as long as a man lives may always hold something worth having.

What I like is to see that you'll have a friendly publisher who will feel some interest in Your success. *M* seems a mighty decent fellow[2] from the tone of his letter.

Come down as soon as you can—or want to. Understand?

We must talk a little of that humourous* Italian book.[3] You have a vein there which may be a paying one. You ought to try and work it.

Without mentioning names (of pub*ers*) I described the transaction to Gibbon who finds that on royalties as secured an advance of £40 is quite fair dealing. When I told him of the Smith proposal he was quite indignant—described it as a pigeon-plucking operation. He understands these things.

Our kindest regards.

Yours

J Conrad.

Your portrait shaving is a sort of idealised likeness which astonished us profoundly.

[1] Another letter about Smith and Dent, answered '8 Nov': Conrad was probably too much out of sorts to have been travelling the previous Friday.

[2] John Nicholas Mavrogordato (1882–1970) worked as an assistant editor at the *English Review* and as a reader for Dent's. Later, he was elected to the Bywater and Sotheby chair in Byzantine and Modern Greek at Oxford; in 1951, he published a translation of Cavafy's poems. He became Douglas's lifelong friend.

[3] An anticipation of Douglas's comic masterpiece, *South Wind* (1917)?

To John Galsworthy
Text MS Forbes; J-A, 2, 122

[letterhead: Capel House]
Tuesday. [8 November 1910][1]

Dearest Jack.

No, I was not taken in.[2] Yes, I thought it might be dangerous; and I wrote with the earnestness befitting the occasion. But I must confess that I was not "wholly serious" (like Mrs Humphrey Ward[3] in her novels) when I compared the public to an ostrich, and an empty sack, and called it sublime.

I am willing to trust without reserves the *nous* of your Manchester readers.[4] The public! We can't get away from it. And in this connection, judging from the extatic* convulsions of the Dly Papers, the *Quaker Girl*[5] is what the public wants just now.

No. Not a single word more (or other) is wanted in your paper. The thing's perfect as it stands even to the last two lines.

Your postscript opens a larger question—a very large question.—It touches upon the very essence of *all* your writing—or I should say the essential principle guiding your art. There is material for much talk there; admitting naturally—(it couldn't be otherwise with you) that the malice is honest (and warranted), and that mystery is a sort of emotional pickle and preservative of the highest things, being—as you say—divine.

I am however a little in doubt of your *precise* meaning. Not much in doubt but just a little. It seems to me at times as though I had, to some small extent, lost intellectual touch with you. Why it should be so, unless from the general weak[en]ing of my grasp on things, of which (rightly or wrongly) I have a dismal consciousness, I don't know. Perhaps it is only that of late we have been physically apart for long stretches of time? There is something in personal contact which clarifies the mists of preconceived ideas each of us carried* about him like a sort of private atmosphere. It is quite possible that I have never understood you

[1] Letterhead one, used until the end of 1911: references to *The Quaker Girl* and the 'radiograph' confirm Jean-Aubry's November dating. The X-ray photograph, taken on the 2nd, would surely have been returned before Friday, the 15th; thus, the 8th is the only possibility.
[2] By 'The Windlestraw'.
[3] In her novels, Mrs Humphry Ward (née Mary Augusta Arnold, 1851–1920) dealt with high theology and high society; *Robert Elsmere* (1888) pleased Mr Gladstone.
[4] Manchester audience? *The Little Dream* was to open there in April.
[5] The very popular musical play had just started what was to be a lengthy run.

thoroughly—a fond—as the French say, or at least as much as it is possible to understand—if so I must have appeared to you more than once as insufferable and even perversely dense. Give my dear love to Ada. The other day I took up Yvette.[1] How well she has done it all!

<div style="text-align:center">Yours ever</div>

<div style="text-align:right">J. Conrad.</div>

PS We haven't yet received the report on the radiograph of Jessie's knee.

To E. L. Sanderson
Text MS Yale; J-A, 2, 123

<div style="text-align:right">[letterhead: Capel House]
17 Nov 1910</div>

Dear old Ted.

Prodigious! Prodigious! The shade of the old Frenchman who has said:—That it is only the unexpected that happens[2]—must be rubbing its hands in the Elysian Fields and nudging the other shades to call their attention to Elstree, here below, where its wisdom is satisfied.[3] But I am not sure that an action for mental and emotional damages would not lie against you people. The amount of thought and sympathy expended in this house on Helen and you during the stormy 13th inst—on the assumption that you were then off the Spanish Coast—is positively ruinous.[4] We felt awfully "sold" when Your letters arrived.

Seriously dear Ted! I rejoice exceedingly at Your taking up this work for which your hardly acquired experience of men and things makes you even more fit than You were before.[5] I don't forget the material improvement which has its great importance; but my most affectionate wishes go to the guardian of the best sort of learning and of the best traditions, taking up the care of young minds in this troubled time of disappearing landmarks.

[1] *Yvette and Other Stories by Guy de Maupassant* (1904), translated by Ada Galsworthy with a preface by Conrad.

[2] Proverbial at least as far back as the Romans: cf. Plautus, *Mostellaria*, 1, 3, 40.

[3] Instead of returning to Africa, Sanderson was going to take over from his brother-in-law as Headmaster of Elstree, a preparatory school with a strong connection to Harrow.

[4] They were probably to have sailed in the *Germany*, which left Southampton on the 12th and ran into very rough weather.

[5] Since he had last taught at Elstree, he had fought in the Boer War, worked for the Transvaal Education Department, and served as Town Clerk of Nairobi.

May all blessings attend you both on this new ground of daily toil, wherein, I know, you will both set up for yourselves the mark of a high ideal. After you are settled a bit I shall be anxious to visit you. It will be like old times to enter again that house with the friendship which has first led me into it now ready to welcome my (somewhat tottering) footsteps.

No more at present except three times three and one more from yours
Ever affectionately
J. Conrad.

Love to Helen and the kiddies from us both. Jessie has been seedy somewhat. She's writing.

To J. B. Pinker
Text Telegram, Berg; Unpublished

[Ham Street]
[22 Nov 1910 1030 am]

Pinker Bookishly London
Don't care much for London Magazine[1] all these men give their third best but if terms allow you make it up to 55[2] for me shall deliver altered MS by Friday[3]

Conrad

To John Galsworthy
Text MS Forbes; Marrot 351 (in part)

[letterhead: Capel House]
22 Nov. 10.

Dearest Jack.

Simply delicious—the descriptions in the Inn of Tranquil[l]ity[4]— nothing less. No one can write that sort of thing with that directness and delicacy, express the truth of natural beauty in such apparently effortless combination of simple words. And when one thinks that it is done as it were by the way at the mere setting of the thesis one can only marvel at your riches—and perhaps envy you a little.

As to thesis—no one could deny the spirit of it.[5] Its form could only

[1] Which had accepted 'A Smile of Fortune'. [2] Pounds or guineas?
[3] The 25th. [4] To be found in the collection of the same name (1912).
[5] Having described a peaceful, beautifully-set Italian inn and its new owner, who has plans to make it garishly modern, Galsworthy decides that he should not, after all,

have come from you. It is as unique as the setting—but whether as perfect? That's another question. But as I could not write a piece like that to save my life I don't know whether I have the right to criticise. Yet as a mere reader, one of many I have a right to state my impression. Shortly it is that the elaboration, the careful sequence of the states of mind, weakens the general effect. At the same time I am not at all sure that the effect could be produced at all by any other means. Perhaps such a train of thought *can not* be suggested and must be *developed* if it is to be conveyed at all? Perhaps——

If I weren't afraid of overstating my position I would say that there is a sensation of neatness. To give a matter of feeling (even if evoked intellectually) a conclusion is a very fine thing but not the finest thing and perhaps not even the most convincing.

But all this is mere rabâchage.[1] The answer to it is that You know what you are doing and that anyhow certain things must be done if the written word is to have any influence on mankind at all.

Gibbon was here on Sunday and told me he has seen you in town and that you propose to come down here before long. If authentic this is great news. I have begun writing again—and time I had too*. A short story.[2] Impossible to do anything with Chance just yet. The London Magazine has taken my long short-story (26000 w). There's glory for you![3] However I am to tinker at it to fit it quite for that exalted destiny.

Our dear love to you both

Ever yours

J. Conrad.

To Edward Garnett
Text MS Indiana; G. 233

[letterhead: Capel House]
22 Nov 1910.

Dearest Edward.

Its ever so good of you to have sent me the Hogarth little book.[4] I knew practically nothing of the man. And I was glad to learn.

I have meditated over some of these small pages where indeed one

despise him: contempt is the enemy of mystery, and mystery is the sweetest part of life.

1 'Repetitious twaddle'. 2 'The Partner'.
3 'A Smile of Fortune' appeared as a 'complete novel' is the February 1911 issue. Earlier complete novelists were Leonard Merrick, Barry Pain, and 'Q'; later, Morley Roberts and H. De Vere Stacpole.
4 In *Hogarth*, written for the Duckworth Popular Library of Art, Garnett praises the great chronicler and satirist for his realism and his defiance of correct eighteenth-century taste.

finds more than what meets the eye. For your critical thought once started leads one to a return upon oneself.

And after all Hogarth was a story teller a critic of life; and then every word of your appreciation seemed to have a double value: illuminative as to the subject—searching as to the reader—this reader.

In addition you are so interesting all the time; its surprising how much characteristic suggestion you have packed into that small compass. But all your criticism that I ever heard or read is infinitely suggestive. I believe my dear Edward that if you started criticising the leg of a table you would end by getting home to our consciences—I mean of us all who have, at least, tried to do something with an honest purpose.

Marwood gave me news of you some time ago and only last Sunday P. Gibbon reported having sighted you in London[1] looking well. But all the same the days slip away. A sort of unholy spell keeps me chained to the desk. And for what? Either for nothing or for rather less than nothing.

But its a fact that the London Mag has accepted a story (longish) of mine which I have written since my illness. You can't say that I haven't "arrived".

A good grip of your friendly hand if only on paper

<div style="text-align:center">Ever yours</div>

<div style="text-align:right">J. Conrad.</div>

To J. B. Pinker
Text MS Berg; Unpublished

<div style="text-align:right">[letterhead: Capel House]
[24 or 25? November 1910][2]</div>

I am disgusted at the silly job but what has been agreed to is performed.

At beginning 5 pp of MS[3] to replace 9 of type

1 1/2 pp. of MS to be inserted on page 112 of type. (A & B)

A few lines of MS at end of story on p 113.

Machine away for repairs prevented me typing the alterations. When preparing the TS for the magazine kindly reproduce the typographical note on first page.

<div style="text-align:right">J. C.</div>

[1] Gibbon was a regular at Garnett's Mont Blanc lunches.

[2] Received 'November 1910': Conrad asked to have 'A Smile of Fortune' back on the 22nd and promised to return it by the 25th.

[3] The MS (Berg) runs to 140 pages.

To J. B. Pinker
Text MS Berg; Unpublished

[Capel House]
30 Nov 10

Dear Sir.

Thanks for the cheque received yesterday.

I hold the cancelled papers of the story for eventual re-insertion in book form.

Am I right in presuming that there will be time before publication here to secure American copyright of that story? I imagine it may be of some value.

Yours obdly

J. Conrad.

To Sir William Robertson Nicoll
Text MS Rosenbach; Unpublished

[letterhead: Capel House]
[late 1910?][1]

Dear Sir William.[2]

I must throw myself on your mercy. I have no photograph I could send you; and only two days ago I refused a request for a portrait from the editor of a magazine where a story of mine is about to appear.[3]

I have preserved consistently this attitude for fourteen years, with one exception, in the case of the *Day's Work*, where a portrait of mine appeared in 1904[4] on condition that it should not be reproduced elsewhere.

The fact is that I have not been photographed more than four times in the course of my existence. I've never in my life bought a photograph of any kind; and if anybody ever took a snapshot of a house of mine it was not for publication.

[1] Written on the first type of Capel House stationery, this letter probably refers to illustrations for Perceval Gibbon's 'Joseph Conrad: An Appreciation', published in the *Bookman*, 39 (January 1911), 177–9.

[2] The Rosenbach has no evidence of destination. The only literary Sir William, however, was Sir William Robertson Nicoll (1851–1923), founder of the *Bookman* in 1886 and still its editor; he also started the *British Weekly* and the *British Monthly*. A Scotsman with strong ties to the Nonconformist churches, Nicoll often wrote as 'Claudius Clear'; his was a powerful influence on late Victorian and Edwardian literary taste. He collaborated with T. J. Wise on *Literary Anecdotes of the Nineteenth Century* (1895–6).

[3] 'A Smile of Fortune' in the *London Magazine* for February 1911?

[4] In the December issue of *World's Work*.

I have no "documents" of that nature. Two old, faded photographs of ships lie somewhere in a drawer: certainly not fit for reproduction. They are not even photographs of the ships I commanded. No doubt the owners of the *Loch-Etive*, the ship in which I began my career as officer of the British Merchant Service, just thirty years ago,[1] have a collection of the photographs of all their ships past and present. But of all the ships in which I served there's not one now remaining afloat[2]. They have been the only home I knew for twenty years; and I think I have paid them the debt of grateful affection in a page here and there. They can say nothing to the eyes of strangers. They are gone and we may well let them rest.

I hope I may be forgiven for the only answer I can make to your, so kindly worded, request.[3] And in this hope I am, dear Sir William,

with the greatest consideration

Yours faithfully

J. Conrad.

To John Galsworthy

Text MS Forbes; Unpublished

[letterhead: Capel House]
Thursday [1 or 8 December
1910][4]

Dearest Jack.

This is good news. Suppose you came on the 17[th] Sat. we could on Sunday (18th) travel by 5.31 or 8.33 to town together, as I have to be in Luton (if I can) on the 19[th] early for B's first communion.

I have ten minutes ago finished a story. Don't feel capable to write any sort of answer to your letter. Only must remark that I didn't use statement in a disparaging sense—nor like M[r] Punch.[5] I meant that each facet being successively turned to the light the single impressive flash-effect of the theme is to a certain extent lost. Everything You write

[1] In August 1880.

[2] Hans van Marle counts six still afloat in 1910.

[3] The cover of the January *Bookman* carried the 1904 photograph of Conrad by G. C. Beresford.

[4] Within the span of the first Capel House letterhead, the combination of a just-finished story and Saturday falling on the 17th occurred in only two months: September and December 1910. The second paragraph echoes a recent commentary on Galsworthy's work: the letter of 22 November provides the obvious point of reference. By 10 December, 'The Partner' was in Pinker's hands.

[5] Who, in his stage rather than his magazine appearances, likes to hit people over the head.

has importance and therefore deserves discussion on a general ground. Our dear love to Ada. But is she not coming too.

<div align="center">Ever Yours</div>

<div align="right">J. Conrad.</div>

To Douglas Goldring
Text MS Indiana; Unpublished

<div align="right">[letterhead: Capel House]</div>
<div align="right">4 Dec 1910</div>

My dear Goldring[1]

My dilatory habits are deplorable. The fact is I put off looking at your verses till I got rid of a piece of work of mine. I ought to have dropped you a line.

Now I have looked I've got to thank you for the kind thought of sending me the little volume[2] and for the pleasure it has given me. I like very much your Country Boy. The spontaneous quality of your verse appeals to me very much. Of the In Sussex "June" I think is the gem. In the Singer's journey the part beginning

"And so from Paradise I turned my feet" pleases me most. But the whole awakens response—the great object of verse.

I won't say more except to repeat the assurance of my appreciation both of your gift and of your performance.

<div align="center">Yours faithfully</div>

<div align="right">J. Conrad.</div>

PS You know I am a writer who has no reserve drawer. I like The Tramp[3] well—but as to contributing I can't promise—tho' I should like to. I have been ill 6 months on end and have to write now for dear life—literally.

[1] Douglas Goldring (1887–1960) worked for Ford in his *English Review* days, later published Ford's poetry, and wrote a study of him, *The Last Pre-Raphaelite* (1948). During his long career, Goldring produced essays, memoirs, poems, and books of travel.

[2] *A Country Boy and Other Poems*, published in June 1910.

[3] A magazine, dedicated to the cult of the open road so popular among fledgling Georgians; Goldring was editor, business manager, and publisher. Contributors included Ford and Wyndham Lewis as well as James Elroy Flecker, Edward Thomas, and W. H. Davies.

To J. B. Pinker

Text MS Berg; Unpublished

[Capel House]
10 Dec 1910

Dear Sir.

I beg to acknowledge receipt of ch: for £40. for story *the Partner*.[1]

I had a letter from M^r Galsworthy. All I can say in this connection is that I hope you will be in a position to negociate* *Chance* MS in hand early in the spring. I cant in this matter be more positive. I am naturally anxious to see that matter go through but I can't get on terms with the thing somehow.

Yours fait[h]fully

J. Conrad.

To Harriet Mary Capes

Text MS Yale; Unpublished

[Capel House]
22 Dec 1910.

Dear Miss Capes

You know in what miserable mental state I am—and you will not be angry with me for putting off answering your most kind, dear and friendly letter till I got a wretched, long "short story" off my chest.

It is infinitely good of you to have taken all this trouble. All I can say at present is that Borys (who sends his love and thanks) is very keen to try,[2] and his present schoolmaster is quite anxious to do his best to prepare him. But in a competitive exam: of that kind it isn't so much what one knows but what sort of competitors one is pitted against which decides the issue. A couple of brilliant boys coming up would destroy B's chances—because, good worker and good player tho' he is, he is not brilliant. Yet it is certain that with such an object in view half a year of real hard work will do him no harm. On the other hand he has enough character not to be demoralised by failure in this most honourable attempt.

I shall write by to night's post to the bookseller in Winchester for the

[1] Finished, according to the letter to Galsworthy of 'Thursday', on either the 1st or the 8th. An undated note to Pinker (Berg), received 'Dec. 1910', reads: 'With M^r J. Conrad's Compliments. About 12000 words. An opportunity to revise the clean copy would greatly oblige.'

[2] Miss Capes, who lived in the city, had evidently suggested he should sit the challenging entrance exam for Winchester School.

papers of last year's exam on which I can in a certain measure form an opinion; and I shall forward them to B's schoolmaster for his judgment. And then we shall see. I shall of course write to you at once of our decision.

I can not tell you how much I appreciate the interest you take in the boy. This fresh proof of your goodwill for us touches us both deeply. Accept our warmest wishes for the coming year. All the house sends its best love. Believe me always

<div style="text-align: right">

Your most grateful and
affectionate friend and servant
J. Conrad.

</div>

To Sir Hugh Clifford
Text MS Clifford; J-A, 2, 123; Hunter (1985, 2)

<div style="text-align: right">

[letterhead: Capel House]
22 Dec., 1910

</div>

My dear Clifford.

We are so much not *du monde* that never looking at the social columns of our noble press we have remained in ignorance of the happy event till a friend came along and enlightened us.[1] Pray receive our belated felicitations none the less hearty for the delay. We are made happy by Your happiness; and Jessie applauds both your wisdom and your good fortune. May a long succession of unclouded years be your lot.

For my part I feel constrained to remonstrate a bit. The appeal to my literary opinion was not scrupulously fair. Suppose I had been in one of my cantankerous hours when the book came?[2] But I daresay you were confident. And with reason. No native or acquired cantankerousness could resist the charm of style, the delicate simplicity of expression, the obvious (and so rare!) "good faith" of the writer, exercising her insight not for the sake of cleverness but in the service of a true feeling for the human beings with whom she deals. These are rare qualities.

I would have written but I kept on thinking—he's coming soon. You know You had promised to come in the autumn. Then I thought—he's writing. And with the book—the great book—in my mind I thought I had better keep quiet till I heard from you. I myself had to write a quantity of dismal rubbish—and so the days went slipping by.

[1] A widower, Clifford had married Mrs Henry de la Pasture, the novelist, on 24 September, in what the press called a 'literary wedding' (information from Hunter).
[2] Clifford had sent his fiancée's novel *Peter's Mother* to Conrad without disclosing any personal connection.

We send you our warmest Xmas wishes. Believe me always

Yours

J. Conrad.

To William Maas

Text MS Yale; Unpublished

Capel House

23 Dec 1910[1]

Dear Mr Maas.[2]

Many thanks for your letter and MS. I was very much interested to read the close analysis of my work so sympath[et]ically written by you. I appreciate it greatly. I turned with equal curiosity to the article on Galsworthy which seems to me eminently just (and judicious) in many respects.[3] I shall dispatch your MS on Tuesday by registered post. Our best wishes for health and prosperity in the coming year.

Yours sincerely

J. Conrad.

To J. B. Pinker

Text MS Berg; Unpublished

[letterhead: Capel House]

23 Dec '10

Dear Sir.

I don't know how Mr T Fisher Unwin came to sell the translation rights of the *Outcast*. I suppose you notified him at the time my agreement with Davray was filed at your office that the Mercure had all the rights. I am writing to Paris at once—but it is a beastly complication.

I heard nothing from Mr T Fisher Unwin[4] about this matter. The only book of which he can dispose as he thinks fit without reference to me is *Almayer's Folly*, which he has bought outright.

The proceeding seems to me inconceivable. That a publisher should go and sell the rights of translation, without any reference to the author, to the first man that offers a little money for it, as if the thing were a piece of dry goods, is simply an outrageous proceeding.

[1] Or 1911: a debatable reading.

[2] William Harold Maas worked for the literary department of the *Daily Chronicle*. Later he contributed to *Punch*, wrote for Northcliffe and, in 1931, became fiction editor, then editor of the *Winner*.

[3] Untraced; not in the *Chronicle*.

[4] Publisher of Conrad's first three books: Conrad had a low opinion of him long before the present incident.

As to the Frenchman in Tonkin[1] the only thing to do is to say that I shall make it very clear, by all the means of publicity I can command, that the only translation authorised by me is the one published by the *Mercure de France*. I can't accept an agreement entered into without as much as "by your leave" from me.

<div style="text-align:center">Yours faithfully</div>

<div style="text-align:right">J. Conrad.</div>

To Sidney Colvin
Text MS Texas; Unpublished

<div style="text-align:right">[letterhead: Capel House]</div>
<div style="text-align:right">24 Dec 1910.</div>

My dear Colvin.

Many thanks. The box has not arrived yet, but it will be infinitely welcome when it does and the contents most carefully used.

It is really very good of you to take all this trouble. Be sure that I appreciate it greatly.

Our best wishes of unclouded days, of health and peace for Mrs Colvin and yourself in this coming year and for many years to come.

Believe me

<div style="text-align:center">yours with the greatest regard</div>

<div style="text-align:right">J. Conrad.</div>

To J. B. Pinker
Text MS Berg; Unpublished

<div style="text-align:right">[letterhead: Capel House]</div>
<div style="text-align:right">24 Dec '10</div>

Dear Sir.

I have three requests to make: first to beg you to inform me definitely whether Mr T. Fisher Unwin had been advised of my arrangement with the *Mercure de France*—(a reputable, well known and highly literary publication)—at the time I entered into it.

Secondly _not_ to receive any money from Mr Fisher Unwin in connection with his transaction with Capt Lebouc of the Tonquinese Sharpshooters.

Thirdly to send me by registered post my agreements with Mr T. Fisher Unwin relating to *Outcast* and *Tales of Unrest* for me to look at.

[1] A note, perhaps by Davray, accompanying the letter of 29 December (MS Texas) identifies him as 'Captain E. Lebouc of the Third Regiment of Tonquin Riflemen (tirailleurs), Commandant of the post at Bac-Lé, Tonkin' (Viet Nam).

My impression is that the agreements do not give M^r T. F. Unwin the *right* to *sell* the rights of translation to anybody that may come along. They give him the right to *one half of the proceeds* and of this I was aware. The wording is clear to that effect. But I very much doubt whether it implies the right for M^r T. F. Unwin to sell without referring to me, regardless of the proposed translator's qualifications, to a person who may be incompetent, or careless, or unsuitable in any other respect. A man whose work is supposed to hold a place in literature is entitled to have a decisive say in such a matter on the ground of an author's moral right to look after his reputation.

<div align="right">Yours faithfully
J. Conrad.</div>

To Arthur Symons
Text MS Virginia; Hunter (1985, 3)

<div align="right">[letterhead: Capel House]
24 Dec 1910.</div>

My dear Symons.

I am most touched by the charming and friendly token of remembrance your wife and Yourself have sent me. It has become a treasured possession; and henceforth not a line of mine will be written but on it.

I am scrawling this in a hurry to catch the post. I pray you both to believe in our affection and in our wishes for your peace and prosperity.

<div align="right">Ever yours
J. Conrad</div>

To John Galsworthy
Text MS Forbes; Unpublished

<div align="right">[Capel House]
Monday ev^g [26 December
1910?][1]</div>

Dearest Jack

Are you (and we <u>do</u> hope dear Ada too) coming to Ham Street?

The question is shall I order the fly from the village?

[1] Speculative: Conrad started 'Freya' on 26 December. A visit earlier in the year seems unlikely, given the remarks about separation in the letter of [8 November]. After 'Freya' Conrad wrote no more stories until May 1912, when the Galsworthys were in the U.S.; by the summer of 1912, they could have been met in Conrad's own car. At the end of 1910 the Galsworthys were in Littlehampton; a cross-country railway journey was awkward but possible.

Or, as there is a wait in Ashford, would you want Hayward New Street Ashford to meet your train at *Ash*? with the little open Darracq[1] which could run you here to Capel in 20 m or so.

Of course if the weather is bad that's not to be thought of.

The distance from Ham St Station is only 1 1/2 miles.

Will you wire or let us know—no! a letter won't do as (having missed tonights post) this won't be delivered to you till the evening. I've begun another story and moiling over the foolish stuff I forgot the time.

Our dearest love

<div style="text-align:center">Ever yours</div>

<div style="text-align:right">J. Conrad.</div>

To H.-D. Davray
Text MS Texas; *L. fr.* 104

<div style="text-align:right">[letterhead: Capel House]</div>
<div style="text-align:right">29 Dec 1910</div>

Mon cher Davray.

Comme je pensais a Vous envoyer un petit mot d'amitié pour le jour de l'an une tuile affreuse me tombe sur la tête. Je viens d'apprendre indirectement que Fisher Unwin a vendu *sans m'en dire un mot* les droits de traduction du *Outcast* au capitaine Lebouc dont la lettre adressée a mon agent vous trouverez ci-incluse.

Moi, pour Vous dire toute la verité, je croyais que vous vous étiez mis en rapport avec F. Unwin depuis longtemps surtout au sujet de l'*Almayer's Folly* qui lui appartient exclusivement. Et d'ailleurs je ne pensais pas qu'il fut capable de me jouer un tour pareil. Car enfin disposer des droits de traduction au premier venu sans consulter l'auteur ni même l'en avertir c'est un peu fort. Malheureusement il parait que par une clause du contrat a laquelle je n'avais pas fait attention il a strictement le droit de le faire.

La question est que dois-je faire moi? Peut être que la traduction de ces vieux livres n'est pas encore mise en train. Dans ce cas vous pourrez sans doute vous arranger avec Lebouc. Ecrivez moi ce que vous en pensez. En attendant je vais me faire envoyer tous mes autres contrats pour les examiner a la loupe; mais je crois pouvoir vous assurer que avec mes autres livres (publiés par *Blackwood* et *Methuen*) il n'y a pas a craindre des complications de cette espèce.

Il parait que Lebouc m'a écrit. J'étais gravement malade quand sa

[1] A Motor-car.

lettre est arrivée. Ma pauvre femme qui m'a soigné toute seule pendant les cinq mois de cette maladie l'a mise de côté et puis n'y pensa plus. Nous ne pouvons même la retrouver a present.

Cette affaire me chagrine et m'inquiète beaucoup car légal[e]ment je n'ai pas de remède contre Fisher Unwin. Tout ce que je peux vous dire est que je suis prêt a abandonner ma part du profit sur les autres livres jusqu'a concurrence des frais que l'action de F. Unwin peut vous causer d'une façon ou d'autre.

 Croyez moi mon cher avec nos meilleurs souhaits

<div style="text-align:right">toujours tout à vous</div>

<div style="text-align:right">J. Conrad.</div>

Translation

My dear Davray,

 Just as I was thinking of writing you a little new year's note of friendship, some rotten luck descended on my head. I've just learned indirectly that, *without saying a word to me about it*, Fisher Unwin has sold the translation rights of the *Outcast* to Captain Lebouc, whose letter addressed to my agent you will find enclosed.

 To tell you the whole truth, I myself believed that you had been in touch with F. Unwin ages ago, above all on the subject of Almayer's Folly, which is his exclusively. Besides, I didn't think he was capable of playing me such a trick. After all, to dispose of the translation rights to the first comer without consulting the author or even alerting him is a little much. Unfortunately it seems that, by a clause in the contract to which I hadn't paid attention, he has the right, strictly speaking, to do so.

 What should I do? Perhaps the translation of these books from the past has not yet started. In that case you can surely come to an arrangement with Lebouc. Write, telling me what you think. In the meantime, I'm going to send for all my other contracts and look at them under a magnifying glass; but I believe I can give you a guarantee that with my other books (published by Blackwood and by Methuen), there's no reason to fear complications of this sort.

 Apparently, Lebouc wrote to me. I was gravely ill when his letter came. My poor wife, who looked after me all by herself for the five months of the illness, put it to one side and thought no more about it. At the moment, we can't even find it.

 This affair vexes and disturbs me, for legally I have no remedy against

Fisher Unwin. All that I can say to you is that I am ready to give up my share of the royalties on the other books to the extent that Fisher Unwin's action may cost you in one way or another.

 With our best wishes, my dear fellow,

<div align="center">Yours ever,</div>

<div align="right">J. Conrad</div>

To J. B. Pinker
Text MS Berg; Unpublished

<div align="right">[letterhead: Capel House]
29 Dec. 10</div>

Dear Sir.

 I return the agreement with thanks.

 Obviously he has the right. There is also such a thing as common decency. I, for instance, have an indubitable right to send a chartered accountant to look at Mr F. U.'s books—if I like.—However I've communicated with Davray and shall write to Lebouc in a day or two.

<div align="center">Yours faithfully</div>

<div align="right">J Conrad</div>

1911

To H.-D. Davray

Text MS Texas; L. fr. 106

[letterhead: Capel House]
9 Jan. 1911.

Cher ami.

J'ai été tout saisi d'apprendre la maladie de Mmme Davray et les angoisses que Vous avez du souffrir. Nous vous prions instamment de nous envoyer un petit mot pour nous rassurer completement sur la convalescence de la malade.

Merci pour la manière amicale dont vous me tranquil[l]isez au sujet de l'affaire Unwin.[1] Oui certainement servez-vous de la traduction Lebouc (commandant du poste de Bac Lé. Tonkin). Il fera le gros de l'ouvrage et pour le reste je me fie a vous. C'est bien compris, mon cher que (comme je vous l'ai écrit dans le temps) le volume: *Typhoon* appartient a Heinemann *absolument*.[2] Je n'ai rien a toucher là-dessus.

Oui. J'ai reçu une lettre de Smet a qui je reponds ce soir-même.

Avec nos meilleurs sympathies pour vous et votre chère malade

je suis bien a Vous

J Conrad.

Translation

Dear friend,

I was distressed to learn about Mme Davray's illness and the agonies you must have suffered. To reassure us about the invalid's recovery, we implore you to send us a brief note right away.

Thanks for your friendly way of setting my mind at rest about the Unwin business. Yes, indeed, make use of the translation by Lebouc (commandant at Bac Lé, Tonkin). He will do the bulk of the work; I depend on you for the rest. As I wrote to you at the time, it's quite understood that *Typhoon*, as a volume, belongs *entirely* to Heinemann. I can't touch it.

Yes, I've had a letter from de Smet, which I shall answer this evening.

With all our sympathies for you and your precious invalid, I am

Yours ever,

J. Conrad

[1] See the letters of 23, 24, and 29 December 1910.
[2] As the following letter shows, Joseph de Smet had been working on a translation.

405

To the Abbé Joseph de Smet
Text L. fr. 106

Capel House.
9 jan. 1911
Cher Monsieur,[1]

Merci de votre amicale lettre. Je suis sûr que la besogne de traduire 'Typhoon' sera bien faite.[2] Peut-être voudriez-vous me permettre de jeter un coup d'oeil sur le 'typescript' (je ne connais pas le terme français) à cause des termes marins dont je pourrais fournir l'exact équivalent. Monsieur d'Humières qui a traduit 'The Nigger of the "Narcissus"' m'a permis de revoir les épreuves à cause de cela même.

Je suis très flatté d'apprendre que je serai le sujet d'une de vos conférences.[3] Mais je ne veux pas vous parler de moi-même. Ce n'est pas fausse modestie. Je ne sais pas. Je ne saurais que dire. L'oeuvre est là. Il faut la prendre en entier. Créative? Peut-être. Je ne possède ni le sens critique ni la faculté littéraire. Mes livres m'ont trop coûté pour que je les aime. Je vais à ma tâche quotidienne comme le forçat à son labeur,—parce qu'il le faut. La vie est un dur maitre. Mais je préfère ne pas en parler.

Translation

Dear Sir,

Thank you for your friendly letter. I am sure that the task of translating 'Typhoon' will be well done. Perhaps you would let me glance over the 'typescript' (I don't know the French term) on account of the sea vocabulary for which I can supply the exact equivalents. M. d'Humières, who translated *The Nigger of the 'Narcissus'*, allowed me to revise the proofs for that very reason.

I am very flattered to learn that I shall be the subject of one of your lectures. But I do not wish to speak of myself. This isn't false modesty. I do not know, I would not know what to say. The work is there. It must be taken as a whole. Creative? Perhaps. I have neither the critical sense

[1] The Abbé Joseph de Smet (1870–1933) was a Belgian priest and writer who became Inspector General of Catholic Education. He felt a great enthusiasm for modern poetry, especially for the work of Emile Verhaeren, of whom he published a study (Malines, 1909). After translating 'Typhoon', de Smet turned to *Nostromo*. His 1912 essay on Conrad in the *Mercure de France* was the first in French.

[2] The translation was to appear in the review *Progrès*.

[3] At the Cercle Artistique in Ghent, according to Jean-Aubry. The letter to Pinker of 28 February refers to an imminent lecture in Paris.

nor the literary faculty. My books cost me too much for me to like them. I go to my daily task as a convict to his labour—because he must. Life is a hard master. But I prefer not to speak of it.

To Edward Garnett
Text MS Free; G. 237

Capel House. Orlestone.
Nr Ashford. 12 Jan. '11.

Dear old boy.

I was glad to hear from you. Don't put off your promised visit too long. Yes it is a far cry from 1894 when this literary child was born to you.[1] For you know You can't get out of it however you may regret it. You are responsible for my existence.

Directly I get 3 instalments or so of the novel together I'll send them to you. My copy of proofs is uncorrected as yet.

Look here. The straight truth of it is that I am now writing a silly story[2] (being near the end of it) and as soon as I am done with the truck[3] and have got over the disgust my writing leaves behind, I shall drop you a postcard asking for the play.[4] I don't ask for it now because I know myself. I would look at it at once and I am not fit to look at anything at present. I am in that state that I would hit Venus of Milo on the nose if anybody showed her to me. I am not trying to be funny I assure you: this state of mind is as near as damn it to cutting one's throat.

And so you've kept my letters! Have you! Ah my dear you'll never meet the man who wrote them, again. I feel as if I had somehow smashed myself. But do come over and look at the pieces. The only thing You'll find uninjured will be my affection for you.

Jessie sends her love to you all. Pray remember me to your wife and David as tenderly as they will let you.

Yours ever

J. Conrad.

[1] In that year Garnett had advised T. Fisher Unwin (whose reader he was) to take *Almayer's Folly*. At their first meeting, Garnett persuaded Conrad to continue with a second novel (*Letters*, 1, p. 178, n. 1).

[2] 'Freya of the Seven Isles'. [3] 'The paltry thing'.

[4] Garnett's *The Trial of Jeanne d'Arc*.

To H. G. Wells

Text MS Illinois; Unpublished

[letterhead: Capel House]
20 Jan '11.

My dear Wells.

This is really great, great in every dimension![1]

After that—which is a cry—there is not much to say. And indeed I will confess to you that at the present moment I am as it were overwhelmed—for the cumulative effect of your pages is enormous. You may believe me if I say that I haven't lost a line. I don't know much but I know how to read you.

Every feeling of admiration being exhausted I won't try to find words just now. Not that I am tired (the stress is too inspiring in a sense to tire one), but because I am as if silenced by the multiplicity of responsive strains within me.

I have read the book yesterday and this evening I re-read it from p 290 to 504.[2] I don't know what a "masterpiece" may be—but I know what master-work is when I see it. And this is it.

I have been sitting for this last (and late) hour thinking in an exclamatory mood, an inarticulate mood. But what does it matter—since the finest words I could find could convey to you no more than the assurance that I am most deeply touched—intellectually and emotionally—by the marvellous quality of the book.

Ever yours with admiring
affection

J. Conrad

To the Abbé Joseph de Smet

Text J-A, 2, 124

Capel House
23rd Jan., 1911

Dear Sir,

It is perfectly correct. I was nineteen before I learned English. I went to sea rather late at the age of seventeen, but I was for two years in the

[1] Wells's novel *The New Machiavelli*, just published, very reluctantly, by Macmillan. Its diaphanously masked portraits of the Fabians and its open acknowledgment of sexual desire provoked a furore.

[2] The book ran to 528 pages.

Mediterranean. I joined my first English ship in March, 1878, I think.[1] Anyway as we went up the Bosphorus we saw the tents of the Russian army at San Stephano.[2] That was the year. In May of the same year[3] I landed in Lowestoft (on the East Coast), knowing no one in England. My first English reading was the *Standard*[4] newspaper, and my first acquaintance by the ear with it was in the speech of fishermen, shipwrights and sailors of the East Coast.[5] But in 1880 I had mastered the language sufficiently to pass the first examination for officer in the Merchant Service, including a viva-voce of more than two hours.[6] But "mastered" is not the right word; I should have said "acquired." I've never opened an English grammar in my life. My pronunciation is rather defective to this day. Having unluckily no ear, my accentuation is uncertain, especially when in the course of a conversation I become self-conscious. In writing I wrestle painfully with that language which I feel I do not possess but which possesses me,—alas!

Thanks for your friendly letter. Pardon the delay in answering it, but I am trying to finish a longish story and I have been so tired at the end of the day that the pen once thrown down I had not the courage to pick it up again for correspondence. There is a pile of letters to answer lying before me now.

Pray rest assured of my deep sense of your sympathetic appreciation and believe me

cordially yours.

[1] The chronology here is confusing. Conrad based himself in Marseilles for three and a half years but spent about eighteen months of that time on voyages to the Caribbean. A passenger, he began his first voyage in the *Mont-Blanc* on 15 December 1874, twelve days after his seventeenth birthday; an apprentice, in the same ship, he began his second voyage on 25 July 1875. He sailed in the *Mavis*, his first English ship, on 24 April 1878; thus, unless Conrad took lessons from his British and American acquaintances in Marseilles, he began to learn English when he was twenty.

[2] Where, in March, the Turks had capitulated after a year of war. By the treaty of San Stefano, Bulgaria, a Russian client state, extended its borders to the Bosporus, a move that the Austrian, British, and German governments found highly suspicious.

[3] On 10 June, from Taganrog (*Lloyd's List*).

[4] The London morning, not the evening newspaper.

[5] On 11 July, Conrad joined the *Skimmer of the Sea* for three voyages up the east coast to Newcastle and back.

[6] Vividly, if not absolutely accurately, recalled in *A Personal Record*, Chapter 6.

To Edward Garnett
Text MS Texas; Copy, Indiana; G. 238[1]

Capel House
Orlestone.
Nr. Ashford.
[17 February 1911][2]

Dearest Edward.

A thousand apologies for delay. A fool girl mislaid the envelope and I was going to write you in despair when it turned up.

Is what I have written sufficient?[3] If you had given me the slightest lead I would have done better.

In haste.

Ever yours,

J. Conrad.

I associate myself with all my heart with the opinion that Mr. W. H. Davies' poetical gift is of the rarest and its expression enriching our literature most deserving of recognition.

Joseph Conrad.

To the Abbé Joseph de Smet
Text L. fr. 108

Capel House.
Fevrier 1911

Cher Monsieur,

Je regrette de ne pas pouvoir vous envoyer les 'Inheritors'. Il semble que ce livre a disparu complètement. Même l'exemplaire que je possédais est égaré. Du reste je puis vous assurer que ce livre n'a aucune importance dans mon oeuvre. Il en est autrement de *Romance* (une seconde collaboration avec Hueffer),—dont la moitié est de ma main,—dans tous les cas.[4]

[1] Text for the letter to Garnett from the Indiana copy, formerly in the Sutton collection; text for the statement of support from Conrad's MS note on the petition, now at Texas.

[2] Documents at Texas confirm Garnett's dating: George Jefferson, *Edward Garnett: A Life in Literature* (Cape, 1982), pp. 134–5.

[3] Edward Garnett and Edward Thomas were circulating a petition to the Government on behalf of W. H. Davies (1871–1940), the Welsh poet and former tramp, author of *Nature Poems* and *Autobiography of a Supertramp* (both 1908). He was granted a Civil List pension of £50.

[4] There is a scholarly consensus that *Romance* was far more Conrad's book than *The Inheritors* was.

Merci de votre bonne lettre. Je serais très heureux de lire votre
critique dans le 'Mercure'.[1] Certainement servez-vous du portrait de
Bookman.[2] Il n'y en a pas de plus récent.

Pardonnez ce gribouillage.

A vous cordialement.

Translation

Dear Sir,

I regret not being able to send you the *Inheritors*. This book seems to
have vanished. Even my own copy has strayed. Anyway, I can assure
you that this book has no importance among my works. It is otherwise
with *Romance* (a second collaboration with Hueffer)—half of which is
from my hand—at least.

Thank you for your good letter. I should be very happy to read your
critique in the *Mercure*. Certainly help yourself to the portrait in the
Bookman. There is nothing more recent.

Forgive this scrawl.

Cordially yours.

To Arthur Symons

Text MS Lohf; J-A, 2, 125

[letterhead: Capel House]
7 Febr 1911.

My dear Symons.

I understand you are all alone for a few days so I drop you this note en
camarade for company's sake, tho' indeed I have nothing memorable
and nothing new to say. I wish I could invent something amusing, but I
feel too stupid just now to try. Moreover to be amusing is not in my line.
That's why the public fights shy of my writing I suppose.

I was glad to see you more alert, more hopeful and altogether better
this time.[3] I expect many fine things from You in the future. My days of
fine things are done I fear. Still one must go on. At any rate I must.

Miss Tobin's passage under our roof left a delightful scent of

[1] The essay on Conrad did not appear until 1 May 1912.
[2] Both on the cover and inside the January number.
[3] Agnes Tobin had driven Symons to Capel House on the 5th (Beckson, *Symons*,
p. 274).

intelligence and charm of a finely humane quality.[1] You are lucky in your friends mon cher. Pray remember us to her in as friendly terms as you can think of.

It's late. I am tired after a day of uphill toil. Now it is always uphill with me. And the worst is that one doesn't seem any nearer the top when the day is done.

Our affectionate regards

Yours

J. Conrad.

To J. B. Pinker
Text MS Berg; Unpublished

[letterhead: Capel House]
8 Febr '11

Sorry for delay.

I have signed the agreement here enclosed with modifications which Harpers if they really care to publish my work should accept.[2] I am averse from signing for the different rates of royalty.

I'll be sending you a longish story in a day or two. I've done also something to *Chance*. And in this connection I presume you'll have no objection to accept batches of 5000 words of that story should it be convenient to me to send in that quantity?

Yours

J. C.

To Stephen Reynolds
Text MS Berg; Unpublished

[Capel House]
14 Febr '11.

Dear Stephen.

Your letter delights me. I've a great confidence in your future—and indeed I've always had it. But somehow the tone of this last missive has warmed me and cheered me. Your plan of contribution to the West[er] Gaz.[3] strikes me as most promising.

[1] They had discussed Poland and California (*ibid.*).
[2] 'The Partner' appeared in the November *Harper's Magazine*.
[3] The *Westminster Gazette*, an evening paper.

Yes. Send the story not that I think your French needs revising but for my pleasure.[1]

Come along here whenever you can—and try to make it soon.

Yours affectionately

J. Conrad

To Warrington Dawson
Text MS Duke; Randall 134

[letterhead: Capel House]
15 Febr '11.

My dear Warrington Dawson

Thanks for your friendly letter. I feel remorseful towards you in this matter of correspondence; but I've grown so shameless that I have forgotten even how to apologise in fitting terms. I prefer to brazen it out and ask for forgiveness as a sturdy beggar asks for alms—with a sort of unholy leer confessing his unworthiness at the very moment he asks for charity.

It is jolly of You to beat my little drum "en bon camarade." I should be delighted to appear in the new magazine.[2] If she wants something of mine complétement inédit I am putting finishing touches to a story, (which I think I'll call *Freya of the Seven Isles*), length about 20 000 words (3 or four instalments) of which I could send her the typescript in say a fortnight.[3] It's quite good magazine stuff, quite Conradesque (in the easier style),—"no blush to the cheek of the young person" sort of thing.[4] Perfectly safe. Eastern sea setting, but not too much setting. I would be glad to hear from the lady.

Tell me mon bon—should Mrs de Lano Demachy write to me—whether I can ask her for 1000 frcs for giving her the *English text* in advance of publication here? I mean that she should get the translation done herself. But I would revise it if she wished it. Qu'en pensez-vous? Of course in confidence I ask you only because I don't want to do anything outrageous. I should think she could get the translation done for 250–250 frcs. Altogether say the stuff would cost her about £50 which does not seem much?

[1] It is possible that the note on p. (313) may refer to this story rather than the sketch about French trawlermen.

[2] *Progrès*, a short-lived Parisian monthly.

[3] The editor, Adeline de Lano Demachy, took de Smet's translation of 'Typhoon' instead; it began in the April number.

[4] It would not offend even the vigilant Mr Podsnap of *Our Mutual Friend*.

It's good news to hear that you are coming over. We can put you up now.[1] So you must come for the night—a night at least—and we shall have a long argumentative talk. I am looking forward immensely to seeing you. My wife sends her most friendly remembrances. Au revoir. A bientôt—then.

<div align="right">Yours ever sincerely</div>

<div align="right">J. Conrad</div>

To John Galsworthy
Text MS Forbes; Unpublished

<div align="right">[letterhead: Capel House]</div>

<div align="right">15 Febr '11.</div>

Dearest Jack.

I would have written before if I had had anything worth saying to put down—I mean as to myself. As to you not even an echo of your existence or activities has reached me, as echoes have sometimes done. Indeed I haven't seen anyone for ages except the regular Marwood who walks the ten miles religiously every Tuesday for a four-hours call.[2]

I had a pretty bad time for a full 3 weeks—no two consecutive ideas, no six consecutive words to be found anywhere in the world. I would prefer a red hot gridiron to that cold blankness, but the choice is not given to me. I expect to finish a longish story in a day or two—but devil only knows. I have been fooled too often by such expectations to put my trust in them.

Have you begun another novel? Are you at work on another play? Je me demande ... And in this connection have you got fitting music for the dream-play[3] of which I've been thinking more than once.

I even don't know where to imagine you. I shall send this to Addon Rd tho' it seems to me you must be in Devon. Drop us a line my dear Jack—the shortest of lines if you are busy, which I suppose you are.

I've heard a vague rumour that that ridiculous English Review was to be prosecuted for indecency.[4] If somebody would kick it for idiocy it

[1] The Aldington lodgings had been too cramped.

[2] The Marwoods lived the other side of Aldington, at Water Farm, Stowting.

[3] *The Little Dream*, with its children's dances, was to open in Manchester on 15 April.

[4] Possibly on account of Arnold Bennett's mildly scandalous 'Paris Nights', in the December and January numbers; the same numbers carried the beginning of *Under Western Eyes*.

would be more to the purpose—but the right thing never gets done in this imperfect world.

Our dear love to you both.

Ever yours

J. Conrad.

To Arthur Symons

Text MS Lohf; Symons 30; J-A, 2, 126

[Capel House]
Wednesday evening [15 February
1911][1]

My dear Symons.

I've just finished reading your touching and sympathetic letter.

No my dear fellow. You have not deserved it;[2] and if any one has the right to ask: Why? you have that right. But if you do such things as your translation of Crimen Amoris out of despair[3]—then, take my word for it, you need not despair.

One survives everything—disaster, annihilation itself, absurd as it seems to say it. Your *désir de vivre* is the best proof that you deserve to live. And you must not forget that you *exist* pour les ésprits d'élite which is the best sort of existence.

To recommend forgetfulness to a man so profoundly tried as you have been tried, would be folly. Yet, as has been said, life is a dream,[4] or, as I should say, a succession of songes doux ou terribles. Well and if it is so then even in terror we may find inspiration once we regain courage enough to turn our eyes away from it. Don't look back for indeed the only way to overcome injustice whether of men or fate is to disregard it.

Yours

J. Conrad.

[1] 1910 according to Symons, but the envelope was postmarked on Thursday, 16 February 1911. The Verlaine reference confirms the later date.

[2] The mental collapse from which Symons was recovering.

[3] During his visit to Capel House, Symons had read a translation of Verlaine's poem (from *Jadis et naguère*, 1884). Conrad called it 'Magnificent' and was 'transported' by an encore (Beckson, *Symons*, p. 274).

[4] Said by Calderón and in *Lord Jim*, Chapter 20, by Conrad himself.

To H.-D. Davray
Text MS Indiana; *L.fr.* 107

[letterhead: Capel House]
[mid February 1911][1]

Cher Davray.

Je vous écris ce mot tout de suite pour ne pas avoir l'air de manigancer des affaires derrière votre dos. Un ami à moi Dawson (journaliste, romancier Americain—peut-être vous connaissez?) m'a mis en relation avec Mme. Demaché,* Revue: *Progrès.* pour une oeuvre de moi. Je suis en train de finir une nouvelle (24000 mots) qui fait l'affaire. Je lui ai cédé (serial rights) le texte (inédit) anglais pour mille frcs. Elle fera faire la traducon. Voilà. Vous concevez mon cher, que je ne suis pas allé chercher cela. Je l'ai fait pour D qui est un bon garçon et voulait me rendre service.

Dans ces circonstances, je propose que nous partageions—c'est il juste, croyez vous? Mais comme j'ai diablement besoin d'argent peut-être voudrez vous bien me débiter les 500 frcs que vous prendrez en compte en reglant ce qui pourra me revenir sur les livres publiés par le Mercure. Voulez vous?

Nous esperons de tout notre coeur que la convalescence de Madame a été heureuse.

Mille amitiés.

Tout à vous.

J Conrad.

Translation

Dear Davray,

I'm writing this note at once so that I don't seem to be intriguing behind your back. Dawson, a friend of mine (journalist, American novelist—perhaps you know him?), has put me in touch with Mme Demachy, of the review *Progrès*, regarding a story. I am in the middle of finishing a long story (24,000 words) that would fit the bill. I've given her serial rights to the unpublished English text for a thousand francs. She will have the translation done. There it is. You understand, my dear fellow, that I didn't go looking for this. I did it for D., who is a good lad and wanted to do me a favour.

[1] After the 15th, when the fee for translating 'Freya' was proposed but not settled, but well before the 28th, when the 24,000 cited here had become 'say 27000'.

In these circumstances, I suggest we share—that's fair, isn't it? But because I am devilishly short of money, perhaps you will debit your five hundred francs against the money that could be coming to me from the books published by the *Mercure*. Would you do that?

We hope with all our hearts that Mme Davray's convalescence has been smooth.

Many regards,

Yours sincerely,

J Conrad.

To J. B. Pinker
Text MS Berg; Unpublished

[letterhead: Capel House]
28 Febr. 1911.

Dear Sir.

Herewith Freya: say 27000. Eastern seas tale—quite a novel in character and quite suitable for serialising.

I beg to point out to you that in common fairness a work of that nature can not come within the definition of short story. I don't suggest that it should be regarded as a novel. It is a short serial of value. It took me nearly three months to write.[1] And what I suggest is that having regard to our agreement it would be but justice to make an advance at the rate of short story and a half—say sixty pounds which would be still *less* than £3 per thous. And the thing is worth 150—if the Point of Honour[2] was worth that amount serially. It is worth more.

Whatever happens I beg to say at once that no suggestion of alteration or curtailment will be entertained. *Not a single word.* And I think that if you look it through you will admit that I am right.

I beg you will kindly return me my corrected typed copy *as soon as the clean one is made.* I would like to send it on to a Belgian[3] who is going to lecture on me and my work in Paris before long.

Yours faithfully

J. Conrad.

[1] Having finished 'The Partner', its predecessor, on 1 or 8 December, he started 'Freya' on the 26th.

[2] 'The Duel', about 30,000 words, became a five-part serial in Britain and a four-part serial in the U.S.

[3] Joseph de Smet.

To Edward Garnett
Text G. 238

[Capel House]
2 March 1911

Dearest Edward,

I got that infernal story out of the house this morning at last![1] Do send me your Joan[2] and believe me if I say that I am asking for her at the earliest possible moment when I feel I can trust myself to read anything.

There's nothing much to tell you. And if there were it would be the old story. So to avoid monotony I take refuge in silence.

I am expecting you here (*we* are) all the time—you know!

Ever yours

J. Conrad

To J. B. Pinker
Text MS Berg; Unpublished

[Capel House]
2 Mch
1911.

Dear Sir.

I beg to acknowledge with thanks the receipt of cheque for £60 on acct/ of MS of *Freya*.

I had the enclosed sent to me some time ago. It struck me that perhaps Prince Roman could be made use of in that direction[3]—not with the view of securing a prize, but on the chance that it may be accepted at a price (vide the underlined passages).

Should you think it advisable it may be better if you would send me a clean copy of *P. R* which I should send as from myself after shortening it a little? You would perhaps also suggest at what price I ought to mark the MS? I put forward this suggestion as it would leave the English market clear for the story.

I must tell you in reference to Freya (I was really too tired to remember when sending off the MS) that I wrote 3 days ago to the Editor of the *Pall Mall Mag*. saying: that I had a story just finished which I thought would be suitable for him as to subject and treatment; I wrote[?] as the *PMM* had published some of my best short writings (*Typhoon. Gaspar. Mirror*.[4] *Duel*) I addressed him directly asking whether

[1] A friendly fiction: the MS of 'Freya' had gone two days earlier.
[2] The MS of Garnett's play *The Trial of Jeanne d'Arc*.
[3] Apparently an American magazine. [4] 17 of the 49 sections.

he would like to have the first look at the story; in which case I would ask for it to be sent to him at once on the understanding that if accepted he would pay £180. serial rights. (I reckoned 5 instalments at 36 each). My idea was, the acceptance by *PMM* barring Harpers in US, to propose to you that I should send the *MS* to my friend Harris Merton Lyon,[1] whose name is probably familiar to you, to try *Hamptons*[2] with it. H. M. L used to be on the staff of Hamptons and though he has thrown up the connection he is apparently on the best of terms with H. and generally he seems to be in touch with various magazines. A year ago he wrote to me offering in a friendly way to do his best to place anything of which I should want to dispose quickly. I don't mean that anything should be done behind Reynolds'[3] back but in those matters a little personal interest may carry a matter through.

However I had no answer from the *PMM.* as yet. I can't imagine that no notice whatever will be taken of my communication. Perhaps the Editor will approach you directly.

In re N. Y. H[erald] offer. It was made after Mr Bennet[t]'s visit to Ceylon where he was staying with the Colonial Secretary Sir Hugh Clifford. I shall be writing to Clifford shortly asking him—if it becomes necessary—not to let the matter drop.

<div style="text-align:right">Yours faithfully</div>
<div style="text-align:right">J. Conrad.</div>

PS In another envelope I return copy of Partner with added paragraph typed and pinned on. Also two loose typed sheets to be pinned to the other copy.

To J. B. Pinker
Text MS Berg; Unpublished

<div style="text-align:right">Capel House</div>
<div style="text-align:right">4 Mch 1911.</div>

Dear Sir.

I have to thank you for Your letter of the 3[d]. No. I have no particular wish to send *P. R.* to M[r] Taylor.[4] I simply mentioned the matter because of the circular.

[1] The editor and short story writer (1883–1916), whom Dreiser called 'De Maupassant, Junior'. *Sardonics* came out in 1908, *Graphics* in 1913.

[2] Successor to the *New Broadway Magazine*.

[3] Paul R. Reynolds, the American agent.

[4] Editor of the American magazine mentioned on the 2nd.

Would you kindly tell me if I am right in thinking that there is in existence a contract between me & Harpers for a work described as a "Mediterranean novel".[1] I only want to know as it might be taken up next after Chance and if so I would want to read up the epoch (1808–10) in which I was thinking of placing it.

I think that the additional 120 words or so improve *The Partner* in so far that now nothing remains unexplained.

Will Harpers send me a proof do you think? Owing to the peculiar narrative style it'll require the author's eye.

Yours faithfully

J. Conrad.

To J. B. Pinker
Text MS Berg; Unpublished

[Capel House]
[March 1911][2]

Dear Sir

Will you kindly forward the enclosed to good old Alden[3] after casting your eye over it. It'll be a beastly job anyhow; and I really don't know how on earth I can shorten the narrative itself. But I'll try.

I beg you earnestly to preserve a typed copy for use in book form when the time comes.

Yours.

J. C

To the Abbé Joseph de Smet
Text L. fr. 109

5 mars 1911

Cher Monsieur,

Merci bien pour la coupure du journal avec le compte-rendu de votre conférence. J'ai la plus parfaite confiance en votre jugement et aussi dans la manière dont vous la prononcez. Je suis très curieux de vous lire dans le 'Mercure'.[4] Merci de la promesse des épreuves.

Bien à vous en tout[e] hâte.

[1] For the agreement, see *Letters*, 3, p. 126; for plans, see also pp. 219 and 409.
[2] Received 'March 1911': after the 4th, when Conrad wondered whether Harper's would send proofs of 'The Partner'.
[3] Henry Mills Alden, editor of *Harper's Magazine*.
[4] The essay on Conrad eventually published in 1912? The *Mercure* carried nothing from de Smet in the first four months of 1911.

Translation

Dear Sir,
Thank you for the newspaper cutting with the report of your lecture. I have the most perfect confidence in your judgment and also in the manner in which you deliver it. I am very curious to read you in the *Mercure*. Thank you for promising me the proofs.
Yours in all haste.

To Edward Garnett

Text MS Rosenbach; G. 239

[Capel House]
Monday. [6 March 1911][1]

Dearest Edward
Phew! This *is* fine. Just one word as the curtain falls for the last time.[2] Fine!
How sternly imagined how tenderly felt, how magnificently conducted! I am glad:—I'll with your leave keep the MS for 3 days before I read it again. I wanted to give the very freshest first impression just now, but won't say more at present. Fine!
Yours

J. Conrad.

To Edward Garnett

Text MS Dartmouth; G. 239

[Capel House]
[7 March 1911][3]

Dearest Edward.
Yes. The impression of the achievement remains, perhaps the stronger from the deep conviction of how incapable I would have been even to attempt that kind of work. Creative? Well, yes. Your doubt on that point I can understand but for myself I have no doubt—even after a long reflexion. It is creative in the sense in which a mystery play[4] is creative. The feeling that there is something in all this more subtle,

[1] Conrad asked for Garnett's play on the 2nd. Only one Monday fell between then and the 12th, when Conrad wrote the second of two longer judgments of the play.
[2] Joan's 'loud, piercing cry' from the stake: 'Jesus!'
[3] Thus dated from postmark when sold by the American Art Association, New York, 24 April 1928.
[4] The context suggests the religious rather than the criminal kind.

stronger and more poignant than the actual sensations and ideas expressed in the words and in the action abides with one all the time. No small triumph for you. For you must understand that I know nothing of Joan of Arc; that is no more than I learned of her as a boy. And as a matter of fact 99% of any audience assembled to see the play will know no more. Therefore you may look upon me as the stodgiest "bourgeois" in the stalls. The only difference is that the "bourgeois" likes the stage and I don't. But one cannot dislike an art so much without understanding something of it if only [in] a prejudiced sort of way. And in this connection what strikes me is that the climax of the action (in fact the only action of the play strictly speaking) the recantation with its cause and effect is perhaps not sufficiently emphasised for the theatre. A supreme moment should be made to stand out supremely especially when as in this case it throws such a searching light on the spiritual situation which is the real subject of the play. It is the revelation of her incredible sufferings, the measure of her nature and the shape of her humanity. And yet this crisis is contained in one short scene.

It is possible that I am wrong, over-anxious. But believing as I do that the control of the public's (audience, readers) attention is in a sense the beginning and end of artistic method I had to confess my uneasiness. You must forgive me. It is really because I do care for your work at least as much as I do for my own. I have told myself insistently that after all the subject is the *Trial* of Joan. But even then ... And don't forget my dear boy that from the nature of things such a subject can not be developed. It can only be unrolled—and it is unrolled with undoubted mastery with a relentless hand. A great consecutive picture—and yet it seems to me that in that one particular part there is something as it were blurred.

I won't say any more just now—except to express my admiration at the art with which you have differentiated all these churchmen. That's a feat! And it proves sufficiently the *creative* quality of your imagination. Very fine—very fine indeed. You must come over soon so that we may have a talk. I am very lame again just now or I would try to get to you. Give our love to your wife and son.

<div style="text-align:center">Yours ever</div>

<div style="text-align:right">J. Conrad.</div>

PS What do you think of Jack's last?[1]

[1] *The Patrician*, published on the 6th. Garnett had disliked the earlier drafts.

To J. B. Pinker

Text MS Berg; Unpublished

[Capel House]
[March 1911]¹

Dear Sir.

I return the proof to you so that you should see that I've really tried to do my very best for old Alden. Will you please dispatch it to Albemarle Street.²

Under the circumstances I doubt whether Alden will incorporate the additional pars: I really don't care—the story being sold on the merits of the first copy. We shall have the full text for book form of course.

I am rather curious to know if Scribners accepted *Freya*.³

I shall be compelled to be in London for 2 or 3 weeks in may. By that time I hope to be at a point with Chance when dictation would do some good to push it forward.

I suppose you would not mind paying Miss Hallowes, should I get her to work with me,⁴ for a couple of weeks, and debit me with the amount against the £100 on delivery of comp^d MS as stipulated in our arrangement.

Yours faithfully

J. Conrad.

To Edward Garnett

Text G. 241⁵

[Capel House]
[9? March 1911]⁶

Dearest Edward,

I send you Norman Douglas' book.⁷ Can you do something to give it a start? I understand that you liked what you had seen of his in the *E. R.*⁸ It is a serious matter for the poor fellow to get decent reviews and if you could give a lead? His opinions would make him acceptable for extra

¹ Received 'March 1911': later than the other letter concerning 'old Alden', and probably before the other mention of Miss Hallowes on [25? March].
² Harper's London office. ³ See the letter of [25? March].
⁴ As she had at various times since 1904.
⁵ The MS was sold by Christie's, 22 November 1985: present location unknown.
⁶ Probably the same day as the letter to Douglas.
⁷ *Siren Land*, published on the 8th.
⁸ The *English Review* had published five essays by Douglas, all of which had been worked into his book.

notice in *Nation* or any other liberal paper.[1] I am so out of everything that I must appeal to you in this matter. And the man is worthy—I think.

<div align="center">Yours ever</div>

<div align="right">J. C.</div>

To Norman Douglas
Text MS Texas; Unpublished

<div align="right">[Capel House]
Thursday. [9 March 1911][2]</div>

My dear Douglas.

I've sent off my copy to E. Garnett at once with the most earnest request to do his best to give a lead to reviewers either himself or get somebody he can trust to make a start. I've also written to one or two men whom I do not know so well asking them to pay attention to the book.

My dear fellow I am no critic. I should not know what to say—and there would be always the trouble of getting printed. No weekly or daily wants me in its columns. My short connection with the Dly Mail was a dismal failure. Dent's a fool.[3] The book's certain to be well noticed—maybe attacked too; but that's no harm. I've been delighted. There are mighty fine things there. But as you said to Dent they must have time. It's not every reviewer's meat. I daren't write to Graves of the Spectator.[4]

<div align="center">Yours ever</div>

<div align="right">J Conrad</div>

To John Galsworthy
Text MS Forbes; J-A, 2, 126

<div align="right">[letterhead: Capel House]
10 Mch 1911[5]</div>

Dearest Jack.

Of course it isn't pure [a]esthetics (only Flaubert's Salammbo amongst novels is that) but even on that ground alone You have done a

[1] Garnett reviewed for the *Nation* and did not hide his political sympathies. Douglas's learned book, however, does not show an especially liberal cast of mind.
[2] Conrad had a reply from Garnett on Saturday the 11th.
[3] But Douglas's publisher, as he would be Conrad's.
[4] Charles L. Graves (1856–1944), assistant editor from 1899 to 1917.
[5] Finished on Saturday the 11th according to the date below the signature. See also the last paragraph of the ensuing letter to Garnett.

very fine thing.[1] There are passages and pages which have an inalterable* beauty. The psychology is masterful the conduct admirable. You have put insides into these people with a vengeance. Do you remember telling me (it's ten or more years ago) that they had no insides.[2] Aha! You are doing such wonders with them now that I can't resist rubbing in that saying a bit—in sheer glee at the completeness of your achievement. Every patrician woman of them all is first rate—the aristocrat, the Pagan the woman of the world, the housewife. They are exquisite. *The* woman of the story is just what she should be I think: with her somewhat mysterious attraction and a sort of shadowy beauty. I consider her a great evidence of your artistic sense. She is very touching in her immobility, with the action of the story revolving round her. Very fine in every attitude, in every shade of expression.

And the men too are exquisitely done including the knightly defender of lost causes. He too is very fine in every attitude, in every word, a touching pendent to the portrait of the woman. They are the only two personages who have some chiaro-scuro* in them. The others are seen as in a mountain atmosphere in a limpid, coloured, but perfectly dry (too dry?) light. And equable! This peculiarity of light and atmosphere in which the figures stand each with its own definite outline was to be seen first in the Country House. Fraternity is a more mellow book[3]—I mean in the action and interaction of its humanity. In the Patrician the effect of this limpid, dry medium on the personages of the story appears intensified; perhaps simply because they all belong to the same family. They seem not so much [to] act and react upon each other as jostle each other. This is no criticism. It is simply a confession of the impression produced upon me.

As to Miltoun he stands out from them in a very striking manner, a very consistently sombre figure. You don't give him a single little gleam. He is to my mind more sombre than Bazarow and almost as plebeian, with his temperamental asceticism, his non-conformist conscience and his passion more like that of a priest in love than anything I could compare to it.[4] He is a strange bird to come out of that nest. However I

1 *The Patrician.*
2 In this, the aristocrats would resemble Conrad's Mr Kurtz. The inwardness of Galsworthy's titled people was the main subject of the dispute with Garnett. To prove the authenticity of his knowledge, Galsworthy sent Garnett a list of 130 aristocrats he had known (Marrot, pp. 288–305, and Dupré, pp. 171–2).
3 *The Country House* (1907) and *Fraternity* (1909).
4 Miltoun is a law and order man, Bazarov (in Turgenev's *Fathers and Sons*) a nihilist, but both, in a chilly way, obsess themselves with politics. Miltoun gives up Mrs Noel to preserve his career.

don't suppose You meant him to be typical. He's a bigger creation than the others but I should not say a greater. He is alive right enough but the reader (this reader) somehow feels that he is what he is because you _will_ _him_ to be so. Whereas the others exist as tho' they had come to life on their own.

Upon the whole this novel is not so large as *Fraternity*; it hasn't got the profound intimacy of feeling of the *Man of property*—and perhaps less suggestiveness than the *Country House*. In technique, in mastery, it is superior to them all. I should like to know what welcome it will get from the world.[1]

There would be a lot more to say if I weren't anxious to catch the post. Our love to you both

Yours ever

J Conrad.

Saturday evening

To Norman Douglas

Text MS Texas; Unpublished

[Capel House]
Sunday night [12 March 1911][2]

Dear Douglas.

I had on Sat a letter from Garnett telling me that he had already written to four reviewers on the daily press. What will come of it God knows.

Call on him at Duckworth's (Henrietta Street near Covt Gdn corner) on Tuesday about 1 o'clock and send in Your name—He'll be pleased to see you I am certain. That, of course, if you feel like it.

Since you left[3] I had a beastly knock out on a certain matter,[4] from which I am just recovering. Come soon—

Yours ever

J Conrad.

[1] Praise from friends and critics, indifference from the public (Marrot, pp. 310–17).
[2] The same date as the letter thanking Garnett for 'taking interest in Douglas'.
[3] Douglas had seen the Conrads on the 7th (Holloway, p. 181).
[4] A financial jolt? The threat of an operation on Jessie Conrad's knee – distressing financially as well as emotionally? On the 28th, Conrad thanked Galsworthy for 'giving me both the material and the moral support I need'. In the letter of [14 May], he told Galsworthy he had written nothing from 5 March to 29 April.

To Edward Garnett
Text MS Indiana; G. 242[1]

[Capel House]
Sunday.
[12 March 1911][2]

Dearest Edward

You won't mind this pencil scrawl—feels less formal.

Thanks infinitely for taking interest in Douglas. Whatever happens I am grateful to you for honouring so handsomely this draft on your friendship. Sorry to learn that you have bad nights. They are the devil.

I ask myself whether I have conveyed to you sufficiently my appreciation of the Jeanne d'Arc. When a thing hits me straight I can only just exclaim without phrases. It's easier to make phrases about things that hit and glance off; and as to things that miss me, of which I only feel the wind so to speak, I could write politely by the yard of them. I also feel a kind of compunction for putting forward my review of the recantation episode. But I wanted to give You *all* my impression—not in a critical spirit at all but as a matter of sincerity.

I am not at all sure that my feeling there was right.

I build no great hopes on the *H. B*[3] I met him once and was talked to by him in honeyed tones. He struck me as an *arriviste* pure and simple. But being a bitter and prejudiced person I may be wrong. In my character of a b and p person I mistrust likewise the public. Will they answer to the spiritual appeal of the play?

You see my dear fellow the état d'âme capable of being moved by such a subject is not a common one. I don't mean to say that a crowd in the auditorium is incapable of it, only that such a mood is a rare one, everywhere. The pretty-pretty of Maeterlinck is much more their mark—I mean the Pink Goose or whatever kind of bird is being preserved at the Haymarket.[4]

That fact I think must be faced, but it's very probable that I make too much of it. The devil is never as black as he is painted. I don't want you to think me presumptuous* or mad. You know that it was from the discussion of the *Tentation de S^t Antoine* that the idea of *Mme Bovary* sprang

[1] In the published text, the last paragraph ends at 'yesterday'.
[2] Garnett wrote the date on the MS.
[3] Although the MS reads '*H. B*', Conrad meant H[erbert] T[rench] (1865–1923), director of the Haymarket Theatre. He rejected the play on the 29th (Jefferson, *Garnett*, p. 125).
[4] Conrad never liked the plays of Maurice Maeterlinck (1862–1949), whose comforting allegory *The Blue Bird* was on display in London: see *Letters*, 3, p. 503.

up in Flaubert's mind. A complete turn about.[1] Why should you not also
execute a change of front and take up a subject where your irony could
find its opportunity your wit an aim for its shafts? Why not write a play
about the literary world which as far as I know has never yet been
lighted by the masked glare of the footlights? Why not read up Scribe
and Sardou (the two good mechanics)[2] a little, and give us a play about
Le Monde ou l'on Ecrit—the World where they write! It would be fair
game. And you you seem to me the hunter pointed out by destiny. You
have heard so many confidences, observed so many illusions, weak-
nesses and struggles of that particular world. You who have a sense of
the comic which would be governed by complete comprehension and
sympathy.

Of course I don't mean anything like poor Gissing's Grub Street[3]—
But really I need not have said that.

The fable does not matter much. I don't think I would base it on the
marital relations of the "world where they write". The efforts to found
say an academy of letters[4] would do as the stuff on which you could
embroider some gorgeous grotesque and beautiful designs. For indeed it
need not be all satire. You could speak the truth not only in jest but also
in earnest. You could have a cut at the frauds but you could also strike a
blow for the good cause. Of course poetical or rather imaginative
realism should be the note. And who better fitted than you?

I will say no more. Think of it dear Edward. There are moments when
I succeed in being "wholly serious"—and this is one of them.

Hint to me something of your opinion of Jack's novel. I wrote to him
about it yesterday but as a matter of fact I feel rather unsettled in my
mind. It seems to me all in the air—or is it I who have not (or have lost)
the ability to get to the bottom of written things? But this *strictly entre
nous*! Love from us both

Yours ever

J. Conrad

[1] Although the third version was the only one published, in 1874, Flaubert finished the
first *Temptation of St Anthony* in 1849. Then, after a visit to Egypt, he set to work on
Madame Bovary, a work whose careful architecture and finish contrasted with its
lyrical, visionary, and disjointed precursor.

[2] Eugène Scribe (1791–1861) and Victorien Sardou (1831–1908), the master artificers
of the well-made play – of what Shaw called 'Sardoodledom'.

[3] George Gissing's *New Grub Street* (1891) gives a sad picture of cynical success and
principled failure in the literary world.

[4] A project often mooted at the time.

To John Galsworthy

Text MS Forbes; Unpublished

[Capel House]
15 Mch. 1911.

Dearest Jack.

I haven't told you half what I thought of the book. While writing I felt still a little "in the air" about it—but after a second reading I feel so no longer. My ideas and feelings are beginning to cristalize.* I shall fire at you a longish page presently—unless you had rather not hear..?

It is practically settled that Jessie is to be operated upon in the first week of May at latest. We'll come up to London when she will enter St Barnabas' Home an institution where the nursing fees are moderate. It is a[n] R.C. home. The fee for the operation will be greatly reduced there too. Dr Mackintosh who has arranged all this for me says that she need not remain there for more than 3 weeks. I will try to get a couple of rooms in the neighbourhood and look after Jack. I am somewhat perturbed at the prospect but not much. I intend to work too—probably dictate to Miss Hallowes in the morning. I hope Chance'll be advanced sufficiently for dictation by then. I am at it now. Slow. Dam' slow—but still.

Mac promised to motor her back here directly she can be moved. That's how things stand at present. P. very decently advanced me 60 for the last story (28000 words) at my suggestion it is true but without the slightest demur.

Our dear love to you both.

Yours ever

J Conrad.

To Norman Douglas

Text MS Colgate; Unpublished

[Capel House]
Thursday. [23 March 1911?]1

Dear Douglas.

Come on Sat *for lunch*. Miss Tobin shall be here and at any rate you'll

1 Answered, according to Douglas's MS note, '24 March', a Thursday (if the reply went off at once) or a Friday. The 24th fell on a Thursday in 1910 and 1921, but in neither year was Douglas in England; the 24th fell on a Friday in 1911 and 1916; Agnes Tobin was in Kent in late March 1911 (Beckson, *Symons*, p. 275).

have a look at each other. Of course You'll stay till Monday or longer—
as long as You like.

Our love

Yours

J Conrad.

To Norman Douglas
Text MS Texas; Unpublished

[Capel House]
[late March 1911?][1]

Dear D.

Of course the woman knows nothing except that you are one of my
two most intimate friends. You just meet by chance.

Then next week I shall go to Wittersham and talk to her.[2] That's the
line.

JC

Try to be charming.

To J. B. Pinker
Text MS Berg; Unpublished

[Capel House]
Saturday. [25? March 1911][3]

Dear Sir.

Thanks for your letter. Either Miss H or some other short-hand writer
will have to be employed.

"Unrelieved gloom" seems to me a bit too strong. Of course the story
is not the stuff for a comic paper; but I've tried to keep the pathetic side
of the tale in the background. The fate of the girl is just sketched in,
hinted at rather than told. Jasper's break-up is merely alluded to, in fact
slurred over. There was material there for a novel as long as Almayer's

[1] Sharing an agenda with the previous letter? Conrad was in Wittersham on the 29th
(Beckson, *Symons*, p. 275).

[2] About possible U.S. publication of Douglas's work, if the woman were Agnes Tobin?
If she were the Hon. Mrs Lyttleton, who had a place in Wittersham, about
favourable notices of his book in the Conservative press?

[3] Received 'March 1911': the letter is about the refusal of 'Freya' by an American
magazine and must therefore belong late in the month. On [29 July]. Conrad wrote
of the rejection's happening in April.

Folly—I mean psychologically. And anyhow the tragic consequences appear only in the last 5000 (or less) words of the story. So there could have been four or three fairly cheerful instalments.[1]

Frankly I thought (given the subject) that I had done a rather delicate piece of work. But perhaps the *tone* of the *writing itself* the *style of telling* is gloomy? Of that I can form no opinion. I don't want to bother you with such a question but as you are the only person who has seen the story in England may I ask whether you think it is so. I certainly didn't mean it to be. It is the tone I wish to avoid for practical purposes.

Believe me

faithfully Yours

J Conrad

To Warrington Dawson
Text MS Duke; Randall 136

Capel House
Orlestone
Nr Ashford
28 Mch 1911.

Cher ami.

Just a word to let you know, in view of your promised visit, that unfortunately in the month of May we shall be in London. It has been decided that another operation is necessary on my wife's knee. What must be, must be.

I'll send you the address in London as soon as I know myself where we shall hang out that troublous time. But we expect to be back here by the first of June. Anyway we must see each other either here or in town.

Mrs Demachy prefers to take the *Typhoon* de Smet's translation—I hope good. Would you mind, when you see the lady, asking her to return me the MS of *Freya* if she still has it in her possession. It may be she has given it to Davray who has arranged with her for the Typhoon.

But don't give yourself any special trouble over the matter. It is not particularly important. Only if occasion offers.

Wife's kindest regards.

Yours cordially

J. Conrad.

[1] At some point between March and July, 'Freya' was turned down by the *Century*, an event which led to the contretemps with Garnett in August. It is not clear whether the letter quoted here came from the *Century* or from *Scribner's*.

To John Galsworthy
Text MS Forbes; J-A, 2, 127

[Capel House]
28 Mch 1911.

My dearest Jack.

You are really infinitely good to me. I don't know how to say the things I would like to say to you. My fibre has become so much softened that I have lost all confidence in the future—in the next day as it were. The only thing which remains to me is the certitude of my tenacity. I know I'll stick to it—but I have no belief in anything ever coming to a good end. I had arranged things in a measure yet I felt that there was no reserve of force in me to meet the unexpected, which in all human arrangements works in the background. Your assistance makes me feel much more easy in my mind; thus giving me both the material and the moral support I need.

How the little play will fare on the stage has occupied my thoughts not a little of late. With my ineradicable mistrust of the theatre as destroyer of all suggestiveness I cannot help wondering whether the involuted (*not* involved) delicacy of the idea will get over the footlights unscathed.[1] But I am avowedly a prejudiced person, and under the fragrant charm of that piece of work there is more than a hint of your native strength to give it the necessary dynamic quality, wherein resides the power of "effect".

I see you are on the way of becoming an object of suspicion to the "*Nation*". Which is amusing to observe.[2] All that page of criticism is rather dense and the marvel is that being so dense it is by no means solid. The truth is that the only foundation on which criticism of your work can be built is *our common humanity*. That and nothing else. I don't see any change in M^r Galsworthy's attitude. But then I am not looking at him from the standpoint of some political or social theory. However the fact must not be shirked that in whatever you do my dear Jack people will look inside or beyond your art for the idea. And it is on the

[1] In this play two men visit the hut of Seelchen ('Little Soul') on their way up a metaphysically intimidating Tyrolean mountain. While the climbers are about their task, Seelchen dreams an allegorical and music-laden dream. Of its opening in Manchester, Galsworthy wrote '*The Little Dream* met with the enthusiastic approval of an audience who obviously didn't understand more than about 30 per cent of it' (Marrot, p. 319).

[2] Since Galsworthy, unlike Conrad, shared that weekly's Liberal beliefs. The reviewer felt that the new novel's sympathies lay too much with the patrician and too little with the people (25 March, 1046–7) – a bias that the author certainly had not intended.

enunciation of the idea that you'll have to put on stress if you want to guide the judgement of your contemporaries. No more at present. Love from us both to Ada and yourself.

<div style="text-align: center">Ever yours,</div>

<div style="text-align: right">J. Conrad.</div>

To Stephen Reynolds

Text MS Berg; Unpublished

<div style="text-align: right">[Capel House]
28 Mch 1911.</div>

My dear Stephen

We are delighted. Do come along for lunch on Saturday. I'll meet you or send the pony trap to cart you and the unnumerable* trunks with which a person of your vast future is obliged to travel, over.

The train arrives at Ham Street S.E.R at 1.4 am.* and unless we hear to the contrary we shall expect you by that one.

Well no more. Au revoir then

<div style="text-align: center">Yours</div>

<div style="text-align: right">J Conrad.</div>

To Ford Madox Ford

Text MS Berg; Unpublished

<div style="text-align: right">[letterhead: Capel House]
29 Mch 1911</div>

My dear Ford.

I can't tell you how happy we are to know you are at peace at last.[1] Thanks for the vol of stories.[2] I haven't looked at it yet, because I am just now trying to make a fresh start with a thing called *Chance* I began some time ago and laid aside. It's a beastly job and I simply daren't look at anyone's writing for the next week or so.

I did not write before simply because there was nothing to write— nothing good, nothing new. I was very seriously ill last year for some 3

[1] According to Ford. He was now living in Giessen, contemplating German citizenship and a divorce from Elsie Hueffer, writing *The New Humpty-Dumpty*, arguing with publishers, and facing – or not facing – the capricious weather of his relationship with Violet Hunt.

[2] Unidentified: not by Ford.

months, but since last June I have been fairly well. Only—no elasticity. Life an awful grind. The feeling that the game is no longer worth the candle.

I've ordered your latest.[1] No doubt my dear fellow the bloom of the fruit is rubbed off in the picking. Haven't we groaned together over this fatality in years not so very distant yet after all. But remembering our talks over your early days, certain as I am of your literary probity in the matter of form, I am confident of finding in your pages a delicate flavour of feeling, a wishfulness which is the charm of things remembered and a perfectly worthy, human appreciation of a phase of art untainted by self-seeking—as pre-raphaelitism of the early time has always seemed to me. What came later—c'est une autre question. I suppose you will have something to say of that and I am very curious to see———

No more at present. I'll drop You another line soon—directly I get free of this damnable worry of making a start with stuff in which I don't believe and yet must go on spinning out myself like a disillusioned spider his web in a gale. Our love.

<div align="right">Yours ever</div>

<div align="right">J. Conrad</div>

To T. Fisher Unwin

Text MS Colgate; Unpublished

<div align="right">[letterhead: Capel House]</div>

<div align="right">26 Ap 1911.</div>

Dear Sir.[2]

I did arrange with Davray for the translation of all my work leaving to him all arrangements and I understand that he has communicated with you on the matter some time ago. All these books are past the ten years limit[3] but if I get anything on the appearance of the volumes You shall of course have the half of the amount whatever it may be.

I did some time ago authorise Mme Poradowska my relation by marriage to translate the *Outpost* which appeared serially in a French

[1] *Memories and Impressions*, also known as *Ancient Lights*, whose centre is Ford's portrait of his Pre-Raphaelite grandfather, Ford Madox Brown.

[2] Thomas Fisher Unwin (1848–1935) published Conrad's first three books. Neither his business practices nor his adherence to the Liberal party endeared him to Conrad.

[3] Specified in the contracts with Unwin: the books in question were *Almayer, An Outcast*, and *Tales of Unrest*.

publication the name of which has escaped me altogether.[1] I don't know whether I have made myself liable to a civil or criminal prosecution by this transaction, but I don't suppose You would wish to crush me in any case. Anyway we are coming to town in May when I promised* myself the pleasure of calling on you. We may talk then all these matters over. I see that the Tales of Unrest are in the Adelphi Lib^y. The vol: looks very well. I only regret I had not the opportunity to make a few corrections.[2]

<div style="text-align:center">Yours faithfully.</div>

<div style="text-align:right">J. Conrad.</div>

To Arthur Symons

Text MS Lohf; Hunter (1985, 3)

<div style="text-align:right">[Capel House]
29 Ap. 1911</div>

My dear Symons.

No end of thanks for the little vol:[3] so charming inside and outside—in its slender body containing a gently melodious soul.

I see quite a new aspect of you in these few delightful pages. What a rich and varied temperament you have! For the spanish inscription I must say muy gracias excellentissimo señor[4] but I can never sufficiently thank you for your Kindness to me which is generous and invariable.

Remember me please to Your wife.[5] Jessie sends affectionate messages to you both.

<div style="text-align:center">Always Yours</div>

<div style="text-align:right">J. Conrad.</div>

Pardon this short scrawl. I am stupefied and wearied with the day's work.[6] We'll be going to town probably on the 4^th for 3 weeks I think.

[1] Marguerite Poradowska had translated 'An Outpost of Progress' in 1900; this translation was considered for a volume of stories projected but not published by the *Mercure de France* and is not known to have appeared elsewhere (*Letters*, 2, p. 269; 3, pp. 391, 400, 402; Rapin, p. 174, n. 5).

[2] Unwin, in other words, had not bothered to consult him about the new edition.

[3] An earlier volume: Symons had not yet resumed publication after his collapse.

[4] Symons had a longstanding passion for Spanish music, dancing, and dancers.

[5] Rhoda Symons (née Bowser, 1874–1936), a violinist; in 1912 she at last fulfilled her ambition to go on the professional stage.

[6] The first day of work on *Chance* since early March: see the letter of [14 May].

To J. B. Pinker

Text MS Berg; Unpublished

[Capel House]
[Summer 1911][1]

Dear sir

It's done. I join to the type a corrected set of galley slips immediately preceeding* the text in case it may come in useful.

I beg you most earnestly—if you can do so—to arrange for the English Rev. setting up slips from *this corrected copy* here. It will save me infinite trouble. I doubt too if I will be able to remember exactly the corrections I've just made.

And please, will you request Methuens to send me proofs (in the usual way double set) in good time. I won't be hustled over that matter. I must have time to read them.

I shall despatch you by rail at least 4000 w. of Chance to-morrow. I have begun last night the 5th thou: of this week's work and shall try to finish it to-night.

Yours faithfully

J Conrad

Am extremely pleased at your successful deal with the O & C Review for Prince Roman.[2] Truly it wasn't everybody's story.

To J. B. Pinker

Text MS Berg; Unpublished

[letterhead: Capel House]
[c. 10 May 1911][3]

Dear Sir.

I have to thank you for the prompt cheque received this morning. To be candid I must say that somehow I imagined that the rate was 4 pounds per thousand in which of course I was mistaken. Owing to this error of mine I have had to ask my wife to type at once 20 of my MS pages containing something over 2000 words (10 pp of type) which I send you with the request that you should be good enough to pay for that

[1] Between the resumption of work on *Chance* at the very end of April and its temporary suspension in August; later dates would be too close to the appearance of 'Prince Roman' and the end of the serial *Under Western Eyes*. Pinker's reply may have prompted the letter of [13 May].

[2] To be published by the Conservative *Oxford and Cambridge Review* in October.

[3] Received 'May 1911': on the 15th, 'next Monday', Conrad sent the first batch of *Chance* submitted under the terms requested here.

small batch; as the twenty pounds I mistakenly reckoned upon were wanted for a special purpose. I regret to trouble you with such a small batch, but I hope to send you 3 thou: words more this week or by next Monday.

For that average—5,000 p. week we may hope. It's no use reckoning on more. I trust that now since the fine weather set in there will be no stoppage. From last July when I first began to write after my illness I have written to date roughly 75000 words. If I can deliver 30 thou: more by end June it will make over 100000 for twelve actual and 10 working months. At that rate we may be able by end July to tell the N. Y. H[erald] to go ahead—with 15–20 thou: words more to write of the end which generally comes to me the easiest of all.

I[n] connection with this I must mention that our sojourn in London may extend to a couple of months. The surgeons who were here on Sunday hope to save the limb by a small operation followed by a long treatment. I am making arrangements to come up directly there is a room vacant in the nursing home.

In view of what lies before me I have looked at our agreement as embodied in Galsworthy's letter to me and I see that practically the rate agreed upon for long novel is £4 per thou (hence my mistake) but the mode of payment is £3 down and £1 deferred till completion of the novel and paid in a lump sum of £100. (This assuming the novel to be about 100000 words)—I wish to ask You whether You would consent to pay me that deferred £1 down on the instalments of the *Chance* MS—if not for the whole then for all copy delivered from now till end of July. Owing to circumstances that pound extra now would be worth infinitely more to me than later on. I don't wish to write 6–7000 words short stories which I suppose, at a pinch, I could do fairly well at £40 apiece. Neither would I attempt to do anything beside *Chance*. It would be fatal to the novel—which after all is the thing most profitable both to you and to me in the end.

I put this before you in order to know in time what arrangements I must make.

Fisher Unwin has been writing to me letters raising all sorts of small points but whose inward purport is to induce me to sell him outright the copyright of Outcast & of Tales. Indeed he is ready to buy outright *any* of my old books. I tell you of this but my feeling is that whatever he might offer (and he would offer probably three pence) there should be *no* such deal on *any account*. Is this your opinion? My work has a future yet. This is not only my opinion but that of others very competent to judge.

In fact I am thinking of a uniform edition. Presently with Raz. & a vol of short stories[1] now ready there will be some 15 vols (including collaborated books). The negociations* might take a year or so. I would like to know how you look at the matter. I don't see why a uniform ed should not be brought out to help pay off my indebt[ed]ness to you, thereby freeing earlier my policies—to my advantage. Will you think it over. After all, long after I am gone the material interests[2] connected with my work will be in your hands and perhaps of your son as well.

<div align="right">Yours faithfully</div>

<div align="right">J. Conrad.</div>

To Arthur Symons
Text MS Virginia; Hunter (1985, 3)

<div align="right">Capel House</div>
<div align="right">Wednesday [10 May 1911][3]</div>

My dear fellow,

I think Jessie is writing to you appointing Friday for your visit.

I just am adding this word to beg you to get rid of all your uneasiness. It afflicts me. There's no reason for it. Everything shall be well with you.

Au revoir

<div align="center">Yours</div>

<div align="right">J. Conrad.</div>

To J. B. Pinker
Text MS Berg; Unpublished

<div align="right">[Capel House]</div>
<div align="right">*Saturday* [13 May 1911][4]</div>

Dear Sir.

Thanks for your letter consenting to my request as to the rate of advance per thou: I am very sensible to all you say in it and am glad to see that my views commend themselves to you.

I appreciate very much Your considerate suggestion in re proofs[5] in the letter received this morning. I shall send you on Monday the text as published in the *ER*, torn out of the numbers and arranged for the

[1] All the stories in *'Twixt Land and Sea* (1912) were now written.
[2] An echo of *Nostromo*.
[3] Envelope postmarked on Thursday the 11th.
[4] Pinker's consent gives a date between the letters of [c. 10] and 15 May.
[5] For the book publication of *Under Western Eyes*.

printers. I wish Methuens to set up from *that*. There would be then no author's alterations—only corrections of misprints.

They can go on as far as it has appeared including June. And for the future I shall correct the 2 sets of Review proofs and send one to you for Methuen to go on setting up from.

Can we possibly get a set of *ER* for Harpers to set up from?[1] Would it cost too much? A small sacrifice would be worth while perhaps in view of the circumstances. This correcting puts me off other work for a day. Perhaps if that's practicable you would stop Harper's setting up till we can send them the *R*. They surely must have old copies of it on their side. And if they set from them they needn't send proofs here at all. Their own readers can look after mere misprints.

<div style="text-align: center">Yours faithfully</div>

<div style="text-align: right">J Conrad.</div>

To John Galsworthy
Text MS Forbes; J-A, 2, 128

<div style="text-align: right">[letterhead: Capel House]
Sunday. [14 May 1911][2]</div>

Dearest Jack.

Having got a slant of fair wind with *Chance* I let Jessie write to dear Ada of the conclusion arrived by the surgeon who has taken up her case. It will be certainly a matter of 3 months in nursing homes in London and in the country but the game is worth the candle.

But we both have come to the conclusion that it should be put off to end of Aug[st]. She wants me to get on with *Chance* without worry—and with the great help her being at hand to type and retype my copy would be to me. She fears too that Jack who is absurdly sensitive to heat would feel the summer in London too much. It would not do him any good I am certain. We dont want him to wilt down from the flourishing state in which we have managed to keep him. She wants also to give Borys the full month of Aug[u]st, out of his holiday, in the country.

All this seems to me sensible enough; not to speak of her desire (no doubt) to have a summer in the country where she can at least sit out in the open air all day long. And indeed I believe I shall find it easier to

[1] The Methuen edition came out on 5 October; the U.S. edition, two weeks later.

[2] News of Conrad's progress gives the date: a fortnight after resuming work on 29 April. The hope of writing 30,000 more words by the end of June also figures in the letter of [c. 10 May].

work here than in dismal London lodgings. I've written to the surgeon proposing this delay.

B is booked to try for a Tonbridge scholarship;[1] the fateful date being June 6[th]. A couple of years there would not do him any harm. I hope he may get it, but he is too much like me in disposition.

Since last July my dear Jack up to date (including the batch of *Chance* now on my table ready for post) I've written as follows: 21-9-30-12-thousand words in short stories[2] and just now 12 000 of *Chance* done in the last fortnight. Say 84 000 in 10 1/2 months of time. In that time I have been three weeks in Dec without writing a line; and now again seven weeks—the most horrible nightmare of an existence—from March 5[th] to April 29 with not a page—not half a page in all that time! How I came out of it with my sanity apparently unimpaired I don't know. When I think that this may happen to me again any day, any time, like being bludgeoned from behind, I feel my courage ooze out of my finger-tips. But there are the words. And, if I can keep up, there will be about 30 000 more by end June. Say 120 000 in a year of 9 1/2 *working* months—the other 2 1/2 months being like the lowest circle of the inferno[3] and not to be thought of, even, without shudders.

You haven't given me the slightest inkling as to the reception of the little play by the M[an]ch[est]er public. Were you pleased with the interpretation?

Our love to You both

<div align="center">Yours ever</div>

<div align="right">J. Conrad.</div>

To J. B. Pinker
Text MS Berg; Unpublished

<div align="right">[Capel House]
15 May '11</div>

Dear Sir.

In reference to a question which I neglected to answer before—Yes;

[1] Among public schools, Tonbridge had two advantages: it was not far away, and Agnes Ridgeway's husband was a housemaster there. Borys failed the exam (*My Father*, p. 73).

[2] As well as 'A Smile of Fortune', 'The Partner', and 'Freya', this tally must include 'Prince Roman', probably first drafted by 9 December 1908 and finished by 1 October 1910.

[3] Where the damned are frozen in perpetual ice.

the old copy and the new copy[1] are fit for the printer and may be typed fair as soon as you wish it. I would only ask for a sight of the fair copy before it goes off to America. But I suppose it won't be for a long time yet. In no case would I keep it longer than 24 hours.

I am sending here a full 4000 words, the first batch under the arrangement you have so obligingly consented to.

If the back N[os] of the *ER* can be obtained for Harpers I am prepared to pay for them myself by deduction from the first money due to me to any reasonable amount for indeed I wish to save myself the necessity of reading for Harpers, which would be a serious interruption.

Yours faithfully

J. C.

To T. Fisher Unwin
Text TS Berg; Unpublished

[letterhead: Capel House]
May 17th. 1911

Dear Mr. Unwin.

Your last letter in its final suggestion requires consideration on my part.

I am now contemplating the publication of a small vol: of reminiscences, not of a gossipy character of course, but which will have its importance both in the life and the work of an author who, whatever his exact merit, has his place in English literature. The text appeared in the first 7 Nos. of the English Review. With an introduction which I propose writing for it, it will amount to about 43000 words—enough for a, say 3/6 vol. It deals, in an unconventional form, with the writing of my first book and with my first contact with the sea. It is a piece of literature, first of all, and also a disclosure of personality.

I was thinking of some such title as *The Double Call: An Intimate Note*—by J. Conrad.

[1] The work done that year and the work done earlier. Accompanying the first sections of the *Chance* MS (Berg) is a note to Quinn beginning: 'This part of Chance consisting of five batches of pinned pages (*1 to 152*) numbered 1 to 5 in red pencil was written in the year *1906* and then laid aside not to be taken up again till the month of June [altered from 'May'] of the year 1911.' The later sections are lettered A to ZZ; Conrad wrote on f.1 of A: 'began here on 3d June 1911'. Unless Conrad was passing off old copy as new, his progress reports to Pinker are more trustworthy than this narrative after the fact. The batch of TS sent [21 or 28 May] brought the tally of 'new copy' to 19,000 and the grand total to 34,000. Thus Conrad assumed that the 'old copy' came to 15,000 words; the pencilled figure '16750' on f.1 of the original five sections probably gives a more accurate total.

I know that there are people who'll want to read it: My public. I also think that if published at a proper time as, for instance, in the months following the issue of a novel of mine it may secure a larger sale. Later on another personal vol. of that sort could be added.

I am, to be frank with you, in negociation* on that point.[1] I was under the impression that you would not care for a work of that kind, tho' indeed it would be fitting for the publisher of my first book to have that one, in which I am trying "to account for myself" publicly. As nothing is concluded, so far, perhaps you'll care to let me know whether you would be disposed to buy it outright, and what would be the sum you would be inclined to offer, either on that or on a royalty agreement. I must warn you that some of the instalments in the English Review have not been copyrighted in the U.S.[2] But the book would be sufficiently protected, I think.

I am dear M^r Unwin

Very faithfully yours,

J. Conrad

To J. B. Pinker
Text MS Berg; Unpublished

[Capel House]
Friday. [19 or 26 May 1911][3]

Dear Sir.

I've forwarded You Harper's proofs—corr^d—complete, for transmission as I haven't here a proper wrapper I could trust.

They extend into *May* N^o of Review, all but 5 pp. Therefore only the N^{os} from May (inclusive) onwards will have to be sent to the US.

Thanks to unexpected assistance of a friend staying with us, the interruption to my current work was not serious.

I'll be sending you a batch on Monday and with that we shall have altogether (old & new) some 34000 words of copy—a full third of the novel.

[1] On 19 June, Conrad told Pinker that Dent and Macmillan were interested in *Under Western Eyes*; perhaps they also took an interest in the autobiography, which was eventually taken by Eveleigh Nash.

[2] To secure U.S. copyright of *Some Reminiscences*, Paul R. Reynolds brought out a minuscule edition of the first instalment.

[3] The 26th, unless Conrad had managed to finish the 'full *7000* words' sent with the next letter (for a total of 'some 34000 words of copy') between the 15th and Sunday the 21st – a prodigious but not an impossible deed.

The text of the Review for Messrs Methuen will reach You by Tuesday at latest.

Yours faithfully

J. Conrad.

To J. B. Pinker

Text MS Berg; Unpublished

[Capel House]

Sunday evening [21 or 28 May 1911][1]

Dear Sir.

I send here full *7000* words, still of part first. Enclosed too a page with the title I propose for book[2] and the half-title page of the part for your remarks if any suggest themselves to you.

We may consider this batch to complete 1st third of the book. Perhaps there will be only two parts; but I shall try to have three, pretty equal. In any case I don't intend to exceed 100 000 words—perhaps *just* under.[3]

My letter to N. Y. H (gone sometime now) acknowledged the courteous and considerate tone of their letters which you forwarded to me, stating that the delay in answering was my fault. Then some complimentary remarks and the point. That by end July there would be I hoped enough copy to begin pub^on if they desired it with only the end (less than 3000 w I trust) to write.[4]

The proofs for the July *ER* are now hanging over my head. I wish I could reach the half of the book without interruption of mood—but that's impossible.[5] I shall send you the dup^te sheets without delay for Harpers.

Yours.

J C.

Pray delay if not too late putting in hand clean typed copy as I want to alter the personal appearance of M^r Powell. But it would not be a great matter—two pars of about 20 lines together to rewrite. If copy already

1 Probably the 28th: see the letter before. In any case, received 'May 1911'.
2 The final title was *Chance: A Tale in Two Parts*.
3 It eventually came to over 130,000 words.
4 For the editor's reply to Conrad, see the letter of 19 June, n. 3.
5 Berg has an undated MS note to Pinker which must belong to this period: 'Dear Sir. Thanks for your assurance. I enclose here slips of *W Eyes* left out by oversight yesterday. In haste Yours J.C.'

begun the two pages containing references to his exterior can be retyped
without great trouble later on.

To Edward Thomas
Text MS Harvard; Unpublished

[letterhead: Capel House]
[early Summer? 1911][1]

My dear Thomas.

Thanks for the little book so full of good things. You know I have a
predilection for your prose with its quiet, flowing felicity of phrase and
what I call "penetrative" power of expression (In contradistinction to
the "shock-power" of another kind of style). The gentle individuality of
the paper is pretty acute too; which, of course, is an added source of
pleasure; and what is fascinating is the total absence of any line that
would look as if written of a set purpose[2]—nor a sign or shadow of
literary verbiage. It is all as natural as grass in the fields or the carpet of
bluebells in a wood—born there (not put there) and yet giving all the
delight of an artistic conception. *A group. Home. July. End of day. Olwen* I
mention specially but as a matter of fact one likes best the paper one is
reading at the time. Hawthornden is delicious—oh! quite. The *Attempt*
very unexpected very curious and suggestive in its psychology.————

And there the word *beauty* comes in resuming the whole. Thanks,
many thanks to Mrs Thomas and yourself for the kind invitation.[3] *Of
course* Mrs Conrad would come. But we have been visited lately by
surgeons & docs.—There is before her a long and wearisome treatment
in the hope of saving the limb. That'll begin in Sept. in a London
nursing home of some sort. Meantime she remains crippled and must
remain quietly at home. As to your grateful servant the fact is I am now
working for dear life to save a much jeopardised contract with the N. Y.
Herald for a serial novel. If I can keep up the pace I am going at now I
shall save it most likely. But you will understand my dear Thomas and
will be able to explain to Mrs. Thomas that this sort of thing unfits me
completely for the society of my kind. I am overstrained and more or less

[1] Duckworth published *Light and Twilight*, the collection of sketches and stories praised
here, in May.

[2] Many of the pieces had already appeared in such places as the *English Review*,
Saturday Review, and *Nation*.

[3] To stay at Wick Green, their cottage near Petersfield, Hampshire. The memoirs of
Helen Thomas (née Noble, 1877–1967) were republished in *Under Storm's Wing*
(Manchester: Carcanet, 1988).

like a lunatic. Besides I can't, positively can't, get away from the table for more than a few hours—and even this with fear and trembling lest it should mean losing my grip (my writing grip—not the musing grip) on the silly subject.

Well, no more, except our very kindest regards to all your house and in the hope of better times the assurance of my most friendly sentiments for you, your work and everything that is yours in that sense,

<div align="center">affect^{ly}</div>

<div align="right">J Conrad.</div>

To J. B. Pinker
Text MS Berg; Unpublished

<div align="right">[letterhead: Capel House]
Thursday evening [1 or 8? June
1911][1]</div>

Dear Sir.

I send you 7000 w. of Chance, and enclose the text of the *ER* from which Messrs: Methuen may begin to set up, continuing from the June no and so on to the end.

The June no may be sent on to Harpers and in a few days I shall send you corrected slips of the *July* instalment for sending to America.

<div align="center">I am faithfully yours</div>

<div align="right">J. Conrad.</div>

I would be very glad if you would send me back my corrd type when done with for the purpose of clean copy as I may want to refer to some passage—or fact—and my MS is not quite satisfactory for that purpose. I mean here only the new stuff sent to you this month.

1 The progress of *Under Western Eyes* through proof and publication suggests early June 1911. Between [21 or 28 May] and 19 June, Conrad wrote 13,000 words of *Chance*; he might have written even more if not interrupted by a cold, probably after telling Sanderson on the 7th of 'sitting tight over the grindstone'. In a likely scenario, Conrad sent the present batch a week after [21 or 28 May] and then took considerably longer over the other 6,000 words. The 15th, however, would not be out of the question.

To Norman Douglas
Text MS Texas; Unpublished

[letterhead: Capel House]
2 June '11

Dear Douglas.

The humour of your letter is exquisite, but there is something, an under-note, in it which does not please me—for your sake, bien entendu.

Cunninghame Graham was here last sunday very full of admiration for Syren-Land and urging me enthusiastically to read it without loss of time. I said I would, at once, for the (about) 14th time. Thereupon we talked of you. He told me that a long, eulogistic review appeared lately in the *Sat Review*;[1] and this is a good sign, so long after publication, that the book is now clear of the ruck of printed matter and has made a name for itself. You *must* publish another this year.

I heard from the cursed Harpers—damn their Yankee eyes![2]

As to Sid Colvin. Well, if these things don't come off as you say the best thing is to let him go on with his notion. Pourquoi pas? He can do no harm. Write him a kind humorous letter—about fleas and Byz[anti]ne Madonnas—that *genre* I mean,[3] and pat him on the back. It can't hurt you and it will please him, and me too—if that's any inducement to you to behave with comparative sanity. And, damn it all man! Where's your diplomacy? Deployez-moi ça je vous prie.[4]

I have been working amazingly of late. I don't say amazingly well—but the quantity is a record. Effects of a sort of dull desperation. Comprenez-Vous?

Our love. Right yourself again if you can and come over here to us. You don't seem to me to feel solid. Why? We can secure for you a fine, fancy little cottage *gratis* for the whole of July. A woman could be found to make the bed and prepare breakfast. Then from lunch on you would be here. Distance 1/2 mile or less.

Now! Consider it. And believe in our affection for you.

Ever yours

J Conrad.

PS Consider seriously the cottage. August could be practicable too, we think. And then you could have Archie and even the *two* boys with you.[5]

[1] 27 May, 651–2. The reviewer found Douglas 'full of humanity, full of the humanities'.
[2] About a plan to help Douglas rather than about *Under Western Eyes*?
[3] The genre of *Siren Land* itself.
[4] 'Put it to use, I beg you'.
[5] Douglas's sons, Archie and Robin.

Really! The cottage is furnished, linen—and everything. 3 bedrooms.
Nice room downstairs to work in. 'Twould be jolly.

To R. B. Cunninghame Graham

Text MS Syracuse; J-A, 2, 129; Watts 175

[letterhead: Capel House]
2 June 1911

Très cher ami.

Thanks very much for the books. You are indeed very good to me.
Hudson's vol is fine, very fine, infinitely loveable and, as one reads on,
one feels one's affection increase at every page.[1] And as mere writing it is
remarkably harmonious, nothing too much, the right note of humanity,
the right tone of expression, a sort [of] earnest quietness absolutely
fascinating to one's mind in the din of this age of blatant expression. He
is a delight—absolutely individual.—It is as if some very fine, very
gentle spirit were whispering to him the sentences he puts down on the
paper. A privileged being. Give him my love when you write to him.

François is quite good.[2] Very genuine touches all along and quite
telling bits here and there. I am grateful to you.

I send you back His Excellency's letter.[3] I wish I could read Spanish
so as not to miss the smallest crumbs of your prose of which I have been
enamoured for years, with a passion I imagine to be inextinguishable
since your pages give me the same emotion as years ago, haunt my mind
with the same persistence, bring in their train the same delight.

Well no more just now. I've been writing late last night and feel slack
and stupid this morning.

Jessies Kind regards

Yours ever

J. Conrad.

[1] Like Graham, W. H. Hudson (1841–1922) had lived in Argentina; his studies of
wild and rural life there and in England won the admiration of Ford, Pound,
Conrad, and Graham. Watts (p. 176) identified the book as Hudson's newly-reprin-
ted novel *The Purple Land*, but now believes it to have been *A Shepherd's Life* (1910);
the tone of Conrad's remarks makes this volume more likely.

[2] George Sand's *François le champi* (1847) or Maupassant's story, 'François'?

[3] As Watts suggests, Santiago Pérez Triana (1860–1916), Colombian Envoy Extra-
ordinary in London and Madrid and owner and editor of *Hispania*, a new review which
had asked for Graham's work. For Triana's influence on *Nostromo*, see *Letters*, 3, pp. 102
and 176.

To Austin Harrison

Text MS Indiana; Unpublished

[letterhead: Capel House]
7 June 1911.

Dear Mr. Harrison.

Shall be glad to see you with F. Harris or alone either by rail, motor or aeroplane. There's a nice bumpy field in front of the house to land on. Give us a day's notice by p-c please.

We shall be able to "exchange ideas" (as they say in the world of diplomats) on this matter of your letter for which thanks. As you know I don't shake out my stuff out of my sleeve, but you may be sure I appreciate greatly your suggestion.

And thanks also for opening the McMillan* matter.[1] Frankly: nothing would please me more. There are however certain complications which would have to be removed first. Do you think I may write to them openly—I mean will they care to hear? for of their discretion, fairness and so on I am perfectly certain, of course.

Yours faithfully

J. Conrad

PS It would be best if you named a day for your run down here. We shall be "At home" to end of August. You must come to lunch of course. Give please my greeting to F. H.

To E. L. Sanderson

Text MS Yale; J-A, 2, 130

[letterhead: Capel House]
Wednesday. 7 June 1911.

Dearest Ted.

Thanks for your letter which has touched us both immensely. Henceforth we look upon Jack as an Elstree boy. You are very good to us.

Last monday I saw Mrs Ridgeway[2] and we had a long and delightful talk—rejoicing together on you being in England in your rightful place[3] and making a success from the very beginning.

My congratulations on the effective use of your influence in high

[1] See the letter of 19 June. [2] Sanderson's sister Agnes.
[3] As Headmaster of Elstree.

places. You did do a fine stroke of work for these young men. May every endeavour of yours be blessed and every task lightened!

I must tell you that before long you shall see it gazetted that Joseph Conrad has been granted a pension of £100 on the Civil List *for his services to Literature.*[1] Wonders shall never cease. Jack started the agitation of course and apparently there was no difficulty. One accepts such recognition with mixed feelings. It is in a sense a confession of failure—but I prefer to look at it from its other and honourable side. At the same time I feel a little ashamed. There are so many deserving men who ought to have pensions and haven't got them!

I am just now in a tolerably effective writing vein, and therefore am sitting tight over the grindstone. Must! Or else I would take a day off to run over to Elstree. A very clever surgeon has been to see Jessie, and lifted the load of our hearts by declaring that the limb can be made serviceable by a long course of treatment. No operation—or only a very slight one. It is arranged that we shall come to town in early Sept*er* for Jessie to go into a nursing home. It may be a matter of 3 months perhaps.

No more for the present. Our dear love to all your house

Yours affectionately and
gratefully
J. Conrad.

To E. L. Sanderson
Text MS Yale; Unpublished

[letterhead: Capel House]
9 June 1911.

Dearest Ted.

Just a word to thank you for your real[ly] friendly letter. In giving you the news I never meant to draw you into correspondence of the congratulatory kind, well knowing how busy you are. Your warming words are the more prized since the time to write them was stolen from your slender stock of leisure.

We are no end sorry to hear of the horrid whoops. An odious complication this. All our sympathies to Helen & yourself.

You are, my dear Ted, under a misapprehension as to Jack's age. He won't be five till next august. A little too young for a preparatory school

[1] Although not announced until July, the grant had been made a year ago: see the letter of [15? August 1910].

of Elstree's distinction. And anyhow I would have to cut Jessie into small pieces before I could take the kid away from her now. But in another 3–4 years' time she will be ready to stand the pang of separation like a sensible woman. By that time too the monkey'll be thoroughly spoiled and Elstree shall be his salvation.

Our dear love to you all

Yours ever

J. Conrad.

T. R. is a real brick as I've always thought,[1] notwithstanding reams of silly bosh written about and around him by the press.

To J. B. Pinker
Text MS Berg; Unpublished

[Capel House]
19 June 1911.

Dear Sir.

It was sheer bad luck. We had to leave the house for a couple of days for the drains to be opened and we went to a seaside village[2] where I caught a severe cold on the sands.

However we have now roughly 47000w—nearly half of the novel.

I send you the N. Y. H[erald] letter received the other day.[3] It is satisfactory. I shall make every effort to be done by end Aug[u]st—but still one's glad to know that a little delay needn't be fatal.

Thanks for the last batch of rough copy which reached me some time ago. Both Dent and McMillans* would be after Western Eyes. The first approached me directly. McM. did so indirectly. I made suitable replies. Book engaged but in the future etc etc.

I am still heavy and slow but trust that 5000w will be ready by end of coronation festivities.[4]

Yours faithfully

J. Conrad.

[1] Ex-President Roosevelt, who professed himself an admirer of Conrad, had known the Sandersons in East Africa.
[2] Dymchurch, about eight miles away.
[3] Dated 7 June, from the Sunday editor of the *Herald* (TS Berg). The editor thanked Conrad for the news that part of *Chance* would reach New York by the end of July. The *Herald*, however, did not want to risk starting an unfinished serial: 'For that reason, we have allowed you until the end of August to complete and deliver your material. This calculation has been made on your assurance that "the end[s] of my novels, so long contemplated, come along pretty quickly."'
[4] By the end of the month? King George was to be crowned on the 22nd.

To Sir Hugh Clifford

Text MS Clifford; J-A, 2, 131; Hunter (1985, 2)

[letterhead: Capel House]
Coronation Day.
[22 June] 1911.

My Dear Clifford.

It would be too long to tell you of the usual botherations to which my life seems condemned. The first 3 months of this year now look to me like the confused recollections of a nightmare—what with the usual (but not very severe) illness—then being chucked out of the house on account of some beastly complications with the drains. We fled to Dymchurch, where fate treated me to something which looked and felt like a cold but of such devilish virulence (and I've never had a "cold." in my life before) that I remained mentally prostrated for weeks. And all the time I was involved in one of my 40000-word "short stories"—which I was unable to throw off my chest. And over it all like a black-winged phantom there was hovering the necessity, the urgent necessity to begin the novel for the New York Herald:[1] a contract which I owe to Your friendship,[2] and much too good to let slip through my fingers.

I had to lay aside this letter. Coronation Day is now in the past. But I won't take a fresh piece of paper to put the date right. What I set out to say was that all these delays vexing as they were gave me the time to read the Downfall of the Gods three times from end to end. As to pages and passages read and re-read and meditated over I can't give you that tale of them even approximately.

What a tremendous subject for a great a really great Opera! And pray don't think it mean praise. No great poem for music has been written yet; subjects of course are lying about. What I mean to say is that here is a subject, the subject of *the* Great Oriental Opera,[3] worked out. Absolutely done! The simplicity of the highly dramatic action, the picturesquely imposing background, the irresistible blind movements of the crowds and the tragic fatality of the "passion charnelle"—all is there to inspire some musician of the future great enough to express the very

[1] If Conrad received Clifford's new novel, *The Downfall of the Gods*, on publication in April, the distorted chronology of this paragraph would be a way of explaining the uncharacteristically slow response.

[2] Clifford had praised Conrad's book to its proprietor, James Gordon Bennett, when he visited Ceylon.

[3] There is a whole sub-genre of Oriental operas, rife with betrayal, divided loyalties, and splendid religious rites. Examples include Delibe's *Lakmé* (1883), Bizet's *Les Pêcheurs de perles* (1863), and Meyerbeer's *L'Africaine* (1865).

spirit of the East in the music of the West. I never thought that the day should come on which I would wish I had been born a great composer. *Then* indeed we would have collaborated—to be abused of course by every yapping musical critic on* the press, but with the certitude of leaving behind us a magnificent achievement. The above you may take as the first impression—of no mean force I can assure you. Then came the other readings—deeper impressions.

Slat the artist, is a great "trouvaille". The girl is amazing, the high Priest quite convincingly alive, and the suggestion of the oppressed, toiling, sweating humanity both in its subjection and in its revolt admirable. It lives, it moves it has its artistic being—it is undeniable. Chun himself is the least distinct; but that perhaps was unavoidable, unless—and here comes the general criticism: the book seems to me too short for the greatness of the conception. Chun should have been more developed. And if you ask me how? I must answer that I don't know how. I have not the critical knack. It's a feeling—an instinct if you like. Chun is weak—not absolutely, of course, but in relation to the strength of all the rest. I admit that all he says and does is right—but there is something wanting. Something that would *impose* him upon our attention. Not a very illuminating criticism—is it? Perhaps it is the girl who extinguishes him. She is truly a creation.

But indeed I am very glad of the book; glad that you have written it. I don't think I've missed anything. It has a great ampleness of conception and many beautiful pages. In those hours I have lived with it I seemed now and then to see as if an allegory draped in Eastern robes of things much nearer to us here in space and time than that gorgeous legendary story of ancient wrongs and ancient revolt, something of the fatality which broods over all popular upheavals.

This is not the tenth part of what I could find to say if I were not growing stupid—or tongue-tied, or something. There are weeks, whole weeks, when I am utterly unable to write a single sentence. I struggle with my thoughts like a man stricken dumb suddenly. But enough of that. I congratulate you. And when I think that it was thrown off as a holiday task—well!

Keep always for us a corner in your thoughts and may all the gods of East and West be propitious to you.

<div style="text-align: center">Yours always</div>

<div style="text-align: right">J. Conrad</div>

To John Galsworthy
Text MS Forbes; Unpublished

[letterhead: Capel House]
26. June 1911.

My dearest Jack.

Thanks for your letter. I haven't been working very well lately but nevertheless there is a rather consoling fact that since the sixth of April I have done about half the novel for the N.Y. Herald, and I may now hope to have it finished some time in Sept*er*. Pinker has volunteered the statement that should I deliver the novel to him quickly he will be disposed to revise the terms of our agreement to my advantage. We shall see.

We are ever so glad to hear that the cure has done Ada some good. I can sympathise with her as an expert in the sort of horrid time she must have had. I only hope that the improvement will be maintained.

I don't think either liberty or literature endangered by the spectator.[1] What *discredits* freedom of expression and liberty of thought is a publication like the *ER* with its equivocal methods of pushing itself and its all but fraudulent contents. I have the regret to see myself there and this month I had the regret to see you within those suspect covers.[2] This is my feeling. And I wouldn't have troubled You with it if you had not mentionned* the subject yourself.

I am horribly tired having sat all day to squeeze a couple of pages out of myself. But I wouldn't sleep without writing to you. Love to dear Ada

Ever Yours

J. Conrad.

[1] The *Spectator* had announced that it would no longer discuss the *English Review* in its monthly survey of the magazines (10 June, 875–6). Two items in particular offended the *Spectator*. The first was a flyer from the self-styled 'Great Adult Review' insisting that 'Our standard is NOT that of the "young person," either the callow lad or raw school-girl'. The second was an essay in the June number by Frank Harris that decried the narrowness of official morality and its bias against women: 'Our vagrant nature is impatient of rigid limits. And the tolerance already extended to one sex should be extended to the other' ('Thoughts on Morals', *English Review*, 8, 441). To this, the *Spectator* replied: 'We happen to hold that the propagation of such views is harmful to the State in the highest degree ... we absolutely refuse to be forced by any canting talk about a censorship into aiding the *English Review* to find readers and disciples for these gross and blear-eyed sophistries' (876).

[2] In the June number, Galsworthy's story 'The Two Looks' appeared alongside D. H. Lawrence's 'Odour of Chrysanthemums', poems by Masefield, Aleister Crowley and others, a translation of some letters by Wagner, several literary, social, medical or political essays including Harris's, and of course a new instalment of *Under Western Eyes*.

To J. B. Pinker

Text MS Berg; Unpublished

[letterhead: Capel House]
27 June 1911.

Dear Sir.

I regret this long delay in writing to you on the subject of the proofs. I think you are under a misapprehension in this matter. I'll try to make it clear. The batch you have received follows on the set of proofs I corrected in *May* last for the *E. R* under the impression that the whole was to go into the *June* inst'. As a matter of fact the June (current) number contained but little more than half of the contents of the *May* slips. That is the reason why the set I have forwarded to you does not "catch on" to the current (*June*) number. The balance of that *May* batch of proofs will appear in the number now about due (*July* N°) with some portion of the text you have in your possession to eke out the instalment. At least I hope so. The instalments have been so short lately that I really don't know when the publication shall be finished at that rate.[1]

The set I have forwarded to you is the *very last* I have had from the *ER*. I expect further proofs before very long and then you may be certain I shan't lose a day in revising and sending you the sheets for Harpers.

The position then is: The *July* N° of the ER. shall be out in a day or two. It will probably contain part of the text You have in your possession or it shall at least be right up to it. If you will then kindly send the July N° and such proof-sheets as are not included in it to Harpers they shall have something to go on with. In a week or so I ought to have more galley slips from the Review, which will be *consecutive* to what you hold now, and I shall transmit them to you for H's without delay.

I must tell you that I've had a pretty sharp passage with M^r Harrison arising from the *Spectator* article.[2] I won't trouble you now with the whole story but you may believe me if I say that I had to resent by very plain speaking what I felt to be a highly improper insistence to draw me into the controversy with which I didn't want to have anything to do.

[1] Whereas the December instalment of *Under Western Eyes* had come to 36 pages, June came only to 20 and July to 19; the serial ran until October.
[2] On 24 June, the *Spectator* published letters, by Ford Madox Ford and Henry Newbolt among others, objecting to its policy of ignoring the *Review*. Harrison may have asked Conrad to write as well. In any case, when the counter-attack against the *Spectator* began with a list of authors recently published in the *Review*, Conrad figured along with Hardy, Shaw, Wells, James, Tolstoy, Chekhov, Yeats, and 88 others (*English Review*, 8 [July 1911], 666–70).

The point is that I must ask you to refrain from offering any of my work to the *ER*, for the present, at least. I am sorry to have to make this request under the circumstances in which I feel you ought to have a completely free hand. On the other hand I am confident that you'll accede to it as I am certain that you would never wish to put me in a false position.

I am going on with *Chance* and shall be sending you a few thousand words before long. I have been much interrupted in one way or another for the last fortnight. I am not at all hopeless of pulling off the thing within the time we have fixed, and in its required size of about 100,000 words.

<div style="text-align:center">Yours faithfully</div>

<div style="text-align:right">J. Conrad.</div>

To Wincenty Lutosławski

Text MS Warsaw; Illg[1]

<div style="text-align:right">[letterhead: Capel House]</div>

<div style="text-align:right">2 July 1911</div>

Dear Sir[2]

I remember your visit of fourteen years ago very well.[3] I also remember your letter, which reached me a few days after your visit, requesting me to keep it strictly confidential. Why and from whom, however, you did not have the kindness to confide.[4] As a man who is not used to hiding anything either in my life or in my thoughts, I have to admit the impression was not very pleasant. Nevertheless, I can assure

[1] Translation by Tadeusz Sławek, revised by Dr Krystyna Dietrich.

[2] Wincenty Lutosławski (1863–1954) was a Polish philosopher and zealous nationalist. He wrote to Conrad while he was studying in London; later he taught in Cracow, Geneva, Lausanne, London, Paris, and Vilnius, where he held the chair of philosophy from 1919 to 1928. In his work, he attempted to combine Platonism with the belief that Poland is the Messiah among nations. His *The Origin and Growth of Plato's Logic* (Longmans, 1897), published in English, established the chronology of Plato's work. An unstable man, he suffered a number of nervous breakdowns.

[3] Probably on Sunday, 13 June 1897: see *Letters*, 1, pp. 359–60; the visit, effected by an introduction from Henry James, bordered on farce. The account published two years later in *Kraj* did some damage to Conrad's Polish reputation. In 1930, Lutosławski explained that his purpose had been 'to win Conrad for Polish literature'; thanks to Conrad's modesty and Lutosławski's immediate awareness that they were astrologically incompatible, the mission failed: 'A Visit to Conrad in 1897', *Blue Peter* (Boston), 10 (1930), 638–40.

[4] 'I disliked the idea of being asked by Henry James, or anybody else, about that fateful visit, which could not be understood by my English friends. Therefore, I wired Conrad the next day asking him to keep my visit secret' (*ibid.*).

you that for all these years I have kept your secret, which was made easier by the fact that no-one has asked me anything. I assure you that your unexpected letter will also remain secret from the entire world.

Respectfully yours

your servant Konrad Korzeniowski

To J. B. Pinker

Text MS Berg; Unpublished

[Capel House]

Tuesday night. [4? July 1911][1]

Dear Sir.

I didn't get home till about seven when it was too late to wire you that evening.

I hope you will agree with me that to enter into this transaction would be saddling ourselves with a needless anxiety.[2] At any rate it would be an added anxiety for me. For you it would mean an immediate disbursement to make. I am indeed very much obliged to you for Your offer to do so, obviously in order to ease my mind, which, I admit, is much concerned by my situation as to Heinemann. But you know how it is. I simply dare not say anything positive. I must devote all my energies to the work in hand and don't want to even *think* of anything else.

Once the general position is improved we may return to that matter. If H. has been told that I am only waiting for his release to go on with the book—it isn't just to me. I hope to finish it for him yet. A good serial contract would enable us to work it off in that way.

Believe me

faithfully Yours

J. Conrad.

PS I trust that you understand how much I appreciate your willingness to enter into this transaction.

[1] Received 'July 1911': probably a few days before the second undated July letter referring to Heinemann, which accompanied 3,000 words of *Chance*; since other correspondence accounts for deliveries later in the month, the first Tuesday in July is the most likely.

[2] Heinemann must have offered Conrad a chance to buy back the rights of *The Rescue*; Pinker had evidently agreed to put up the necessary £360.

To J. B. Pinker
Text MS Berg; Unpublished

[Capel House]
[July 1911][1]

Dear Sir.

Your letter just to hand. Thanks. I never meant that *you* said anything "awkward" to M^r H. But somehow I had the impression the* Doubleday may have done so.[2]

Herewith 3000 w. Bad enough but I've been much interrupted. And yet one can't shut everybody out [of] one's life.

Yours

J Conrad.

To Professor Tadaichi Hidaka
Text Hidaka (with facsimile)

[letterhead: Capel House]
11 July 1911.

Dear Sir.[3]

I am sorry my answer to Your letter has been delayed so long. I am very much flattered by the interest you show in myself and my work. It is obviously impossible for me to tell you the story of my life; but if I ever complete a work of autobiographical character I shall send you a copy.[4]

Now I can only tell you that I have led a sea-life for 22 years and have been writing for fully 15 years more. As to my view of life it is contained in my books which are the sincere expression of my thoughts and feelings. But I have formulated no doctrine either for my own use or for the information of the world. I respect courage, truth, fidelity, self-restraint and devotion to the ancient ideals of mankind; and am sorry that, like most men, I fail in the practice of these simple virtues. I beg

[1] Received 'July 1911': the reference to 'M^r H[einemann]' points to a connection with the letter of [4? July 1911].

[2] As successor to McClure, Doubleday held North American book rights to *The Rescue*.

[3] Tadaichi Hidaka (c. 1875–1955) was Professor of English and American Literature at Waseda University in Japan. In 1922 he visited Conrad at Oswalds. Hidaka published a bilingual edition of *Some Reminiscences and Amy Foster* in 1929, a volume on *The Background of English and American Literature* in 1933, and *Essays on English and American Literature* in 1937.

[4] Conrad hoped to place *A Personal Record*; to accompany his reminiscences, in August or September, he wrote the 'Familiar Preface', echoing the principles expressed here. Until he read the reminiscences, Hidaka assumed that Conrad was English-born information from Professor Takahisa Nishimura).

you to believe in my friendly sentiments towards your nation and yourself.

<div style="text-align: center">Yours faithfully</div>

<div style="text-align: right">Joseph Conrad.</div>

To J. B. Pinker

Text MS Berg; Unpublished

<div style="text-align: right">[Capel House]
Thursday ev^g [13 July 1911]¹</div>

Dear Sir.

I send you here 3000 words only of Chance. There are more but not typed and indeed not fit to be typed yet. Next week I hope will be better as to quantity.

Thanks for the acct received today. The payments for the book-form of Western Eyes ought to make some impression on the amount of my debt. I don't really know how much Meth: & Harpers are contracted to pay for that book.

Methuen might have spoken about the title ten months ago. They knew of the book then. Now I have established the text of the work in the *ER*. And the text includes the title which must stand. Let them look to the danger. It's their business. What is this sort of talk?² A novel by Conrad is a novel by Conrad. It will be advertised as a novel listed by the libraries as a novel reviewed as a novel. I am not an obscure beginner. In what that title is worse* than *Temporal Power* of Miss Corelli or *The Master Builder* of Ibsen? Did anyone take the first for a theological or polemical book,³ or the second for a pamphlet on putting up walls? Did any one take the *Green Carnation* for a treatise on the cultivation of that flower? or the *New Moon* for a hand-book of Selenography? Or the

¹ Received 'July 1911': an immediate reply to Methuen's request was likely; in any case, the MS deliveries and letters of [21 July] – if correctly dated – and [28 July] would rule out the 20th or the 27th.

² Algernon Methuen had written to Pinker on the 11th: 'I see that Conrad proposes to call his novel "Under Western Eyes". I know that he is rather sensitive, but I hope he can be induced to alter it. The title gives promise not so much of a novel, as a book of descriptive impressions. I expect that you may agree with me, and be willing to put this before Mr. Conrad' (TS Methuen). See Keith Carabine, 'Conrad, Pinker, and *Under Western Eyes: A Novel', The Conradian*, 10 (1985), 144–53; this article includes parts of Conrad's letter.

³ 'Marie Corelli' (Mary Mackay) herself? Her novel, a defence of monarchy, came out in 1902. Ibsen's play appeared in 1892.

New Machiavelli for a series of political essays?[1] Let Mr Methuen attend to his business and not talk of "danger". If he does his part as well as I do mine there will be no danger. When I settled on *Typhoon* for the title of that vol of stories, (just that one word, which is an accepted meteorological term) Heinemann did not talk to me of the danger of it being mistaken for a work on atmospheric disturbances in the China Sea. However if M likes to put *A Novel* in sub-title he may do so with my blessing.[2]

You know that I am not unreasonably touchy about suggestions. If M. had spoken in time I would have done my best to consider the matter not from any regard for him but out of consideration for you who have made advances on that book. Not that I believe the book to be endangered by its title if it's handled properly. But I can't really at this period of my career allow a work of mine to appear under two different titles. It isn't a thing to do.

> Yours faithfully
>
> J. Conrad.

To Edward Garnett

Text MS Colgate; G. 245

[letterhead: Capel House]
18 July 1911

My dear Edward.

It was good to see Your handwriting again. When! Oh when! shall we set eyes on each other? We are not growing younger.

Glad you have got the Century.[3] Gibbon told me some time ago that there was something of the sort in the wind. That talented buccaneer will come down to Dymchurch for six weeks and I expect to see him pretty frequently.[4]

No my dear boy. I haven't a single thing to send you. Moreover I don't think the Century shop wants me at all. If I am not mistaken they have refused in March last a very tolerable long-short-story of mine.[5] But I may be mistaken. It might have been Scribners. I am very hazy as

[1] Robert Smythe Hichens, *The Green Carnation* (1894); 'C. E. Raimond' (Elizabeth Robins), *The New Moon* (1895); H. G. Wells, *The New Machiavelli* (1911): a satire on aestheticism, an occult romance, and a novel of life among the intelligentsia.

[2] The solution adopted.

[3] A commission to find English authors for the *Century Magazine*.

[4] The Gibbons would be about eight miles away.

[5] The *Century* had refused 'Freya'.

to what happens to my work after I've sent it out of the house with a curse. I am now pelting along with a novel (God save the mark!) for the New York Herald. It's being made to measure no less than 90000 words—and I won't let you know what I think of it. I only mention it at all so that you should know that I am not likely to do any short stories, either decent or indecent, for some months to come.

How are you? Gibbon gave us a tolerably good report of you some time ago. I am immensely excited about your wife's trans: of Dostoievski.[1] Give her my most respectful regards—and a greeting to David from one of his oldest friends.

<div style="text-align:center">Yours ever</div>

<div style="text-align:right">J. Conrad.</div>

To Agnes Tobin
Text Tobin 81

<div style="text-align:right">Capel House,
21 July 1911</div>

My dear Inez[2]

Listen to the wisdom of a man of mature years and no longer a thrall to illusions. The Mermaid is a darksome, earthy hole.[3] By Allah it is! I have always mistrusted it. I think you shall find Mrs. Prothero's[4] friend a very tolerable if not a positively pleasant company*. And then the Mermaid will be there still as a stand-by should the other arrangement fail to work. Whereas if you go first to the Mermaid and discover (as I believe) that it is a whited sepulchre a move the other way would not be so easy to make.

The above proves the interest, the vivid interest, I take in the prospect of having you near us for some time. It *doesn't* prove that I like to have my finger in every pie. I am not a meddlesome person.

I have been hard at work except on Tuesday when I went to see the St.

[1] Constance Garnett's translation of *The Brothers Karamazov*, the first in English, appeared in 1912. Between then and 1920, she published twelve more volumes of Dostoevsky's work.
[2] Using the Spanish form of her name paid tribute to Agnes Tobin's background. Although her parents were Irish by descent, both had lived in Chile, and her mother was born there. Her father had been bilingual secretary to the first Roman Catholic Archbishop of San Francisco.
[3] The Mermaid Inn, Rye? Nearness to Ham Street (rather than any invidious reference to its mediaeval atmosphere) makes the identification likely.
[4] Mary Frances, wife of the editor and historian G. W. Prothero?

Augustine's Abbey School in Ramsgate.[1] I am awfully in arrears with my N.Y. H[erald] novel; and it makes me anxious. But all my writing life has been one long anxiety. There are days when I daren't confess to myself my infinite, soul-crushing weariness. Il faut marcher—toujours il faut marcher—but it is confoundedly difficult sometimes to put one foot before the other.

I don't write generally to people in that tone. With you I am frank—but this frankness is for you only. Vous comprenez? It wouldn't do to let the world in behind the scenes. Even Jessie herself is not always admitted when darkness descends upon the stage. A quoi bon l'inquieter? N'est-ce pas?

I remember Ethel Clifford[2] very well. We had a long talk once, years ago. Tempi passati[3], my dear Inez. She was charming, with something unconsciously mysterious in her charm. I remember also being appallingly stupid that evening. Therefore I hoped that she had forgotten all about it! But perhaps it's better to be remembered anyhow. Yes it is better. And so I commend myself to your memory, defects, crimes and all—and with love from us all, am always

<div style="text-align: right">your friend and servant</div>

<div style="text-align: right">J. Conrad</div>

To J. B. Pinker

Text MS Berg; Unpublished

<div style="text-align: right">[letterhead: Capel House]</div>

<div style="text-align: right">Friday [July or October? 1911][4]</div>

Dear Sir.

I have been in bed. There's no help for it. And all the same this batch completes full 55 thou: words (new copy) since May (incl). I would be glad if you found it convenient to post me a cheque to day.

<div style="text-align: right">Yours</div>

<div style="text-align: right">J.C.</div>

[1] Where Borys might finish his education?

[2] Lady Dilke (died 1959), author of *Songs of Dreams* (1903) and *Love's Journey* (1905). Her mother was Mrs W. K. Clifford, the playwright and novelist.

[3] 'Bygone times'.

[4] Pinker wrote on the MS 'Please send him a cheque' and 'July 1911'; if the month is correct, the 21st might fit the circumstances, counting old copy with new. A dating of 20 October, however, corresponds more closely to the state of Conrad's health and the progress of 'new copy'.

To J. B. Pinker

Text MS Berg; Unpublished

[letterhead: Capel House]
25 July 1911.

Dear Sir.

Thanks for cheque received on Monday. The Nn Newspaper Syndte Kendal are everlastingly writing to me.[1] I mention this to you tho' I don't suppose it's much use.

I have an idea that you are in possession of the only existing copy of Rescue. Hueffer lost mine—tho' he says he didn't.[2] Anyway I haven't got a single scrap or fraction of that work. Perhaps—Chance being happily got rid of before very long—you will let me have the MS to look at and get on terms with, while I am writing the 2 or 3 short stories I intend to turn to after Chance. Just now I can't allow anything to interrupt—or rather interfere—with my concentration on the book in hand.

Yours faithfully

J Conrad

To John Galsworthy

Text MS Forbes; Unpublished

[letterhead: Capel House]
28 July 1911.

Dearest Jack.

There's nothing new to say of myself. I have been at work more or less successfully all this month. There is no gout—neither am I particularly well. Life is a dead pull now all the way, but I am beginning to get used to it. Jessie has been very tolerably well in general health and has even walked better of late. Jackolo is more sprite-like than ever—all skin and bone and mischief. But he does not seem to feel the heat as we feared he would; and as long as his health is good we are not much concerned about his morals which are distinctly of the pagan kind. At this present moment he's chasing his tame rabbit all over Jessie's flower-beds (such as they are) with exulting shrieks. I warrant you that there's a fellow who isn't sorry to be alive—not like poor B who at the age of five wished "he had never been borned".

[1] The Northern Newspaper Syndicate placed stories and articles in provincial newspapers and magazines. The chief editor, John Watson, had been asking Conrad for contributions since 1902.

[2] Either the MS or a copy had gone to Ford in January 1903 (*Letters*, 3, p. 4).

Borys however has got rid of his pessimism. He's just back after his last term in Luton very fit and cheerful. After much anxious cogitation I think that I shall send him to the HMS *Worcester* the nautical school-ship in the Thames.[1] Not that either he or I think of his going to sea but from other considerations. We had a long talk the very first evening and he falls in with my idea enthusiastically. The Worcester is a good school of general education (not classical). The course is of two years but very few boys go through it in that time. Still, even giving B a term extra he shall be not more than sixteen when he leaves with (I hope) a first-class leaving certificate. This would fit him either to enter some technical school or, which is more likely to happen under the circumstances, the draughtsmen's office or the workshops of some engineering works, where he would be earning his living while educating himself for higher qualifications. I am thinking of the Thames Shipbuilding Co or the Port of London Engineering deptnt. On the other hand should he manage to get well up in the list he may elect the sea-life. There are always cadetships in the Navy (2 every year I think) for the top-boys, commissions in the R[oyal] N[aval] R[eserve] nominations for the Indian Marine and Bengal Pilot Service and other advantages.

What do you think dearest Jack? Beyond communicating with the secretary I've done nothing yet. I am sending you the prospectus to look at. I would be glad to see him started on his life's-work (whatever it may be) and if he takes this course I may reasonably hope to live long enough to see how he shapes. I am sending you the prospectus, because I imagine you know nothing of the school.

We do hope dear Ada has been free from pain in this dry weather. Have you been doing a lot? Our dear love to you both

Yours ever

J. Conrad.

[1] The *Worcester*, the Thames Nautical Training College, was moored off Greenhithe, between Dartford and Gravesend. It had the advantage of being closer to home than the *Conway*, the training ship moored off Birkenhead that Conrad so much admired.

To J. B. Pinker

Text MS Berg; Unpublished

[Capel House]
Friday. [28 July 1911][1]

Dear Sir

I send You some further copy—a full 3000 words. I trust you will not mind if I ask you to send the cheque by the 5 o'clock post. Your last letter tho' dated on the 21st did not reach me till Monday. It did not matter in the least then; but this week I have promised to make a payment on Sat: and shouldn't like to fail.

Do you think my suggestion as to B'woods any good? Of course there is no hurry except as to serialising *Freya*—because the vol could never appear before Mch. or Ap. next year.

Edward Garnett reads now for the Century people and has asked me if I have anything for him to look at. I mention this to you only for information. You are no doubt in touch with the Century.

I am Yours faithfully

J. Conrad.

To Edward Garnett

Text MS Bryn Mawr; G. 246

[Capel House]
[29 July 1911][2]

Dearest Edward.

Pink writes he has sent you Freya to look at. So it can't be the Century which has refused same in April last. It must have been Scribners—on the ground that: "its *overpowering gloom* makes it impossible for serialisation".[3] All I can say is that I hope You won't be overpowered by the "gloom" to the point of swallowing a dose of prussic acid after reading the copy. Let me entreat you to bear up—to react—to be a man! And do write to me—so that I know You are still alive after the terrific experience which, I understand, has nearly killed the Scribners' man.

Seriously my dear fellow, I've tried to do a magazine-ish thing with some decency. Not a very high purpose; yet it seems I've failed even in that! All this is very comical—if not exactly amusing.

I wanted P to send the story to B'wood. After all the "Maga" public was yet the one to catch on best to my stuff. I suppose I am myself a

[1] Received 'July 1911': the date of 'Your last letter', the arrival of a cheque on the 29th, and the reference to Garnett point to the month's end.
[2] Date from postmark. [3] Cf. the letter of [25? March].

"horrible bourgeois" at bottom. But all the same it only shows your almost devilish (or diabolic?) cleverness; for it is You—and no other—who turned Karain (you remember?) on to Maga—so many years ago—with inspired judgement.[1]

If only for the sake of old days don't bring your heaviest guns against the thing. It's but tissue-paper after all. Love from us all.

<div style="text-align:center">Yours ever</div>

<div style="text-align:right">J. Conrad.</div>

To J. B. Pinker

Text MS Berg; Unpublished

<div style="text-align:right">[Capel House]
Saturday. 29 July [1911][2]</div>

Dear Sir.

Thanks for the cheque received to-day.

I am glad you think B'wood plan feasible. As I have said it's the sort of public I should like to keep in touch with. Gibbon was talking to me about the Century but I haven't a clear idea whether they serialise in *both* countries. If that is so then I think that B'wood won't particularly care to publish the book-form.[3]

I was pleased to hear that G. was doing the last Gregory story[4] and meant to finish it by Sunday. I see him fairly often. He has some subjects for short stories and also two subjects for novels of the most promising sort. Especially the novels. He has no doubt mentionned* them to you. But what I am most pleased at is the way he intends to treat them. I think they are certain to win a real success. Of his great, *very great* talent there's no doubt—in my mind.[5] What I am anxious for is that he should use it in a "large" way.

<div style="text-align:center">Yours faithfully</div>

<div style="text-align:right">J. Conrad.</div>

[1] In 1897, Garnett encouraged him to revise 'Karain' and advised Unwin to send it to *Blackwood's*, thus beginning Conrad's connection with that magazine (*Letters*, 1, pp. 352–3, and Blackburn, pp. 3–4).

[2] Received '1911'.

[3] After the *Century* fiasco, on 9 August, Pinker sent 'Freya' to Messrs Blackwood (Blackburn, p. 197); the company showed interest neither in this story, long enough for a serial, nor in a collection.

[4] Gibbon collected these tales of a resourceful traveller as *The Adventures of Miss Gregory* (1912); they were written mostly for *McClure's*.

[5] Gibbon was another Pinker client.

To Warrington Dawson
Text MS Duke; Randall 137

[letterhead: Capel House]
1 Augt 1911.

My dear Dawson.

We shall be delighted. Why not take Your ticket from Paris only to Dover or Folkestone. A train which stops in *Ashford* leaves half an hour or so after the Continental mail train. If you let me know I shall meet you in Ashford. You could sleep here and continue to London say after lunch next day—by the fast afternoon train.

Wife sends kind regards.

Yours cordially

J. Conrad.

Marwood just been and sends you greetings.

Drop us a line in time. For wire: *Conrad Hamstreet* is sufficient address. S[outh] E[astern] R[ailway]. *Change in Ashford.*

To John Galsworthy
Text MS Forbes; Unpublished

[Capel House]
Tuesday evening [1 or 8 August
1911][1]

My dearest Jack.

I was glad to get your letter and to see that you approve the idea on the whole. Meantime I have been on board and had an interview with Wilson-Barker,[2] to whom I could speak openly as a fellow-seaman. He assured me that there were on board a good many boys destined for an engineering career (I don't mean mechanical engineering) and that he thought it was a good preparatory schooling. And I don't know where to look for an authoritative opinion. But I reason like this: the boy is young yet—too young for any technical institute. He would have to put in a couple of years in some school or other—then why not in this one where at any rate they lay themselves out to teach mathematics. I am of course

[1] Between 28 July, when Conrad wrote about his plans for Borys, and 12 August when Norman Douglas's illness disrupted life at Capel House. By [18 August], Galsworthy had given some advice on 'where to look for an authoritative opinion'.

[2] David Wilson Barker (1858–1941; knighted 1920), Captain-Superintendent of the Nautical Training College from 1892 to 1919.

thinking of civil engineering; but I cannot hope for him the possibility of following long studies and getting a degree in C.E. (which I believe is granted now by the London University) at 23 or thereabouts. It's no good even dreaming of this. An apprenticeship to a Rway or some works is more likely—indeed is my highest hope. By working hard in his spare time he may fit himself to pass the exams of the I.C.E.[1] as other men before him have done.

I have talked with the boy and I believe he understands the position thoroughly. He's a good fellow and there's the stuff of a *responsible* man in him. But in truth dearest Jack I feel so uncertain of the next day, so completely at the mercy of the first ill wind that may blow that I am not capable of thinking much of the future. I simply dread it; and the only way for me to keep at work (God save the mark) is to forget that there is such a thing as next morning to come.

I have arranged with Nash to publish the E.R series of my reminiscences in book form this autumn.[2] A 5/- vol on which he agrees to give a 20% royalty and an advance of £60 on pubon. It will pay B's first term, and go a long way towards his outfit—at least I hope so.

Our dearest love to you both.

<div style="text-align:center">Yours ever</div>

<div style="text-align:right">J. Conrad.</div>

PS. It's late and I have 800 words to write yet before I sleep.

To J. B. Pinker

Text MS Berg; Unpublished

<div style="text-align:right">[letterhead: Capel House]
1st Augst. [1911][3]</div>

Dear Sir.

I am ready to do anything necessary to carry through the publication without delay. But couldn't you propose to H. to set up *at once* from typed copy in their possession and send me over galley slips.[4] I shan't detain them more than a couple of days and they could go back to them

[1] The Institute of Civil Engineers.

[2] Eveleigh Nash (1873–1956) brought out *Some Reminiscences*, later known as *A Personal Record*, in January 1912. The contract, now at Indiana, was signed 27 July.

[3] The contents give the year.

[4] On 5 July, F. W. Slater of the Harper & Brothers London office told Pinker that no publication date for *Under Western Eyes* could be given until final copy reached New York (TS Berg).

by the return boat. I would prefer this arrangement if possible—one corrects better on the printed page—quicker too.

If they are quick about it they may have the whole matter settled and the corrected proofs with them by middle Sept.—or even before.

But I repeat I'll do what You think is best to save time and trouble. I have been much concerned myself on that very point.

I am about to send you further copy of *Ch*: either today or tomorrow. I had a letter from Garnett which I've answered. Hasn't the *Century* Co refused the story some time ago?

Pray continue *if you can* to advance me £4.[1] I am going on well so far—my health seems improved and I think that the contract (N.Y.H.) is fairly safe. By the time the book is finished I shall have received $\frac{1}{2}$ proceeds of the serial which is all I expect from that work. And with any luck in book-form terms we shall be able to write £800 off my debt. Then perhaps the Mediterranean novel may be started at once. But I am afraid that I should have to "read up" a little for that subject.

I hope you'll be successful with B'woods.

<div align="right">Yours faithfully</div>

<div align="right">J. Conrad.</div>

To J. B. Pinker

Text MS Berg; Unpublished

<div align="right">[Capel House]</div>

<div align="right">Thursday. [3 August 1911][2]</div>

Dear Sir.

Thanks for the cheque for £12 which reached me this morning.

We may consider a full half of the book done now. If the rest comes off in six weeks from this I shall be pleased with myself.[3]

I am rather sorry you send* Freya to EG. He should not have asked for it, either. It had been refused once and that was enough. This between ourselves—but there's more in this than meets the eye.

<div align="right">Yours faithfully</div>

[1] Per thousand words of *Chance*.

[2] On the 1st, Conrad promised to send more MS that day or the next. 'The cheque for £12' must have been payment for that batch. The unfolding of the *Century* affair confirms the date.

[3] Even without the batch accompanying the problematic note of [21 July?], the count had now reached at least 59,000 words. For a possible much higher figure, see p. 482, n. 1.

To Edward Garnett

Text MS Yale; J-A, 2, 133; G. 247

[Capel House]
[4 August 1911][1]

My dear Edward.

I have expressed to Pinker my view of his sending to you a story rejected already by the Century. It was not fair either to you or to me. As to faking a "sunny" ending to my story I would see all the American Magazines and all the american Editors damned in heaps before lifting my pen for that task.[2] I have never been particularly anxious to rub shoulders with the piffle they print with touching consistency from year's end to year's end.

The story itself, I suppose, is not "done" since it has failed to convince you. It is the story of the *Costa Rica* which was not more than five years old when I was in Singapore.[3] The man's name was Sutton. He died in just that way—but I don't think he died of Slav temperament.[4] He was just about to go home to marry a girl (of whom he used to talk to everybody and anybody) and bring her out there when his ship was run of* a reef by the commander of a Dutch gunboat whom he had managed to offend in some way. He haunted the beach in Macassar for months and lies buried in the fort there.

Only 18 months ago Charles Marris master and owner of the *Araby Maid* island-trader, came to see me in Aldington.[5] He was in England to see his people who farm in Somersetshire. He said to me: "We are all reading your books out there". We had a long talk about men and things of the Archipelago. He said: "You ought to write the story of the *Costa Rica*. There's a good many of us left yet who remember Sutton." And I said I would, before long.

[1] Date from postmark.
[2] For Garnett's opinion of the ending, see n. 1 to the following letter.
[3] Here is another story prompted in all likelihood by the visit of Captain Marris, who had served on the *Costa Rica* (letter to Conrad, 18 July 1909, MS Yale). In 1891, her skipper, John Bolton Carpenter, was arrested by the Dutch authorities and taken to Macassar in a dispute over several casks of gin retrieved from a derelict proa. The case, an international cause-célèbre, was eventually decided in Carpenter's favour. In 'Freya', threads of the affair are woven with the misfortunes of Sutton (otherwise unknown), the fate of a ship stranded off Macassar, and memories of Conrad's own days as a gun-runner. For a fuller account, see G. J. Resink, 'Jozef Korzeniowski's voornamste lectuur betreffende Indonesië', *Bijdragen tot de taal-, land- en volkenkunde*, 117 (1961), 209–37.
[4] Conrad found Garnett over-fond of this mystification.
[5] See the letter of [11 or 18 September? 1909].

That's how Freya came to be written. But of course facts are nothing unless they are made credible—and it is there that I have failed.

<div align="center">Yours ever</div>

<div align="right">J Conrad</div>

To J. B. Pinker

Text MS Berg; Unpublished

<div align="right">[letterhead: Capel House]</div>
<div align="right">9 Aug 1911.</div>

Dear Sir.

I have your letter of the 8th. All this business upsets me rather. I thought that showing a story already rejected by the Century to E. G. (newly appointed reader for the C.) was not a safe thing to do. E. G. could not under the circumstances accept it for publication. He ought to have felt this himself and refrained from asking to see it.

What makes me sick—positively sick—is the *thundering lie* he told you—God only knows why—that he had seen the story *years ago*!!!¹ I can produce Gibbon to whom I talked of the story in Dec. 1910 and who has <u>seen</u> me writing it in Jan-Febr and March of this present year during his fairly frequent visits to my house. There is also M^r Marwood my friend and neighbour who calls every Tuesday regularly. He has seen the MS on my table growing from week to week—the very ink wet on the page as I rose from my writing table to shake hands with him. And there is the MS itself which does not look as if written years ago. I declare to you solemnly that not a line of that story—*neither sketch, synopsis or even a mere note on that subject*—has been written before the 26th of Dec 1910 when I wrote the first page and then laid it aside till the 10th of Jan 1911 being utterly unable to write a line during all the intervening days—as it happens to me sometimes. Why G. made that monstrous false statement to you I can't imagine.² I am too indignant to think of it calmly. I can only hope that you think me incapable of sending you an old work

¹ On 26 July, Garnett wrote to Pinker (MS Berg) as follows:

> I am returning to you 'Freya of the Seven Isles' with many thanks. The story is undoubtedly very fine. (I remember reading it years ago.)
>
> I don't often agree with the enthusiasts for 'a happy ending', but I do feel a certain weakness in the manipulation of the tragedy at the close. If I write to JC on the matter I will *suggest* that he should have another look at the MS. I don't suppose he would alter the end, but if he did so, I would put it before the Century C° again.

² Surely not from malice but from absent-mindedness: his consumption of stories and novels was gargantuan.

accompanied by circumstantial lies as to the time it took me to write it—and so on—in order to get from you an increased advance, which you at once granted. This is the point which distresses me. Finally I can tell you that since *Lord Jim* (pub. in 1900) EG has not seen a single line of my work before publication. *Not a line! Not a scrap.*[1] I look again at your letter and can't believe my eyes.

<div align="right">Yours faithfully</div>

<div align="right">J Conrad.</div>

(pray treat this as confidential till I obtain an explanation from G.)

PS I'll be sending you further copy of *Chance* on Friday by rail.

To Warrington Dawson

Text MS Duke; Randall 137

<div align="right">[letterhead: Capel House]</div>

<div align="right">17 Aug. 1911.</div>

My dear Dawson.

I am no end sorry to have acted tactlessly. I had not read the whole book. I knew that G[ibbon] was no negrophile in the common meaning of the word.[2] Neither is he a man *"out after dollars"*. I quite understand all you say and so will he when I show him your letter (he's in Paris just now)—and pray believe in my most genuine regard for your opinions, for your feelings for your judgement and your sincerity.

In fact my dear fellow neither he nor I would have had anything to say had you printed Your letter to me as an article, or made a most condemnatory analysis of the book in your paper. Your hands are free now.

I would have written at once but there is a most tragic affair going on in our house. A friend arrived last *Sat* for a week end[3]—and now is lying

[1] When Conrad wrote to Pinker on [28? July 1908], Garnett was about to look at the early stages of 'Razumov'.

[2] The OED examples signify activity in rather than sympathy for the cause of African or African-American rights. On the strength of his upbringing in Charleston, S.C., and his few months in East Africa, Dawson considered himself an authority on the 'Negro problem'. He had taken exception to Perceval Gibbon and his novel *Margaret Harding*, a South African story of friendship across the lines of race and gender, which was dedicated 'To Jessie and Joseph Conrad'. The book was controversial in South Africa itself: P. D. Williams (ed.), Introduction, *Margaret Harding* (Cape Town and Johannesburg: David Philip, 1983), p. xxiii.

[3] In Norman Douglas's version of events, he was already very ill: 'There came a lucid moment when I thought: this must end. All my friends being out of town, I went to

dangerously ill in our house. The worry and strain drives* me almost crazy. There are also other circumstances which make this affair particularly poignant.[1] I can say no more just now. Pray pardon the delay in answering your letter, and believe always in my inalterable* feelings of friendship and regard.

<div style="text-align:center">Yours in haste</div>

<div style="text-align:right">J. Conrad.</div>

Wife sends kindly greetings.

To John Galsworthy

Text MS Forbes; J-A, 2, 133

<div style="text-align:right">[letterhead: Capel House]
Friday 11 am. [18 August 1911][2]</div>

Dearest Jack.

Providence is looking after me with a vengeance. Last Saturday Norman Douglas (who had returned to London from Italy 4 days before) came for a week end. But he arrived in a state of high fever and hardly able to stand. We put him to bed and sent for a doctor. On Monday we sent for a nurse (after Jessie and I had been up with him for two nights and a day). To day he does not recognise anybody, his temp after most appalling ups and downs has reached 105°.—and here we are.

His "oldest friend" (a solicitor in London) and his brother in Scotland[3] return evasive answers to my letters and telegrams. They say they are "shocked". And the "friend" has bolted off somewhere north for his holiday without sending me his address. He is "very sorry".

All we know *for certain* of D's illness is that it is not typhoid.[4] At first we thought it was a heat-stroke. Now we doubt it. The doctor says—how can I tell? There are no other symptoms but fever. And suppose it is brain fever. He can't be moved and indeed where could one move him? One can hear him moaning and muttering all over the house. We keep Jack outside all day—or as much as we can. Borys begins to look hollow-eyed—his room is just across the passage—six feet from the sick

Joseph Conrad near Ashford – or rather found myself, somehow or other, at his home' (Holloway, p. 185).
[1] Douglas's apparent friendlessness, the absence of his young sons, his efforts to sustain a literary career?
[2] The Friday after Douglas's arrival.
[3] William George Fraser Nelson, Douglas's legal adviser and the mainstay of his sons, and John William Edward James Douglas, 16th laird (Holloway, *passim*).
[4] It was malaria, contracted that summer in Calabria.

man's door which is kept open for air. I've never seen Jessie look so strained. She knows what it means for all of us. Last week I haven't written a line. My head swims—and in truth I am as near distraction as is consistent with sanity.

Should he die I shall have to bury him I suppose. But even if he recovers (which we still hope for) it will be a matter of weeks. All my work, all our plans and our little pitiful hopes seem knocked on the head. I have seen and tended white men dying in the Congo[1] but I have never felt so abominably helpless as in this case. As Jessie said last night—this is like a nightmare.

Well—I felt I must tell you. For the rest I've sold the MS of *Outcast* to an American collector for £30.[2] This will come extremely handy now, or else I wouldn't have sold it for the price. In pursuance of your Suggestion I have made inquiries as to the *Worcester* in the Education Dept. A man called Hornell—a friend of Lady Ritchie.[3] He assured me it was a very good school generally and a good preparation for any technical course in the future.

I think this is all—rather catastrophic isn't it? Love to You both.

<div style="text-align:center">Yours ever</div>

<div style="text-align:right">J Conrad.</div>

To Henry Mills Alden
Text MS Morgan; Unpublished

<div style="text-align:right">[letterhead: Capel House]
23 Augst 1911.</div>

Dear Mr Alden.

Many thanks for Your friendly letter. At present I am engaged on a rather long novel; but I hope to have time before the end of the year to take up one or two subjects (for short stories) now reposing at the back of my head.

I need not tell you how highly I appreciate your request couched in such flattering terms.[4] Perhaps you will have the kindness to tell me (at

[1] Including Georges Antoine Klein (1863–1890), who had at least some part in the making of Kurtz (Sherry, *Conrad's Western World*, pp. 72–8).

[2] John Quinn: see the letter of 24 August.

[3] Anne Isabella, Lady Ritchie (1837–1919) wrote fiction and literary essays and edited the works of her father, William Makepeace Thackeray. Her husband, Sir Richmond, was Permanent Under Secretary at the India Office. W. W. Hornell was a Junior Examiner at the Board of Education.

[4] A request from its editor for contributions to *Harper's Magazine*.

your leisure) whether you would be disposed to consider a three-numbers story, say 12 to 15 thousand words.

Believe me, dear Mr Alden, with the highest consideration,

cordially yours

J. Conrad.

To Elsie Hueffer

Text MS Yale; Unpublished

[letterhead: Capel House]
24 Aug 1911.

My dear Señora.

We have been very much startled at your news.[1] We do hope all is well with you now and all your invalids on the high road to recovery. We had Douglas here ill with something like a heat stroke. It looked alarming for a few days. Jessie's rather done up—but as you know—she picks up again quickly. I have been simply distracted.

We had no idea you were being so severely tried; not a whisper reached us from Aldington; which is strange as news more or less like truth do travel over the country.[2]

Jessie sends her dear love to you and the chicks in which I hope I may be allowed to join. I write this for her (and for myself) as she's gone to Ashford to see Douglas.[3] You shall hear from her soon, and meantime she wishes to express her compunction at not having written at once. Do drop us a line as to you all. We trust you haven't been overstrained. This, since the invalids are better, is our immediate concern. Always dear Elsie

Your friend and servant

J Conrad.

[1] Estranged from Ford, who was in Germany with Violet Hunt, Elsie Hueffer lived on in Aldington with her daughters, who had both been ill. No doubt word from Germany had added to her miseries.

[2] The Conrads lived only four miles away.

[3] He had been moved to the hospital there on the 19th and was about to return for a few days at Capel House (Holloway, p. 186).

To John Quinn

Text MS NYPL; Unpublished

[letterhead: Capel House]
Thursday 24 Aug 1911.

Dear Mr Quinn.[1]

I am sending off to-day properly packed and registered two MS

An Outcast of the Islands	1895.	516 pp.
Freya of the Seven Isles	1911.	226 pp.

one of my earliest and the latest completed. I've declared the packet as of *no commercial value*, but have insured it with our post office for £60 as there's no saying what may happen at sea.

I regret not having been able to send you the MS of my first novel. We hunted it up but discovered at the last moment that the whole of Chap. ix was missing. However, apart from that, the MS of the *Outcast* is a much better specimen—tho' it is far, far from beautiful to look upon. *Freya* of course is cleaner.

I have joined to these two the MS of the suppressed preface to the *Nigger of the Narcissus*. The late Mʳ Henley insisted on publishing it in the New Review; but except for that it has not been put before the public.[2] It will never be published now, unless perhaps in a complete edition of my work—when that comes to pass. The little printed pamphlet I have distributed to a few friends and have enclosed a copy in the envelope containing the 11 pp of MS, which perhaps you may care to join to your collection as a sort of curiosity.

I have to thank you for your most obliging promptness in this affair in which our friend Miss Tobin has been good enough to act as intermediary. Believe me, dear Sir,

very faithfully yours

J. Conrad.

[1] John Quinn (1870–1924), the son of Irish immigrants, came from Ohio. As a New York lawyer, he had a highly lucrative practice in commercial and financial law, particularly regarding tariffs. As a supporter of the arts, he won an exemption for artists from sales taxes and built up a great collection of modern painting and sculpture. He also collected modern literary manuscripts, buying extensively from Conrad as he later did from Joyce and Pound; Eliot made him a present of the MS *Waste Land*. When Quinn auctioned off his Conradiana in 1923, several years after relations between patron and author had chilled, manuscripts and inscribed volumes bought for a total of $10,000 fetched $110,000.

[2] The Preface had made a second public appearance as 'The Art of Fiction' in *Harper's Weekly*, 13 May 1905; there was also the pamphlet mentioned below, which appeared in 1902 in a private edition of 100 copies. The 1914 Doubleday, Page edition of the novel was the Preface's first appearance in book form.

To Warrington Dawson
Text MS Duke; Randall 138

[Capel House]
Friday. [August? 1911][1]

My dear Warrington Dawson

Just a word to say that the negotiation with Progrès "a abouti"—
thanks to your friendly offices, tact, wisdom and diplomacy. What could
be more admirable than your speeches to Mme D[emachy]!

Yours is a jolly letter. What activity, what go there is in you. What
mental alertness. You are a wonderful fellow. Yes. You can do anything
you like I believe. And why I should be supposed to be in the way I want
to know. *Your* individuality will make your work. When you touch Africa
you shall make it yours—and yours will be better no doubt than
mine—and at any rate very different—not so much in the shadows as
the *H[eart] of D[arkness]* is.

Marwood sends his regards.

Au revoir—a bientôt

Yours

J Conrad.

To Norman Douglas
Text MS Texas; Unpublished

[letterhead: Capel House]
[early September 1911][2]

My dear Douglas.

We are no end sorry to hear of the return of the fever. This looks like
malaria. Let us know how you get on.

Yours

J. C.

[1] The date '24-8-11' given by Randall is not in Conrad's hand; 24 August, moreover,
was a Thursday. Conrad was negotiating with Mme Demachy, editor of *Progrès*, in
March; nevertheless, he may have negotiated again about the final arrangements for
publishing 'Typhoon' towards the end of the year.

[2] '7 Sept.' in Douglas's hand gives the date of reply; Douglas left Capel House on 19
August and was taken ill again in London (Holloway, p. 186).

To J. B. Pinker

Text MS Berg; Unpublished

[letterhead: Capel House]
13 Sept^{er} 1911.

Dear Sir.

I have acknowledged by card the receipt of cheque for £12 yesterday.[1] I am writing now to tell you first that I am extremely sorry at the pause in Chance. Not my fault in a sense. We had a terrible upset here—a friend coming for a week-end, falling suddenly and dangerously ill and giving us no end of anxiety. That affair over I felt quite unwell myself. Altogether a piece of bad luck. However I still hope we shall not be unduly late with Chance.

On M^r Gordon Bennet[t]'s personal instructions an interviewer of the N. Y. H[erald] asked me to receive him—which I consented to do.[2] He went away apparently satisfied with my amiability. Should the N. Y. H's people get restive I think I could write personally to M^r Bennett. That's of course in case of absolute necessity. But I trust it'll not be necessary.

I want also to inform you in a friendly way that I have arranged for the publication of my Reminiscences (E. R. articles) this autumn.[3] The vol: will be entitled *"A Personal Note"* or something of that kind. I think—in fact I am certain that it will *not* interfere with the sale of the novel. On the contrary. Those who will read the Personal Note will no doubt wish to see the novel. I am not so sure of the vice-versa but it may very well be. It will be a vol: of 43000 words, 5/- net. 20% roy. and I get £60 advance from M^r Nash.

What decided me to put out the work (or fragment) at this particular time were two considerations. The first purely personal, which I will not enter into at length, merely stating that I wished to explain (in a sense) how I came to write such a novel as *Under Western Eyes* (I shall say that much in the preface) so utterly unlike in subject and treatment from anything I had done before. That *Personal Note* will make it intelligible to such people—my public—who care for and attach some importance to my work. The second reason is that my eldest boy is joining this term the

[1] For 3,000 words of *Chance*, perhaps the first batch since 1 or 2 August?

[2] The interview appeared in the 'Sunday Magazine', 14 January, p. 3. The reporter's visit can be dated to 18 August by the references to a railway strike and the presence of a sick friend (i.e. Douglas).

[3] Eveleigh Nash's publication of *Some Reminiscences* was planned for 19 October but later postponed till January. Clearly Conrad understood his current arrangement with Pinker as applying only to fiction.

Nautical School *H. M. S. Worcester* and that I absolutely needed that amount of money to fit him out and pay the first term. It will just do it. Whatever you may think of my first incentive you'll see that the second had some force.

From a few words dropped by Gibbon when I saw him last I gather you have been annoyed by the Methuen muddle. Surely not with me! I didn't want to bother you with it at all. I telegraphed strongly to them as indeed I had a right to do. If M. imagine they are doing an author a favour by publishing him they are mistaken. At least I won't take it as a favour. It's true that in the first moment of irritation at such an instance of carelessness I told them that I would not return the proofs in hand till I had a complete set in my possession; but the very next day (at their request) I returned them the first batch and the day after the whole lot right up to the page where the omission occurred. When I got the amended proofs at last I didn't keep them more than 48 hours. There was no delay on my part. As far as you are concerned I must say that all through you have done everything possible to spare me all extra trouble in revising both text and proof. I state this so that there should be no doubt in your mind about my feelings in the matter.

The Chance copy will be coming in now as fast as I can write it.[1] I am feeling better. Will you tell me if the B'wood negociation* has come to anything?[2]

<div style="text-align:right">Yours faithfully</div>

<div style="text-align:right">J. Conrad.</div>

To John Galsworthy

Text MS Forbes; J-A, 2, 134[3]

<div style="text-align:right">[letterhead: Capel House]</div>
<div style="text-align:right">23 Sept 1911.</div>

My dearest Jack.

Yesterday at 5.30 I went on shore leaving Borys looking after me from the gangway grating of the *Worcester*. The painful part of it was that he had to join in spectacles. Almost at the last minute the medical

[1] On 14 September, Conrad wired: 'Proofs and letters just received. Yes breviary Hodder and Stoughton if they will agree advertise well and give Chance success' (Berg).

[2] Negotiations over 'Freya'.

[3] Leaving out all but the first sentence of paragraph one.

examination discovered his sight to be defective.[1] It was all right when he first went to school and if it had been watched the mischief might have been stopped perhaps by giving him glasses say at eleven years of age to wear for desk-work during a couple of years. It is my fault to a certain extent but I think still more of his headmaster in Luton. I had no warning of any sort, and somehow even the possibility of his becoming short-sighted never occurred to me. He has been playing his games, cycling quite expertly at night and so on. It came on gradually. Only last Easter a friend of his a Naval cadet came for the day and they amused themselves shooting at tins floating on the moat, and B shot quite as well as the other boy. However, here it is—a deplorable fact. We were both considerably upset and the boy shut himself up in his room and had a good cry. Next day I rushed him to Maidstone where there is a very good oculist (head of the Ophthalmic hospital). The only comfort is that we were still in time to preserve for him a normal eyesight—with glasses of course. I am thankful for that small mercy. It would have been awful to see him go through life peering through thick lenses. He is putting a good face on the matter and I have been chaffing him on his learned appearance in spectacles, but neither of us felt very lighthearted.

I spent an hour and a half on board. I was struck very favourably by the appearance of the boys both as to their physique and the faces. I must have looked at a hundred of them at least out of the full complement of 158. The instructors are all Naval petty-officers. There are seven masters. I had a long talk with the head-master and liked him very well. He came up on deck with me and was very nice to the boy. M^r May, the Chief Officer promised me to put him through his course of drill and seamanship instruction exactly as if there were nothing the matter with his eyes. Of course he can't expect now to get any of the many prizes given by various shipping companies. Were he ever so proficient it would not be fair to the other boys; but that does not trouble me much as long as he gets a first-class leaving certificate at the end of two or 2 1/2 years.

Poor Mons. B looked to me a very small and lonely figure on that enormous deck in that big crowd where he didn't know a single soul. It is an immense change for him. Yes. He did look a small boy. I couldn't make up my mind to leave him and at last I made rather a bolt of it. I can't get him out of my eyes. However there are over twenty new boys

[1] For Borys Conrad's account of this time, see *My Father*, pp. 73–9. Set down almost sixty years after the event, Borys's recollection that his myopia was diagnosed before the interview with Captain Barker (letter of [1 or 8 August]) must be wrong.

and all their hammocks are slung together aft on the port side of the lower deck so he shall have some companions in the first few days of misery. I went ashore in the 14 oared second cutter and I have never seen a nicer boat's-crew. Having more than an hour to wait in Maidstone I wrote a letter to B which I am certain it must have comforted him to receive this morning.

To day putting away some things in his room I discovered carefully preserved all the postcards dear Ada used to send him when he was ill with scarlet fever six years ago or more in London.[1] It would be kind, it would be very dear of both, or either, of you to drop him a few words in the course of the next week or so. Cadet A. B. Conrad. H.M.S. Worcester. Greenhithe. Kent.

I haven't been very bright these last 2 months. I don't think I have written more than 10 thou: words in all that time. This is very bad. I hope to make a start soon for the time is running out. The novel[2] is advertised for the 5[th] Oct. and the Rem: will come out a fortnight later. Our dear love to you both

<div style="text-align:center">Yours ever</div>

<div style="text-align:right">J Conrad.</div>

To John Quinn
Text MS NYPL; Unpublished

<div style="text-align:right">[letterhead: Capel House]
25 Sept 1911.</div>

Dear Mr Quinn.

Many thanks for your friendly and interesting letter. I have heard a long time ago of your noble collection of modern MS[3] and am very proud of having a place in it.

The MS of *Under Western Eyes* will have to be checked and arranged, being in a state of great confusion and scattered in various receptacles. It consists of upwards of 1300 pp and contains a great deal more text than has appeared in print. I have been cutting down that novel ruthlessly. The full copy forms an enormous pile. Almost twice the size of the *Outcast* MS.

You are right in your conclusion that *Freya* has not been published yet. I propose to publish that story in book-form next spring together

[1] November and December 1905. [2] *Under Western Eyes.*
[3] He had already built strong collections of Yeats, Synge, Lady Gregory, George Moore, 'Æ', and William Morris.

with two other longish stories: *The Secret-Sharer* and *A Smile of Fortune*. It will make a moderately thick vol; but Freya by herself would have been too slender.

It occurs to me, in this connection, that should you care to include the MSS of the two companion stories to *Freya* in your present proposal, I suppose that the same terms as for our first transaction would not seem to you exorbitant. I base my suggestion on the number of pages which in that case would amount to a full *1600 pp* at least. You would be then in possession of two MS novels of *750 pp* and *1300 pp* respectively[1] and one set of three MS stories of say *620 pp*.

I am ignorant of the manner in which MSS are preserved in a notable collection like yours. But taking the three stories (Freya & two more) as *One MS* the above will give you three substantial Conrad items for the catalogue at the average outlay of £40 each.

However pray don't think you have fallen upon a shark. I shall dispatch you the *Under Western Eyes* by the end of this month anyhow.

Miss Tobin has been staying with us for a week lately. I am dedicating the novel to her. The date of pubon is the 5th Oct and I think it's the same on your side.[2] A small vol of personal reminiscences will follow in a fortnight or so. You will allow me to send you a signed copy as a small token of my regard. Believe me, dear Sir,

very sincerely yours

J. Conrad.

To John Galsworthy

Text MS Forbes; Unpublished

[letterhead: Capel House]
28 Sept. 1911.

My dearest Jack.

You are great dears Ada and you to have written to the boy. I asked you because that day you two were the only people he spoke of asking me if You knew where he was going and remarking that he had not seen either of you for some years. You seem to know him better than I do and I can only hope that the confidence you have in his good sense will always be justified. I have had a note from the head-master telling me

[1] Quinn wrote on the MS: 'Western Eyes 1300 + 2 short stories 400 = 1600 +' and identified the novels as '(Outcast)' and '(Western Eyes)'. The MS of *An Outcast* is now in the Rosenbach; as Conrad reported on 24 August, it has 516 pages, not the 750 cited here.

[2] Harper & Brothers published it on the 19th.

that on examination (last Sat, I suppose) he had a place which gives him a "very good start". I heard yesterday from the captain, just a line, to let me know that he had "settled down comfortably". From himself we had a letter and two pcards, the last of which contained only the words: "I have been aloft yesterday". So everything seems all right.

My dearest Jack I am bitterly ashamed to hang on to you so unconscionably. But what can I do? In the last 7 weeks I wrote only 4.000 w of *Chance* and 3000 w preface for the Reminiscences. I can't depend on myself for any amount of work in any given time. It's a very cruel feeling. Still I hope.

The novel of course is Western Eyes in book form. I haven't an idea what reception that sort of thing is likely to get. Of *Chance* I have 60 000w—all but—written; such as it is; of which about 45 since last april.[1] I shall have a desperate try to start on again. Of course there is also a thick *vol* of short stories written since my illness. So, after all, I have done something.

I am dead lame just now but not in pain unless I stand or walk. Otherwise but for a silly cough I feel fairly well.

Our dear love.

Yours ever

J. Conrad.

To Warrington Dawson

Text MS Duke; Randall 139

[letterhead: Capel House]
30 Sept '11

My dear Warrington Dawson

Just a line on this scrap of paper to thank you for your letter which gave me immense pleasure and to thank you still more for your friendliness to my boy. He joined the school-ship just a week ago and you shall hear from him before long.

[1] On 15 September the Sunday editor of the *Herald* wrote to Pinker acknowledging a first instalment of about 75,000 words and asking when the rest would arrive (TS Berg). On 19 June, Conrad, who was unlikely to understate his achievement, had reached a tally of 47,000 words, new and old. Beyond that date, too many gaps and puzzles make it impossible to be sure whether either or neither September sum is right, but the rhythm of Conrad's work, the evidence of the MS, and his apologies to Pinker make his own figure of 60,000 words more plausible. See also the letters of [21 July?] and 13 September, which provide unreliable evidence for swelling the total by a few thousand words.

I am no end flattered by the Princesse's appreciation of the Duel[1] and much honoured by the gracious invitation. Please say so at a fitting opportunity. It looks to me as tho' You were determined to make me a success in the *grand monde* in which you move. I am instructing Methuen's to send you a copy of Western Eyes due to appear on the 5[th] Oct. You shall also have a little later on a small vol of Reminiscences which will be published by Nash in 3 weeks or so.

I am only so so. Can't work. Wife sends her friendly regards.

Tout à Vous

J. Conrad.

To Stephen Reynolds
Text MS Berg; Unpublished

[letterhead: Capel House]
Saturday. [30? September 1911][2]

My dear Reynolds.

I have devoured the prawns with infinite thankfulness and a great appreciation of their goodness and intense admiration for your benevolence which prompted you to send them to us. I don't know whether You will take it as a compliment but there is something Christianlike in it—a touch of love and charity (I don't mean it in the eleemosynary sense) and a picturesquely evangelistic aspect—distribution of fishes (*not* in the scientific sense) almost as unexpected as a miracle. (The loaf I have managed to provide). In my state of dreamy repletion (the miracle was curried for my lunch) Your figure acquires—what with your remoteness in space and time and your occupations of fishing and preaching[3]—an Apostolic and en-haloed aspect. Is it possible that without knowing it I have been, I am, in communion with the Peter of a new dispensation in whom our future creed shall be founded on as on a rock?

Yes O! Apostle-like man! I ought to have written to you months ago. But you know that I am one who is possessed by a dumb devil. No doubt if he could be driven out his shape would resemble that of a swine.[4] But

[1] Randall identifies her as the Princesse Lucien Murat (née Marie de Rohan-Chabot); Dawson was staying at the Breton chateau of her parents, the Duc and Duchesse de Rohan.

[2] The month before *Under Western Eyes* came out 'on the fifth' of October, but 'two months, nearly' since the arrival of Douglas threw *Chance* off course.

[3] The gospel of social renewal.

[4] For the Biblical references in this letter see, e.g., Mark 6.36–44 (the loaves and fishes), Matthew 13.18 (Peter), Mark 5.1–13 (the Gadarene swine).

he cannot be driven out. Sometimes he slumbers and then my tongue is untied—but not much. No. Never very much. And that's no joke since I have to live by my loquacity. Thirteen vols in 15 years is not enough loquacity to live on.

For two months, nearly, I haven't written a line; brooding in the blackest depths of utter impotence. Voilà. It seems to be passing off now; but I assure you that the simplest letter cost me a day's effort—and such an effort that no mental torture could be equal to it.

I have read the two July articles just before that period began.[1] Evidently my dearest boy it *is* your synthesis, of course sketched in merely. When one is in complete agreement with the underlying feelings of an expressed opinion, view or theory, it is difficult to write at length about it. You know that I have a strong conviction of your soundness. I think that yours is a good morality and a good philosophy—and good too in the sense that it is now very much wanted not only as a remedy but as an antidote. More I wouldn't know how to say. But I imagine you don't need a more extended assurance of being understood as far as my capacity can guage* your meaning. Glad to hear the Seems So vol is coming out.[2] My novel appears on the fifth. I shall dispatch you a copy at the earliest moment. Our love to you

<div align="right">Yours affect^{ly}</div>

<div align="right">J Conrad.</div>

To Ford Madox Ford
Text Violet Hunt's copy, Cornell; Unpublished

<div align="right">Capel House
Orlestone, N^r Ashford.
Friday night. [6 October 1911?][3]</div>

My dear Ford,

I was touched by your congratulatory telegram and yet it might have been ironic too! That sort of recognition is the consecration of failure, for even talent must be appreciated by the standards of the world we live in. On receiving the gift I glanced back and what I said most clearly then is that there hasn't been a book published for 3 years![4] And then I understood how much I deserved the recompense.

[1] Untraced: Reynolds contributed to a broad range of newspapers and magazines.
[2] The volume of political commentary written with Bob and Tom Woolley, his friends and fellow workers.
[3] A reply to a congratulatory telegram about *Under Western Eyes*, published on Thursday, 5 October?
[4] Since *A Set of Six*, October 1908.

All this is for your ears only. It would be in the highest degree unbecoming for me to voice such sentiments. It would be ungrateful too! I say that seriously. It would be. It is only to you you know my manner of speech so well, that this may be said—*le fin fond de la pensée*[1]—without fear of being misunderstood.

I am living in a state of savage exasperation with myself, unfit to talk, unfit to write. And this too you'll may be* understand. I am writing, however, spasmodically, with long intervals of absolute dumbness. *Quel enfer!* I composed one or two letters to you which have remained unwritten, on which, really you may congratulate yourself. I hear of you—favourable reports—from M[arwood] who comes over now and then.

<div align="center">Yours</div>

<div align="right">J. Conrad.</div>

To Arthur Symons

Text MS Lohf; Unpublished

<div align="right">[letterhead: Capel House]
Saturday. [14 or 21? October
1911][2]</div>

My dear Symons.

Sorry for delay; it was not my fault. It was very good of you but as a matter of fact I haven't a copy of the play;[3] and I very much doubt whether I have the MS: Will you kindly explain to Mrs Lyttelton.[4] I am delighted to hear you have written both verse and prose since we last saw each other. I do hope You will have good weather for your visit to Wales. Drop me a line when You come back.

<div align="center">Yours affectionately</div>

<div align="right">J. Conrad.</div>

[1] 'Innermost thoughts'.
[2] Letterhead one: Symons went to Wales late in October (Beckson, p. 275).
[3] *One Day More?* Cf. letters of 21 and 29 August 1908.
[4] The aristocratic playwright Edith Lyttelton, Symons's neighbour in the country.

To John Galsworthy
Text MS Forbes; J-A, 2, 135

[letterhead: Capel House]
1911
15 Oct. 11 pm

My dearest Jack.

Yes. There is no arguing against what you say. One could attempt to explain certain things but it would be an unprofitable occupation.

You know there are about 30000 words more than the printed text.[1] Revising while ill in bed I am afraid I have struck out whole pages recklessly. The other day I looked at the MS: 1357 pp averaging about 120 words per page. There are passages which should have remained. I wasn't in a fit state to judge them. Well—it's done now and let the critics make what they can of it. I have ordered no press-cuttings, not because I am afraid of them but that I am really indifferent to what may be said—or left unsaid. However Marwood sent me the review out of the Morning Post which he takes in.[2] It was all right; but there was a passage in it which is incomprehensible unless meant as a hint that I, being a Jew, am especially fit to hold the balance between East & West![3] I believe that some time ago that preposterous Papist Belloc has been connecting me with Father Abraham, whether to hurt me or to serve me, or simply because he's an idiot—I don't know.[4] Anyhow I heard it from somebody a year or more ago. It's an absurd position to be in for I trust I have no contemptible prejudices against any kind of human beings— and yet it isn't pleasant to be taken out of one's own skin, as it were, by an irresponsible chatterer. I wrote a friendly note to the Critic giving him my surmise as to the passage in question and begging him should he hear any statement of the kind to contradict it positively.

[1] See Higdon and Sheard, 'Conrad's "Unkindest Cut"'.

[2] 12 October: reprinted in *Critical Heritage*, pp. 231–3.

[3] This passage actually refers to the narrator: 'The professor, we cannot help fancying, must have been a Jew, holding the balance between the West and the East. However that may be, he does succeed in making us see a difference so large that it requires a large mind to appreciate its existence. Those of us who are but shallow observers of national distinction are apt to strain at a gnat and swallow a camel.'

[4] While indulging exuberantly in fiction, controversy, travel, politics, and wine, Hilaire Belloc (1870–1953) found time to be literary editor of the *Morning Post*. Conrad suspected Belloc's hand in the offending review because he had written an unsigned notice of *A Set of Six* for the same paper, but also because his anti-Dreyfusard obsession with the Jews was notorious. A connection with the patriarch Abraham would imply Jewish ancestry.

I have been revising the Rem^ces book. I don't know when it will appear. I think that the evil spell is broken at last. I've just written 500 words of Chance in a couple of hours. It's about time. Over two months—indeed nearly three without (practically) a line!

Well. Bonsoir dear Jack. Our dear love to you both

Yours ever

J. Conrad.

To Norman Douglas
Text MS Colgate; Unpublished

[Capel House]
Monday night [16 or 23 October 1911][1]

My dear Douglas

I was expecting to hear you were coming here when Jessie told me that you were already in Leigh[2]—settled for writing, but apparently with no address other than the post office.

I don't know if she has written to you yet asking you to come over. Anyway I hope you will come whenever you feel like it. I've had a bad time of it as usual. I haven't written a line all Aug^st Sept. and half Oct. I am only fit to die—for this state of nervous exasperation with myself unfits me for this world. I feel ill too now and again. Queer sensations. But that's between ourselves. I've got to stick out my time to the end. I have begun again to write but of course I have to pay the bank overdraft first. Never, never a moment to breathe and forget. Never. Look here you helped me once—perhaps you will do it again. I don't want to ask M'wood and Gibbon is hard up I happen to know. If you would send me 10 pounds I will repay you in two instalments in the course of Nov. I expect also to sell another MS in the states but that takes time.

Your copy of West: Eyes is lying in store here till you come. I don't suppose you yearn to read the damn'd thing now while you are having lots of writing to do. Have you any news as to publication of *Tunis*.[3]

I am off to bed—done up after writing since 9. It's one o'clock now—Tuesday.

Yours ever

J. Conrad.

[1] Conrad started writing again around the middle of the month. Douglas answered this letter on the 27th, and Conrad wrote again on [30 October].

[2] With his twelve-year-old friend Eric, Douglas spent two months in rooms at Leigh-on-Sea, Essex.

[3] Published in 1912 as *Fountains in the Sand*.

Jessie went to bed to night feeling seedy. Another terror added to life. I am by no means easy about her.

To Edward Garnett
Text MS Indiana; G. 248

[letterhead: Capel House]
20 Oct 1911.[1]

My dear Edward.

I don't understand your picturesque allusions to packing spinach into the saucepan and the hell broth that's supposed to be the result of that culinary operation. There's just about as much or as little *hatred* in this book as in the Outcast of the Islands for instance.[2] Subjects lay* about for anybody to pick-up. I have picked up this one. And that's all there is to it. I don't expect you will believe me. You are so russianised my dear that you don't know the truth when you see it—unless it smells of cabbage-soup when it at once secures your profoundest respect.[3] I suppose one must make allowances for your position of Russian Embassador* to the Republic of Letters. Official pronouncements ought to be taken with a grain of salt and that is how I shall take your article in the Nation[4] which I hope to see to morrow evening when the carrier comes back from Ashford. But it is hard after lavishing a "wealth of tenderness" on Tekla and Sophia, to be charged with the rather low

[1] Handwriting of a later period and an incompatible date dissociate the note at Indiana headed 'Tuesday' from its current envelope, postmarked 19 October 1911, a Thursday. A letter of this date, therefore, has vanished: according to the catalogue of the Garnett sale, 24 April 1928, it was about arrangements to meet.

[2] Conrad's reply apart, clues to the contents of Garnett's letter have two sources: his review of *Under Western Eyes* in the *Nation*, 21 October, pp. 140–2 (reprinted in *Critical Heritage*, pp. 237–9), and his annotations in a copy of the novel now in the Free Library, Philadelphia. David Leon Higdon discusses these annotations in 'Edward's Garnett's copy of *Under Western Eyes*', *The Conradian*, 10 (1985), 139–43.

[3] The annotations include comments such as '*not* good: *not* Russian' (on p. 252) and 'good picture – Russian!' (on p. 287).

[4] In the review Garnett finds a few faults and many virtues: 'If to Western eyes his material seems to be eked out here and there with guess-work, to be fragmentary and puzzling, the artist has wrought it into meaning curves and a highly original pattern.' Garnett does discuss the question of Russianness: 'The artistic intensity of the novel lies, however, less in the remarkable drawing of characteristic Russian types than in the atmospheric effect of the dark national background.' Writing for publication, Garnett does not accuse Conrad of hating everything Russian; rather, the animus is directed at specific groups, the aristocrats and the conspirators: 'There is something almost vitriolic in Mr. Conrad's scathing rejection of the shibboleths of humanitarian lovers of their kind'.

trick of putting one's hate into a novel.[1] If You seriously think that I
have done that then my dear fellow let me tell you that you don't know
what the accent of hate is. Is it possible that You haven't seen that in this
book I am concerned with nothing but ideas, to the exclusion of every-
thing else, with no arrière pensée of any kind. Or are you like the Italians
(and most women) incapable of conceiving that anybody ever should
speak with perfect detachment, without some subtle hidden purpose, for
the sake of what is said, with no desire of gratifying some small personal
spite—or vanity.[2]

As to discussing Russia it's the most chimeric of enterprises since it is
there for anyone to look at. "La Russie c'est le néant" Prince Bismarck
said in 1864—and forthwith proceeded to prove it by 20 years of the
most contemptuous policy towards that "Great Power".[3] C'est le néant.
Anybody with eyes can see it.

And anyhow if hatred there were it would be too big a thing to be put
into a 6/- novel. This too might have occurred to you, if you had
condescended to look beyond the literary horizon where all things
sacred and profane are turned into copy.

> Yours ever
>
> J. Conrad.

To Olivia Rayne Garnett

Text MS Indiana; G. 250

[letterhead: Capel House]

20 Oct 1911

Dear Miss Garnett[4]

You are a good critic. That girl does not move. No excuse can be
offered for such a defect but there is an explanation. I wanted a pivot for

[1] In the review, Garnett finds 'the admirable figure of Sophia Antonovna' to be
evidence that Conrad's 'merciless picture' of revolutionary politics is not entirely
'vindictive art'.

[2] In his Author's Note (1920), Conrad refers to the 'scrupulous impartiality'
demanded by his project.

[3] Manipulating Russia, in his quest for European hegemony, sometimes as an ally,
sometimes as an enemy, but always as a pawn. No friend to Poland either, Prince
Otto von Bismarck (1815–1898), future Chancellor of Germany, was Minister-
President and Foreign Minister of Prussia when he made his scornful remark during
the Schleswig-Holstein crisis; he had been ambassador to Russia between 1859 and
1862. The association of Russia with blankness or nothingness figures in *Under
Western Eyes* and 'Autocracy and War'.

[4] The Bobbs-Merrill edition of the letters to Garnett identifies the recipient as
Constance Garnett; the Nonesuch, as Olivia Rayne Garnett. Either woman might
well have written to Conrad about *Under Western Eyes*, but in MS the salutation reads

the action to turn on. She had to be the pivot. And I had to be very careful because if I had allowed myself to make more of her she would have killed the artistic purpose of the book: the development of a single mood. It isn't that I was afraid or ignorant of her possibilities. Indeed they were very tempting. But it had to be a performance on one string. It had to be. You may think such self-imposed limitation a very stupid thing. But something of the kind must be done or else novel-writing becomes a mere debauch of the imagination. No doubt if I had taken another line the book would have been richer. But what I aimed at this time was an effect of virtuosity before anything else—and even to the exclusion of everything else. Still I need not have made Miss Haldin a mere peg as I am sorry to admit she is. Result of over caution.

Your kind appreciation of the book gives me great pleasure and I am glad you think it is true—as [. . .][1] goes. I am quite aware it does not go very far. But the fact is that I know extremely little of Russians. Practically nothing. In Poland we have nothing to do with them. One knows they are there. And that's disagreeable enough. In exile the contact is even slighter if possible if more unavoidable.[2] I crossed the Russian frontier at the age of ten.[3] Not having been to school then I never knew Russian. I could not tell a Little Russian from a Great Russian to save my life. In the book as you must have seen I am exclusively concerned with ideas.

Yes. I had a letter and some books from Mr Lutoslawski.[4] I ought to have written to him before—tho' really and truly I don't know what he wants with me. I don't understand him in the least. His illumination seems to me a very naïve and uninteresting thing. Does he imagine I am likely to become his disciple? He worries and bores me. But I won't tell him that when I write (as I must do in common decency) because I believe he is a good man—though confoundedly inquisitive.

We had a letter from Elsie[5] the other day. She seems quite well now. We don't see much of her because of the distance. But we had Xna[6] staying with us for a few days during the holidays.

'Miss' rather than 'Mrs'. Olivia (or Olive) Garnett (1871–1957) was Edward's sister. She published *Petersburg Tales* (1900). As a friend of Stepniak and other political refugees, she was familiar with the background to Conrad's novel.

[1] A hiatus caused by turning the page: 'as [far as it] goes'.

[2] In 1899, Conrad pleaded his inability to join Cunninghame Graham on the platform of an anti-Tsarist 'peace meeting' because 'Il y aura des Russes. Impossible!' (*Letters*, 2, p. 158).

[3] Early in 1868, he crossed into Galicia, then under Austrian rule.

[4] A reply to Conrad's letter of 2 July?

[5] Hueffer. [6] Christina Hueffer, her daughter.

Thanks once more for your friendly and very interesting letter. I assure you I am very sensible to all the kind things you say of my work. Believe me with great regard

<div style="text-align:center">Yours faithfully</div>

<div style="text-align:right">J. Conrad.</div>

To Warrington Dawson
Text MS Ozarks; Randall 142

<div style="text-align:right">[letterhead: Capel House]
21 Oct. 1911.</div>

My dear fellow

You have warmed me through and through with your wonderfully appreciative letter.[1] I just drop you these few lines to thank you without delay for a great and rare pleasure. I have been beastly seedy for days. Wife has told you—didn't she.[2] I am most grateful for your invitation so truly brotherly but I can't jump at it (as I would like to do) just now.

Mille amities. The house sends its love.

<div style="text-align:center">Yours always</div>

<div style="text-align:right">J. Conrad</div>

To J. B. Pinker
Text MS Berg; Unpublished

<div style="text-align:right">[letterhead: Capel House]
Sat. [21 October 1911][3]</div>

Dear Sir.

Thanks for cheque (£16) which reached me safely to-day.[4]

I was just informed that a certain actor manager thinks of approaching me for rights of dramatisation of Razumov.[5]

[1] About *Under Western Eyes*, 17 October: Randall (pp. 140–2) provides the whole text from a carbon copy. Given the dispute with Garnett, Conrad might especially have liked the praise of his political evenhandedness, 'the advantage of many years of detachment from it all'.

[2] Her letter of 11 October is also in Randall, pp. 139–40. In it, she passes on Conrad's regrets for being unable to visit Dawson in France.

[3] Between the *Standard* review and the 24th, when Conrad forwarded Laurence Irving's letter.

[4] Evidence of renewed work on *Chance*.

[5] Laurence Sidney Brodribb Irving (died 1914), son of Sir Henry, wrote to Conrad on the 18th (MS Berg). After reading a review of *Under Western Eyes*, Irving had sent for the book, thinking that it would make a powerful drama. He thought Razumov might be just as good a part as Raskolnikov, the role he had taken in a recent stage

The idea is rather odious to me. But I have to look at this practically. Will you tell me if there is a chance of making anything by such a transaction? Is it worth while? Pray drop me a line on receipt as I shall very likely hear something on Tuesday and want to answer according to your advice. If yes I shall write to him accordingly and refer him to you for negociations*.

<div align="center">Yours</div>

<div align="center">J. C.</div>

Have you seen the *Standard* of the 20th? Colvin writes me there's a good review by H. Walpole.[1] I understand Garvin intends to write himself a long review for the *Observer*.[2] I hope he will do it. By the by I had an absurd letter from F Unwin which I'll forward to you. Its mislaid now. I am going on with the copy.—

To J. B. Pinker
Text MS Berg; Unpublished

<div align="right">[Capel House]
Tuesday. [24 October 1911][3]</div>

Dear Sir.

Thanks for your letter which I answer at once on this scrap of paper,[4] enclosing the communication from Laurence Irving. You will see for yourself how the matter stands. I wrote to him saying that I was willing and asking him to drop me a line as soon as he has read the book.

If this takes shape I'll have no hand in the work at all. Let him do it. I can see a play in the novel quite well but to make L. I. see it in my way is a job which I would not like to tackle. So from the artistic point of view there would be nothing to settle. The business end you will look after of course. I must concentrate on Chance now entering upon its last lap. And it will be the very devil. I am going to send you on Friday morning ab. 5 or perhaps 6 thou: words of copy. You won't mind if I ask you for

version of *Crime and Punishment*. Irving, who had translated Gorky's *The Lower Depths*, had spent three years in Russia.

[1] Hugh Walpole (1884–1941), the novelist and critic, began his career as a reviewer for the *Standard*. He published a short book on Conrad in 1916 and came to be on good terms with him. In the unsigned review (20 October, p. 5), Walpole praised Conrad's novel for its Dostoevskian qualities.

[2] J. L. Garvin (1868–1947) edited the *Observer* from 1908 to 1942. His review did not appear.

[3] Received 'October 1911': the first Tuesday after Irving's letter.

[4] Paper originally destined for *Chance*: the sheet bears the cancelled number '532'.

cheque on receipt; I have had a stoppage for a good 2 months and consequently I am bothered by a small overdraft at the bank which I must cover at once. Thanks for returned rough copy.

<div align="center">Yours faithfully</div>

<div align="right">J. Conrad.</div>

To J. B. Pinker

Text MS Berg; Unpublished

<div align="right">[letterhead: Capel House]
[25 October? 1911][1]</div>

Dear Mr Pinker.

I send you three thou: words of copy and would be glad to have cheque as I explained in my last. I hope to have another 2 thou by Thursday night ready which I shall sent* on by rail.

I should suggest that beginning with this batch you should simply hold the rough copy till the book is done when I can correct the lot in one day or say two days. You must understand that the uncorrected copy is (barring misprints) fit for the printer anyhow. It *is* the novel. I contemplate no alterations in it for *serial* at any rate. I may touch it up for book form later on.

So from p 285† please have no clean copy made till we reach the end when I shall correct that portion in one lot and then the clean copy can be finished.

I am feeling better. No word from Irving yet. Are you feeling for an opening of serialising Chance in UK? Every little would help. We must squeeze every penny out of that book for I shall want a couple of months' reading for my Mediterranean novel of which I am already thinking at odd times.

<div align="center">Yours</div>

<div align="right">J. C.</div>

†the present batch 285–299

[1] The next letter after [24 October], the request for speedy payment written on what would have been f. 532? According to a note on the MS, f. 531 corresponded to TS p. 299, the last of the batch delivered here. Taken with the one announced for 'Thursday night' (the following day), this delivery would come close to the 5 or 6,000 words promised for Friday the 27th. On [30 October?], Conrad said he was working at a thousand words a day.

To Carlo Placci

Text MS Mursia; Angeleri (with facsimile)

[letterhead: Capel House]
26 Oct 1911.

My dear Sir.[1]

Pardon this delay in acknowle[d]ging your most amiable note and the newspaper which reached me safely.

Unluckily, as is too often the case with me, I was rather unwell. These are the first words I trace on my return to my writing-table.

I must thank you sincerely for the article of such friendly tone. I am very sensible to the generosity of your appreciation tempering the most just criticism. On the great question of form there really is no defence to offer. An explanation I believe may be given. In that involved form of narrative which so often seduces me away from the straight path what I am looking for is the effect of the *living word*. That quest fascinates me against my better judgement. And yet you who know my work with such completeness—you know that I can do also the other thing. What leads me astray is the ineradicable conviction that it is in the living word que l'on saisit le mieux la forme du rêve. Therefore with stupid obstinacy I am always trying for the effect of the living word in the hope of coming as near as possible to that fleeting, ever elusive form.

You seem to have read not only every line ever written by me but also a good many lines written about me. I am surprised and charmed—and a little abashed too. Tout ça c'est si peu de chose—and the hour when all dreams must cease is approaching with disconcerting swiftness.

But my gratitude for the recognition of merit implied in your distinguished article is very real. Pray believe me

Very sincerely Yours

J. Conrad.

PS The Reminiscences are coming out early in January in a small volume. You will let me send you a copy in which I shall write your name and mine.

[1] Carlo Placci (1861–1941), a literary critic, musicologist, and poet, lived in Florence. He wrote articles on Conrad for the *Corriere della Sera* and *Il Marzocco*. On 3 November 1909 (MS Indiana), Violet Paget ('Vernon Lee') wrote to tell Conrad of Placci's interest, describing him as 'a well known Italian polyglot & critic'; she lent Placci her copy of *Nostromo*.

To J. B. Pinker

Text MS Berg; Unpublished

[Capel House]
Saturd[ay]
29 [28] Oct. [1911]¹

Dear Sir.

Thanks for cheque duly received this morning.

Herewith agreement with Tauchnitz which I have signed tho' as I have said before I dont care to be included in their collection.² English books are being sold on the continent now in English edition[s].

I would suggest that when Tauchnitz pays up you should let me have ten pounds instead of crediting the lot (less com:) to my acct. It would be very convenient just now if you can see your way to do so.

Thanks for taking the precaution of writing to New-York*. It will be all right³ but it is an anxious time with me.

Yours faithfully
J. Conrad.

To Norman Douglas

Text MS Macpherson; Unpublished

[letterhead: Capel House]
Monday morning [30 October?
1911]⁴

My dear fellow

Many thanks. I believe that Tauchnitz wants the novel for his library and if so I shall be able to repay you in a very few days.

I am sorry you are so discouraged. Don't give way to the feeling of having written yourself out. That will pass off and my dear it's really unreasonable to give the game up before its fairly begun. You have only published one book after all. We can't possibly tell how far you may be successful. At any rate you may just as well keep on with that as fold your hands. Colvin is always enquiring most tenderly about you. But as

¹ Saturday was the 28th. The 29th fell on a Saturday in 1910, but the Tauchnitz and New York references indicate 1911.

² In October 1907, Conrad made a vehement case against the Leipzig publisher and his paperback reprints of books in English (*Letters*, 3, pp. 497–8). The new proposal was for a continental edition of *Under Western Eyes*.

³ The serial of *Chance* in the *Herald*.

⁴ Holloway prints about half the text (p. 187); his suggested date, based on Douglas's circumstances, also matches Conrad's: the expected payment from Tauchnitz and the burst of effort on *Chance*.

you do not seem to care to let him do anything I did not keep him up to the mark. What is it precisely you would like? Anything is difficult to get but one could try. I am now a month behind with my novel and am pushing at 1.000 words a day just at present. It's absurd. It unfits me for seeing or talking with anybody, wife and kids included. But of course it won't last. Jess will be sending you the novel and 2 Nos of Eng[lis]h Rev. to read by this evening's post.

<div style="text-align: right">Yours ever</div>

<div style="text-align: right">J. Conrad</div>

To Henry James
Text MS Indiana; Unpublished

<div style="text-align: right">[letterhead: Capel House]</div>
<div style="text-align: right">[October? 1911][1]</div>

Cher et bon Maître[2]

Merci du beau cadeau. Il est bien vraiment beau. Depuis un an en pensant à Vous je me sentais attristé et effrayé. Je n'ai pas écrit. Car a quoi bon? Avec la meilleure volonté du monde on risque d'être importun. Et puis, il est trop naturel que mon affection (sentiment bien intime pour moi), Vous semble une chose lointaine et presque etrangère.

En lisant avec délices, cette petite oeuvre qui brille d'un éclat si doux j'ai pu pour un moment oublier la fuite des temps. Je me sentis rajeuni regaillardi dans le renouveau de mon admiration que* ne Vous a jamais manqué. Jamais. Comme Vous savez ramasser l'action et établir vos personnages dans toute leur subtile verité! Quelle vigeur étonnante et quelle delicatesse merveilleuse! Et dans ce petite* volume on a aussi le sentiment de légereté, de parfaite aisance. Ça semble fait en se jouant dans un moment de gaité un peu malicieuse. C'est charmant. Et c'est fort. Ah! Il n'y a que Vous; il n'y a que Vous!

J'envoie ceci au soins de Methuen Ltd (quelle sacré boutique mon Dieu!) car je ne sais pas ou Vous Vous trouvez en ce moment-ci[3] et cela me semble encore le plus court chemin pour vous trouver.

[1] Letterhead one: James's novel came out in October.
[2] There is no external sign of the recipient's identity, but the letter's context and tone make James the obvious choice. Few other writers would have earned Conrad's 'Cher et bon Maître'. Although not usually a Methuen author, James had taken *The Outcry*, a short work well-supplied with 'gaité un peu malicieuse' to that 'sacré boutique'. A copy of *The Outcry* was in the Hodgson sale of Conrad's books, 13 March 1925.
[3] James was dividing his time between London and Rye.

Croyez en mon inaltérable affection

<div style="text-align:center">Votre devoué</div>

<div style="text-align:right">J. Conrad</div>

Translation

Dear and good Master,

Thank you for the fine present. It is truly fine. Thinking of you for the last year, I've felt sad and apprehensive. I haven't written. What good would it do? With the best will in the world, one risks being tiresome. And then it's all too natural that my affection (a very intimate feeling for me) seems to you something distant and almost strange.

While reading delightedly this little work which shines with so soft a brightness, I have for a moment been able to forget the passage of time. I feel myself restored to youth, made fresh again by the renewal of the admiration for you that has never left me. Never. How you know the way to bring all the action together and establish your characters in all their subtle truth! What astonishing vigour and what marvellous delicacy. And in this little volume one also has a feeling of lightness, of perfect ease. It appears to be done playfully, in a moment of rather mischievous gaiety. It's charming, and it's strong. Ah, there is no one but you—no one!

I'm sending this care of Methuen's (my God, what a damnable shop!) because I don't know where you are at the moment, and that seems the shortest way of finding you.

With unalterable affection,

<div style="text-align:center">Your devoted</div>

<div style="text-align:right">J. Conrad</div>

To William Maas
Text MS Rosenbach; Unpublished

<div style="text-align:right">[letterhead: Capel House]
Wednesday [1 November 1911][1]</div>

Dear Mr Maas.

We shall expect you on Tuesday next and I hope you will have a fine day for a rather wearisome journey. 11 o'clock from Char + is *the* train; but you must take your ticket to *Hamstreet* changing in Ashford for that

[1] Date from postmark.

station which is only about a mile from here; whereas Ashford is 5 1/2 miles. And that makes a long drive.

A small pony trap shall meet your train in Hamstreet (due 1.4 pm).

<div align="right">Yours faithfully</div>

<div align="right">Joseph Conrad.</div>

P.S. Could you procure for me the N° of the Chronicle containing the review of my novel?[1] It would be right friendly of you. I don't know the date.

To J. B. Pinker

Text MS Berg; Unpublished

<div align="right">[letterhead: Capel House]</div>

<div align="right">2 Nov. 1911.</div>

Dear Sir.

Herewith 4000 words all I could manage this week having been interrupted in one way or another. One really can't shut one's door in people's faces.

Would you mind paying me in *two* cheques one for £5 the other for £11 for this lot.

No word from L. Irving. I imagine he has dropped the idea but he should have sent me a line. He may do so yet.

Pray tell me if B'woods have rejected the Freya story.[2] A thing like that does not seem to require much thinking over.

I heard from Mr Maas. He's coming next Tuesday to lunch.

Have you planned next year's publications? Do you think that *Chance* should appear in the autumn? The vol of short stories (3)[3] is ready—if only Freya gets serialised in time—for, say, next May. These stories are not bad.

I see the 3ᵈ Ed. of U. W. E. advertised (last week's literary page of Telegraph) but that may mean anything. Still I would like to know what sort of sale the book had up to now.

<div align="right">Yours faithfully</div>

<div align="right">J. Conrad.</div>

[1] By W. H. Chesson, it appeared on 13 October. Maas himself worked for the *Daily Chronicle*.

[2] Pinker had sent them the story on 9 August; on 3 November, Conrad knew that it had been taken instead by the *London Magazine*.

[3] 'The Secret Sharer', 'A Smile of Fortune', and 'Freya of the Seven Isles'.

The *Partner* in Harpers[1] is sadly mangled in the last 3 pages. Have you a typed copy in Your office?

To John Quinn
Text MS NYPL; Unpublished

[letterhead: Capel House]
3 Nov. 1911

Dear Sir.

As it has happened to me that a registered letter to New York (to Messrs Harpers) has not been received by the addressee I would be glad to know if you have safely received the MS of Under Western Eyes. It was posted in our village p office, registered, on the 28 Sept. in time to catch the mail-packet *Saxonia* on the 1st Oct.[2] It is not the sort of package likely to slip into a crevice and be overlooked but still one never knows what may happen; and I am such a generally unlucky person that you must forgive my request for just a word on a post-card acknowledging receipt—or non-receipt as the case may be.

My little autobiographical volume which was to be pubd in October is held back till January. I tell you this not particularly interesting piece of news so that you should not think I have forgotten my promise to send you a signed copy.

Freya is to appear serially in the London Magazine before very long[3] and I am thinking of pubg that story by itself in a 2/- volume in the spring if I can arrange it with the Nelson the publisher.

Believe me

sincerely Yours

Joseph Conrad

To J. B. Pinker
Text MS Berg; Unpublished

[Capel House]
Saturday. [4 November 1911][4]

Dear Sir.

Thanks for your letter with the two cheques received to day.

I am sorry *Freya* has done no better. Under the circumstances to

[1] *Harper's Magazine*, 123 (November 1911), 850–65.

[2] Because of delays at the New York Custom House, Quinn received the MS only on 13 November (Quinn to Conrad, 15 November, TS copy NYPL).

[3] It was delayed until July 1912.

[4] Received 'Nov 1911': Conrad requested the two cheques on Thursday the 2nd.

publish that story by itself in a 2/- vol seems the best thing to do, if it can be arranged.

Secret-Sharer. Smile of Fortune Partner & *Prince Roman* would make almost a vol by themselves and certainly with one more story. But it hardly seems worth while writing stories except for Harpers. Alden wrote me twice asking for stories. He meant however shorter ones than Freya. Still in his last letter he mentionned* that they would be ready to consider 2 or even 3 instalment stories from me.

Do you mean *Freya* to be the spring vol:? The little book of Reminiscences I have fixed for early January. Now the papers are crowded with Xmas books reviews.

Thanks for type of *Partner*. I shall add a couple of pages to that story for book form. I wish I could get the text I sent to Harpers. It's slightly different and in parts longer than the one you have sent me. Could you when (and if) you write to them ask if it['s] possible to get it?

Yours faithfully

J. Conrad.

To H.-D. Davray
Text L. fr. 109

Capel House.
6 Nov. 1911

Cher Ami,

Merci. Je viens de recevoir la somme de frs 400. J'ai bien remarqué les coupures dans le feuilleton de l'*Agent*.[1] J'ai pensé que ces gens là avaient votre permission. Je n'ai rien dit, car au bout du compte le texte du feuilleton signifie peu de chose.

Je suis très heureux de savoir que vous allez le rétablir.[2] Du reste mon cher j'ai la plus parfaite confiance en vous.

Imaginez-vous que je suis en train de finir un long roman commencé seulement cette année. J'ai marché à toute vapeur depuis le mois d'avril. Je suis exténué—mais je marche toujours.

Tout à vous.

Translation

Dear Friend,

Thank you. I have just received the sum of 400 francs. Indeed I noticed cuts in the serial of the *Agent*. I thought that these people had

[1] Cf. the letters of 27 June and 10 August 1910.
[2] For book publication by *Mercure de France* and Gallimard in 1912.

your permission. I said nothing, for in the long run the serial text means little.

I am very happy to know that you are going to restore it. Besides, my dear fellow, I have the most perfect trust in you.

You should know that I am in the midst of finishing a long novel, begun only this year. I have worked at full speed since April. I am exhausted—but I keep working.

<div align="center">Sincerely yours.</div>

To J. B. Pinker

Text MS Berg; Unpublished

<div align="right">Capel House</div>
<div align="right">Thursday. [9 November 1911][1]</div>

Dear Sir.

I beg to acknowledge the returned letter and insce ticket. I didn't dream of the possibility of any explanation. It was a matter of yes or no simply. But I trust that under the circumstances you won't mind me putting to you the request to forward the payment for the encld 5000 w. of Chance by rail from Char + all the way. There is a train at 4.25 arriving at 6.9 here which will give me time to catch our last post. I will send to the station at that time and warn the station-master. The station is *Hamstreet*. I believe they want a string tied round the envelope.

The nearness of Sunday obliges me to ask you to do that and I hope You will excuse for this once the inconvenience I may be causing you.

———————

I am glad you think of trying Freya in US.[2] I have really a reputation there. Various people who ought to know tell me that Harpers are not doing justice to the possibilities of my work. However they pay decently for stories.

I will be writing to you soon in the matter of next year's publications.

Pray tell me at your leisure if in your opinion the contract you entered into with Harpers (Mediterran Story) still stands? For if so I am greatly inclined to start that novel right away (after Chance). It has been in my mind a good deal of late.

<div align="right">Yours faithfully</div>
<div align="right">J. Conrad.</div>

[1] Received 'Nov. 1911': followed by the letter of 'Friday evng', which acknowledges the cheque's arrival by passenger train.
[2] Where the *Metropolitan Magazine* published it in April 1912.

To J. B. Pinker

Text MS Berg; Unpublished

[Capel House]
Friday evng [10 November 1911][1]

Dear Sir.

I have to thank you for the trouble you have been good enough to take in sending by rail the cheque which reached me this evening.

The rest of this letter you will perhaps read and consider at your leisure.

I will be very frank with you in this matter. I don't like my position with Methuen. It's a very modern manufactory of books, no doubt with very up to date methods (or used to be) but without any sort of literary associations or tradition. Methuen's is a shop. In this opinion I am not alone. It is a very good business—for the firm. I don't question the policy of your action when you engaged me for 3 novels to them—but as a matter of fact we could have had the same terms for book-form from other people. There was a consideration of £50. for the signature, I know, but I doubt whether that sum compensates us for being strictly bound. It is not as if M were a firm owning an old established magazine from whom one could expect some advantages in the way of serial publication. A very important point which we have secured to a certain extent with Harpers. And that's why I share your opinion that we should keep in with Harpers whatever their shortcomings as a publishing house may be. After all they paid under the contract you have negociated* as much hard cash for one novel as M will pay for three.

I really don't see the advantages of the Methuen connection. They paid 120 for book-form of the *Set of Six*. Well I had that amount years before for the *Youth* vol. from B'woods besides the serial payments for all the stories. As to their ability to push sales I do not see any special evidences of it. One gets the advance and there's the end. I don't question the fact that they sell a lot of books—probably more than any other firm—but then look at their list. It's much too big. I don't like to be lost in the I won't say ruck—but in the number. What can they care about any individual author? With them its numbers that tell not the authors; and their policy can never be to push any particular man

[1] Received 'Nov 1911': the *Daily Telegraph* advertisements restrict possible dates to the 10th and 17th; in view of Conrad's remark on the 21st that he had not expected an immediate answer to this 'long letter', an ascription to the 17th would not make sense.

forward. I don't care for their advertising. I am an individual writer and I prefer to go to a publisher who will think it worth his while to treat me accordingly. His money would be just as good. And really they are irritating. They bother one to write pars for their list about one's own work. I told them plainly twice to attend to their own business and try to do it half as well as I do mine. I also told them as plainly on the occasion of the proof muddle[1] that if they could do no better than that they had better leave my books alone. Their imprint has no particular distinction; their proceedings are queer.

A fortnight ago I saw myself advertised as in the 3d ed: To-day I happened to look at the ad: page of the *Telegraph* and I saw my book advertised as in the *second*. What is it? A game? Sheer contempt for common decency? This is not the way to handle work such as mine. It prejudices it from a merely business point of view. Unless the contention is that it's a trifle, that ads mean nothing and that nobody ever looks at them.

I must decline to believe that there is no publisher worth talking to in London besides M—no publisher that can sell a book and treat his author's* somewhat better than if they were factory hands. Under the circumstances I have no faith whatever in M.['s] *keenness* about my work and I feel extremely unwilling to sign any contract with that firm. I had the pleasure of seeing Mr Methuen once. He had the impudence to advise me what to write. I prefer to deal with men who know better than to talk like that to an author who has always stood on his own feet, quite alone both in vision and expression.

Three novels they must have and they shall have them but not a line more if I can help it; and I must tell you openly that I have always expressed my feelings as to *M* freely in speech and writing. Plenty of people are aware of them. And I did this for the reason that when I am free at last I don't want it to be said that M. got rid of me. It is *I* who do not *want* the connection.

In the matter of next year's publications I'll tell you frankly what I should like to be done:—

If you are successful in placing Freya in US on terms which will enable you to credit me with a decent amount I would very much like to have *Sharer—Smile* & *Freya* published in one vol, say in Aug: (& July). These three stories are a set of which I am not ashamed. They have a common character—something slightly different from any short stories

[1] Blunders in the proofing of both *The Secret Agent* and *Under Western Eyes* infuriated Conrad. See, e.g., *Letters*, 3, pp. 439–40.

I ever wrote. It's my second manner, less forcible, more popular than the Typhoon set and in another tone than the Six.

You see what I mean? Whereas *Sharer, Smile Partner* & *Roman* won't make a homogeneous vol. And it would be a pity. I know I made the suggestion myself but I would be sorry all the same.

Then I would like Chance to come out early in 1913—spring, instead of autumn 1912 as you suggest. I don't think it's to the advantage of my novels to appear before Xmas. They want longer reviews than the papers can give them at that season of the year.

But I am aware of the importance of the money for *Chance* coming in as soon as possible. So if you consider that your plan must stand I shall make no objections—except always as to Methuen. Pardon this over-long screed.

Yours faithfully

J. Conrad.

To Warrington Dawson
Text MS Duke; Randall 143

[Capel House]
Saturday [11 or 18 November 1911?][1]

My dear fellow.

You will pardon the delay. I am pushing on desperately with my novel now six weeks overdue. I am not going to write you exhaustively for the same reason—and I know you will not take it amiss.

I have read the MS.[2] I have read it twice. And I can safely say that I have appreciated it without missing any material point. The question before us is however the question of expediency.

On meditating it over carefully I discover, stated shortly, that what stands in the way of that work is this: that the treatement* is not light enough. It is witty and in places there is even profundity (in the comments)—but no lightness. There is I must say a sort of discord

[1] Although Dawson himself noted that this letter concerns *The True Dimension*, finished in May 1914, Randall (p. 143, n. 1) argues that it assesses either an earlier version of that work or another story, 'Exiles of Elysium'. In either case, the letter of 25 November, pulling back from earlier criticism of an unspecified MS, may be seen as a sequel to this one. Conrad had hoped to finish *Chance* by the beginning of October; thus, by mid November, he was 'now six weeks overdue'.

[2] Since the work at issue was long enough to submit for book publication, a draft of *The True Dimension* ('The Purser's Shilling') seems a more probable candidate than 'Exiles of Elysium'.

between the subject and the style which is the style of the man who wrote the *Scar* & the *Scourge*.[1] And this [it] is which puts off publishers and editors. They don't see its high qualities. They only feel that it does not fit in with their idea of what the treatment of such a subject should be.

I don't agree with them "au fond". My conclusion however is that the MS should be kept back as material for future use in a mood of the frankest *fun*. You, mon cher, in my view, are not only a serious artist but an artist *dans le genre sérieux*. At any rate at present. And I think that a man who has written such two books as those you have published may well forego the immediate publication of this MS. Later on when the things near your heart, and therefore in accord with Your temperamental manner of expression, have been uttered, *then* you may take up a lighter vein and no doubt you will find in Yourself a more light-hearted mood. Voilà. This briefly is le vrai fond de ma pensée. I think that abstention just now is the more dignified policy. You ought to try to *faire grand*. It is in you. Keep to that gift. There will be always time enough to discover yourself as an excellent jester. Think of the public which you have yet to conquer. It mustn't be put in doubt of what you are really. A matter of policy. I tell you all this in the fulness of the sincerity which is due to you as écrivain and of my affection for the man

 Yours ever

 J Conrad.

[1] Reviewing *The Scar* (2 April 1910, p. 183), the *New York Times* referred to its 'gray, forbidding picture' of Virginia life (Randall, p. 20). *The True Dimension* is the Fourth Dimension, a subject that the co-author of *The Inheritors* took less seriously than Dawson.

To J. B. Pinker

Text MS Berg; Unpublished

[Capel House]
Sunday. [12 or 19 November
1911][1]

Dear Sir.

I've been thinking of the matter. We have now unpublished in book form in this country.

	*The Secret Sharer.	—	about 11.000.
	*Smile of Fortune.	—	—"— 20 000
*pub serially already	Freya of the Islands		—"— 38 000
	*The Partner.		—"— 8 000
	*The Black Mate.	(?)	6 000
	Prince Roman.		—"— 6 000

What would you think of the *Smile* and *Freya* being pubd in a volume title:—

A Smile of Fortune
and
Freya
by
J—— Conrad.

perhaps with Nelson at 2/6 or preferably with some other puber at 3/6, next Spring; that is if Freya can be serialised in time.

Perhaps B'woods would publish Freya serially if the other story is given them to make a vol: at 3/6. I regret Maga.[2] One was in decent company there and had a good sort of public. There isn't a single club and messroom and man-of-war in the British Seas and Dominions which hasn't its copy of Maga—not to speak of all the Scots in all parts of the world. I would even let them have the *Secret Sharer* if they preferred a 6/- vol. Would you have any objection to approach B'wood with the proposal?

I put forward this idea of the two (or even three) longest stories being published first in view of the future. After finishing *Chance* I shall probably fill in the year's work by writing 2 or 3 short stories. At least I hope so. We shall then have another vol. of short stories ready to be published at a convenient time—say after the vol: form of *Chance*.

[1] Received 'Nov 1911': between proposing a schedule for publication on [10] and telling Pinker not to pursue Blackwood on 21 November.

[2] This passage apparently implies that if the editor of *Blackwood's* had second thoughts about 'Freya', Conrad would withdraw it from the *London Magazine*.

What do you propose to do with the *Set of Six* stories (*less* the Point of Honour) in US? With the *Smile*, say (instead of the Duel) they will make a vol: I think of full size. I think they ought to be published over there under the same title.

Thanks for your letter in the matter of the E[nglish] R[eview]. Though I had no doubt I am not the less sensible to what you say.

<div align="right">Yours faithfully</div>

<div align="right">J. Conrad.</div>

To J. B. Pinker
Text MS Berg; Unpublished

<div align="right">[letterhead: Capel House]</div>

<div align="right">Monday. [20 November 1911][1]</div>

Dear Sir.

Herewith 3 thous w. of copy.

I only wish I could work quicker—not that I am tired of the story—on the contrary. It positively pains me not being able to do with the end what I should like to do. However I don't think it will be bad.

You haven't answered my question as to the Tauchnitz payment. I should like to know one way or the other so I venture to remind you.

<div align="right">Yours faithfully</div>

<div align="right">J. Conrad.</div>

To J. B. Pinker
Text MS Berg; Unpublished

<div align="right">[Capel House]</div>

<div align="right">21 Nov. 1911.</div>

Dear Sir.

Thanks for Your letter and cheque for £23.5. (£12 against copy and £11.5 half of Tauchnitz payment) which reached me this morning.

I am sorry to hear of your influenza and hope you are now recovering. As to the long letter I did not expect it to be answered at once. I wrote you all I had in my mind, and while writing I was fully aware that there are many arguments to be advanced on the other side.

[1] Received 'Nov 1911': the following day Conrad acknowledged a cheque covering 3,000 words of *Chance* and the payment from Tauchnitz. The present note's regretful tone suggests that this was the batch in question. A delivery on the 6th or 13th, close to those of 2 and 9 November, would not have called for regrets.

I am very pleased at your willingness to accept my suggestion as to dates of publications. I would like what you propose best. But material considerations are important too. My feeling is that as B'woods refused serialising *Freya* they need not have the book. Reynolds who was here for week end had a letter from M^r B'wood with very friendly message for me. But I don't want them to think they are doing us a favour. Couldn't we suspend the matter of pub^er for the 3 stories for a while? McMillans* at one time seemed to wish to enter into communication with me through Harrison. I fancy they would be willing to take over all my books if the thing could be negociated*. Perhaps it wouldn't be a bad thing. These people have money. I asked Reynolds who was to call on Sir Frederick[1] to say that I was open to such a proposal. But I haven't heard anything from him or them yet. I don't know what you think of the practicality of such a transaction. The notion at the back of my head is that if they made a move in that sense we could perhaps let them have the 3 stories vol as a sort of encouragement to proceed. Even if nothing came of it in the end there would be no harm in having a vol with McMillans. I'll keep you informed of what (if anything) happens.

<div style="text-align:right">Yours faithfully</div>

<div style="text-align:right">J Conrad.</div>

To Henri Ghéon

Text MS Private collection; Cap

<div style="text-align:right">[letterhead: Capel House]</div>
<div style="text-align:right">22 Nov. 1911</div>

Cher Monsieur.[2]

Merci de votre livre,[3] si juste, si intéressant, si touchant—pourquoi ne le dirai-je puisque j'en ai été touché?

On est toujours heureux de se découvrir un ami inconnu; et quand cet

[1] Sir Frederick Macmillan (1851–1936), chairman of the family firm, had published *Seems So!*

[2] Henri Ghéon was the pseudonym of Henri-Léon Vangeon (1874–1944), poet, critic, painter, and playwright. He published his first collection, *Chansons d'aube*, in 1897; his later work included *Algérie* (another collection of poems) and more than sixty plays. From 1901 to 1909, Vangeon practised medicine in Bray-sur-Seine, his native town. His intimate friendship with André Gide began in 1898. In 1900, they travelled together in Tunisia and Algeria; the two of them were among the founders of the *Nouvelle Revue Française* in 1908. His experiences as a military doctor in World War One turned Vangeon towards Christianity, and he later worked with Claudel.

[3] *Nos directions*, a collection of articles from the *Nouvelle Revue*, published on the 7th.

ami est un écrivain qui exprime avec force et délicatesse en même temps (vous savez les hommes forts sont généralement doux) je ne dirais pas les pensées mais les sentiments qu'on a sur les choses littéraires, on se sent doublement fortuné. En lisant votre volume je me disais: comme c'est ça! Voilà, vous êtes entré dans mes sympathies pas "comme dans une maison vide" mais comme dans une maison habitée par très peu de critiques. Je vous assure que ne fait pas ce tour qui veut. Il ya a là (je veux dire dans ma maison) une confusion perpétuelle et un demi-jour sur les choses de l'esprit. Mais je sais fort bien qui je veux entendre. Je vous ai écouté avec un vrai plaisir. C'est bien ça!

Dites je vous prie à Gide—qui est bien de vos amis, n'est-ce pas?—que je vais me présenter à sa porte un de ces jours, en chemise de nuit, pieds nus et la corde au cou.[1] Il comprendra. Surtout si vous ajoutez que ce misérable Conrad a écrit un long (et bête) roman depuis sa visite.[2] C'est *dégoûtant* meme à dire—pensez ce que c'était à faire! J'en ai gagné un degout de moi-même, de* papier de l'encre—de tout! Et il y a encore une quarantaine de pages à barbouiller! Quand j'y pense la plume me tombe des mains.

Encore une fois merci. Vous m'avez ouvert un peu l'esprit. Vous avez donné un peu d'air dans cet endroit, autrefois respectable, qui commence à sentir le renfermé. Que voulez-vous! J'ai le travail si difficile que je n'ai jamais le temps d'ouvrir ma fenêtre. C'est la dure vérité. Et puis pour ce qu'on trouve à respirer ici—!

Croyez moi cher Monsieur

bien à vous

Joseph Conrad

P.S. Please give my love to Gide and tell him I am really ashamed of myself for not having written to him yet.

Translation

Dear Sir,

Thank you for your book, so judicious, so interesting, so touching— why shouldn't I say so when I have been touched?

[1] Wearing metaphorical if not actual garments of penitence, Conrad wrote to Gide on 26 December.
[2] Agnes Tobin brought Gide, Valery Larbaud, and Arthur Symons to visit Conrad on 22 July. They drove over from Wittersham after lunch and stayed for dinner: Cecily

One is always glad to discover an unknown friend; and when that friend is a writer who expresses both forcefully and tenderly (strong men, you know, are usually gentle) I won't say one's thoughts, but one's feelings about literary questions, one feels doubly lucky. Reading your volume I said to myself: 'How right that is!' So there, you have entered into my sympathies not as into an empty house but as into a home frequented by very few critics. I assure you that not everyone who wants to achieves this feat. There (I mean in my house) there is confusion about spiritual matters for ever and a day. But I know exactly whom I want to understand. I have listened to you with real pleasure. Truly!

I beg you to tell Gide—who is a friend of yours, no?—that I'm going to turn up at his door one of these days in a nightshirt, barefoot, with a rope round my neck. He will understand. Especially if you add that the wretched Conrad has written a long (and stupid) novel since his visit. It's *disgusting* even to talk about it; just imagine what writing it was like! It's made me disgusted with myself, with paper, with ink—with everything! And there are still forty or so pages to scrawl out! When I think of it, the pen falls from my hand.

Thanks again. You have opened my spirit a little. You have brought some air into this once respectable place, which was beginning to smell musty. What can you expect? My work's so difficult that I never have time to open my window. It's the hard truth. And what there is to breathe here—!

Believe me, dear sir,

<div style="text-align: right">Yours sincerely,</div>

<div style="text-align: right">Joseph Conrad</div>

PS Please give my love to Gide and tell him I am really ashamed of myself for not having written to him yet.

To Warrington Dawson

Text MS Duke; Randall 144

<div style="text-align: right">[letterhead: Capel House]</div>
<div style="text-align: right">25 Nov '11.</div>

My dear Warrington Dawson.

I am distressed by your letter; but I don't think I am guilty as much as you seem to think. If there is any man I would wish to help it is you. But

Mackworth, *English Interludes* (Routledge & Kegan Paul, 1974), pp. 183–4. By late July, Conrad had written about one third of *Chance*.

my dear fellow you are mistaken if you think I have the slightest influence. I don't know really who are the men of whom you speak. I certainly got some reviewing to do for my friend Douglas some time ago.[1] But that was purely be* the accident of meeting once or twice the editor of a newspaper whom I have not seen since.[2] My dear fellow I am profoundly unknown here—or at any rate completely uninfluential. My own stories get refused. I have a little vol now[3] which I have been unable to place for months.

Reading your letter (the one which came with the MS[4]) I saw that the MS had been already offered to several publishers; and amongst them those of whom I had been thinking. I don't know many of them. To go to them again would have been to go to meet a rebuff both for you and me. And having lately got some few knocks on my own account I knew I would do no good. I am now having a row with Methuen about certain matters connected with the publication of that miserable novel of mine. I have been so outspoken with that beastly firm that any interference of mine in favour of your work would be simply fatal to its chances.

I am very sorry for having offered my opinion on the MS. I can see its quality. I can also see why these men have declined it. But indeed my dear fellow I had no idea you attached so much importance to the immediate placing of that MS. From our conversation[5] I imagined you had other works ready or at any rate not far from being finished. I don't know how I got that impression. I can only repeat that I am sorry. I wrote to you in all sincerity if under a complete misapprehension of the real state of affairs. And now I can only express my profound contrition at having disappointed Your expectations. Whether you will forgive me my clumsiness I don't know. But whether or no I can assure You of my unalterable regard and sympathy

<div align="center">Yours always</div>

<div align="right">J Conrad.</div>

[1] The earliest identified reviews came out in the *English Review* during 1912; some of them were written late in 1911 (Holloway, p. 187, and Cecil Woolf, *A Bibliography of Norman Douglas* [Hart-Davis, 1954]).

[2] R. A. Scott-James, literary editor of the *Daily News*? Cf. the fourth paragraph of the letter to Reynolds (p. 517).

[3] The protean collection of stories.

[4] An early version of *The True Dimension*? See the letter of [11 or 18 November 1911?]

[5] In August.

To the Abbé Joseph de Smet

Text L. fr. 110

[Capel House]
26 novembre 1911

Cher Monsieur,

Voilà de bonnes nouvelles. Je suis très content que cela soit vous qui allez traduire *Nostromo*.[1]

Ne pensez-vous pas que l'on pourrait raccourcir un peu ce long livre? Pas ôter des episodes de l'action elle-même,—non! mais je veux dire enlever les mots superflus. Il y a dans ce volume trop de phrases. Phrases d'analyse, phrases descriptives aussi. Cela pourra aider les lecteurs français à avaler un si gros livre. Ce sarclage,—émondage, si vous voulez,—doit être fait par moi-même et sur le texte anglais. Si vous voulez m'envoyer votre exemplaire de 'Nostromo', je m'engage à ne le garder que huit jours et à vous le renvoyer marqué légèrement au crayon. Qu'en pensez-vous? En tout peut-être cinq à six pages de moins. Je ne pense pas que Davray fasse des objections.

Merci bien du livre que vous avez eu l'amabilité de m'envoyer.[2] Je l'attends avec impatience. Je vais vous renvoyer les épreuves du *Typhon*[3] dans le plus court delai possible. Je pense que je les recevrai lundi prochain. Croyez à mes sentiments les plus sincères.

Tout à vous.

Translation

Dear Sir,

What good news. I am very happy that it should be you who will translate *Nostromo*.

Don't you think that this long book could be abridged a little? Not removing episodes of the action itself—no! But removing superfluous words: that's what I have in mind. There are too many phrases in that volume. Analytical phrases, descriptive phrases too. It will help French readers to swallow such a large book. This weeding—pruning, if you like—should be done myself and on the English text. If you would send me your copy of *Nostromo*, I undertake to keep it no more than a week, returning it to you lightly marked in pencil. What do you think? In all perhaps five to six pages fewer. I don't think Davray will have any objections.

[1] Philippe Neel's translation of *Nostromo* was published in serial in 1924. The Abbé de Smet's plans were frustrated by the war (*Lettres françaises*, p. 111, n. 2).
[2] His book on Lafcadio Hearn, recently published by *Mercure de France*.
[3] As a serial, it had already appeared in *Progrès*.

Thank you for the book you have kindly sent off to me. I wait for it impatiently. I shall return the proofs of 'Typhoon' with the shortest possible delay. I think I'm going to have them next Monday. Believe me most sincerely

Yours sincerely.

To J. B. Pinker
Text MS Berg; Unpublished

[letterhead: Capel House]
Thursday [30? November 1911][1]

Dear Sir.

Many thanks for the trouble you have been good enough to take in the matter of the Partner.

Yes. I see. But there is some mystery there. I did write about $1\frac{1}{2}$ additional pages at the end of the copy sent to me for revision at Harpers request. The copy I have received from You this morning is not however (neither did I expect it to be) the copy on which the revision was made. However pray do not trouble about it any more. I am sorry I spoke at all about the matter. I know what I did write and I can put in the additional pars when preparing the text for book form.

Sorry there has been another check with Chance. I have been in bed for five days with some internal trouble. I am up since yesterday. You can't imagine how anxious I feel to bring the end off at last, now, that it is in sight I may say.

Yours faithfully

J. C.

[1] Received 'Nov 1911': nearness to recent deliveries of *Chance* rules out the 9th and the 23rd. Conrad and Pinker discussed versions of 'The Partner' early in the month, but obtaining 'The copy received ... this morning' may have required time-consuming correspondence with New York. Since this letter answers one from Pinker, his illness around the middle of the month makes the 16th the less likely date.

To John Quinn
Text MS NYPL; Unpublished

[letterhead: Capel House]
30 Sept [November] 1911[1]

Dear Mr Quinn.

Many thanks for draft (£60) which I received by the last mail. The book has arrived too. It was very kind of You to think of sending it to me. As everything that Professor James ever wrote it's most suggestive and interesting and morally valuable.[2]

I am sorry for all the trouble you have had with the MS. Your Customs seems to be a most precious institution. I assure you I had nothing to do with any Express C°. In fact I must confess I don't know very well what an Express C° is. I mailed the parcel in the usual way at our village Post Office where I transact all my postal business. They made me sign the usual declarations and I thought there could be no trouble. However I think all this complication arises from my insuring for the full value. I shan't do it again. I'll simply register the MSS which I shall be sending to you in a few days. It will be safe enough I dare say. I am not fit to travel to London; but I shall write to your consulate sending particulars and asking for a certificate as you desire me to do.

Pardon this hurried scrawl. I have just got out of bed and feel abominably shaky yet. I am dear Sir

very faithfully Yours
Joseph Conrad.

PS I would much rather You had my MS now than any one else—later on. I regret that the autobiographical MS is not in existence. All

[1] Quinn's reply (11 February 1912, TS copy NYPL) reads in part: 'Your letter was dated September 30th, but it must have been written November 30th. It is so post-marked and it acknowledges my draft (for sixty pounds) which I sent you about the middle of November.' In the same letter, Quinn noted receipt of the three stories listed in the PS.

[2] The works of Henry's brother William James (1842–1910), Professor of Philosophy at Harvard, included *The Principles of Psychology* (1890), *The Will to Believe and Other Essays* (1897), *The Varieties of Religious Experience* (1902), *Pragmatism* (1908), *The Meaning of Truth* (1909), *A Pluralistic Universe* (1909), and, posthumously, *Some Problems in Philosophy* (1911). 'The Stream of Thought', a chapter in the *Principles* (1, 9) has many echoes in modern fiction, as in the remark so close to the description of Marlow's story-telling in 'Heart of Darkness': 'The significance, the value, of the image is all in this halo or penumbra that surrounds and escorts it'. Quinn had sent Conrad the posthumous collection *Memories and Studies* (1911): B. L. Reid, *The Man from New York* (New York: Oxford University Press, 1968), pp. 113–14.

the text almost was dictated and then worked upon in typed copy.[1] But should you like to have something more I have preserved the MS of my *first* novel *Almayer's Folly*. Unfortunately however one whole chapter (Chap IX) is missing. Can't imagine how it happened. We have looked for it without success so far. But it may turn up yet.[2] If you care to have it as it is I would be happy to send it to you on the same terms (owing to its incomplete state).

I have also the MS of *Karain* (the very first short story I've ever written[3]) complete. (In the Tales of Unrest. The first of the vol) £20. The MS of the *Secret Agent* about 640 pp. complete £40.

I shall be sending you to complete the Freya item:

1. The Secret-Sharer. 125 pp. (ser: Harpers. last year.)
3. The Partner. 86 pp. (ser: Harpers. this november n°.)
3 Il Conde. 56 pp. (pub: in Hampton's mag: 3 years ago and included in the vol of Set of Six my only Italian story)

I add it to the other two to make up your Freya item to about 500 pp of MS. the other two stories contain less pages than I thought they did.

Since you seem to want some autobiographical MS of mine I am sending you the only bit of autobiographical MS I possess. It is out of the *Mirror of the Sea* (which was mostly dictated) the part called Initiation. Please accept it a mark* of my regard. I shall send it to you together with the signed portrait out of the *New Review* next week at the latest.[4]

[1] Dictated to Ford or to Miss Hallowes and typed by her.
[2] To judge by the sale catalogue of his library (Anderson Galleries, New York, 13 November 1923), Quinn never received the missing chapter.
[3] With the possible exception of 'The Black Mate'.
[4] On 15 November, Quinn had asked for a signed copy of the latest *English Review*, carrying a Rothenstein portrait drawing of Conrad. The *New Review* had published *The Nigger* in 1897.

To Stephen Reynolds
Text MS Berg; Unpublished

[Capel House]
Thursday. [late November or
December 1911]¹

My dear Reynolds

The volume is very emphatically *all right*.² In many respects better than I expected. That is it puts the point more clearly than I should have thought it possible in that form. Perhaps I mean more consecutively. On the other hand the form is very dangerous. It does away with a certain amount of force and authority. That is perfectly apparent in contrast with the preface which indeed from every point of view, is a very fine, effective and sympathetic statement of your moral and intellectual position in the face of modern events—or modern manipulations, if you like. Yes. I like the preface immensely. It's first rate literary Reynolds. The ease and point of expression are quite fascinating.

What I regret are the quotations from other works in the last third of the book. A production of that kind should have been written as if there had been no other book in the world. Your volume is professedly a first hand thing—living words. Then why drag in these dead lists of books? Can the opinions of Miss X and Messrs: X Y Z add an atom of authority to what is supposed to come out of the warm lips of men? Their intrusion damages the simplicity and the sincerity of the scheme and in so far is shocking to my sensibilities. You might have said all you wanted to say on the points dealt with in these quotations without disfiguring the book by a single line not coming from the three authors. And it would have been more effective if not so easy to do.

I am telling you these things on which I might have honestly held my tongue because I am concerned as to the *integrity* of your work—any of your work—as much as you can possibly be. And that in the merest trifles even. For obviously my remarks in view of the general quality of the work are of no particular importance. *Quality* is not the right word. General sentiment of the book I should have said. It is in what they say,

¹ The collaborative volume was published in November. On the 21st, Conrad had had no word about Reynolds's approach to Macmillan. The earliest possible Thursday, then, would be the 23rd, and a later one, such as 30 November, 7 or 14 December, is more likely.

² *Seems So! A Working-Class View of Politics* by Reynolds and his fellow fishermen, Bob and Tom Woolley; most of the contents had previously appeared in the *English Review, Evening Standard, Fortnightly Review, Nation, New Age, Quarterly Review, T.P.'s Magazine, Spectator,* and *The Times.* In 1909, Reynolds described his politics as 'Tory-Democratic' (Wright, p. 123).

you all say, and you say alone a most right and valuable expression of stark humanity confronted by problems and theories fabricated within four walls of some sort or other.

I wonder very much what reception you will get. I imagine i[t] can't be but good. What I want is to see it *exceptional* and that of course is uncertain. Let me know how things go. I really am anxious to know what are the signs. If you send me any cuttings Jessie will see to it that they are returned to you at once. I am truly grateful to you for trying to put some work in D[ouglas]'s way. Does Scott-James know his address? I do hope he will find enough work to keep body and soul together. Of course a modest mission to the East would be the making of him in a sense. For the D. N.[1] he could write also about Italy—social and political and historical. Artistic too, for he knows more than one would give him credit for. Anyway whatever happens, if only the humblest kind of reviewing, you have my thanks. To him I shall say nothing of your action as he is a deplorably skittish animal tho' not devoid of proper feeling—in the end. Well my dear more power to your elbow. You have made a fine start. I still think that the short stories Vol should be a thick one.[2] A severe sifting but everything that will go through the sieve should be given out at once. And soon! I think it important that it should be soon.

Give my regards and congratulations to your collaborator and to Bob also on the other kind of authorship, with wishes of all possible luck to the newcomer. Jessie has begun to knit a coat already.

I didn't write before as I knew You were on your wanderings. This I suppose will meet you on your arrival home.

<div style="text-align:center">Yours always</div>

<div style="text-align:right">J. Conrad.</div>

Thanks for the McM mission. I quite see. It's bound to be a long affair if it ever comes off, which I doubt somewhat. It seems P had some sort of conversation with G. McM.[3] lately.

[1] R. A. Scott-James was literary editor of the *Daily News*, a Liberal paper.
[2] *How 'Twas*, a collection of stories dedicated to the Conrads, appeared in 1912.
[3] George A. Macmillan (1855–1936), a director of the family firm.

To the Abbé Joseph de Smet
Text J-A, 2, 136

[Capel House]
30 November, 1911.

Dear Sir.

You have succeeded admirably with the *Typhoon*—the most difficult piece of my work to render into French, with perhaps the exception of the *Nigger*. I repeat it's done admirably, and I beg you to believe in my gratitude for all the toil and trouble you have undertaken.

The few suggestions I have made, you will see, are of a trifling nature, but I wished to show you that I took an earnest interest in your work.

You will find *Nostromo* infinitely easier to translate. Of that I am certain. I shall prune that novel of all redundant phrases as much as I can.

Your book about Hearn delighted me greatly by its appreciative tone and its sympathetic view of that remarkably fine nature.[1] It is in every way worthy of its subject and I beg to congratulate you on your achievement. Many thanks for the copy, which I shall prize greatly.

To H.-D. Davray
Text MS Yale; *L. fr.* 111

[letterhead: Capel House]
[December 1911][2]

Cher Ami.

Merci de votre bonne lettre. Je viens de recevoir un mot de de Smet. Je lui propose de faire moi-même quelques coupures dans *Nostromo*. Il y a des phrases superflues dans ce gros livre! Oui! Il y en a. Helas! Tel paragraphe, tel passage d'analyse ne perdrait rien a avoir une phrase sur deux enlevée. Je voudrais bien émonder cette prose. En tout peut-être cinq a six pages de raccourcissement. Voulez-vous? Moi je ne pense qu'a mes lecteurs Français—Voyez-Vous. C'est long—cette machine. Et un peu lent aussi.

Enfin c'est à Vous de dire.[3]

[1] Lafcadio Hearn (1850–1904) was born in the Ionian Islands to Greek and Irish parents; he worked as a journalist in the United States from 1869 to 1887 and in Martinique from 1887 to 1889. He spent the rest of his life in Japan, becoming a citizen in 1895. He wrote many studies, stories, and sketches of Japanese and Antillean life.

[2] Dated on the 16th by Jean-Aubry, who may have seen an envelope; soon, in any case, after the letters to de Smet of 26 and 30 November.

[3] On behalf of *Mercure de France*.

Rappelez nous a l'aimable souvenir de madame Davray. Vous verra-t-on en Angleterre l'année prochaine?

A vous affectueusement.

J. Conrad.

Translation

Dear Friend,

Thanks for your kind letter. I've just had word from de Smet. I suggested to him that I myself should make some cuts in *Nostromo*. There are some superfluous phrases in that stout volume! Yes, there are. Alas! Such paragraphs, such passages of analysis would lose nothing by having one phrase in two removed. I should very much like to trim the prose. In all, an abridgment of five or six pages. Would you like it so? I'm thinking only of my French readers—do you see? It's long drawn out, that contrivance. And a little slow as well.

But it's up to you to decide.

Remember us to Madame Davray. Shall we see you in England next year?

Affectionately yours,

J. Conrad

To J. B. Pinker
Text MS Berg; Unpublished

[letterhead: Capel House]
5 Dec 1911.

My dear Sir.

In the matter of Dent's offer I agree with Your remark. It's not much use placing the stories vol with him. Unless you should consider that the terms you can obtain make it worth while?

As to the Mirror of the Sea I must say that I do not quite understand the drift of Methuen's proposal. The book is now in its 6/- form (which means that it can be bought for 4/6) on which I get a royalty of 20%.

They propose to republish it at 5/- net and reduce my royalty to 13%. I ask myself—why? If there is a demand for the book people will buy it at 4/6. The plates can not be worn out yet. If there's no demand then I don't see how resetting it, raising the price and cutting down my royalty is to create a fresh demand. In this ignorance I prefer leaving things as they are.

Yours faithfully

J. Conrad.

To Edward Garnett
Text MS Colgate; G. 252

[Capel House]
Wednesday [6? December 1911][1]

Dearest Edward.

I haven't* turned over the 3d page when I let out a whistle of respectful admiration. Frankly I never suspected in M^r Byrne that power of "haut comique".[2] For it is that—the comic just trembling on the verge of poignancy. And the wit: not the wit of repartee (which always gets on my nerves in a play) but the whole conception of the play being so witty! I have had there a most delightful surprise going on from page to page from act to act—a true effect of art—for never, not for a single moment, has my conviction wavered. After the first half of the first act I went on with a sense of secure anticipation without a check.

I admire the exposition of the first act and the inventiveness of the last. The second in its way is perfect. I don't know if the third act does not suffer from a certain effect of summariness. Mind—I don't mean to say that there is anything in it that isn't triumphantly right in the lightness of touch and truth of feeling. No. One can question nothing; but one wonders if one more turn of screw—or even half-a-turn—something more from Catherine—something in the nature of a cri-de coeur, a glimpse of humanity under her admirably rendered femininity would not give the supreme touch of poignancy to that creation of "grand comique". For, obviously, she *is* human.

But I may be wrong. Perhaps anything more would have been out of tone.

But anyhow to the very end the impression of the first-ratedness* of the work persists, and survives a critical meditation.

Thanks my dear fellow for sending me the little book. I can hardly tell you how pleased I am with it: the deft touch, the perfect mastery of intention, the felicity of phrase (*not* picturesqueness) disclosing character (the amazingly true mother-in-law) I have taken it all in and cherish it greatly. Oh it is good! Well.

Our dear love and tenderest wishes to you three. Tell me something of

[1] Dated 7 December, a Thursday, when sold by the American Art Association.

[2] Garnett's play *Lords and Masters* was produced and published (in 1911) under the pseudonym 'James Byrne' lest connections be made between the principal male character, who hangs on to his working-class mistress while encouraging another woman to leave her husband, and anyone in the author's circle: David Garnett, *The Golden Echo* (New York: Harcourt, Brace, 1954), p. 135. Disillusioned with husband and lover, the married woman leaves them both.

David when you write next. I expect I shall come to town in January and shall invade you at Duckworths for a long talk.

> Yours ever. With affectionate
> exultation in M^r Byrne's work
> J Conrad.

To J. B. Pinker

Text MS Berg; Unpublished

> [letterhead: Capel House]
> 8 December 1912 [1911][1]

Dear Sir.

Thanks for the cheque and for the account for the 1/2 year received this morning. My congratulations on the brilliant manner in which you have placed Freya in the US.[2] To tell you frankly I was feeling unhappy a little about that story—which I thought good and which seemed so difficult to place. The fact that you have also found a home over there for Prince Roman gives me pleasure.[3]

Pray tell me at Your leisure who took Freya in America and if I may hope to see proofs from there.

I am driving on. In haste.

> Yours
> J Conrad.

To John Quinn

Text MS NYPL; Unpublished

> [letterhead: Capel House]
> 11 Dec 1911.

Dear Mr Quinn.

Herewith the certificate which I hope will end the difficulties with the Customs.

I trust you have received my two packages by reg^d post. One containing a bit of autobiographical MS[4] and the other containing MS of *Secret-Sharer*. I will send you the *Partner* this week and *Il Conde* (to complete set to go with Freya) before New-year's day.

My best wishes for the coming Xmas.

> Yours cordially
> Joseph Conrad.

[1] Conrad must have meant '8 Dec 1911'; publication of the stories early in 1912 makes his date impossible.

[2] *Metropolitan Magazine* (NY), April 1912. [3] *Metropolitan Magazine*, January 1912.

[4] 'Initiation' from *The Mirror of the Sea*.

To Arthur Symons
Text MS Lohf; J-A, 2, 137

[letterhead: Capel House]
11 Dec 1911.

My dear Symons.

You must think me an unspeakable brute. Well, I can only hang my head and trust in your charity. The letter you wrote me about the novel is the only real satisfaction I got from my work—my desperate work at it. It's impossible to thank you adequately. You haven't missed a single point I verily believe—not a single phrase. But readers like you are the only ones for whom it is worth while to write.

I have been continually seedy all nov—up to last week. I am feeling a little better now. Your letter has saddened me. I understand perfectly how you feel. But what can one say. Words are poor comfort. Of one thing you may be certain and that is of my comprehension and sympathy. For the rest I can only say to you what I am saying to myself: Courage—courage—quand même.[1]

I am trying to finish a beastly novel which ought to have been done with last Oct*er*. I am sick of the pen.

Yours ever

J. Conrad.

To J. B. Pinker
Text MS Berg; Unpublished

[letterhead: Capel House]
12 Dec 1911.

Dear Sir.

Whatever I might have thought of publishers there could never have been in my mind any thought of the "stupidity" of my agent. You know that I am invariably guided by you. Your letter on the matter expressed no opinion and rightly or wrongly I imagined that you looked coldly on Methuen's proposal,[2] yourself. I voiced a natural feeling of dislike at having my royalty reduced; but if you believe that there is some advantage for us both in the plan, why I am ready to agree if you say distinctly that in your judgement I ought to do so.

I don't remember the terms of the agreement but it seems to me that

[1] In the same month, Symons wrote to Augustus John: 'How useless, may it not be, to go on doing thing after thing, without any remaining idea of fame, ambition, or hope of publishing anything' (Beckson, p. 276).
[2] For a five-shilling edition of *The Mirror of the Sea*.

the reduction is very considerable. I think that 15% roy. would not be extravagant even if the book has to be reset. However, as I understand the advantage for me would lie in the publicity of the name (I take this to be your argument) I won't insist unduly. The question which arises in my mind is whether a real cheap edition say at 2/6 or 3/6 which M. have a right to publish would not do more for me in the way of publicity than a 5/- net edition—which would not be a cheap edition under the contract.

If the plan is to be carried out I wish to have the opportunity to revise the text a little—mainly for misprints of which there are a few. I should like also to be given an opportunity to see how the book will look as to size shape and get up. For obviously that edition will be the "definitive" edition except for anything which may be done in the future in the way of collected works.

One more stipulation I would mention. I don't wish that edition to appear earlier than say end March.

Sorry that there are only 3000 words in this batch of copy; but indeed I have been too seedy to do better. Of course there are a great many pages more written but I am sending you only what is (barring misprints and slight verbal corrections) fit for the printer. I *see* my end right enough but the putting it down with some effect is the very devil. And of course I have ominous twinges of tooth-ache. Ever since Lord Jim (inclusive) the end of every long novel has cost me a tooth. I wouldn't mind losing two teeth to get this end done quickly. But it isn't so simple as that I am sorry to say. Thanks for your explanatory letter which made the matter clear to me.

Yours faithfully

J. Conrad.

To the Abbé Joseph de Smet
Text L. fr. 112

[Capel House]
16 décembre 1911

Cher Monsieur et ami,

Je suis bien fâché d'apprendre que vous avez été souffrant. J'espère que vous êtes complêtement rétabli et je serais heureux de le savoir par un petit mot de réponse à ceci.

Le passage que vous citez est *parfaitement* rendu. Je partage absolument vos idées, au sujet de la traduction et j'ai la plus grande confiance en vous personnellement comme traducteur. Vous n'avez qu'à suivre votre idée et votre inspiration et tout sera pour le mieux.

Mille pardons d'avoir gardé le volume si longtemps. Je le renvoie par le même courrier avec ce petit mot.

Croyez, cher Monsieur, à mes sentiments les plus amicaux.

Tout à vous.

Veuillez accepter mes meilleurs souhaits pour la nouvelle année.

Translation

Dear Sir and friend,

I am very upset to learn that you have been unwell. I hope that you are completely recovered, and I should be happy to know it by a brief word in answer to this.

That passage that you quote is *perfectly* rendered. I share absolutely your ideas on the subject of the translation, and I have the greatest confidence in you personally as a translator. You have only to follow your idea and your inspiration and all will be for the best.

A thousand apologies for having kept the volume such a long time. I return it by the same post as this short note.

Believe me, dear Sir, with most friendly feelings,

Sincerely yours.

Please accept my best wishes for the new year.

To Ford Madox Ford

Text MS Berg; *Listy* 317; Original unpublished

[letterhead: Capel House]
21 Dec 1911.

My dear Ford

You may find it hardly credible but as a fact I did not read your article in the ER till yesterday.[1] I do not read the lit: ads in papers; they did not send me the Nº of course, and no one I know thought it necessary to tell me. A mere allusion to it from a Belgian (who is translating Nostromo) put me on the track: "le charmant article que Monsieur F. M. Hueffer vous consacre dans la E. R".

———————

I am infinitely touched by what you say and by the accent you have

[1] 'Joseph Conrad', *English Review*, 10 (December 1911), 68–83; reprinted in *Critical Heritage*, pp. 240–50.

found to express what may be critically just and true but to a certainty is the speech of a friend. What touches me most is to see that you do not discard our common past.[1] These old days may not have been such very "good old days" as they should have been—but to me my dear Ford they are a very precious possession. In fact I have nothing else that I can call my own. And had you put them aside in your fortunate present I should have felt distinctly the poorer for it.

By the same post with the ordered copy of the ER arrived the charming cahier des vers inscribed to us both.[2] I have been turning over its pages ever since, in a manner of speaking, perfectly fascinated with its feeling and music. It's you—very characteristic—and yet with a difference—how shall we say it? A sort of deeper vibration. One is interested by that something additional and glad to find you unchanged. Pray thank your wife[3] from us both for the inscription and beg her to accept our most sincere wishes for the coming year and all the years to come. And may they be many for you both in peace and happiness and in the recognition of the fine work you both are doing.[4]

Borys asks to be remembered to you. He has just come for his holidays. He's a Worcester cadet now. Not that he wishes to go to sea; indeed the poor devil has got to wear glasses; but it is a good mathematical school and he seems to like the life very much.

With affectionate regards from us both

Yours as ever

J. Conrad.

[1] 'I knew at one time very well a writer who collaborated with Conrad in one or two books, and has very kindly presented me with the manuscript of these works'. Ford goes on to quote extensively from the MS of *Romance*, comparing his technique with Conrad's.

[2] Ford's new collection, *High Germany*, inscribed 'With all good wishes from Ford and Violet Hueffer' (copy listed by Edgar H. Wells, a New York dealer, in his May 1928 catalogue).

[3] Violet Hunt. Ford told his friends that he had married her in Germany (James T. Boulton, ed., *The Letters of D. H. Lawrence*, Vol. 1 [Cambridge University Press, 1979], p. 309 and Mizener, pp. 218–19). Under British law, however, Ford was still married to Elsie Hueffer, who refused to give him a divorce.

[4] Violet Hunt's most recent novel was *The Doll* (1911), dedicated to Ford's mother; she was now finishing her own mother's novel, *The Governess* (1912). Ford was at work on *The Panel* (1912).

To Jacques Copeau
Text MS Texas; Unpublished

[letterhead: Capel House]
26 Dec 1911.

Cher Monsieur[1]

Je vous remercie infiniment de la bonne et amicale idée que vous avez eu de m'envoyer les Frères Karamazow.[2]

Je suis tout simplement émerveillé de voir comme vous et votre collaborateur[3] avez réussi d'arracher, comme qui dirait, le coeur même de ce gros livre et le mettre a nu dans vos cinq actes.

Apart l'interêt de la piece et le langage simple et poignant que vous avez trouvé pour exprimer les profondeurs embrouillés de toute cette psychologie[4] j'ai ressenti aussi ce plaisir special d'ouvrier devant la besogne bien faite. Elle est admirablement bien faite. Mes felicitations les plus chaleureuses,

Agréez je vous en prie mes meilleurs souhaits de la nouvelle année et croyez moi

a vous bien cordialement
Joseph Conrad

Translation

Dear Sir,

Very many thanks for your kind and friendly notion of sending me *The Brothers Karamazov*.

I am quite simply astonished to see how you and your collaborator have succeeded in tearing out, so to speak, the very heart of that stout book, laying it bare in five acts.

Aside from the interest of the work itself and the simple, poignant language that you find to express the deep complications of all that psychology, I have also felt the special pleasure of a [fellow] worker before a task well done. It is admirably well done. My warmest congratulations.

[1] Jacques Copeau (1879–1949) was an actor, director, and playwright bent on ridding the Parisian stage of triviality and banality. He founded the Théâtre du Vieux-Colombier; for a brief period in 1940–41, he was administrator of the Comédie-Française. Like Gide and Ghéon, he was one of the founders of the *Nouvelle Revue Française* and a contributor to *L'Ermitage*.

[2] Copeau's dramatisation, staged at the Théâtre des Arts in 1913. [3] Jean Croué.

[4] When Conrad read Constance Garnett's translation of *The Brothers Karamazov* in 1912, he told Edward Garnett 'I don't know what D stands for or reveals, but I do know that he is too Russian for me' (27 May).

Please accept my best wishes for the new year, and believe me
Very cordially yours,
Joseph Conrad

To André Gide
Text MS Gide; *L. fr.* 113

[letterhead: Capel House]
26 Décembre 1911

Mon cher Gide—[1]

Je ne sais pas si vous me jugez digne de vous écrire—mais un homme
de votre intelligence ne peut être que miséricordieux. Enfin.
J'ai prié M. Ghéon de vous expliquer les raisons de mon criminel
silence. A part le travail j'ai eu aussi un tas d'embêtements de toute
sorte qui m'ont ôté, je ne dis pas, l'envie mais la possibilité d'écrire a
coeur ouvert. Et le travail n'est pas encore fini.

Je vous avoue enfin que j'ai lu et admiré *l'Immoraliste*[2] il y a bien deux
ans de ça. C'est Davray qui me l'a donné. Je n'ai rien dit car mon
exemplaire a été subtilisé par quelqu'un—et puis je voulais tenir ce livre
de Vous. Quant au vol de critique,[3] tout ce que je puis vous dire est,
que je me sens tellement d'accord avec le sentiment de ce livre que ma
sympathie—permettez moi de dire l'affection—que j'ai ressentie pour
vous dès le premier moment, en est infiniment augmentée.

Pardonnez Moi mon cher Gide, toutes mes scélératesses. L'autre jour
j'ai changé de bureau (je veux dire le meuble) et voilà que je ne peux pas
mettre la main sur la feuille avec votre adresse. J'envoie ceci au
Mercure.

Tout à vous.

PS—Ma femme se rappelle à votre bon souvenir, avec ses meilleurs
souhaits de nouvelle année. Je vous la souhaite bonne et heureuse.

[1] Of all the literary friends of Conrad's later years, André-Paul-Guillaume Gide
(1869–1951) was the most distinguished and the most artistically remarkable. A
born-again pagan and a recidivist puritan, his strengths lay both in intimate
autobiography and in ironic fiction. Among his works are *Les Nourritures terrestres*
(1897), *La Porte étroite* (1909), *Les Caves du Vatican* (1912), and *Les Faux-monnayeurs* (1926).
He first met Conrad in July 1911 and dedicated *Voyage au Congo* (1928) to his memory.
[2] Dedicated to Henri Ghéon, Gide's brief and resonant novel first appeared, in an
edition of only 300 copies, in 1902.
[3] Jean-Aubry identifies this as *Prétextes* (1903); it might equally well have been
Nouveaux prétextes (1911).

Translation

My dear Gide,

I don't know if you deem me worthy of writing to you, but a man of your intelligence can be only merciful. So...

I asked M. Ghéon to explain to you the reasons for my criminal silence. Besides work, I have also had a heap of nuisances of every kind, which have taken away, I do not say the wish, but the possibility of writing with an open heart. And the work is not yet finished.

I admit, then, that I read and admired *The Immoralist* all of two years ago. Davray gave it to me. I have not said anything, for someone has filched my copy; and I wanted to get this book *from You*. As to the volume of criticism, all I can tell you is that I am so much in accord with the sentiment of this book that the sympathy—permit me to say, affection—that I felt for you from the first moment is infinitely increased.

Forgive, my dear Gide, all my villainies. Having changed desks the other day, I can't lay my hands on the note with your address. I send this to the *Mercure*

Sincerely yours.

J. Conrad

PS—My wife wishes to be remembered to you, with her best wishes for the new year. I wish you a prosperous and happy one.

To Ford Madox Ford

Text Violet Hunt's copy, Cornell; Unpublished

Capel House
Orlestone
nr Ashford
Tuesday
Dec. 27 [26?] 11[1]

My dear Ford

We can't leave Hope very well alone and Miss Tobin has announced herself for Friday. We have told her to come along. All this is awkward. But perhaps the car which you so kindly offer to send for us could bring you here to lunch say on Saturday.[2] Jessie's gone upstairs with an awful

[1] The 27th was a Wednesday.

[2] Violet Hunt and Ford were staying either in Sandgate or in Littlestone-on-Sea (Mizener, p. 559, n. 22), both within easy motoring distance.

headache (a rare thing with her) so I scrawl these few words to tell you she will be writing to your wife to-morrow in that sense.

<div style="text-align: center;">Yours</div>

<div style="text-align: right;">J. Conrad</div>

To Edward Garnett
Text G. 254

<div style="text-align: right;">[Capel House]
28 Dec. '11</div>

My dear Edward,

On re-reading and thinking it out I see that the 3d act is not summary. It is rapid only—for only think how much happens in it in comparison with the first two. I mean here the mere comings and goings. It is indeed an excellent act; cleverly invented and finely imagined. The animation of it is quite extraordinary (given the situation) and I envy you the power* which could conceive and create all the successive "scenes" of* (in the French sense).[1]

But it is the exposition of the first and the development of the third act which strike me as masterly. If I don't go into special ecstacies* over the mother it is simply because I can see how fine the others are; the husband, the truly marvellously rendered friend—how good that incidental figure is, how tactfully done!—and the flawless Milly.[2] Don't be annoyed at my enthusiasm. It is perfectly sincere if artless—and perhaps a bit egotistic. I always thought you could do that sort of thing if you only tried. And to see my secret opinion so triumphantly vindicated is very delightful.

Meditating over the play in the light of your letter I feel that you want only (if you would condescend) to adopt some sort of fable, story, anecdote (the commonest* the better) to serve as a vehicle for your wit and psychology, in order to get hold of success in the popular way. It would no doubt be a concession to the depraved beast—but I question whether one does not owe such a concession to one's own gift. I venture to speak like this my dearest Edward because in all soberness I am very much impressed by the play. You won't take it ill, because I don't presume to offer advice; I am expressing to you my feeling which is the sort of thing for which one is not responsible. It seems to me I could back

[1] According to French tradition, a new scene begins every time a character exits or enters.

[2] Molly Frant, the mistress of Brian Harding.

it up with arguments—but enough for this time. Also of Catherine[1] one can better talk than write. Don't imagine I am not alive to her excellence. Rather! But of that some other time. Love from us all

<div align="center">Yours ever</div>

<div align="right">J Conrad</div>

P.S. Thanks for your invitation dear boy. I am very much interested by the little you tell me of David. By the bye: Marwood tells me he has asked you to run down here, but when I saw him yesterday he said he had no answer from you yet. Sacrifice a couple of days—give him one, and give one to us. Anyhow I shall certainly make a dash to town before long just to see you. But there is a novel in the way. The last 2000 words! Horrors!

To Warrington Dawson
Text MS Duke; Randall 145

<div align="right">[letterhead: Capel House]</div>
<div align="right">29 Dec '11</div>

Dear Warrington Dawson.

Our best wishes of health and prosperity for the coming year. Thanks for your card. I am immensely flattered by your choice for the "conference" but I feel profoundly how unworthy I am of the distinction.[2] But still I would come over for the pleasure of hearing you speak (if at the cost of enormous blushes) if I could possibly manage it. But it is not possible. On ne peut pas lutter contre la force des choses.[3] Everybody (including the two boys) sends most affectionate greetings.

<div align="center">A vous de coeur</div>

<div align="right">J. Conrad.</div>

[1] Catherine Henderson, the married woman.
[2] On 3 March, Dawson was to lecture on Conrad in Paris; the audience was the Club St Geneviève, which probably met at the library of that name.
[3] 'One can't contend with circumstances'.

To Norman Douglas
Text MS Texas; Unpublished

[letterhead: Capel House]
[late 1911]¹

Dear D.

I am writing in haste. It is difficult to advise you. I thought that you were going to try Heinemann. It's a question of publicity rather than money. But the publisher you mention may be a very good man.² I've never heard of him.

Of the general principles of negotiation I dare say You know more than I do. I had £20 for my first book 40 for the second, fifty for the third. And they were novels—always a sporting chance. You ought to get 60 for Tunis. Ask for more. Just now you can afford to have a try all round.

What does Dent say? An offer from him would give you some idea how the first book went. You need not accept it, of course.

Your symptoms don't surprise me after such a bout of fever. You can't get well all at once. Keep up your pecker.

Yours

J. Conrad

To the *New York Herald* 'Sunday Magazine'
Text New York Herald, 14 January 1912, Magazine, p. 3³

[Capel House]
[late? 1911]⁴

[it gives me the keenest pleasure when I find that womankind appreciates my work, and in] writing the story for the N. Y. H. I aimed at

¹ Between Douglas's illness and the switch to letterhead two at the new year. Douglas wrote '2' on the MS, showing that he had replied on the 2nd – probably of December or January.
² Late in 1911 and early 1912, Douglas negotiated with Murray, Heinemann, and Dent (Holloway, p. 193, and letters from Conrad to Douglas). The unknown publisher would have been Martin Secker (1882–1978), who had started his own company in January 1911 and accepted *Fountains in the Sand* in February 1912.
³ To publicize the first instalment of *Chance*, which would appear the following Sunday, the *Herald* printed a long interview with the author; it was embellished with photographs, the neighbourly opinions of drinkers at the local pub, and the verso of Conrad's letter in facsimile. Although the interview as a whole was not a fake (see the letter of 13 September 1911), most of the opening statement corresponds almost verbatim to the letter and the rest must come from the unpublished recto. The second paragraph may also be drawn from this source: 'What is the name of the novel? It is entitled "Chance." It deals with the life of a seaman and a woman, and it is while they are on board ship that, if I may say so, the situations develop that, I think, will appeal strongly to my readers.' In the present text, the passage in square brackets is taken from the body of the interview, the rest from the facsimile.
⁴ Probably written well after the reporter's visit to Capel House on 18 August.

treating my subject in a way which would interest women. That's all. I don't believe that women have to be written for specially as if they were infants. Women as far as I have been able to judge have a grasp of and are interested in all the facts of life. I am not speaking of mere dolls of course. Such exist—even in a democracy—just as dummy-men exist. But any woman with a heart and a mind knows very well that she is an active partner in the great adventure of humanity on this earth and feels an interest in all its episodes accordingly.[1]

<div align="center">yours faithfully</div>

<div align="right">Joseph Conrad</div>

[1] Conrad's remarks served a double purpose; they canvassed for new readers, and they establish his distance from Marlow's grumpy misogyny. Cedric Watts highlights Conrad's shrewd positioning here between old audience and new: *Joseph Conrad: A Literary Life* (Macmillan, 1989), pp. 114–19.

SILENT CORRECTIONS TO THE TEXT

The following slips of the pen have been silently corrected.

Missing full stop supplied

7 Jan. 1908: after 'with all my work'; 16 Jan. 1908: after '£1.4 wages', after 'to Dec last', after 'or if possible', after 'proportion of the month', after 'let me know'; [3 or 24? Feb. 1908]: after 'some time ago'; 5 Feb. 1908 (to Poradowska): after 'avec la coqueluche'; 17 Feb. 1908 (to Galsworthy): after 'may be dangerous'; [late Feb. 1908]: after 'arranged for me'; 29 Feb. 1908: after 'country folk etc etc'; [early? March 1908]: after 'immediately to my work'; [early? April 1908]: after 'interruptions'; 23 March 1908: after 'his bill (enclosed)'; 31 March [1908] (to Pinker): after '£ 18.10', after '2.13.3'; [19? March 1908]: after 'want to write'; 18 April 1908: after 'a great serenity'; [15? May 1908]: after 'in the *USA*'; [c. 19–21? May 1908]: after 'short stories in US', after 'unpleasant surprise'; 16 June 1908: after 'as much as possible'; [16? July 1908] (to Galsworthy): after 'her *feeling*'; [28? July 1908]: after 'interests him greatly'; 18 Aug. 1908: after 'out of my thoughts'; 19 Aug. 1908: after 'sheets of MS paper'; [23 Aug. 1908]: after '"amazing phenomena etc etc"'; 29 Aug. 1908: after 'understand already'; [2–3 Sept. 1908]: after 'can be managed somehow'; 18 Sept. [1908]: after 'to call on you', after 'necessity for some space', after '6 months notice', after 'on Nov. 25th', after 'this country as well'; 19 Sept. 1908: after 'in some way'; [25 Sept.] 1908 (to Rothenstein): after 'the doctor to-day'; 8 Oct. 1908 (to Douglas): after 'obscure scrawl'; 9 Oct. 1908: after '*A Set of Six*'; 13 Oct. 1908: after 'tomorrow evening's post', after '25th Jany '09'; [21 or 28] Oct. 1908: after 'hour away from *Raz*'; 3 Nov. 1908 (to Poradowska): after 'cette semaine-ci'; 4 Nov. 1908: after '*XIX Century*'; 20 Nov. 1908 (to Galsworthy): after 'Nevinson is a dear'; [24 or 25 Nov. 1908?]: after 'intermediate typing'; 25 Nov. 1908: after '4th paper of *Reminces*', after 'Engsh Review'; [7 Dec. 1908] (to Pinker): after 'Remces No IV'; 17 Dec. 1908 (to Pinker): after 'pressing necessities'; 29 Dec. 1908: after '"*Conrad aged 10 years*"'.

26 Jan. 1909: after '*less than* 250'; [24 Feb. 1909]: after 'at Smeeth'; 6 March 1909 (to Douglas): after 'appearing in the *ER*'; 6 March 1909 (to Reynolds): after 'before I look at anything', after 'the horizon of publicity'; [7 March 1909]: after 'Anyway my apologies', after 'take chances'; [11 or 18 March 1909]: after 'may come later'; [19 March 1909]: after 'into the parcel'; [25? March 1909]: after 'Postman at door'; [1? April 1909]: after 'the sort of thing'; 30 April 1909: after 'forgotten all about it'; 18 May 1909 (to Douglas): after 'with[in] seven days'; [13 June 1909] (to Pinker): after 'hanging over his head'; 14 June 1909: after 'authority of the *Spectator*'; [30 June or 7 July 1909]: after 'hands *at once*'; 2 July 1909 (to Benjamin): after 'possible success'; 2 July 1909 (to Douglas): after 'sick in mind'; [17 July 1909]: after '(Ford's brother in law)'; 19 July 1909 (to Pinker): after 'a little money'; 31 July 1909 (to Ford): after '*Ragged condition*'; 31 July 1909 (to Reynolds): after 'disagreeable impression'; [11 October 1909]: after 'letter of Wednesday'; 10 Nov. 1909: after '"book must be finished"'; 19 Nov. 1909 (to Galsworthy): after 'many re-readings'; 19 Dec. 1909 (to Gibbon): after 'yet swiftly enough'; 22 Dec. 1909 (to Galsworthy): after '*sat* at it'; [22 Dec. 1909] (to Pinker): after 'in Engd'; 31 Dec. 1909: after 'rigour of my solitude'.

[7 April 1910]: after 'one hour at a time'; 23 May 1910: after 'no discourtesy was intended'; 17 Aug. 1910: after 'approach them myself'; 25 Sept. 1910: after 'sometime in October'; [20? Oct. 1910]: after 'your country house', after 'against Smith'; 27 Oct. 1910 (to Galsworthy): after '(once owner of the Saturday)'; 29 Dec. 1910 (to Davray): after 'vous en pensez'.

7 Feb. 1911: after 'done I fear'; [mid Feb. 1911]: after 'faire la traducon'; [6 March 1911]: after 'the last time', after 'at present'; [9? March 1911] (to Garnett): after 'I think'; [9 March 1911] (to Douglas): after 'pay attention to the book'; [12 March 1911] (to Garnett): after '*H. B.*'; 15 May 1911: after 'a serious interruption'; 2 June 1911 (to Douglas): after 'our affection for you'; 2 June 1911 (to Graham): after 'stupid this morning'; 27 June 1911: after 'the *June* instt'; [13 July 1911]: after 'acct received today'; 20 Oct. 1911 (to Edward Garnett): after 'that "Great Power"'; [21 Oct. 1911] (to Pinker): after 'Its mislaid now'; 29 [28] Oct. [1911]: after 'received this morning'; 5 Dec. 1911: after 'a royalty of 20%'; 21 Dec. 1911: after '"dans la E. R"'; 27 [26?] Dec. 1911: after 'to come along'; [late 1911?] (to *New York Herald*): after 'mere dolls of course'.

Dittography
28 March 1908: a second 'to' after 'If you care'; 15 Aug. 1908: a second
'must' before 'be mad to go on'; 25 Nov. 1908: a second 'of' after 'I will
think'; 26 Jan. [1909]: a second 'and' after 'advance it now'; 5 May 1909
(to Pinker): a second 'the' after 'no delay beyond'; [13 June 1909] (to
Pinker): a second 'it' after 'I thought that'; 22 Dec. 1909: a second 'with'
after 'often worked'; 3 May 1910: a second 'd'avoir' after 'j'ai bien
besoin'; 17 May 1910: a second 'and' after 'with biggish rooms'; 28 June
1910: a second 'me' before 'what has been done'; [March 1911]: a
second 'use' before 'in book form when'; [c. 10 May 1911]: a second
'than' after 'infinitely more to me'; [18 Aug. 1911]: a second 'can' before
'hear him moaning'; [30? Sept. 1911] (to Reynolds): a second 'the' after
'in communion with'; [10 Nov. 1911]: a second 'the' after 'the advance
and there's', before 'do not *want* the connection'; 25 Nov. 1911: a second
'to' after 'already offered'; 11 Dec. 1911: a second 'to' before 'last week'.

Other

Quotation marks supplied:
7 Jan. 1908: after 'do this or that'; 7 Oct. 1908: after 'The Art and the
Life'; 6 March 1909 (to Douglas): see p. 197, n. 1; 29 Oct. 1909: before
'Que voulez vous'; 31 Oct. 1909: cf. 6 March (to Douglas); 4 Dec. 1910:
before and after 'And so from Paradise I turned my feet'.

Bracket supplied:
2 Feb. 1908: after 'suggested by yourself'; 26 Jan. [1909]: after 'say the
word'.

Hyphen supplied:
29 July 1910: before 'scène'.

Dash supplied:
[13 July 1910] (to Galsworthy): after 'I take'.

Comma supplied:
4 Nov. 1908: after 'Hueffer is editing'.

Semi-colon supplied:
21 Dec. 1911: after 'ads in papers'.

Colon supplied:
20 Feb. 1908 (to Ford): after 'occasion to say'.

Question mark supplied:
[9 Dec. 1908]: after 'snapshot portrait'.

CORRIGENDA

Volume 1

Page 219, n. 1: Henry Norman (1858–1939) of the *Daily Chronicle*.
304, letter to Unwin, address: the contents of the PS show that the
Conrads had now returned to London.
(Index) 443: add Henley, 321.

Volume 2

159, n. 2: these parallels were first noticed by Paul Kirschner in
Conrad: The Psychologist as Artist (Edinburgh: Oliver & Boyd, 1968).
342, n. 3: for 14 read 19 July.
(Index) 481: MacArthur, James; 482; add *Daily Telegraph*, 342.

Volume 3

(Chronology) xxi: Serial of *The Secret Agent* finished 15 December.
(Biographies) xxxviii: Bryan Palmes: described by Norman Douglas
(*Looking Back*, 1933) as 'Close-fisted . . . an entertaining talker, a good
Russian scholar, and possessor of a noble erotic library'; Alice
Rothenstein died 1957.
75, l. 5: 'esthétique'.
122, l. 1: 'the delay; but'. 122, to Garnett: [19 or 26 March]. 124, n. 3:
Lilian, not Lillian.
204, l. 8: no italics. 234, n. 2: Pietkiewicz (1823–1903). 248, n. 2: *My
World*.
317, PS, l. 3: 'Peyrou'. 361: written at Pent Farm? 395, translation, l.
2: 'from the street'. 370, telegram: add note: At 1:16, Jessie Conrad
wired 'Messenger lost train end left 1. 37 train' (Berg).
437, n. 2: 12 September. 482: [13 October] the likeliest date.
504, l. 4: 'medicine nauseous*'.
(Index) 523: Ford; delete 158; 525: Bible, add Colossians, 495; delete
hyphens after Borel; 526: add 'Inland Sea', 286; 526: Conrad, Works,
Nostromo; add 17, 34, 119, 129, 202; 527: Cortés, Hernán; add
Cumberland & Sons, 471; Ducailar; 528: add Ford, 509; add Gals-
worthy, 506; Hallowes, Lilian; add Hawkhurst, 428, 457; 529:
Humières; add Hythe, 428; add Jackson, 211: add James, 184; Keen,

William Brock; (London II: add Hampstead Station, 471; Kentish Town, 513; West Hampstead, 507); 530: Nałęcz arms; add Newbolt, 246; add Ninnes, 320; O'Connor, 91 only, T.P., not T.F.; (Periodicals: *Illustrierte*; add *Standard*, 295); 531: Pług, Adam (Antoni Pietkiewicz); add Rothenstein, Alice, 468; add Rothenstein family, 352; add Rowlstone & Co., 320; add Sauter, Georg; 18, 532: add Stanford, 404, 421.

INDEX I

In Index I, which identifies recipients, only the first page of each letter is cited.

In Index II, an index of names, run-on pagination may cover more than one letter. References to ships are consolidated under 'Ships'; references to newspapers and magazines under 'Periodicals'. References to works by Conrad appear under his name. A full critical index will appear in the final volume.

Recipients

INDEX II